Instructor's Edition

Invitation
THIRD EDITION

*Contextes, culture
et communication*

Gilbert A. Jarvis
The Ohio State University

Thérèse M. Bonin
The Ohio State University

Diane W. Birckbichler
The Ohio State University

HOLT, RINEHART AND WINSTON, INC.
New York • Chicago • San Francisco • Philadelphia
Montreal • Toronto • London • Sydney • Tokyo

Publisher • Vincent Duggan
Acquisitions Editor • Laura McKenna
Developmental Editor • Jacqueline Rebisz
Production Manager • Lula Als / Priscilla Taguer
Design Supervisor • Renée Davis
Text Design and Layout • York Production Services
Composition and Camera Work • York Graphic Services
Printing and Binding • Von Hoffmann Press, Inc.

Photographic credits appear at the end of the book.

Library of Congress Cataloging-in-Publication Data
Jarvis, Gilbert A.
    Invitation : contextes, culture et communication / Gilbert A. Jarvis, Thérèse M. Bonin, Diane
W. Birckbichler. — 3rd. ed.
    p.   cm.
English and French.
    Rev. ed. of : Invitation : French for communication and cultural awareness / Gilbert A. Jarvis
. . . [et al.]. 2nd ed. 1984.
    Includes index.
    ISBN 0-03-004973-3
    1. French language — Textbooks for foreign speakers — English. 2. French language —
Grammar — 1950- I. Bonin, Thérèse M. II. Birckbichler, Diane W. III. Invitation.
IV. Title.
PC2129.E5J37   1988   87-28660
448.2'421 — dc19   CIP
ISBN 0-03-004973-3 Student Edition
Instructor's Edition : ISBN 0-03-004974-1

ISBN 0-03-004974-1

8 9 0 1   032   9 8 7 6 5 4 3 2

Holt, Rinehart and Winston, Inc.
The Dryden Press
Saunders College Publishing

Introduction to the Instructor's Edition

Invitation : Contextes, culture et communication and its supplements (*Invitation à écouter et à écrire*, the combined workbook and laboratory manual, the tape program and the testing program) are a complete beginning college French program. As the title indicates, the book invites students from the first moments to communicate meaningfully in French and at the same time to understand better the daily life and attitudes of French-speaking people. *Invitation* is designed to accommodate diverse instructional needs rather than to impose a single methodology : its flexible format can be easily adapted to different teaching styles, student preferences, and course objectives and to varying amounts of instructional time. Although equal time is given to the four language skills, this flexibility allows instructors who so desire to emphasize a particular skill or group of skills. The book is organized to capitalize on the organizational efficiency provided by awareness of grammar but immediately provides functional and communicative uses of the pattern in diverse situations.

The third edition of *Invitation* is a true revision. More than half of the introductory and end-of-chapter conversations and readings have been changed or modified ; the number of chapters has been reduced to eighteen to allow more time to be devoted to the development of the student's language proficiency ; the thematic vocabulary sections (now called *Les mots et la vie*) at the beginning of each chapter have been enhanced ; changes in the sequencing of grammar have been made ; communicative activities (now called *Communication et vie pratique*) have been expanded to include a wider range of communication and survival situations ; and finally, numerous language functions and sociolinguistic settings are illustrated in the *Mise en situation* conversations that accompany each structural topic and in the accompanying role-playing situations (*C'est votre tour*).

True proficiency has been the goal of *Invitation* since it was first published; the third edition carries on this tradition and, through the changes outlined above, expands and enhances the student's communicative potential.

The goal of communication

The primary goal of *Invitation* is to help students to acquire proficiency in communicating within culturally significant contexts. "Communication" refers not only to the ability to express ideas orally or in writing but also the capacity to comprehend linguistic and cultural meaning while reading or listening to French. To achieve these communication aims with the greatest possible flexibility, *Invitation* includes the following features as an integral part of its organization.

1. *Communication and role-playing activities accompany all grammar presentations.*

   Varied activities provide for immediate meaningful practice of every new grammar structure. Communication, therefore, takes place at once rather than at some unspecified time in the future.

2. *Cultural insights are presented throughout the book.*

   Cultural content is not limited to scattered cultural notes but is integrated into various activities throughout the book: in culturally authentic dialogues and reading passages; in contextualized activities that have a cultural or situational setting; and in various communication activities. Many notes in the Instructor's Edition explain cultural allusions in the text or present additional cultural information.

3. *Language learning takes place in context.*

   Context is an integral part of every stage of the learning process. For example, the *Mise en situation* conversations that accompany each structural topic take place in an authentic situational or functional context designed to illustrate real-life use of the topic. Grammar exercises are also placed in a context to demonstrate ways in which the structures could be used in authentic cultural settings or in communication situations typically encountered in daily life. In addition, the role-playing situations that accompany the *Mises en situation* further illustrate language functions and potential contexts for communication. Additional contextual support is provided through the use of authentic documents and through readings that have been excerpted and adapted from French magazines and newspapers.

4. *Chapters are thematically organized.*

   Readings and grammar are related to a broad chapter theme to maximize communicative potential and facilitate learning. Attitudes, values, and concerns of people from all parts of the French-speaking world are reflected in the reading passages and cultural notes. In addition, each introductory passage is followed by a special communication section that provides vocabulary and expressions related to the chapter theme.

5. *Presentation of each grammar topic is sequenced for greatest efficiency.*
Each grammar structure is presented comprehensively with ample examples, practiced in carefully structured drills and preparation activities, and then applied meaningfully in communication activities.

6. *Chapter sequencing encourages successful communication at the earliest possible time.*
Because topics and structures are sequenced in terms of learning difficulty and usefulness in communication, early chapters allow students to acquire quickly a genuine feeling of being able to speak French.

7. *Considerable cognate vocabulary is used to provide maximum communication potential with minimal learning loads.*
The book capitalizes, especially in early chapters, on the large number of French words that resemble English words. Drills are included to accommodate the special pronunciation problems of cognate vocabulary.

8. *Grammar coverage is comprehensive.*
The most common structures and patterns of French are included in the book, although all need not be covered. Flexibility in the coverage of topics is therefore possible.

9. *Vocabulary is presented in context.*
Principal noncognate vocabulary is presented in the reading passages, which are followed by communication sections that immediately illustrate its use in an appropriate context. Important vocabulary words are listed at the end of each chapter.

10. *Options are presented throughout the book.*
Abundant drills and activities are provided so that instructors and students can select those that are best suited to their purposes. Others can be omitted with no resulting confusion. In addition, the organization of the book itself is flexible, and each section can be used in a variety of ways.

Organization of the book

The third edition of *Invitation* has a preliminary chapter, eighteen regular chapters, a final chapter that focuses on the *passé simple* (*Invitation à la lecture*), and appendixes. Each of the eighteen chapters includes the following sections.

Mise en scène

Introduction : These introductory conversational passages of varying subject matter and format (e.g., dialogues, interviews, newscasts, monologues) provide diverse contexts for the development of speaking skills and introduce the general chapter theme. New noncognate vocabulary is glossed in the margin to ensure immediate comprehension of unfamiliar words.

Compréhension :   The comprehension check evaluates the student's understanding of the introductory passage.

Notes culturelles :   Cultural topics related to the chapter theme and the introductory passage are discussed in this section. The cultural notes are in English in the first seven chapters of the book and in French thereafter.

Les mots et la vie :   This section introduces new vocabulary centered around a topic that is related to the chapter theme. Varied communication activities involve the student in the active use of this newly presented vocabulary.

Explorations

Each chapter introduces four grammar topics that are presented, practiced, and expanded upon in the following phases.

Présentation :   This section introduces the grammar topic and its functional use and presents sample sentences that illustrate the structure.

Mise en situation :   The *Mise en situation* conversations that accompany each structural topic not only show how a particular structure can be used in a real-life setting but also introduce numerous language functions, cultural settings, and conversational patterns that can be used by students.

Préparation :   The grammar is then practiced in structured, lifelike situations. Many exercises are set in cultural contexts, thereby reinforcing the authenticity of the language used and its potential value for real-life communication while providing, at the same time, insights into francophone cultures. The Instructor's Edition contains simple mechanical drills for each topic.

Communication et vie pratique :   The varied formats in this section give students the opportunity to communicate about a wide variety of topics. In addition to the personal communication of some formats, students are also given different types of survival situations and role-plays that enable them to see how well they would get along in a French-speaking country.

Intégration et perspectives

Lecture :   This reading recombines and integrates the grammar and vocabulary used in the chapter and provides additional cultural and / or human interest perspectives. It also provides reading practice and introduces new words in context. *Compréhension* and *Notes culturelles* sections follow this end-of-chapter reading.

Communication et vie pratique :   This final section presents communication and survival situations that are related to the chapter theme and which require students to further integrate and use in new contexts the language they have already learned. The use of realia and authentic documents and the inclusion of survival and role-playing situations are an important aspect of these activities. The range of survival and communication situations and the varied cultural settings in which they take place help develop the student's range of expression.

Prononciation et orthographe

The most significant features of spoken French (and their written counterparts) are described in each of the first ten chapters. Practice of both individual sounds and longer sentences containing critical sounds is included.

Vocabulaire du chapitre

Each chapter is followed by a list of vocabulary words intended for active use in that chapter and in subsequent chapters. The lists contain the most important noncognate and cognate vocabulary used in the lesson or page references for thematically grouped vocabulary. Where appropriate, the vocabulary lists are organized in thematic clusters (e.g., sports, food).

Appendice

The appendix contains a key to the phonetic alphabet, a glossary of grammar terminology, verb charts for regular, irregular, and spelling-changing verbs, vocabularies (French-English ; English-French), and a grammar index. Because students are not always aware of appendix material, it may be a good idea to point out the different components. The glossary of grammar terms may be particularly helpful to students who lack a knowledge of such terminology.

The supplementary materials

Student workbook / laboratory manual and tape program

The combined workbook and laboratory manual (*Invitation à écouter et à écrire*) contains written and oral activities for each of the book's eighteen chapters. The first half of each chapter contains writing activities ; the second half oral exercises.

The workbook component has been designed to expand the student's ability to communicate in writing. Each chapter of *Invitation* has accompanying exercises in the student workbook section of this manual. A series of exercises and communication activities ranging from simple to more complex is coordinated with each section of the chapter and with each structural topic. This sequencing allows the instructor to assign all or part of the exercises, depending upon the needs of the class or individual students. Workbook assignments can be made on a daily basis, used for end-of-chapter review, or given to students experiencing difficulty with a specific topic.

The tape program and laboratory section of the manual have been designed to provide students with the opportunity to practice their oral skills outside class. Each chapter in *Invitation* has accompanying taped material which includes : (1) readings of the *Mise en scène* and the *Intégration et perspectives* passages ; (2) two or three activities for each grammar topic ; (3) readings of the *Mise en situation* conversations ; (4) a listening comprehension passage based on the chapter theme that integrates chapter grammar and vocabulary. In addition, a pronunciation section (Chapters 1 – 10), a short thematic dictation, and a series of thematically related personal questions are included.

The lab section of the manual is the student guide to the tape program. Like the workbook, each chapter of the main text has accompanying exercises in the tape program. The lab section includes directions and models for listening tasks that involve writing in the manual. Space is provided for students to complete the listening tasks, write out dictation sentences, and answer the comprehension questions on the listening passage. Page references are given for those exercises and pronunciation sections that are taken from *Invitation*. These exercises are marked with an asterisk.

Answer keys for the workbook and lab exercises as well as the tape script for the tape program are available from the publisher.

The instructor's edition

In addition to the more general introduction, the Instructor's Edition contains the complete Student Edition of *Invitation* accompanied by marginal notes. The marginal notes are not intended to be prescriptive or all-inclusive but are simply suggestions for ways in which various sections, exercises, and activities in the text can be used, modified, or elaborated upon. Implementation of these suggestions will depend to a large degree upon individual instructional preferences and teaching style, students' interests, course objectives, and the amount of class time available. In many cases, however, they may function as a time-saver for the instructor. Where appropriate, the marginal notes also offer additional pertinent cultural information.

Testing materials

A testing program completes the ancillary materials available for *Invitation*. The following tests and quizzes are available in a separate booklet : (1) ten-minute vocabulary quizzes for each chapter ; (2) fifty-minute unit tests for every two chapters ; and (3) speaking tests for every six chapters. In all cases, the focus is on the communicative use of the structures and vocabulary studied rather than on discrete-point grammar items. Each of the tests contains a listening comprehension section ; a reading section, which often includes materials excerpted and / or adapted from authentic sources and questions dealing with French culture ; and a writing section, which usually includes a more open-ended composition topic.

Using each section of *Invitation*

Except for its emphasis on encouraging the meaningful use of language, *Invitation* imposes few constraints and can be used in many ways. It is not intended that every section be used *throughout* or that all exercises and activities always be completed ; rather, it is assumed that each instructor will choose sections or activities that best suit his or her purposes. The extent to which a given section of a chapter is emphasized and utilized will depend upon course goals, the amount of instructional time available, teacher preferences, and the needs and interests of the class or individual students. Although specific suggestions and options for using individual activities are given in the marginal notes of the Instructor's Edition, varied ways to use the different sections of the book can be delineated.

Chapitre préliminaire

The purpose of the *Chapitre préliminaire* is to give general language-learning strategies, to introduce the student to useful classroom expressions and every-day conversational phrases, to present useful classroom objects and numbers from 1 to 20, and to give a brief overview of different francophone countries. Although designed to be completed before beginning *Invitation,* the content of this chapter can be spread across the first several days of instruction.

Mise en scène

Because the *Mise en scène* introductory dialogue or text is intended as a vehicle for the presentation of the chapter's theme and of new vocabulary and cultural information rather than the presentation of new grammar structures, it functions best as the first assignment in a lesson. As the first assignment, the *Mise en scène* and the *Compréhension* can be used as a basis for class discussion. The *Mise en scène* can also serve as an out-of-class reading assignment with the *Compréhension* prepared in writing. Various techniques can be used to enhance student comprehension :

- Students can be asked to look at the title and try to guess what the passage is about.
- The photographs and the illustrations that accompany the passages can be used to elicit comments about what students think the passage is about and for discussing the cultural differences and similarities evoked by the *Mise en scène.*
- A brief introduction in French or in English can help "set the scene."

- The content of the *Mise en scène* can be related to students' lives. For example, Chapter 7 deals with the theme of television. Students might be asked in this instance : **Avez-vous une télé ?** or **Qu'est-ce que vous aimez regarder ?**
- Students may be asked to anticipate content by looking over the *Compréhension* before reading or listening to a passage.
- Present new vocabulary through visuals, gestures, French synonyms or paraphrases, and English translation. The marginal glosses can serve as a reference point if students do not remember the meanings of the new words.
- Put the *Mise en scène* without glosses on duplicating masters and see if students can understand the general meaning of the passage. Then have them guess the meaning of new vocabulary words. Students will not only learn the new vocabulary but will also gain valuable skill in contextual guessing.
- If the passage is assigned as homework, students can be told to study the marginal glosses before beginning and to make sure they think about the meaning as they study it.

After learning the new vocabulary and having an idea about the content of the introductory passage, students will be better able to read and understand the entire passage. Depending on student abilities and available time, the *Mise en scène* can be presented in one day or spread out across several days. The presentation and practice of the *Mise en scène* can take several forms. Instructors can present visuals and transparencies that illustrate the passage before students see it in writing. Students can listen to the taped version of the passage before seeing it. The passage can be assigned as homework and gone over in class the next day. Although it is not necessary that students memorize these passages, it is important that they be given the opportunity to say the lines either in class and / or in the language laboratory.

Compréhension

Although individual or whole-class repetition of a dialogue or reading helps pronunciation of new vocabulary and structures, it does not ensure comprehension of content. The *Compréhension* can be used to determine whether or not students have understood meaning. In addition to assigning the *Compréhension* as homework or asking the questions orally in class, instructors might use these questions for guided comprehension practice by asking students to read or listen to the conversation in order to find just one piece of information or the answer to a single comprehension question. They can subsequently be asked to find other bits of information. Although time-consuming, this focused comprehension allows students gradually to make sense of a passage and reduces frustration, especially in early stages of language learning. Students can also be asked to read the passage once (or more, depending on the time available) and then write in English (or French) all that they remember from the passage. A perusal or discussion of what they have recalled will help identify those areas (e.g., vocabulary, grammar, culture) that have interfered with comprehension. Responsibility for finding the answers to questions and reporting back to the class may be assigned to individual students or to small groups of students. Other comprehension techniques require students to use the content of the passage in slightly new ways :

- Having students make up a new title for the reading (in English in early chapters and later in French) or choose a title from among several offered by the teacher.
- Having students create a new beginning or end of the passage.
- Having students rewrite the material relating it to their lives or from a different perspective.
- Having students summarize the passage in French or in English.
- Providing students with a résumé of the passage with misinformation and then having them choose only those sentences that summarize it accurately.
- Having students play the role of a character or characters in a conversation and having other students ask them questions.
- Having students choose adjectives that describe the people in conversations or readings, verb phrases that indicate their activities and occupations, particular words that reveal their moods and preoccupations, and phrases that indicate the particular viewpoint of the author.

Notes culturelles

The *Notes culturelles,* which appear in both *Mise en scène* and *Intégration et perspectives* sections, can be assigned as out-of-class supplementary reading or used for discussion in class with the instructor illustrating them with additional information or personal anecdotes, depending upon his or her experience or course objectives. The notes can also be illustrated or enhanced by drawing attention to the photographs and realia in the book or by using slides, songs, and other such materials. In addition, each cultural topic can be elaborated upon by assigning supplementary readings, research projects, or *exposés.* Suggestions for specific activities and discussions appear in the Instructor's Edition.

Les mots et la vie

The *Les mots et la vie* section that follows the introductory dialogue or text not only presents through visuals and interesting contexts vocabulary related to the chapter theme but also provides a variety of communication activities for immediate practice with these words. Using visuals, gestures, synonyms, or English equivalents can help students master this vocabulary ; it may also be assigned as homework. Possible ways to complete these activities are described in the *Encouraging communication* discussion later in this section.

Explorations

The grammar explorations form a logical progression from understanding a particular grammar topic to practicing it in meaningful contexts and last, but most important of all, to using these forms in communicative situations. Users of *Invitation* are encouraged to view the *Présentations* as a way to access the language and not as an end in and of itself. Thus, lengthy discussions of grammar and lectures about the structure of French should be avoided so that class time can be spent using the language.

Présentation

Each *Présentation* is given in English and is basically a deductive grammar explanation; that is, it is based on information the student already knows in English or in French and proceeds to new material. This type of presentation does not preclude, however, discussing the grammar topic in French should the instructor or the class so desire. In addition, many grammar topics easily lend themselves to inductive presentations in which the instructor leads the students to discover the pattern and rules through judicious comparisons of examples and asking of appropriate questions. If an inductive approach is used, students can use the explanation in the book to check their understanding. Because the grammar patterns are thoroughly illustrated with abundant examples, the instructor can also assign the *Présentation* as homework, thereby preserving valuable class time for oral, especially communication, practice. Each explanation is divided into subsections, thus allowing all or part of a topic to be assigned, depending on the amount of coverage desired. The *Présentations* can also be used for review or remedial work.

Mise en situation

The *Mise en situation* conversation that follows each presentation of a structural topic is designed to give the student an immediate application of the grammar structure in question, to provide additional conversational patterns useful in communication, and to introduce the student to a wide variety of language functions used in different cultural settings. Students can prepare to use these conversations in class in several ways. First, they can be assigned as homework in the lab where students can listen to the taped version of the conversation and practice repeating the conversation. Instructors might also want to do this familiarization phase in class, perhaps using the taped version as a model. (Note that these conversations are not intended to be memorized; rather, students should become familiar with the exchanges through laboratory and in-class work.) After listening to the conversation, students can be asked several comprehension questions to make sure that they have understood the meaning of the exchange. Students can then be asked to repeat and dramatize the conversations as a class or in small groups. If time permits, students might want to tape or videotape the *Mise en situation*. Vocabulary, functions of language, and cultural information contained in the *Mises en situation* can be used as the basis for class discussion. *C'est votre tour,* the role-playing situations based on the *Mise en situation,* are found at the end of the *Communication et vie pratique* section. Although in some cases, the *C'est votre tour* can be completed when the *Mise en situation* is first introduced and practiced, students will generally be better prepared for the role-playing situations at the end of the practice sequence.

Préparation

The mechanical drills provided in the Instructor's Edition are intended to give students initial practice in manipulating grammar structures and making rapid responses to controlled language stimuli. The number of drills used will depend upon student needs, class and laboratory time available, the complexity of the grammar topic, and instructional preferences. A given exercise may be used entirely, or partially, or not at all. If students learn a particular structure rapidly, few exercises will be necessary, and students can move on to *Communication* activities.

The *Préparation* exercises are intended as a bridge between simple manipulative practice, where the establishment of structural patterns and grammatical accuracy is the goal, and free communication, where the transmission or understanding of ideas is emphasized. They provide a realistic context for the structure but do not yet engage the student personally in that context. It is possible to use these realistic transitional exercises instead of manipulative exercises, moving back to drills if students seem to be experiencing difficulty with a structure. On the other hand, if the instructor is satisfied with the understanding and fluency that students have demonstrated in the Instructor's Edition drills, the *Préparation* activity can be omitted. Because these exercises range from easy to more complicated, instructors may choose to complete selected exercises rather than the entire section in class. The selection of exercises depends on student abilities, class time, the difficulty of the grammar topic, and the extent of student comprehension of the particular grammar topic. In some cases, it may be possible to skip both drills and *Préparation* sections and move directly to *Communication* sections, reserving the omitted exercises for remedial work.

Various approaches can be used with the *Préparation* exercises : instructors can give cues and have students respond individually or as a class ; students can be divided into small groups, each with a leader who has the correct answers and the teacher circulating to help each group ; students can role-play certain activities, especially those where two individuals are engaged in a simulated conversation. Additional suggestions for use of the *Préparation* section are found in the Instructor's Edition.

Although most *Préparation* activities can be completed with books closed, instructors may ask students to keep their books open until they are familiar with the pattern. These activities can then be repeated with books closed. It is important that instructors use the contexts provided so that students associate responses with the situation. Attention should be drawn to model sentences so that students clearly understand their tasks.

Préparation exercises are generally designed to prepare students better for oral communication tasks. This does not, however, preclude their being assigned as written homework should class time be limited or should students need additional practice. Some of these exercises can be completed orally in class without prior preparation; others require advance written work.

Communication et vie pratique

The *Communication et vie pratique* follows the sequenced series of exercises designed to prepare students for communication tasks. It is not intended that each activity be used or that each question or item be fully discussed but rather that instructors and students choose *Communication* activities that best suit their needs and interests.

Because students, especially in early stages of language learning, can be frustrated by totally unstructured communication tasks, many activities are designed to provide both a framework of language structures and a set of ideas from which the student can draw. Thus, to successfully communicate an idea, less able or secure students may choose ideas from those provided. A question mark invites and encourages others to venture beyond the suggestions provided and to create their own responses. Should an instructor wish, many of these structured tasks can be made more open-ended by having students complete the activity with their books closed. In addition to the guided communication activities, many are less structured and require the student to produce both the necessary language and ideas. Ways of encouraging communication and explanations of how to use the communication activities in *Invitation* are outlined later in this introduction.

C'est votre tour

The *C'est votre tour* role-playing activities are based on the *Mise en situation* conversations presented earlier in the sequence. Some of these role-plays are fairly close to the *Mise en situation*; others (especially later in the book) are more open-ended. All are designed to give the students the opportunity to try out their language skills in a variety of survival and communication situations. Although spontaneous language use is the desired outcome of the *C'est votre tour*, it may be difficult for students to react spontaneously, especially in the initial stages of language learning. Thus, it is important that students be prepared carefully for the *C'est votre tour* role-plays. As a first step, the *Mise en situation* conversation can be repeated and dramatized by students. Especially at early stages in the book, it would be useful to model the suggested role-play with a good student in front of the class to give other students an idea of the direction that the role-play might take. (If possible, you might want to tape or videotape a model role-play to use in class.) You may want to assign the *C'est votre tour* as homework or give students some preparation time in class. Preparation can also consist of reviewing relevant vocabulary, listing phrases that might be useful in the situations described, sketching out in greater detail the situation, or planning an outline of the conversation to guide students as they play their assigned roles. Role-plays can be acted out in front of the class with other students assigned to listen and answer questions about what took place. Students can also be given a limited amount of class time to enact the role-plays in groups of two or three with the instructor circulating among groups.

Intégration et perspectives

The *Intégration et perspectives* is intended to reinforce and integrate the content of a given chapter and to develop the student's reading skill. Some new cognate and noncognate vocabulary is also introduced. The *Intégration et perspectives* can be given as a regularly scheduled class assignment to be used as a basis for oral or written discussion, or it can be assigned as supplementary reading. If instruction time is limited, the *Intégration et perspectives* can be omitted, provided that students are held responsible for the end-of-chapter vocabulary lists.

The *Communication et vie pratique* section following the reading passage can be used after reading the text, although many activities can be used to supplement communication practice of previous grammar topics. Although the entire final *Communication et vie pratique* section or some of its activities could be omitted, this section allows students to apply their cumulative knowledge of grammar and vocabulary while exploring their reactions to a wide variety of topics and situations.

Prononciation

The main purpose of the pronunciation section (included in Chapters 1 – 10) is to provide a systematic presentation of important aspects of French pronunciation. These end-of-chapter pronunciation sections can be used in several ways. They can be completed (1) before beginning a chapter, (2) spread throughout a chapter, or (3) in their entirety at the end of a chapter. The drills provided in these sections can be used for brief but intensive pronunciation practice in class, or they may be completed in the laboratory outside class. The instructor plays an important role, however, in explaining how to form these sounds, in modeling correct pronunciation, and in giving feedback to students.

Invitation à la lecture

The final chapter in *Invitation* has been designed to introduce the forms of the *passé simple* so that students can begin to enjoy literary and historical material that uses the *passé simple*. In addition to presenting the forms of the *passé simple* for recognition purposes, the chapter also contains activities and illustrative readings. This chapter can be done after completing the core chapters in *Invitation* — or taken up earlier should instructors wish to add supplementary reading materials that use the *passé simple* to their course content.

Encouraging communication

Error correction

Both students and instructors contribute to the creation of an atmosphere in which communication is likely to occur. In a communicative classroom, the student becomes an active participant in the communication process rather than a passive recipient of information about language or a rote manipulator of grammatical forms. If the student's role is defined so that he or she feels comfortable in expressing an idea, then communication is likely to occur. This implies not only that students should be encouraged to express their thoughts but also that what they communicate should be valued and respected. When students feel comfortable, they are more likely to take the necessary risks to express their ideas.

The amount of error correction an instructor undertakes during communication activities will vary. Because no definitive research exists to guide in the correction of student errors, instructors must rely instead on their experience, common sense, intuition, and knowledge of the individuals in the class. Some believe that students generally need not be corrected during communication and prefer to make corrections only during manipulative practice. Still others point out only errors that impede communication or that might be offensive to a native speaker. This does not imply, however, that structure and guidance are not necessary. It implies, rather, that a delicate balance be maintained, allowing students to speak freely and take risks in using French (especially when communicating) while at the same time having standards that will develop students' language abilities to the fullest.

Errors can often be pointed out to students in discreet and unobtrusive ways. The student's statement **Je suis dix-huit** can be rephrased **Ah, vous avez dix-huit ans,** or the instructor can react to the student's statement by using a variation of the correct structure — **C'est vrai ? Moi, je n'ai pas dix-huit ans.** In addition, frequently recurring mistakes can be pointed out to the entire class. Whatever strategies are used, the learning environment should encourage students to take risks, be willing to make errors, and test their limits of self-expression in the second language.

Small-group work

Small-group work is also useful in encouraging communication and coopera-tion for the following reasons : (1) communication is more lifelike in small groups because real-life communication usually takes place among a small group of people ; (2) students are more at ease in small groups ; (3) the amount of communication increases because each student talks more frequently ; and (4) the teacher, in addition to providing vocabulary or help when needed, can participate in conversations rather than merely direct them.

The instructor is very important if small-group work is to be effective. First, the students' tasks should be clear so that they know exactly what they are to do. Second, the time allotted should be clearly indicated. Third, students should be responsible for the information found out during the activity. If they are to ask other students questions, they can report back to the class what they learned about the student(s) interviewed. They can also write a short report of their interview to submit to the instructor.

Types of communication activities

Invitation contains a rich variety of communication activities and role-playing situations that can be used to help develop the student's language proficiency. Below are some of the typical communication activities in *Invitation* and possi-ble ways to use them as whole-class or small-group activities.

Questions / Interview

This consists of a series of questions that students answer or use to interview another student (see Chapter 4, p. 101).

1. Où est-ce que tu aimes aller en vacances ?
2. Qu' est-ce que tu aimes faire en vacances ?
3. Est-ce que tu préfères voyager en été ou en hiver ?
4. Quels pays est-ce que tu désires visiter ?
5. Est-ce que tu désires visiter la France un jour ?
6. Quelles villes françaises est-ce que tu désires visiter ?
   etc.

Students can prepare questions for homework so that they are better able to answer in class. If the questions are used for small-group interviews, various follow-up activities encourage students to be responsible for the information they learned. Students can share with the class information they learned from their partner (e.g.,**Michel désire visiter la France un jour**); they can take brief notes on their partner's answers and submit them as an informal composition; or instructors can ask for information that students learned in their small-group interviews (e.g., **Est-ce que Caroline préfère voyager en été ou en hiver ?**). This format can also be used for guided composition practice.

Interviews

This activity type consists of a series of cues that students transform into questions that they will then use to interview other students. Though similar to *Questions / Interview,* this format requires the student to formulate and ask questions (see Chapter 4, p. 88).

Exemple   aller à la bibliothèque
             Est-ce que tu vas aller à la bibliothèque le week-end prochain ?

1. aller au concert   **5.** aller au cinéma
2. manger dans un bon restaurant   **6.** étudier pour un examen
3. aller à la campagne   etc.
4. parler avec des amis

Students can use the phrases to ask each other questions in small- or large-group activities, or they can interview another student about the items listed. Interview sheets can be given to students to record the results of their interviews. These interview sheets, which contain the cues and a place for students to mark their partner's answers, can be put on dittos and distributed to students. They can therefore more easily remember their partner's responses for follow-up, whole-class discussions. The cues can also be transformed into questions asked by the instructor (**Est-ce que vous allez à la bibliothèque le week-end prochain ?**) or directed dialogues (**Demandez à Michelle si elle va à la bibliothèque le week-end prochain**) and used as a whole-class activity.

Students can also be asked to role-play interviews in both structured activities where cues are provided or in free-response role-plays. For example, in Chapter 11, students are asked to role-play a conversation between a patient and his or her doctor, who diagnoses the illness and prescribes a remedy.

Students can prepare their answers as homework or in class. They can then role-play the situation in small groups, taking first the role of the patient and then the doctor. Selected groups can then present their conversations to the class, which can diagnose the problem and prescribe appropriate remedies. A variation would entail a three-person group where two students role-play the situation while a third student listens and takes notes so that he or she can report to the class the patient's symptoms and the doctor's prescription. If videotaping equipment is available, these role-plays can be recorded and played back to the class.

Surveys

Students are asked to answer survey questions in an activity or a reading (see example 1 from Chapter 17, p. 437) or are asked to prepare their own survey questions.

(1) **Et vous, aimez-vous le cinéma ?** Répondez vous-même aux questions du sondage présenté dans *Intégration et Perspectives.* Ensuite, comparez vos réponses à celles des autres étudiants ou bien à celles des Français.

(2) Make up questions that you would include on a survey of television viewing habits and preferences. Then use these questions to interview another student or group of students.

These questions can be asked by the instructor in a whole-class activity with a student tallying the results. Students can also work in pairs and take turns asking each other the questions or work in groups of five or six where one student asks the questions and tabulates the responses of his or her group. In both cases, the results are reported back to the rest of the class. In addition, student interviewers can be given responsibility for one or two questions. After they have interviewed as many students as possible within a given time frame, each reports his or her findings to the whole class. Students can also respond to the survey questions as a homework assignment, then turn in their answers to be tabulated by the instructor (or a volunteer student) so that the results can be used for subsequent reading practice (by putting the results on a ditto) or for listening-comprehension practice. Survey activities such as those illustrated in the first example provide an excellent way to have students compare their culture with francophone cultures.

Agree / Disagree

Students respond to a series of statements by indicating whether or not the sentences are true for them. The example below (see Chapter 12, p. 305) asks students to react to statements made by an opinionated person.

1. C'est en France qu'on boit les meilleurs vins du monde.
2. Les Françaises sont les plus belles femmes du monde.
3. Pour être heureux, il faut travailler le moins possible et s'amuser le plus possible.
4. Les hommes sont plus intelligents et plus capables que les femmes.
5. La cuisine française est la meilleure du monde.
   etc.

Agree / Disagree activities can be used in a variety of ways. The statement can be transformed by the teacher or by the student into direct questions (**À votre avis, est-ce que la cuisine française est la meilleure du monde ?**) and used for whole-class or small-group activities. Students can prepare the activity for homework and be asked to explain their answers.

Completions

Students complete sentences in ways that are personally meaningful. ***Que feriez-vous ?*** (see Chapter 15, p. 380) asks students to tell what they would do in various situations.

1. S'il n'y avait pas de cours aujourd'hui...
2. Si j'avais besoin d'une nouvelle voiture...
3. Si je pouvais être une autre personne...
4. Si j'avais soixante ans...
5. Si j'étais millionnaire...
   etc.

Students can complete the statements as homework or in class; in either case, prior preparation is helpful. Students can offer their reactions in response to teacher questions (e.g., **S'il n'y avait pas de cours aujourd'hui, que feriez-vous?**) or in small-group activities where the students elicit information from each other. Depending on the abilities of individual students or the class in general, completion of items can be used for making short statements or as the basis for longer sentences with explanations and elaborations.

Sentence builders

Students combine items from different columns to make complete sentences that describe their opinions on various topics or typical activities (see Chapter 7, p. 164).

Exemple   Hier j'ai invité des amis à dîner.

		envoyer une lettre à
hier		mes parents
lundi		dîner chez mes amis
mardi		manger au restaurant
mercredi	j'ai	avoir un examen difficile
jeudi	mes amis ont	étudier le français
vendredi	mes amis et moi, nous avons	inviter des amis à dîner
samedi	?	regarder un film à la télé
dimanche		écouter de la musique
la semaine dernière		préparer le dîner [etc.]
		?

Instructors can ask students to volunteer statements about their activities or can elicit responses by using one of the columns given (**Qu'est-ce que vous avez fait mercredi?** or **Est-ce que vous avez regardé un film à la télé vendredi? Et vos amis, qu'est-ce qu'ils ont fait?**) After students have volunteered their statements (or the teacher has asked questions), class members can be asked to remember who did various activities (e.g., **Qui a invité des amis à dîner dimanche?**).

Using scales

Students use a scale or a continuum to indicate the degree to which they like something or agree with an idea or opinion (see Chapter 9, p. 208).

1 = très important   3 = pas très important
2 = assez important   4 = sans importance

Exemple   La sécurité de l'emploi est assez importante pour moi.

1. _____la sécurité de l'emploi
2. _____un salaire assez élevé
3. _____de bonnes conditions de travail
4. _____des horaires souples
5. _____la liberté et la place à l'initiative personnelle
etc.

Students can give their preference orally and ask for the opinion of another student in small-group or whole-class situations (**Un salaire assez élevé est très important pour moi. Et pour toi ? Est-ce que c'est important aussi ?**). In addition, instructors can solicit student opinions by transforming these items into direct questions (e.g., **La sécurité de l'emploi, est-ce important pour vous ?**). This activity can also be transformed into a ranking activity where students are asked to rank a list of items in the order of their preference. They can then compare and contrast their choices with those of other students (**Mon premier choix est la liberté et la place à l'initiative personnelle. Quel est ton premier choix ?**). Note that as soon as comparatives and superlatives have been presented, they can be used instead of ordinal numbers.

Planning a course syllabus

As already indicated, *Invitation* consists of eighteen chapters plus a *Chapitre préliminaire* and a final chapter called *Invitation à la lecture*. In some semester programs, the content of *Invitation* can be divided equally so that nine chapters are covered each semester. In a quarter system, six chapters can be assigned for each quarter. Because of the way the chapters are designed, however, coverage can be organized and altered in many ways. In a quarter system, for example, one may elect to teach seven chapters the first quarter, six the second, and five the third so that supplementary readers may be added in the second and third quarters. In order to achieve more in-depth mastery or to include additional cultural or reading material, the content can also be spread over a greater number of terms in both semester and quarter programs. It is also possible to omit one or more of the last chapters of the book or to skip sections of the later chapters. A large number of structures have been included; those of lesser importance have, however, been placed in the later chapters so that their omission from the curriculum will not create serious problems.

Sample lesson plans

The sample lesson plans in this section suggest ways in which the material in specific chapters of *Invitation* can be organized and presented. Ultimately, of course, lesson planning, like other aspects of classroom organization, will depend upon the individual needs of the instructor and the class.

Whether lesson plans are prepared in great detail or consist simply of a list of activities and exercises to be covered, it will be important to keep in mind certain guidelines :

1. Plan specific objectives for each class period.
2. Plan activities that relate to course objectives. If the course emphasizes conversation, a correspondingly large portion of class activities should be geared toward developing speaking skill.

3. Plan a variety of activities that sustain students' interest and that give them the opportunity to develop the skills emphasized in the course.
4. Involve students as much as possible. Teaching a skill course implies that students should use that skill rather than talk — or be told — about it.
5. Plan to systematically review material from the chapter you are working in and from previous chapters.

The sample lesson plans that follow are prepared for a four-skill course that meets four times a week. They do not include specific suggestions for use of the supplementary course materials. The first set of plans includes the preliminary chapter and Chapter 1 and covers six days of instruction. The second set of plans deals with Chapter 12, which is an all-French chapter. The third set of plans is for Chapter 17, chosen because students are more sophisticated linguistically at this point and capable of more open-ended and creative classroom activities. The textbook assignments have been kept relatively short in the third set of plans to allow for supplementary cultural or literary readings.

For classes that meet three days a week or five days a week, the division of course material will obviously be different. Suggestions for emphasizing or deemphasizing given sections according to class needs have been discussed in the preceding section. General guidelines — for those who have to condense the course material and for those who, contrariwise, have more time — follow the sample lesson plans.

Chapitre préliminaire

First day

1. Explain course goals, evaluation procedures, organization of the book (including appendix material), course syllabus, and other administrative matters.
2. Call roll, having students respond **présent** or **présente**.
3. Greet a student by saying **Bonjour, monsieur** or **mademoiselle** and shaking hands. Have the student greet you in turn. Greet several students in this way and then have them greet each other.
4. Help students get to know each other by giving your name and asking a student his or her name (**Je m'appelle... Et vous ?**). After students are familiar with the pattern, go around the class until each student has given his or her name.
5. Begin teaching the words for classroom objects in the *Dans la salle de classe* section. Point out various objects and have students repeat each word. If students catch on rapidly, ask **Qu'est-ce que c'est ?** and see if they can provide the appropriate classroom object.
6. Begin teaching the numbers 1 – 20 by having students repeat them. If time is available, count different classroom objects or students present.
7. Begin teaching the alphabet by having students repeat in sequence the letters of the alphabet.

Assignment   *Chapitre préliminaire*

Second day

1. As a warm-up activity, greet students and have them greet each other by using the informal **ça va** pattern.
2. Have students ask each other in turn what their names are and how they are. Go around the class until each student has volunteered this information.
3. Finish teaching the alphabet and then spell the names given in the **alphabet français** section and have students write down what they hear. Briefly review accents in French and then have students spell French names (including some with accents such as **Thérèse, Hélène, Joël,** etc.). If students are ready, have them spell their own names.
4. Review (and or finish presenting) numbers from 1 – 20 and complete the related activities in the numbers section of this chapter.
5. Have students identify various classroom objects by asking **Qu'est-ce que c'est ?**
6. Have students repeat the useful classroom expressions and then complete the related activity (*Dans la salle de classe*).
7. Ask students to give you in English the names of countries where French is spoken. Write the equivalent on the board. Then refer students to the map of the French-speaking world and have them locate those countries and note other countries where French is spoken.
8. Ask students to give the gist of the newspaper headlines presented in *Faites le premier pas*. Point out the usefulness of cognates and contextual guessing as well as the need to avoid word-for-word translations. Then tell students they can make use of cognates and contextual guessing as they listen to the passage that they have for the next class meeting. Read them the *Mise en scène* for the first chapter and have them volunteer what they have understood about the conversation.

Assignment   Mise en scène, Compréhension, and Les mots et la vie, Chapitre 1.

Chapitre 1 — Préférences

First day

1. As a warm-up activity, greet several students and have them greet each other and ask how they are. An alternative warm-up would be a quick review of classroom objects, perhaps having students point at various objects, asking other students to identify them.
2. To begin the *Mise en scène*, ask the *Compréhension* questions orally, having students respond **C'est vrai** or **c'est faux** and correct the sentence if it is false. Then have students repeat the sentences in chorus and then individually so that they become familiar with the vocabulary and structures used. (Optional : Dictate several sentences from the *Mise en scène* and have students check their sentences.)

3. Review the vocabulary for school subjects (*Les mots et la vie, A, Qu'est-ce que vous étudiez ?*). Have students repeat the words and ask for an English equivalent from time to time to ensure meaningful processing. Then have students tell what subjects they are currently studying.

4. Review the vocabulary in *Les mots et la vie (B, Activités)*. Then name an activity and have students indicate whether or not they like or dislike the activity (**écouter la radio ? Moi, j'adore écouter la radio**). Then have students work in small groups and ask each other *Qu'est-ce que vous aimez et qu'est-ce que vous détestez ?* If time permits, complete *Les mots et la vie, C, Activités et préférences*.

5. Have students work in small groups and rewrite the *Mise en scène* by using words from the *Les mots et la vie* section. (Optional : Encourage students to ask for other words that they might like to use in rewriting the conversation.) Ask students to hand in their work so that it can be checked informally.

6. Begin the pronunciation section by completing section A (syllabication).

7. Present definite articles deductively or inductively, using *Préparation A* to introduce the forms.

Assignment   *Présentation* of the definite article, *Préparation*, and *Communication et vie pratique*.

Second day

1. As a warm-up activity, read one or several students' rewritten conversations for listening practice, adding several comprehension questions.

2. Begin the definite article section by asking students what the definite articles are and how they are used in French. Then complete *Préparation A (Les études universitaires)* as a class activity with books closed. After that, go over *Préparation B (Opinions)* as a class activity, assigning the roles of Véronique and Gérard. Give them the first word and have Véronique respond affirmatively while Gérard takes the opposite point of view. (Optional : Prepare copies of correct answers and divide students into groups of three. The group leader is given the correct answers and helps the students who are playing the roles of Véronique and Gérard.)

3. Complete *Communication A (Réactions)* as a class activity with books closed. Give a word and have students offer their opinions by using one of the verb forms suggested. Then do *Communication B (Questions)* by having students first create the questions as a class and then ask each other these questions in groups of two and record their partner's answers on interview sheets.

4. Include personalized writing practice by having students (individually or in small groups) create slogans for famous people or for different groups of people (e.g., politicians, professors, students). Students can work at the board or in their seats. Introduce **Vive** and **À bas**.

5. Pick a good student and model the *C'est votre tour* role-play with him or her. Then ask other students to role-play the situation with you. If time permits, have students role-play the situation in small groups. (Optional: Give each student who is answering questions the names of two or three buildings or types of buildings on your campus to use in the role-play.)
6. Complete the next section of the *Prononciation et orthographe* section (B, vowel enunciation).
7. Briefly present first conjugation verbs and negation.

Assignment Les verbes de la première conjugaison et la négation. Write out *Communication et vie pratique B (Faisons connaissance)* in first conjugation verbs and *Communication et vie pratique B (Pas moi !)* in negative.

Third day

1. As a warm-up activity, give statements about your own interests and ask students to give their preferences (for example, **Moi, j'aime les sports. Et vous ?**)
2. Complete the Instructor's Edition drills for *-er* verbs very rapidly and then ask students to write the forms from memory. Complete *Préparations A* and *B* with books closed. Then go over *Préparation C* with books open.
3. Start working with the negative by first completing the Instructor's Edition drills as a closed-book class activity and then the *Préparation (Contradictions)*. If time permits, give a short listening-comprehension test. Read sentences from *Contradictions* (or others) — putting some in the negative, others in the affirmative — and have students indicate whether the sentence is affirmative or negative.
4. Give a short transformational dictation. Have students write the sentence and then make the indicated changes.
   a. **Je voyage beaucoup.** (Change the subject to **nous** and then put the sentence in the negative.)
   b. **Vous aimez la télévision.** (Change the subject to **je** and then put the sentence in the negative. If desired, ask students to change this statement so that it applies to them personally.)
   c. **Paul déteste faire la cuisine.** (Change the subject to **tu** and then put the sentence in the negative.)
5. Complete the *Communication (Rarement ou souvent)* for first conjugation verbs by having students ask others how often they do different activities. Encourage students to use the negative in giving their ideas. Then ask students to volunteer information they remember about the activities of members of the class.
6. Complete the pronunciation section.
7. Have students complete the *C'est votre tour* for the negative in small groups. As preparation, have students first think of different activities they might ask questions about and then practice answering these questions in the negative.

8. Briefly introduce the interrogative and, if time permits, go over *Préparation A (N'est-ce pas ?)*. If desired, introduce the new vocabulary from the *Intégration et perspectives* reading and read it aloud to students.

Assignment   *L'interrogatif* (write out *Préparation B*) and *Intégration et perspectives* reading (write out *Compréhension*). Complete *Communication et vie pratique A* and *B*.

Fourth day

1. As a warm-up activity, ask personal questions integrating grammar previously studied or read the listening comprehension passage from the tape program and ask students questions about it.
2. Begin the interrogative section by quickly completing *Préparation A* and *B* as closed-book activities. Then complete *Communication A (Interview)* as a whole-class activity by giving a cue (**aimer danser ?**) and having students make up questions to ask other students (**Est-ce que tu aimes danser ?**).
3. Have students complete the *C'est votre tour* in small groups after asking them to come up with a variety of questions to ask in this situation.
4. Ask the comprehension questions on the *Intégration et perspectives* reading. Then dictate several sentences from the reading and have students check their sentences.
5. Discuss briefly the *notes culturelles*, showing slides of Paris and / or other areas mentioned if available.
6. Then have several students introduce themselves to the class using their written homework as a guide. If time permits, have students introduce themselves to each other in small groups.
7. After completing *Communication A (Petites announces)*, have students role-play *Communication C (Situation)* in small groups.

Assignment   *Mise en scène, Les mots et la vie,* and *Le verbe être et l'utilisation des adjectifs (Chapitre 2)*

Chapitre 12 — L'apparence

First day

1. Review the clothing and color vocabulary presented in *Les mots et la vie* by having students imagine that they are at an outdoor café and are describing people they see (clothing, hair, eyes, etc.). Then have them describe each other.
2. Ask students the comprehension questions on the *Mise en scène* dialogue; then ask them to repeat these conversations in chorus and / or in small groups. Then have students role-play the second activity in *Les mots et la vie,* using in particular the vocabulary given in *Les commentaires et les compliments*.

3. Briefly discuss the *Notes culturelles*, having students give the names of French and American fashion designers. If time permits, have students look through current French magazines for ads of various fashion products. They then describe the clothing or other products shown in the ads.

4. Begin the indirect object pronouns by completing the Instructor's Edition drills and the *Préparation* section, using as many exercises as necessary for student mastery.

5. Have students complete *Communication A (Interview)* by working in small groups and asking each other questions. Have students report back orally the results of their conversations. If time permits, complete *Communication B (J'ai une autre suggestion)*.

6. Have students repeat in chorus and dramatize the *Mise en situation*. Then model the role-play with a student in the class and then have students role-play the *C'est votre tour* situation in small groups. (Optional : Prepare lists that contain the names of members of imaginary French families and their friends (ages, interests) that students can use as a basis for the role-play.)

7. Introduce inductively or deductively the comparative and **mettre** for the next class meeting.

Assignment Les verbes conjugués comme mettre and Le comparatif.

Second day

1. As a warm-up, give a series of statements and have students tell whether the person has made the right choice of clothing or not (e.g., **Marie-Louise va faire du camping ce week-end; elle va porter une robe rose**). Activity A in *Les mots et la vie* could also be used here.

2. Begin working with **mettre** verbs by completing the Instructor's Edition drills and *Préparation A (Qu'est-ce qu'on va mettre ?)* with books closed. Then use the sentences in *Préparation B (Promesses)* for a short dictation. Students can then work in small groups to make lists of five things that they would permit their students to do and five that they would not allow them to do (*Communication A, On change de rôle*). Sentences can be shared orally or placed on the board as a follow-up activity.

3. If students have no questions on the comparative, have them complete *Préparations A (Paris et la province)* and *B (Le nouveau prof)* and then work in small groups to go over *Préparation C (Évian ou Vittel ?)*. A student leader is given the correct answers to *Préparation C* so that student responses can be checked for accuracy.

4. Have students interview each other in small groups by using the questions in *Communication A (Questions / interview)* and taking notes on their partner's answers for a brief exchange of information after the interviews are completed.

5. With books open, have students create sentences comparing the different items in *Communication B (Comparaisons)*. Cue words could also be given orally or placed on the board with student books closed. If time permits, ask students to give items that they would like to compare and have the class make up sentences.

6. After choral and individual repetition and dramatization of the *Mise en situation* given for the comparative, have students role-play the situation given in *C'est votre tour*.

7. Present inductively or deductively the superlative.

Assignment Le superlatif (Write out *Communication A* and *C*; also prepare in writing five questions to ask in the game described in the *C'est votre tour* section).

Third day

1. As a warm-up, give comparative sentences and ask students to agree or disagree with the statements (e.g., **Le français est plus facile que les maths**).

2. Give a short dictation on the superlative, using the sentences from *Préparation A (Vendeur aux Galeries Lafayette)*: e.g., **Nous avons de bons prix. Nous avons les meilleurs prix.** Then complete *Préparations B (Paris)* and *C (Le chou-chou du prof)* orally with books closed.

3. Have students complete *Communication A (À votre avis)* in small groups, with instructions to note their partner's answers on interview sheets so that a class tally of answers can be made as a follow-up activity. Use the answers to encourage students to discuss the merits of various choices: e.g., **Mais non! New York n'est pas aussi beau que San Francisco. San Francisco est la plus belle ville des États-Unis.**

4. Use *Communication B (Le plus et le moins)* as a whole-class activity, again encouraging students to explain and discuss their responses.

5. Have students work together to begin making a list of **"les meilleurs aspects de la vie universitaire"** that they might give to a new student. If time permits, have students share their ideas.

6. Have students separate into two to four teams to play the game described in the *C'est votre tour* section. Begin by asking instructor-prepared questions and then ask students to ask the questions that they have prepared for today's homework.

Assignment Intégration et perspectives (reading, comprehension, and *Communication et vie pratique C (Portraits)*.

Last day

1. Read the statements in *Communication et vie pratique C (Vérité ou chauvinisme)* for the superlative and ask students to indicate whether they agree or disagree with the statements.
2. To evaluate student comprehension of the reading *(Mannequin ou maçon)* have students describe Laurence (age, interests, jobs, etc.). Then discuss the questions in *Communication et vie pratique A (Opinions)*.
3. Dictate several sentences from this reading and have students check their work.
4. Have students discuss the information given in the *Notes culturelles*. Ask them to tell the government position responsible for women's issues, the percentage of women in the active work force, the percentage of women in various types of jobs, etc.
5. Have students role-play the situation described in *Communication B (Description)*. One student will play the role of the **agent de police;** one or two others the person being interviewed. Give each group of interviewees a picture of the "suspect" that they can use in the role-play.
6. Complete *Communication et vie pratique D (Les opposés)* by having students write down items about the town where they are living.
7. Ditto or make photo copies of a short written paragraph that describes an illustration or photo of an individual (also included on the copy). Have them elaborate and expand upon the description using the vocabulary they have learned about appearance, clothing, etc.

Lesson 17 — L'Humour et les arts

First day

1. To evaluate student comprehension of the reading about Bretécher, go over the *Compréhension* or ask students to describe Bretécher and her work. Have them describe (or give a **"monologue intérieur"**) for the Bretécher cartoon included in this chapter.
2. Begin discussing the *Notes culturelles* and show samples of paintings by well-known French artists; ask students to describe both the content of the painting and their reaction to it.
3. Have students ask each other the questions in *Les mots et la vie A (Interview)* in small groups; have them prepare a written summary of the conversation.
4. Have students repeat in chorus and in small groups the *Mise en situation* for the subjunctive with impersonal expressions. Have them identify the examples of the subjunctive contained in the conversation. Then have them complete as many of the *Préparation* exercises as necessary to assess whether they understand this topic. They can then work at their seats or at the board and write out *Communication A (Décisions)*.

5. Have students complete the role-play in the *C'est votre tour*. If available, bring in the entertainment page from a French magazine to use in completing the activity.

Assignment   *Le subjonctif avec les verbes de volition* (write out *Préparation C* and *Communication A*) and *Les pronoms démonstratifs* (write out *Communication A*)

Second day

1. Use *Les mots et la vie B (Connaissez-vous la musique?)* as a warm-up activity. Then play samples of French classical music as a point of departure for a brief discussion about the *Notes culturelles*.
2. Complete the *Préparation* activities (as needed) for the subjunctive and *Communication (Êtes-vous d'accord?)*. Then repeat and dramatize the *Mise en situation* in chorus and in small groups.
3. Ask students to volunteer their answers for *Communication A (Préférences)*; if they seem to be having difficulty, go back over Instructor's Edition drills and *Préparation* exercises as necessary. Repeat and dramatize the *Mise en situation* for demonstratives.
4. Divide the class into two groups. The first group will subdivide into groups of two and will enact the *C'est votre tour* (subjunctive); the second half of the class (also in groups of two) will complete the role-play for demonstratives. After they have worked on the role-plays, select two or three from each group to present their conversations to the class. The other students will listen and answer questions on the role-plays.

Assignment   *Les pronoms possessifs* (write out *Préparation A*)

Third day

1. Have students work in small groups to complete *Communication C (Une soirée musicale)* in the *Intégration et perspectives* section. Give them a limited amount of time to make their decision and ask them to report back their choice to the class.
2. Review the uses of the subjunctive by completing a transformational dictation that requires choosing between the subjunctive or the indicative. For example, **il est possible que Chantal aille au concert ce soir**; change to **il est probable**, then **je ne suis pas sûre que**, etc.
3. Complete *Préparation* exercises for the possessive pronouns as necessary before asking students to work in small groups to answer the questions in the *Questions / interview*.
4. Have students repeat and dramatize the *Mise en situation* for possessives before completing the role-play in the *C'est votre tour* section. Give the

"neat" person a list of items that the "messy" roommate leaves lying round. It is then up to the "accused" to defend himself or herself.

Assignment *Intégration et perspectives* reading (*Comment va le cinéma français ?*); have students complete the *Compréhension* and the *Et vous, aimez-vous le cinéma* activity that follows the *Compréhension*.

Last day

1. Give selected students a card with one of the survey questions on it. These students circulate, asking other students their question. They then give a brief oral report of the results of the survey. While not being interviewed, students can be asked to prepare comprehension questions to ask about the reading and the *Notes culturelles*.
2. Discuss **le cinéma français** by having students ask each other the questions that they have prepared on the *Compréhension* for the reading and the *Notes culturelles*. If available, have students examine and answer questions about the movie page of a French newspaper or magazine.
3. Ask the questions in the *Testez vos connaissances* activity in the *Intégration et perspectives* section. If possible, show examples of the work of some of the individuals included in the test. Then give students a few minutes to prepare their own cultural questions to ask the instructor or other students.
4. Read the listening comprehension passage from the tape program, asking students to retell what they have heard. If time permits, give them the tape program dictation and have them check their work in class.
5. Use the remaining time for chapter review.

Classes meeting three times a week

Because *Invitation* is a book of options, its organization allows instructors to delete or deemphasize sections, exercises, and activities without harming the logic of the instructional process. In a four-skill course meeting three times a week, it may be necessary, for example, to spend less time discussing the *Mise en scène* and *Intégration et perspectives* readings and to assign them instead for out-of-class reading. Instructors will, on the other hand, need to devote proportionally more class time to working with the grammar concepts.

If laboratory facilities are available, much of the manipulative practice of each grammar topic can be completed outside class, allowing more class time to develop the student's ability to communicate. If not, instructors may wish to make a judicious selection of *Préparation* and *Communication et vie pratique* activities to be prepared as homework. In addition, it is possible to delete all or portions of the later chapters in the book, thus allowing students to progress through the remaining material at a more leisurely pace.

Classes meeting five days a week

Under such a system, a more in-depth coverage of the different sections of the book will be possible. Many of the optional activities and follow-up suggestions given in the marginal notes of the Instructor's Edition can be implemented. In addition, the instructor can provide more opportunities to develop listening, reading, writing, and speaking skills as well as to discuss in greater detail the *Notes culturelles*.

Instructor's Edition

Invitation
THIRD EDITION

Contextes, culture
et communication

Gilbert A. Jarvis
The Ohio State University

Thérèse M. Bonin
The Ohio State University

Diane W. Birckbichler
The Ohio State University

HOLT, RINEHART AND WINSTON, INC.
New York • Chicago • San Francisco • Philadelphia
Montreal • Toronto • London • Sydney • Tokyo

Publisher • Vincent Duggan
Acquisitions Editor • Laura McKenna
Developmental Editor • Jacqueline Rebisz
Production Manager • Lula Als / Priscilla Taguer
Design Supervisor • Renée Davis
Text Design and Layout • York Production Services
Composition and Camera Work • York Graphic Services
Printing and Binding • Von Hoffmann Press, Inc.

Photographic credits appear at the end of the book.

Library of Congress Cataloging-in-Publication Data
Jarvis, Gilbert A.
    Invitation : contextes, culture et communication / Gilbert A. Jarvis, Thérèse M. Bonin, Diane W. Birckbichler. — 3rd. ed.
    p.   cm.
    English and French.
    Rev. ed. of : Invitation : French for communication and cultural awareness / Gilbert A. Jarvis... [et al.]. 2nd ed. 1984.
    Includes index.
    ISBN 0-03-004973-3
    1. French language — Textbooks for foreign speakers — English. 2. French language — Grammar — 1950- I. Bonin, Thérèse M. II. Birckbichler, Diane W. III. Invitation. IV. Title.
PC2129.E5J37   1988
448.2'421 — dc19
ISBN 0-03-004973-3 Student Edition   87-28660
Instructor's Edition : ISBN 0-03-004974-1   CIP

ISBN 0-03-004973-3

8 9 0 1   032   9 8 7 6 5 4 3 2

Preface

Invitation : Contextes, culture et communication, a basic French textbook, is a vehicle for the development of proficiency in French. Despite this practical goal, it has not lost sight of the value of language study in helping people understand the meaning of being human, the richness and diversity of cultures, and the wonder of the communicative process. The third edition retains the successful features and conceptualization of the first two editions while incorporating new developments in learning theory, sociolinguistics, and language curriculum design. It has also benefited from the insights and recommendations of the many students and instructors who have used previous editions.

In presenting the basic patterns of French, *Invitation* capitalizes on the pedagogical efficiency that structural patterns provide the learner. At the same time, it immediately engages the learner in functional use of French in contexts that relate the patterns to genuine communicative situations and needs.

Invitation is designed for use in two-year and four-year colleges and universities and is equally suitable for semester and quarter systems. It accommodates students who benefit from considerable practice as well as those who prefer the cognitive shortcuts provided by concise descriptions of language structure. Accompanying the student textbook are an Instructor's Edition, a tape program, and a combined workbook and laboratory manual (*Invitation à écouter et à écrire*).

The third edition of *Invitation* is a true revision. The components entitled *Mise en scène, Les mots et la vie, Mise en situation,* and *Communication et vie pratique* all represent new elements and reconceptualizations of second-edition components. Hundreds of language functions are depicted in the *Mise en situation* conversations that accompany each structural topic. Thus, the student gains the organizational efficiency provided by awareness of grammar and immediately sees the functional role of the new pattern in diverse authentic situations. New learning activities have been added; grammar has been streamlined and resequenced to enhance communicative proficiency.

Invitation is unique in that it provides, for every grammar concept, a sequence of practice that leads the student from simple manipulative drills through practice within authentic contexts to meaningful and communicative use of the concept in everyday communication situations. The meaningful use of French is not relegated to end-of-chapter personalized questions or to drills disguised as communication; it is present on every page. Instead of promising students that they will be able to communicate someday, *Invitation* creates the opportunity to communicate immediately.

Invitation also offers insights into French-speaking cultures and an understanding and appreciation of differences and similarities among individuals and cultures in a pluralistic, interdependent world. Cultural content is not limited to a few cultural notes but is integrated throughout the text.

Each student enrolls in a French class with his or her own purposes, goals, and interests. Each instructor likewise has instructional goals that, within the context of a particular course and school, mean "learning French." *Invitation* has been carefully engineered to accommodate this diversity. It is a textbook that maximizes options.

Organization of the Book

The third edition of *Invitation* has a preliminary chapter, eighteen regular chapters, a final chapter that focuses on the passé simple *(Invitation à la lecture),* and appendixes. Each of the eighteen chapters includes the following sections.

MISE EN SCÈNE

Introduction : These introductory conversational passages of varying subject matter and format (e.g., dialogues, interviews, newscasts, monologues) provide diverse contexts for the development of speaking skills and introduce the general chapter theme. New noncognate vocabulary is glossed in the margin to ensure immediate comprehension of unfamiliar words.

Compréhension : The comprehension check evaluates the student's understanding of the introductory passage.

Notes culturelles : Cultural topics related to the chapter theme and the introductory passage are discussed in this section. The cultural notes are in English in the first seven chapters of the book and in French thereafter.

Les mots et la vie : This section introduces new vocabulary centered around a topic that is related to the chapter theme. Varied communication activities involve the student in the active use of this newly presented vocabulary.

EXPLORATIONS

Each chapter introduces four grammar topics that are presented, practiced, and expanded upon in the following phases.

Présentation : This section introduces the grammar topic and its functional use and presents sample sentences that illustrate the structure.

Mise en situation : The *Mise en situation* conversations that accompany each structural topic not only show how a particular structure can be used in a real-life setting but also introduce numerous language functions, cultural settings, and conversational patterns that can be used by students.

Préparation : The grammar is then practiced in structured, lifelike situations. Many exercises are set in cultural contexts, thereby reinforcing the authenticity of the language used and its potential value for real-life communication while providing, at the same time, insights into francophone cultures. The Instructor's Edition contains simple mechanical drills for each topic.

Communication et vie pratique : The varied formats in this section give students the opportunity to communicate about a wide variety of topics. In addition to the personal communication of some formats, students are also given different types of survival situations and role-plays that enable them to see how well they would get along in a French-speaking country.

INTÉGRATION ET PERSPECTIVES

Lecture : This reading recombines and integrates the grammar and vocabulary used in the chapter and provides additional cultural and / or human interest perspectives. It also provides reading practice and introduces new words in context. *Compréhension* and *Notes culturelles* sections follow this end-of-chapter reading.

Communication et vie pratique : This final section presents communication and survival situations that are related to the chapter theme and which require students to further integrate and use in new contexts the language they have already learned. The use of realia and authentic documents and the inclusion of survival and role-playing situations are an important aspect of these activities. The range of survival and communication situations and the varied cultural settings in which they take place help develop the student's range of expression.

PRONONCIATION ET ORTHOGRAPHE

The most significant features of spoken French (and their written counterparts) are described in each of the first ten chapters. Practice of both individual sounds and longer sentences containing critical sounds is included.

VOCABULAIRE DU CHAPITRE

Each chapter is followed by a list of vocabulary words intended for active use in that chapter and in subsequent chapters. The lists contain the most important noncognate and cognate vocabulary used in the lesson or page references for thematically grouped vocabulary. Where appropriate, the vocabulary lists are organized in thematic clusters (e.g., sports, food).

Supplementary Materials

STUDENT WORKBOOK / LABORATORY MANUAL AND TAPE PROGRAM

The combined workbook and laboratory manual (*Invitation à écouter et à écrire*) contains written and oral activities for each of the book's eighteen chapters. The first half of each chapter contains writing activities ; the second half oral exercises.

The workbook component has been designed to expand the student's ability to communicate in writing. Each chapter of *Invitation* has accompanying exercises in the student workbook section of this manual. A series of exercises and communication activities ranging from simple to more complex is coordinated with each section of the chapter and with each structural topic.

The tape program and laboratory section of the manual have been designed to provide students with the opportunity to practice their oral skills outside class. Each chapter in *Invitation* has accompanying taped material which includes : (1) readings of the *Mise en scène* passages ; (2) two or three activities for each grammar topic ; (3) readings of the *Mise en situation* conversations; (4) a listening comprehension passage based on the chapter theme that integrates chapter grammar and vocabulary. In addition, a pronunciation section (Chapters 1 – 10), a short thematic dictation, and a series of thematically related personal questions are included.

Acknowledgments

Special thanks are owed to the students, instructors, and teaching assistants at The Ohio State University who have used the first two editions of *Invitation* and whose reactions and comments have been helpful in this revision. Among those we wish to thank especially are Patricia Myhren and Vicki Steinberg. Additional thanks are owed to the native speakers of French who were consulted on various language and cultural matters — in particular, Professor Micheline Besnard, Martine André, Céline Phillibert, The Ohio State University, and the exchange students from the École supérieure de commerce de Nantes, especially Emmanuel Chesneau. Professor Josette Wilburn of Dennison University also provided many valuable comments and suggestions.

We would also like to thank the following reviewers, whose comments helped to shape this revision of *Invitation*: Wendy Allen, St. Olaf College; Elizabeth Anglin, University of Southern Mississippi; Betsy Barnes, University of Minnesota; Richard Barnett, Chatham College; Lillian Bulwa, Northeastern University; Dominick DeFilippis, Wheeling College; Nathaniel Dubin, St. John's University; Jon Hassel, University of Arkansas; Claudine Hastings, Golden West College; Denise Jones, University of Southwestern Louisiana; John Joseph, University of Maryland; Jean Knecht, Texas Christian University; Laurey K. Martin, University of Wisconsin; Mary Jo Muratore, University of Missouri; Robert O'Reilly, Syracuse University; Fred Toner, Montana State University; Benné Willerman, University of Texas at Austin.

Table des matières

TROIS   La famille et les possessions   60

QUATRE   En vacances   82

CINQ   La vie quotidienne : la nourriture et les repas   104

SIX   La vie quotidienne : logement et activités   128

SEPT   Le temps passe   152

HUIT   La pluie et le beau temps   178

NEUF   Choix et décisions   204

DIX   Français ! Achetez et
consommez !   234

ONZE   Santé et habitudes personnelles   260

DOUZE   L'apparence   284

TREIZE   Le passé et les souvenirs   310

Saint-Pierre-et-Miquelon

Sénégal

Belgique

Martinique

Québec

Découverte du monde francophone

Learning French will allow you to communicate with people in many parts of the world. French is the main language of 130 million people and is widely spoken in north and west Africa, southeast Asia, and the Caribbean. It is also an official language of Belgium, Switzerland, Luxembourg, and Canada. In Canada alone, there are more than five million French speakers in the province of Quebec. In the United States, there are two and one-half million people who speak French, especially in the Northeast and in Louisiana.

French was the language of diplomacy for centuries. Today it is an official language of the United Nations and of many other international organizations. It is also the first language of the European Common Market. The world map on pages 4–5 shows those countries in which French is an official or an important language.

Have students name in English as many French-speaking countries as they can. Give the French equivalent of these countries and have students pronounce them. Students can then find these countries on the world map.

3

Le Français dans le monde

Give the number of a country and have students give the name and locate it on the map.

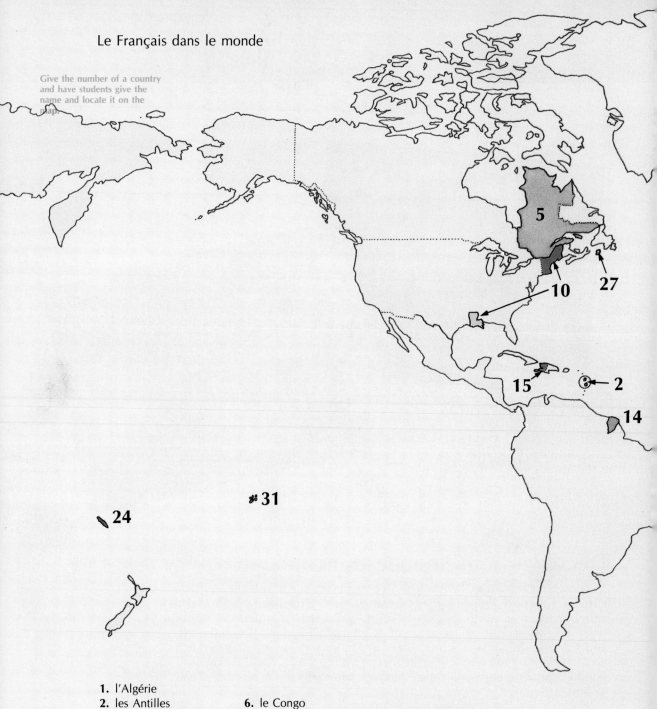

1. l'Algérie
2. les Antilles
   (la Guadeloupe,
   la Martinique,
   Saint-Martin)
3. la Belgique
4. le Cameroun
5. le Canada (le Québec)

6. le Congo
7. la Corse
8. la Côte-d'Ivoire
9. le Bénin
10. les États-Unis
    (la Louisiane,
    la Nouvelle-Angleterre)

11. la France
12. le Gabon
13. la Guinée
14. la Guyane
15. Haïti
16. le Burkina Faso

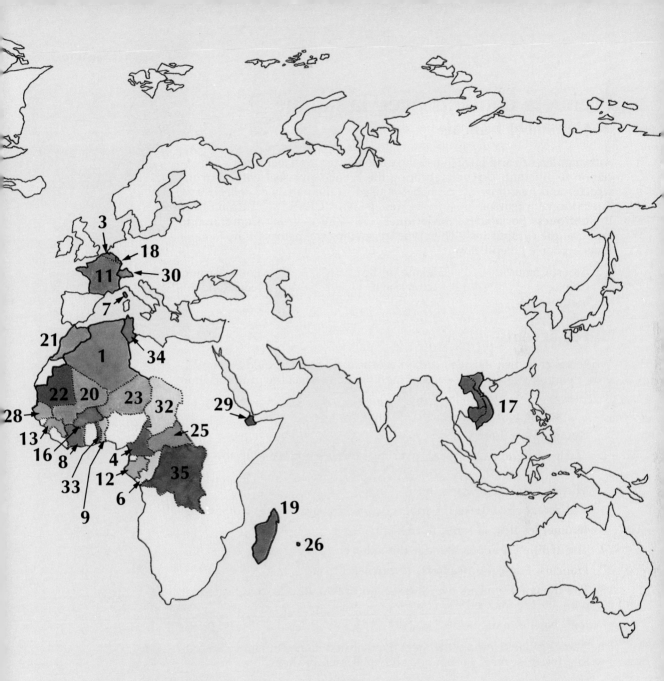

17. l'Indochine
(le Cambodge,
le Laos,
le Viêt-Nam)
18. le Luxembourg
19. Madagascar
20. le Mali
21. le Maroc

22. la Mauritanie
23. le Niger
24. la Nouvelle-Calédonie
25. la République Centrafricaine
26. la Réunion
27. Saint-Pierre-et-Miquelon
28. le Sénégal

29. Djibouti
30. la Suisse
31. Tahiti
32. le Tchad
33. le Togo
34. la Tunisie
35. le Zaïre

5

Premiers contacts avec la langue
✤ L'alphabet français

Although French and English use the same written alphabet, their pronunciation is different. Practice repeating the French alphabet with your instructor and note how the alphabet is used in the names of countries or international organizations (e.g., **les USA, l'URSS — l'Union des Républiques Socialistes Soviétiques, la CEE — la Communauté économique européenne**). Then practice spelling the names of the famous French people given below.

Albert Camus	Simone de Beauvoir	Louis Pasteur
Colette	Victor Hugo	Jean Renoir
Marie Curie	Lafayette	

Have students tell why each of these people are well known; then have them see if they can identify other famous French figures.

✤ Les accents

Written French also includes certain accent marks that should be considered a part of spelling. These accent marks usually affect the pronunciation of the letter with which they appear.

1. The **accent aigu (´)** appears over the vowel **e**:

   Gérard, Véronique

2. The **accent grave (`)** appears over the vowels **e** and **a** and in the word **où**:

   Michèle, Hélène, à Paris, où

3. The **accent circonflexe (^)** appears over the vowels **a, e, i, o,** and **u**:

   Jérôme, les îles, la forêt, le château

4. The **cédille (¸)** appears under the letter **c**:

   François, Françoise, français, le garçon

5. The **tréma (¨)** appears over the second of two vowels to indicate that both are pronounced:

   Joël, Noëlle, naïf

The names given below are the most popular first names in France according to a recent survey. Pronounce and spell each of them.

Filles		**Garçons**	
1. Janine	6. Françoise	1. Daniel	6. Philippe
2. Jacqueline	7. Jeanne	2. René	7. André
3. Nathalie	8. Isabelle	3. Bernard	8. Pierre
4. Catherine	9. Monique	4. Jacques	9. Jean
5. Sylvie	10. Marie	5. Alain	10. Michel

Practice repeating the names of the countries on pages 4–5 with your instructor.

❧Faites le premier pas

What you know about English can help you as you begin to study French. First, see if you can get the general ideas in the following material from a French-Canadian newspaper.

La famille, premier bastion de la société

POLITIQUE CANADIENNE

EDITORIAL
La longue marche du Parti libéral du Québec

$1000 À GAGNER — LOTO BINGO

Petite histoire d'un grand festival

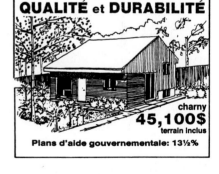

QUALITÉ et DURABILITÉ

charny
45,100$
terrain inclus

Plans d'aide gouvernementale: 13½%

Restauration de la résidence du Gouverneur général

carrières et professions

A good example of the head start that you have in learning French is the large number of words that are similar in French and English. These words (e.g., **famille**, **société**, **festival**, **éditorial**) are called cognates. You may also have noted the need to be flexible when you encounter an unfamiliar word. In the ad for homes, for example, you see the word **terrain**, which would not be the English word used in this context. A synonym that makes more sense in this context is *ground* or *land*. Learning to guess the meanings of words is also important. In the item about Loto Bingo, for example, a noncognate word, **gagner**, appears. In this particular context you know that the idea of winning money is important. Thus, from the context, you can guess that **gagner** means *to win*.

Premiers contacts avec les gens
✿Petites conversations

You can use the following phrases to begin speaking French with your instructor and with other students in your class. Model your teacher's pronunciation of these phrases.

● Two students greet each other and introduce themselves.

MICHELINE	Salut. Je m'appelle Micheline. Et toi?
CLAUDE	Je m'appelle Claude.

Greet and introduce yourself to the person next to you in class.

● Madame Durand greets two students and asks their names.

MADAME DURAND	Bonjour, monsieur. Comment vous appelez-vous?
CLAUDE	Bonjour, madame. Je m'appelle Claude Legrand.
MADAME DURAND	Et vous, mademoiselle? Comment vous appelez-vous?
MICHELINE	Je m'appelle Micheline Dubourg.

Greet your professor and introduce yourself.

● Micheline asks her friends how they are.

MICHELINE	Comment ça va?
CLAUDE	Ça va bien, merci. Et toi?
MICHELINE	Pas très bien. Et toi, Gérard, ça va?
GÉRARD	Assez bien.

Ask another student how she or he is. The student in turn asks how you are.

● Micheline greets Madame Durand and asks how she is.

MICHELINE	Bonjour, madame. Comment allez-vous?
MADAME DURAND	Très bien, merci. Et vous?
MICHELINE	Ça va très bien.

Greet your instructor and ask how he or she is.

- Claude says good-bye to Gérard and indicates that he will see him later.

  CLAUDE   Au revoir. À tout à l'heure.
  GÉRARD   Au revoir.

  Say good-bye to another student and say that you will see him or her later.

- Micheline says good-bye to her instructor who tells her that she will see her tomorrow.

  MICHELINE   Au revoir, madame.
  MADAME DURAND   Au revoir, Micheline. À demain.

  Say good-bye to your instructor and say that you will see him or her tomorrow.

  Faisons connaissance. Use the phrases you have learned to get acquainted with other students and your instructor. For example, you might want to ask another person what his or her name is and how he or she is. You could also greet someone you already know and ask how things are.

Dans la salle de classe

Qu'est-ce que c'est? The following illustration shows objects typically found in a classroom. Name them when your instructor or another student asks you what they are.

Exemple   Qu'est-ce que c'est? → **C'est une chaise.**

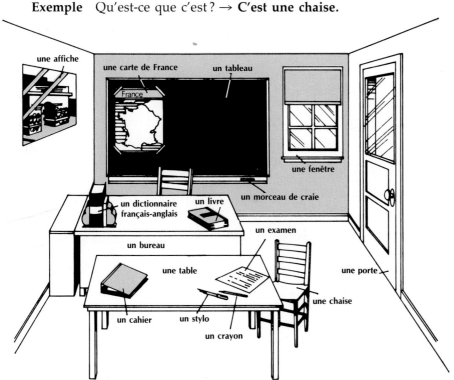

une affiche
une carte de France
un tableau
France
une fenêtre
un morceau de craie
un dictionnaire français-anglais
un livre
un examen
un bureau
une table
une porte
un cahier
un stylo
une chaise
un crayon

Make a ditto or copies of this illustration. Have students write in the names of each of the classroom objects.

✣ Les nombres de 1 à 20

With your instructor, practice repeating the numbers from one to twenty.

1	un	6	six	11	onze	16	seize
2	deux	7	sept	12	douze	17	dix-sept
3	trois	8	huit	13	treize	18	dix-huit
4	quatre	9	neuf	14	quatorze	19	dix-neuf
5	cinq	10	dix	15	quinze	20	vingt

Have students count from 1 to 20 by ones, then by fives. Give a number and have students give the next number. Simple math problems can be done by introducing plus / moins / ça fait. (Un plus trois ? — Ça fait quatre.)

A. Quelques adresses. Read the following addresses.

Exemple   14, rue Berlioz → **quatorze, rue Berlioz**

1. 3, place de Rome
2. 6, rue du Pavillon
3. 8, rue des Remparts
4. 19, rue du Palais
5. 12, boulevard Victor-Hugo
6. 5, rue Pasteur
7. 16, avenue Maréchal-Foch
8. 1, rue Émile-Zola

B. À la librairie. Some students are asking the price at a bookstore near Laval University. Give the salesperson's response.

Exemple   un livre de maths / $15 → **Quinze dollars.**

1. cinq crayons / $1
2. deux cahiers / $4
3. un stylo / $2
4. six affiches / $20
5. un dictionnaire / $18
6. une carte de France / $11

C. Codes postaux. Read aloud the following Canadian postal codes.

1. M3C 2T8
2. V5A 1S6
3. G1G 1P2
4. G1R 3Z3
5. H4T 1E3
6. H3A 1Y2
7. H3A 2J4
8. J3L 2M1
9. M1P 2J7
10. L4C 3G5

✿ Quelques expressions utiles

The following are typical expressions that you and your professor will need to use in class to communicate with each other.

Student comprehension can be checked by having students follow directions given by the instructor (or other students).

Est-ce que vous comprenez?	*Do you understand?*
Oui, je comprends.	*Yes, I understand.*
Non, je ne comprends pas.	*No, I don't understand.*
Je ne sais pas.	*I don't know.*
Répétez, s'il vous plaît.	*Please repeat.*
Qu'est-ce que ça veut dire?	*What does that mean?*
Ça veut dire...	*That means . . .*
Comment dit-on... en français?	*How does one say . . . in French?*
On dit...	*One says . . .*
Épelez ce mot, s'il vous plaît.	*Spell this word, please.*
Merci.	*Thank you.*
De rien.	*You're welcome.*
Allez au tableau.	*Go to the board.*
Écrivez votre nom.	*Write your name.*
Ouvrez votre livre.	*Open your book.*
Fermez votre livre.	*Close your book.*
Écoutez bien.	*Listen well (carefully).*
Asseyez-vous.	*Sit down.*
Levez-vous.	*Stand up.*
Remettez vos devoirs.	*Hand in your homework.*
Pardon.	*Pardon me.*
Excusez-moi.	*Excuse me.*

Dans la salle de classe. What would you or your teacher say in the following situations?

1. You don't understand what your teacher has said.
2. Your teacher wants you to go to the board.
3. You want to ask how to say "computer" in French.
4. You want to say that you don't know the answer to a question.
5. Your teacher wants the class to listen carefully.
6. You want to ask what something means.
7. You want your teacher to repeat something.
8. You want to thank someone.
9. You want someone to sit down.
10. Your teacher wants you to open your book.

CHAPITRE UN

CHAPITRE UN

Communication objectives

Discussing school-related activities and
preferences

1. Naming objects and activities
2. Expressing actions and opinions

3. Disagreeing or making negative
   statements
4. Asking others about their activities and
   preferences

Structures

Les mots et la vie : Activités et préférences

    L'article défini et le nom

    Les verbes de la première conjugaison et
    les pronoms sujets

    La forme négative

    La forme interrogative

Point de départ

Mise en scène

Premiers contacts

Point out that although *le*, *la*, *les* usually mean *the*, no article is used here in English.

Jacqueline and Patrick, both students at the University of Strasbourg, are getting acquainted.

JACQUELINE	*Moi, j'étudie les langues.* Et vous?	I (emphasis) / study / languages
PATRICK	*Tiens, moi aussi!*	Say / me too
JACQUELINE	Vous étudiez *l'anglais*?	English
PATRICK	Oui. *Mais j'aime mieux l'espagnol.*	But / prefer / Spanish
JACQUELINE	Vous aimez *voyager*?	to travel
PATRICK	Oui, *beaucoup.* Mais je déteste les voyages *en* groupe.	a lot / in a
JACQUELINE	*Pas* moi. Moi, j'*aime bien* voyager en groupe. Je *trouve ça* intéressant.	Not / enjoy / find / that

Compréhension. Est-ce que les phrases suivantes sont vraies ou fausses selon les renseignements donnés? *(Are the following statements true or false according to the information given?)*

1. Jacqueline étudie les langues.
2. Patrick étudie aussi les langues.
3. Patrick étudie l'anglais et l'espagnol.
4. Patrick aime mieux l'espagnol.
5. Patrick aime bien les voyages en groupe.
6. Jacqueline déteste les voyages en groupe.

Scramble the sentences of the conversation between Jacqueline and Patrick and have students put them in the appropriate order.

13

Notes culturelles : *Les universités en France*

There are seventy-six universities in France, thirteen of which are located in the Paris area. Three general types of higher education are offered within the university system: (1) Technological studies, which take place in the **instituts de technologie**; (2) Medical or health-related studies; and (3) General university studies, which are composed of three cycles. The first of these cycles takes two years and leads to the **Diplôme d'Études Universitaires Générales (D.E.U.G.)**. This diploma is roughly equivalent to a Bachelor's degree. In this cycle, the curriculum is somewhat general and can be composed of many different combinations of disciplines. In the second cycle, which lasts one or two years, students specialize in one field. This cycle leads to the **licence** or the **maîtrise**, which is similar to a Master's degree. The third cycle (one to five years), which is highly specialized and research-oriented, leads to a **doctorat du 3ᵉ cycle** (similar to a Ph.D.) and a **doctorat d'état**, which is the highest academic degree awarded. In addition to the public university system, many schools and institutes as well as the prestigious and highly selective **Grandes Écoles**, offer advanced training in fields ranging from architecture and business administration to public and military service. The percentage of students in each of these different fields is indicated in the following table.

Étudiants *inscrits* dans les universités : 852 000

Droit	15,8%	Médecine	16,8%
Sciences économiques	6,6%	Pharmacie	4,3%
Sciences	15,2%	Instituts universitaires	
Lettres	30,8%	de technologie	6,1%
Dentaire	1,4%	Divers	3 %

Étudiants inscrits dans des écoles et instituts spécialisés: 259 000
Total: 1.111.000
(Source: *Le Nouveau Guide France*, 1983)

Ask students if they think American students have the same preferences.

enrolled

law

humanities
dentistry

L'université de Paris

You may find it useful to follow these guidelines in using the *Les mots et la vie* section: Present the words and their meanings and have students pronounce each of them; then assign the section (or portions of it) as homework, asking students to complete the assigned activities. In class the next day, go over the meaning and pronunciation of the words, repeat the model sentences, and then have students give their own sentences.

Les mots et la vie: *Activités et préférences*

A. Qu'est-ce que vous étudiez? Tell which of the following subjects you are currently studying.

Exemple   **J'étudie le français, les mathématiques et l'histoire. J'étudie...**

le français
l'anglais
l'espagnol
la géographie
la littérature
l'histoire

la philosophie
la musique
les sciences
les mathématiques
l'informatique *(computer science)*
l'éducation physique

B. Activités. Tell whether you like or dislike the following activities.

Exemple   **J'adore écouter la radio, mais je déteste regarder la télévision.**

For listening practice, prepare a short paragraph in which you describe the courses a French student is taking. Although the description should be simple, students do not need to understand every word as their task is to listen for the courses mentioned. Student responses can also be used in a similar way, e.g., students listen as another student tells what s/he is studying and they write down those courses. If you happen to have the weekly *emploi du temps* of a French high school student, you may want your students to study it as a reading and report back on the major subjects studied.

travailler

étudier la littérature

parler français

marcher

manger

écouter la radio

regarder la télévision

danser

nager

voyager

This activity can also be done with *j'aime bien, j'aime mieux,* and *j'aime beaucoup.*

Have students name one thing they like or dislike and ask another student his or her opinion: *J'adore parler français. Et toi?*, etc.

C. Activités et préférences. Make a list of things you like to do. Another student will use the adjectives below to give his or her reaction to each item on the list.

Exemple — J'aime regarder la télé.
            — Moi aussi. Je trouve ça intéressant.
    ou : — Pas moi. Je trouve ça ennuyeux.

facile *(easy)*   intéressant *(interesting)*   désagréable *(unpleasant)*
agréable *(pleasant)* difficile *(hard)*   ennuyeux *(boring)*

Explorations
⚜ Naming objects and activities
L'article défini et le nom

Présentation

All nouns in French are either masculine or feminine. The French definite article, which corresponds to *the* in English, has different forms for masculine or feminine and singular or plural.

Les articles définis		
	Singular	*Plural*
Masculine before a consonant	le professeur	les professeurs
Feminine before a consonant	la classe	les classes
Masculine or feminine before any	l'étudiant (m)	les étudiants
vowel sound	l'étudiante (f)	les étudiantes

When a masculine or feminine noun begins with a vowel or vowel sound (i.e., a mute **h** as in **histoire**), the **s** in **les** is linked to the next word with a **z** sound : **les amis** — / le zami / . This liaison will be marked with ‿ in the first few chapters to remind you of it.

Note that the plural of most nouns is formed by adding **s**, except when the noun already ends in an **s** or an **x**. Because final consonants are usually not pronounced, the **s** is silent. The article therefore indicates number in spoken language.

A. Useful nouns that relate to campus life are :

l'université (f)   l'étudiante (f) *(student)*
le campus   le professeur
la bibliothèque *(library)*   les sports (m pl)
la résidence universitaire *(dorm)* la note *(grade)*
le restaurant universitaire   les vacances (f pl) *(vacation)*
le cours *(class)*   le week-end
l'étudiant (m) *(student)*   la leçon *(lesson)*

B. The definite article can be used much like *the* in English:

Je regarde **le** livre.
J'aime écouter **la** radio.

It also precedes nouns used in a general sense and abstract nouns.

J'aime **les** sports	*I like sports.*
J'étudie **le** français.	*I am studying French.*
J'aime **la** politique.	*I like politics.*

Repetition : Have students repeat the nouns in Part A of the *Présentation* (and, if time allows, the school subjects in *Les mots et la vie*). *Substitution :* Then give these same nouns without the article, having students provide the noun with its appropriate article (e.g., *livre* → *le livre*). Then give a singular noun and have students provide the plural (e.g., *le professeur* → *les professeurs*).

Mise en situation

Monique is showing a friend around the University of Strasbourg and is telling her what various buildings are. Practice repeating her conversation.

MONIQUE	Regarde. *Voilà* la résidence *où* j'*habite*.
ANNE	Et ça, qu'est-ce que c'est ?
MONIQUE	C'est la bibliothèque.
ANNE	Et ça ?
MONIQUE	C'est le restaurant universitaire.
ANNE	Tu aimes *la vie à* l'université ?
MONIQUE	Oui, assez.

After repeating the conversation chorally, students can practice it in small groups ; the instructor can circulate among groups helping students as needed. Common pronunciation and / or intonation problems can be discussed or worked on with the class where needed.

Here is, There is / where / live

life / at

Students are asked to adapt this conversation in *C'est votre tour*, a role-playing activity in the *Communication et vie pratique* section below.

Préparation

A. Les études universitaires. Several students are telling what subjects they are currently studying. Using the cues provided, tell what they say.

Modèle   histoire → **J'étudie l'histoire.**

1. maths
2. anglais
3. espagnol
4. littérature
5. philosophie
6. géographie
7. musique
8. histoire
9. informatique
10. sciences

During the *premier cycle* (the first two years), university students take courses in several related areas (e.g., *sciences humaines* — *philosophie, histoire, sciences sociales*). After passing the *D.E.U.G.*, they choose an area of specialization.

B. Opinions. Véronique and Gérard, students at the Saint-Martin-d'Hères campus of the University of Grenoble, disagree about various aspects of university life. Tell what each says.

Modèle   campus
  VÉRONIQUE   **J'aime le campus.**
  GÉRARD   **Moi, je déteste le campus.**

1. université
2. professeurs
3. bibliothèque
4. résidences
5. examens
6. étudiants
7. restaurant universitaire
8. cours

Although French universities have traditionally been located in the center of town, many have also built new campuses on the outskirts of town to accommodate increasing numbers of students.

Communication et vie pratique

A. Réactions. Tell how much you like different courses and then ask another student his or her opinion. Use the scale below to help formulate your ideas.

Exemple   maths
— **Moi, j'aime beaucoup les maths. Et vous ?**
— **Moi, je déteste les maths.**

Je déteste	J'aime bien	J'aime beaucoup	J'adore

1. maths
2. anglais
3. sciences
4. philosophie
5. informatique

6. éducation physique
7. littérature
8. musique
9. histoire
10. géographie

B. Questions. Use the following suggestions to ask other students how much they like or dislike various aspects of campus life.

Exemple   université
— **Vous aimez l'université ?**
— **Oui, j'aime beaucoup l'université. Et vous ?**

1. université
2. campus
3. professeurs
4. examens
5. résidences

6. étudiants
7. restaurant universitaire
8. cours
9. week-ends
10. bibliothèque

C'est votre tour. Imagine that a French-speaking friend (played by another student in your class) is asking you about various buildings on your campus. Using the **Mise en situation** as a guide and using vocabulary you know, answer your friend's questions.

✿ Expressing actions and opinions

Les verbes de la première conjugaison et les pronoms sujets

Présentation

Verb endings change according to the subject of the verb. One large group of verbs, called the first conjugation (**la première conjugaison**), has infinitives that end in **-er** and the following endings in the present tense.

travailler			
(I)	je travaille*	(we)	nous travaill**ons**
(you)	tu travaill**es**	(you)	vous travaill**ez**
(he / she / one)	il / elle / on travaille	(they)	ils / elles travaill**ent**

étudier			
(I)	j'étudie	(we)	nous étudi**ons**
(you)	tu étudi**es**	(you)	vous étudi**ez**
(he / she / one)	il / elle / on étudie	(they)	ils / elles étudi**ent**

All the singular forms and the **ils / elles** form have the same pronunciation; the endings add no sound. When the verb begins with a vowel sound, **je** becomes **j'** and **nous, vous, ils, elles** all link to the verb with a **z** sound.

A. Voyager, manger, and other verbs ending in **-ger** are like first conjugation verbs, except that in the **nous** form an **e** is added before the **ons** ending.

> Nous mang**e**ons beaucoup.
> Nous voyag**e**ons en France.

Despite their spelling irregularities (which need not be overemphasized at this point), *voyager* and *manger* are very useful in communication.

B. The subject pronouns shown in the verb chart can replace nouns as the subjects of sentences.

- **Tu** is used to address a close friend, a relative, a child, or a pet; **vous** is used otherwise and always when addressing more than one person.

  Tu danses bien, Pierre!
  Paul et Nicole, **vous** travaillez beaucoup!
  Vous parlez anglais, madame?

- **On** is an impersonal pronoun like *one, they, we,* or *people,* and in conversational French is often used in place of **nous**.

  On parle français en Belgique. *They speak French in Belgium.*
  On aime mieux écouter la radio. *We prefer to listen to the radio.*

---

*The present tense in French can express several meanings: *I work; I am working; I do work.*

- **Il** and **ils** replace masculine nouns; **elle** and **elles**, feminine nouns. A mixed group of masculine and feminine nouns is replaced by **ils**.

Alain et Patrick regardent la télé.   **Ils** regardent la télé.
Monique et Catherine parlent anglais.   **Elles** parlent anglais.
Henri et Julie étudient les maths.   **Ils** étudient les maths.

The meanings of verbs can be modified by adverbs. An adverb usually follows the verb in a sentence.

rarement   *(rarely)*   Ils étudient **rarement**.
quelquefois *(sometimes)*   Nous écoutons **quelquefois** la radio.
souvent   *(often)*   Vous regardez **souvent** la télévision.
tout le temps *(all the time)*   Tu travailles **tout le temps**.
toujours   *(always)*   Ils voyagent **toujours** en groupe.
bien   *(well)*   Elle nage **bien**.
mal   *(badly)*   Il danse **mal**.

Mise en situation

Aline is calling a friend to find out what she is doing. Practice repeating their conversation.

ALINE   *Allô*, Michèle?

MICHÈLE   Oui, j'écoute.

ALINE   *Qu'est-ce que tu fais?*

MICHÈLE   Je travaille.

ALINE   Et Denis?

MICHÈLE   Il travaille *avec* moi.

ALINE   Ah, vous étudiez *ensemble*?

MICHÈLE   Oui, nous étudions souvent ensemble.

Have students note the different spellings of the sound /e/ in this conversation: *j'écoute*; *la télé*; *et*; *étudier*; *étudiez. C'est votre tour* (below in *Communication et vie pratique*) asks students to adapt this conversation and then to role-play it.

Hello (on the phone)

What are you doing?

with

together

Préparation

A. Activités. Solange is telling what she and her friends do. Using the cues provided, tell what she says.

> **Modèle** nous / étudier → **Nous étudions**.

1. Michel / nager
2. je / travailler
3. Paul et Luc / écouter la radio
4. vous / parler anglais
5. tu / étudier
6. nous / regarder la télé
7. on / manger
8. vous / danser

Repetition: Have students repeat the conjugations of *travailler, aimer, étudier*. *Substitution*: (1) Je regarde la télévision. (*vous / tu / nous / Marie / Gérard et Robert*) (2) On parle français. (*je / Marc / vous / tu / je / les étudiants*) (3) Alain et Michel adorent voyager. (*nous / tu / Sylvie et Anne / je / vous*)

B. Et vous? Using the cues provided, tell how much or how often the following people do certain activities.

> **Modèle** Elle parle français. *(well)* → **Elle parle bien français.**

1. Nous regardons la télé. *(often)*
2. Michel travaille. *(all the time)*
3. Tu écoutes la radio. *(sometimes)*
4. Nous parlons ensemble. *(always)*
5. Je voyage en groupe. *(rarely)*
6. Chantal danse. *(well)*

Review: If necessary, remind students that the adverbs used here will follow the verb.

C. Occupations. Based on the illustrations given below, tell what each of the following is doing.

> **Modèle**

Paul et Luc... →
Paul et Luc regardent la télé.

Option: Put visuals on an overhead transparency and complete activity orally.

2. Vous...

3. Nous...

1. Je...

4. Frédérique et Pascale...

5. Tu...

6. Michelle...

Communication et vie pratique

Activity can be done as whole-class activity (with instructor or student asking questions) or in pairs. If completed as a small-group activity, have students record their partner's answers and report back to the class orally or in writing.

A. Rarement ou souvent? Use the cues below to ask another student how often he or she does the following activities. Use the words **rarement**, **quelquefois**, and **souvent** in your questions and answers.

Exemple   parler français?
      — **Tu parles souvent français?**
      — **Je parle rarement français.**

1. étudier?
2. regarder la télé?
3. écouter la radio?
4. travailler?
5. nager?
6. parler français?
7. marcher?
8. voyager?

B. Faisons connaissance. Imagine that you have just met some French-speaking students and want to tell them the following information. Using vocabulary you know, what would you say?

1. Tell them two subjects that you are studying now.
2. Tell them whether you prefer watching television or listening to the radio.
3. Tell them two things that you like and two that you don't like.

Have students work in pairs to adapt the conversation in the *Mise en situation*. They can then role-play their completed conversation in small groups or selected groups can present their conversation to the class. If done as a presentation to the class, have other students listen and be prepared to ask questions on the conversation presented.

> **C'est votre tour.** Imagine that you are calling a French friend (played by another student) to find out what he or she is doing. Use the **Mise en situation** as a guide to role-play the situation with another student.

❧ Disagreeing or making negative statements
La forme négative

Présentation

Have students note the variations of the negative that they can now use: *not, not at all, never.*

To make a sentence negative, **ne... pas** is used. **Ne** precedes the conjugated verb, and **pas** follows it. To indicate the meaning *not at all*, **ne... pas du tout** is used. To indicate *never*, **ne... jamais** is used.

Affirmative	Negative
Vous parlez bien.	Vous **ne** parlez **pas** bien.
Nous nageons souvent.	Nous **ne** nageons **pas** beaucoup.
Nous parlons espagnol.	Nous **ne** parlons **pas du tout** espagnol.
Tu travailles tout le temps.	Tu **ne** travailles **jamais**.
Michel écoute toujours.	Michel **n'**écoute **jamais**.

A. When a verb begins with a vowel sound, **ne** becomes **n'**.

Je **n'**aime pas l'histoire.
Vous **n'**écoutez pas.

B. When an infinitive follows a conjugated verb, **ne... pas** surrounds the conjugated verb.

Nous **n'**aimons **pas** voyager.
Gilbert **n'**aime **pas** danser.

Mise en situation

Alain is trying to call Serge. Michèle, who answers, doesn't feel like talking. Practice repeating their conversation.

ALAIN	Allô, allô, Serge ?
MICHÈLE	Non, *c'est Michèle à l'appareil.*
ALAIN	Serge travaille *ce soir* ?
MICHÈLE	Non, il ne travaille pas.
ALAIN	Vous regardez la télé ?
MICHÈLE	Non, je n'aime pas regarder la télé.
ALAIN	Vous ne regardez jamais la télé ?
MICHÈLE	Non, jamais.

it's Michèle speaking (on the phone)
this evening

Have students conjugate the following in the negative: *Je ne travaille pas beaucoup; Je n'aime pas voyager; Je ne regarde jamais la télé; Je ne danse pas bien.*

Préparation

A. Contradictions. Each time that Monique makes a statement, Serge disagrees with her. Tell what Serge says.

> **Modèle** Nous aimons parler anglais.
> **Non, nous n'aimons pas parler anglais.**

1. Nous regardons la télé.
2. Les étudiants travaillent beaucoup.
3. Nous aimons les professeurs.
4. Ils voyagent beaucoup.
5. On aime marcher.
6. Hélène travaille beaucoup.
7. On parle anglais en classe.
8. Richard déteste les examens.

B. Non, malheureusement. Jean-Michel is asking Monique how well she and her friends like university life. Unfortunately, as her answers show, things are not going well. Use the cues provided to tell what she says.

Review: If necessary, review the meanings of the different adverbs.

> **Modèle** Tu aimes l'université ? *(no... not much)*
> **Non, je n'aime pas beaucoup l'université.**

1. Tu aimes les professeurs ? *(no)*
2. Tu aimes le cours d'anglais ? *(no... not much)*
3. Tu parles bien anglais ? *(no... not well)*
4. Tu étudies souvent ? *(no)*
5. Tu regardes quelquefois la télé ? *(no... never)*
6. Les étudiants écoutent en classe ? *(no... not often)*
7. Régine aime le restaurant universitaire ? *(no... not at all)*
8. Caroline aime la résidence où elle habite ? *(no... not at all)*
9. Fabien et Anne aiment la classe d'histoire ? *(no... not much)*

Communication et vie pratique

A. Oui ou non? Answer the following questions. If you disagree, make your answers negative by using **ne... pas**, **ne... pas du tout**, or **ne... jamais**.

> **Exemple**   Vous voyagez beaucoup?
> **Non, je ne voyage pas beaucoup.**
> *ou:*   **Non, je ne voyage jamais.**

1. Vous travaillez tout le temps?
2. Vous aimez étudier?
3. Vous étudiez beaucoup?
4. Les étudiants aiment beaucoup les examens?
5. Vous parlez bien français?
6. Vous aimez beaucoup les maths?
7. Les étudiants écoutent toujours le professeur?
8. Vous nagez bien?

B. Pas moi! Using vocabulary you know, tell what things you and the other people mentioned below don't do or never do.

> **Exemple**   Les étudiants... → **Les étudiants n'aiment pas les examens.**

1. Moi, je...
2. Les étudiants...
3. Les Français...
4. Les Américains...
5. Nous, les étudiants, nous...
6. Les professeurs...

Written preparation may be helpful. Option: Have students work in small groups to prepare sentences for one or several of the items in this activity. Their responses can then be shared with the class.

C'est votre tour. Imagine that you are in a bad mood and a friend calls to find out what you are doing. Each time your friend asks a question you respond in the negative. Use the **Mise en situation** as a guide to role-play this situation.

Preparation: Have students use vocabulary they know to come up with negative statements that a person in a bad mood might make.

❧ Asking others about their activities and preferences
La forme interrogative

Présentation

There are three ways to ask yes-or-no questions in French.

- By intonation only
  - → **Vous parlez anglais?**
    Il aime étudier?

- By placing **est-ce que** before a statement
  - → **Est-ce que** vous parlez anglais?
    Est-ce qu'il aime étudier?

Tell students that Section D of the Prononciation at the end of the chapter deals with intonation patterns in questions. Remind students that the voice goes down at the end of a statement and that the voice goes up slightly at the end of a question by intonation.

Point out that the voice rises mostly on est-ce que (and only slightly on the last word).

● By adding **n'est-ce pas** to a statement

→ Vous parlez anglais, **n'est-ce pas**?
Il aime étudier, **n'est-ce pas**?

In colloquial language, *n'est-ce pas* is often replaced by *hein*.

Note that before a vowel sound **est-ce que** becomes **est-ce qu'**, and that confirmation questions are simpler in French than in English. In French the form is always **n'est-ce pas**? but it varies in English:

You're tired, aren't you?
He doesn't speak French, does he?

Mise en situation

Marcelle has just found out that Brigitte has an American roommate and is asking questions about her. Practice their conversation, paying particular attention to intonation patterns.

MARCELLE   Est-ce qu'elle parle bien français?
BRIGITTE   Oui, assez bien.
MARCELLE   Elle aime bien l'université, n'est-ce pas?
BRIGITTE   *Je pense que oui.*
MARCELLE   Vous parlez anglais ensemble?
BRIGITTE   Oui, quelquefois.

I think so. (Je pense que non = I don't think so)

Préparation

A. N'est-ce pas? Marie-Claude is fairly certain what subjects her friends are studying but, to be sure, she asks them. Give her questions.

Modèle   Michel / philosophie
Michel étudie la philosophie, n'est-ce pas?

1. tu / littérature
2. vous / les maths
3. Véronique / anglais
4. Michel et Roger / sciences
5. tu / géographie
6. vous / histoire
7. François / informatique
8. Daniel / philosophie

Have students change the following to questions with *est-ce que*: *(1) Chantal étudie beaucoup; (2) Vous aimez le cinéma; (3) Georges et Jean voyagent souvent; (4) Monique danse bien.* Have students change the following to questions with *n'est-ce pas*: *(1) Vous aimez le cinéma; (2) Chantal étudie l'anglais; (3) Brigitte ne mange pas beaucoup; (4) Ils aiment mieux la littérature.*

B. Faisons connaissance. Pauline is talking with Marc and wants to find out about him and his roommate Georges. What questions would she ask to find out the following information?

Modèle   if he enjoys music → **Est-ce que tu aimes la musique**?
if Georges is studying math → **Est-ce que Georges étudie les maths**?

1. if he works a lot
2. if they like the university dining hall
3. if Georges studies often
4. if they like the teachers
5. if they like sports
6. if they watch television often
7. if Georges speaks English well
8. if they travel a lot

Option: Have students use vocabulary they know to make up questions that they might ask a prospective roommate. They could then use these questions to role-play an interview with a prospective roommate.

Communication et vie pratique

A. Interview. Use the words provided to make up questions to ask another student. Begin your questions with **est-ce que**.

Exemple écouter souvent la radio
— **Est-ce que tu écoutes souvent la radio?**
— **Non, je n'écoute pas souvent la radio.**

1. aimer nager
2. étudier tout le temps
3. voyager souvent
4. étudier la philosophie
5. regarder souvent la télé
6. aimer les sports
7. travailler beaucoup
8. aimer le campus

Have students interview each other in small groups and then report the results orally or in writing. Remind them that they are encouraged to ask additional questions based on vocabulary they already know.

B. Vérification. Based on what you know about other students in your class, see if you can identify some of their activities or interests. Use **n'est-ce pas** in your questions. They will confirm whether you are right or not.

Exemple — **Tu aimes beaucoup les sports, n'est-ce pas?**
— **Oui, j'aime beaucoup les sports.**
— **Non, je n'aime pas du tout les sports.**

C. Petite conversation. Using vocabulary you know, make up questions that you would ask another student about his or her likes and dislikes, typical activities, and courses that he or she is taking.

Exemple **Est-ce que tu regardes souvent la télé?**
ou: **Est-ce que tu étudies l'histoire?**

Preparation: Written preparation may be helpful.

C'est votre tour. Imagine that another student in your class has a French friend, Alain, and you want to find out more about this person. Use vocabulary you know to ask questions similar to those in the **Mise en situation.** You might want to ask your friend if Alain speaks English well, if they speak French together, if they like to watch television, if Alain swims well, etc. Another student will answer your questions.

Have the class come up with as many questions as they can for this activity, reminding students to include questions from the *Chapitre préliminaire.* Have students interview each other in small groups and then report the results orally or in writing.

Intégration et perspectives

Faisons connaissance

Several students from different French-speaking countries are getting acquainted at a neighborhood café in Paris.

TAHAR (de Tunis)

Je m'appelle Tahar. J'étudie la médecine *ici* à Paris. J'aime beaucoup Paris, *surtout* le Quartier latin. Mais je déteste le climat. Je ne regarde jamais la

here
especially

The café is still an important meeting place for French people. Many students like to sit in their favorite café to study or talk with friends.

télévision, mais j'écoute quelquefois la radio. J'aime beaucoup la musique classique.

ANNE-MARIE DUCLERC (de Lausanne)
Moi, je m'appelle Anne-Marie Duclerc. J'adore Paris. Je travaille ici comme secrétaire bilingue. La vie à Paris — les films, les monuments, les concerts, les *musées* — je trouve ça *formidable*.

museums / great

MONIQUE ET ANDRÉ DUCHEMIN (de Québec)
Nous habitons *maintenant* à Paris. André étudie l'informatique et moi, j'étudie le droit et les sciences politiques. Nous aimons bien Paris, mais nous préférons* la vie à Québec.

now

CATHERINE SIMON (de Saint-Étienne)
Est-ce que je préfère Paris *ou* Saint-Étienne? Paris, *bien sûr*! J'adore marcher *dans* les *rues*, regarder les *gens* et les *magasins*. Mais je déteste le *métro*.

or / of course
in / streets / people / stores / subway

Compréhension. For each of the students described in the reading, give the following information:

1. nom
2. pays d'origine
3. études
4. activités
5. préférences

Faisons connaissance. Using the reading as a guide and using vocabulary you know, introduce yourself to another student in your class.

---

*Préférer is a regular -er verb except that, in writing, the second accent changes in all singular forms and in the ils / elles form: **je préfère, tu préfères, il / elle préfère, ils / elles préfèrent**; but **nous préférons, vous préférez.**

Notes culturelles : *Paris et le reste de la France*

The richness of Parisian history and the diversity of its cultural and intellectual life have always attracted visitors, students, and artists from all over the world. Among the well-known attractions of Paris are its famous museums (**le Louvre, le Jeu de Paume, le centre Pompidou**); its landmarks (**la tour Eiffel, Notre Dame, le Sacré-Cœur, l'Arc de Triomphe**); its prestigious schools (**la Sorbonne, l'École polytechnique**); its world-renowned restaurants (**la Tour d'Argent, Maxim's**); and its interesting areas (**le Quartier latin, Montmartre**). This same diversity exists in its population, which includes native Parisians and **provinciaux** who have moved to Paris from the provinces and people of various nationalities. Sizable groups of Indochinese, North Africans, and black Africans are among the most recent ethnic groups to establish themselves in Paris.

Despite considerable decentralization of economic, political, and cultural affairs in France in recent years, Paris still remains the hub of most aspects of French life. Although there are a number of urban centers throughout France — 32 cities have a population of more than 100,000 — many French people and foreigners still tend to think of areas outside Paris as **en province** and to equate Parisian culture with French civilization itself.

France is geographically varied, including high mountains in the south (the **Pyrénées** form a natural boundary with Spain) and in the east (the Jura and the Alps form the boundary with Switzerland and Italy). **Mont Blanc**, the highest mountain in Europe (4,810 meters), is located in the French Alps, just south of the Swiss city of Geneva.

Montmartre

Communication et vie pratique

A. Petites annonces. The following ads were placed on bulletin boards by students looking for (**chercher** — *to look for*) roommates. After reading each of them, match them with the descriptions of the American students who are also looking for roommates. Notice how easily you recognize the cognates found in these ads.

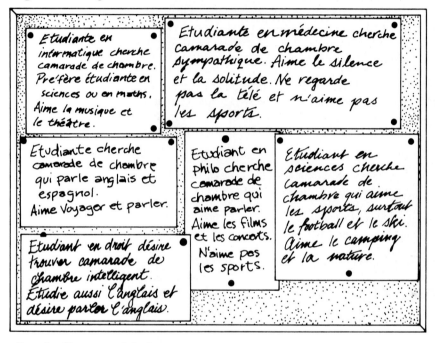

Etudiante en informatique cherche camarade de chambre. Préfère étudiante en sciences ou en maths. Aime la musique et le théâtre.

Etudiante en médecine cherche camarade de chambre sympathique. Aime le silence et la solitude. Ne regarde pas la télé et n'aime pas les sports.

Etudiante cherche camarade de chambre qui parle anglais et espagnol. Aime voyager et parler.

Etudiant en philo cherche camarade de chambre qui aime parler. Aime les films et les concerts. N'aime pas les sports.

Etudiant en sciences cherche camarade de chambre qui aime les sports, surtout le football et le ski. Aime le camping et la nature.

Etudiant en droit désire trouver camarade de chambre intelligent. Etudie aussi l'anglais et désire parler l'anglais.

Les étudiants américains :

1. Richard likes sports and the outdoors, especially camping.
2. Katie wants a roommate who shares her interests in languages and in traveling.
3. Michael is somewhat intellectual and wants to enjoy various cultural activities while in France.
4. Susan is nearing the end of her year of study in France and needs to have peace and quiet while studying for her exams.
5. Joseph has just arrived in France and is looking for a roommate who speaks some English.
6. Elizabeth is majoring in math. In addition to her interest in computer science, she enjoys movies and music.

B. Lettre. Choose the student that you would prefer to room with and then write a letter in which you introduce yourself to that person. Include information about the interests that you share. Begin your letter with **Chère...** (for a feminine name) or **Cher...** (for a masculine name), then end the letter with **Cordialement** and your signature.

Have students make up their own bulletin board of real or imaginary roommate ads. They could then try to find out if there are any suitable matches among the descriptions provided.

It may be useful to have students prepare the letter as homework or give them time to work on their letters in class.

La tour Eiffel

C. Situation. Choose the student that you would find the most compatible and then have another student play the role of that student as you get acquainted.

D. Impressions. Review the ways in which you can express varying degrees of intensity, quality, and frequency and then complete the activity given below.

1. l'intensité

j'adore
j'aime beaucoup
j'aime bien
j'aime assez

je n'aime pas du tout
je déteste

2. la qualité

Elle danse bien.

Elle ne danse pas bien.
Elle danse mal.

3. la fréquence

Il travaille tout le temps.	Ils voyagent toujours en groupe.
Il travaille quelquefois.	Ils voyagent quelquefois en groupe.
Il ne travaille jamais.	Ils ne voyagent jamais en groupe.

Now use the above expressions to give a general description of Americans. Then compare your impressions with those of other students.

Exemple   marcher
Les Américains ne marchent pas beaucoup.
Les Américains n'aiment pas marcher.

1. voyager
2. parler français
3. regarder la télé
4. aimer les sports

5. marcher
6. nager
7. travailler
8. aimer la musique

• *Prononciation et orthographe*

The French vowel system differs from the English system in significant ways. Contrary to English, French is essentially a vocalic language, i.e., vowels play a more important role. This affects the language in several ways.

A. Syllabic division of words. In French, syllables within a word generally end in a vowel sound.

Compare:

English	French
A-mer-i-can	*A-mé-ri-cain*
Am-a-zon	*A-ma-zone*
her-i-tage	*hé-ri-tage*
in-ter-est	*in-té-rêt*

B. Vowel enunciation. A clear differentiation in vowel sounds is much more important in French than in English. French vowels are never "glided" or "swallowed" as English vowels are.

Compare:

English	French
key	qui
may	mais
oh	oh
probable	probable
sensible	sensible
probability	probabilité

The pronunciation section is divided into four parts. Each section can accompany an *Exploration* (e.g., Part A with the first *Exploration*, *L'article défini*, etc.) or the sections can be grouped together and completed at the end of the chapter.

C. Accentuation. The sharp differentiation among vowels is partly due to the fact that French is *not* a stressed language, whereas English is. In an English word, one particular syllable is stressed and it remains stressed, regardless of the position the word occupies in a group of words. In French the last syllable in a word or group of words is the only accentuated syllable.

Compare:

English	**French**
music	la musique
residence	la résidence
university	l'université

Repeat:

Bonjour.
Bonjour, monsieur.
Bonjour, Monsieur Delaporte.

D. Note the difference in the intonation patterns of different types of sentences.

1. In a declarative sentence or statement, the voice goes down at the end.

Les étudiants travaillent beaucoup.

2. In yes-or-no questions by intonation, the voice goes up.

Les étudiants travaillent beaucoup?

3. In yes-or-no questions with **est-ce que**, the emphasis is on **est-ce que** and the voice goes up again slightly at the end of the sentence.

Est-ce que les étudiants travaillent beaucoup?

• *Vocabulaire*

Noms

la vie universitaire (voir p. 16)

les études

    l'**anglais** (m) *English*
    le **droit** *law*
°   l'**éducation physique** (f)*
    l'**espagnol** (m) *Spanish (language)*
° la **géographie**

° l'**histoire** (f)
    l'**informatique** (f) *computer science*
    la **langue** *language*
° la **littérature**
° les **mathématiques (maths)** (f pl)
° la **médecine**
° la **musique**
° la **philosophie**
° les **sciences** (f pl)

---

*The degree signs in the chapter vocabularies indicate words whose spelling and meaning are identical or similar in French and English.

d'autres noms

°   la **classe**
°   le **climat**
°   le **concert**
°   le **film**
    les **gens** (m pl) *people*
°   le **groupe**
    le **magasin** *store*
    le **métro** *subway*
    le **musée** *museum*
    la **note** *grade, mark*
°   la **radio**
    le **restaurant universitaire**
        university food service
    la **rue** *street*
° le, la **secrétaire**
°   la **télévision (télé)**
    la **vie** *life*
    le **voyage** *trip*

Verbes

adorer *to adore, to like a great deal*
aimer *to like, to love*
aimer bien *to like*
aimer mieux *to prefer, to like better*
° **danser**
détester *to hate*
étudier *to study*
habiter *to live*
manger *to eat*
marcher *to walk*
nager *to swim*
parler *to speak, to talk*
° **préférer**
regarder *to watch, to look at*
travailler *to work*
trouver *to find*
voyager *to travel*

Adjectifs

agréable *pleasant*
bilingue *bilingual*
° **classique**
désagréable *unpleasant*
difficile *difficult, hard*

ennuyeux, ennuyeuse *boring*
facile *easy*
formidable *great, wonderful*
° **intéressant(e)**
° **politique**

Adverbes

aussi *also, too*
beaucoup *a great deal, much, many*
ensemble *together*
ici *here*
maintenant *now*
mal *badly*
ne... jamais *never*
ne... pas *not*
ne... pas du tout *not at all*
quelquefois *sometimes*
rarement *rarely*
souvent *often*
surtout *especially*
toujours *always*
tout le temps *all the time*

Divers

les pronoms sujets (voir p. 19)
à *at, to*
à l'appareil *speaking, on the phone*
allô *hello (on the phone)*
avec *with*
bien sûr! *of course!*
ça *that*
c'est *it's*
ce soir *this evening*
comme *like, as*
dans *in*
je pense que non *I don't think so*
je pense que oui *I think so*
mais *but*
moi *me, I*
n'est-ce pas? *right? isn't it so?*
ou *or*
où *where*
oui *yes*
tiens *hey, look*
tu fais *you are doing*
voici *here is, here are*

2

CHAPITRE DEUX

Communication objectives

Telling who we are

1. Telling who we are, where we are from, and what we are like
2. Identifying objects and people
3. Describing people and objects
4. Counting

Structures

Les mots et la vie : Profession et état civil

Le verbe **être** et l'utilisation des adjectifs

Les articles indéfinis

Les adjectifs qualificatifs

Les nombres de 20 à 99

Identité

Mise en scène
Demande de travail

Have students note the communication strategies used by the speaker when (1) she doesn't understand the question about her date and place of birth and (2) how this information as well as the address is shown when the person does not have the necessary language to give it. Similar strategies are outlined in the *Communication et vie pratique* section of the *Intégration et perspectives*.

application / work, job

Ann, an American student, is applying for a job in a French hotel during her stay in France.

L'EMPLOYÉE	*Nom* et *prénom*, s'il vous plaît?	last name / first name
ANN	Pardon?	
L'EMPLOYÉE	Quel est votre nom? Comment vous appelez-vous?	
ANN	Je m'appelle Ann.	
L'EMPLOYÉE	Et votre nom de famille, c'est *quoi*?	what
ANN	Manchester... MANCHESTER.	
L'EMPLOYÉE	Vous êtes *mariée* ou *célibataire*?	married / single
ANN	*Je suis* célibataire.	I am
L'EMPLOYÉE	Nationalité?	
ANN	Américaine.	
L'EMPLOYÉE	Profession?	
ANN	Je suis étudiante.	
L'EMPLOYÉE	Date et *lieu* de *naissance*?	place / birth
ANN	*Pouvez-vous* répéter, s'il vous plaît?	Can you
L'EMPLOYÉE	Où et *quand êtes-vous née*?	when / were you born
ANN	C'est *indiqué* ici, *sur mon* passeport.	shown / on / my
L'EMPLOYÉE	*Domicile habituel*?	usual address
ANN	Je suis de Saint Louis. Voici l'adresse.	

Students are asked to fill out a registration form in *Communication B (Demande de carte d'étudiant)* in the *Intégration et perspectives* section.

35

Compréhension. Indiquez si les phrases suivantes sont vraies ou fausses selon les renseignements donnés dans le texte. Si la phrase est fausse, corrigez-la. *(Indicate whether the following sentences are true or false according to the information given in the text. If the statement is false, correct it.)*

1. Le nom de famille d'Ann est Manchester.
2. Elle est mariée.
3. Ann est française.
4. Elle est professeur de français.
5. Ann est de Saint Louis.
6. Elle habite maintenant en France.

Les mots et la vie: *Profession et état civil*

The **cartes de visite** of various people are shown below. Describe each of these people by giving the information required in the **Renseignements à donner** section.

Have students prepare their own cartes de visite or have them make up one for a French person that they create. Other students can interview them to find out the information on the card.

Renseignements à donner

NOM ET PRÉNOM	**Il / elle s'appelle...**
ADRESSE	**Il / elle habite...**
PROFESSION	**Il / elle est...**
VILLE D'ORIGINE	**Il / elle est de...**

Anne-Marie Journeau
Ingénieur
44, rue de la Poste
33018 Bordeaux

Denis Journeau
Comptable
44, rue de la Poste
33018 Bordeaux

Christine Latour
Vétérinaire
55, boulevard de la
République
59002 Lille

Jacques Lebrun
Dentiste
93, avenue de Saxe
69006 Lyon

Sabine Mercier

Psychologue
39, promenade des
   Anglais
06002 Nice

Jacqueline Bertrand

Journaliste
68, rue du Port
13001 Marseille

Armand Simon

Avocat
18, cours Franklin-Roosevelt
44005 Nantes

Sylvie Jobert
Architecte
3, quai Saint-Hubert
45001 Orleans

André Seguin
Commerçant
79, rue du Mont-Blanc
74061 Annecy

JEAN-CLAUDE ANDRÉ
MÉDECIN
25, AVENUE JEAN-JAURES
29421 BREST

Notes culturelles: *Les Français: Qui sont-ils?*

France has a population of about 55 million people, a large percentage of which (73.3%) live in urban areas. Paris alone claims over 2 million inhabitants and the Paris region has 10 million people. Almost 30 percent of France's population is under 20 years of age and close to 20 percent is 60 or older.

Despite regional differences and some separatist movements (especially in Brittany and in Corsica), the French have long been a people united by a common history and a shared pride in their cultural heritage. The current French population is descended from the intermingling of different ethnic groups that settled long ago on French territory: the Gauls, the Celts, the Romans, the Francs, and the Vikings. In addition, France has a long tradition of attracting substantial numbers of foreigners who even today account for eight percent of the population.

These varied origins may account for the complexity of the French character and its many contradictions: independent and individualistic yet respectful of tradition and social protocol; warm and sociable yet very private; dynamic and inventive yet fascinated by the past.

When asked in a recent survey which characteristics best described the French people, the qualities most often mentioned by the people interviewed were tolerance, generosity, equality, and above all, freedom. They also recognized that they are prone to being overly patriotic.

Explorations
৬Telling who we are, where we are from, and what we are like
Le verbe *être* et l'utilisation des adjectifs

Présentation

The irregular verb **être** *(to be)* can be used to tell who or where you are, where you are from, or what you are like.

être	
je **suis**	nous **sommes**
tu **es**	vous **êtes**
il / elle / on **est**	ils / elles **sont**

— Est-ce que vous **êtes** étudiant?
— Non, je **suis** professeur.

— Ils **sont** à la bibliothèque?
— Non, ils ne **sont** pas à la bibliothèque.

A. Adjectives agree in number and gender with the nouns they modify. Some adjectives (including several that you know already, such as **formidable**, **agréable**, and **facile**) have identical masculine and feminine forms and simply add **s** for the plural.

Je suis optimiste.
Tu es optimiste.
Il / Elle / On est optimiste.

Nous sommes optimiste**s**.
Vous êtes optimiste**(s)**.
Ils / Elles sont optimiste**s**.

Other useful adjectives of this type are:

optimiste	pauvre *(poor)*	triste *(sad)*	sévère *(strict)*
pessimiste	juste *(fair)*	possible	timide
célèbre *(famous)*	injuste *(unfair)*	impossible	honnête
modeste	sympathique *(nice)*	moderne	irrésistible
riche	bête *(stupid)*	simple	

An adjective usually follows the noun it modifies.

Il n'aime pas les examens **faciles**.
Nous préférons la musique **moderne**.

C'est is used to refer to a general idea or situation. A following adjective is always in the masculine singular because there is no specific noun referred to.

C'est facile.
Ce n'est pas possible.
J'aime bien parler français, mais **ce n'est pas facile**.

B. Adjectives can also be modified by adverbs.

pas assez	assez	très	trop
not enough	fairly	very	too much

Il est **assez** timide.
Les professeurs sont **trop** sévères.
Ce n'est pas **assez** moderne.

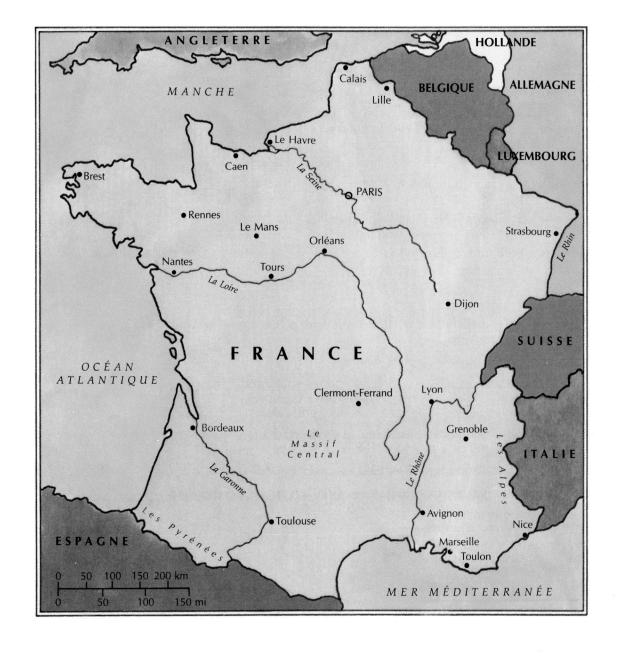

Le Tour de France

Mise en situation

Une interview avec Serge Lambert. A reporter is interviewing a participant in the famous bicycle race, **le Tour de France**.

LE REPORTER	Serge Lambert, c'est vous, n'est-ce pas ?
SERGE	Oui, *c'est moi.*
LE REPORTER	Vous êtes français ?
SERGE	Non, je suis *belge.*
LE REPORTER	Et Claude Joris, il est belge aussi ?
SERGE	Oui, nous sommes de la *même ville.*
LE REPORTER	Et le tour, *ça marche bien* ?
SERGE	Oui, je suis assez optimiste.

it's me

Belgian

same / city
it's going well

Préparation

A. Professions et métiers. Tell what the following people do for a living. Use the cues provided.

Modèle   je / dentiste → **Je suis dentiste.**

1. je / médecin
2. tu / avocat
3. elle / comptable
4. nous / étudiants
5. vous / ingénieur
6. ils / professeurs

B. Descriptions. Georges is describing himself and various people he knows. Using the cues provided, tell what he says.

Modèle   Paul / assez timide → **Paul est assez timide.**

Mireille / pas très modeste → **Mireille n'est pas très modeste.**

1. je / trop pessimiste
2. Pascale / très sympathique
3. nous / pas assez modestes
4. tu / pas très riche

5. Richard et Jean / pas sympathiques
6. vous / assez optimistes
7. Madame Lagrange / pas trop sévère
8. Robert / pas très honnête

C. À la résidence universitaire. Students at Laval University are trying to find out where some of their friends are from. What do they say?

Have students locate these cities on a map of Quebec.

Modèle   Geneviève / Trois-Rivières
   Est-ce que Geneviève est de Trois-Rivières?

1. tu / Québec
2. vous / Saint-Jean
3. Robert / Jonquières
4. François et Jacques / Montréal
5. elle / Toronto
6. vous / Beauport

Communication et vie pratique

A. Descriptions. Using the scale below, tell whether you never, rarely, sometimes, or always have the qualities given below.

Have students give a sentence describing themselves and ask another student if the same is true for him or her: *Moi, je suis toujours optimiste. Et toi?*

jamais	rarement	quelquefois	toujours

Exemple   pessimiste → **Je suis rarement pessimiste.**

1. optimiste
2. pessimiste
3. désagréable
4. honnête
5. modeste
6. triste
7. injuste
8. irrésistible

B. Opinions. Using the cues provided, ask other students their opinions about various aspects of campus life. Use adverbs such as **assez**, **très**, and **trop** in your answers.

Have students guess the home towns of other students in the class. Students can also pretend that they are from one of the French cities on the map on p. 39. Other students will try to guess which city they are from.

Exemple   professeurs / sympathiques
   — Est-ce que les profs sont sympathiques?
   — Oui, les profs sont assez sympathiques.
   ou: **— Non, les profs ne sont pas très sympathiques.**

1. français / facile
2. étudiants / sympathiques
3. cours / difficiles
4. profs / sévères
5. examens / difficiles
6. campus / moderne
7. climat / agréable
8. restaurants universitaires / formidables

C'est votre tour. Imagine that you are a famous sports figure (or a film or television star) and are being interviewed by a French reporter (played by another student). Using the **Mise en situation** as a guide, make up answers to the reporter's questions.

Before students role-play this situation, it would be helpful to give a model interview in which a student plays the role of a reporter and asks the instructor the questions given in the *Mise en situation*. If possible, it would be useful to tape an adaptation of the *Mise en situation* to use for listening comprehension practice and to give students an additional model to use in their role-plays. Students can then interview each other and selected groups can present their interviews to the class.

ॐ Identifying objects and people
Les articles indéfinis

Présentation

The indefinite articles correspond to *a*, *an*, and *some* in English.

Les articles indéfinis		
	Singular	**Plural**
Masculine	**un** étudiant	**des** étudiants
Feminine	**une** fenêtre	**des** fenêtres

A. To ask what something is, use the question **Qu'est-ce que c'est?** To ask the identity of persons, use **Qui est-ce?** To answer, use **c'est** (*it / he / she is*) or **ce sont** (*they are*) followed by a noun with the correct indefinite article or a proper name.

> — **Qu'est-ce que c'est?**
> — **C'est** un musée. **Ce n'est pas** un magasin.

> — **Qui est-ce?**
> — **C'est** Jacques. **C'est** un étudiant.

B. To identify people or talk about their professions, the following vocabulary is important.

un homme *(man)*
un garçon *(boy)*
un(e) enfant
une femme *(woman)*
une fille *(girl)*

When talking about people's professions, nationalities, and religions, the indefinite article must be used with **c'est** and **ce sont**. It is also used whenever the profession is modified by an adjective.

C'est **un** professeur.
Mme Lebury est **un** professeur formidable.
Ce sont **des** professeurs belges.

The indefinite article is not used when the name of the profession follows any other pronoun or a noun and the verb **être**.

Catherine est journaliste.
Elle est journaliste.

Mise en situation

Jean and Marianne are school friends who have not seen each other for a
long time. They are talking about what they and their friends are doing.

JEAN	Qu'est-ce que tu fais maintenant?
MARIANNE	Je suis ingénieur.
JEAN	Où ça? Ici, à Lyon?
MARIANNE	Oui, je travaille dans *une usine* de la région. Et toi?
JEAN	Je travaille dans *un bureau*.
MARIANNE	C'est un travail intéressant?
JEAN	Non, pas très... Et Céline?
MARIANNE	Elle est *infirmière* dans un hôpital *pour* les enfants.

factory

office

nurse / for

Préparation

A. Qu'est-ce que c'est? Identify each of the following objects.

Modèle — **Qu'est-ce que c'est?**

— **C'est un livre.**

ou: — **Ce sont des livres.**

1.
2.
3.
4.

5.
6.
7.
8.

B. **Professions.** What is the profession of each of the people shown below?

1.
2.
3.

Modèle   **C'est un comptable.**

4.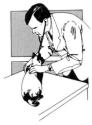
5.
6.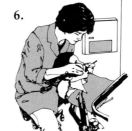
7.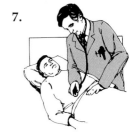

C. **Identité.** Robert is describing what some of his friends are doing and where they are working. Tell what he says.

> **Modèle**   Vincent? (médecin / Toronto)
> **C'est un médecin. Il est médecin à Toronto.**

1. Michelle? (avocat / Paris)
2. Roger? (journaliste / Montréal)
3. Anne? (professeur / Grenoble)
4. David? (comptable / Bordeaux)
5. Martine? (médecin / Bruxelles)
6. Sophie? (architecte / Lyon)

Communication et vie pratique

A. **Qu'est-ce que c'est?** Use the cues provided to identify each of the following Parisian monuments and buildings.

> **Exemple**   le centre Pompidou / musée
> **C'est le centre Pompidou. C'est un musée.**

1. la Sorbonne / université
2. la Tour d'Argent / restaurant
3. la Bibliothèque nationale / bibliothèque
4. les Galeries Lafayette / magasin
5. le Louvre / musée
6. les Champs-Élysées / rue

Point out that *Galeries Lafayette*, *Le Printemps*, and *la Samaritaine* are some of the main Parisian department stores. One can also find discount stores such as *Monoprix* and *Prisunic*.

B. **Dans la classe de français.** Point to an object and ask another student to identify it.

    Exemple   — **Qu'est-ce que c'est?**
                   — **C'est une affiche.**

C. **Célébrités.** Make a list of famous people or television characters who have the following professions. As you name them, other students will identify their profession. Categories: **professeur, médecin, ingénieur, journaliste, avocat, architecte**

C'est votre tour. Imagine that you meet one of your current classmates five years from now. S/he asks you about yourself and others in the class. Using the **Mise en situation** as a guide, answer his or her questions.

Preparation: Have students think about how they would answer these questions before doing the role-plays. They can also be given (or can make up) a French identity (e.g., name, where they live, where they are working, and where a friend lives and works).

❧ Describing people and objects
Les adjectifs qualificatifs

Présentation

French adjectives agree in number (an **s** is usually present in the plural form) and in gender (an **e** is usually present in the feminine form) with the noun or pronoun they describe.

Les adjectifs qualificatifs		
	Singular	**Plural**
Masculine	patient	patient**s**
Feminine	patient**e**	patient**es**

If the masculine singular form ends in **s** or **x**, no additional **s** is added in the plural form.

    Il est **français**.
    Ils sont **français**.

An adjective that describes a combination of masculine and feminine nouns is always masculine plural.

    Alain et Yvonne sont **intelligents**.

A. The masculine and feminine forms of an adjective are pronounced the same for all adjectives that have a masculine form ending in a pronounced vowel.

> Paul est **fatigué**.
> Jeanne est **fatiguée**.

Useful adjectives of this type are:

compliqué(e) *(complicated)*	poli(e) *(polite)*
fatigué(e) *(tired)*	vrai(e) *(true)*

B. When the masculine singular form ends in an unpronounced consonant, the consonant in the corresponding feminine form is pronounced.

> Marc est patient, mais Monique n'est pas patiente.
> C'est une femme très intéressante.

Useful adjectives of this type are:

amusant(e)	fascinant(e)	intelligent(e)
compétent(e)	fort(e) *(strong)*	intéressant(e)
content(e)	français(e)	parfait(e)
excellent(e)	impatient(e)	passionnant(e) *(exciting)*
prudent(e) *(careful)*	embêtant(e) *(annoying)*	indépendant(e)
violent(e)		

C. Some adjectives do not fit into the general pattern but can be grouped into specific patterns.

	Singular	Plural
Masculine	impulsif	impulsifs
Feminine	impulsive	impulsives

actif, active
naïf, naïve
sportif, sportive *(athletic)*

	Singular	Plural
Masculine	sérieux	sérieux
Feminine	sérieuse	sérieuses

ambitieux, ambitieuse
courageux, courageuse
heureux, heureuse *(happy)*
paresseux, paresseuse *(lazy)*

	Singular	Plural
Masculine	parisien	parisiens
Feminine	parisienne	parisiennes

ancien, ancienne *(old)*
canadien, canadienne
italien, italienne

	Singular	Plural
Masculine	naturel	naturels
Feminine	naturelle	naturelles

exceptionnel, exceptionnelle
intellectuel, intellectuelle
personnel, personnelle
quel, quelle *(what or which)*
sensationnel, sensationnelle

Mise en situation

Students are asked to play this game in the *C'est votre tour* section.

C'est un jeu. Denise and Robert are playing a game that consists of guessing the identity of the person or object the other person is thinking about.

DENISE	Je pense à une femme.
ROBERT	Est-ce que c'est une femme célèbre?
DENISE	Oui.
ROBERT	Est-ce qu'elle est française?
DENISE	Non.
ROBERT	Est-ce qu'elle est très sportive?
DENISE	Oui.
ROBERT	C'est une *championne* américaine?
DENISE	Oui.
ROBERT	Je *parie* que c'est Chris Evert...
DENISE	Oui.

champion

bet

Point out *champion* (masc.) and *championne* (fem.).

Préparation

Have students give the masculine form of the following adjectives: *contente, parfaite, française, ambitieuse, courageuse, active, impulsive, parisienne, canadienne, paresseuse, intellectuelle.* Have them give the feminine form of the following adjectives: *compliqué, heureux, naïf, intéressant, modeste, violent, italien, compréhensif, ancien, sincère, amusant, exceptionnel, ennuyeux.*

A. Égalité. Hubert is convinced that men are superior to women. His friend Suzanne does not agree. Tell what she says.

> **Modèle** Les hommes sont ambitieux.
> **Les femmes aussi sont ambitieuses.**

1. Les hommes sont sérieux.
2. Les hommes sont sportifs.
3. Les hommes sont intelligents.
4. Les hommes sont courageux.
5. Les hommes sont exceptionnels.
6. Les hommes sont indépendants.
7. Les hommes sont amusants.
8. Les hommes sont parfaits.

In French a male chauvinist is a *phallocrate.* Explain that *chauvinistic* comes from *Chauvin* (an extreme patriot).

B. Curiosité. A friend is asking Martine how well she is getting along at the University of Bordeaux. Use the cues provided to formulate her questions.

> **Modèle** les professeurs / intéressant
> **Est-ce que les professeurs sont intéressants?**

1. les examens / difficile
2. les professeurs / sympathique
3. les cours / intéressant
4. les étudiants / amusant
5. la bibliothèque / excellent
6. la classe de géographie / intéressant
7. tu / content
8. tu / fatigué

C. **Qualités et défauts.** Alain is telling which of his friends fits the following categories. Tell what he says.

Modèle   pas très patient ? (Hélène) → **Hélène n'est pas très patiente.**

1. assez naïf ? (Catherine)
2. très patient ? (Marc)
3. très ambitieux ? (Janine)
4. pas très content ? (Brigitte et Luc)
5. trop sérieux ? (Claudine et Roger)
6. très intelligent ? (Josette)
7. pas très sympathique ? (Michel)
8. pas très intellectuel? (Anne-Marie)

Communication et vie pratique

A. **Préférences.** Ask other students what type of teachers, classes, books, etc. they prefer. They will answer using adjectives they know.

Exemple   les professeurs
— **Quelle sorte de professeurs aimez-vous ?**
— **J'aime les professeurs amusants; je n'aime pas les professeurs trop sérieux.**

1. les professeurs   3. les femmes   5. les films   7. les journalistes
2. les hommes   4. les cours   6. les enfants 8. les examens

Written preparation may be helpful. Students can be asked to compare and contrast their answers. *Moi, j'aime les professeurs amusants. Et toi ? Moi, j'aime mieux les professeurs sérieux,* etc.

B. **Description.** Using adjectives you know, describe yourself or someone you know. Use words like **en général, rarement, souvent, assez, trop,** etc. in your description.

Exemple   **En général, je ne suis pas très modeste, mais je suis honnête,** etc.

C. **Interview.** Ask questions to find out if other students think the following adjectives describe their personalities. Make sure that your adjectives agree with the person you are talking with.

Exemple   ambitieux
— **Marie, est-ce que tu es ambitieuse ?**
— **Oui, je suis assez ambitieuse.**

1. ambitieux   3. exceptionnel   5. sportif   7. paresseux
2. prudent   4. impatient   6. impulsif   8. indépendant

Students can also describe a well-known person. Activity can be used for written homework and student papers used (with their permission and without using names of individuals) for listening comprehension practice.

Option: Give each student a card containing an adjective. Their task is to circulate, asking other students if they have that characteristic (e.g., *Roger, est-ce que tu es sportif ?*). The student's name is recorded on the back of the card. At the end of the activity, students report back the results of their survey (e.g., *Roger et Caroline sont sportifs ; Robert et Anne ne sont pas sportifs.*)

C'est votre tour. Imagine that you are at a French party. In groups of three or four students (or as a class), play the guessing game presented in the **Mise en situation.** The first student starts : « **Je pense à un homme (une femme)... »** Other students ask yes-or-no questions until they guess the person's identity.

Have students prepare a description of what Americans are like and share it with the class. Other possible topics are *les étudiants, les professeurs, les hommes, les femmes.*

❧ Counting
Les nombres de 20 à 99

Présentation

The numbers from 20 to 59 are:

20	vingt	28	vingt-huit	42	quarante-deux
21	vingt et un	29	vingt-neuf	…	
22	vingt-deux	30	trente	50	cinquante
23	vingt-trois	31	trente et un	51	cinquante et un
24	vingt-quatre	32	trente-deux	52	cinquante-deux
25	vingt-cinq	…		…	
26	vingt-six	40	quarante	59	cinquante-neuf
27	vingt-sept	41	quarante et un		

See Prononciation C for information and drills on pronunciation of numbers.

The numbers from 60 to 99 follow a slightly different pattern:

60	soixante	80	quatre-vingts
61	soixante et un	81	quatre-vingt-un
62	soixante-deux	82	quatre-vingt-deux
…		…	
70	soixante-dix	90	quatre-vingt-dix
71	soixante et onze	91	quatre-vingt-onze
72	soixante-douze	92	quatre-vingt-douze
79	soixante-dix-neuf	99	quatre-vingt-dix-neuf

A. To ask how much something costs, use the question **Combien est-ce que ça coûte?** or the more colloquial **Combien est-ce que ça fait?** *(How much does that make?)*, **Ça fait combien?** or **C'est combien?**

— **Combien est-ce que ça coûte?**
— **Ça coûte huit francs.**

— **Combien est-ce que ça fait?**
— **Ça fait douze francs.**

Although combien can be combined with coûter to ask prices (Combien coûte cette affiche?), the questions given in the text are more typical of everyday speech.

B. For basic mathematical operations, **plus** is used for *plus*, **moins** for *minus*, **fois** for *times*, and **divisé par** for *divided by*. **Ça fait** *(that makes)* is used to express the result.

— Neuf **plus** cinq? Combien est-ce que **ça fait**?
— **Ça fait** quatorze.

— Dix-huit **moins** huit? **Ça fait** combien?
— **Ça fait** dix.

Mise en situation

Demande d'emploi. Laurence Rivière is applying for a job. The employer who is interviewing her wants to know where he can get in touch with her.

job application

L'EMPLOYEUR	Quelle est votre adresse ?
LAURENCE	75, rue Voltaire.
L'EMPLOYEUR	*Code postal ?*
LAURENCE	69006
L'EMPLOYEUR	*Numéro de téléphone ?*
LAURENCE	C'est le 78.22.44.62.
L'EMPLOYEUR	Nom et adresse de votre employeur précédent ?
LAURENCE	Agence Publicis, 63, rue de la République. Téléphone 78.91.35.33.

zip code

phone number

(1) Have students count from 1 to 20. (2) Write numbers on the board and have students read them. (3) Call out a number and have students write it down. (4) Have students write down the numbers from 1 to 20. Read aloud in random order all the numbers except one. Students check all numbers except the one that was not read. Repeat 1–3 with numbers 20–59.

Préparation

A. Distances. A group of French students who commute each day to the university are comparing the distances they have to travel. Tell what they say.

Modèle   25 → **J'habite à vingt-cinq kilomètres de l'université.**

1. 99	**3.** 25	**5.** 61	**7.** 42	**9.** 91
2. 34	**4.** 77	**6.** 86	**8.** 93	**10.** 39

« J'habite à 20 kilomètres... »

Aux Galeries Lafayette

B. Mais non! A salesclerk at **les Galeries Lafayette** in Paris is not doing a good job making change. Play the roles of the clerk and the customers.

Make up supplementary math problems to give to students or have them make up problems to give to each other.

Modèle   20 − 3 = 15
　　　　　— **Vingt moins trois, ça fait quinze.**
　　　　　— **Mais non! Ça fait dix-sept.**

1. 15 − 1 = 3
2. 20 − 5 = 16
3. 68 − 10 = 57
4. 29 − 5 = 23

5. 45 − 5 = 41
6. 12 + 3 = 16
7. 50 − 6 = 43

8. 13 + 7 = 17
9. 39 + 10 = 48
10. 60 − 2 = 55

C. Le téléphone. Assume that you are a telephone operator working at a switchboard. Give your customers the numbers they request. Note that French phone numbers are said as four pairs of numbers (eight digits). The first two digits represent the local exchange.

Modèle   Madame Martin (29.43.32.15)
　　　　　C'est le vingt-neuf, quarante-trois, trente-deux, quinze.

1. Monsieur Humbert (74.82.53.46)
2. Mademoiselle Lacoste (40.96.75.84)
3. Madame Seurat (21.49.13.79)
4. Monsieur Picot (28.45.41.99)
5. Mademoiselle Granville (94.69.71.17)
6. Madame Arnaud (53.51.81.85)

Provide scores of sports events (in the US, Canada, or France) and have students give the scores. Students could also give the scores of games played recently.

Communication et vie pratique

A. Sondage d'opinion. Take an opinion poll to find out the favorite singers, writers, actors, actresses, school subjects, etc. of students in your class. Write a list of possible candidates on the board and then count in French the number of votes for each candidate.

Point out that there are six major railroad stations in Paris, each serving different regions of France. *La gare Saint-Lazare*, one of the largest stations, is located in the middle of Paris and along with *la gare Montparnasse* has trains that leave for and arrive from the West. Southwest trains are at *la gare d'Austerlitz*; southeast trains at *la gare de Lyon*; east-bound trains from *la gare de l'Est*; and north-bound trains at *la gare du Nord*.

B. À la gare Saint-Lazare. You are at the Saint-Lazare station in Paris and are trying to locate the following places. Use the map and legend given below and tell where the following are located.

Exemple   a pharmacy → **C'est au numéro quarante et un.**

1. a taxi stand
2. a bus stop
3. a policeman
4. a subway station

5. a restaurant
6. a bank
7. a place to change money
8. a travel agent

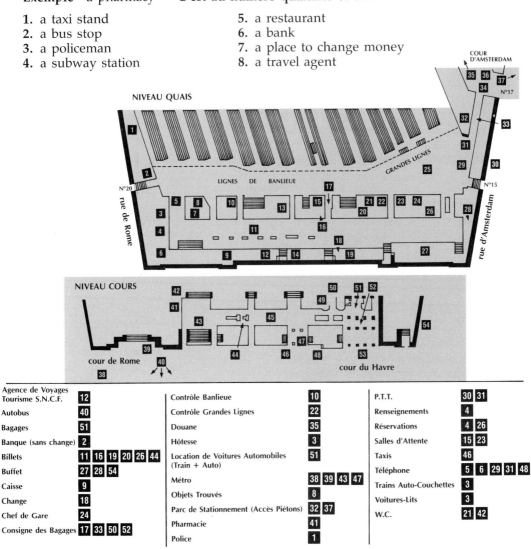

Agence de Voyages Tourisme S.N.C.F.	12	Contrôle Banlieue	10	P.T.T.	30 31
Autobus	40	Contrôle Grandes Lignes	22	Renseignements	4
Bagages	51	Douane	35	Réservations	4 26
Banque (sans change)	2	Hôtesse	3	Salles d'Attente	15 23
Billets	11 16 19 20 26 44	Location de Voitures Automobiles (Train + Auto)	51	Taxis	46
Buffet	27 28 54	Métro	38 39 43 47	Téléphone	5 6 29 31 48
Caisse	9	Objets Trouvés	8	Trains Auto-Couchettes	3
Change	18	Parc de Stationnement (Accès Piétons)	32 37	Voitures-Lits	3
Chef de Gare	24	Pharmacie	41	W.C.	21 42
Consigne des Bagages	17 33 50 52	Police	1		

C'est votre tour. Imagine that you are applying for a job in a French firm. The employer (played by another student) asks you questions similar to those in the **Mise en situation**. Answer these questions based on your own situation.

Intégration et perspectives

Identité   For possible further discussion, see the questions and answers within the song.

The song below was written by Claude Gauthier, a French-Canadian singer. Its words evoke, with great simplicity, what it is like to be a French-Canadian. It also reveals the need that many French-Canadians feel to find their own identity and cultural heritage apart from the rest of Canada.

Je suis de lacs et de rivières.   from

Q: Are there many lakes and rivers in Quebec? Which are the main ones? A: Yes. Lake Ontario, St. Lawrence River, Lake Winnepeg.

Je suis de gibier, de poissons.   wild game / fish

Q: Is there much hunting and fishing in Quebec? Why? A: Yes, because of numerous waterways and untamed land.

Je ne suis pas de grandes moissons.   large / harvests

Q: Are large amounts of wheat produced in Quebec or on the plains of Alberta and Saskatchewan? A: On the plains of Alberta and Saskatchewan.

Je suis de sucre et d'eau d'érable,   sugar / maple sap

Q: In what season is the maple sap collected? A: Late winter, when the sap runs.

de pater noster, de credo.   Roman Catholic prayers

Q: What is the main religion in Quebec and why? A: Catholic, because of French ancestors.

Je suis de dix enfants à table.

Q: Why have French-Canadians tended to have large families? A: Because of Catholic traditions.

Je suis de janvier sous zéro.   January / below

Q: What are winters like in Quebec? A: Cold, snowy.

Je suis d'Amérique et de France.

Q: In what ways is Quebec a blend of French and American cultures? A: The *Québécois* have guarded their French traditions, but proximity to the U.S. has affected their culture (e.g., American TV).

Je suis de chômage et d'exil.   unemployment

Q: When were the Acadians exiled from Canada? A: In the early 18th century after the Treaty of Utrecht (1713), when Acadia was ceded to the British.

Je suis d'octobre et d'espérance.   hope

Q: Are French-Canadians generally happy with their relationship with the rest of Canada? A: It depends. The *Québécois* voted down the resolution for a separatist Quebec but still seek more cultural autonomy.

Je suis l'énergie qui s'empile d'Ungava à Manicouagan.   that piles up

Q: Why is Canada so rich in hydroelectric energy? A: Many waterways—i.e., natural resources for electricity.

Je suis Québec mort ou vivant.   dead / alive

« Je suis de lacs et de rivières… de *pater noster*, de *credo*… »

A. Compréhension. Tell whether the statements below are true or false based on Claude Gauthier's song and what you know about Quebec. In each case, give the line that justifies your response.

1. Quebec is a land of many lakes and rivers.
2. Wild game is still plentiful in Quebec.
3. There are large grain harvests in Quebec.
4. Making maple sugar is a traditional activity in Quebec.
5. Quebec is noted for its mild winters.
6. The Catholic religion has had little influence on the life of French-Canadians.
7. Quebec is a blend of French and American cultures.
8. French-Canadians are torn between a sense of futility and hope for the future.
9. The production of electricity is an important aspect of Quebec's economy.
10. French-Canadians feel a sense of pride in and loyalty for their heritage.

Using Gauthier's song as a guide, have students (alone or in groups) prepare similar poems about the United States.

B. Qu'est-ce que c'est? The following names are familiar to French-Canadians. Can you identify them and match them with the appropriate description from the list of possibilities?

The new cognates in this activity are not part of the chapter's active vocabulary.

Exemple   Trois-Rivières → **C'est une ville.**

1. le Saint-Laurent
2. le Québec
3. Québec
4. Saint-Jean
5. Chicoutimi
6. Champlain
7. pater noster
8. Maria Chapdelaine
9. le château Frontenac
10. Laval
11. Pierre Trudeau

A. un lac
B. une rivière
C. une prière catholique
D. une tribu indienne
E. un homme politique
F. une université
G. un film
H. un explorateur
I. une province
J. un monument historique
K. une région
L. une ville
M. un livre

Office de la langue française
Québec

Notes culturelles: *Vive le Québec*

« **Je me souviens** » *(I remember)* is the official motto of Quebec, and even today, many French-Canadians have not forgotten that their province was for many years under British rule. « **Vive le Québec libre** » *(Long live a free Quebec)* is the rallying cry of the Quebec separatist movement and the **parti québécois** is the political party that is working toward independence for Quebec. For the separatists, the preservation of their French culture and heritage is an important goal. Perhaps the most serious problems facing French-Canadians are the lack of social mobility and the difficulty of gaining access to high-paying jobs that have traditionally been given to English-speaking Canadians. In a book entitled *Les Nègres blancs d'Amérique*, Pierre Vallières compared the situation of French-Canadians to that of Black Americans. On the other hand, there are those who believe that the separatist movement will lead to cultural and economic isolation. In their opinion, certain businesses have left Quebec because of laws establishing French as the only official language in Quebec.

« Vive le Québec »

Communication et vie pratique

A. Le système « D ». Le système « D » refers to the ability to find creative ways of getting out of difficult situations. As a language learner, you may find yourself in situations where you do not know or have forgotten a word you need to know. For instance, how would you answer questions about your date of birth or your address when you can count only up to 99? After consulting the strategies suggested below, work with other students and take turns asking and answering these questions.

Point out that *le système « D »* is related to the adjective *débrouillard(e)* and to the verb *se débrouiller.*

Stratégies :

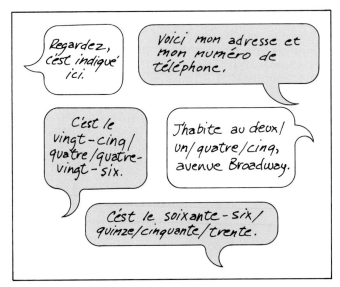

Regardez, c'est indiqué ici.

Voici mon adresse et mon numéro de téléphone.

C'est le vingt-cinq / quatre / quatre-vingt-six.

J'habite au deux / un / quatre / cinq, avenue Broadway.

C'est le soixante-six / quinze / cinquante / trente.

Show your passport or some other form of identification and say:

Regardez, c'est indiqué ici.

Write the needed information on a piece of paper and say:

Voici mon adresse et mon numéro de téléphone.

Give your date of birth, being sure to note the way dates are given in French. April 25, 1986 becomes 25 / 4 / 86.

C'est le vingt-cinq / quatre / quatre-vingt-six.

Give the numbers of your address one by one. For instance, if your address is 2145 Broadway, you would say:

J'habite au deux / un / quatre / cinq, avenue Broadway.

You can give telephone numbers by saying the number one by one or by doing it the French way, i.e., grouped in twos. If the number where you are staying in France is 66.15.50.30 you would say:

C'est le soixante-six / quinze / cinquante / trente.

B. Fiche d'inscription. Imagine that you are planning to study in France. Another student will play the role of the clerk who is asking you questions in order to fill out the registration form given below.

```
FICHE D'INSCRIPTION
REGISTRATION FORM

à remplir par l'étudiant
(to be filled in by the student)
                                                        ┌─────────────┐
NOM : M. Mme Mlle,..................................     │             │
(Surname)                                               │    Photo    │
NOM DE JEUNE FILLE.................................      │  d'identité │
(Maiden name)                                           │             │
PRÉNOM..............................................    │             │
(First name)                                            └─────────────┘
NATIONALITE........................ SEXE ...............
(Nationality)
DATE DE NAISSANCE ....................................
(Date of birth)      JOUR (day)        MOIS (month)        AN (year)
ADRESSE DANS VOTRE PAYS ..............................
(Home address)
              Nº RUE ..................................
              (Nº, street)
              VILLE ...................................
              (Town)
              PAYS ....................................
              (Country)
Désire participer à la session de : (wishes to attend the following session)
1ère SESSION : 7 au 31 JUILLET          2ème SESSION : 4 au 28 AOUT
ou une quinzaine du : ...................... au .......................
(or two weeks, from:              to)
```

● *Prononciation et orthographe*

A. Liaison refers to a consonant sound that is added to link one word to another. In French a **liaison** may occur when a word that normally ends in a silent consonant (e.g., **s**, **t**, **x**, or **n**) is followed by a word that begins with a vowel sound. For a liaison to occur, the first word must in some way modify or qualify the second.

Articles

les étudiants
un Américain
les examens

Adverbs or adjectives

très intéressant
bien agréable
mon adresse

Être (3rd person singular)

C'est intéressant.
C'est assez facile.
Il est optimiste.

Subject pronouns

vous êtes
ils habitent
on aime

Numbers

deux hommes
trois Anglais
six enfants

B. Note the difference in pronunciation between **un** /œ̃/ and **une** /yn/. Note also how a /n/ sound is added to **un** when it is followed by a word that begins with a vowel sound. No change occurs in the feminine because the **n** is already pronounced.

Masculine	Feminine
/œ̃/	/yn/
un commerçant	une commerçante
un journaliste	une journaliste
un Français	une Française
/œ̃/ + /n/	/yn/
un‿employé	une employée
un‿avocat	une avocate
un‿infirmier	une infirmière

C. Masculine and feminine adjectives differ in sound as well as in spelling. The spoken form of the feminine adjective ends in a pronounced consonant; the consonant sound is dropped in the masculine. Note, however, that there is no difference in pronunciation between the masculine and feminine forms of adjectives that end in **-el** / **-elle** (**naturel** / **naturelle**).

Feminine	Masculine
/ɑ̃t/	/ɑ̃/
amusante	amusant
prudente	prudent
/øz/	/ø/
sérieuse	sérieux
courageuse	courageux
/ɛn/	/ɛ̃/
canadienne	canadien
italienne	italien

D. Note the patterns of pronunciation of the following numbers.

deux	cinq /sɛ̃k/	huit /ɥit/
deux enfants	cinq‿enfants	huit‿enfants
deux livres	cinq livres	huit livres
trois	six /sis/	dix /dis/
trois‿enfants	six‿enfants	dix‿enfants
trois livres	six livres	dix livres

Note the pronunciation of the following numbers. (Unpronounced consonants are crossed out.)

vingt̸	quatre-vingt̸s̸	soixante et onze
vingt et un	quatre-vingt̸-un	quatre-vingt̸-onze
vingt-deux	quatre-vingt̸-deux	

• *Vocabulaire*

Noms

les gens/les professions

l'**Américain(e)** (m, f)

l'**architecte** (m)

l'**avocat(e)** (m, f)   *lawyer*

° le **champion, la championne**

le, la **commerçant(e)**   *small-business person, shopkeeper*

le, la **comptable**   *accountant*

° le, la **dentiste**

° l'**employeur** (m)

l'**enfant** (m, f)   *child*

° la **famille**

la **femme**   *woman*

la **fille**   *girl*

le **garçon**   *boy*

l'**homme** (m)   *man*

l'**infirmier** (m), l'**infirmière** (f)   *nurse*

l'**ingénieur** (m)   *engineer*

° le, la **journaliste**

le **médecin**   *physician, medical doctor*

° le, la **psychologue**

° le, la **vétérinaire**

d'autres noms

° l'**adresse** (f)

le **bureau**   *office*

le **code postal**   *zip code, postal code*

° la **date**

la **demande**   *application, request*

le **domicile**   *residence, home*

l'**emploi** (m)   *employment, job*

° l'**énergie** (f)

° l'**hôpital** (m)

° le **lac**

le **lieu**   *place*

la **naissance**   *birth*

° la **nationalité**

le **nom**   *name, last name*

le **numéro**   *number*

° le **passeport**

le **prénom**   *first name*

° la **profession**

° la **région**

° la **rivière**

° le **téléphone**

le **travail**   *work, job*

l'**usine** (f)   *factory*

la **ville**   *city*

° le **zéro**

Verbes

coûter   *to cost*

être   *to be*

parier   *to bet*

Adjectifs (voir pp. 38, 45–46, 49)

belge   *Belgian*

célibataire   *unmarried*

° **compliqué(e)**

fatigué(e)   *tired*

habituel, habituelle   *usual*

° **indiqué(e)**

marié(e)   *married*

même   *same*

° **patient(e)**

poli(e)   *polite*

précédent(e)   *preceding, former*

vrai(e)   *true*

Adverbes

combien   *how much, how many*

trop   *too much, too many*

Divers

ça fait   *that makes*

ça marche bien   *it's going well*

des   *some*

divisé par   *divided by*

êtes-vous né(e)   *were you born*

fois   *times*

moins   *minus, less*

plus   *plus, and*

pour   *for*

pouvez-vous…?   *can you . . .?*

quand   *when*

qui est-ce?   *who is it? who is that?*

quoi   *what*

sur   *on*

un(e)   *a, an*

3

CHAPITRE TROIS

Communication objectives

Naming possessions

1. Indicating what we have
2. Identifying relationships and ownership

3. Expressing possession and relationships
4. Describing our surroundings

Structures

Les mots et la vie : Les possessions

Le verbe **avoir**

Identification : la famille et les possessions

Les adjectifs possessifs

Quelques adjectifs prénominaux et les pièces d'une maison

Background information : Like American students, French students have stereos and enjoy listening to music. Although they prefer *la musique pop* or *le rock*, many enjoy traditional ballads. French students are very familiar with American singers and musicians. The typical French student does not have very much money; few have part-time jobs. Most depend upon modest but readily available government scholarships and subsidies. Annual tuition is inexpensive (from fifty to sixty dollars) and also entitles students to complete medical coverage. Meals in university dining halls are also inexpensive (about a dollar and a half) and though in great demand, university housing is modestly priced. Unlike American dormitories, most rooms are single rooms. Because of limited space, large numbers of students live in apartments and rooms, which tends to be very expensive. Others live at home and commute daily from suburbs or surrounding towns. A small but growing number of students have cars, often an inexpensive and economical *2 CV* (*Deux Chevaux*).

La famille et les possessions

Mise en scène

C'est la vie

Patrick is thinking about various aspects of his life.

J'ai dix-neuf *ans*.	years
J'ai un *frère* et une *sœur*.	brother / sister
J'ai des parents qui sont formidables.	
J'ai une *petite amie* qui est très *gentille*.	girlfriend / nice
J'ai des cours intéressants et des profs assez sympathiques.	
J'ai des *amis*.	friends
J'ai deux *camarades de chambre*.	roommates
J'ai une guitare et une *chaîne-stéréo*.	stereo
J'ai un *vélomoteur qui marche* bien	moped / that / runs
et un *magnétophone* qui ne marche pas!	tape recorder
J'ai un bon *travail*.	job
Je suis en *bonne santé*.	good health
J'ai quelquefois des problèmes — comme *tout le monde*.	everyone
Mais, c'est la *vie*, n'est-ce pas?	life

Compréhension. Est-ce que les phrases suivantes sont vraies ou fausses selon les renseignements donnés dans le texte? Corrigez le sens de la phrase s'il est faux.

1. Patrick possède une chaîne-stéréo.
2. Patrick aime la musique.
3. Le vélomoteur de Patrick ne marche pas bien.
4. Les parents de Patrick sont sympas.
5. Patrick est professeur.
6. Patrick est assez heureux.

61

Notes culturelles: *La famille française*

Many changes in recent years are altering the way French people view the family, marriage, and divorce. The family of the future, for example, will probably consist of an average of two children. There has been a 73% increase in the number of unmarried couples living together in the last ten years, and the number of unwed mothers has increased from 6% in 1968 to 14.2%. In addition, changes in divorce laws have altered the traditional marriage. In 1960, for instance, one out of ten marriages ended in divorce; today that figure is one out of three.

Despite these changes, young people remain optimistic. There is an increased interest in establishing a family and in staying close to one's parents and grandparents. In addition, the French government has continued its support of the family, offering financial benefits such as **allocations familiales** and the **complément familial**. (The **allocations familiales** are money given to families by the government; the amount varies depending on the number of children in the family and its income. The **complément familial** is an additional subsidy given to families with more than three children or with a very young child.)

Les mots et la vie : *Les possessions*

The items in the categories shown below represent things that you are likely to have. After studying these words, tell which items you have (**j'ai**) and which you would like to have (**je voudrais avoir**).

Exemple   J'ai une chaîne-stéréo. Je voudrais avoir un magnétoscope.

1. logement

une chambre

une maison

un appartement

2. équipement de bureau

une machine à écrire

un téléphone

un micro-ordinateur

une calculatrice

3. meubles

un lit

une lampe

une commode

un placard

6. animaux domestiques

un chien

un chat

4. moyens de transport

un vélo

une voiture

une moto

5. audio-visuel

un téléviseur

une chaîne-stéréo

un magnétophone

des vidéocassettes

un appareil-photo

des cassettes

une radio

une caméra

des disques

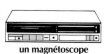
un magnétoscope

Explorations
✾Indicating what we have
Le verbe *avoir*

Présentation

Avoir (*to have*) is an irregular verb.

avoir	
j'**ai**	nous **avons**
tu **as**	vous **avez**
il / elle / on **a**	ils / elles **ont**

Est-ce que tu **as** un frère ?
Nous **avons** trois chats.

A. When the verb **avoir** is used in the negative, an indefinite article (**un**, **une**, **des**) that follows it becomes **de** or **d'**.

Il a **une** moto.	Il n'a pas **de** moto.
J'ai **des** amis.	Je n'ai pas **d'**amis.
Nous avons **un** appartement.	Nous n'avons pas **d'**appartement.

Point out that the same rule applies to *posséder*, *acheter*, and other verbs that indicate possession or acquisition.

B. Avoir is used in many common expressions such as **il y a** (*there is* or *there are*) and in talking about someone's age.

Il y a vingt étudiants dans la classe.	*There are twenty students in the class.*
Il n'y a pas de métro à Québec.	*There isn't any subway in Quebec.*
Quel âge est-ce que vous **avez** ?	*How old are you?*
J'ai dix-neuf ans.	*I'm nineteen years old.*

Repetition : (1) *J'ai un vélo, tu as un vélo, etc.* (2) *Je n'ai pas d'appartement, tu n'as pas d'appartement, etc. Substitution :* (1) *J'ai un frère.* (nous / Serge / Robert et Solange / vous / tu) (2) *Est-ce que tu as un stylo?* (Marc / vous / le professeur / tu / Cécile et Patrick) *Transformation :* Have students put these sentences in the negative. *J'ai un téléviseur. Nous avons trois cours. Marc a des disques. Tu as un appartement. Il y a un métro à Strasbourg. Ils ont une voiture.*

Mise en situation

Au magasin de disques. Barbara is buying some records and is talking with the clerk at a record store.

BARBARA	Est-ce que vous avez des disques canadiens ?	
LE MARCHAND	Oui, nous avons des disques de *tous* les *pays*. Qu'est-ce que vous *cherchez* ?	all / countries looking for
BARBARA	J'ai un ami qui a un disque de Claude Gauthier. C'est l'album où il y a la *chanson* « Je suis de lacs et de rivières... » Est-ce que vous avez ça ?	song
LE MARCHAND	Un instant, s'il vous plaît, je regarde... Non, *je regrette*. Nous n'avons pas de disques de Claude Gauthier. Regardez à Discorama. Ils ont *peut-être* ça...	am sorry perhaps

Recent statistics indicate the following record-buying patterns : French — 45% ; American / British — 20% ; classical music — 16% ; orchestra music — 5% ; children's records — 5% ; jazz — 5% ; comedy — 2% ; misc. — 2%.

Au magasin de disques

Préparation

A. Une soirée sympa. Some friends are planning a party. Tell what each has to bring.

> **Modèle** Richard / chaîne-stéréo
> **Richard a une chaîne-stéréo.**

1. nous / disques
2. Michel et Hélène / radio
3. tu / guitare
4. vous / cassettes
5. André / magnétophone
6. je / magnétoscope

B. Une salle de classe impossible. Geneviève is complaining about the overcrowded, sparsely furnished room where she is taking an English class. Based on the illustration below, tell whether or not the following items are found in the classroom.

Point out that very few students take beginning language classes at the university. Many arrive with several years of language study. Common languages taught are English, German, Italian, Spanish, some Russian, Latin and Greek.

> **Modèle** tableau → **Il y a un tableau.**
> carte → **Il n'y a pas de carte.**

1. fenêtre
2. porte
3. affiches
4. carte
5. magnétophone
6. table
7. chaises
8. bureau

Have students make similar statements about their classroom.

C. **Sondage.** Monsieur Lebrun is taking a survey of the types of audiovisual equipment that families have. Give his questions and the answers of the person being interviewed.

> **Modèle**   téléviseur (oui)
>
> MONSIEUR LEBRUN   **Est-ce que vous avez un téléviseur?**
> MADAME DUPONT   **Oui, nous avons un téléviseur.**

1. magnétoscope (non)
2. micro-ordinateur (oui)
3. chaîne-stéréo (oui)
4. machine à écrire (non)
5. caméra (non)
6. appareil-photo (oui)

Have students role-play this exercise, using these same cues or those from other categories (e.g., office equipment, vehicles).

Communication et vie pratique

A. **Interview.** Ask questions to find out if other students have the following things. Report the results of your conversation to the class.

> **Exemple**   un chien ou un chat
> — **Est-ce que tu as un chien ou un chat?**
> — **Je n'ai pas de chien, mais j'ai deux chats.**

1. un chien ou un chat
2. une chambre dans une résidence ou un appartement
3. un vélo ou une voiture
4. une machine à écrire ou un micro-ordinateur
5. des disques ou des cassettes
6. un magnétoscope ou un magnétophone
7. un frère ou une sœur
8. un appareil-photo ou une caméra

Using known vocabulary, have students ask each other about their possessions (*Est-ce que tu as un chat? une voiture*, etc.) until they find five things that they have in common. Students can use the vocabulary on pp. 63 or a list of suggestions can be put on the board. Another alternative is to prepare cards with the names of different items. Each student must go around the room and ask questions until s/he finds an owner for each item.

B. **Les étudiants américains.** Imagine that some French friends have asked you about things that American students typically have. Give information about students in general and about yourself. Include information about the following categories : **logement, meubles, équipement audio-visuel, moyens de transport, animaux domestiques.**

> **Exemple**   **En général, les étudiants américains ont une chambre dans une résidence ou un appartement en ville. Moi, j'ai une chambre dans une résidence.**

Useful for written homework. Another option is to have small groups of students (at their seat or at the board) write this description. They can then compare and contrast their descriptions.

C'est votre tour. Imagine that you are in a French record shop and want to buy a record whose title you have forgotten. Using the **Mise en situation** as a guide, explain to the salesperson (played by another student) what you are looking for.

Have students use vocabulary and numbers they know to make up true-false statements about the number of people or objects found in different places (e.g., classroom, university, town). Other students will agree or disagree with the statements : *Il y a quarante étudiants dans la classe. Non, il y a vingt-deux étudiants dans la classe*, etc.

❧Identifying relationships and ownership
Identification : La famille et les possessions

Présentation

Important words for identifying family members are :

la mère (*mother*)	l'oncle (*uncle*)	la grand-mère (*grandmother*)
le père (*father*)	la tante (*aunt*)	le grand-père (*grandfather*)
le fils (*son*)	le (la) cousin(e)	les grands-parents
la fille (*daughter*)	le mari (*husband*)	
la sœur (*sister*)	la femme (*wife*)	
le frère (*brother*)		

Other family members : le beau-père (step father or father-in-law), la belle-mère, etc. ; le petit fils ; la petite fille ; la nièce ; le neveu ; l'arrière grand-père, etc. You may want to point out the following : le grand-père — pépé ; la grand-mère — mémé.

A. To express relationships between people, **de** is used.

C'est le père **de** Suzanne.
Les parents **de** Patrick sont sympas.

B. De is also used to express possession.

C'est la chambre **de** Claire.
Le vélo **de** Jean-Louis ne marche pas bien.

C. De is used to express many relationships among things. Note the combinations of **de** with the definite article.

de + **le** becomes **du**	C'est la porte **du** bureau.
de + **les** becomes **des**	Voici la chambre **des** enfants.
de + **la** remains **de la**	C'est une amie **de la** mère de Monique.
de + **l'** remains **de l'**	Où est la voiture **de l'**oncle Jean ?

Mise en situation

Où sont les clés ? Marianne and Daniel are returning home from a trip and cannot find their house keys.

MARIANNE	Tu as la *clé* de la maison ?	key
DANIEL	Non, j'ai la clé des *valises*, mais je n'ai pas la clé de la maison.	suitcases
MARIANNE	*Alors*, elle est *encore* dans la chambre de l'hôtel !	so, then / still
DANIEL	*Qu'est-ce qu'on va faire ?*	What are we going to do?
MARIANNE	*Entre par* la porte du garage…	go in / by, through
DANIEL	Impossible ! Elle est *fermée*.	closed
MARIANNE	Tu n'as pas la clé du garage ?	
DANIEL	Non, elle est sur la table du bureau !	

Préparation

A. Arbre généalogique. Based on the information given in Pierre's family tree, give the relationship between Pierre and each of the people shown.

Modèle   Simone Lefèvre est la tante de Pierre.

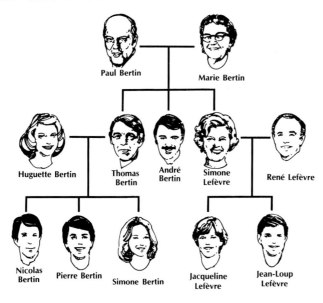

B. Trousseau de clés. Michel Dumas is labeling his keys. Use the cues provided to tell what he says.

Modèle   bureau → **C'est la clé du bureau.**

1. maison
2. valises
3. garage
4. hôtel
5. voiture
6. chambre

Communication et vie pratique

A. Votre famille. Tell another student about various members of your family.

Exemple   **J'ai deux frères et une sœur. J'ai une tante et un oncle qui habitent à New York et des cousins à San Francisco.**

B. Qui est-ce? Give the names of well-known people and have other students tell how that person is related to or identified with another famous person.

Exemple   Caroline Kennedy → **C'est la fille de Jacqueline Onassis.**
Phil Donahue → **C'est le mari de Marlo Thomas.**

C'est votre tour. Imagine that you are traveling by car with a friend (played by another student) and you discover that you have locked your keys inside the car. Using the **Mise en situation** as a guide, role play the conversation between you and your friend.

⚜ Expressing possession and relationships
Les adjectifs possessifs

Présentation

Ownership or relationship is often indicated with a possessive adjective (like *my*, *your*, *their*, etc. in English). A possessive adjective, like all French adjectives, agrees in gender and number with the noun it modifies.

Les adjectifs possessifs			
	Singular		**Plural**
	Masculine	Feminine	Masculine and Feminine
my	**mon** frère	**ma** sœur	**mes** parents
your	**ton** frère	**ta** sœur	**tes** parents
his / her / its / one's	**son** frère	**sa** sœur	**ses** parents
our	**notre** frère	**notre** sœur	**nos** parents
your	**votre** frère	**votre** sœur	**vos** parents
their	**leur** frère	**leur** sœur	**leurs** parents

A. Mon, ton, and **son** are used not only with masculine singular nouns but also with feminine singular nouns that begin with a vowel or vowel sound.

  Est-ce que tu aimes **mon affiche**?
  Ton amie Françoise est très sympathique.
  Son appartement est très moderne.

B. Possessive adjectives agree with the noun modified rather than with the possessor. This difference is especially important with **son, sa,** and **ses** — each of which can mean *his, her, its,* or *one's.*

Robert travaille avec **son** frère et **sa sœur**.	*Robert works with his brother and his sister.*
Annick travaille avec **son** frère et **sa sœur**.	*Annick works with her brother and her sister.*

Mise en situation

Qui est-ce ? Jacques is showing his mother some photos of his new friend, Catherine Dupré, and her family.

SA MÈRE   Tu as des photos de sa famille ?

JACQUES   Oui, regarde. Voici ses parents. Sa mère est prof d'anglais.

SA MÈRE   Et son père ?

JACQUES   Il travaille avec ses deux frères. Ils ont un magasin de *vêtements*.   clothing

SA MÈRE   Et ici, c'est la maison des Dupré ?

JACQUES   Non, ce n'est pas leur maison. C'est la maison de leurs cousins. Ils habitent dans le *même quartier*.   same / neighborhood

Préparation

A. **Album de photos.** Joëlle and Brigitte are looking at Joëlle's photo album. Give Joëlle's answers to Brigitte's questions.

    Modèle   C'est la maison de tes parents ? → **Oui, c'est leur maison.**

    1. Ce sont tes parents ?
    2. C'est ton frère ?
    3. C'est l'appartement de ta sœur ?
    4. C'est la voiture de tes parents ?
    5. C'est le vélo de ton frère ?
    6. Ce sont les amis de tes parents ?
    7. C'est votre chat ?
    8. Ce sont vos chiens ?

B. **Descriptions.** Jean-Paul is talking about his relatives. With the model as a guide, use the appropriate form of the possessive adjective to complete his descriptions.

    Modèle   Mon oncle et ____ tante habitent à Strasbourg.
            Mon oncle et ma tante habitent à Strasbourg.

    1. J'ai un cousin qui est avocat. ____ femme est journaliste.
    2. Le fils de mon oncle Pierre travaille à Montréal. ____ fille est étudiante à l'Université Laval.
    3. Mes grands-parents habitent dans notre quartier. ____ grand-père aime parler avec ____ amis et ____ grand-mère aime marcher et nager.
    4. Mon oncle Robert a deux enfants. ____ fils est étudiant et ____ fille travaille comme médecin à Bruxelles.
    5. Mon oncle et ____ tante ont deux enfants. ____ fille Geneviève est étudiante en droit à Paris et ____ fils Maurice étudie l'informatique.

Substitution : Have students give each noun with the appropriate possessive adjective. (1) (*mon, ma, mes*) le livre, la voiture, le chien, les disques, les amis. (2) (*ton, ta, tes*) la moto, la camarade de chambre, les frères, le stylo. (3) (*son, sa, ses*) les disques, la chaîne-stéréo, la guitare, l'affiche. (4) (*notre, nos*) les parents, la sœur, les vêtements, le professeur. (5) (*votre, vos*) les amis, le magnétoscope, l'appareil-photo, les disques. (6) (*leur, leurs*) l'appartement, les examens, les parents, la chambre.

Short translations are also useful with possessives, especially in the third-person singular : *his sister, her brother, his car, her car, his roommate, her mother, his mother, my books, your* (familiar) *aunt ; our mother ; their house ; her room,* etc.

C. Réunion de famille. David has been invited to Marie-Claire's family reunion. Marie-Claire is identifying family members. Use the cues provided to tell what she says.

Have students note that this exercise combines possessive adjectives and the possessive with de.

Modèle   (my father's brother) → **C'est le frère de mon père.**

1. (my grandmother's sister)
2. (Micheline's children)
3. (my aunt's daughter)
4. (our uncle from Nice)
5. (my aunt's friend)
6. (my brother's girlfriend)
7. (my cousin's children)
8. (our cousins from Strasbourg)
9. (her two sons)
10. (her American friends)

Communication et vie pratique

A. Interview. Use the following words and phrases to ask other students questions about things they have or about people they know.

Have students interview each other in groups of three. Two students ask and answer questions; the third student records their answers and after verifying the accuracy of his / her notes, reports briefly to the whole class.

Exemple   classes / intéressantes
  Est-ce que tes classes sont intéressantes?

1. amis / amusants
2. chambre / agréable
3. camarade de chambre / sympathique
4. cours / intéressants
5. professeurs / sévères
6. examens / difficiles
7. travail / intéressant
8. frères et sœurs / gentils

B. **Opinions.** Comment on each of the following by making statements about yourself or someone else.

Prior preparation may be helpful. Each topic can also be used as the basis for a short written composition.

   Exemple   vos cours
                **Mes cours sont très intéressants, mais ils sont assez dif-
                ficiles.**
        ou: **Mon ami Jean n'aime pas beaucoup ses cours mais il trouve
                ses profs assez sympas.**

   1. votre université
   2. vos professeurs
   3. vos cours
   4. vos amis (camarades de chambre)
   5. votre appartement ou votre chambre
   6. vos possessions (voiture, vélo, cassettes, vidéo-cassettes, etc.)

C. **Famille et amis.** Describe your family and friends to another student, including information about what they do and what they are like.

   Exemple   **J'ai un frère et deux sœurs. Mon frère a dix-huit ans et il est
                aussi étudiant à l'université.**

C'est votre tour. Imagine that a friend (played by another student) is asking you about your new college roommate. Using the **Mise en situation** as a guide, show him / her some pictures and describe the people and places in the photos.

Students could also talk about a friend or relative.

❧ Describing our surroundings
Quelques adjectifs prénominaux et les pièces d'une maison

Présentation

The adjectives **grand** (*tall, large*), **petit** (*small*), **joli** (*pretty*), **beau** (*handsome, beautiful*), **bon** (*good*), **nouveau** (*new*), **jeune** (*young*) and **vieux** (*old*) are very useful in descriptions. These adjectives, which are usually placed before the noun rather than after it, have irregular forms. Note that **beau**, **nouveau**, and **vieux** have irregular forms.

Les adjectifs prénominaux

Masculine	Masculine before a vowel sound	Feminine
un **petit** magasin	un **petit** appartement	une **petite** maison
un **grand** magasin	un **grand** appartement	une **grande** maison
un **joli** magasin	un **joli** appartement	une **jolie** maison
un **beau** magasin	un **bel** appartement	une **belle** maison
un **bon** magasin	un **bon** appartement	une **bonne** maison
un **nouveau** magasin	un **nouvel** appartement	une **nouvelle** maison
un **vieux** magasin	un **vieil** appartement	une **vieille** maison

The liaison sound for **grand** is **t**, and **bon** followed by a vowel sound is pronounced the same as **bonne**.

A. In formal French, when one of these adjectives precedes a plural noun, the indefinite article **des** becomes **de** : **de bons magasins**, **de vieilles maisons**.

You may want to point out that in colloquial French, *des* is often used instead of *de*.

B. These adjectives and others you already know are useful in describing the parts of a home or apartment.

You may wish to note the common ways of asking for the restroom : *Où sont les W.C. ? Où sont les toilettes ?*

    C'est une belle maison de sept pièces (rooms).
    La salle de séjour est très jolie.

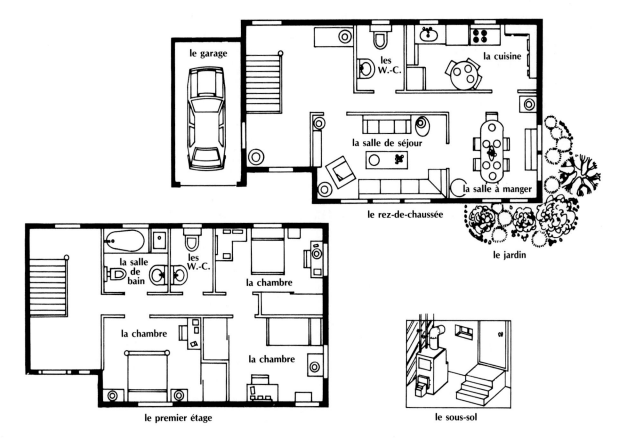

le garage   les W.-C.   la cuisine

la salle de séjour

la salle à manger

le rez-de-chaussée

le jardin

la salle de bain   les W.-C.   la chambre

la chambre

la chambre

le premier étage

le sous-sol

Mise en situation

De vieux amis. Laurent and Nicolas are catching up on each other's news.
Laurent notices a new car parked nearby.

LAURENT	Qu'est-ce que tu fais maintenant ?
NICOLAS	Je travaille dans un grand magasin.
LAURENT	Tu as une nouvelle voiture ?
NICOLAS	Non, j'ai *encore* ma vieille Renault. Elle n'est pas belle, mais elle marche bien.
LAURENT	Mais, *dis-moi*, qu'est-ce que tu fais ici ?
NICOLAS	Je cherche un nouvel appartement.
LAURENT	Il y a un petit appartement *à louer* dans mon *immeuble*. Je pense que c'est *meublé*. Parle au *propriétaire*, c'est un vieil ami de mes parents.
NICOLAS	C'est une bonne idée.
LAURENT	Alors, *bonne chance*.

still

say

for rent / apartment building
furnished / owner

good luck

Préparation

A. Description. Régine is describing her apartment to her friends. Based
on the floor plan below, tell what rooms she has and how many.

Modèle   Il y a une petite cuisine, etc.

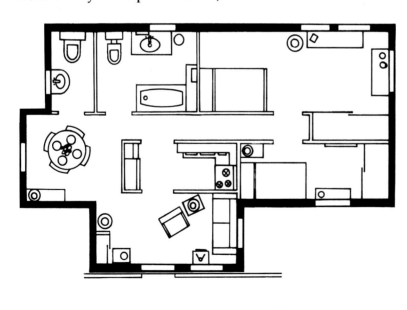

Substitution : (1) C'est un bon ami. *(appartement / livre / film / vélo)* (2) Ils ont une grande cuisine. *(garage / salle à manger / bureau / salle de séjour)* (3) C'est un vieux monsieur. *(homme / musée / maison / appartement / magasin)*

B. Agent immobilier. A real estate agent is showing some clients through a home and comments on various rooms of the house. Tell what the clients say.

> **Modèle**   La cuisine est très grande.
> **Oui, c'est une très grande cuisine.**

1. La salle de séjour est très petite.
2. Le bureau est assez petit.
3. La salle à manger est belle.
4. Le jardin est joli.
5. La chambre est petite.
6. La maison est assez vieille.
7. Le garage est nouveau.
8. Le sous-sol est assez grand.

Have students role-play an agent immobilier trying to sell a house to a reluctant customer.

C. Conversation. Patrick is just getting settled at the university. A friend, Robert, is asking him how he is doing. Using the cues provided, give Patrick's answers.

> **Modèle**   ROBERT   Est-ce que tu as un appartement?
> PATRICK   (petit) **J'ai un petit appartement.**

ROBERT	Est-ce que tu as un appartement?
PATRICK	(très beau)
ROBERT	Tu as des camarades de chambre?
PATRICK	(sympathique)
ROBERT	Tu as un travail?
PATRICK	(bon)
ROBERT	Tu as des profs sympas?
PATRICK	(très bon)
ROBERT	Tu as une voiture?
PATRICK	(vieux)
ROBERT	Tu as une chaîne-stéréo?
PATRICK	(nouveau)
ROBERT	Est-ce que tu as des amis?
PATRICK	(très intéressant)

Have students note that this exercise combines adjectives that precede and adjectives that follow nouns. Have students ask each other the questions in this exercise.

Communication et vie pratique

A. Votre chambre. Use vocabulary you know to describe your room, apartment, home, or the home you would like to live in some day.

B. Réflexions. Using the **Mise en scène** on p. 61 as a guide, prepare a description of the things you have and people you know. Enrich your description by using as many adjectives as you can.

> **Exemple**   **J'ai des livres intéressants.**
> **J'ai une nouvelle chaîne-stéréo et de bons disques.**

C. **Compliments.** Imagine that you are with a French friend and want to compliment him about the following. Use the examples as a guide.

Exemples   appartement
            Tu as un très bel appartement.
    ou: **Ton appartement est très beau.**

1. parents
2. sœur
3. frère
4. maison

5. ville
6. amis
7. grands-parents
8. chambre

C'est votre tour. Imagine that you have just run into a French friend (played by another student) that you have not seen for a long time. Ask your friend . . .

if s/he still lives at the same address
if s/he has a new car
if it works well
if s/he has a new job
if it's a good job

Intégration et perspectives

La vie de Louis Duvivier

Sa vie ? Il travaille, il *dort,* il mange. Il habite un petit appartement à Paris. Il est marié et il a trois enfants — Michel, dix ans, Anne-Marie, sept ans, et Paulette, deux ans. Duvivier, qui a trente-quatre ans, travaille dans une usine d'automobiles. Sa vie est simple et tranquille. Il est assez content.

    Sa femme ne travaille pas maintenant ; elle *reste* à la maison avec les enfants. Elle aussi est assez contente. « Nous ne somme pas riches, c'est vrai, mais nous ne sommes pas pauvres. Nous avons trois enfants qui sont adorables et un appartement qui est modeste mais confortable. Nous habitons dans un quartier agréable et nos *voisins* sont assez gentils. »

    Les Duvivier possèdent l'essentiel : une auto, un grand réfrigérateur, une *machine à laver,* et une télévision en couleur. Ils aiment regarder la télévision et inviter leurs amis à dîner. Oui, ils ont une vie confortable. Oui, ils sont assez satisfaits, mais ils sont aussi résignés à la monotonie de leur vie. « Je suis trop fatigué pour être ambitieux, » *explique* Duvivier. Leur *rêve* est de posséder une petite maison à la *campagne.*

sleeps

stays

neighbors

washing machine

explains
dream / country

A. Compréhension. Répondez aux questions suivantes selon les renseignements donnés dans le texte. (*Answer the following questions according to the information given in the text.*)

1. Où est-ce que Louis Duvivier habite?
2. Est-ce qu'il a des enfants?
3. Quel âge ont-ils?
4. Où est-ce qu'il travaille?
5. Est-ce que sa femme travaille aussi?
6. Est-ce que les Duvivier sont riches?
7. Qu'est-ce que les Duvivier possèdent?

B. Et vous? Give the following information about yourself.

1. Où vous habitez
2. Votre âge
3. Votre lieu de travail
4. Votre situation de famille
5. Vos possessions
6. Votre rêve

Have students prepare questions to ask each other on the reading. In addition, students could be asked to prepare questions to ask Louis Duvivier and his wife, played by other students. Have students try to describe in French an American worker's life and possessions. Have them note any similarities and differences between a worker's life in the U.S. and in France.

Notes culturelles: *La classe ouvrière*

The expression **métro-boulot-dodo** (*subway-work-sleep*) is often used to symbolize the working-class person's frustration with the predictable routine of daily life in a large city.

The standard of living of French working-class and middle-class families has steadily improved since the end of World War II. For a long time, housing was expensive and in short supply, but many of these families are now able to live in **cités ouvrières** (*housing developments*) or in **H.L.M.**'s (**habitations à loyer modéré**). The **H.L.M.**'s are government-sponsored, moderate-rent apartment buildings that have been built on the outskirts of French cities during the last thirty years. Individual apartments are small — averaging three rooms per family — but even in the most modest, a refrigerator and a washing machine are now considered necessities rather than luxuries as they once were.

Many French employees belong to labor unions. The three major unions are based on political affiliation rather than on craft or industry as in the United States. One is communist-led; another is militantly socialist in outlook; a third is moderately socialist. Some major firms, however, including leading automobile manufacturers, have nonpolitical "house" unions.

H.L.M.

Communication et vie pratique

A. Plan d'une maison. Imagine that you have some French friends who are planning to work in the United States for a year. You have found a house for them and need to describe it to them. Include as much information as you can based on the floor plans already given.

Exemple   C'est une assez grande maison. Il y a huit pièces., etc.

B. Choix. Look at the following ads for rooms and apartments taken from a French newspaper. Then decide which apartment or room you would like to rent and why.

Californie, Bas Fabron, studio récent, cuisinette équipée, bains, 1.500 + 200. GERANCE IMMOBILIERE, CNAB, 38, rue de France, 93.87.78.74, Nice.

Frédéric-Mistral, studio impeccable, 32 m2, séjour et vraie cuisine sur terrasse ensoleillée, vue mer, cave, 1.800 + charges. MICHAUGERANCE, Nice, 93.87.10.88.

Hauts Vaugrenier : superbe 60 m2, jardin, vue, situation privilégiée, 4.400 charges comprises. SAINT-PIERRE, 93.07.40.20.

Promenade : beau 2 pièces 68 m2, excellent état, grands balcons, bains, dressing, cave, garage, 3.000 plus charges.   LOCASSISTANCE, 93.82.01.02, Nice.

Haut Cessole, studio avec cuisinette, balcon, 1er étage, 1.350 + charges. BARTOLOTTA, 93.84.08.74, Nice.

Victor-Hugo Alphonse-Karr : bel appartement, 2e, sud, balcon, 2.600 + charges. URBANICE, 93.44.76.47, Nice.

Parc Chambrun Saint-Maurice : beau 2 pièces, garage, cave, 2.500 F + charges. Tél. 93.84.90.72, Nice.

Have students guess the meaning of abbreviations and new vocabulary from context. It might also be useful to have students write out in complete sentences one or several of the ads.

C. Louez un appartement. Imagine that you are going to talk with the owner about renting the room or apartment that you have selected. Another student will play the role of the owner. Use the questions below to help you role-play the situation.

Questions du client :
— Est-ce que l'appartement est meublé ?
— Combien de pièces est-ce qu'il y a ?
— Est-ce que les pièces sont grandes ?
— Est-ce qu'il y a un garage ?
— Est-ce que c'est dans un quartier agréable ?

Questions du propriétaire
— Est-ce que vous avez un(e) camarade de chambre ?
— Est-ce que vous travaillez ?
— Est-ce que vous êtes étudiant(e) ?
— Est-ce que vous avez un chien ou un chat ?
— Est-ce que vous êtes marié(e) ?
— Est-ce que vous êtes une personne tranquille ?

• *Prononciation et orthographe*

A. In French the letter **a** is pronounced /a/ . Compare the pronunciation of the following pairs of words, each containing the letter **a**, and practice repeating the French words.

English	**French**
Barbara	Barbara
Daniel	Daniel
lake	lac
patient	patient
education	éducation
geography	géographie
radio	radio

B. Note the difference between the third person plural of **avoir** (**ils ont** with a /z/ sound) and the third person plural of **être** (**ils sont** with an /s/ sound). Practice repeating the following :

Ils ont des amis; ils sont contents.
Ils ont vingt ans; ils sont jeunes.
Ils ont des problèmes; ils sont tristes.

C. There are three basic nasal vowel sounds in French : /ɔ̃/ as in **mon** ; /ɛ̃/ as in **magasin** ; and /ɑ̃/ as in **étudiant**. Practice repeating words containing the sound /ɔ̃/ .

mon	maison	mon livre	mon ami
ton	leçon	ton vélo	ton oncle
son	concert	son chien	mon affiche

D. Note the difference between the pronunciation of **bon** /bɔ̃/ with a nasal sound and **bonne** /bɔn/ . Note also that **bon** /bɔ̃/ becomes /bɔn/ (the same pronunciation as the feminine form **bonne**) when it is followed by a vowel sound.

/ɔ̃/	/ɔn/	/ɔn/
un bon prof	un bon élève	une bonne classe
un bon camarade	un bon hôtel	une bonne amie
un bon travail	un bon emploi	une bonne santé

• *Vocabulaire*

Noms

les possessions

°   l'**album** (m)
     l'**appareil-photo** (m)   *camera*
°   l'**appartement** (m)
°   l'**automobile** (f)
     la **calculatrice** (f)   *calculator*

la **caméra**   *movie or video camera*
la **cassette**
la **chaîne-stéréo**   *stereo*
le **chat**   *cat*
le **chien**   *dog*
la **clé**   *key*
la **commode**   *chest of drawers, cabinet*

le **disque** *record*
° l'**équipement** (m)
° la **guitare**
° la **lampe**
le **lit** (m) *bed*
la **machine à écrire** *typewriter*
le **magnétophone** *tape recorder*
le **magnétoscope** *video recorder*
la **maison** *house*
les **meubles** (m pl) *furniture*
le **micro-ordinateur** *microcomputer*
la **moto** *motorcycle*
° la **photo**
le **placard** *closet*
° le **réfrigérateur**
la **valise** *suitcase*
le **vélo** *bicycle*
le **vélomoteur** *moped*
les **vêtements** (m pl) *clothing*
la **voiture** *automobile*

la maison et l'appartement (**voir p. 73**)

les membres d'une famille (**voir p. 67**)

d'autres noms

l'**ami(e)** (m, f) *friend*
° l'**animal** (m)
l'**an** (m) *year*
le, la **camarade de chambre** *roommate*
la **chance** *luck*
la **chanson** *song*
° la **couleur**
° l'**hôtel** (m)
° l'**idée** (f)
l'**immeuble** (m) *apartment building*
l'**instant** (m) *instant, moment*
le **logement** *housing*
le **moyen** *means*
le **pays** *country*
le **petit ami** *boyfriend*
la **petite amie** *girlfriend*
la **pièce** *room*

le, la **propriétaire** *owner*
le **quartier** *neighborhood*
le **rêve** *dream*
la **santé** *health*
le **transport** *transportation*

Verbes

avoir *to have*
chercher *to look for, to seek*
dîner *to have dinner*
entrer *to enter, to go in*
expliquer *to explain*
° **inviter**
louer *to rent*
marcher *to run, to walk*
regretter *to be sorry, to regret*
rester *to stay, to remain*

Adjectifs

les adjectifs possessifs (**voir p. 69**)
° **audio-visuel, audio-visuelle**
beau, bel, belle *beautiful, handsome*
bon, bonne *good*
confortable
fermé(e) *locked*
gentil, gentille *nice*
grand(e) *tall, large*
jeune *young*
joli(e) *pretty*
meublé(e) *furnished*
nouveau, nouvel, nouvelle *new*
petit(e) *small, short*
satisfait(e) *satisfied*
sympa (short for
sympathique) *nice*
tranquille *calm, peaceful*
vieux, vieil, vieille *old*

Divers

alors *so, well, then*
il y a *there is, there are*
par *by, through*
peut-être *perhaps*
qu'est-ce qu'on va faire? *what are we going to do?*
qui *that, who*
tout le monde *everyone*

4

CHAPITRE QUATRE

Communication objectives

Making travel plans

1. Indicating our destination and / or intentions
2. Telling where we are or where we are going
3. Telling when something is taking place
4. Identifying people and countries

Structures

Les mots et la vie : Les voyages

    Le verbe **aller**

    Les prépositions et les noms de lieux

    Les jours, les mois et les saisons

    Les nationalités

En vacances

Mise en scène

Bonnes vacances!

Note that the abbreviations for *Madame (Mme)* and *Mademoiselle (Mlle)* do not have a period; the one for *Monsieur (M.)* does. You may want to mention the traffic jams on French highways on the days that many French families leave on vacation, especially on the *Autoroute du Sud*, which goes to the *Côte d'Azur*.

Paris, le 31 *juillet*. Un reporter *pose* des questions aux automobilistes qui *quittent* la *ville*.

LE REPORTER	Bonjour, monsieur. Bonjour, madame. Où est-ce que vous *allez* en vacances *cette année*?
M. BLANC	Nous *allons* à Antibes, sur la *Côte d'Azur*.
LE REPORTER	C'est la *première fois que* vous allez à Antibes?
MME BLANC	Oui. *D'habitude*, nous *passons* nos vacances en Bretagne.
LE REPORTER	Eh bien, *bonnes vacances*!
LE REPORTER	Bonjour, madame. Bonjour, monsieur. Vous allez en vacances cette année?
MME ARLAND	Oui, mais pas *aujourd'hui*. Nous allons à la *campagne*.
LE REPORTER	Est-ce que vous allez passer vos vacances en France ou dans un *pays étranger*?
MME ARLAND	Dans un pays étranger. Cette année, nous allons en Italie et l'année *prochaine*, nous désirons visiter la Grèce et la Yougoslavie.
LE REPORTER	*Alors*, bon voyage!

Glosses (right margin):
July / asks, poses
are leaving / city

are going / this / year
are going / Riviera
first / time / that
usually / spend
have a good vacation

today / country, countryside
country / foreign

next

well, then

Compréhension. Selon les renseignements donnés, est-ce que les phrases suivantes sont vraies ou fausses ? Corrigez le sens de la phrase s'il est faux.

1. D'habitude, Monsieur et Madame Blanc passent leurs vacances sur la Côte d'Azur.
2. C'est la première fois qu'ils visitent Antibes.
3. Ils ne passent jamais leurs vacances en Bretagne.
4. Monsieur et Madame Arland passent le week-end à la campagne.
5. Cette année, les Arland passent leurs vacances dans un pays étranger.
6. Cette année, ils visitent la Grèce et la Yougoslavie.

Option : Have students make up other titles for the *Mise en scène* and / or for its two subsections.

Notes culturelles: *En vacances*

Vacations are sacred for most French people. Every employee is guaranteed by law a minimum of five weeks' paid vacation. Unlike Americans, very few spend their vacation time working to earn extra money. For most French people the preferred vacation time is in the summer (usually in the month of August) and the preferred vacation spot is the beach. It has been said that in August, the only people in Paris are tourists. To avoid the high cost of hotels, up to eight million people also choose to camp during their vacations. Other people prefer newer types of vacations. For example, winter sports vacations are becoming increasingly popular as are different forms of rediscovering the French countryside on foot, on horseback, on bicycle, on river barges, and even by horse-drawn carriage. Others rent old houses in the many villages that dot the countryside or stay with a farm family.

You may want to point out the following : *Quand les Français vont en vacances : mai — 4,8% ; juin — 8,6% ; juillet — 40,3% ; août — 39,1% ; septembre — 7,2%. Où ils vont en vacances : mer — 45,5% ; campagne — 23,1% ; montagne — 16,1% ; ville — 8,4% ; circuit — 6,9%.*

La plage à Nice

For children and teenagers, a variety of summer camps, called **colonies de vacances**, are available. These are sponsored and subsidized by government agencies, industries, cities, and religious or social groups. Students can also attend summer camps sponsored by the **Ministère de la Jeunesse et des Sports**, where they participate in such activities as sailing, mountain climbing, scuba diving, and spelunking. The tradition of summer jobs, so popular with American high school students, is less common in France.

Les mots et la vie : *Les voyages*

Imagine that you are at a travel agency to plan a trip. Another student will play the role of the travel agent who will ask you the following questions. Possible answers that you might give are also provided.

1. Où est-ce que vous préférez passer vos vacances ?
   à la montagne   à la campagne   à la plage   en ville
2. Comment est-ce que vous préférez voyager ?
   en voiture   par le train   en avion   en moto   à bicyclette   à pied
3. Avec qui est-ce que vous préférez voyager ?
   seul(e)   en groupe   avec vos amis   avec votre famille
4. Où est-ce que vous préférez voyager ?
   dans votre pays   à l'étranger
5. Quand vous voyagez, quelles sont vos activités préférées ?
   aller au concert, au cinéma ou au théâtre   parler avec les gens
   visiter des musées et des monuments   manger au restaurant
   marcher dans les rues   acheter des souvenirs
6. Où est-ce que vous préférez rester ?
   à l'hôtel   chez des amis
   dans une auberge de jeunesse   dans un camping
   dans une pension de famille

Vocabulaire

la montagne *mountain*
la plage *beach*
en avion *by plane*
à pied *on foot*
seul(e) *alone*

à l'étranger *abroad*
chez *at the home of*
*acheter *to buy*
l'auberge de jeunesse *youth hostel*
la pension de famille *rooming house*

*Acheter is a regular -er verb except that an **accent grave** is added in all but the **nous** and **vous** forms : **j'achète, tu achètes, il / elle / on achète, nous achetons, vous achetez, ils / elles achètent.**

Explorations
❧ Indicating our destination and / or intentions
Le verbe *aller*

Présentation

The verb **aller** (*to go*) is irregular and is used to indicate movement or travel to a place, or to express future plans or intentions.

aller	
je **vais**	nous **allons**
tu **vas**	vous **allez**
il / elle / on **va**	ils / elles **vont**

Remind students that aller is used in phrases they already know : Comment allez-vous ? Ça va ?

Vous **allez** à Genève ?
Non, nous **allons** à Lausanne.

A. When used to express future plans or intentions, a conjugated form of **aller** is followed by an infinitive.

Nous **allons voyager** par le train.
Il **va faire** des études à Montpellier.
Je **vais acheter** un micro-ordinateur.

Some useful expressions in talking about future plans or intentions are :

aujourd'hui (*today*)
demain (*tomorrow*)
pendant les vacances (f)
  (*during vacation*)

la semaine prochaine
  (*next week*)
le week-end prochain
  (*next weekend*)

You may want to point out that in French huit jours refers to one week and quinze jours to two weeks.

B. To indicate movement to a place, **aller** is often used with the preposition **à** (*at, to*). Note how **à** combines with the definite article, whether it is used with **aller** or with other verbs.

à + **le** become **au**	Je vais **au** concert.
à + **les** become **aux**	Il parle **aux** enfants.
à + **la** remain **à la**	Nous restons **à la** maison.
à + **l'** remain **à l'**	Ils sont **à l'**hôtel.

Repetition : (1) Je vais à la plage, tu vas à la plage, etc. (2) Je ne vais pas au concert, tu ne vas pas au concert, etc. Substitution : (1) Nous n'allons pas rester à la maison. (je / mon frère / vous / tu / mes amis / nous) (2) Monsieur Durand va visiter le Portugal. (tu / votre ami / vous / tes parents / Anne) (3) Je vais à la plage. (bibliothèque / campagne / montagne / théâtre / café / cinéma / musée)

Point out that many restaurants, small shops, businesses, and even large factories close for a period of time, ranging from two weeks to a month, every year for the *fermeture annuelle*. Although these dates vary, most occur during the months of July and August.

Mise en situation

Fermeture annuelle. It is the second week of August and a client is wondering when the neighborhood pharmacy will close this summer.

LA CLIENTE	Vous n'allez pas *fermer* cette année?	**to close**
MME DUBOURG	Si! On va fermer la semaine prochaine.	
LA CLIENTE	Vous avez des *projets* pour vos vacances?	**plans**
MME DUBOURG	Mon mari et moi, nous allons *chaque* année sur la Côte.	**each, every**
LA CLIENTE	Et vos enfants?	
MME DUBOURG	Ma fille va aller à la montagne et les garçons vont *faire du camping* avec des *copains*.	**to go camping** **friends (slang)**

Préparation

Point out that *une copine* is used for a female friend.

A. Projets. Danielle and her friends all have plans for this weekend. Using the cues provided, tell where they are going.

Activity could be repeated using all verb forms: *je / restaurant, vous / plage, etc.*

Modèle   Catherine / concert → **Catherine va au concert.**

1. Rémi / plage
2. Bernard / restaurant
3. Christiane / bibliothèque
4. Frédéric / cinéma
5. Julie / théâtre
6. Martine / musée
7. Robert / montagne
8. Serge / campagne

B. La fête du travail. Several students are talking about their plans for the Labor Day holiday (May 1st). Tell what they are going to do.

Modèle   Serge / rester à la maison
Serge va rester à la maison.

1. nous / faire du camping
2. Claudine / aller à la plage
3. mes amis / aller au théâtre
4. vous / regarder la télé
5. je / rester à la maison
6. tu / aller chez tes parents
7. mon frère / aller à la montagne
8. ma camarade de chambre / étudier

Communication et vie pratique

A. Le week-end prochain. Ask other students if they plan to do these things next weekend.

Have students report the results of their conversation to the class : *Robert va aller au concert, mais il ne va pas aller au cinéma.*

Exemple   aller à la bibliothèque
Est-ce que tu vas aller à la bibliothèque ?

1. aller au concert
2. manger dans un bon restaurant
3. aller à la campagne
4. parler avec des amis
5. aller au cinéma
6. étudier pour un examen
7. écouter des disques
8. regarder la télé
9. aller chez tes parents
10. rester à la maison

B. Suggestions. Imagine that you and some friends are making plans for the weekend. Ask them if they would like to do the following things. They will indicate whether or not they like the idea.

Exemple

—**On va à la montagne ?**
—**Oui, c'est une bonne idée.**
ou: —**Non, je préfère rester ici.**

1.

3.

6.

2.

4.

7.

5.

8.

C'est votre tour. With another student, role-play and adapt the **Mise en situation**. Ask and give information about (1) where you usually go during the weekend ; (2) your particular plans for this weekend ; (3) your usual plans for winter or spring break ; and (4) your particular plans for this winter or spring break.

Written preparation would be helpful.

⚜ Telling where we are or where we are going
Les prépositions et les noms de lieux

Présentation

The preposition used to indicate a location or destination depends on the kind of place :

à + city	**à Paris** **à Chicago**
en + feminine country	**en France** **en Belgique**
au + masculine country	**au Canada** **aux États-Unis**

chez + person's name
       + person
       + pronoun
       + person's profession
         or business
	chez Madame Ménard
	 chez des amis
	 chez moi
	 chez le dentiste

En is used with feminine provinces (*en Alsace*) and with feminine states (*en Californie*).

One says *dans le* for masculine provinces (*dans le Périgord*) and for masculine states (*dans le Colorado*).

A. Most countries ending in **e** are feminine, except **le Mexique** and **le Zaïre**. Others are masculine singular, except **les États-Unis** (*the United States*), which is masculine plural.

Point out that although *Israël* is masculine, it does not take an article (*Je vais visiter Israël*) and one says *en Israël*. *À* is generally used with islands (fem. — *à la Martinique, à la Réunion* and masc. — *à Cuba*).

Point out that the definite article is used with *visiter* : *Je vais visiter le Canada.*

Quelques pays féminins

		Quelques pays masculins
l'Algérie	la Hollande	le Brésil
l'Allemagne (*Germany*)	l'Inde	le Canada
l'Angleterre (*England*)	l'Irlande	le Danemark
l'Australie	l'Italie	les États-Unis
l'Autriche (*Austria*)	la Norvège	le Japon
la Belgique	la Pologne (*Poland*)	le Maroc
la Chine	la Russie ou l'U.R.S.S.	le Mexique
l'Égypte	la Suède (*Sweden*)	le Portugal
l'Espagne (*Spain*)	la Suisse (*Switzerland*)	le Sénégal
la France	la Tunisie	le Viêt-nam
la Grèce	la Yougoslavie	le Zaïre

B. En is also used with continents, which are feminine : **l'Afrique, l'Amérique du Nord, l'Amérique du Sud, l'Antarctique, l'Asie, l'Australie, l'Europe.**

Mise en situation

Projets. Neighbors in a Parisian apartment building are comparing their plans for Easter (**Pâques**) weekend.

MONSIEUR SIMON   Vous restez à Paris pendant le week-end?

MADAME PESSIN   Non, nous allons chez mes parents.

MONSIEUR SIMON   Ils habitent en province?

MADAME PESSIN   Oui, ils ont une petite maison en Bourgogne. Et vous, vous avez des projets?

MONSIEUR SIMON   *Pas vraiment*. Ma femme est en *voyage d'affaires* au Danemark et les enfants sont en *voyage scolaire* en Angleterre.

Substitution : (1) Nous allons à Paris. *(Madrid / Genève / Montréal / Dakar)* (2) Ils habitent en France. *(Belgique / Allemagne / Chine / Suède / Australie / Espagne)* (3) Je voudrais voyager au Portugal. *(Mexique / Maroc / Japon / Canada / États-Unis / Zaïre)*

not really / business trip

school trip

Préparation

A. Quels pays visiter? Agnès is talking about the countries she would like to visit. What does she say?

Modèle   Italie → **Je voudrais aller en Italie.**

1. Portugal	5. Chine	9. Russie
2. Grèce	6. Norvège	10. Sénégal
3. Mexique	7. Canada	11. Égypte
4. Japon	8. Tunisie	12. États-Unis

B. À l'auberge de jeunesse. Some students have met in an **auberge de jeunesse** (*youth hostel*). Using the model as a guide, tell how each introduces himself or herself.

Modèle   Brigitte / Nice / France
             Je m'appelle Brigitte et j'habite à Nice en France.

1. Pablo / Séville / Espagne
2. Maria / Lisbonne / Portugal
3. Juanita / Acapulco / Mexique
4. Karl / Vienne / Autriche
5. Théo / Athènes / Grèce
6. Érik / Oslo / Norvège
7. Djenat / Alexandrie / Égypte
8. Bob / Philadelphie / États-Unis
9. Miko / Tokyo / Japon
10. Amadou / Dakar / Sénégal

Give students a card with this or similar information and have them introduce themselves to other students or have students find out their name, city of origin, and country by asking questions.

C. Projets de voyage. Where are the following people going this summer? Use the cues provided to tell what they say.

Have students note that the preposition, even when the same, is repeated : *Je vais en Algérie et en Tunisie.*

Modèle   Henri / Espagne et Portugal
Henri va en Espagne et au Portugal.

1. mes amis / Sénégal et Zaïre
2. Monsieur Robert / Suisse et Italie
3. je / Norvège et Danemark
4. nous / Canada et États-Unis
5. vous / Pologne et Russie
6. tu / Angleterre et Irlande
7. mon frère / Algérie et Maroc

Communication et vie pratique

A. Je voudrais aller... Decide which countries you would like to visit. Then find out if another student would like to visit those countries too.

Exemple   — **Je voudrais aller en Grèce. Et toi?**
— **Pas moi. Je voudrais aller en Suède et en Norvège.**

B. Bonnes vacances! What would be a good vacation spot abroad for the following people?

Written preparation may be helpful. Have students compare their answers.

Exemple   Pour ma camarade de chambre, des vacances...
Pour ma camarade de chambre, des vacances en Italie.

1. Pour mon prof de français, un voyage...
2. Pour ma famille, quinze jours...
3. Pour mes amis, trois semaines...
4. Pour les étudiants de notre classe, des vacances...
5. Pour moi, des vacances...

C. Villes et pays. Tell where the following cities are located. Then give the names of other cities and see if other students can give the name of the country where each is located.

Exemple   Dakar
— **Où est Dakar?**
— **C'est au Sénégal.**

1. Bruxelles
2. Genève
3. Londres
4. Berlin
5. Moscou
6. Montréal
7. Alger
8. Strasbourg
9. Rome
10. Lisbonne

C'est votre tour. Imagine that you are an experienced world traveler and that friends have asked you « **Vous avez des projets pour vos vacances?** » Tell them the different places you usually visit and where you stay. Describe also your vacation plans for this year and next year. You may also mention some of the destinations of your "jet-set" friends and relatives.

❧Telling when something is taking place
Les jours, les mois et les saisons

Présentation

The French words for the days of the week, the months, and the seasons are not capitalized and are all masculine :

Les jours de la semaine	Les mois de l'année		Les saisons
lundi	janvier	juillet	l'automne
mardi	février	août	l'hiver
mercredi	mars	septembre	le printemps
jeudi	avril	octobre	l'été
vendredi	mai	novembre	
samedi	juin	décembre	
dimanche			

Point out that août is pronounced /u/ or /ut/.

Point out the major holidays in France : le 1er janvier — le Jour de l'An ; Pâques et le lundi de Pâques ; le 1er mai — la fête du Travail ; le 8 mai — fin de la 2e Guerre mondiale ; 40 jours après Pâques — l'Ascension ; le 7e dimanche après Pâques — la Pentecôte ; le 14 juillet — la Fête nationale ; le 15 août — L'Assomption ; le 1er novembre — la Toussaint ; le 11 novembre — l'Armistice ; le 25 décembre — Noël. On April 1st, one says poisson d'avril instead of April Fool's.

A. To ask what day it is, one says :

Quel jour est-ce aujourd'hui ?	*What day is it today ?*
Quel jour sommes-nous ?	*What day is it today ?*
C'est lundi.	*It's Monday.*
C'est aujourd'hui lundi.	*Today is Monday.*

B. To indicate that an event is occurring on a particular day, use the day without any preposition or article.

Il y a un match de football samedi.	*There is a soccer game (on) Saturday.*

To indicate that an event occurs repeatedly or regularly on a certain day, the definite article and the singular form of the noun are used.

J'ai une classe de français **le** mardi.	*I have a French class (on) Tuesdays.*

C. To ask what the date is, one says :

Quelle est la date aujourd'hui ?	*What is today's date ?*
C'est le 11 février.	*It's the 11th of February.*
C'est aujourd'hui le premier mai.	*Today is the first of May.*

Note that dates are expressed by **le** plus a number, except for the first of the month, where **le premier (le 1er)** is used. Note also that the day always precedes the month ; thus, 6/1/88 refers to January 6, 1988.

Have students repeat in order the months of the year and days of the week. Give a day of the week (or month of the year) and have students give the next month. Give a month and have students tell what season it is in : *juillet — c'est en été*, etc. Have students give the days of the week (*C'est aujourd'hui dimanche*, etc.) and the date (*C'est le 1ᵉʳ janvier*, etc.).

D. En is used to indicate that an event occurs in a particular month or season, except for **le printemps** where **au** is used.

En quel mois est son anniversaire ?	*In what month is his birthday?*
Son anniversaire est **en** novembre.	*His birthday is in November.*
Je n'aime pas voyager **en** hiver.	*I don't like to travel in (the) winter.*
Nous avons dix jours de vacances **au** printemps.	*We have ten days of vacation in the spring.*

Mise en situation

C'est quand ton anniversaire ? Danielle is trying to guess when Alain's birthday is.

DANIELLE	En quel mois est ton anniversaire ?
ALAIN	*Devine.*
DANIELLE	Est-ce que c'est au printemps ?
ALAIN	Non.
DANIELLE	Est-ce que c'est en automne ?
ALAIN	Oui.
DANIELLE	Est-ce que c'est au mois d'octobre ?
ALAIN	Non, ce n'est pas en octobre.
DANIELLE	Je parie que tu es un scorpion.
ALAIN	Oui, *je suis né* le 15 novembre.

guess *(command form)*

Students are asked to guess each other's birthday in *C'est votre tour*. You may also want to give students the French names for the signs of the zodiac and have them give the corresponding dates.

I was born

Préparation

A. C'est quand ta fête ? Many French people celebrate their saint's day (**la fête**) as well as their birthday. Tell when the following have their **fête**.

Use additional saint's days if additional practice is needed.

Modèle   Didier 23 / 5 → **La fête de Didier est le vingt-trois mai.**

1. Gilles 1/9
2. Germaine 15/6
3. Jacqueline 8/2
4. Vincent 22/1
5. Albert 15/11
6. Valérie 28/4
7. Dominique 7/8
8. Colette 6/3
9. David 30/12
10. Serge 7/10
11. Olivier 12/7
12. Yves 19/5

Marché à Dakar

B. Une semaine à Dakar. You and your friends are visiting Dakar, the capital of Senegal, and are planning your week's activities. Tell what you are going to do each day.

Have students plan a week's activities for a group of French-speaking students who are visiting their city.

> **Modèle** Dimanche? (visiter des monuments)
> **Dimanche, nous allons visiter des monuments.**

1. Dimanche? (marcher dans les rues de la ville)
2. Lundi? (manger au restaurant)
3. Mardi? (visiter l'université)
4. Mercredi? (visiter le musée)
5. Jeudi? (acheter des souvenirs)
6. Vendredi? (aller au théâtre)
7. Samedi? (aller chez des amis)

C. **Activités.** Michel is asking when his friends do various things. Using the cues provided, give their answers.

Modèle   Quand est-ce que tu vas en vacances? *(in August)*
            En août.
    ou: **Au mois d'août.**

1. Quand est-ce que Monique va partir en vacances? *(in December)*
2. Quand est-ce que ta famille va à la campagne? *(on Sundays)*
3. Quand est-ce que Marc va au ciné? *(Friday)*
4. Quand est-ce que Marie-Louise va partir en Suisse? *(in the spring)*
5. Quand est-ce que tu vas inviter tes amis à dîner? *(Saturday)*
6. Quand est-ce que tes amis italiens vont arriver? *(next week)*
7. Quand est-ce que ton frère va en Bretagne? *(in May)*
8. Quand est-ce que tu vas chez tes parents? *(on Saturdays)*
9. Quand est-ce que ta famille va à la plage? *(in the summer)*
10. Quand est-ce que tu vas au concert? *(Wednesday)*

Communication et vie pratique

Questions / Interview. Answer the following questions or use them to interview another student.

Students may take notes on each other's responses, then write a paragraph combining the answers.

1. Quel jour de la semaine est-ce que tu préfères?
2. En quel mois est ton anniversaire?
3. Quelle(s) saison(s) de l'année est-ce que tu préfères?
4. Quel mois est-ce que tu préfères?
5. D'habitude, qu'est-ce que tu fais le samedi et le dimanche?
6. Qu'est-ce que tu fais le vendredi soir?
7. Quand est-ce que tu as tes différents cours?
8. Qu'est-ce que tu aimes faire en été?
9. En quelle saison est-ce que tu aimes voyager?

C'est votre tour. Ask yes-or-no questions to try to find out the birthdays of other students in your class. Use the **Mise en situation** as a guide.

✸ Identifying people and countries
Les nationalités

Présentation

Terms for nationalities have four basic endings :

Pays	Habitants

● la France   → les Français / les Françaises

    l'Angleterre   les Anglais / les Anglaises
    l'Irlande   les Irlandais / les Irlandaises
    la Hollande   les Hollandais / les Hollandaises
    le Japon   les Japonais / les Japonaises
    le Portugal   les Portugais / les Portugaises
    le Sénégal   les Sénégalais / les Sénégalaises

● le Canada   → les Canadiens / les Canadiennes

    la Tunisie   les Tunisiens / les Tunisiennes
    l'Égypte   les Égyptiens / les Égyptiennes
    l'Italie   les Italiens / les Italiennes
    le Brésil   les Brésiliens / les Brésiliennes
    l'Autriche   les Autrichiens / les Autrichiennes
    l'Inde   les Indiens / les Indiennes
    l'Australie   les Australiens / les Australiennes
    la Norvège   les Norvégiens / les Norvégiennes

● le Mexique → les Mexicains / les Mexicaines

    l'Amérique   les Américains / les Américaines
    le Maroc   les Marocains / les Marocaines

● la Chine   → les Chinois / les Chinoises

    la Suède   les Suédois / les Suédoises
    le Danemark   les Danois / les Danoises
    le Zaïre   les Zaïrois / les Zaïroises

Other nationalities do not follow these patterns :

    l'Allemagne   les Allemands / les Allemandes
    l'Espagne   les Espagnols / les Espagnoles
    la Grèce   les Grecs / les Grecques
    la Russie   les Russes / les Russes
    la Belgique   les Belges / les Belges

Two patterns can be used to indicate someone's nationality :

C'est + INDEFINITE ARTICLE
+ NOUN (capitalized)

C'est un Français.
C'est une Italienne.
Ce sont des Belges.

NOUN or PRONOUN + *être*
+ ADJECTIVE (not capitalized)

Il est français.
Elle est italienne.
Ils sont belges.

Mise en situation

La saison marche bien ? Two hotel clerks on the **Côte d'Azur** are comparing notes.

M. DUJARDIN	La saison marche bien ?
MME CHRISTOPHE	Oui, l'hôtel est *complet*. Nous avons un grand nombre de clients étrangers. Et vous ?
M. DUJARDIN	Nous avons surtout des Anglais et des Hollandais.
MME CHRISTOPHE	Chez nous, il y a surtout des Allemands, des Norvégiens et des Suédois.
M. DUJARDIN	Les gens qui parlent au *patron*, ce sont des Italiens ?
MME CHRISTOPHE	Oui et non. Le mari est italien mais sa femme est espagnole.

full

boss, owner

Transformation : (1) Have students give the masculine form for each of the following: *Elle est française.* → *Il est français.* Elle est belge. Elle est mexicaine. Elle est japonaise. Elle est canadienne. Elle est russe. Elle est anglaise. Elle est égyptienne. (2) Have students repeat, giving the feminine form. *Il est français.* → *Elle est française.* Il est américain. Il est suisse. Il est danois. Il est tunisien. Il est marocain. Il est espagnol. Il est sénégalais.

Un grand hôtel à Nice

Préparation

A. À la résidence internationale. The staff of the **résidence internationale** is counting the number of students from different countries who are living there. Tell what they say based on the following information.

Modèle   Angleterre (3) → **Il y a trois Anglais.**

1. Belgique (9)
2. Espagne (4)
3. Sénégal (6)
4. Zaïre (7)
5. États-Unis (14)
6. Norvège (3)
7. Autriche (1)
8. Maroc (8)
9. Japon (5)
10. Allemagne (10)
11. Russie (2)
12. Hollande (11)

B. À l'auberge de jeunesse. Yves and Gisèle are talking about where different people at the youth hostel are from. What do they say?

Repeat, using *C'est une Anglaise* and having students give *Elle est anglaise*, etc.

Modèles   Elle est anglaise? → **Oui, c'est une Anglaise.**
　　　　　　 Ils sont norvégiens? → **Oui, ce sont des Norvégiens.**

1. Elle est suédoise?
2. Ils sont algériens?
3. Il est allemand?
4. Elle est italienne?
5. Ils sont japonais?
6. Il est brésilien?
7. Elles sont canadiennes?
8. Il est portugais?
9. Elle est australienne?
10. Ils sont américains?

C. Cours d'été pour étrangers. The following foreign students have registered for summer courses in a French university. Based on the information given, tell what their nationality is.

Modèle   David Martin (États-Unis) → **C'est un Américain.**

1. Richard Walter (Australie)
2. Anne Dubé (Canada)
3. Eirik Aasland (Norvège)
4. Suzanne Long (États-Unis)
5. Werner Schmidt (Autriche)
6. Diana Harris (Angleterre)
7. Yvonne Fleur (Hollande)
8. Maria Sanchez (Mexique)
9. Luciano Botelli (Italie)
10. Bridget O'Casey (Irlande)

Communication et vie pratique

Contacts internationaux. Using the following categories, tell about people from other countries with whom you have contact.

Give (or have students give) the names of well-known people from other countries. Students will give this person's nationality.

Exemple   dans votre université
　　　　　　 Dans mon université, il y a des Français, des Allemands, des Espagnols et des Japonais.

1. dans votre université
2. dans votre famille
3. dans votre ville
4. dans votre région
5. dans votre pays
6. dans votre résidence

C'est votre tour. Imagine that you are among a small group of hotel managers (played by several other students) who are bragging about their international clientele. The first person names two nationalities currently represented in his or her hotel : « **Chez nous, il y a des ... et des ...** » The second says that they have the same nationalities plus two more : « **Chez nous il y a non seulement des ... et des ... ; il y aussi des ... et des ...** » See how long you can continue bragging.

Intégration et perspectives

À la douane

Madame Lévêque rentre au Québec après un voyage en France. Elle parle avec le douanier.

— Bonjour, madame. Qu'est-ce que vous avez à déclarer ?
— Rien de spécial.
— Est-ce que vous avez des cigarettes ?
— Oui, j'ai dix paquets de Gauloises. C'est permis, n'est-ce pas ?
— Oui, ça va. Est-ce que vous avez des *vins* et des *liqueurs* ?   **wine / liquors**
— Oui, j'ai deux bouteilles de cognac.
— Très bien, vous êtes dans les limites permises.
— Je comprends, monsieur.
— Qu'est-ce qu'il y a dans votre valise ?
— Des vêtements, des livres, des souvenirs de voyage.
— Ouvrez votre valise, s'il vous plaît.
— Mais oui, monsieur.
— Et ça, qu'est-ce que c'est ?
— C'est un appareil-photo.
— Et ça, sous les vêtements, qu'est-ce que c'est ?
— Ça, euh… c'est *une autre* bouteille de cognac…   **another**

Compréhension. Répondez par une phrase complète aux questions suivantes selon les renseignements donnés dans le texte.

1. Est-ce que Madame Lévêque est française ?
2. Où est-ce qu'elle est maintenant ?
3. Selon elle, qu'est-ce qu'elle a à déclarer ?
4. Combien de cigarettes est-ce qu'elle a ?
5. Est-ce qu'il est permis d'avoir des cigarettes ?
6. Est-ce qu'elle a une caméra ?
7. Qu'est-ce qu'il y a dans sa valise ?
8. Et sous les vêtements, qu'est-ce qu'il y a ?

Notes culturelles: *Comment voyager en France*

Traveling in France is relatively easy and fast because of France's extensive network of railroads, highways, and airlines. Paris is the transportation hub of France, and it is very easy to go from there to other points in the country.

Railroads continue to be a popular way to travel and to transport goods. This popularity is, to a large extent, due to the excellent reputation of the **SNCF (Société Nationale des Chemins de Fer)** whose trains run frequently and on time. The **TGV (train à grande vitesse)** line between Paris and Lyon is so successful that several other similar lines are in the planning stage.

Because of its flexibility, road travel remains the preferred method of everyday and vacation travel. Most of France's major highways are now four-lane expressways (**autoroutes**) or tollways. The speed limit is 130 kilometers an hour on freeways.

There are three major airlines in France : **Air France**, **UTA**, and **Air Inter**, which is limited to domestic flights. France is ranked fifth in the world for passenger airline travel, with domestic flights accounting for one third of the total number of passengers.

Have students note differences and similarities between transportation systems (and preferences) in the U.S. and France.

Le TGV

Communication et vie pratique

A. **En vacances!** Answer the following questions or use them to interview another student.

1. Où est-ce que tu aimes aller en vacances?
2. Qu'est-ce que tu aimes faire en vacances?
3. Est-ce que tu préfères voyager en été ou en hiver?
4. Quels pays est-ce que tu désires visiter?
5. Est-ce que tu désires visiter la France un jour?
6. Quelles villes françaises est-ce que tu désires visiter?
7. Quels monuments parisiens est-ce que tu désires visiter?
8. Quel est le voyage de tes rêves?

Options : (1) Use as guided composition for writing practice. (2) Have students interview each other in small groups and report the results of their interviews orally or in writing.

B. **Situation.** You are working for a French travel agent who has asked you to make travel arrangements for some clients. What questions would you ask to find out the following information?

1. What countries they are going to visit
2. If they are going to travel by train or by plane
3. If they are going to rent a car
4. If they have their passports
5. In what month they prefer traveling
6. If they are going to stay in a small or a big hotel
7. If they are going to leave on Friday or Saturday

C. **Vous êtes à la douane.** Imagine that you have just arrived in France (Canada) and are going through customs. Another student will play the role of the customs agent (**le douanier**) and will ask you what you have to declare. Use the reading from the **Intégration et perspectives** section as a guide in role-playing this situation.

• *Prononciation et orthographe*

A. Note that the letters **a** + **n** or **m** (or **e** + **n** or **m**) combine to form the nasal vowel /ɑ̃/ as in **danser**. Note also the main spelling patterns associated with this sound.

vacances	camping	enfant	employé
chanson	chambre	parents	ensemble
Angleterre	lampe	intelligent	embêtant

If, however, a vowel follows the **n** or **m** or if there is a double **n** or **m**, the vowel is not a nasal sound.

Annie	Amélie	homme

B. Note the difference in the pronunciation between the **-ent** ending when it is the third-person plural verb ending, where it is silent (e.g., **ils voyagent**) and when it is the last syllable of a noun (e.g., **appartement**), adjective (e.g., **content**), or adverb (e.g., **vraiment**). Practice repeating the following phrases.

> Ils dansent; ils sont contents.
> Ils étudient; ils sont prudents.
> Ils pensent; ils sont intelligents.
> Ils achètent un appartement.
> Ils aiment vraiment leurs parents.

C. Practice repeating the nasal sound /ɛ̃/ as in **province** and note the different letter combinations associated with this sound.

matin	impossible	copain	chien
médecin	simple	train	bien
intéressant	sympathique	prochain	

D. Note the difference in the pronunciation of the masculine and feminine forms of nouns and adjectives whose masculine form ends in /ɛ̃/ . This change occurs whenever **-in**, **-ain**, or **-ien** is followed by a vowel or by another **n** or **m**.

/ɛ̃/	/ɛn/	/ɛ̃/	/in/
américain	américaine	cousin	cousine
mexicain	mexicaine	voisin	voisine
marocain	marocaine	un médecin	la médecine
italien	italienne		
canadien	canadienne		
tunisien	tunisienne		
pharmacien	pharmacienne		

● *Vocabulaire*

Noms

les pays (voir p. 89)

les jours de la semaine (voir p. 92)

les mois de l'année (voir p. 92)

les saisons (voir p. 92)

les voyages

  l'**auberge de jeunesse** (f)   *youth hostel*
  l'**avion** (m)   *plane*
° la **bicyclette**
  la **campagne**   *country*
  le **camping**   *campground*

la **colonie de vacances**   *summer camp*
la **Côte d'Azur**   *Riviera*
la **douane**   *customs*
le **douanier**   *customs official*
la **montagne**   *mountain*
° le **monument**
le **pays**   *country*
la **pension de famille**   *rooming house*
la **plage**   *beach*
° la **province**
° le **souvenir**
° le **théâtre**
° le **train**

d'autres noms

° l'**activité** (f)
l'**année** (f) *year*
l'**anniversaire** (m) *birthday*
l'**automobiliste** (m, f) *motorist*
la **bouteille** *bottle*
° la **cigarette**
le **client**, la **cliente** *customer*
le **copain**, la **copine** *pal, friend*
la **fête** *saint's day*
le **jour** *day*
° la **limite**
le **mois** *month*
° le **nombre**
le **paquet** *package*
le **patron**, la **patronne** *boss*
le **pied** *foot*
le **projet** *plan, project*
° la **question**
° le **reporter**
la **saison** *season*
la **semaine** *week*
le **vin** *wine*

Verbes

acheter *to buy*
aller *to go*
° **déclarer**
désirer *to want, to desire*
faire du camping *to go camping*
fermer *to close*
partir *to leave*
passer *to spend (time)*
poser *to ask (a question)*
quitter *to leave*
° **visiter**

Adjectifs

autre *other*

chaque *each*
complet, complète *full, complete*
étranger, étrangère *foreign*
permis(e) *permitted*
préféré(e) *favorite*
premier, première *first*
prochain(e) *next*
scolaire *school*
seul(e) *alone, only*
° **spécial(e)**

Adverbes

aujourd'hui *today*
d'habitude *usually*
demain *tomorrow*
vraiment *really, truly*

Divers

à l'étranger *abroad*
alors *well then*
à pied *on foot*
bonnes vacances! *have a good vacation!*
cette année *this year*
chez *at the home of, at the business of*
d'affaires *business*
eh bien *well, well then*
en *to, at, in, by*
je voudrais *I would like*
je suis né(e) *I was born*
pendant *during*
que *that*
quel jour est-ce aujourd'hui? *what day is it today?*
quel jour sommes-nous? *what day is it today?*
quelle est la date? *What is the date?*
quinze jours *two weeks*
si *yes*

CHAPITRE CINQ

CHAPITRE CINQ

Communication objectives

Naming the foods we eat

1. Pointing out objects and people
2. Buying and consuming food
3. Choosing and ordering foods
4. Specifying quantities

Structures

Les mots et la vie : La nourriture et les repas

Les adjectifs démonstratifs

Le partitif

Le verbe **prendre** et le verbe **boire**

Nombres, poids et mesures

La vie quotidienne : La nourriture et les repas

Mise en scène

The traditional two-hour lunch is becoming less common, especially in large cities where people often live too far away to go home for lunch and prefer instead *la journée continue*.

On mange ici ?

Suzanne et Monique travaillent dans un bureau qui ferme à *midi*. Elles ont une heure pour déjeuner. — noon

SUZANNE	On mange ici ? Ça *a l'air* sympa. — looks, seems
MONIQUE	*D'accord*. Mais c'est *complet*… non ? — okay, agreed / full
SUZANNE	Non, regarde, il y a une table *libre* dans le *coin*. — free / corner
MONIQUE	Alors, c'est parfait. Voici la *carte*. — menu Qu'est-ce que tu vas *prendre* ? — to have, take
SUZANNE	Le *plat du jour*, c'est quoi ? — daily special
MONIQUE	Une *côtelette de porc* avec des *pommes de terre* et des tomates provençales. — pork chop / potatoes
SUZANNE	Humm… Ça a l'air bon. C'est *ce que* je vais prendre. Et toi ? — what
MONIQUE	La même *chose*. Qu'est-ce qu'on va *boire* ? — thing / drink
SUZANNE	On *commande* une petite carafe de vin *rouge* et une bouteille d'*eau* minérale ? — order / red / water
MONIQUE	D'accord.

Recent statistics indicate that the French are eating less bread and fewer potatoes because of concerns with fitness.

Point out that a carafe implies house wine. The French are generally drinking less *vin ordinaire* in favor of more expensive and higher quality wines or other beverages such as beer and carbonated drinks.

Compréhension. Répondez aux questions suivantes selon les renseignements donnés dans le texte.

Option : Have students write in French a short *résumé* of the conversation (e.g., *Monique et Suzanne vont manger ensemble. Le restaurant a l'air sympa, etc.*)

1. Où est-ce que Monique et Suzanne travaillent?
2. Combien de temps ont-elles pour déjeuner?
3. Comment est le restaurant où elles vont manger?
4. Où est-ce qu'elles trouvent une table libre?
5. Qu'est-ce que Monique va prendre?
6. Et Suzanne, qu'est-ce qu'elle va prendre?
7. Qu'est-ce qu'elles vont boire?

Notes culturelles: *La nourriture et la vie moderne*

Food and its preparation continues to occupy an important place in the lives of French people despite noticeable changes in their eating habits. For instance, the French now tend to take less time for lunch, which used to be the main meal of the day. Because of the increasing popularity of **la journée continue**, the traditional two-hour lunch break is often reduced to an hour or less because few people have the time to go home for lunch. Neighborhood restaurants, **brasseries**, cafés, snack-bars, and other fast-food outlets do a booming lunch business. In the last several years alone, 500 new fast-food restaurants opened in France.

The increasing numbers of women who work and the availability of high-quality processed or frozen foods have brought about a gradual decrease in the amount of time spent preparing daily meals. In addition, a growing concern for health and physical fitness has led to a reduction in the richness and variety of foods served. Yogurt and **la cuisine minceur** (*lean cuisine*), for instance, are increasingly popular, and, conversely, the consumption of bread and table wine are on the decline.

In addition, more and more French people are eating in restaurants than in the past. Because choosing a restaurant that serves fine food is still a priority, diners often consult the *Guide Michelin*, especially in an unfamiliar city. This world-famous restaurant guide indicates the price range, the specialties of the restaurant, and the number of **étoiles** (*stars*) that its cuisine merits. Only the very best restaurants receive the much

sought-after four stars. In most restaurants, one has the choice of eating **à la carte** (*choosing from the menu*) or ordering one of the **menus**, i.e., a set of courses with choices within each category. Most of the time, the 15% surcharge for service will be included in the **addition** (*the bill*) ; however, it is customary to leave a small additional tip if the service has been especially good.

Despite changes in eating habits, the French still have a great deal of pride in their cuisine. More than 75% of the French people surveyed recently indicated that France was the country that had the best food. When ranking foods from other countries, the French preferred Italian, Spanish, and Moroccan cuisine.

Les mots et la vie : *La nourriture et les repas*

Study the food vocabulary presented below. Then use the scale below to tell how much you like various foods.

Je déteste	Je n'aime pas	J'aime assez	J'aime beaucoup	J'adore

les légumes (m) (*vegetables*)
les artichauts (m) (*artichokes*)
les carottes (f)
les épinards (m) (*spinach*)
les haricots verts (m) (*green beans*)
les oignons (m)
les petits pois (m) (*peas*)
les pommes de terre (f) (*potatoes*)
les tomates (f)

les fruits (m)
les bananes (f)
les cerises (f) (*cherries*)
les oranges (f)
les pêches (f) (*peaches*)
les poires (f) (*pears*)
les pommes (f) (*apples*)

les boissons (f) (*beverages*)
la bière (*beer*)
le café (*coffee*)
le jus d'orange
l'eau (f) (*water*)
l'eau minérale
le lait (*milk*)
le thé (*tea*)
le vin

les viandes (f) (*meats*)
le bœuf (*beef*)
le jambon (*ham*)
le poisson (*fish*)
le porc (*pork*)
le poulet (*chicken*)
le veau (*veal*)

quelques autres aliments (m)
(*some other foods*)
le beurre (*butter*)
la confiture (*jam*)
les frites (f) (*French fries*)
le fromage (*cheese*)
le gâteau (*cake*)
la glace (*ice cream*)
les œufs (m) (*eggs*)
le pain (*bread*)
le poivre (*pepper*)
le sel (*salt*)
la salade
la soupe
le sucre (*sugar*)

les repas (m) (*meals*)
le petit déjeuner (*breakfast*)
le déjeuner (*lunch*)
le dîner (*dinner*)

Point out that there is no liaison with *haricots*.

Contrast the pronunciation of *un œuf* /œ̃ nœf/ and *des œufs* /dezø/.

Point out that there are two types of *eau minérale* : *gazeuse* (e.g., Perrier and Vichy) and *non-gazeuse* ou *plate* (e.g., Evian and Vittel). *Options* : Have students interview each other to find out their favorite vegetables, fruits, drinks, and meats (*Quels légumes préfères-tu ?*). Have students imagine that they are commenting on the quality of various foods (e.g., *le vin → Le vin est bon.*).

Explorations
❧ Pointing out objects and people
Les adjectifs démonstratifs

Présentation

Demonstrative adjectives (*this*, *that*, *these*, and *those* in English) are used to point out objects or people. Like all adjectives, they agree in number and gender with the noun modified.

Les adjectifs démonstratifs		
	Singular	Plural
Masculine before a consonant	**ce** restaurant	**ces** restaurants
Masculine before a vowel sound	**cet** hôtel	**ces** hôtels
Feminine	**cette** maison	**ces** maisons

Ce soir, je vais chez Alain.	*This evening I'm going to Alain's house.*
Cet hôtel est complet.	*This (that) hotel is filled.*
Est-ce que **cette** table est libre?	*Is this (that) table available?*
Ces haricots verts ne sont pas bons.	*These (those) green beans are not good.*

When it is necessary to make a distinction between *this* and *that* or *these* and *those*, the suffixes **-ci** and **-là** are added to the noun. The suffix **-ci** conveys a meaning similar to *this* and *these*; **-là** is similar to *that* and *those*.

Est-ce que tu préfères **ces** vêtements-**ci** ou **ces** vêtements-**là**?	*Do you prefer these clothes or those clothes?*

Mise en situation

Chez le marchand de fruits et de légumes. Madame Humbert is shopping at the market and stops at her favorite fruit and vegetable stand.

LE MARCHAND	Bonjour, madame. Vous désirez...
MME HUMBERT	*Qu'est-ce que vous avez de bon* aujourd'hui?
LE MARCHAND	Ces pêches-ci sont excellentes. Ces pêches-là ont l'air bonnes aussi, mais elles ne sont pas assez *mûres*.
MME HUMBERT	*À votre avis*, est-ce que ce melon-ci est assez mûr?

Transformation : Donnez la forme appropriée de l'adjectif démonstratif. (le gâteau → ce gâteau) : (1) le vin, (2) le fromage, (3) le café, (4) le restaurant, (5) la table, (6) la salade, (7) l'hôtel, (8) l'eau, (9) les oignons, (10) les poires, (11) les haricots, (12) les cerises. Mettez les mots suivants au singulier (ces gâteaux → ce gâteau) : (1) ces fruits, (2) ces légumes, (3) ces hommes, (4) ces femmes, (5) ces étudiantes, (6) ces examens, (7) ces boissons, (8) ces hôtels.

Open-air markets, which are set up several times a week, are still common in both small and large cities. Covered markets (*les halles*) are found in large cities.

What do you have that is good

ripe

in your opinion

Note that the adjective (*bonnes*) agrees with the subject (*pêches*) when *avoir l'air* means *sembler*.

French people tend to value fresh (versus frozen or canned) produce and are more likely to be aware of and buy those fruits and vegetables that are in season.

LE MARCHAND	Oui, il a l'air *extra*.
MME HUMBERT	Vous n'avez pas de cerises ?
LE MARCHAND	Non, pas en cette saison.
MME HUMBERT	Alors, je vais prendre ces trois artichauts, ce melon et ces haricots.

super, excellent

Préparation

A. Au restaurant. While eating out, several friends comment on the quality of what they are eating.

> **Modèle** vin / exceptionnel → **Ce vin est exceptionnel.**
> viande / pas bonne → **Cette viande n'est pas bonne.**

1. petits pois / excellents
2. veau / parfait
3. café / pas très bon
4. fromage / extra
5. poulet / pas bon
6. glace / très bonne
7. fruits / pas assez mûrs
8. dessert / irrésistible

Option : Have students imagine that they are in a restaurant and are commenting on the good food they are eating. Then have them pretend that the food is not at all good.

B. Indécision. Philippe and Solange can't decide what to buy. Use the cues provided to tell what they say.

> **Modèle** vin → **Est-ce qu'on va acheter ce vin-ci ou ce vin-là ?**

1. confiture
2. gâteau
3. vin
4. légumes
5. poisson
6. bière

C. Regarde ! Some friends are taking a walk and are pointing out to one another what they see. Use the cues provided to tell what they say.

> **Modèle** (beautiful car) → **Regarde cette belle voiture.**

1. (pretty houses)
2. (old store)
3. (new hotel)
4. (beautiful apartments)
5. (little boy)
6. (new poster)
7. (little children)
8. (new café)

Option : Bring in photos that contain familiar vocabulary and have students comment on what they see : *Regarde ces belles montagnes.* Students can also imagine that they are sitting outside at a café and are mentioning things they see.

Communication et vie pratique

A. Au marché. Imagine that you are at a market where you comment on the quality of various items and ask the merchant how much each costs. Another student will play the role of the merchant and will use the information in the photo above to respond to your questions.

Option : Have students open stands and prepare signs that indicate the produce they have for sale, including prices. If available, ads from French or Canadian stores can be used here. Students can also be asked to pay for their items, thus practicing counting and making change.

> **Exemple** — **Ces pêches ont l'air bonnes. Elles coûtent combien ?**
> — **Trois francs trente le kilo.**

After you have made your selections, tell the merchant which items you have chosen.

> **Exemple Je vais prendre ces pommes et ces petits pois.**

B. Compliments et commentaires. Imagine that you are in the following situations and want to compliment your French-speaking friends about various things. What would you say ?

> **Exemple** Vous mangez dans un bon restaurant avec vos amis.
> **Ce restaurant est très bon.**
> *ou:* **J'aime bien ce restaurant.**

1. Vous visitez leur ville.
2. Vos amis préparent un bon dîner.
3. Vous regardez un film ensemble.
4. Vous allez au concert avec vos amis.
5. Vous êtes au marché avec vos amis.
6. Vous visitez le quartier où ils habitent.

110

> **C'est votre tour.** Use the **Mise en situation** as a guide to role-play a conversation at the market between a merchant who praises his or her products and a client who finds fault with everything.

As preparation, have students imagine that they are the merchant and make up things they might say about their high-quality produce. Then have them come up with the negative comments the client might make. These sentences will help them in role-playing the situation.

❧ Buying and consuming food
Le partitif

Présentation

Some items (e.g., coffee, sugar, patience) cannot be counted. In English, we often use the words *some*, *no*, *any*, or no article at all with such words. One says, for example : *I would like some coffee* ; *we don't have any time* ; *he has no patience* ; *we have money.* In French, the partitive article conveys these meanings.

Les articles partitifs			
	Before a masculine noun	**Before a feminine noun**	**Before a noun beginning with a vowel sound**
Affirmative	**du** café	**de la** salade	**de l'eau** minérale
Negative	**pas de** café	**pas de** salade	**pas d'eau** minérale

Partitive articles, like indefinite articles, change to **de** or **d'** in the negative.

Elle a **du** travail à faire, mais elle n'a pas **d'**énergie.
Je voudrais **de l'**eau, s'il vous plaît.
Nous ne mangeons jamais **de** viande.

A. It is important to know when to use the definite article and when to use the partitive. As you have learned, the definite article is used to refer to general categories, as when talking about likes and dislikes. The partitive is used to indicate an unspecified amount of a noncountable item.

J'aime **le** poisson.	↔	Je mange **du** poisson.
Je préfère **la** viande.	↔	Je vais acheter **de la** viande.
J'adore **la** glace.	↔	Je voudrais **de la** glace.
Je n'aime pas **la** bière.	↔	Il n'y a pas **de** bière dans mon réfrigérateur.

B. Especially when talking about buying and eating food, one has to decide whether to use a partitive or an indefinite article. The partitive is used when food cannot be counted or comes in bulk, or when one talks about buying or eating an unspecified amount of a food item.

> Je mange souvent **de la** viande.
> Je voudrais **du** lait, s'il vous plaît.
> Nous allons acheter **du** beurre.

But when food items are counted as separate items (*an artichoke, an orange*) or used in the plural (*some green beans, some fruits*), the indefinite article is used.

> Je voudrais deux glaces et **un** gâteau.
> Nous allons manger **des** petits pois et **des** carottes.

Mise en situation

À la maison. Henri has just come home from school and wants to have his after-school snack (**le goûter**). Unfortunately, there is not much to eat.

HENRI	Maman, je voudrais du pain et du chocolat pour mon goûter.
LA MÈRE	Il *n'y a plus* de pain. Mais je vais *faire les courses avant* le dîner.
HENRI	Qu'est-ce que tu vas acheter ?
LA MÈRE	Du pain, de la viande, des légumes et des fruits… *comme d'habitude.*
HENRI	*C'est tout ?*
LA MÈRE	Regarde dans le frigo. Est-ce qu'il y a *encore* du lait ?
HENRI	Il y a encore du lait, mais il n'y a plus de fromage.

no more / to go shopping / before

as usual

that's all

still

Préparation

A. **Au marché.** Monique and Alain are shopping in their neighborhood stores. Tell what they are going to buy.

> **Modèle**   poisson → **On va acheter du poisson.**

1. poulet	6. bière
2. bœuf	7. glace
3. confiture	8. sucre
4. pain	9. lait
5. vin rouge	10. eau minérale

B. **Qu'est-ce qu'il y a au menu ?** Several students are talking about the foods served in the student dining hall. Tell what they say.

> **Modèle**   soupe (souvent) → **Il y a souvent de la soupe.**

1. viande (souvent)	6. eau minérale (toujours)
2. poisson (rarement)	7. vin (toujours)
3. glace (quelquefois)	8. fromage (souvent)
4. salade (souvent)	9. légumes (toujours)
5. pain (toujours)	10. fruits (rarement)

Point out that *le goûter* is used specifically for an after-school snack; *un casse-croûte* refers to a morning snack eaten by workers. *Un snack-bar* is a cafeteria-style restaurant. Among the more popular after-school snacks are *un morceau de pain et de chocolat*; *un petit pain au chocolat*; *une tartine de confiture.*

Have students imagine that Monique and Alain are not going to buy the items listed (e.g., *On ne va pas acheter de poisson*).

Have students repeat the following nouns, replacing the definite article with the partitive article : *le pain, le fromage, le vin, le thé, le lait, la viande, la soupe, la salade, la glace, la bière, l'eau minérale. Transformation :* Have students change the following sentences. *J'aime le poisson. → Je mange du pain.* (1) Nous aimons le pain. (2) Ils aiment le poulet. (3) Monique aime la glace. (4) Tu aimes la salade. (5) Vous aimez le fromage. (6) Mon frère aime la confiture.

Have students tell what foods are served in their student dining hall and how often.

C. À la bonne soupe. Fabienne and Céline are eating in a small neighborhood café with a limited menu. Give the waiter's responses to their questions.

> **Modèle** Est-ce que vous avez de la soupe aujourd'hui ? (non)
> **Non, nous n'avons pas de soupe.**

1. Est-ce que vous avez du porc ? (oui)
2. Est-ce que vous avez du poisson ? (non)
3. Est-ce que vous avez des haricots verts ? (oui)
4. Est-ce que vous avez de la salade ? (non)
5. Est-ce que vous avez du fromage ? (oui)
6. Est-ce que vous avez de la glace ? (non)

Point out that some *cafés* and *bistros*, though not restaurants, have limited menus ; others offer sandwiches.

Communication et vie pratique

A. Préférences et habitudes. Tell how well you like and how often you eat the following foods.

> **Exemple** la glace
> **J'aime beaucoup la glace et je mange souvent de la glace.**

1. le poisson
2. le pain français
3. le fromage français
4. la soupe
5. la viande
6. la glace
7. la salade
8. le dessert

Students can give an answer and then ask another student his / her preferences (e.g., *J'aime beaucoup la glace et je mange souvent de la glace. Et toi ?*). Other food items can be added to the list.

J'aime beaucoup le fromage…

B. **Interview.** Ask other students how often they eat various foods.

> **Exemple** le poisson
> — **Est-ce que tu manges souvent du poisson?**
> — **Non, je mange rarement du poisson.**

C. **C'est vous le chef!** Tell which ingredients are necessary to make the following dishes. The question mark in item 6 is an invitation to include one of your favorite dishes.

> **Exemple** Qu'est-ce qu'il y a dans une fondue suisse?
> **Il y a du fromage et du vin.**

1. dans une pizza
2. dans une salade
3. dans un sandwich
4. dans une soupe aux légumes
5. dans une omelette
6. ?

D. **Contrastes.** The pictures below illustrate three typical French meals. Describe what is served at each meal and then tell if Americans eat the same foods.

> **Exemple** **Pour le petit déjeuner, les Français mangent...**
> **Pour le petit déjeuner, nous mangeons...**

C'est votre tour. Imagine that you have stopped at a small French country store to get some food supplies. Unfortunately, the store is almost out of everything, but the owner (played by another student) is determined to sell you the few items that are left. Use the suggestions below as you role-play this situation.

Le client	**Le marchand**
Je voudrais…	Je regrette, mais nous n'avons plus de…
Est-ce que vous avez…	Oui, nous avons encore…
Je ne mange pas…	Est-ce que vous aimez…

Practice role-playing this situation with one or two groups before having students act it out. It might also be useful to ask students to prepare short written versions of the situation.

ꙮ Choosing and ordering foods
Le verbe *prendre* et le verbe *boire*

Présentation

Prendre (*to take*) is an irregular verb. When used with food or beverages, it means *to have*.

prendre	
je **prends**	nous **prenons**
tu **prends**	vous **prenez**
il / elle / on **prend**	ils / elles **prennent**

The singular forms are all pronounced /prɑ̃/ , but the third-person plural is pronounced /prɛn/.

Comme légumes, je **prends** des carottes.
Qu'est-ce que vous allez **prendre** comme dessert?

Note that the equivalent of *to make a decision* is **prendre une décision**.

Quand est-ce que tu vas **prendre une décision**?

Other common verbs conjugated like **prendre** are **comprendre** (*to understand*) and **apprendre** (*to learn*).

The verb **boire** *(to drink)* is also irregular.

boire	
je **bois**	nous **buvons**
tu **bois**	vous **buvez**
il / elle / on **boit**	ils / elles **boivent**

Qu'est-ce que vous **buvez**?
J'aime **boire** du café le matin.

The following expressions and names of beverages are useful in a French café or restaurant.

boissons

un apéritif (*before-dinner drink*)

un café crème (*coffee with cream*)

un café noir (*black coffee*)

une carafe de vin (*a carafe of wine*)

un chocolat chaud (*hot chocolate*)

un citron pressé (*fresh lemonade*)

un demi (*mug of beer*)

une eau minérale (*mineral water*)

expressions

On va **boire un pot**? On va **prendre un verre**?

Apportez-moi **un café**, s'il vous plaît.

L'addition, s'il vous plaît.

À votre santé!

Bon appétit!

Let's go have a drink. Shall we have a drink?

Bring me a coffee, please.

The bill (check), please.

Cheers! (To your health!)

Have a good meal!

Repetition : Je prends un café, tu prends un café, etc. Substitution : Monique apprend l'anglais. *(Jean / les enfants / je / vous / tu / nous)* Nous comprenons bien. *(les étudiants / je / Alain / vous / tu / nous)* Repetition : Je bois de l'eau, tu bois de l'eau. Substitution : Chantal ne boit pas de café. *(nous / tu / Serge / vous / mes parents / je)*

Mise en situation

Au restaurant. Madame Robert has been shopping in the neighborhood boutiques. She meets a friend and her children and they decide to have lunch.

LE GARÇON	Vous êtes *prêtes* à commander?
MME ROBERT	Oui, nous prenons le menu à 85 francs.
LE GARÇON	Et comme boisson, qu'est-ce que vous prenez?
MME ROBERT	Moi, je bois toujours du vin rouge. Et vous, Denise, qu'est-ce que vous buvez?
MME CHAMBON	Du vin aussi. Mais les enfants ne boivent pas de vin. Ils aiment mieux le coca-cola.
LE GARÇON	Et comme dessert?
MME CHAMBON	D'habitude, je ne prends pas de dessert, mais la *tarte* aux cerises est bien *tentante*…

ready

In well-to-do circles, it is not uncommon for friends and acquaintances to use the *vous* form. These two women are typical of the *B.C.B.G.* (*bon chic, bon genre*) type, similar to American yuppies.

pie, pastry

tempting

Préparation

A. Préférences. Use the cues provided to tell what the following people generally drink with their dinner.

Have students put the sentences in the negative (e.g., *Michel ne boit pas de vin*).

Modèle   Michel / vin → **Michel boit du vin.**

1. je / thé
2. Véronique / eau minérale
3. nous / vin rouge
4. les enfants / lait
5. vous / bière
6. son fils / jus d'orange

B. Au restaurant. Monsieur Monot is asking his guests what they are having. Give his questions.

> Vary the question by using *est-ce que* (e.g., *Est-ce que Marc prend une boisson ?*).

> **Modèle**   Marc / boisson
> > **Qu'est-ce que Marc prend comme boisson ?**

1. Catherine / apéritif **3.** tu / légumes **5.** les enfants / dessert
2. nous / boisson **4.** vous / viande **6.** Marc / digestif

Communication et vie pratique

A. Qu'est-ce que vous buvez ? Using the scale below, tell how often you drink various beverages.

> *Option :* These cues can also be used for questions asked by the instructor or students : *café → Est-ce que tu bois souvent du café ?*, etc.

jamais   rarement   souvent
⊢_____⊢_____⊣

> **Exemple**   café
> > **Je ne bois jamais de café.**
> *ou:*   **Je bois rarement du café.**

1. le café **3.** le coca-cola **5.** l'eau **7.** le jus d'orange
2. le vin **4.** le lait **6.** l'eau minérale **8.** la bière

B. Préférences. Imagine that you are telling some French friends about your food and beverage preferences. Give them the following information.

> Useful for written practice.

1. what you generally drink for breakfast, lunch, and dinner
2. what your favorite drinks are
3. what you like to eat for breakfast
4. what you generally eat at noon
5. what you eat for dinner

C. Dans un café français. The waiter (**le garçon**) or the waitress (**la serveuse**) in a French café asks you and your friends what you want to drink. Role-play the situation with another student.

> It might be useful to have students prepare a list of *boissons* to be used in role-playing this situation.

> **Exemple**   LE GARÇON : **Qu'est-ce que vous prenez aujourd'hui ?**
> > LE CLIENT : **Je vais boire un café.**
> > LE GARÇON : **Un café crème ou un café noir ?**
> > LE CLIENT : **Un café crème.**

C'est votre tour. Imagine that you and several friends are in a small family restaurant and are going to order your dinner from the menu below. One student can play the role of the waiter or the waitress who asks the customers what they would like.

Exemple   LA SERVEUSE : **Est-ce que vous prenez la salade de tomates ou la soupe à l'oignon ?**
          LE CLIENT :   **Je pense que je vais prendre la soupe à l'oignon.**

Chez Mimi
Menu à 58 francs
Salade de tomates   ou   Soupe à l'oignon
Rôti de porc   ou   Bœuf bourguignon
Carottes Vichy   ou   Tomates provençales
Glace au chocolat   ou   Fruits
Vin rouge   ou   Vin blanc

Role-play the situation several times and then ask students to form groups of three or four. The waiter takes the order and reports back to the class (or instructor) ; the clients verify the accuracy of the order.

Specifying quantities
Nombres, poids et mesures

Présentation

Numbers in the hundreds follow a regular pattern.

100	cent
101	cent un
102	cent deux
200	deux cents
201	deux cent un
202	deux cent deux
300	trois cents
1 000	mille

Point out that *cent* is followed by *-s* only when used alone (*deux cents* vs. *deux cent vingt*).

A. To indicate distance, length, or weight, the following terms (or their abbreviations) are used :

centimètre (cm)
mètre (m)
kilomètre (km)

un gramme (g)
un kilogramme ou un kilo (kg)
une livre (½ kg) (*a pound*)

B. Other useful terms for indicating quantity are :

un verre de (*a glass of*)
une boîte de (*a can of, a box of*)
une bouteille de (*a bottle of*)
une tasse de (*a cup of*)

un litre de (*a liter of*)
une tranche de (*a slice of*)
un paquet de (*a package of*)
un morceau de (*a piece of*)

Mise en situation

Au supermarché. Like most French people, Madame Mathiot usually does her daily food shopping in the neighborhood stores, but occasionally she also goes to a large supermarket. She is going through the check-out line.

LA CAISSIÈRE *Voyons* ce que vous avez…
Quatre boîtes de petits pois,
deux litres de lait,
deux kilos de sucre en *morceaux*,
une livre de café,
une bouteille d'*huile*,
deux boîtes de *champignons*,
six tranches de jambon,
un paquet d'épinards *surgelés*.
C'est tout ?

MME MATHIOT Oui, c'est tout.

LA CAISSIÈRE Vous payez par chèque ou *en espèces* ?

MME MATHIOT Par carte de crédit, *si* possible.

LA CAISSIÈRE Je regrette, mais nous n'acceptons pas les cartes de crédit.

MME MATHIOT Alors, par chèque, s'il vous plaît.

let's see

lumps

oil

mushrooms

frozen

in cash

if

Have students count by 100's to 1,000. Have students count by ten's from 300 to 400. Write random numbers between 100 and 1,000 on the board and have students read them aloud. *Substitution :* Je vais acheter deux kilos de pommes. *(250 grammes de beurre / trois bouteilles de vin / une boîte de haricots verts / un morceau de fromage / quelques tranches de jambon / une livre de café) Translation :* three bottles of milk, a glass of orange juice, three slices of meat, a can of soup, two pounds of bananas, 500 grams of sugar.

Préparation

A. Attention aux calories! The following table indicates the caloric content per 100 grams of various foods. Give the calorie count of each.

Exemple l'huile
Dans 100 grammes d'huile, il y a huit cent quatre-vingt-quinze calories.

Valeur calorifique de quelques aliments			
l'huile	895	la crème fraîche	255
le beurre	760	les œufs	162
la margarine	752	le poulet	147
le chocolat	500	le veau	124
le sucre	399	les pommes de terre	89
le camembert	312	le lait	67
le pain	259	les oranges	40

B. À l'épicerie. Monsieur Legros has his shopping list ready and gives his order to the grocer. What does he say?

Modèle beurre (250 g)
Je voudrais deux cent cinquante grammes de beurre.

1. café (1 livre)
2. jambon (3 tranches)
3. eau minérale (3 bouteilles)
4. vin rouge (1 litre)
5. petits pois (4 boîtes)
6. tomates (1 kg)
7. pêches (2 kg)
8. cerises (500 g)

Communication et vie pratique

A. Monsieur Tout-le-Monde. The following table indicates the recommended amount of different foods for the average man. Based on that table, tell how much he should eat each week of the following foods. Then give the recommended amount for Madame Tout-le-Monde.

Exemple   la viande → **560 grammes de viande par semaine**

COMMENT NOURRIR
Monsieur
Tout-le-Monde

Proportions théoriques de base.		
	PAR SEMAINE	PAR REPAS EN MOYENNE
	(g)	(g)
Viande	560	80
Poisson	105	15
Œufs	140	20
Lait	2 450	350
Fromage	280	40
Beurre	105	15
Graisse	105	15
Huile	105	15
Pain	2 800	400
Farineux	245	35
Pommes de t. ...	2 100	300
Légumes frais ...	2 100	300
Légumes secs ...	175	25
Fruits frais	1 050	150
Fruits secs	35	5
Sucre	280	40
Confitures	140	20
Chocolat	70	10
Vin	1 l. 3/4 à 3 l. 1/2	1/4 à 1/2 l.

Ces moyennes concernent les hommes.
Pour une femme, les quantités sont
à diminuer de 10 à 15 %.

1. le poisson
2. le lait
3. le fromage
4. le pain
5. les pommes de terre
6. les légumes frais
7. les fruits frais
8. le chocolat

B. Qu'est-ce qu'on va acheter? *Prepare shopping lists for one or more of the following situations :* (1) vos provisions habituelles pour la semaine ; (2) un repas spécial pour quelques amis que vous désirez impressionner ; et (3) un repas typiquement américain pour des amis français.

C'est votre tour. Use the **Mise en situation** as a guide and imagine that you are at a neighborhood grocery store where you give the grocer your order. Another student will play the role of the grocer, asking you questions to clarify your order if necessary. The grocer will then ask you how you are going to pay.

Option : As a class project, plan a trip to a French restaurant if possible or prepare a French dish in class. Bring in other simple recipes in French if available for further practice.

122

CHAPITRE CINQ

Intégration et perspectives

Le poulet aux champignons et à la crème.

Point out to students that the infinitive is often used as an imperative in recipes and instruction manuals.

Poulet Aux Champignons

Recette pour quatre personnes.   recipe

Il faut :   1 joli poulet de 1 kg ou 1 kg 500   you need
             250 grammes de champignons
             2 *cuillères à soupe* de beurre   tablespoons
             1 grand verre de crème *fraîche*   fresh
             2 cuillères à soupe de sauce béchamel
             1 *échalote*   shallot
             1 verre de vin *blanc*   white
             1 petit verre de *madère*   a sweet wine
             du sel et du poivre

Couper le poulet en quatre morceaux. *Mettre* le beurre dans une *casse-*   cut / put
role. Quand il est bien *chaud, ajouter* les morceaux de poulet et *laisser*   pan / hot / add / let, leave
mijoter pendant environ trente-cinq minutes. Quand le poulet est   simmer
presque cuit, ajouter les échalotes et le vin blanc. *Ensuite, faire cuire* les almost / cooked / then / cook
champignons dans du beurre. Quand ils sont prêts, placer les cham-
pignons *autour du* poulet et ajouter le verre de madère. Laisser cuire   around
encore pendant quinze minutes. Ajouter la crème et la sauce bé-
chamel. Le poulet est prêt. Bon appétit!

Compréhension. La recette du poulet aux champignons n'a pas été recopiée correctement. Re-
mettez-la dans le bon ordre. (*The recipe for chicken
with mushrooms was not copied correctly. Put it back in
the right order.*)

Correct order : 4 ; 3 ; 8 ; 6 ; 5 ; 7 ; 1 ; 10 ; 2 ; 9

1. Placer les champignons autour du poulet.
2. Ajouter la crème et la sauce béchamel.
3. Mettre le beurre dans une casserole.
4. Couper le poulet en quatre morceaux.
5. Ajouter les échalotes et le vin blanc.
6. Laisser mijoter pendant trente-cinq minutes.
7. Faire cuire les champignons dans du beurre.
8. Ajouter les morceaux de poulet.
9. Le poulet est prêt.
10. Laisser cuire encore pendant quinze minutes.

Notes culturelles: *Les repas*

French adults generally eat three meals a day. **Le petit déjeuner**, eaten early in the morning, is different from an American breakfast. It normally consists of **café au lait** served in a bowl along with **tartines**, buttered French bread, or **biscottes**, similar to melba toast. Although doctors stress the importance of a nutritional breakfast, this already light meal is often skipped altogether or reduced to a quick cup of coffee **sur le pouce** (*on the run*).

Lunch is usually between noon and 2:00 P.M. and is more and more frequently eaten outside the home. On weekends or during vacation, **le déjeuner** regains its full importance and is a more elaborate meal. A traditional **déjeuner** — either at home or in a restaurant — is similar to an American Sunday dinner. However, dishes are not served all at once but are brought out in courses : **les hors-d'œuvre** (*light appetizers*) ; soup ; fish or meat (in more elaborate meals, fish is served first and is then followed by a meat dish) ; one or several vegetable dishes ; salad ; **le plateau de fromages**, a tray of cheeses ; and then dessert or fruit. Coffee is not served until after the meal and can be followed by a **digestif**, i.e., brandy or a liqueur.

When eaten at home, **le dîner** is a lighter meal than lunch, often consisting of soup, an omelette, cheese or fruit, and bread. It is usually served around 8:00 P.M. and is an important time for the family to get together and talk.

The delight that the French take in preparing fine foods and in sharing them with family and friends is evident in the more elaborate **repas de fête** and the **repas entre amis**. Food is chosen, prepared, and presented with great care so that it will be a joy to the eye as well as to the palate. The meal is accompanied by one — or on special occasions several — carefully selected wines that will enhance the taste of the food.

Chez le poissonnier

Communication et vie pratique

A. Questions / Interview. Answer the following questions or use them to interview another student.

1. Quels sont tes légumes préférés ?
2. Quels sont tes fruits préférés ?
3. Quelles boissons est-ce que tu aimes ?
4. Quel est ton dessert préféré ?
5. Qu'est-ce que tu manges d'habitude pour le petit déjeuner ? le déjeuner ? le dîner ?
6. D'habitude, qu'est-ce que tu aimes boire avec tes repas ?
7. Qu'est-ce que tu aimes manger quand tu vas au restaurant ?

B. Bon appétit ! Some French friends want you to prepare a typical American dish for them. They will buy the groceries. Decide what dish you want to prepare, then tell your friends what items they need to buy and how much of each is needed.

It might be useful to have students complete this activity in small groups. Find simple recipes in English that students can explain in French.

C. Qu'est-ce qu'il y a au menu ? Look at the following menu and then tell what types of food are available for the following : **hors-d'œuvre, entrées, légumes,** and **dessert.**

Menu du jour   63 francs

Hors-d'œuvre
   Artichauts à la vinaigrette
   Salade de tomates
   Jambon de Parme
   Céleri rémoulade
Viandes
   Poulet en sauce
   Bœuf bourguignon
   Côtelette de porc
   Poisson grillé
Légumes
   Haricots verts
   Carottes à la crème
   Gratin de pommes de terre

Desserts
   Fromage
   Salade de fruits au kirsch
   Crème au caramel
   Tarte aux cerises
Boissons
   Vin rouge ou vin blanc
   Bière
   Eau minérale

D. Au restaurant. Imagine that you are ordering from the above menu. What would you select for each course ? One student can play the role of the waiter (**le garçon ou la serveuse**) and ask the clients what they want to order.

• *Prononciation et orthographe*

A. The French /r/ is very different from the *r* sound in English. It is pronounced at the back of the mouth — almost in the throat —and resembles the sound one makes when gargling. It is also similar to the sound produced when saying the name of the German composer Bach, pronounced with a guttural *ch*. To learn the pronunciation of the French /r/, one can (1) start with a familiar sound, as in Bach, or (2) start with words where the sound that precedes or follows the **r** is also pronounced toward the back of the mouth : /a/ as in **garage**, or /k/ as in **parc**.

Now practice repeating the following words that end with an **r** sound.

bar	père	beurre	porc
car	mère	heure	sport
par	terre	moteur	d'accord
épinards	dessert	sœur	avoir
guitare	bière	docteur	boire

B. Practice repeating the following pairs of words, starting with words where the **r** is in final position, then moving to words where the **r** is in the middle.

bar	→ barrage	mort	→ morceau
par	→ parent	sport	→ sportif
gàre	→ garage	père	→ personne
car	→ carottes	mère	→ merci
terre	→ terrain	pour	→ pourquoi
faire	→ fermer	sur	→ surtout

C. Practice repeating words where the **r** is preceded by another consonant sound.

agréable	étranger	chambre
géographie	entrer	nombre
adresse	poivre	votre
patron	sucre	peut-être
métro	prendre	

D. Practice repeating words that start with an **r** or with a CONSONANT + **r**. Using the definite article to break down the difficulty can also be helpful. For instance, if the initial **r** in **région** is too hard, say the word as follows : **la — lar — laré — larégion**.

la région	le rouge	le groupe
le réfrigérateur	la rue	le crayon
le raisin	le fromage	le train
la radio	les fruits	le travail

• *Vocabulaire*

Noms

la nourriture et les repas (voir p. 107)

d'autres noms

l'**addition** (f)   *check (restaurant)*
l'**aliment** (m)   *food item*
l'**apéritif** (m)   *before-dinner drink*
la **boisson**   *drink*
la **boîte**   *can, box*
la **bouteille**   *bottle*
le **café**   *coffee, café*
° la **carafe**
la **carte**   *menu*
° la **carte de crédit**
la **casserole**   *pan*
° le **centimètre**
le **champignon**   *mushroom*
° le **chèque**
° le **chocolat**
la **chose**   *thing*
le **citron pressé**   *lemonade*
° le **coca-cola**
le **coin**   *corner*
la **côtelette**   *chop*
° la **crème**
la **cuillère**   *spoon*
le **demi**   *mug of beer*
° le **dessert**
le **digestif**   *after-dinner drink*
l'**échalote** (f)   *shallot*
le **frigo**   *refrigerator*
le **goûter**   *after-school snack*
° le **gramme**
l'**huile** (f)   *oil*
° le **kilogramme**
° le **kilomètre**
° le **litre**
la **livre**   *pound (500 grams)*
la **madère**   *madeira wine*
° le **melon**
° le **menu**
° le **mètre**
midi   *noon*
le **morceau(-x)**   *piece, lump*
l'**orangeade** (f)   *orange drink*

le **paquet**   *package*
le **plat du jour**   *daily special*
la **recette**   *recipe*
° la **sauce**
la **tarte**   *pie, tart*
la **tasse**   *cup*
la **tranche**   *slice*
le **verre**   *glass*

Verbes

° **accepter**
ajouter   *to add*
avoir l'air   *to look, seem, appear*
boire   *to drink*
commander   *to order*
couper   *to cut*
cuire   *to cook*
faire les courses   *to go shopping*
laisser   *to let, leave*
mettre   *to put, place*
mijoter   *to simmer*
prendre   *to take, have*

Adjectifs

blanc, blanche   *white*
cent   *hundred*
chaud(e)   *hot, warm*
complet, complète   *full*
cuit(e)   *cooked*
extra   *super, excellent*
frais, fraîche   *fresh*
libre   *free*
mille   *thousand*
° **minéral(e), -aux, -ales**
mûr(e)   *ripe*
noir(e)   *black*
prêt(e)   *ready*
provençal(e), -aux, -ales   *from Provence*
quelques   *some, a few*
rouge   *red*
surgelé(e)   *frozen*
tentant(e)   *tempting*

Adverbes

encore   *still, yet, again*
ensuite   *then*
presque   *almost*

Divers

à votre avis *in your opinion*
à votre santé *cheers, to your health*
autour de *around*
avant *before*
bon appétit *have a good meal*
c'est tout *that's all*
ce que *that which, what*

comme d'habitude *as usual*
d'accord *OK, agreed*
en espèces *in cash*
environ *about, approximately*
ne... plus *no more, no longer*
si *if*
voyons *let's see*

CHAPITRE SIX

Communication objectives

Describing our surroundings

1. Talking about our daily activities
2. Finding our way: giving and receiving directions
3. Indicating sequences and proportions

4. Telling how much, how many, and when

Structures

Les mots et la vie: La ville et le quartier

Le verbe **faire**

Les prépositions

Les nombres ordinaux, les fractions et les pourcentages

Les nombres supérieurs à 1 000 et les dates

La vie quotidienne: logement et activités

Mise en scène

Après le travail

Laurent et Alain, qui travaillent dans la même compagnie, parlent de ce qu'ils vont faire ce soir.

ALAIN   On prend un pot avant de *rentrer*?

LAURENT   Non, je n'ai pas le *temps* aujourd'hui. J'ai des *courses* à *faire* en ville.

ALAIN   Qu'est-ce que tu vas acheter?

LAURENT   *Rien de spécial*. Les enfants *ont besoin de* différentes choses pour *l'école*. *Après* ça, je vais aller à la *poste* pour acheter des *timbres*.

ALAIN   Tiens, moi aussi. J'ai des lettres à *envoyer*.

LAURENT   Il y a un bureau de poste dans le quartier?

ALAIN   Oui, au coin du boulevard Gambetta et de la rue Lamartine.

LAURENT   C'est *loin*?

ALAIN   Non, pas du tout. Tu prends l'avenue Pasteur, tu vas *jusqu'au* coin et tu tournes à *droite*. La poste est à cent cinquante mètres.

It is not uncommon for people to stop for an *apéritif* on their way home from work.

go home

time / errands / to do

nothing special / need
school / after / post office
stamps

send

far

as far as
right

You might want to point out that stamps can be purchased at the post office and in *bureaux de tabac*.

French streets are often named after literary, historical, and scientific figures or after descriptive landmarks (*rue de la Gare, avenue de Lyon,* etc.)

129

Compréhension. Répondez aux questions suivantes selon les rensei-gnements donnés dans le texte.

1. De quoi est-ce que Laurent et Alain parlent?
2. Pourquoi est-ce que Laurent n'a pas le temps d'aller prendre un pot avec Alain?
3. Qu'est-ce que Laurent a besoin de faire ce soir?
4. Qu'est-ce qu'il va acheter?
5. Qu'est-ce que Laurent va faire au bureau de poste? Et Alain?
6. Où est le bureau de poste?
7. Est-ce que c'est loin?
8. Quelle avenue est-ce qu'on prend pour aller à la poste?

Option : Have students write in French a short *résumé* of the conversation.

Notes culturelles: *La ville française*

A tourist visiting a French city is likely to be struck by certain contrasts with most American cities. French cities, for example, are not always clearly divided into downtown business districts and residential areas. The downtown area (**centre-ville**) usually remains a highly desirable place to live. In general, streets are lined with buildings three to six stories high, with small shops on the street level and apartments of various sizes on the upper levels. Some apartments are rented; others are owned by their occupants. As a result, within each neighborhood there may be considerable intermingling of diverse socioeconomic groups. In some cases, part of the downtown area is restricted to pedestrian traffic in order to enhance the appeal of downtown shopping and living. Despite the existence of supermarkets, the French still like to buy fresh meat, bread, and produce daily from their neighborhood stores. The many small shops where people do their daily shopping also facilitate personal contact. Life in French cities is not, however, free of problems. City dwellers must contend with increased traffic, noise, and pollution. The rising crime rate and terrorist activity are also becoming a concern, especially in certain areas.

Have students compare the downtown areas of French and American cities.

St. Maurice

Nice

Les mots et la vie : *La ville et le quartier*

The following words can be used to describe a town or neighborhood. After studying them, complete the activities below.

Option : Have students rewrite the *Mise en scène* using the new vocabulary in this section.

Le plan de la ville

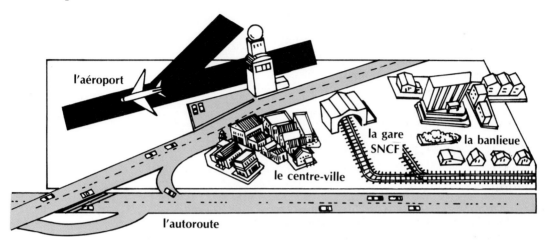

Les transports
le train
l'avion (m)
l'autobus (m)
le métro
la voiture

la gare
l'aéroport (m)
l'arrêt (m) d'autobus
la station de métro
le parking public

Point out that Paris, Lille, and Lyon have subways and that France has an excellent railway system (*la S.N.C.F.*).

Les lieux et services publics
la banque
l'école (f) (*school*)
le bureau de poste
la bibliothèque
le parc
le stade (*stadium, athletic field*)
la piscine

l'église (f) (*church*)
le musée
l'hôpital (m)
la mairie (*city hall*)
les W.C. publics (m)
le poste de police

Le poste de police is a neighborhood police station; *la préfecture de police* refers to the main police station.

Les magasins d'alimentation
la boulangerie
la charcuterie (*pork shop*)
la boucherie (*butcher shop*)

l'épicerie (f) (*grocery*)
la pâtisserie

Autres magasins et services
le cinéma
le garage
le grand magasin
   (*department store*)
la librairie (*bookstore*)

le magasin de chaussures
   (*shoe store*)
le magasin de vêtements
   (*clothing store*)
la pharmacie

A. Où est-ce qu'on va pour…? Tell where one goes to buy or to do the following.

Exemple   Où est-ce qu'on va pour acheter de la viande?
On va à la boucherie.

Où est-ce qu'on va pour acheter…?

des livres   du porc
du pain   des vêtements
du bœuf   un gâteau
des chaussures   du sucre

Où est-ce qu'on va pour…?

prendre l'autobus (le train, le métro, l'avion)
nager
faire du sport
envoyer une lettre
acheter des livres
jouer ou marcher

B. Un quartier français. Use the words and phrases given in **Les mots et la vie** to describe the following street scenes from French towns.

C. Et vous? Describe your own home town, indicating whether it is a large or small town, the types of transportation, shops, and other places of interest in the town.

Explorations
✤ Talking about our daily activities
Le verbe *faire*

Présentation

Faire (*to do, to make*) is an irregular verb.

Point out that all the singular forms of *faire* have the same pronunciation /fɛ/, but that *nous faisons* is pronounced /nufəzɔ̃/.

faire	
je **fais**	nous **faisons**
tu **fais**	vous **faites**
il / elle / on **fait**	ils / elles **font**

Je **fais** mon travail.
Qu'est-ce que tu **fais** dimanche?
Qu'est-ce qu'on va **faire** demain?

Faire is used in the following idiomatic expressions.

faire du sport (*to participate in sports*)
faire du ski (*to go skiing*)
faire du camping (*to go camping*)
faire le ménage (*to do the housework*)
faire son lit (*to make one's bed*)
faire sa chambre (*to clean one's room*)
faire la vaisselle (*to do the dishes*)
faire des courses (*to run errands*)
faire ses devoirs (*to do one's homework*)
faire la cuisine (*to cook, to do the cooking*)
faire le marché (*to go grocery shopping*)
faire des achats (*to go shopping*)
faire un voyage (*to take a trip*)
faire une promenade (*to go for a walk*)

Repetition: (1) Je fais du sport, tu fais du sport, etc. (2) Je ne fais pas le marché, tu ne fais pas le marché, etc. Substitution: (1) Nous faisons souvent du ski. (je / Marc / mes amis / tu / vous / nous) (2) Qu'est-ce que tu fais ce soir? (Michel / vous / vos amis / Luc / tu) Translation: (1) Monique is doing her homework. (2) Jean-Paul is going to make his bed. (3) We are going to run some errands this afternoon. (4) My brother is taking a trip this summer. (5) Are Charles and Josette going camping this weekend? (6) You're doing the cooking tonight, aren't you?

Mise en situation

C'est la vie. La majorité des femmes françaises travaillent. Mais ce n'est pas toujours facile quand on a des enfants encore jeunes.

LE REPORTER	Comment *arrivez*-vous *à* tout faire ?
MME LANIER	Ce n'est pas facile mais je *fais de mon mieux* et nous *partageons* les responsabilités. Je fais la cuisine et mon mari fait la vaisselle — ou vice versa.
LE REPORTER	Qui fait le ménage ?
MME LANIER	Nous faisons le ménage ensemble. Les enfants font leur chambre et nous faisons le reste.
LE REPORTER	Vous faites aussi les courses ensemble ?
MME LANIER	Quelquefois. Je fais les achats dans les magasins du quartier. Mais souvent, pendant le week-end, nous allons au supermarché ou au *centre commercial*. *Ça fait* une *sortie* pour toute la famille.

succeed in

do my best / share

Point out to students that there are increasing numbers of supermarkets and shopping centers in France, though people still like to shop in their neighborhoods.

shopping center / it makes / outing

Préparation

A. Questions. Jean-Jacques is asking his friends about their plans. Give his questions.

Have students ask each other what they plan to do at various times.

> **Modèle**   Fabien / samedi → **Qu'est-ce que Fabien fait samedi ?**

1. tu / maintenant
2. Jacques / l'année prochaine
3. Pierre et Sylvie / l'été prochain
4. vous / dimanche
5. nous / demain
6. Véronique / lundi soir

B. Qu'est-ce que tu fais cet après-midi ? Some friends are talking about what they are doing this afternoon. What do they say ?

Have students repeat the activity in the negative: *Sylvie ne fait pas le marché.*

> **Modèle**   Sylvie / faire le marché → **Sylvie fait le marché.**

1. je / faire mes devoirs
2. tu / faire une promenade
3. Monique et Simon / faire le ménage
4. vous / faire des courses
5. Micheline / faire la vaisselle
6. nous / faire du sport

Communication et vie pratique

A. Activités. Tell how often you do the following activities and then ask another student how often he or she does the same activity.

Have students ask each other questions about their activities (e.g., *Est-ce que tu fais souvent le ménage ?*).

> **Exemple**   faire le ménage
> — **Je fais rarement le ménage. Et toi ?**
> — **Moi, je fais souvent le ménage.**

ne... jamais   rarement   quelquefois   souvent

1. faire le ménage
2. faire une promenade
3. faire du sport
4. faire du camping

5. faire mes devoirs	7. faire un voyage	9. faire des courses
6. faire la cuisine	8. faire la vaisselle	10. faire du ski

B. Négociations et compromis. You are sharing an apartment with several students. Decide who is going to do each of the following household tasks. The following suggestions can help you.

Suggestions: j'accepte de… ; je refuse de… ; je regrette, mais… ; je n'ai pas le temps de… ; je n'aime pas… ; je préfère… ; d'accord, je…

Exemple   J'accepte de faire le ménage si tu fais la vaisselle.

1. faire le ménage	3. faire les courses	5. faire le marché
2. faire la vaisselle	4. faire la cuisine	6. faire les lits

> It might be helpful to role-play this situation with one or several students before putting students in small groups. As additional preparation, have students jot down their reactions to each of the tasks mentioned. Once in small groups, have one student in charge of taking notes and presenting the group's decisions orally or in writing.

C. Et les Américains…? Imagine that some French friends are asking about typical activities of Americans. How would you answer?

> Useful for written homework and/or for class discussion of cultural differences.

1. Est-ce que les Américains font souvent du camping ?
2. Est-ce que les Américains aiment faire des promenades en voiture le dimanche après-midi ?
3. Est-ce qu'ils font souvent leur marché dans les supermarchés ?
4. Est-ce que les Américains font souvent du sport ?
5. En général, est-ce que ce sont les femmes, les hommes, ou les enfants qui font la vaisselle ?
6. Est-ce que les enfants américains font des devoirs chaque soir ?
7. Est-ce que les Américains aiment faire des promenades à pied pendant le week-end ?

C'est votre tour. Imagine that you have been asked the same questions that were asked of Madame Lanier (asked by another student playing the role of a reporter). Use the **Mise en situation** as a guide to explain the different things you do and how you manage to do them all.

> *Variation :* Role-play the situation again ; this time Madame Lanier's responses reflect the lack of cooperation and help from her family.

❧Finding our way: giving and receiving directions
Les prépositions

Présentation

Prepositions are useful in indicating the location of a person, object, or place.

A. Certain prepositions directly precede the noun.

dans (*in*)	La voiture est **dans** le garage.
sur (*on*)	Ses livres sont **sur** la chaise.
sous (*under*)	Le chien est **sous** la table.
devant (*in front of*)	L'arrêt d'autobus est **devant** l'épicerie.
derrière (*behind*)	La pharmacie est **derrière** la poste.
entre (*between*)	Trois-Rivières est **entre** Québec et Montréal.

B. Other prepositions contain **à** or **de** and contract with **le** or **les**.

jusqu'à (*as far as, up to*)	Il faut aller **jusqu'au** café.
au milieu de (*in the middle of*)	L'université est **au milieu de la** ville.
loin de (*far from*)	La banque est **loin de** l'hôtel.
près de (*near*)	L'hôtel est **près de la** gare.
à côté de (*beside, next to*)	La boulangerie est **à côté du** cinéma.
en face de (*facing, across from*)	La librairie est **en face du** musée.

Substitution : (1) La pharmacie est derrière la bibliothèque. (*cinéma / épicerie / banque / théâtre*) (2) Ils habitent à côté de la gare. (*le bureau de poste / le restaurant / l'épicerie / la pâtisserie / la librairie*) (3) Nous sommes en face de la bibliothèque. (*à côté de / près de / derrière / devant / loin de*)

C. The following expressions are also useful when giving directions.

Traversez la rue.	*Cross the street.*
Allez jusqu'à la pâtisserie.	*Go as far as the pastry shop.*
Allez tout droit.	*Go straight ahead.*
Tournez à gauche.	*Turn left.*
Tournez à droite.	*Turn right.*
Prenez l'autobus numéro sept.	*Take bus number seven.*
Descendez place Carnot.	*Get off at Carnot Square.*

Mise en situation

Excusez-moi, monsieur l'agent... Monsieur et Madame Rollet *cherchent* l'hôtel Beauséjour. Ils parlent avec un *agent de police*.

are looking for
police officer

M. ROLLET	Excusez-moi, monsieur l'agent... Nous cherchons l'hôtel Beauséjour... C'est loin d'ici ?
L'AGENT	Non, c'est à trois ou quatre rues d'ici, à côté de l'église Saint-Vincent.
MME ROLLET	C'est dans quelle direction ?
L'AGENT	Sur votre gauche. Vous prenez la rue Sully, là-bas, en face de vous. Vous continuez jusqu'à la place Kléber, vous traversez la place, vous passez derrière l'église et vous tournez à droite. L'hôtel est entre l'église et le cinéma Rex.

Have students note how the police officer is addressed.

Have students note that the word block does not have a direct equivalent in French. Have them note also how the agent expresses this idea.

Préparation

A. C'est où ? Éric doesn't know his way around his new neighborhood yet. Thérèse is telling him where various places are. What does she say?

Option : Provide different cues for each response.

Modèle Où est ton appartement ? (*across from the church*)
C'est en face de l'église.

1. Où est l'arrêt d'autobus ? (*across from the movie theater*)
2. Le restaurant universitaire est près d'ici ? (*no, far from here*)
3. Tes amis habitent près de la poste ? (*yes, next to the post office*)
4. Où est la station de métro ? (*behind the museum*)
5. Où est le musée ? (*in the middle of the park*)
6. Où est la pharmacie ? (*between the bakery and the grocery store*)

B. Où est-ce qu'ils habitent? Emmanuel is telling where his friends live. Tell whether or not his statements are true. The numbers on the map below indicate the approximate locations of his friends' apartments.

> **Modèle** 7. François habite près de la piscine.
> **Non, il n'habite pas près de la piscine.**

1. Solange habite en face de l'école.
2. Catherine habite à côté de l'hôtel de la Gare.
3. Jean-Luc habite entre la poste et le musée.
4. Julien habite derrière l'église.
5. Nadine habite assez loin de la gare.
6. Véronique habite rue de la Poste.

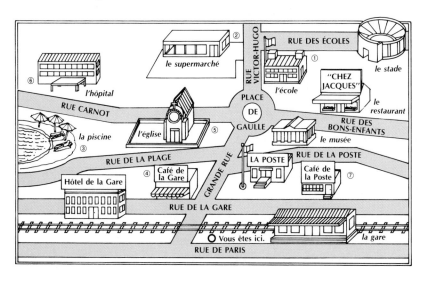

Communication et vie pratique

A. Excusez-moi... While you are at the railroad station, people ask you how to get to various places in town. Using the map above, what would you tell them?

> **Exemple** de la gare à l'école
> **Prenez la Grande Rue. Allez tout droit et tournez à droite à l'école.**

Donnez les indications nécessaires pour aller...

1. de la gare à l'hôpital
2. du café de la Poste au stade
3. du stade à l'hôtel de la Gare
4. du supermarché au restaurant de la rue des Bons-Enfants
5. de la piscine à la gare
6. de l'hôtel de la Gare à la poste

Have students tell where they and their friends live: *J'habite assez loin du campus. Mon ami Richard a un appartement près d'ici.*

Option: Have students decide where they are (e.g., *derrière la poste, près d'un supermarché*); other students will guess their precise location.

B. **Votre quartier.** Describe the neighborhood where you live, including as much information as you can about the locations of what is found in your area. If you live in a dormitory, describe where your dorm is located and what buildings surround it.

Exemple   **J'habite un petit appartement assez près du campus. En face de chez moi, il y a une épicerie et une pharmacie. Il y a aussi une très bonne librairie à quatre rues d'ici. Au coin de la rue, il y a un petit restaurant où je vais manger de temps en temps.**

C'est votre tour. Imagine that a French person (played by another student) asks you where a particular building on campus or in town is located. Using the **Mise en situation** as a guide, answer his or her questions.

Indicating sequences and proportions
Les nombres ordinaux, les fractions et les pourcentages

Présentation

Ordinal numbers (*first, second, third,* etc.) are given below. **Premier, première** and **dernier, dernière** agree with the noun modified. Other ordinal numbers always end in **-ième.**

premier, première (1er, 1ère)	neuvième*	seizième*
deuxième (2e or 2ème)	dixième	dix-septième
troisième	onzième*	dix-huitième
quatrième*	douzième*	dix-neuvième*
cinquième*	treizième*	vingtième
sixième	quatorzième*	vingt et unième
septième	quinzième*	etc.
huitième		

Ils habitent au **cinquième** étage.
C'est la **troisième** rue à gauche.

A. Ordinal numbers are not used with kings and rulers except for **premier.**

François Ier   François **premier**
but
Louis XIV   Louis **quatorze**
Napoléon III   Napoléon **trois**

B. Ordinal numbers are always used to identify a century (**un siècle**).

le **dix-neuvième** siècle
le **vingtième** siècle

---
*Some ordinal numbers involve spelling changes.

C. The most commonly used fractions are:

½   demi- (*adj.*)   Je voudrais une **demi-livre** de petits pois.
      la moitié (*n.*)   La **moitié** des étudiants sont ici.
⅓   un tiers
⅔   deux tiers
¼   un quart
¾   trois quarts

Have students note the use of *la moitié* where in English the indefinite article (*a half*) is used.

Other fractions are expressed with an ordinal number in the denominator:

⅕   un cinquième
5/7   cinq septièmes

D. To indicate a percentage (**un pourcentage**), **pour cent** is used.

Quel est **le pourcentage** de Français qui habitent dans une maison individuelle?
En ce moment, 54% (cinquante-quatre **pour cent**) des Français habitent dans une maison et 46% (quarante-six **pour cent**) dans un appartement.

Ordinaux: Give a cardinal number and have students give the corresponding ordinal number (e.g., 5 — cinquième). Have students count from 1 to 25 using the appropriate ordinal number. *Substitution*: le deuxième jour (leçon / visite / fois / chapitre / rue / année) *Pourcentages*: Put the following percentages on the board and have students read them: 5%; 25%; 87%; 33%; 100%; 10%; 67%; 56%; 13% *Fractions*: Put the following fractions on the board and have students read them: ½; ¾; 5/6; 9/10; 7/8; ⅔; ⅛; 3/20

Periods and commas are reversed in French and English numbers. Thus, commas are used in French to indicate decimals.

8,5%   huit **virgule** cinq pour cent
75,6%   soixante-quinze **virgule** six pour cent

Mise en situation

Résidence et *lieu* **de travail.** Paris is divided into twenty administrative districts called **arrondissements.** In addition, the city is surrounded by many suburbs. Jean-Pierre and Michelle live far from their work.

place

JEAN-PIERRE	Dans quel arrondissement vous habitez?
MICHELLE	Dans le 19ᵉ, près de la Porte des Lilas.
JEAN-PIERRE	Et vous travaillez dans le centre?
MICHELLE	Oui, je travaille dans le 7ᵉ, près des Invalides.
JEAN-PIERRE	Ça prend *combien de temps* en métro?
MICHELLE	Ça prend *environ* une demi-heure ou trois quarts d'heure.
JEAN-PIERRE	C'est direct?
MICHELLE	Non, *il faut* changer *plusieurs* fois.

how much time

about

it is necessary / several

Préparation

A. Arrondissements. Different people in Paris are telling which district they are from. Tell what they say.

Exemple   19^e
> **Nous habitons dans le dix-neuvième.**

1. 3^e	**3.** 14^e	**5.** 1er	**7.** 20^e	**9.** 2^e
2. 6^e	**4.** 18^e	**6.** 4^e	**8.** 16^e	**10.** 15^e

B. Quelques statistiques. An employee of the census bureau is answering an interviewer's questions by giving approximate instead of precise figures. Give the employee's answers.

Modèle   48,2% → **environ la moitié**

1. 30%	**3.** 19,8%	**5.** 24%
2. 73,2%	**4.** 50%	**6.** 67%

Communication et vie pratique

A. Le budget des Français. Using the table below, tell what percentage of their budget French people spend on the following categories. Then estimate what percentage you spend on each category.

Exemple   nourriture 27%
> **La nourriture représente vingt-sept pour cent de leur budget. Pour moi, ça représente environ vingt pour cent de mon budget.**

Catégorie	Pourcentage
1. Nourriture	27%
2. Vêtements	9%
3. Maison ou appartement	22%
4. Santé et hygiène	13%
5. Transports et téléphone	11%
6. Cinéma, théâtre, concerts, etc.	9%
7. Hôtels, restaurants, cafés, etc.	9%

B. La France du confort. Using the following information, tell what percentage of French people own the appliances given below. In your opinion, what percentage of American families own these same appliances?

Appareil électroménager	Pourcentage
Réfrigérateur	96,4%
Congélateur (*freezer*)	32,8%
Machine à laver	82,7%
Lave-vaisselle	20,6%
Téléviseur	91,2%
Téléviseur en couleurs	61,4%
Magnétoscope	3,8%

Have students note that each *arrondissement* is governed by a mayor who is selected by the government. Paris is also divided into nine electoral units which elect the *Conseil de Paris*; the presidency of the council is primarily an honorary position.

The French statistical bureau is called the *I.N.S.E.E.* (*Institut national de la statistique et des études économiques*). It has generally the same functions as the U.S. Census Bureau.

C'est votre tour. Imagine that you are living in Paris. An acquaintance (played by another student) asks where you live. Using the **Mise en situation** as a guide and the maps of Paris on pp. 139 and 147, answer his or her questions.

Have students decide ahead of time what section of Paris they are going to choose. They might want to look up some information on this area.

❧ Telling how much, how many, and when
Les nombres supérieurs à 1 000 et les dates

Présentation

Number above 1 000 (**mille**) are expressed in the following ways:

1 351	**mille trois cent cinquante et un**
3 000	**trois mille**
19 300	**dix-neuf mille trois cents**
541 000	**cinq cent quarante et un mille**
2 000 000	**deux millions**

Note that **mille** is never spelled with an **s**, but **million** has an **s** when it is plural.

Two patterns are used with dates:

in 1789　　**en mille sept cent quatre-vingt-neuf**
　　　　　　　　　　or
　　　　　en dix-sept cent quatre-vingt-neuf

To distinguish between B.C. and A.D., **avant Jésus-Christ** and **après Jésus-Christ** are used.

52 **av. J.-C.**　　　　845 **apr. J.-C.**

Point out that *million* is followed by *de* when counting a group of people or things: *deux millions d'habitants.* Have students note that *mille* is never preceded by *un.*

Mise en situation

Achat d'une voiture. Diane needs a new car and asks the salesperson for advice.

DIANE	Pour une voiture *d'occasion* en bonne condition, il faut *compter* combien?
LE VENDEUR	*Ça dépend de* l'année et du modèle. Mais pour une voiture assez récente, il faut compter entre 12 000 et 20 000 francs.
DIANE	Cette Peugeot, elle coûte combien?
LE VENDEUR	22 600 francs.
DIANE	C'est *plutôt* cher!
LE VENDEUR	Oui, mais elle a seulement 12 000 km. Elle est pratiquement *neuve*.
DIANE	Et cette petite Renault, elle coûte combien?
LE VENDEUR	Seulement 9 750 francs. C'est une bonne *affaire*.

Point out the difference between *neuf / neuve* (*brand-new*) and *nouveau* (*new to the individual*): *Marc a acheté une nouvelle voiture* (*new to him*). *Elle est neuve.* Point out also that the major manufacturers of French cars are *Peugeot, Renault,* and *Citroën.*

secondhand / to count, to expect

It depends on

rather

brand-new

deal

Préparation

A. Populations. Students from various cities in France are telling how large their home towns are. What do they say?

> **Modèle**   Lyon (1 150 000 h)
> **Lyon est une ville d'un million cent cinquante mille habitants.**

1. Toulouse (500 000 h)
2. Le Havre (265 000 h)
3. Bordeaux (590 000 h)
4. Nice (440 000 h)
5. Grenoble (390 000 h)
6. Strasbourg (360 000 h)
7. Tours (235 000 h)
8. Clermont-Ferrand (225 000 h)

B. Leçon d'histoire. Mademoiselle Lanson is asking her students the dates of the reigns of some of the rulers of France and the dates of governments in recent years. Give her students' responses.

> **Modèle**   Charlemagne (768 – 814)
> **de sept cent soixante-huit à huit cent quatorze**

1. François 1er (1515 – 1547)
2. Henri IV (1589 – 1610)
3. Charles VIII (1483 – 1498)
4. Louis XIV (1661 – 1715)
5. Louis XVI (1774 – 1792)
6. Napoléon 1er (1804 – 1815)
7. Napoléon III (1852 – 1870)
8. la 3e République (1875 – 1940)
9. la 4e République (1946 – 1958)
10. la 5e République (1958 – présent)

Nombres : Put the following numbers on the board and have students read them : (A) *100, 1000, 10 000, 100 000* (B) *3 000 ; 15 000 ; 55 000 ; 175 000 ; 3 700 000* (C) *1 200 ; 9 110 ; 69 821 ; 238 402 ; 248 669 120. Dates :* Put the following dates on the board and have students read them : *1291 ; 1412 ; 1566 ; 1670 ; 1789 ; 1822 ; 1900 ; 1943 ; 1989 ; 2000.*

These figures are for *agglomérations,* which include the city and its suburbs. Have students locate these cities on a map of France.

Have students tell what they know about these historical figures and governments of France and/or have them look up information.

Le couronnement de Napoléon

Communication et vie pratique

A. C'est combien ? How much do each of the luxury apartments described in the following ads cost ? Which would you prefer ?

Exemple Le premier appartement coûte deux cent trente-deux mille francs.

1.

2.

3.

4.

5.

6.

7.

8.
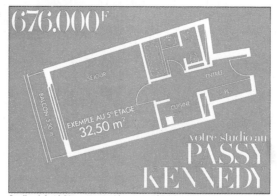

B. Quelques statistiques. Using the following graph, give the number of students (**élèves**) in both public and private junior high schools (**collèges**), high schools (**lycées**), apprenticeship programs, and trade schools (**lycées d'enseignement professionnel**).

Exemple   Il y a 588 980 élèves dans les collèges privés.

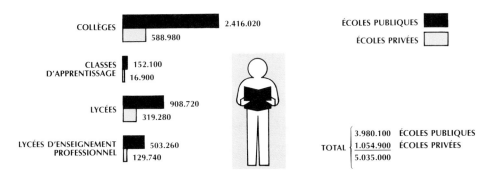

COLLÈGES   2.416.020
                588.980

ÉCOLES PUBLIQUES
ÉCOLES PRIVÉES

CLASSES
D'APPRENTISSAGE   152.100
                  16.900

LYCÉES   908.720
                319.280

LYCÉES D'ENSEIGNEMENT
PROFESSIONNEL   503.260
                129.740

TOTAL   3.980.100 ÉCOLES PUBLIQUES
        1.054.900 ÉCOLES PRIVÉES
        5.035.000

C'est votre tour. Imagine that you are in France and want to buy one of the cars advertised below. Using the **Mise en situation** as a guide, ask about the price and mileage of the different cars. The salesperson (played by another student) will answer your questions.

Intégration et perspectives

Où habiter : banlieue ou centre-ville ?

Est-ce qu'on est heureux quand on habite en *banlieue*? *Selon* un récent *sondage* d'opinion, deux Français *sur* trois *pensent* que oui. Les autres sont *sceptiques*. La réalité est *que* pour certains, c'est un paradis mais pour d'autres, c'est un *cauchemar*.

suburb / according to   **survey, poll / out of / think**   **skeptical / that**   **nightmare**

Banlieue = cauchemar

Myriam Lebeau, qui habite dans une *H.L.M.*, trouve la banlieue ennuyeuse et *laide*. Mère de trois enfants, elle ne travaille pas. Elle n'a pas de voiture et l'arrêt d'autobus est trop loin. Résultat: elle est prisonnière.

low-cost housing   **ugly**

René Pannier est *ouvrier*. Il faut une heure pour aller de son appartement à l'usine où il travaille. Résultat : deux heures d'autobus à *ajouter* à la fatigue du travail.

worker   **add**

Banlieue = paradis

Hervé et Marie-Louise Jacalot habitent une petite maison beige au milieu de *milliers* d'autres petites maisons beiges. Chaque maison a son petit jardin et sa *pelouse*. En comparaison avec l'H.L.M., c'est un rêve.

thousands   **lawn**

Pierre et Catherine Pélissier habitent une jolie maison au milieu des *arbres* à 20 kilomètres du Vieux Port de Marseille. On *respire* le parfum des *fleurs* et des herbes de Provence. Le tennis et la piscine ne sont pas loin.

trees / breathe   **flowers**

Brigitte et Jean-Claude Clément possèdent une grande maison dans un vieux village près de Lille. Il y a des fleurs *partout*. Ils sont *ravis*.

everywhere / delighted

Les résultats du sondage confirment que pour les Français les principaux avantages de la banlieue sont le calme et la possibilité d'avoir un jardin, mais le principal inconvénient est le temps qu'il faut pour aller à son travail.

« au milieu d'autres petites maisons… »   « il y a des fleurs partout… »

H.L.M.

Compréhension. Répondez aux questions selon les renseignements donnés dans le texte.

1. Est-ce que tous les Français pensent que la vie en banlieue est idéale?
2. Est-ce que Myriam trouve la vie en banlieue amusante? Pourquoi?
3. Où est-ce qu'Hervé et Marie-Louise Jacalot habitent?
4. Comment sont les maisons de leur quartier?
5. Est-ce que Pierre et Catherine Pélissier aiment leur maison? Pourquoi?
6. Est-ce que Brigitte et Jean-Claude Clément sont contents de leur maison? Pourquoi?
7. Quel est le principal avantage de la vie en banlieue?
8. Quel est son principal inconvénient?

Have students imagine that they are one (or several) of the people described and write a description of their reactions to where they live (e.g., *Je m'appelle René Pannier et j'habite loin de l'usine où je travaille...* , etc.

Notes culturelles: *La banlieue*

The destruction of 450,000 homes and apartments during World War II created severe housing shortages in France. Much of the replacement construction was on the outskirts of the cities and included both individual family houses and high-rise apartments. Both have been attractive to affluent middle-class French people. Some sections of the suburbs, called **cités ouvrières**, contain more modest homes. Other housing has created new problems. Large clusters of low-cost apartment buildings called **H.L.M. (Habitations à loyer modéré)**, for example, have been criticized for their concrete sterility, crowded conditions, and lack of convenient shopping and recreational facilities. One such cluster contains 1,800 apartments in a small two-block area. These conditions have been blamed for a high crime rate, particularly juvenile crime. Because of these problems and because of a desire for a better quality of life in a more pleasant environment, an increasing number of French people (especially workers and those from the lower middle class) are moving to small towns and rural areas as soon as it is economically feasible for them to do so.

Have students compare American suburbs with the description of *la banlieue*.

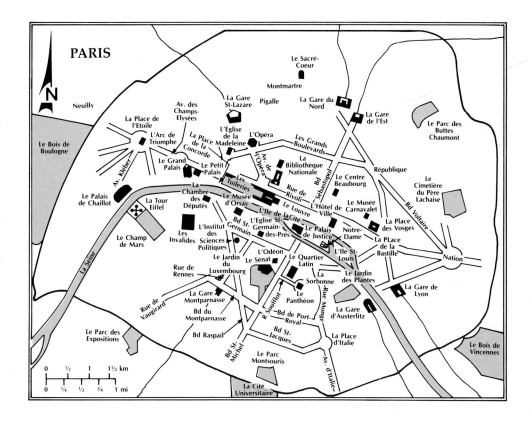

Communication et vie pratique

A. **Connaissez-vous Paris?** Indicate whether the following statements based on the map of Paris are true or false. If a statement is false, reword it to make it true.

1. Les Tuileries sont à côté de la tour Eiffel.
2. Le Grand Palais est a côté du Petit Palais.
3. La cité universitaire est près de la Sorbonne.
4. La Bibliothèque nationale est sur le boulevard Saint-Germain.
5. La gare de l'Est est loin de la gare de Lyon.
6. L'église de la Madeleine est derrière le Sacré-Cœur.

B. **Excusez-moi, monsieur l'agent...** Imagine that you are a tourist in Paris and want to find out how to get to the following places. Another student will play the role of the **agent de police** and tell you where each is located.

1. Où est l'Opéra? le Sénat? la gare du Nord? le musée du Louvre?
2. la tour Eiffel? le jardin du Luxembourg? le Sacré-Cœur?
3. le Centre Pompidou? la place de la Bastille? Notre-Dame?

C. **Plan du métro.** You are staying with a group of students in a hotel located on the Left Bank near the subway station **Saint-Michel**. Other students ask you how to go to different places. Using the **plan du métro** shown below, give them the following information.

1. Quelle ligne il faut prendre.
   Exemple **Pour aller à la gare du Nord, il faut prendre la ligne Porte d'Orléans–Porte de Clignancourt, direction Porte de Clignancourt.**

Note that subway lines are generally identified by their two extremities, framed in yellow on the map. The metro lines can also be referred to by their number. Once you have found the line, you must make sure you are headed in the right direction.

2. Si c'est direct ou non.
   Exemple **Pour aller au Louvre, il faut changer au Châtelet.**

3. Où il faut descendre.
   Exemple **Pour l'Arc de Triomphe, il faut descendre à l'Étoile.**

Suggestions: les Invalides, la place de la Concorde, Pigalle, le bois de Boulogne, la gare de Lyon, l'Opéra, la gare d'Austerlitz

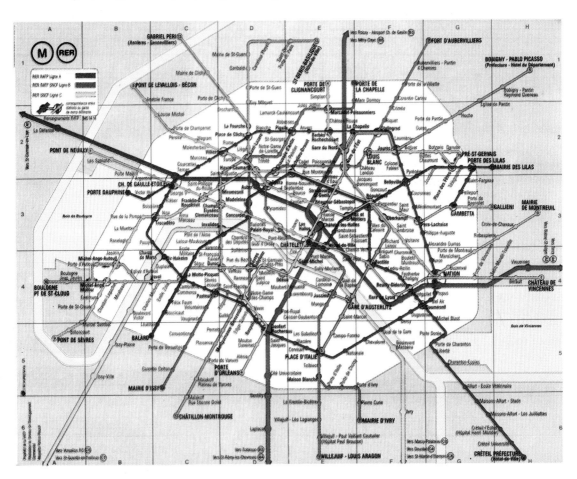

● *Prononciation et orthographe*

A. Some vowels like /i/ in **ici** are pronounced with the lips spread; others like /y/ in **tu** are produced with the lips tightly rounded. Both of these are pronounced in the front of the mouth, with the tongue almost touching the teeth. Thus /i/ and /y/ differ only by the shape of the lips. In fact, if you have difficulty pronouncing the French /y/, try saying /i/ with your lips rounded.

Compare and repeat:

si	su	mais si	c'est sûr
di	du	dis	c'est dur
vi	vu	la vie	la vue
ni	nu	ni	numéro
ti	tu	petit	habitude
ri	ru	le riz	la rue

B. Practice repeating words and phrases containing the sound /y/. Remember to have your lips tightly pursed and reaching forward as if you were going to whistle or give a kiss.

Salut!	le bureau
la voiture	le sucre
la musique	l'usine
impulsif	naturel
l'avenue	la rue

Quelle rue?
La rue Sully, bien sûr.
Tu es sûr?
Absolument sûr.

C. Note the difference between the sound /y/ as in **tu** and the sound /u/ as in **tout** which is also pronounced with the lips rounded, but with the tongue more toward the back of the mouth.

Compare and repeat :

su	sou	sur	sous
tu	tou	tu	tout
bu	bou	nu	nous
mu	mou	vu	vous
lu	lou	la rue	la roue

D. The following summarizes the differences in the way /i/, /y/, and /u/ are produced. Practice contrasting these sounds and repeat the words and phrases below.

Point of articulation (i.e., position of the tongue):	front	front	back
Shape of the lips:	spread	rounded	rounded
	/i/	/y/	/u/
	si	su	sou
	ti	tu	tou
	vi	vu	vou
	li	lu	lou

Du sucre, s'il vous plaît.
Comment trouves-tu la musique de Debussy?
Tu fais du ski avec nous?
D'habitude, nous allons sur la Côte d'Azur.
Tu tournes ici et tu continues jusqu'à la rue Sully.

• *Vocabulaire*

Noms

les transports (voir p. 131)

les lieux et services publics (voir p. 131)

les magasins d'alimentation (voir p. 131)

autres magasins et services (voir p. 131)

d'autres noms

   l'**achat** (m)   *purchase*
° l'**activité** (f)
   l'**affaire** (f)   *deal*
   l'**agent de police** (m)   *police officer*
   l'**arbre** (m)   *tree*
   l'**arrondissement** (m)   *district of Paris*
   l'**autoroute** (f)   *freeway*
° l'**avantage** (m)
° l'**avenue** (f)
   la **banlieue**   *suburb*
° le **boulevard**
° le **calme**
   le **cauchemar**   *nightmare*
   le **centre commercial**   *shopping center*
   le **centre-ville**   *downtown area*

° la **comparaison**
   les **courses** (f)   *errands, races*
   la **droite**   *right*
° la **fatigue**
   la **fleur**   *flower*
   la **gauche**   *left*
   l'**herbe** (f)   *grass, herb*
   l'**inconvénient** (m)   *inconvenience*
° la **lettre**
   le **lieu**   *place*
   le **logement**   *housing*
   un **millier**   *a thousand (approximately)*
° un **million**
   la **moitié**   *half*
° l'**opinion** (f)
° le **paradis**
° le **parfum**
   la **pelouse**   *lawn*
° la **possibilité**
   la **poste**   *post office, job*
° le **pourcentage**
° le **prisonnier**
   le **quart**   *quarter*
° la **réalité**
   le **résultat**   *result*
° le **service**

le **sondage** *poll*
la **sortie** *outing*
le **temps** *time, weather*
° le **tennis**
le **tiers** *third*
le **timbre** *stamp*

Verbes

expressions avec **faire** (voir p. 133)

ajouter *to add*
arriver à *to succeed in (doing)*
chercher *to look for*
compter *to count, to expect*
° **confirmer**
envoyer *to send*
faire *to do, to make*
faire de son mieux *to do one's best*
partager *to share*
penser *to think*
rentrer *to go home*
respirer *to breathe*
tourner *to burn*
traverser *to cross*

Adjectifs

° **beige**
demi- *half*
d'occasion *used, second-hand*
ennuyeux, ennuyeuse *boring*
laid(e) *ugly*
neuf, neuve *brand-new*
ordinal(e), -aux, -ales *ordinal*
plusieurs *several*
premier, première *first*
principal(e), -aux, -ales *main*
quotidien, quotidienne *daily*

ravi(e) *delighted*
° **récent(e)**
sceptique *skeptical*
° **spécial(e), -aux, -ales**

Adverbes

là-bas *over there*
loin *far, far away*
partout *everywhere*
plutôt *rather*
tout droit *straight ahead*

Prépositions

à côté de *beside, next to*
après *after*
au milieu de *in the middle of*
derrière *behind*
devant *in front of*
en face de *across from, facing*
entre *between*
jusqu'à *up to, as far as, until*
loin de *far from*
près de *near*
selon *according to*

Divers

autour *around*
avoir besoin de *to need*
ça dépend (de) *that depends (on)*
ça fait *it makes*
certains *some people*
d'autres *others*
environ *about, approximately*
il faut *it is necessary*
pour cent *percent*
prendre un pot *to have a drink*
que *that*

7

CHAPITRE SEPT

Communication objectives

Selecting TV programs

1. Telling what time it is
2. Talking about past events
3. Telling when something begins and ends

4. Talking about past events

Structures

Les mots et la vie : La télévision

L'heure

Le passé composé avec **avoir**

Finir et les verbes de la deuxième conjugaison

Le passé composé avec l'auxiliaire **être**

Le temps passe

The following is a composite of the weekly description of television programs that appears in French magazines. As such, it represents a selection of programs but does not include the wide range of programs appearing on French television.

Mise en scène

Télévision : Les sélections de la semaine

Laisse *béton* is an example of *verlan*, a code language used by young people in which syllables are inverted. Thus, *verlan* means *l'envers* (*the other side*).

Quelles émissions de télévision est-ce que vous allez regarder cette semaine ?... Voici notre sélection des meilleurs programmes du soir qu'on va montrer cette semaine sur les différentes chaînes.

VENDREDI SOIR
Sur TF1 : « Champs Élysées », un *spectacle* de variétés avec la participation de *Julien Clerc* et de la *chanteuse* canadienne Édith Butler.
Sur FR3 : Pour les enfants, une série de films de Walt Disney.

> show
> popular French singer / singer

SAMEDI SOIR
Sur FR3 : « De la démocratie en Amérique ». Un *reportage* sur la situation politique aux États-Unis.
Sur Canal + : « Laisse béton », un film de Serge Le Péron. « Laisse béton », *c'est-à-dire* « *Laisse tomber* » dans le langage des jeunes. C'est l'histoire de deux enfants, fatigués de la vie dans leur H.L.M. et pour qui le grand rêve est d'aller à San Francisco.

> report
> that is to say / drop it
> Point out that Canal+ is a cable subscription channel.

DIMANCHE SOIR
Sur A2 : « Les *Carnets* de l'Aventure ». L'ascension de l'Annapurna par des *alpinistes* allemands.
Sur la Cinq : « Subway », un film policier de Luc Besson avec Christophe Lambert et Isabelle Adjani. Un film différent. Un film qu'on aime ou qu'on déteste.

> notebooks
> mountain climbers

LUNDI SOIR
Sur A2 : « Apostrophes ». La religion et les hommes.
Sur FR3 : « Musiclub ». Émission spéciale sur Mozart, sa vie et sa musique.

153

La Cité des sciences et de l'industrie (the largest museum of its type in the world) is located in Paris on the former site of the slaughterhouses of la Villette. It is divided into four major sections : De le Terre à l'Univers ; l'Aventure de la vie ; Matière et travail de l'homme ; and Langage et Communication.

MARDI SOIR	Pour les *passionnés* de football, la *coupe* d'Europe de football sur TF1. Et sur Canal + , « La Dictée », un *feuilleton* en six épisodes de Jean-Pierre Marchand.	fans / cup mini-series
MERCREDI SOIR	Sur TF1 : « Voyage dans la Cité des Sciences ». Un reportage spécial sur ce passionnant musée.	
JEUDI SOIR	Sur A2 : « C'est la vie » : Les pères divorcés, un reportage de Jean-Claude Allanic et Catherine Ceylac. Sur TF1 : « Les enfants du rock » avec la participation de trois groupes de musiciens martiniquais.	

Compréhension. Indiquez quelles sont les différentes émissions susceptibles d'intéresser les personnes suivantes. (*Indicate which programs might be of interest to the following people.*)

Ask students which of the television programs described they would choose and why.

1. Jean-Louis aime seulement les émissions culturelles et les débats politiques.
2. Michel aime mieux les émissions amusantes et les sports.
3. Stéphanie a seulement onze ans, mais elle rêve d'être un jour une grande alpiniste.
4. Alain et Marie-Claire ne vont pas souvent au concert, mais ils adorent la musique classique.
5. Sylvie pense qu'on ne montre pas assez de bonnes émissions scientifiques.
6. Chantal et Pierre sont contents quand il y a un bon film à la télé.
7. François est un passionné de rock.

Notes culturelles: *La télévision française*

French television viewers have a choice of several channels. Some are publicly owned stations ; others are privately owned. These stations broadcast throughout much of the day on weekdays and all day on weekends. Luxembourg and Monte Carlo have independent stations that can be seen throughout most of French-speaking Europe. **Eurovision**, a new form of television programming, broadcasts special programs simultaneously via satellite in multiple countries — each with its own sound track in the appropriate language.

The government-controlled **R.T.F. (Radio-Télévision France)** is financed by special taxes paid by owners of radio and television sets. Consequently, **R.T.F.** enjoys financial autonomy and is relatively free of commercials. Advertising does not usually interrupt programs but occurs between them. French television can thus offer a greater variety of programs and appeal to a wider range of interests than can American commercial stations. On the other hand, the top officials of **R.T.F.** are appointed by the **Conseil des Ministres**, which is similar to the American president's Cabinet, and these close ties with the government have led to charges of biased programming that favors the official point of view.

Recent statistics indicate that on the average, the French watch television 2 hours and 45 minutes daily, which is similar to other European countries. The average daily viewing time in the U.S. is four hours. More than 17 million households own televisions (64% are color sets) and about 14% have two televisions. The French are generally satisfied with TV's ability to provide news and information to its viewers ; they are less satisfied with it as a means of entertainment.

Les mots et la vie : *La télévision*

Listed below are vocabulary words that are useful for talking about television and other types of entertainment. Study these words and then answer the related questions.

L'équipement audio-visuel
le téléviseur en couleurs ou en noir et blanc
le magnétoscope
les vidéo-cassettes

Les différents types d'émission
les matchs télévisés et les reportages sportifs (*games and sports shows*)
les émissions scientifiques ou culturelles
les feuilletons (m) (*mini-series, soap operas*)
le bulletin météorologique / la météo (*weather report*)
les spectacles (m) de variétés (*variety shows*)
les documentaires (m)
les films et les téléfilms
les dessins animés (*cartoons*)
les causeries (f) (*talk shows*)
les jeux télévisés (*game shows*)
la publicité (*advertising*)
les actualités (f) / le journal télévisé / les informations (*news*)
les pièces (f) de théâtre (*plays*)
les séries (f)

Le monde du spectacle (*show*)
une vedette (*male or female star*)
un acteur / une actrice (*actor / actress*)
un chanteur / une chanteuse
un comédien / une comédienne
le début (*beginning*)
la fin (*end*)
les personnages (*characters*)
l'histoire (*story*)
le sujet (*subject, topic*)
le héros / l'héroïne
jouer un rôle (*play a part*)

In 1977, 7,000 households had VCRs; today the number has risen to 1,800,000. More than 60% of those owning VCRs belong to *vidéoclubs* and generally rent films about once a week.

Give the name of a program and have students place it in a category : *Wheel of Fortune ? C'est un jeu télévisé.* Give a category and have students name a program in that category.

A. Vos programmes préférés. Use the scale below to tell how well you like the different types of television programs listed above.

je déteste   **je n'aime pas beaucoup**   **j'aime**   **j'aime beaucoup**   **j'adore**

Put different types of programs on separate note cards and have students go around the room, asking others for their opinion. They then report back to the class : *Dix étudiants aiment beaucoup les feuilletons; sept détestent les feuilletons.*

Exemple   **J'aime beaucoup les documentaires mais je déteste les jeux télévisés.**

B. **Opinions.** Make a list of popular American television shows. Then use the following rating system shown in a popular French magazine to rate the quality of these programs.

À mon avis (*in my opinion*)…

*** C'est une émission à ne pas manquer.
(*It's a program that shouldn't be missed.*)

** C'est une émission à regarder si vous êtes chez vous.
(*It's a program to watch if you're at home.*)

* C'est un navet.
(*It's a loser.* [literally, *a "turnip"*])

Exemple **À mon avis, « Nova » est une émission à ne pas manquer.**

C. **Les vedettes de la télévision et du cinéma.** Who are your favorite stars in each of the following categories? Use one or more adjectives to describe each star.

Exemple **J'aime Garfield. Il est très amusant.**

1. un héros ou une héroïne de dessins animés
2. un acteur ou une actrice
3. un présentateur ou une présentatrice du journal télévisé (*anchorperson*)
4. un chanteur ou une chanteuse

Explorations
❧ Telling what time it is
L'heure

Présentation

To ask what time it is, ask : **Quelle heure est-il ?** (*What time is it ?*) or, more informally, **Vous avez l'heure, s'il vous plaît ?** (*Do you have the time, please ?*) To answer these questions, use :

A. On the hour :

Il est une heure. Il est quatre heures. Il est midi (m). (*noon*)
Il est minuit (m). (*midnight*)

B. On the half or quarter hour :

Il est trois heures
et demie.

Il est midi et demi.

Il est deux heures
et quart.

Il est huit heures
moins le quart.

C. Minutes after or before the hour :

Il est une heure dix.

Il est neuf heures cinq.

Il est midi vingt.

Il est six heures vingt.

Il est midi moins cinq.

Il est quatre heures
moins dix.

Il est neuf heures
moins vingt.

Il est minuit moins
vingt-cinq.

D. To ask or indicate at what time an event takes place, the following patterns are used :

— **À quelle heure** est-ce que le téléfilm commence ?
— Il commence **à dix heures**.

Notice that **heure(s)** is never omitted in French, whereas in English we often omit the word *o'clock*.

> Because of the use of digital watches and clocks, one hears increasingly *huit heures quarante-cinq* instead of *neuf heures moins le quart*.

E. The French system does not use A.M. and P.M. In conversation, use :

du matin (*in the morning*)
de l'après-midi
du soir

Il est onze heures **du matin**.
Je vais partir à quatre heures **de l'après-midi**.
Nous dînons à sept heures et demie **du soir**.

F. In official time schedules (for example, schedules for planes, trains, buses, radio, or television programs), the twenty-four-hour system is used.

Official time	**Conventional time**
zéro heure trente (0 h 30)	minuit et demi
trois heures cinq (3 h 05)	trois heures cinq
douze heures (12 h)	midi
quinze heures quinze (15 h 15)	trois heures et quart
vingt-trois heures cinquante-cinq (23 h 55)	minuit moins cinq

(1) Beginning at 1 o'clock, have students give the time at one-hour intervals until they reach noon. (2) Beginning with 3 o'clock, have students give the time at fifteen-minute intervals until they reach 5 o'clock. (3) Beginning with 6 o'clock, have students give the time at five-minute intervals until they reach 7 o'clock.

G. Additional expressions used in discussing time are :

arriver à l'heure	*to arrive on time*	Il est tôt.	*It's early.*
être en retard	*to be late*	Il est tard.	*It's late.*
être en avance	*to be early*		
vers midi	*around noon*		

Point out that France has an excellent railroad system (*la SNCF — la Société Nationale des Chemins de Fer*). The *TGV (train à grande vitesse)* is generally viewed as state-of-the-art in rail transportation.

Mise en situation

Au bureau de *renseignements*. Monsieur Josserand is calling the information desk at the **gare de Lyon** in Paris to find out when the next train for **Lyon** is scheduled to leave.

information

M. JOSSERAND	Allô, allô, je voudrais *savoir* à quelle heure il y a un train pour Lyon.	to know
L'EMPLOYÉE	Le prochain train est à onze heures cinq.	
M. JOSSERAND	Il est maintenant dix heures et quart et *il faut* une demi-heure pour aller à la gare…	it takes, one needs
L'EMPLOYÉE	Ça va être *trop juste*. *Il vaut mieux* prendre le *suivant*.	too close / it's better following (next) one
M. JOSSERAND	Il est à quelle heure ?	
L'EMPLOYÉE	À midi dix, mais ce n'est pas un TGV.	
M. JOSSERAND	Ça fait une *grosse* différence ?	big
L'EMPLOYÉE	Bien sûr ! Avec le TGV, ça prend seulement deux heures. Le train de midi dix n'arrive pas avant cinq heures.	
M. JOSSERAND	Et quand est le prochain TGV ?	
L'EMPLOYÉE	À treize heures trente.	

Horaire DU 28 Sept. 1986 AU 30 Mai 1987

SNCF

Paris - Lyon

- Paris
- Laroche Migennes
- Montbard
- Dijon
- Beaune
- Chagny
- Chalon-sur-Saone
- Tournus
- Macon
- Villefranche-sur-Saone
- Lyon

Cette fiche ne comporte que les horaires pour les relations de départ d'une localité ● à destination des localités ●

521A

Point out to students that in France one can generally travel *première ou deuxième classe* and that seats are reserved ahead of time. Sleeping cars (*couchettes*) are also available at an extra cost. Students might also be interested in knowing about Eurail passes, which allow them to ride any trains in France (and the rest of Europe) for a fixed price during a specified length of time.

Préparation

A. Quelle heure est-il? The announcers on radio give the time at various intervals. Use the watches to tell what they say.

1. 12:00
2. 7:30
3. 4:45
4. 2:50
5. 1:10

6. 5:00
7. 9:20
8. 10:05
9. 8:05
10. 3:30

B. À l'aéroport. At Charles de Gaulle airport in Paris, flights are being announced using the twenty-four-hour system. Use the more common twelve-hour system to tell when each flight leaves.

Modèle   22 h 45 → **onze heures moins le quart**

1. 8 h 30	**3.** 16 h 20	**5.** 3 h 15	**7.** 12 h 05	**9.** 5 h 25
2. 20 h 35	**4.** 13 h 50	**6.** 17 h 35	**8.** 23 h 55	**10.** 0 h 15

C. Emploi du temps. Charles is telling what he is going to do today. Use the information on the calendar to tell what he says.

Modèle   **À neuf heures, je vais prendre un café avec Roger.**

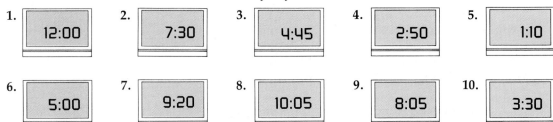

MARDI **12**

9 h - prendre un café avec Roger
10 h 15 - aller au cours d'histoire
12 h 30 - déjeuner avec Nathalie
2 h 30 - aller à la bibliothèque
4 h 45 - parler au professeur Godard
7 h - dîner avec tante Élisabeth
9 h 35 - regarder la Dictée à la télé

Communication et vie pratique

A. **Questions / Interview.** Use the words and phrases below to ask another student questions. Find out when he or she usually does the following.

Exemple   quitter la maison le matin
— **À quelle heure est-ce que tu quittes la maison le matin ?**
— **En général, je quitte la maison à 7 h 30.**

1. prendre ton petit déjeuner
2. quitter la maison le matin
3. arriver à l'université
4. avoir ton premier cours
5. avoir ton dernier cours
6. rentrer à la maison
7. dîner
8. commencer à faire tes devoirs

B. **Qu'est ce qu'il y a à la télé ?** The evening television schedule below is taken from *Nice Matin*, a French newspaper. Answer the questions based on the information in the schedule.

18.00	**HUIT ÇA SUFFIT** Série en 104 épisodes. (N° 92). La nuit des lauréats (2ᵉ partie).
18.25	**MINI JOURNAL**
18.45	**LA ROUE DE LA FORTUNE**
19.10	**SANTA BARBARA** Série en 120 épisodes. (N° 89).
19.40	**COCORICOCOBOY** Avec : *Kassav*.
20.00	**LE JOURNAL DE LA UNE**
20.30	**COLUMBO** Série en 20 épisodes. (N° 16) Immunité diplomatique.
21.50	**L'ENJEU** Magazine économique et social proposé par François de Closets, Emmanuel de La Taille et Alain Weiller. Réalisation Jean-Vincent Fournis.
23.05	**UNE DERNIÈRE**
23.25	**PREMIER PLAN SUR CANNES** Présenté par Alain Bévérini.

18.05	**ALINE ET CATHY** Avec : *Susan St James (Cathy), Jane Curtin (Aline), Air Meyers (Emma Mc Ardle)*.
18.30	**C'EST LA VIE** Préparez vos examens.
18.50	**DES CHIFFRES ET DES LETTRES**
19.15	**ACTUALITÉS RÉGIONALES**
19.40	**LE NOUVEAU THÉATRE DE BOUVARD** Avec Michel Hidalgo.
20.00	**LE JOURNAL**
20.30	**D'ACCORD, PAS D'ACCORD**

20.35	**POURQUOI PAS VOUS ?** Film français de Michel Berry (1981).
21.55	**CANNES NOIR SUR BLANC** Emission réalisée par François Chalais.
22.55	**EDITION DE LA NUIT**
23.10	**HISTOIRES COURTES**

18.00	**IL ÉTAIT UNE FOIS L'ESPACE**
18.30	**CAP DANGER** N° 23 : Une question de vie ou de...
18.57	**JUSTE CIEL**
19.00	**19-20**
19.15	**ACTUALITÉS RÉGIONALES**
19.35	**19-20 (SUITE)**
19.55	**ULYSSE 31**
20.04	**LA CLASSE** Emission proposée par Guy Lux et Jacques Antoine. Présentée par Fabrice. Avec Gilles Lacoste.
20.30	**D'ACCORD, PAS D'ACCORD**
20.35	**LA FEMME DU BOULANGER** Film de Marcel Pagnol (1938).
22.50	**SOIR 3**
23.15	**FESTIVAL DE CANNES**
23.30	**DÉCIBELS** Emission présentée par Jan Lou Janeir.

CANAL+

18.00	**FLASH D'INFORMATIONS** (◆)
18.05	**MAXITÊTE** (◆) Présenté par Sophie Favier.

18.10	**LA GUEULE DE L'EMPLOI** (◆) Emission jeu présentée par Sophie Garel.
18.40	**TOP 50** (◆) Présenté par Marc Toesca.
19.10	**SPÉCIAL ZÉNITH AU FESTIVAL DE CANNES** (◆) Présenté par Michel Denisot, qui reçoit ce soir Corinne Charby et Caura.
19.55	**FLASH D'INFORMATIONS** (◆)
20.05	**STARQUIZZ** Présenté par Philippe Risoli.
20.35	**ABATTOIR 5** Film fantastique américain de George Roy Hill (1971).
22.20	**FLASH D'INFORMATIONS**
22.30	**LA PARTIE DE CHASSE** Film dramatique anglais de Alan Bridges (1984). Rediffusion.

TMC

19.00	**C'EST FASTOCHE** Emission pour les enfants.
19.15	**JEUNES DOCTEURS** N° 117.
19.40	**SPÉCIAL « JEUX DES PETITS ETATS D'EUROPE »**
19.45	**T.M.C. NEWS** Suivi de la météo.
20.00	**CINÉNIGMES** Soirée cinéma. Animée par José Sacré.
20.25	**LE TREFLE A 5 FEUILLES** (1971). Réalisateur : Edmond Moustaki.
21.55	**JEUX CINÉNIGMES** (Suite).
22.30	**T.M.C. NEWS**
22.35	**HOROSCOPE** Par Maria Duval.

1. À quelle heure commencent les dernières émissions sur les différentes chaînes ?
2. Est-ce qu'il y a un feuilleton sur Télé Monte Carlo (TMC) ? À quelle heure ?
3. À quelle heure sont les actualités sur les différentes chaînes ?
4. Combien de films est-ce qu'il y a à la télé ce soir ? Sur quelles chaînes et à quelle heure ?
5. Est-ce qu'il y a un jeu télévisé sur TF1 ? À quelle heure ?
6. Est-ce qu'il y a des reportages sur le festival de Cannes ? Sur quelles chaînes et à quelle heure ?
7. À quelle heure est-ce qu'il y a une émission pour les enfants sur Télé Monte Carlo ?

C'est votre tour. Vous travaillez au bureau de renseignements de l'aéroport de Lyon. Des clients téléphonent pour savoir l'heure du départ ou de l'arrivée de différents avions. Donnez les renseignements demandés par les clients (joués par les autres étudiants de la classe).

Exemple — À quelle heure est-ce qu'il y a un avion pour Londres ?
— À quinze heures.

After modeling the conversation with a student, have students role-play the situation in groups of two or three. Circulate to give help as needed. If you have a U.S. airline or train schedule, have students role-play a situation where a French tourist needs information about schedules.

❧Talking about past events
Le passé composé avec *avoir*

Présentation

To express a completed past action, the **passé composé** is used. It can express the same meaning as three different English constructions : *I traveled, I have traveled, I did travel.*

A. The **passé composé** of most verbs is formed by using the present tense of **avoir** plus a past participle. The past participle of **-er** verbs is formed by dropping the **-er** ending of the infinitive and replacing it with **é** : **parler** → **parlé, étudier** → **étudié**. The form of **avoir** must correspond to the subject.

Le passé composé avec *avoir*	
j'ai regardé	nous **avons regardé**
tu **as regardé**	vous **avez regardé**
il / elle / on **a regardé**	ils / elles **ont regardé**

Elle **a travaillé** toute la journée.
Nous **avons regardé** un match télévisé.

B. Avoir, être, prendre, boire, and faire have irregular past participles :

avoir	eu	boire	bu
être	été	faire	fait
prendre	pris		

Nous **avons eu** des difficultés.
Vous **avez été** trop imprudent.
Est-ce que tu **as fait** tes devoirs ?

C. In the negative, **ne** precedes and **pas** (or **jamais**) follows the form of **avoir**.

Elle **n'**a **pas** trouvé de travail.
Ils **n'**ont **jamais** visité la Belgique.

D. Useful expressions for referring to past events are :

hier	*yesterday*
hier soir	*last evening*
hier matin	*yesterday morning*
la semaine dernière, la semaine passée	*last week*
samedi dernier, samedi passé	*last Saturday*
l'année dernière, l'année passée	*last year*
déjà	*already*
pas encore	*not yet*

Note that short adverbs are placed between the auxiliary verb and the past participle.

> — Est-ce que tu as **déjà** fait tes devoirs?
> — Non, je n'ai pas **encore** eu le temps.

Mise en situation

Vous avez été sages? After they return home from an evening with some friends, Monsieur and Madame Lemoine ask their children if they have been good.

M. LEMOINE	Vous avez été *sages*?
DIDIER	Bien sûr, papa.
MME LEMOINE	Vous avez fait vos devoirs?
ISABELLE	J'ai étudié ma leçon d'histoire, mais je n'ai pas eu le temps de finir mes maths.
MME LEMOINE	Et toi, Didier, tu as appris ta table de multiplication?
DIDIER	Non, maman.
MME LEMOINE	*Pourquoi* pas?
DIDIER	*Parce que j'ai oublié* mes *affaires* à l'école.

Préparation

A. **Activités et occupations.** Sylviane is talking about some of the things she did on her day off. Use the cues to describe her activities.

Modèle   10 h / téléphoner à Suzanne → **À dix heures, j'ai téléphoné à Suzanne.**

1. 9 h / commencer à travailler
2. 11 h 30 / envoyer une lettre à mes parents
3. 12 h 15 / quitter la maison pour aller en ville
4. 12 h 30 / manger au restaurant avec des amis
5. 3 h / faire des courses
6. 4 h 45 / avoir la visite de Raymonde
7. 5 h 15 / acheter les provisions pour le dîner
8. 7 h 45 / regarder les actualités

B. **Encore et toujours des excuses!** Some students are talking about why they aren't prepared for class today. What are their excuses?

Modèle   Micheline / avoir le temps de faire ses devoirs
Micheline n'a pas eu le temps de faire ses devoirs.

1. nous / acheter les livres pour le cours
2. Michelle et Juliette / écouter en classe
3. tu / être sérieux
4. je / trouver mon cahier
5. vous / avoir le temps d'étudier
6. Pierre / faire ses devoirs

Communication et vie pratique

A. La semaine dernière. Create sentences expressing what you and your friends did during the past week by combining one element from each column.

Exemple   Hier, j'ai invité des amis à dîner.

		envoyer une lettre à mes parents
		dîner chez des amis
		manger au restaurant
		avoir un examen difficile
		étudier le français
hier		inviter des amis à dîner
lundi		regarder un film à la télé
mardi	je	écouter de la musique
mercredi	mes amis	préparer le dîner
jeudi	mes amis et moi	avoir la visite d'un(e) ami(e)
vendredi	mon ami(e)	
samedi	?	être en retard pour mon cours de français
dimanche		nager
la semaine dernière		faire une promenade
		faire le ménage
		passer l'après-midi à la bibliothèque
		faire des courses
		acheter des provisions

B. Et hier ? Using the suggestions provided in **Communication A**, ask questions to find out what other people in your class did yesterday.

Exemples   Est-ce que tu as fait des courses ?
Qu'est-ce que tu as acheté ?

C. Questions / Interview. Use the following questions to interview another student. If the answer to the numbered question is affirmative, ask the lettered questions. If the answer is negative, move on to the next numbered question. Each main question has a series of related questions to help you gain skill in sustaining a conversation in French.

1. Est-ce que tu as regardé la télé hier soir ?
   a. Est-ce que tu as regardé les actualités ?
   b. Est-ce que tu as regardé un film policier ?
   c. Est-ce que tu as écouté le bulletin météorologique ?
   d. Qu'est-ce que tu as regardé à la télé ?
2. Est-ce que tu as écouté des disques hier soir ?
   a. Est-ce que tu as écouté de la musique classique ?
   b. Quel disque est-ce que tu as écouté ?
   c. Quel est ton chanteur préféré ?
   d. Est-ce que tu achètes souvent des disques ?
   e. ?

3. Est-ce que tu as mangé à la maison hier soir?
   a. Est-ce que tu as fait la cuisine?
   b. Qu'est-ce que tu as préparé?
   c. Est-ce que tu as invité des amis?
   d. À quelle heure est-ce que tu as mangé?
   e. Qui a fait la vaisselle?
   f. ?
4. Est-ce que tu as mangé au restaurant universitaire ou dans un restaurant de la ville hier soir?
   a. Qu'est-ce que tu as mangé?
   b. Avec qui est-ce que tu as mangé?
   c. Est-ce que tu as aimé le repas?
   d. ?

Have students tell what television programs they watched last week (day, hour, program, and their opinion of the program) : *Dimanche à sept heures, j'ai regardé Soixante Minutes ; c'est un programme à ne pas manquer.*

C'est votre tour. Imaginez que vous n'avez pas eu le temps (ou que vous avez oublié) de faire vos devoirs de français. Expliquez à votre professeur que…

vous avez été très occupé(e)
vos parents (camarade de chambre, etc…) ont invité des amis à dîner
vous avez mangé très tard et vous n'avez pas eu le temps d'étudier
vous avez étudié la leçon mais vous n'avez pas fait les exercices
ce matin vous avez quitté la maison très tôt et vous avez oublié votre livre sur la table de la salle à manger
?

❧ Telling when something begins and ends
Finir et les verbes de la deuxième conjugaison

Présentation

A group of French verbs has infinitives that end in **-ir**. The present tense of many of these verbs is formed by dropping the **-ir** from the infinitive and adding the endings shown. The past participle is formed by dropping the **r** from the infinitive.

finir	
je fin**is**	nous fin**issons**
tu fin**is**	vous fin**issez**
il / elle / on fin**it**	ils / elles fin**issent**
passé composé : j'**ai fini**	

Other useful verbs conjugated like **finir** are :

réussir *to succeed, to pass*   J'**ai réussi** à mon examen de
   (*a test*)   français.
réfléchir (à) *to reflect, to*   Vous ne **réfléchissez** pas
   think   assez.
choisir *to choose*   On **a choisi** un film de Truffaut.
grandir *to grow* (*up*)   Elle **a grandi** au Maroc.
obéir (à) *to obey*   Ils ont refusé d'**obéir**.
désobéir (à) *to disobey*   Il **désobéit** à ses parents.
punir *to punish*   **Punissez**-vous vos enfants
                                quand ils désobéissent ?
rougir *to blush, to get red*   Pourquoi **rougissez**-vous ?
accomplir *to accomplish*   Qu'est-ce que vous **avez**
                             accompli ?

Mise en situation

On va au ciné ? Denis and Valerie are trying to convince their friends to go
see a film tonight.

Point out that although movie
theaters in France have been
hurt by the increasing use of
VCRs, moviegoing still
remains very popular.

DENIS	Vous finissez à quelle heure ce soir ?
CHRISTINE	Moi, je finis à six heures comme d'habitude, mais Pierre ne finit pas avant huit heures.
VALERIE	*Ça ne fait rien.* On va à la deuxième *séance.* Elle commence à neuf heures.
CHRISTINE	Oui, mais elle ne finit pas avant onze heures. Ça va être difficile de trouver *quelqu'un* pour *garder* les enfants.
DENIS	Écoutez… Vous choisissez le film et moi je trouve *une gardienne* pour les petits. C'est d'accord ?
PIERRE	Eh bien, *dans ce cas*, c'est d'accord !

*it doesn't matter / show,
showing*

someone / watch over

baby-sitter

in that case

Point out that *les petits* means
"the kids" and that *les gosses*
(colloquial) is also commonly
used.

Répétition : (1) Je finis à cinq
heures, tu finis à cinq heures,
etc. (2) J'ai choisi un bon vin.
(tu / mon ami / ses parents /
vous / nous / je) *Substitution :*
(1) Elle ne réfléchit pas assez.
(tu / vous / nous / je / Marc /
ses amis) (2) Il a réussi à
l'examen. (nous / je / les
étudiants / Pierre / vous / tu)

Préparation

A. À quelle heure? Several students are planning to go out this evening and want to find out when the others are through with their classes.

Modèle   Marc / à 6 h → **Marc finit à six heures.**

1. Monique / à 2 h
2. je / à 5 h 30
3. nous / à 4 h
4. tu / avant 7 h
5. vous / assez tôt
6. les autres / vers 5 h

B. Lieu de naissance. The following people are talking about the places where they grew up. What do they say?

Modèle   ma grand-mère / à Nice → **Ma grand-mère a grandi à Nice.**

1. tu / dans une grande ville
2. nous / à la campagne
3. Pierre / dans un pays étranger
4. ma tante / en Italie
5. vous / au Canada
6. mes cousins / en Belgique

C. Petits et grands succès. The Monots are talking about some of the things that they have accomplished lately. Tell what they say.

Modèle   Madeleine / réussir à son examen d'anglais.
             Madeleine a réussi à son examen d'anglais

1. je / apprendre à nager
2. tu / voyager à l'étranger
3. mes amis / réussir à trouver du travail
4. nous / être très occupés
5. vous / accomplir des choses importantes
6. je / faire des progrès en maths

Communication et vie pratique

A. Il faut de tout pour faire un monde. People do well in certain subjects and not so well in others. What about you and people you know?

Exemple   **Mon frère réussit bien en maths mais il n'est pas très fort en littérature.**

B. Questions / Interview. Answer the following questions or use them to interview another student.

1. Où est-ce que tu as grandi?
2. Quand est-ce que tu as fini tes études au lycée?
3. Est-ce que tu as déjà choisi tes cours pour le trimestre prochain?
4. Quels sont les cours où tu réussis bien?
5. Quand est-ce que tu vas finir tes études?
6. Est-ce que tu as déjà choisi ta future profession?
7. Qu'est-ce que tu as accompli ce trimestre?

Have students interview each other in small groups and write in French a summary of their conversation.

> **C'est votre tour.** You have been asked by neighbors if you could baby-sit for their two-year-old child one night a week, but you don't really want to do it. Your neighbors (played by other students in the class) are trying to find some time when you would be free. Using the **Mise en situation** as a guide, explain why you are not free.
>
> Exemple — Est-ce que vous êtes libre le mardi soir ?
> — Non, le mardi soir mes cours ne finissent pas avant neuf heures et demie.

❧ Talking about past events
Le passé composé avec l'auxiliaire *être*

Présentation

Some French verbs use **être** instead of **avoir** as their auxiliary verb. They are usually verbs of motion or transition. Only four of these verbs have been presented thus far : **aller**, **rester**, **rentrer**, and **arriver**.

Le passé composé avec *être*	
je **suis allé(e)**	nous **sommes allé(e)(s)**
tu **es allé(e)**	vous **êtes allé(e)(s)**
il / on **est allé**	ils **sont allés**
elle **est allée**	elles **sont allées**

Note that the past participles of these verbs agree in gender and number with the subject.

Je suis allé au cinéma hier soir.
Est-ce que **Marie est allée** à Genève ?
Nous ne sommes pas restés à la maison.
Est-ce que **vous êtes arrivés** en retard ?
Ils ne sont pas encore **rentrés**.

Mise en situation

Pendant le week-end. Alice, Serge, and Claude are talking about what they did last weekend.

ALICE   Vous avez passé un bon week-end ?

SERGE   Oui, pas *mauvais*... Et vous, vous êtes restés en ville ?   bad

CLAUDE   Non, on est allé faire une promenade en voiture.   Note that agreement of the
                                                                          past participle with *on* is
SERGE   Où est-ce que vous êtes allés ?   optional (*on est allé* or *on est
                                                                          allés*).

Le château de Fontainebleau

CLAUDE	À Fontainebleau. On est arrivé assez tôt le matin et on a pique-niqué dans *la forêt*…
ALICE	Oui, et après, nous avons visité *le château*. Nous sommes rentrés vers six heures du soir.
SERGE	C'est bête, je ne suis jamais allé à Fontainebleau. *Pourtant* c'est *tout près* de Paris !

forest

castle

yet

very near, quite near

Préparation

A. Pendant le week-end. Some students are telling where they went last weekend. Use the cues to tell what they say.

Exemple   Robert / café → **Robert est allé au café.**

1. tu / restaurant
2. Micheline / théâtre
3. Raoul et Marie / concert
4. nous / cinéma
5. vous / match de football
6. Henri / piscine
7. Roger et Jean-Marc / supermarché
8. Viviane et Louise / plage

B. **Où aller?** Monsieur and Madame Lafleur want to take a different vacation trip this year, so they're trying to find out where their friends have already been. What do they ask?

You may want first to review prepositions with the place names given in this exercise.

Modèle   les Monet / Grèce
    Est-ce que les Monet sont déjà allés en Grèce?

1. Marie-Claire / Italie
2. tes amis / Mexique
3. tu / Brésil
4. Monsieur Lemaître / États-Unis
5. tes voisins / Canada
6. les parents de Monique / Tunisie
7. vous / Norvège

C. **Occupations d'une étudiante française.** Here are some activities of Juliette Cordier, a French political science student. Tell what she did yesterday, making sure to use the correct form of **avoir** or **être**.

Note that this exercise integrates verbs conjugated with *être* and *avoir*.

Modèles   étudier à la maison → **Elle a étudié à la maison.**

ou: rester à la maison jusqu'à 9 h → **Elle est restée à la maison jusqu'à neuf heures.**

1. arriver à l'université à 10 h
2. manger au restaurant universitaire
3. aller au café avec des amis
4. avoir son cours d'histoire
5. rester à la bibliothèque jusqu'à 6 h
6. quitter l'université à 6 h 30
7. acheter ses provisions
8. rentrer à la maison
9. faire la cuisine
10. dîner avec un ami

Communication et vie pratique

A. **Trouvez un(e) étudiant(e)...** Ask questions to find out who in your class has gone to the following places. Either ask questions of individual students: **Jean, est-ce qu tu es allé à la plage?** or address the whole class: **Qui est allé au cinéma?**

See *Le passé composé avec avoir,* Préparation B (*Encore et toujours des excuses*), and have students use verbs they know to create additional excuses.

Trouvez un(e) étudiant(e)...

1. qui est allé(e) à la montagne en hiver
2. qui est allé(e) au bord de la mer l'été passé
3. qui est allé(e) en Floride pendant les vacances de printemps
4. qui est allé(e) au théâtre la semaine dernière
5. qui est allé(e) chez ses parents samedi dernier
6. qui est allé(e) dans un pays où on parle français
7. qui est allé(e) en Amérique du Sud
8. qui est allé(e) en Russie

Put each sentence on a note card and have students go around the room, marking who has gone and who has not gone to the places indicated. Results can be presented in the form of written or oral résumés.

B. **Qu'est-ce que vous avez fait?** Create sentences describing what you did last weekend, last night, or during your vacation last year. Choose from the suggestions below or add your own comments. You may want to add what your friends, roommates, etc., did.

Exemple **Pendant les vacances d'été, je suis allé(e) au bord de la mer et j'ai passé quelques semaines chez mes cousins.**

1. Pendant les vacances d'été…

   faire un voyage / visiter un pays étranger / aller au bord de la mer / passer un mois à la campagne / passer l'été avec ma famille / travailler dans un restaurant / dans un bureau / dans une usine

2. Pendant le week-end…

   rester à la maison / manger au restaurant / acheter des vêtements / aller au cinéma / regarder la télé / étudier

3. Hier soir…

   aller au concert / inviter des amis à dîner / emmener mon ami(e) au cinéma / faire la cuisine / regarder un bon film à la télé / aller à la bibliothèque / finir mes devoirs

Note that this activity integrates verbs conjugated with avoir *and* être. *You may want to discuss each of the sections in this activity separately, thus allowing for the development of more cohesive conversations. One or more of the sections could also be used for writing practice. Elicit information through the use of direct questions or through directed dialogue (*Est-ce que tu es allé au concert hier soir?*).*

C. **Huit heures dans la vie d'un(e) étudiant(e).** Tell what you did yesterday, using the questions below as a guide.

À quelle heure est-ce que vous êtes allé(e) à l'université?
À quelles classes est-ce que vous êtes allé(e) et à quelle heure?
Est-ce que vous avez étudié à la bibliothèque?
Où est-ce que vous avez mangé et avec qui?
À quelle heure est-ce que vous avez quitté le campus?
Est-ce que vous avez regardé la télé?
À quelle heure est-ce que vous avez commencé à étudier?
Quand est-ce que vous avez fini vos devoirs?

C'est votre tour. Vous êtes terriblement en retard. Excusez-vous et expliquez les raisons de votre retard. Utilisez les suggestions suivantes.

At what time you left your house
What means of transportation you used
Where you went first
At what time you got there
How long you stayed
Where you went next, etc.

Intégration et perspectives

Huit heures dans la vie d'un agent de police

Un agent de police fait son *rapport* à la fin de sa journée de travail.　　report

18 h 05　Pendant notre inspection du quartier, nous avons trouvé un jeune homme en pyjama, *sans* adresse et sans papiers d'identité. Un *amnésique* probablement. Nous avons *emmené* le jeune homme à l'hôpital psychiatrique.

without

amnesia victim / took

20 h 15　Accident de moto, rue de Sèvres. Nous avons transporté la victime, une jeune fille de dix-huit ans, à l'hôpital.

21 h 00　Dans un restaurant de la rue d'Alger, un client *ivre* a refusé de payer l'addition. Le patron a téléphoné à la police. Quand nous avons interrogé le client, il a *commencé* à *raconter* ses exploits en Indochine. Nous avons emmené l'homme au poste de police.

drunk

began / tell

22 h 10　Des *cambrioleurs* ont *volé* l'argent d'une dame de soixante-quinze ans. Nous avons *montré* des photos des suspects à la victime. Elle a identifié les cambrioleurs.

burglars / stole

showed

23 h 45　Le patron d'un bar a téléphoné pour *signaler* une *bagarre*. Nous avons séparé les adversaires et nous avons emmené les victimes à l'hôpital.

report / brawl

0 h 45　Un monsieur de la rue des Arcades a téléphoné pour signaler une *surprise-partie* trop *bruyante*. Nous avons *demandé* aux participants d'être moins bruyants.

party / noisy / asked

1 h 30　Nous avons trouvé un homme *à genoux* au milieu de la rue. Nous avons interrogé l'homme. Il a expliqué : « Je parle avec la *Vierge Marie*. » Nous avons persuadé l'homme de continuer la conversation sur le *trottoir*.

on his knees

Virgin Mary

sidewalk

Compréhension. Selon les renseignements donnés, est-ce que les phrases suivantes sont vraies ou fausses ? Corrigez le sens de la phrase s'il est faux.

Have students also describe eight hours in the life of a campus police officer, a professor, etc.

1. À 18 h 05 les agents de police ont trouvé un homme ivre dans la rue.
2. À 21 h 15 un jeune homme a eu un accident de moto rue des Arcades.
3. Les agents ont transporté la victime chez ses parents.
4. Le patron du restaurant de la rue d'Alger a téléphoné à la police parce qu'un client a volé son argent.
5. La dame de soixante-quinze ans a identifié les cambrioleurs qui ont volé son argent.
6. À 23 h 45 le patron d'un bar a téléphoné pour signaler une surprise-partie trop bruyante.
7. Les agents de police ont participé à la bagarre.
8. À 0 h 45 un monsieur de la rue d'Alger a téléphoné pour inviter les agents de police à une surprise-partie.
9. Les agents ont persuadé les participants de continuer leur surprise-partie.
10. À 1 h 30 les agents ont trouvé un homme à genoux au milieu de la rue.

Notes culturelles: *Les agents de police*

A typical eight-hour shift of the blue-uniformed French **agents de police** who patrol city streets and direct traffic is similar to that of their American counterparts. Unlike most American police who patrol their areas in cars, French police generally cover their beat on foot. They are always armed with a revolver and a white nightstick. In France, as in most Western countries, the crime rate has risen dramatically in recent years, making the police officer's job more difficult today than in the past. Given the French love of independence and individualism, the **flics**, as police are called, have traditionally been an easy target for jokes and a certain amount of resentment.

Gendarmes, who wear tan uniforms, are responsible for maintaining order in rural communities. **Motards**, dressed in blue motorcycle uniforms and helmets, patrol France's highways.

Un agent de police

Un gendarme

Communication et vie pratique

A. Ce n'est pas moi ! Il y a eu un crime dans votre quartier. Vous êtes interrogé(e) par la police. Expliquez…

à quelle heure vous avez quitté votre maison
où vous êtes allé(e)
à quelle heure vous êtes arrivé(e) à votre destination
ce que vous avez fait et avec qui vous avez parlé
combien de temps vous êtes resté(e)
à quelle heure vous êtes rentré(e) chez vous
ce que vous avez fait après votre retour

Students can role-play this activity, one student taking the role of the police officer and the other the person being questioned.

B. À la gare. Vous êtes à Paris et vous désirez visiter différentes villes françaises. Posez des questions à un(e) employé(e) de la S.N.C.F. (joué par un(e) autre étudiant(e)) pour obtenir les renseignements désirés.

Vous désirez savoir…

s'il y a un train qui va à X…
si c'est direct ou s'il faut changer
à quelle heure est le prochain train pour X…
combien de temps ça prend
à quelle heure le train va arriver à X…
à quelle heure il y a un autre train pour X…
?

C. Il faut choisir. Vous avez décidé d'aller au cinéma avec vos amis Anne et David (joués par d'autres étudiants de la classe), mais vous avez de la difficulté à trouver une heure où vous êtes tous libres et vous avez des goûts très différents. Quel film allez-vous choisir ?

Voici les éléments de la situation :

Anne travaille dans un magasin et elle ne finit jamais avant huit heures.
David a des examens cette semaine et il désire rentrer tôt pour étudier.
Les films qu'on joue et l'heure de chaque séance sont indiqués dans le journal.

GAUMONT. — Une histoire d'amour dans le sud de la France : **L'Eté en pente douce,** avec Jacques Villeret et Pauline Laffont. 13.40, 15.50, 18.00, 20.10, 22.20.

GAUMONT. — Oscar de la meilleure actrice pour Marlee Matlin dans **Les Enfants du silence.** avec également William Hurt. 13.50, 16.30, 19.10, 21.50.

MÉLIÈS. — Claudia Cardinale, Lambert Wilson dans le nouveau film de Luigi Commencini : **La Storia** (V.O.). Film à 17.00 et 19.35 ; dim. 14.40, 17.30.

MERCURY. — César du meilleur acteur : Daniel Auteuil dans **Jean de Florette,** avec Yves Montand et Gérard Depardieu. Film à 14.40, 19.20, 21.40 ; dim. 14.40, 17.00, 19.25.

MERCURY. — Césars 87. Emmanuelle Béart dans **Manon des Sources,** avec Yves Montand et Daniel Auteuil. Film à 14.40, 19.20, 21.40 ; dim. 14.40, 17.00, 19.25.

MERCURY. — Un grand dessin animé de Walt Disney : **Les 101 Dalmatiens.** 19.00 (mer., sam., dim. 14.30 et 19.00).

PATHÉ 1. — Crocodile Dundee, quinzième semaine de triomphe ! 14.15, 16.15, 18.15, 20.15, 22.15.

PATHÉ 2. — Festival de Cannes 1987 : **Good Morning Babylone,** un film de Paolo et Vittorio Taviani. 14.10, 16.45, 19.20, 21.55.

PATHÉ 3. — Eddie Murphy : **Golden Child, l'enfant sacré du Tibet.** 14.05, 16.05, 18.05, 20.05, 22.05.

PATHÉ 4. — Festival du film policier Cognac 87 : **Le Sixième Sens,** un film de Michael Mann. 14.00, 16.35, 19.10, 21.45.

• *Prononciation et orthographe*

A. Some consonant sounds are pronounced slightly differently in French and in English. In particular, / p /, / t /, and / k / are not "exploded" or released with the same force as in English. The French pronunciation of these sounds is similar to their pronunciation in English when they follow an *s*. (Compare : *pair — spare, top — stop, kit — skit*.)

Listen and repeat :

patient	télévision	confortable
police	talent	colonie
petit	téléphone	commander
pays	travailler	capitale

B. To pronounce the French /l/, the tip of the tongue is placed against the upper front teeth rather than on the ridge behind the teeth as in English.

Listen and repeat :

le	valise	ville
la	milieu	tranquille
loin	village	salle
liberté	soleil	hôtel
livre	aller	quelle

C. In French, all consonant sounds occurring at the end of a word (i.e., when there is a written consonant followed by the letter **e**) are pronounced with much more clarity than in English. Notice also how the pronunciation of the final consonant distinguishes the feminine from the masculine form of many adjectives.

Listen and repeat :

content / contente	parfait / parfaite	sérieux / sérieuse
patient / patiente	grand / grande	heureux / heureuse
petit / petite	français / française	blanc / blanche

D. When the letter **s** occurs between two vowels, it is pronounced /z/ as in **poison**. When there are two **s**'s, the sound is always /s/ as in **poisson**. The sound /s/ also corresponds to the following spellings : **ç, c** followed by **i** or **e, t** in the **-tion** ending (**ça, ceci, nation**).

Compare and repeat :

ils ont / ils sont	nous avons / nous savons
poison / poisson	deux heures / deux sœurs
désert / dessert	

Repeat the following phrases :

La cuisine française a une excellente réputation.
Voici la maison de nos voisins.
Nous savons qu'ils ont de la glace comme dessert.
J'ai l'impression que vous aimez ça.

• *Vocabulaire*

Noms

la télévision (voir p. 155)

d'autres noms

° l'**accident** (m)
° l'**acteur** (m)
° l'**actrice** (f)
  les **affaires** (f) *things, belongings*
    l'**alpiniste** (m, f) *mountain climber*
    l'**après-midi** (m) *afternoon*
    l'**argent** (m) *money*
  le **cambrioleur** *burglar*
  le **carnet** *notebook*
  la **chaîne** *channel*
  le **chanteur,** la **chanteuse** *singer*
  le **château** *castle*
° le **comédien,** la **comédienne**
  la **coupe** *cup*
  la **dame** *lady, woman*
  le **début** *beginning*
° la **démocratie**
  la **fin** *end*
  le **football** *soccer*
  la **forêt** *forest*
  la **gardienne d'enfants** *baby-sitter*
° le **héros**
° l'**héroïne**
    l'**heure** *hour, o'clock*
    l'**histoire** (f) *story*
° l'**identité** (f)
  la **journée** *day*
  le **langage** *language, speech*
  le **matin** *morning*
    minuit (m) *midnight*
° le **musicien,** la **musicienne**
° le **papier**
  le **passionné,** la **passionnée** *fan*
  le **personnage** *character*
  le **présentateur,** la **présentatrice** *anchorperson*
  le **programme** *program (list of offerings)*
  le **rapport** *report*
° la **religion**
  les **renseignements** (m) *information*
  le **rock** *rock music*

  le **rôle** *role, part*
  la **séance** *showing*
° la **situation**
  le **soir** *evening*
  le **sujet** *subject*
  la **surprise-partie** *party*
  le **téléviseur** *television set*
  le **trottoir** *sidewalk*
  la **vedette** *star, celebrity*
° la **victime**
  la **vidéo-cassette** *videotape*

Verbes

accomplir *to accomplish*
choisir *to choose*
commencer *to start*
demander *to ask, to ask for*
désobéir *to disobey*
emmener *to take along, to lead*
finir *to finish*
garder *to keep, to watch over*
grandir *to grow, to grow up*
° **identifier**
interroger *to question*
jouer *to play*
montrer *to show*
obéir *to obey*
oublier *to forget*
° **payer**
° **persuader**
punir *to punish*
raconter *to tell, to relate*
réfléchir *to reflect, to think*
° **refuser**
réussir *to succeed, to pass (a test)*
rougir *to blush*
savoir *to know*
séparer *to separate*
signaler *to report*
tomber *to fall*
° **transporter**
voler *to steal*

Adjectifs

bruyant(e) *noisy*
dernier, dernière *last*

divorcé(e) *divorced*
gros, grosse *large*
juste *close, tight*
malade *ill*
meilleur(e) *better, best*
passé(e) *last, past*
policier, policière *police, detective*
sage *well-behaved*
suivant(e) *next, following*

Adverbes

déjà *already*
hier *yesterday*
probablement *probably*
seulement *only*
tard *late*
tôt *early, soon*
tout *quite*

Prépositions

sans *without*
vers *toward*

Divers

à l'heure *on time*
ça ne fait rien *it doesn't matter*
c'est-à-dire *that is to say*
en avance *early*
en retard *late*
il vaut mieux *it's better*
je voudrais *I would like*
parce que *because*
pourquoi *why*
pourtant *however, yet*
quelqu'un *someone*
tomber malade *to become ill*

CHAPITRE HUIT

Communication objectives	**Structures**

Communication objectives

Talking about weather

1. Expressing reactions, feelings, and opinions

2. Talking about coming and going

3. Getting information

4. Talking about changes in location, state, health, etc.

Structures

Les mots et la vie : Le temps qu'il fait

Les expressions idiomatiques avec **avoir**

Les verbes conjugués comme **partir** et comme **venir**

Les questions par inversion et les mots interrogatifs

Les verbes conjugués avec **être**

La pluie et le beau temps

Mise en scène

Bulletin météorologique du vendredi 22 février

Nuages **dans le** *nord*, *soleil* **dans le reste de la France**

En France aujourd'hui

Aujourd'hui, une zone de mauvais temps va progresser de l'*Ouest* à l'*Est*. Dans le Nord et le Centre, le *ciel* va *devenir* nuageux ou très nuageux. Dans le *Midi* il va continuer à faire beau.

Les *vents*, *faibles* et variables le matin, vont devenir modérés dans la partie nord du pays.

Dans le Nord, les températures assez *froides* le matin vont *monter* jusqu'à dix degrés pendant la journée. Dans le reste de la France, les températures vont rester stables.

Demain

Demain, il va faire beau dans le Sud-Ouest de la France. Dans le reste du pays, le temps va rester variable. Possibilité de *pluie* et de *neige* dans les Alpes. Danger de *verglas* sur les routes.

Compréhension. Répondez aux questions suivantes selon les renseignements donnés dans le texte.

1. Est-ce que le mauvais temps va progresser de l'Est à l'Ouest ou de l'Ouest à l'Est ?
2. Est-ce que le ciel va être nuageux ou est-ce qu'il va faire beau dans le Nord ?
3. Est-ce que les vents vont devenir modérés ou violents pendant la journée ?

Point out that *la météo* is commonly used as a short form of *le bulletin météorologique*.

clouds / North / sun

West

East / sky / to become
South
winds / light, weak

cold / go up

rain / snow
ice

Point out that *jour* refers to a specific day (*Quel jour allez-vous partir ?*) ; *journée* refers to a length of time (*J'ai passé toute la journée à la plage.*) You might also want to indicate the differences between *soir* / *soirée* and *matin* / *matinée*.

4. Dans le Nord, est-ce que les températures vont rester stables ou est-ce qu'elles vont monter ?
5. Demain, est-ce qu'il va faire beau ou mauvais dans le Sud-Ouest de la France ?
6. Est-ce qu'il y a des possibilités de pluie et de neige dans le Sud-Ouest du pays ou dans les Alpes ?

Notes culturelles: *Le relief et le climat de la France*

Située entre le 42ᵉ et le 51ᵉ parallèle nord, et avec une large façade sur la mer, la France est un pays au climat modéré et varié. La variété de son *relief* contribue aussi à la variété du climat et des *paysages* naturels. Si vous consultez la carte, vous *pouvez* distinguer les grandes régions naturelles :

1. Les régions montagneuses qui *comprennent* des montagnes jeunes aux sommets élevés (les Alpes, les Pyrénées et le Jura) et des montagnes anciennes aux sommets *arrondis* (le Massif central, le Massif armoricain et les Vosges).
2. Les plateaux et les plaines situés surtout dans le Nord et l'Ouest du pays : le Bassin parisien et le Bassin aquitain.
3. La vallée du Rhône entre les Alpes et le Massif central.

Vous pouvez aussi noter les *principaux fleuves* : la Seine, la Loire, la Garonne, et le Rhône.

En ce qui concerne le climat, on distingue quatre zones climatiques différentes :

1. Le climat atlantique (à l'Ouest) qui est caractérisé par ses *hivers doux* et humides et ses pluies fréquentes en toute saison.
2. Le climat continental (dans le Nord) aux contrastes plus marqués : hivers froids, étés assez chauds.
3. Le climat montagnard (surtout dans les Alpes) où les hivers sont longs et très froids et où il neige beaucoup.
4. Le climat méditerranéen en Provence et dans le Languedoc. Il est marqué par ses hivers très doux et ses étés chauds et *secs*. La Côte d'Azur a un climat particulièrement agréable car les Alpes *la protègent* contre le Mistral, un vent si *puissant* qu'il est capable de *renverser* une voiture.

topography / scenery

can

include

rounded

grandes rivières

winters / mild

dry

protect it / strong
overturn

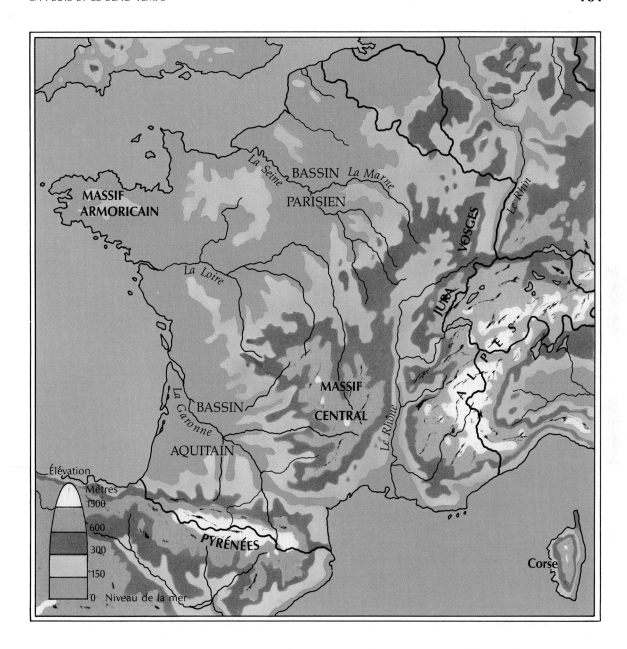

MASSIF ARMORICAIN

La Seine

BASSIN PARISIEN

La Marne

Le Rhin

VOSGES

JURA

La Loire

A L P E S

MASSIF CENTRAL

Le Rhône

La Garonne

BASSIN AQUITAIN

Élévation
Mètres
1500
600
300
150
0 Niveau de la mer

PYRÉNÉES

Corse

Les mots et la vie : *Le temps qu'il fait*

Learn the following weather expressions and then complete the activities below. Note that these expressions are generally formed with the impersonal subject pronoun **il** and the verb **faire**.

Quel temps fait-il ?	*How is the weather ?*
Il fait beau.	*It's nice. (The weather is nice.)*
Il fait chaud.	*It's warm.*
Il fait froid.	*It's cold.*
Il fait frais.	*It's cool.*
Il fait mauvais.	*The weather is bad.*
Il fait du vent.	*It's windy.*
Il fait du soleil.	*It's sunny.*
Il fait (il y a) du brouillard.	*It's foggy.*
Il va pleuvoir.	*It's going to rain.*
Il pleut.	*It's raining.*
Il a plu.	*It rained.*
Il va neiger.	*It's going to snow.*
Il neige.	*It's snowing.*
Le ciel est couvert.	*It's cloudy.*
Il y a un orage.	*There is a storm.*
La température est de 15°.	*The temperature is 15 degrees (Celsius).*

Option: Introduce the following expressions : *Il pleut à verse ; il fait lourd ; il fait un froid de canard ; il fait un temps à ne pas mettre un chien dehors.*

Have students tell what they like to do in various weather conditions (e.g., *Quand il fait beau, j'aime aller à la plage. Quand il neige, je préfère rester à la maison, etc.*).

A. Le temps en France aujourd'hui. Using the following weather map, tell what the weather is like in each of the French cities given below.

Exemple   Paris → **Le ciel est couvert.**

1. Bordeaux
2. Lille
3. Marseille
4. Strasbourg
5. Limoges
6. Lyon

If available, bring in other weather maps and reports from French newspapers and have students summarize the weather conditions. Copies of weather reports from American newspapers can also be given to students who can be asked to give the gist of the report in French.

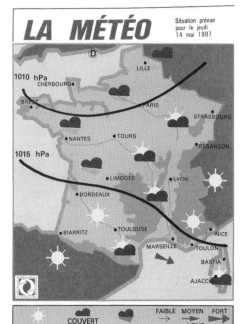

B. **Quel temps fait-il ?** A Paris newspaper reported the following temperatures and weather conditions around the world. Describe the weather in each city.

Exemple   Berlin 10° PV
À **Berlin la température est de dix degrés. Il pleut et il fait du vent.**

Températures et conditions météorologiques			
N = neige P = pluie V = vent S = soleil C = couvert O = orage			
Paris	10° VP	Melbourne	25° OV
Madrid	14° S	Oslo	7° S
New York	2° N	Berlin	10° PV
Londres	8° C	Rome	13° SV

C. **Bulletin météorologique.** Use the **bulletin météorologique** in the **Mise en scène** as a guide to prepare your own weather report. Indicate yesterday's and today's weather and predict what tomorrow's weather will be like. Your forecast might be for your own town, for a city or town in the French-speaking world, or for a country where the climate is either ideal or miserable.

Explorations
✻Expressing reactions, feelings, and opinions
Les expressions idiomatiques avec *avoir*

Présentation

The verb **avoir** occurs in many idiomatic expressions used to indicate reactions, feelings, needs, and intentions. The most useful of these are :

A. Reactions and feelings

avoir froid *to be cold*	Nous **avons froid**.
avoir chaud *to be hot*	J'**ai** trop **chaud**.
avoir faim *to be hungry*	Est-ce que tu **as faim** ?
avoir soif *to be thirsty*	Nous **avons** très **soif**.
avoir sommeil *to be sleepy*	Il est tard et ils **ont sommeil**.
avoir peur *to be afraid*	Elle n'**a** pas **peur** des chiens.
avoir honte *to be ashamed*	Moi, je n'**ai** pas **honte**.
avoir mal *to hurt*	J'**ai mal** partout.

B. Opinions

avoir raison *to be right*	Tu **as raison** d'être très prudent.
avoir tort *to be wrong*	J'**ai eu tort** de faire ça.
avoir l'air *to appear, to look (seem)*	Il n'**a** pas **l'air** content.
avoir de la chance *to be lucky*	Tu **as eu de la chance**!

C. Intentions and needs

avoir l'intention de *to intend*	J'**ai l'intention de** rester à la maison.
avoir envie de *to want, to feel like*	Est-ce que tu **as envie de** lire ce livre?
avoir besoin de *to need*	J'**ai besoin de** prendre des vacances.
avoir l'occasion de *to have the chance, to have the opportunity*	**As**-tu déjà **eu l'occasion de** voyager à l'étranger?

D. Avoir also occurs in such idiomatic expressions as **avoir lieu** (*to take place*) and **avoir... ans** (*to be . . . years old*).

Le concert **a eu lieu** dimanche après-midi.
Çe garçon **a dix-sept ans**.

E. Note that **avoir envie de** and **avoir besoin de** can be followed by an infinitive (j'ai besoin de **travailler**), by a noun (il a besoin d'**argent**), by a definite article (elle a besoin de **la** voiture ce soir), or by an indefinite article (nous avons besoin d'**un** nouvel appareil-photo).

Mise en situation

Une excursion en montagne. C'est la première fois que les amis de Francis ont l'occasion de faire une excursion en montagne. Tout le monde est fatigué.

FRANCIS   Ça va, Pierre ? Tu as l'air fatigué…

PIERRE   Oui, j'ai chaud et j'ai mal partout.

ARMAND   Nous aussi, on est fatigué et on a faim ! On a besoin de manger quelque chose.

FRANCIS   Vous avez raison, on va faire une petite pause.

SABINE   Une petite pause ? Tu as l'intention de marcher encore *longtemps* ?

FRANCIS   Il faut choisir. *Soit* on continue jusqu'au chalet, *soit* on passe *la nuit dehors*… Alors, qu'est-ce que tu as envie de faire ?

a long time

either / or

the night / outside

Substitution : (1) J'ai froid. (nous / tu / vous / Marc / ces touristes) (2) Est-ce que tu as faim ? (chaud / froid / peur / sommeil / soif) (3) Ils ont besoin de travailler. (envie / l'air / raison / tort / l'intention)

Préparation

A.   Descriptions. Using the following illustrations, describe the reactions and feelings of each of the people below.

Modèle

Robert… → **Robert a chaud.**

1. Suzanne…

2. Nous…

3. Vous…

4. Marcel et Roger…

5. Mon frère…

6. Le concert…

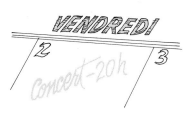

7. Je…

8. Son ami…

B. **Suivez le guide, s'il vous plaît!** Serge, who is studying English, works during the summer as an assistant tour guide for English-speaking tourists in Paris. He has to report some of their complaints and comments to the tour director. What does he say?

You might also want to include sentences about weather to illustrate the difference between *avoir* idioms and weather expressions.

Modèle   We are hungry and thirsty. → **Nous avons faim et soif.**

1. Mrs. White needs to go to the bank.
2. We are cold and hungry!
3. You are lucky to live in Paris.
4. Mr. Collins does not feel like visiting Versailles.
5. Mr. Wolf is afraid to go shopping alone.
6. The others are very sleepy.
7. I am thirsty.
8. You look very tired.

Communication et vie pratique

A. **Petits dialogues.** Complete each of the following dialogues with an appropriate **avoir** expression. Then alone, or with another student, create similar exchanges with **avoir** expressions.

Have students present their *petits dialogues* to the class with the option of having other students provide the *avoir* idiom that fits the situation given.

Modèle   MARC   On va au café?
             PIERRE   Oui, je…
             Oui, j'ai soif.

1. LA MÈRE   Il faut manger ta viande, mon petit!
   L'ENFANT   Mais, maman, je…
2. L'ÉTUDIANT   New York est la capitale des États-Unis.
   LE PROFESSEUR   Mais non, vous…
3. M. DUPONT   Où est-ce que vous allez en vacances cette année?
   MME LECLERC   Je ne suis pas sûre, mais nous… aller sur la Côte d'Azur.
4. JEAN-LUC   Je voyage toujours en avion — c'est très rapide.
   CLAUDE   Pas moi! Je n'aime pas les avions; je… d'avoir un accident.
5. PAUL   Est-ce qu'on va danser ce soir?
   CHANTAL   Non, pas ce soir, J'ai travaillé jusqu'à minuit hier soir et je…
6. LE PROFESSEUR   Vous n'avez pas encore fait vos devoirs?
   L'ÉTUDIANT   Non, monsieur. Mais je… travailler aujourd'hui.

B. **Questions / Interview.** Answer the following questions or use them to interview another student.

Have students prepare related questions to use in small-group interviews.

1. Qu'est-ce que tu as envie de faire ce soir?
2. Qu'est-ce que tu as l'intention de faire pendant le week-end?
3. Qu'est-ce que tu as l'intention de faire pendant les prochaines vacances?
4. Quand tu as très faim, qu'est-ce que tu aimes manger?
5. Et quand tu as soif, qu'est-ce que tu bois d'habitude?
6. Est-ce que tu as déjà eu l'occasion de voyager dans un pays étranger?

7. Est-ce que tu as envie d'habiter dans un pays étranger ? Si oui, dans quel pays et pourquoi ?
8. Quelle région des États-Unis est-ce que tu as envie de visiter ?

C'est votre tour. Vous faites une excursion à bicyclette avec un groupe d'amis (joués par trois ou quatre étudiants). Deux personnes sont super-enthousiastes et ne sont jamais fatigués ; les deux autres ne sont jamais contents. Imaginez la conversation et jouez la scène.

❧ Talking about coming and going
Les verbes conjugués comme *partir* et comme *venir*

Présentation

The present tense forms of several **-ir** verbs like **partir** (*to leave*) and **sortir** (*to go out*) do not follow the regular pattern of second conjugation verbs like **finir**. **Partir** and **sortir** are conjugated with **être** in the **passé composé**.

partir	
je **pars**	nous **partons**
tu **pars**	vous **partez**
il / elle / on **part**	ils / elles **partent**

passé composé : je **suis parti(e)**

À quelle heure **partez**-vous ?
Ils **sont partis** ce matin.
Ce soir **je sors** avec des amis.
Est-ce que Chantal **est sortie** avec Gérard ?

Venir (*to come*) is also irregular. It is also conjugated with **être** in the **passé composé**.

venir	
je **viens**	nous **venons**
tu **viens**	vous **venez**
il / elle / on **vient**	ils / elles **viennent**

passé composé : je **suis venu(e)**

Elle n'**est** pas **venue** en classe aujourd'hui.

* — Est-ce qu'il **vient** du Maroc ?
— Non, il **vient** de Tunisie.

---

*Note that masculine and plural countries are preceded by **du** or **des** ; feminine countries by **de**.

A. Other verbs that are similar to **venir** in the present tense (and that also require **être** in the **passé composé**) are :

devenir	*to become*	Le ciel **est devenu** nuageux.
revenir	*to come back, to return*	Je **suis revenu** à onze heures.

B. Venir de, when followed by an infinitive, means *to have just done something*.

Je **viens de trouver** du travail.	*I just found a job.*
Nous **venons d'arriver.**	*We (have) just arrived.*

C. Thus, there are three ways in addition to the present tense to express actions that relate closely to the present time :

1. **aller** + INFINITIVE is used to indicate that an action is about to take place.

   Anne **va préparer** le dîner.

2. **être en train de** + INFINITIVE is used to express an action in the process of taking place.

   Anne **est en train de préparer** le dîner.

3. **venir de** + INFINITIVE is used to express an action that has just taken place.

   Anne **vient de préparer** le dîner.

Mise en situation

Qu'est-ce que tu deviens ? Mathieu *rencontre* son vieil ami Raymond. Ils échangent des *nouvelles.*

MATHIEU	Alors, *qu'est-ce que tu deviens* ?
RAYMOND	Je voyage beaucoup ces temps-ci. Aujourd'hui, je reviens de Milan et la semaine prochaine, je pars à Londres. Ça devient *fatigant.*
MATHIEU	Si tu as envie de passer une *soirée* tranquille, viens dîner chez nous ce soir.
RAYMOND	Impossible, je sors avec Natacha.
MATHIEU	Ingrid et toi, vous ne sortez plus ensemble ?
RAYMOND	Non, c'est fini. Elle est repartie en Allemagne. Mais... et vous deux, comment ça va ?
MATHIEU	Nous venons d'acheter une maison, et... je vais *bientôt* être papa !
RAYMOND	Eh bien, félicitations !

Répétition : Je pars en vacances, tu pars en vacances, etc. Je suis sorti vendredi soir, tu es sorti vendredi soir, elle est sortie vendredi soir, etc. *Substitution* : (1) Tu sors avec des amis ce soir. *(nous / Véronique / je / Robert et Michel / vous / tu)* (2) Ils ne sont pas partis hier. *(je / vous / mon père / nous / les autres / tu)*

Répétition : Je viens de Paris, tu viens de Paris, etc. Je suis revenu à 11 heures, tu es revenu à 11 heures, elle est revenue à 11 heures, etc. *Substitution* : (1) Nous venons d'acheter une maison. *(nous / tu / je / Marianne / vous / mes cousins)* (2) Il n'est jamais revenu. *(nous / je / ma sœur / ses amis / tu / vous)*

meets

news

what are you up to these days?

Je pars pour Londres is also possible.

tiring

evening

Point out that *viens dîner* means *come and eat.*

Have students note that *vous ne sortez plus ensemble* means that they are not dating anymore.

soon

Have students note the *re* prefix on *repartir* and how it relates to other words (e.g., *revenir, reprendre, refaire,* etc.).

Préparation

A. Activités. Marc and his friends are talking about what they are going to do today. What do they say?   *Repeat in the passé composé.*

Modèle   Marc / partir en vacances → **Marc part en vacances.**

1. je / partir en vacances aussi
2. mes amis / partir en voyage
3. vous / sortir avec des amis
4. Éliane / partir à la campagne
5. tu / venir au cinéma avec nous
6. nous / sortir ensemble ce soir

B. D'où viens-tu? Students taking the **cours pour étrangers** at the **Université de Bordeaux** are telling each other where they are from. What do they say?

Remind students that feminine countries take de (e.g., Je viens de Suisse) and that masculine countries take du (Je viens du Portugal).

Modèle   Mounir / Tunisie → **Mounir vient de Tunisie.**

1. Brahim / Maroc
2. je / Canada
3. nous / Allemagne
4. Marc et Élise / Suisse
5. tu / Belgique
6. vous / Sénégal

C. Départs. Several neighbors are discussing when they left on vacation this past summer. Tell what they say.

Modèle   Véronique / 31 juillet
Véronique est partie le trente et un juillet.

1. vous / 5 août
2. je / 30 juin
3. les Legrand / vers la fin de juin
4. Michel / au début de juillet
5. tu / au printemps
6. nous / 1er août

Véronique est partie le 31 juillet.

D. Avant, pendant, et après. Use the model as a guide to tell what Robert Lefranc and his friends are going to do, are doing, and have just done.

Modèle

Il va manger à midi.   Il est en train de manger.   Il vient de manger.

1.

2.

3.

4.

5.

Communication et vie pratique

A. **Questions / interview.** Answer the following questions about university life or use them to interview another student.

1. Est-ce que tu viens de commencer tes études ici?
2. De quelle ville est-ce que tu viens?
3. Est-ce que tu as été obligé(e) de quitter ta famille pour venir faire tes études ici?
4. Et tes amis du lycée (*high school*), qu'est-ce qu'ils sont devenus?
5. À ton avis, est-ce que les études deviennent plus faciles après la première année?
6. Est-ce que tu vas revenir à l'université l'an prochain?
7. Est-ce que tu as le temps de sortir pendant la semaine?
8. Est-ce que tu es sorti(e) le week-end passé? Si oui, où es-tu allé(e)?

C'est votre tour. Un(e) de vos ami(e)s téléphone pour vous inviter à sortir. Malheureusement, vous êtes très occupé(e) (ou vous n'avez pas envie de sortir). Quelles excuses allez-vous invoquer? Voici quelques suggestions. Choisissez les excuses qui correspondent à votre situation et expliquez à votre ami(e) que…

1. vous allez avoir un examen demain et vous êtes en train d'étudier
2. vous venez de rentrer et vous n'avez pas encore eu le temps de manger
3. vous êtes sorti(e) cet après-midi avec des amis
4. vous allez partir en voyage demain
5. vous avez envie de passer une soirée tranquille à la maison
6. vous avez sommeil et vous avez besoin de dormir
7. vous êtes obligé(e) de rester à la maison parce que des amis vont arriver d'une minute à l'autre
8. vos parents vont arriver demain et vous avez besoin de faire le ménage

---

⚜ Getting information
Les questions par inversion et les mots interrogatifs

Présentation

In Chapter 1, you learned to ask questions by using intonation, **est-ce que** and **n'est-ce pas**. A fourth way of asking questions is to invert (reverse) the subject pronoun and verb and link them with a hyphen. Questions by inversion are commonly used in written and formal language, but less often in conversation. Inversion is not normally used with **je**. Inversion may occur :

A. when the subject of a sentence is a pronoun. In the third-person singular, **-t-** is added when the verb does not already end in **t** or **d**.

You may want to point out that the parts of the negative do not change position in inversion (e.g., *Ne venez-vous pas demain ?*).

Il pleut souvent.	**Pleut-il** souvent ?
Vous venez demain.	**Venez-vous** demain ?
C'est un climat agréable.	**Est-ce** un climat agréable ?
Ils préfèrent sortir.	**Préfèrent-ils** sortir ?
On montre souvent des films étrangers.	**Montre-t-on** souvent des films étrangers ?
Il y a du verglas.	**Y a-t-il** du verglas ?

B. when the subject of the sentence is a noun. The noun subject is not inverted, but a subject pronoun of the same number and gender is added for inversion.

Pierre part-il aujourd'hui ?
Charles et Julien sont-ils ici ?
Votre télévision marche-t-elle bien ?

C. after question words such as the following :

qui (*who, whom*)	**Avec qui sors-tu ?**
que (*what*)	**Que faites-vous** lundi soir ?
où (*where*)	**Où vont-ils ?**
quand (*when*)	**Quand partez-vous ?**
comment (*how*)	**Comment allez-vous** voyager ?
pourquoi (*why*)	**Pourquoi prennent-elles** le train ?
combien (*how much*)	**Combien pariez-vous ?**

All these question words can also be used with *est-ce que* (e.g., *Où est-ce que tu es allé ?*) ; *que* becomes *qu'est-ce que*.

D. in compound tenses such as the **passé composé** where only the conjugated verb is inverted.

Avez-vous eu l'occasion de voyager en Chine ?
Où Serge **est-il allé ?**
Comment Michel et Denise **ont-ils trouvé** le climat ?

Mise en situation

Arrivée à l'hôtel. Madame et Monsieur Delporte ont décidé à la dernière minute d'aller passer le week-end dans *une station de ski*. Le problème est de trouver un hôtel.   **ski resort**

M. DELPORTE	Avez-vous une chambre libre ?
L'EMPLOYÉ	Pour combien de personnes ?
M. DELPORTE	Trois personnes. Deux adultes et un enfant.
L'EMPLOYÉ	Désirez-vous une chambre *à deux lits* ou deux chambres séparées ? **with two beds**
MME DELPORTE	Une chambre à deux lits.
L'EMPLOYÉ	Avec ou sans salle de bain ?

France has a variety of hotel accommodations ranging from large hotel chains of the American type to hotels with limited facilities. In the most modest hotels, it is not uncommon to find rooms with only a wash basin and bidet in the room and a common bathroom down the hall. Prices reflect the degree of comfort offered. Breakfast is usually included. Many hotels offer a *demi-pension* (breakfast and one meal a day) or *pension complète*.

Station de ski dans les
Alpes français

Substitution : (1) Quand revient-il ? *(tu / elles / nous / il / vous / elle)* (2) Vos amis regardent-ils souvent la télé ? *(vos parents / sa sœur / ton professeur / leurs amis)* *Transformation :* Have students put these sentences in the interrogative with inversion. (1) Il y a une banque ici. (2) C'est une grande ville. (3) Tu vas à Paris. (4) Elles sont ici. (5) Vous écoutez souvent la radio. (6) Elle part aujourd'hui. (7) Il vient de manger.

MME DELPORTE	Avec salle de bain si ce n'est pas trop *cher*. Combien est-ce pour la nuit ?
L'EMPLOYÉ	325 francs.
M. DELPORTE	Le petit déjeuner est-il *compris* ?
L'EMPLOYÉ	Oui, tout est compris.
M. DELPORTE	*Dans ce cas-là*, c'est d'accord.

expensive

included

in that case

Préparation

A. Questionnaire. The **Chambre de Commerce** of Lyon is preparing a questionnaire to give to people who stay in their city. Convert the **est-ce que** questions in the rough draft of their questionnaire to questions with inversion.

Written preparation may be helpful in these exercises.

Modèle Est-ce que c'est la première fois que vous venez à Lyon ?
Est-ce la première fois que vous venez à Lyon ?

1. Combien de temps est-ce que vous êtes restés à Lyon ?
2. Quel jour est-ce que vous êtes arrivés ?
3. Dans quel hôtel est-ce que vous êtes restés ?
4. Comment est-ce que vous avez trouvé l'hôtel ?
5. Dans quels restaurants est-ce que vous avez mangé ?
6. Comment est-ce que vous avez trouvé les repas ?
7. Est-ce que vous avez visité le vieux Lyon ?
8. Est-ce que vous avez envie de revenir à Lyon ?

B. À l'agence de voyage. Like increasing numbers of French people, Monsieur Barennes is making plans to go to a warmer climate for a winter vacation. Using the travel agent's answers as a guide, give the questions Monsieur Barennes asked about Guadeloupe.

Modèle   Oui, il y a de très bons hôtels.
             Y a-t-il de bons hôtels ?

1. Il fait très chaud là-bas en hiver.
2. Non, il ne pleut presque jamais.
3. Oui, les hôtels sont assez chers en cette saison.
4. Oui, il y a de très bons restaurants.
5. Il y a deux Clubs Med à la Guadeloupe.
6. Le voyage en avion coûte environ quatre mille francs.
7. Un séjour de quinze jours va coûter environ 10.500 francs.
8. Les plages sont sensationelles.

C. Projet de séjour en France. Suzanne is planning to study at Aix-en-Provence for a year and has prepared a list of specific questions to include in a letter to the **Syndicat d'Initiative**. Use the suggestions given to prepare her questions.

Modèle   si la ville est agréable → **La ville est-elle agréable ?**

1. si c'est une grande ville
2. s'il y a un aéroport
3. s'il y a une piscine
4. quel temps il fait en hiver
5. quand les cours pour étrangers commencent
6. où il y a des résidences universitaires
7. si les chambres et les appartements en ville sont chers
8. quels monuments il y a à visiter

Have students note that most French towns have a *Syndicat d'Initiative*, which provides information about hotels, restaurants, and town attractions to tourists. Have students think of other questions that Suzanne might ask in this situation.

Communication et vie pratique

A. Au Syndicat d'Initiative. Imagine that you have just arrived in Nice on the Côte d'Azur and are at the tourist bureau. What kinds of questions would you ask about Nice (e.g., weather, hotels, tourist attractions, cultural events, university) ?

Exemple   Y a-t-il un bon hôtel près d'ici ?

Written preparation may be helpful.

B. Interview. Choose a topic and then prepare a series of questions to ask another student. Ask the student your questions and then he or she will ask you questions on the same or another topic. Possible topics : **la vie universitaire ; la télévision ; le climat ; la nourriture et les repas.**

Exemple   — **Quels légumes préfères-tu ?**
             — **Moi, je préfère les haricots verts. Et toi, que préfères-tu ?**

Give students time to prepare the questions related to the chosen topic.

If appropriate for your class, introduce a complication to the role-playing situation (e.g., there are no more rooms in the hotel).

C'est votre tour. Imaginez que vous voyagez avec deux amis. Vous venez d'arriver à Marseilles et vous cherchez une chambre pour la nuit. Vous entrez dans l'Hôtel de la Gare et vous parlez avec l'employé(e) joué(e) par un(e) autre étudiant(e). Utilisez la **Mise en situation** comme guide et imaginez la conversation.

❧ Talking about changes in location, state, health, etc. Les verbes conjugués avec *être*

Présentation

Certain verbs like **aller** and **rester** are conjugated with **être** in the **passé composé**. These verbs can be categorized in the following way :

A. Verbs indicating a change of state :

naître (*to be born*)	Elle **est née** le 12 octobre.
mourir (*to die*)	Ils **sont morts** dans un accident.
tomber malade (*to become ill*)	Elle **est tombée** malade.
devenir (*to become*)	Elle **est devenue** célèbre.
	Qu'est-ce qu'elles **sont devenues** ?
arriver (*to happen*)	Qu'est-ce qui **est arrivé** ?

B. Verbs indicating actions related to location (coming, going, remaining, leaving, etc.) :

entrer	Elle **est entrée** seule dans la salle.
aller / venir	Je **suis allée** chez vous mais vous n'**êtes** jamais **venu** chez moi.
partir / arriver / rester / revenir / sortir	Ils **sont partis** le 15 août et ils **sont arrivés** le 16. Ils **sont restés** deux semaines sur la Côte et ils **sont revenus** le 1er septembre. Le 2 septembre ils ne **sont** pas **sortis** de la maison.
monter / descendre	Une personne **est montée** dans l'autobus ; deux autres **sont descendues**.
aller / retourner	Susan **est allée** en France cette année. Elle espère **retourner** en France l'an prochain.
rentrer	Nous **sommes rentrés** à l'hôtel à minuit.
passer	Nous **sommes passés** devant l'Opéra.

Have students note that *revenir* means *to come back to one's starting point* ; *retourner* means *to go back again*.

Substitution : (1) Nous sommes rentrés à midi. (*tu / elle / les autres / vous / je*) (2) En quel mois est-ce que ta sœur est née ? (*vous / tu / ta mère / Monique / Paul*) (3) Elle est tombée malade. (*nous / tu / son père / je / Anne / les enfants*) (4) Elles ne sont pas encore parties. (*ses cousins / je / vous / Serge / tu / nous*) Transformation : Je viens à huit heures. Je suis venue à huit heures. (1) Nous retournons en Europe. (2) Il part à six heures. (3) Est-ce que vous entrez ? (4) Pourquoi est-ce qu'elle ne vient pas ? (5) À quelle heure arrivent-elles ? (6) Elle sort de la maison. (7) Je descends de l'autobus. (8) Tu montes dans ta chambre.

Note that the past participles of verbs conjugated with **être** agree in number and gender with their subjects. Note also these past participles :

naître	né
mourir	mort
descendre	descendu

Mise en situation

Chaque année un grand nombre de Français — et d'*étrangers* — vont sur la Côte (la Côte d'Azur) pour *profiter du* soleil et de *la mer*. Cette année Monsieur et Madame Richard, des Bruxellois, ont décidé de passer leurs vacances à Antibes. Mais leur *séjour* n'a pas été très agréable.

UNE AMIE	Vous n'êtes pas descendus sur la Côte cette année?
MME RICHARD	Si, mais nous ne sommes pas restés longtemps.
L'AMIE	Quand êtes-vous partis?
MME RICHARD	Samedi dernier.
L'AMIE	Et vous êtes déjà rentrés? Qu'est-ce qui est arrivé?
MME RICHARD	Nous avons eu *toutes sortes* d'*ennuis*. Nous sommes passés par les Alpes et la voiture *est tombée en panne*. Nous sommes arrivés à 3 heures du matin!
L'AMIE	Il a fait beau pendant votre séjour?
MME RICHARD	Non, le jour après notre *arrivée* le temps est devenu mauvais. Alors, nous sommes revenus à Bruxelles.

foreigners

enjoy, take advantage of / sea

stay

Remind students that *la Côte d'Azur* is one of the most popular vacation spots for the French and is, therefore, extremely crowded during vacation periods.

all kinds / troubles, difficulties / broke down

arrival

Préparation

A. Il y a des gens qui travaillent... The driver of a sightseeing bus in Monaco is reporting what happened earlier today. Using the cues provided, tell what he says.

Modèle   je / arriver à l'hôtel à midi → **Je suis arrivé à l'hôtel à midi.**

1. les touristes / sortir de l'hôtel
2. ils / monter dans le bus
3. nous / partir à midi et quart
4. nous / passer devant le casino
5. nous / arriver au Palais à deux heures
6. les touristes / descendre de l'autobus
7. ils / entrer dans le Palais
8. je / revenir à la gare
9. je / rester là pendant deux heures
10. je / retourner chercher les touristes
11. nous / rentrer à l'hôtel
12. je / rentrer chez moi vers huit heures

Form complete sentences and read as listening comprehension practice. Point out that Monaco is an independent principality on the Mediterranean in the southeast of France. It is ½ square mile in area and has a population of around 29,000.

B. Et d'autres qui voyagent. Jean-Luc and his brother Alain took a trip to Canada last summer. Using the cues provided, create sentences describing their trip. Be sure to use the correct auxiliary verb (**avoir** or **être**) in each sentence.

Repeat with *ils* (e.g., *Ils sont partis de Paris le premier août*, etc.).

Modèles   partir de Paris le 1ᵉʳ août
          Nous sommes partis de Paris le 1ᵉʳ août.
    ou: quitter Paris le 1ᵉʳ août
          Nous avons quitté Paris le 1ᵉʳ août.

1. aller à l'aéroport d'Orly
2. arriver à Montréal à midi
3. déjeuner à l'aéroport
4. aller à l'hôtel
5. monter dans notre chambre
6. téléphoner à des amis canadiens
7. sortir pour visiter la ville
8. entrer dans un café
9. rencontrer d'autres Français
10. boire une bière ensemble
11. rentrer à l'hôtel

Communication et vie pratique

A. Expériences communes. Interview other students in your class in order to find one or several students who have done the following things. Then report your findings to the rest of the class.

Ask as questions or adapt as directed dialogue.

Trouvez un ou plusieurs étudiants…

1. qui sont sortis tous les soirs cette semaine
2. qui sont nés le même jour
3. qui ne sont jamais montés dans un avion
4. qui sont arrivés à l'université à sept heures et demie ce matin
5. qui sont venus en classe tous les jours la semaine dernière
6. qui sont rentrés à la maison à deux heures du matin
7. qui sont allés dans un pays étranger
8. qui sont déjà allés au Maroc, en Algérie ou en Tunisie

B. Votre emploi du temps. Using verbs you know, describe what you did yesterday or on a day when you were particularly busy.

Encourage students to use time expressions they know in preparing their description (e.g., *ensuite, après cela, quelques minutes plus tard*).

Exemple   **Je suis sorti(e) de chez moi à sept heures et quart.**
          J'ai rencontré quelques amis dans la rue et nous sommes allés prendre un café ensemble.

C. **Une vie.** Tell about the life of a real or imaginary person (e.g., ancestor, an early pioneer, a famous person). Use the suggestions below to tell about this person's life.

où et quand il ou elle est né(e)
en quelle année il ou elle a quitté son pays
quand il ou elle est venu(e) aux États-Unis
combien de temps il ou elle est resté(e) dans différentes villes ou régions
s'il (si elle) est retourné(e) dans son pays d'origine
où il ou elle a rencontré son mari (sa femme)
s'il (si elle) a eu des enfants
ce que ses enfants sont devenus
quand il ou elle est mort(e)

C'est votre tour. Tell about a trip you have taken recently ; include information about where you went, with whom, what you did, where you stayed, what the weather was like, the problems you had, etc.

Option : Have students role-play a situation describing a spring break trip to Florida where everything went wrong.

Intégration et perspectives

Adieu la pluie, bonjour le soleil

Mme Magnien vient de *recevoir* une lettre de son *neveu* Daniel qui fait son service militaire à la Réunion, un des départements français *d'outre-mer* situé dans l'océan Indien.

Saint-Pierre, le 25 avril

Chère tante,

Ça fait deux mois que je suis à la Réunion où je fais mon service militaire dans la coopération. Je suis arrivé dans cette magnifique *île* le 23 janvier, au milieu de « notre » hiver. Mais quel contraste ! *Adieu* la pluie, la neige et le froid. Bonjour le soleil, la végétation tropicale, le surfing !

Eh oui, je suis devenu un passionné de ce sport ! Les *vagues* sont si *hautes* et si régulières que c'est un paradis pour les surfistes. *Par contre*, les belles plages de *sable* blanc sont rares car la côte est très *découpée* et très *sauvage. En fait*, l'île est très montagneuse. C'est une succession de canyons, de *coteaux couverts* de plantations de vanille, et de forêts. Il y a *même* plusieurs volcans qui sont encore en activité.

Je profite de mon temps libre pour visiter l'île (qui est très petite en comparaison avec la France). En voiture, il est possible de *faire le tour de* l'île en trois heures. Mais, en réalité, le *paysage* est si beau et si varié qu'on a envie de *s'arrêter* partout. J'ai déjà pris des *centaines* de photos.

The new words in this text are not glossed. You are asked instead to try to guess the meaning of these words from their context. Be sure to read not only what precedes the new word but also what follows it. Word families can also be helpful (e.g., *chanter — chanteur, chanteuse, chanson*). If you are really unsure of the meaning of a word, look it up in the chapter vocabulary list.

Réunion

Des copains de Lyon sont venus passer huit jours ici. Pendant leur séjour, nous avons fait l'ascension d'un des volcans. Nous sommes partis à pied et nous avons marché et campé dans la nature pendant trois jours. Quel *souvenir* merveilleux!

Mon travail est assez agréable. Je suis *conseiller* technique dans une coopérative agricole. Je suis *vite* devenu ami avec les autres employés et les gens ici sont très *accueillants*. Je suis sûr que mes deux années à la Réunion vont passer très vite.

Je viens de recevoir une lettre de mes parents. Ils ont l'intention de venir ici l'an prochain. Quelle surprise ça va être pour *eux* qui n'ont jamais quitté la France!...

Je pense souvent à *toi* et j'*espère* que tu es en bonne santé.

Grosses bises,
Daniel

Point out that other French-speaking countries in the Indian Ocean with official or unofficial ties with France are *l'île Maurice* (east of Madagascar), *les Seychelles* (a group of islands northeast of Madagascar) and *Madagascar*, the fourth largest island in the world.

Compréhension. Les commentaires suivants ont été attribués à Daniel. À votre avis, est-ce qu'ils sont plausibles ou non? Basez-vous sur le contenu de sa lettre pour décider. (*The following statements have been attributed to Daniel. In your opinion, are they statements that he could have made or not? Base your decisions on the contents of the letter.*)

1. « Je suis ravi de mon séjour à la Réunion. »
2. « Je passe mes week-ends et mon temps libre à regarder la télé. »
3. « Le paysage ici est très monotone et très ennuyeux. »
4. « Les habitants de la Réunion sont froids et distants. »
5. « Mes parents n'ont jamais eu l'occasion de voyager à l'étranger. »
6. « J'ai encore vingt-deux mois à passer ici. »
7. « Je voudrais bien visiter l'île mais c'est impossible parce que ça prend trop longtemps. »
8. « Mes copains ont beaucoup aimé leur visite ici. »
9. « Je suis assez content de mon travail. »
10. « Je n'ai pas encore eu l'occasion de rencontrer des gens du pays. »

Notes culturelles: *La France métropolitaine et les départements d'outre-mer*

La France est divisée en 96 départements, *c'est-à-dire* en 96 unités administratives. Ces départements sont aussi groupés en régions économiques. *En plus des* départements de la France métropolitaine, la République française *comprend* cinq départements d'outre-mer (les DOM) : (1) la Guadeloupe et la Martinique qui sont toutes deux situées dans les Caraïbes ; (2) la Guyane française en Amérique du Sud ; (3) la Réunion située dans l'océan Indien ; (4) Saint-Pierre-et-Miquelon, deux îles situés dans l'Atlantique près de *Terre-Neuve.*

La République française comprend aussi quatre territoires d'outremer (les TOM) qui ont un *statut* plus indépendant. Les plus importants de ces territoires sont la Polynésie française et la Nouvelle-Calédonie.

La France *garde* avec ses *anciennes* colonies, avec le *Tiers Monde* et avec ses départements et territoires d'outre-mer, des relations amicales. En plus de l'aide financière accordée à ces pays, il y a 17.000 coopérants français qui travaillent dans ces pays : 13.000 *enseignants* et 4.000 techniciens. *Ainsi,* un certain nombre de jeunes Français choisissent de faire leur service national dans la coopération à la place du service militaire qui dure 12 mois. Le service national est obligatoire mais les étudiants peuvent obtenir un *sursis.*

Locate countries on the world map located in the *Chapitre préliminaire.*

that is to say

In addition to
includes

Newfoundland

status

keeps / former / Third World

teachers
thus

deferment

Martinique

St-Pierre-et-Miquelon

Communication et vie pratique

A. Souvenirs de voyage. Imagine that you were one of Daniel's friends who visited him in **la Réunion**. Using Daniel's letter as a guide, tell about your trip. Include information such as the following.

date d'arrivée	moyens de transports utilisés
sites visités	moments passés avec Daniel
activités	et ses amis de la Réunion
réactions	date du départ

B. Quel temps fait-il ? Prepare a description of the weather in your area in different seasons, including the types of weather that characterize each season and typical seasonal activities.

C. Il faut attirer les visiteurs. Imagine that you are a travel agent. Some French-speaking people want to visit your country. Try to persuade them to come to the area where your college or university is located.

Have students prepare in French a travel brochure about their town or area.

D. Questionnaire. Prepare a questionnaire to be given to French-speaking tourists on their arrival in your area. Find out the length of their visit, the accommodations they would like, the activities they prefer, the types of visits they like, etc. Use inversion in formulating your questions (**combien de temps allez-vous rester ?**). Then have another student play the role of a French-speaking tourist and fill out the form. Based on his / her responses, role-play a conversation in which you plan a week's activities for this person.

● *Prononciation et orthographe*

A. Vowels can be distinguished from one another not only by the shape of the lips (spread vs. rounded) or by the position of the tongue (front vs. back), but also by the degree of opening of the mouth. For example, the vowels **e**, **eu**, and **o** each have two pronunciations that differ only by the degree of opening of the mouth. First, note that the written forms may not even differ. Then note that, in general, closed vowels tend to occur in syllables ending in a vowel sound, whereas open vowels are found in syllables ending in a consonant sound.

Study the examples below and repeat the following pairs of words.

	Closed vowels	Open vowels
e	/e/ les	/ɛ/ l'air
eu	/ø/ deux	/œ/ heure
o	/o/ nos	/ɔ/ note

/e/ vs. /ɛ/	/ø/ vs. /œ/	/o/ vs. /ɔ/
thé / tête	peu / peur	vos / votre
ses / cette	jeu / jeune	sot / sotte
premier / première	ceux / seul	beau / bord

B. Practice repeating words containing the sound /e/, and notice the different spellings associated with this sound.

été	mes	aimer	boulanger
clé	chez	écoutez	épicier
idée	et	préférer	pâtissier

C. Practice repeating words containing the sound /ɛ/ and notice the different spellings associated with this sound.

mère	faire	être	modeste
infirmière	chaîne	tête	vert
terre	chaise	bête	cet / cette
mer	j'aime	vous êtes	quel / quelle
cher / chère	maire	avec	vers

D. Practice repeating words and phrases containing both the sound /e/ and the sound /ɛ/. Note the role of the contrast of the /e/ and /ɛ/ in distinguishing the masculine versus the feminine form of some nouns and adjectives.

/e/	/ɛ/	/ɛ/	/e/
premier	première	cet	été
boulanger	boulangère	cette	clé
épicier	épicière	quel	thé
	célèbre	quelle	idée
	sévère		fermer
	je préfère		chercher

• *Vocabulaire*

Noms

le temps et la météo (voir p. 182)

d'autres noms

- °   l'**adulte** (m, f)
-     l'**arrivée** (f) *arrival*
-     le **cas** *case*
-     la **centaine** *about a hundred*
- °   le **centre**
-     le **conseiller** *advisor*
- °   le **contraste**
-     la **côte** *coast*
-     le **coteau (-x)** *small hill*
- °   le **danger**
- °   le **degré**
- °   le **département**
- °   l'**employé(e)** (m, f)
-     l'**ennui** (m) *trouble, difficulty*

l'**est** (m) *east*
l'**été** (m) *summer*
l'**étranger** (m), l'**étrangère** (f)
    foreigner
les **félicitations** (f) *congratulations*
le **fleuve** *river*
l'**hiver** (m) *winter*
l'**île** (f) *island*
la **mer** *sea*
le **Midi** *South of France*
la **nature** *nature, outdoors*
la **neige** *snow*
le **neveu** *nephew*
le **nord** *north*
les **nouvelles** (f) *news*
le **nuage** *cloud*
la **nuit** *night*
l'**ouest** (m) *west*

° la **pause**
le **paysage**   *countryside*
° la **personne**
la **pluie**   *rain*
° le **problème**
° le **reste**
la **route**   *road*
le **sable**   *sand*
le **séjour**   *stay*
la **soirée**   *evening*
la **sorte**   *sort, type*
le **souvenir**   *memory*
° la **surprise**
la **vague**   *wave*
le **verglas**   *ice*

Verbes

expressions avec avoir (voir pp. 183–184)

arriver   *to happen*
comprendre   *to include*
° **continuer**
° **décider**
descendre   *to go down*
devenir   *to become*
échanger   *to exchange*
espérer   *to hope*
monter   *to go up, to climb*
mourir   *to die*
naître   *to be born*
profiter   *to profit, to take advantage*
recevoir   *to receive*
rencontrer   *to meet*
retourner   *to return, to go back again*
revenir   *to come back, to return*
s'arrêter   *to stop*
sortir   *to go out*
venir   *to come*
venir de...   *to have just . . .*

Adjectifs

accueillant(e)   *friendly, hospitable*
cher, chère   *dear, expensive*

compris(e)   *included*
couvert(e)   *cloudy, covered*
découpé(e)   *indented, irregular*
faible   *weak, light*
fatigant(e)   *tiring*
frais, fraîche   *cool*
froid(e)   *cold*
haut(e)   *high*
° **magnifique**
mauvais(e)   *bad*
merveilleux,
   merveilleuse   *marvelous*
° **militaire**
modéré(e)   *moderate*
° **régulier, régulière**
sauvage   *wild*
sec, sèche   *dry*
situé(e)   *situated, located*
technique   *technical*

Adverbes

bientôt   *soon*
dehors   *outside*
longtemps   *a long time*
même   *even*
vite   *quickly*

Divers

adieu   *good-bye*
d'outre-mer   *overseas*
en comparaison   *in comparison*
en fait   *in fact*
être en train de   *to be in the process of*
eux   *them*
grosses bises   *much love*
par contre   *on the other hand*
que   *what*
soit... soit   *either . . . or*
toi   *you*
tomber en panne   *to break down*

CHAPITRE NEUF

9

CHAPITRE NEUF

Communication objectives

Talking about career choices

1. Talking about what we want to do, can do, and have to do
2. Referring to something or someone already mentioned
3. Referring to someone already mentioned
4. Talking about what it is necessary to do or better to do

Structures

Les mots et la vie : Professions et métiers

Le verbes **vouloir**, **pouvoir** et **devoir**

Les pronoms compléments d'objet direct : **le**, **la**, **les**

Les pronoms compléments d'objet direct : **me**, **te**, **nous**, **vous**

Le subjonctif avec **il faut que...** et **il vaut mieux que...**

Choix et décisions

Mise en scène

Qu'est-ce que vous faites dans la vie?

Une *société* de sondages d'opinion a organisé une *enquête* pour savoir si les Français sont satisfaits de leur travail et pour faire un *classement* des « *métiers* » heureux ». Des enquêteurs parlent avec des gens de différentes professions.

company / survey
ranking
occupations

Monsieur Panneau, *plombier* à Lyon :

plumber

L'ENQUÊTRICE	Quel est votre métier, monsieur?
M. PANNEAU	Je suis plombier.
L'ENQUÊTRICE	Vous êtes content de votre métier?
M. PANNEAU	Oui, j'aime ce que je fais et je *gagne* bien ma *vie*. Je suis mon *propre* patron. J'aime ça.
L'ENQUÊTRICE	Vous travaillez beaucoup?
M. PANNEAU	Oui, il faut être *là* à toutes les heures du jour et de la nuit. Mais j'ai de la chance, le chômage est le dernier de mes *soucis*!

earn / living
own

there

worries, cares

Madame Aubourg, médecin à Strasbourg :

L'ENQUÊTEUR	Vous aimez votre travail?
MME AUBOURG	Oui, c'est un travail passionnant. Il faut faire de longues études pour être médecin, mais ça *en vaut la peine*.

is worth the trouble

Have students scan the descriptions of Monsieur Panneau and Madame Aubourg and give one reason why each is happy with his or her present job.

205

L'ENQUÊTEUR	Qu'est-ce qui compte le plus pour vous?	
MME AUBOURG	Le contact humain, le sentiment d'aider les autres.	
L'ENQUÊTEUR	Quels sont les inconvénients de votre métier?	
MME AUBOURG	Les longues heures de travail. Souvent je travaille dix et	

MME AUBOURG Les longues heures de travail. Souvent je travaille dix et même douze heures par jour et quand je suis *de garde*, c'est **on call** vingt-quatre heures sur vingt-quatre. Ça ne laisse pas beaucoup de temps pour la famille et les *loisirs*. **leisure activities, recreation**

Compréhension. Répondez aux questions suivantes selon les renseignements donnés dans le texte.

1. Quel est le métier de Monsieur Panneau?
2. Est-il satisfait de son travail? Pourquoi?
3. Est-ce qu'il travaille beaucoup? Quel est le principal inconvénient de son métier?
4. Pourquoi pense-t-il qu'il a de la chance?
5. Et Madame Aubourg, qu'est-ce qu'elle fait dans la vie?
6. Pourquoi aime-t-elle son travail?
7. Quels sont les inconvénients de son métier?

Have students write short paragraphs describing Monsieur Panneau and Madame Aubourg.

Notes culturelles: *Choix d'un métier*

« Pour vous, qu'est-ce qui compte le plus dans le choix d'un métier? » C'est la question qu'on a posée aux jeunes Français au cours d'un récent sondage. Voici leurs réponses. Notez les différences d'opinion entre les filles et les garçons.

	Garçons	Filles	
Salaire	71,7%	57,7%	
Temps *consacré* à la famille	56,3	65,6	**devoted**
Stabilité d'emploi	56,0	56,8	
Contacts humains	24,7	40,9	
Activités de loisir	28,9	26,7	
Avantages sociaux	26,9	16,2	**benefits**
Intérêt des *tâches*	17,2	22,6	**tasks, duties**
Possibilité de promotion	10,3	4,8	
Prestige social	1,8	1,6	

En général, pour les filles, la considération la plus importante est le temps libre pour la famille. Cette différence reflète le double rôle que les femmes jouent dans la société moderne. Elles travaillent et elles désirent avoir une carrière intéressante mais elles *savent* que, *malgré* les énormes **know / despite** progrès accomplis, les responsabilités familiales *reposent* surtout sur les **rest** femmes. Le sondage révèle aussi que les filles acceptent plus *volontiers* **willingly** les responsabilités dans leur travail *aussi bien que* dans la famille. Les **as well as** contacts humains sont aussi *plus* importants pour les filles *que* pour les **more / than** garçons. La majorité des femmes continuent à travailler dans des domaines *tels que l'enseignement*, les professions para-médicales, les services sociaux et les services publics. Il faut mentionner *cependant* que toutes les professions sont ouvertes aux femmes et qu'un nombre de plus en plus grand de femmes choisissent des professions non traditionnelles. Les garçons, par contre, ont tendance à préférer les carrières dans l'industrie, la technologie, les sciences et le commerce.

such as / teaching
however

Les mots et la vie : *Professions et métiers*

Choix et décisions. Answer the questions about careers, choices, and working conditions. Pay special attention to the new vocabulary.

A. Avez-vous l'intention de travailler dans… ?

— l'industrie
— le commerce
— l'agriculture
— l'administration et les services publics

B. Préférez-vous… ?

— faire un métier manuel (comme plombier ou mécanicien) ou exercer une profession libérale (comme médecin ou avocat)
— être fonctionnaire (*civil servant*) ou être employé(e) dans une entreprise privée
— être votre propre patron

Artisane

Futurs ingénieurs

Professeur d'université

The first eleven items on this list were given as important job characteristics by 2,500 French people surveyed. The items are given in the order of their importance and the percentages accorded to each are indicated. Students might want to compare their own (or their class) rankings with those given in the survey. They could also make up a comparative ranking for Americans.

C. Qu'est-ce qui compte le plus pour vous dans le choix d'une profession ou d'un emploi ? Examinez les avantages suivants et dans chaque cas, indiquez si…

1 = c'est très important
2 = c'est assez important
3 = ce n'est pas très important
4 = c'est sans importance

Exemple   La sécurité de l'emploi… ?
   Oui, c'est assez important pour moi.

1. _34%_ la sécurité de l'emploi (*job*)
2. _29%_ un salaire (*salary*) assez élevé (*high*)
3. _24%_ de bonnes conditions de travail
4. _24%_ des horaires (*schedules*) souples (*flexible*)
5. _24%_ la liberté et la place à (*room for*) l'initiative personnelle
6. _24%_ un travail intéressant
7. _20%_ le prestige social
8. _10%_ le contact humain
9. _8%_ la possibilité de participer aux décisions
10. _6%_ un emploi facile
11. _5%_ la possibilité de promotion
12. ___ un travail qui laisse du temps libre (*free*) pour la famille et les loisirs
13. ___ la possibilité de voyager

D. Au cours d'un sondage, on a demandé aux Français de choisir les professions qui, à leur avis, apportent le plus de satisfaction aux personnes qui exercent ces professions. La liste suivante représente leurs choix. Examinez cette liste et choisissez les métiers que vous trouvez intéressants et indiquez vos raisons. Indiquez aussi les métiers qui ne vous intéressent pas et expliquez pourquoi.

Although the fifty professions are not all listed, those included are given in the order of their importance.

Give brief descriptions of what one does in each of these professions and have students tell which job is being described or have them describe each profession.

Exemples   **Je voudrais être vétérinaire parce que j'aime les animaux.**
   ou: **Je ne voudrais pas être comptable parce que je trouve les maths difficiles.**
   ou: **Je voudrais bien être professeur mais je ne suis pas assez patient(e).**

Option : (1) Have students tell what profession they have chosen and why. Have them use the job characteristics given in C *(Qu'est-ce qui compte le plus... ?)* in their oral or written description. (2) Have students use the *Mise en scène* as a guide to create similar interviews with people in other professions.

chirurgien, chirurgienne (*surgeon*)
professeur d'université (m)
dentiste (m, f)
avocat(e)
médecin (m)
comptable (m, f) (*accountant*)
vétérinaire (m, f)
publicitaire (m, f) (*advertising agent*)
chercheur scientifique (m) (*scientific researcher*)

psychologue (m, f) (*psychologist*)
cadre commercial (m) (*business executive*)
ingénieur (m)
instituteur, institutrice (*elementary school teacher*)
commerçant(e)
mécanicien, mécanicienne
artisan(e)
chauffeur de taxi (m) (*taxi driver*)
secrétaire (m, f)

Have students categorize the professions given insofar as possible into the categories given in B : *un métier manuel ; une profession libérale ; un poste dans une entreprise privée ; un travail où on est son propre patron.* They can also be asked to use the items given in C *(Qu'est-ce qui compte le plus... ?)* to describe the professions given here. For example, *Un instituteur a la sécurité de l'emploi, mais il n'a pas un salaire très élevé, etc.*

Explorations
❧ Talking about what we want to do, can do, and have to do
Les verbes *vouloir*, *pouvoir* et *devoir*

Présentation

The verbs **pouvoir** (*to be able, can, may*) and **vouloir** (*to want, to wish*) have similar irregularities of form.

pouvoir		*vouloir*	
je **peux**	nous **pouvons**	je **veux**	nous **voulons**
tu **peux**	vous **pouvez**	tu **veux**	vous **voulez**
il / elle / on **peut**	ils / elles **peuvent**	il / elle / on **veut**	ils / elles **veulent**
passé composé : j'**ai pu**		passé composé : j'**ai voulu**	

Contrast /ø/ of *peux / veux* with the /œ/ of *peuvent / veulent*.

Est-ce que je **peux** sortir ?	*May I go out ?*
Ils **peuvent** faire ce qu'ils **veulent**.	*They can do what they want.*
Nous ne **voulons** pas rester ici.	*We don't want to stay here.*

Remind students that they already know *Qu'est-ce que ça veut dire ?*

A. Pouvoir and **vouloir** are often used to make requests. In the present tense, these requests are very direct, almost blunt :

Pouvez-vous… ?	*Can you . . . ?*
Voulez-vous… ?	*Do you want . . . ?*
Je veux…	*I want . . .*

Point out that in formal style, *puis-je* can replace *est-ce que je peux*.

To be less direct or more polite, the following forms are used :

Pourrais-tu… ? ⎫ Pourriez-vous… ? ⎭	*Could you . . . ?*
Voudrais-tu… ? ⎫ Voudriez-vous… ? ⎭	*Would you . . . ?*
Je voudrais…	*I would like . . .*
Je pourrais…	*I could . . .*

The phrases in the conditional are included to give students a more polite way of making requests ; they should be learned as vocabulary items at this point. If desired, you may want to point out that *pourrais*, etc. are in the conditional, which will be presented later.

*B. In the **passé composé, pouvoir** and **vouloir** have special meanings.

Elle n'**a** pas **voulu** obéir.	*She refused to obey.*
Ils n'**ont** pas **pu** venir.	*They were not able to come (though they tried).*
Elle **a pu** trouver un bon travail.	*She succeeded in finding a good job.*

---
*For recognition only

Cluny was the site of the Benedictine Abbey of Cluny, constructed in the 10th and 11th centuries and largely destroyed during the French Revolution. The church itself was the largest in the world at that time. Cluny was one of Europe's most important religious and cultural centers, and its monks were responsible for far-reaching reform movements during the Middle Ages. At its height, the Abbey was second only to the Papacy as the chief religious force in Europe, with nearly 1,000 houses located all over Europe.

C. Devoir (*to have to, must*) is also an irregular verb.

Devoir	
je **dois**	nous **devons**
tu **dois**	vous **devez**
il / elle / on **doit**	ils / elles **doivent**
passé composé : j'**ai dû**	

Nous **devons** gagner notre vie.	*We must earn our living.*
Tu **dois** rentrer maintenant.	*You have to go home now.*
J'**ai dû** parler au patron.	*I had to talk to the boss.*
Ils **ont dû** oublier.	*They must have forgotten.*

Point out that the present tense of *devoir* is similar to the English *to have to, must,* or *to be supposed to.* Have them note that *devoir* can also mean *to owe* (*je dois de l'argent à mon ami*). The *passé composé* is similar to *had to* or *must have.*

Mise en situation

Un petit service. Emmanuel et sa famille habitent à Macon, une petite ville de Bourgogne. Emmanuel voudrait emprunter la voiture de sa sœur Sylvie pour aller voir une amie qui habite à Cluny, une autre ville de la région.

EMMANUEL	Dis, Sylvie, est-ce que je pourrais *emprunter* ta voiture dimanche ?	borrow
SYLVIE	Et pourquoi veux-tu emprunter ma voiture ? Pour *impressionner* tes petits copains ?	to impress
EMMANUEL	Non, je voudrais *aller voir* une copine qui habite à Cluny.	to go and see
SYLVIE	Tu ne peux pas prendre *le car* comme tout le monde ?	bus (between cities)
EMMANUEL	Non, je ne peux pas, il y a une *grève* des transports publics.	strike
SYLVIE	Demande à papa et à maman...	
EMMANUEL	Ils ne peuvent pas. Ils doivent aller à Lyon. S'il te plaît, Sylvie...	
SYLVIE	Voyons ce que je peux faire... Le soir, je dois *aller chercher* des amis à la gare. Mais je n'ai pas besoin de ma voiture l'après-midi.	to go and pick up
EMMANUEL	Si tu veux, je peux *être de retour* avant cinq heures...	to be back
SYLVIE	Alors, *je veux bien.*	j'accepte

Point out that *l'autobus* is a bus used within a town ; *l'autocar* (*le car*) is for bus travel between cities.

Préparation

A. Possibilités. Marc and some friends are talking about possible part-time jobs. What do they say ?

Modèle   David / travailler dans une colonie de vacances
   David peut travailler dans une colonie de vacances.

1. je / travailler dans un bureau
2. nous / travailler dans un restaurant
3. tu / garder des enfants
4. mes frères / faire un travail manuel
5. Véronique / donner des leçons d'anglais
6. vous / faire le ménage chez les gens

Option : Redo, having students say that Marc and his friends want various part-time jobs : *David veut travailler dans une colonie de vacances.*

Repetition : (1) Est-ce que je peux sortir, est-ce que tu peux sortir, etc. (2) Je veux manger maintenant, tu veux manger maintenant, etc. *Substitution :* (1) Je ne peux pas sortir. (*Marc / nous / tu / mes amis / je / vous*) (2) Qu'est-ce qu'il veut faire ? (*tu / je / nous / vos parents / vous / Marianne*) (3) Elle n'a pas pu dormir. (*je / vous / mon frère / les enfants / tu / nous*)

B. Intentions. The following people are talking about what they want to do this weekend. What do they say?

Modèle   Laurent / aller au cinéma → **Laurent veut aller au cinéma.**

1. je / inviter des amis à dîner
2. tu / regarder la télévision
3. nous / aller voir des amis
4. vous / aller à la campagne
5. Virginie et Marc / faire du camping
6. Mireille / aller au théâtre

Option : Repeat in the negative (e.g., *Laurent ne veut pas aller au cinéma*).

C. Obligations. What do Pascale and her friends have to do this weekend?

Modèle   Pascale / ranger sa chambre
Pascale doit ranger sa chambre.

1. Marc / faire ses devoirs
2. nous / faire des courses
3. mes amis / aller au travail
4. tu / aller voir tes amis
5. je / faire la vaisselle
6. Véronique / préparer le dîner

Option : Repeat in the *passé composé* (e.g., *Pascale a dû ranger sa chambre*).

D. Un travail d'été. Richard is thinking about getting a summer job and is examining his wishes, possibilities, and obligations. Using **pouvoir, vouloir,** or **devoir,** tell what he says.

Modèle   (possibilité) faire un travail manuel
Je peux faire un travail manuel.

1. (désir) ne pas travailler dans un bureau
2. (possibilité) travailler dans l'usine de mon oncle
3. (possibilité) commencer vers la fin du mois de mai
4. (obligation) revenir à l'université au mois de septembre
5. (obligation) gagner de l'argent pour payer mes études
6. (obligation) travailler pendant tout l'été
7. (désir) ne pas passer tout mon temps à travailler
8. (désir) ne pas faire un travail trop difficile

Have students talk about their summer job plans, including information about their wishes, possibilities, and obligations.

Communication et vie pratique

A. Trouvez un(e) étudiant(e)... Ask questions to find out who in your class can, wants to, or has to do the following things.

Trouvez un(e) étudiant(e)...

1. qui veut aller dans un pays étranger
2. qui veut être journaliste
3. qui veut être riche et célèbre
4. qui peut raconter des histoires amusantes
5. qui peut persuader le prof de changer la date de l'examen
6. qui doit étudier pour un examen ce soir
7. qui doit travailler ce soir

Option : Use as questions or directed dialogue (e.g., *Demandez à Alice si elle veut aller dans un pays étranger*).

B. **Conflits.** Make a list of the things you (or people you know) have to do next week and then tell whether you want to or can do these things.

> **Exemples** **Je voudrais faire du ski, mais je ne peux pas. Je dois travailler.**
>
> *ou:* **Mon camarade de chambre doit étudier pour un examen de mathématiques, mais il n'a pas envie d'étudier.**

C. **Vouloir, c'est pouvoir.** Using the suggestions below or adding ideas of your own, create sentences that describe what you want to do now or later.

> **Exemple** **Je veux avoir une profession intéressante, mais je ne veux pas habiter dans une grande ville.**

Follow-up : Have students contrast their plans with those of other students.

avoir des enfants / être heureux (heureuse) / voyager dans des pays étrangers / faire le tour du monde / avoir une vie simple et tranquille / aider les autres / habiter à la campagne / avoir une belle maison / continuer mes études / avoir un travail intéressant / ?

C'est votre tour. Vous désirez emprunter la voiture de vos parents pour sortir avec des amis. Essayez de persuader vos parents. Ils ne sont pas faciles à persuader. Utilisez **la Mise en situation** comme modèle.

Preparation : Have the class come up with reasons why they would need the car and ways to persuade parents. Then have them find reasons why parents would not want to lend them the car.

✵Referring to something or someone already mentioned
Les pronoms compléments d'objet direct : *le*, *la*, *les*

Présentation

In French, third-person direct-object pronouns have the same forms as the definite article (**le** — *him, it* ; **la** — *her, it* ; and **les** — *them*). They agree in gender and number with the nouns they replace.

Elle fait **le ménage**.	Elle **le** fait. (*masculine singular*)
Elle fait **la vaisselle**.	Elle **la** fait. (*feminine singular*)
Elle fait **les courses**.	Elle **les** fait. (*masculine or feminine plural*)

A. Direct object pronouns are placed immediately before the verb not only in affirmative sentences (as shown above) but also in negative and interrogative sentences. When the verb begins with a vowel or vowel sound, however, **le** and **la** change to **l'**.

Est-ce qu'il aime **la géographie** ?	Est-ce qu'il **l'**aime ?
Il aime **le sport**.	Il **l'**aime.
Il n'aime pas **les sciences**.	Il ne **les** aime pas.

Note that direct object pronouns can also replace proper nouns or nouns introduced by possessive or demonstrative adjectives.

Nous trouvons **Alice** intéressante.	Nous **la** trouvons intéressante.
Mon frère ne comprend pas **sa femme**.	Il ne **la** comprend pas.
Elles font bien **leur travail**.	Elles **le** font bien.
Préférez-vous **cet appartement**?	**Le** préférez-vous?

B. With compound tenses such as the **passé composé**, direct object pronouns precede the auxiliary verb. Past participles agree in number and gender with a preceding direct object; thus, they always agree with direct object pronouns.

Est-ce qu'elle a fait **ses études** en France?	Est-ce qu'elle **les** a fait**es** en France?
Ils n'ont pas invité **leurs amis**?	Ils ne **les** ont pas invité**s**?
Avez-vous fini **vos devoirs**?	**Les** avez-vous fini**s**?

Point out the pronunciation of faites /fɛt/ .

C. When an infinitive has a direct object, the direct object pronoun immediately precedes the infinitive.

Je vais acheter **ce livre**.	Je vais **l'**acheter.
Il n'a pas envir de quitter **cette ville**.	Il n'a pas envie de **la** quitter.

D. Direct object pronouns can also be used with **voici** and **voilà**.

Voici **Paul**.	**Le** voici.
Voilà **la patronne**.	**La** voilà.
Voilà **vos amis**.	**Les** voilà.

Mise en situation

Travail et famille. En France, les femmes ont seize semaines de *congé de maternité* pour la naissance d'un bébé et leur emploi est assuré pendant un an. Madame Seguin, qui vient d'avoir son deuxième enfant, a décidé de reprendre son travail. Elle parle avec son mari.

maternity leave

Point out directeur *(masc.) and* directrice *(fem.).*

MME SEGUIN	J'ai parlé avec la directrice du *jardin d'enfants*. Je la trouve très bien... Elle a accepté de prendre Corinne.
M. SEGUIN	Ils peuvent la garder toute la journée?
MME SEGUIN	Oui, je peux la *déposer* le matin, et toi, tu peux aller la chercher le soir après ton travail.
M. SEGUIN	Et le bébé?
MME SEGUIN	Je pourrais le mettre dans une *crèche*, mais maman a accepté de le garder.
M. SEGUIN	Comment l'as-tu persuadée de faire ça?
MME SEGUIN	C'est elle qui l'a proposé.
M. SEGUIN	C'est vrai qu'elle aime les enfants...
MME SEGUIN	*Tu veux rire*... Elle ne les aime pas; elle les adore.

kindergarten

drop off

daycare center

Point out that more than 40% of the French work force is composed of women.

you're kidding, joking

Transformation I : (1) Je fais mon travail. → Je le fais. (1) Je fais mes études à Paris. (2) Il finit ses devoirs. (3) Nous regardons le match. (4) Tu achètes tes provisions. (5) Vous regardez ces photos. (6) Ils font la vaisselle. (7) Qui fait le ménage? (8) J'invite mes amis à dîner. *Transformation II :* Repeat the sentences in Transformation I in the negative *(Je ne fais pas mon travail. → Je ne le fais pas.)*. Repeat in the *passé composé* *(J'ai fait mon travail. → Je l'ai fait)* and in the negative *passé composé (Je n'ai pas fait mon travail. → Je ne l'ai pas fait)*. Then repeat in the near future *(Je vais faire mon travail. → Je vais le faire)*.

Préparation

A. **Compatibilité.** Anne-Marie is deciding whether or not she and Monique would get along as roommates. Give Monique's answers to her questions.

Modèle   Est-ce que tu aimes la musique classique ? (oui)
         Oui, je l'aime.

1. Est-ce que tu écoutes souvent la radio ? (oui)
2. Est-ce que tu regardes la télé tous les soirs ? (non)
3. Est-ce que tu achètes tes provisions au supermarché ? (non)
4. Est-ce que tu fais le ménage toutes les semaines ? (oui)
5. Est-ce que tu invites souvent tes amis ? (non)
6. Est-ce que tu trouves cet appartement agréable ? (oui)

B. **En classe d'anglais.** Georges has missed a week of his English class and is asking Monsieur Bacquet how to catch up on his work. Using the cues provided, tell what his teacher suggests.

Modèle   Il faut étudier les verbes ?
         Oui, vous devez les étudier.

1. Est-ce qu'il faut étudier cette leçon ?
2. Est-ce qu'il faut acheter ces livres ?
3. Est-ce qu'il faut étudier les verbes ?
4. Est-ce qu'il faut écouter les cassettes ?
5. Est-ce qu'il faut faire cet exercice ?
6. Est-ce qu'il faut finir cette leçon aujourd'hui ?

C. **Pense-bête.** Richard is checking off the various items on his reminder list (**pense-bête**). What does he say ?

Modèles   faire le ménage (oui) → **Je l'ai déjà fait.**
     ou: écouter les informations (non)
         Je ne les ai pas encore écoutées.

1. acheter les provisions (oui)
2. ranger ma chambre (oui)
3. fermer les fenêtres (oui)
4. faire la vaisselle (oui)
5. laver ma voiture (non)
6. faire mes devoirs (non)
7. préparer le dîner (non)
8. finir ce travail (non)

Communication et vie pratique

A. Conversations. Answer the following questions or use them to interview another student. Choose one or more of the following topics.

Options : (1) Use one or two sets of questions daily to spread practice across several days. (2) Assign different topics to different pairs of students. After asking each other the questions, students can be assigned (or can choose) another topic. (3) Put questions for each topic on separate interview cards and distribute to members of the class for paired conversation practice.

Nourriture et repas

1. Est-ce que tu aimes les fruits? Et les légumes?
2. Est-ce que tu aimes le poulet? Et le poisson?
3. Est-ce que tu aimes le fromage français? Et le pain français?
4. Est-ce que tu aimes le café? Et le thé? Et l'eau minérale?
5. ?

Activités de loisir

1. Est-ce que tu écoutes souvent la radio?
2. Est-ce que tu aimes regarder la télé?
3. Est-ce que tu aimes faire la cuisine?
4. Est-ce que tu invites souvent tes amis à dîner?
5. ?

Obligations

1. Est-ce que tu as appris tes leçons pour aujourd'hui?
2. Est-ce que tu as fait le ménage cette semaine?
3. Est-ce que tu as fait la vaisselle hier soir?
4. Est-ce que tu as fait ton lit ce matin?
5. ?

Vacances

1. Où est-ce que tu as passé tes vacances l'été dernier?
2. Où est-ce que tu vas passer tes vacances cette année?
3. Est-ce que tu as déjà visité le Canada? le Mexique? l'Europe?
4. Est-ce que tu as envie de visiter la France un jour?
5. ?

B. Il faut les aider! Some first-year students seem to be puzzled about various things. What advice would you give them?

Exemple   nos devoirs / les faire maintenant ou plus tard?
    Il faut les faire maintenant.

1. nos leçons / les étudier chaque jour ou le jour avant l'examen?
2. nos provisions / les acheter dans les petits magasins ou au super-marché?
3. le ménage / le faire chaque semaine ou seulement une fois par mois?
4. la vaisselle / la faire tous les jours ou seulement quand c'est néces-saire?
5. nos amis / les inviter tout le temps ou seulement pendant le week-end?
6. nos devoirs / les faire le matin ou le soir?

C'est votre tour. Vous avez décidé d'aller passer le week-end dans une autre ville. Vous avez un chien et un chat et vous avez besoin de quelqu'un pour les garder. Vous demandez aux autres étudiants de la classe s'ils peuvent le faire. Tout le monde a des excuses. Mais n'abandonnez pas avant d'avoir trouvé quelqu'un.

Preparation : Have students come up with reasons to convince someone to take care of the pets. Have them also find a variety of excuses for not wanting to take care of them.

🪶 Referring to someone already mentioned
Les pronoms compléments d'objet direct : *me*, *te*, *nous*, *vous*

Présentation

The first- and second-person direct object pronouns are used only to refer to people. The table below shows both subject and direct object pronouns.

Les pronoms compléments d'objet direct			
Singular		**Plural**	
Subject	Direct object	Subject	Direct object
(je)	**me (m')** Ils **me** cherchent.	(nous)	**nous** Ils **nous** cherchent.
(tu)	**te (t')** Ils **te** cherchent.	(vous)	**vous** Ils **vous** cherchent.
(il)	**le (l')** Ils **le** cherchent.	(ils)	**les** Ils **les** cherchent.
(elle)	**la (l')** Ils **la** cherchent.	(elles)	**les** Ils **les** cherchent.

A. Like **le**, **la**, and **les**, these pronouns are placed directly before the conjugated verb or the infinitive of which they are the object.

> Elle **te** cherche.
> Tu ne **nous** comprends pas.
> Elle va **les** emmener à la gare.

Point out that chercher and écouter take direct objects in French.

B. As you have already learned, the past participle of a verb in a compound tense agrees with a preceding direct object. Therefore, the past participle of a verb in the **passé composé** agrees with the direct object pronoun.

> Il ne **m'**a pas regard**é(e)**.
> Elle ne **nous** a pas aid**é(e)s**.

C. Some useful verbs that are often used with these direct object pronouns are :

accepter	embêter (*to annoy*)
admirer	insulter
apprécier	intéresser
critiquer	respecter

Mise en situation

Have students note that one can say aux États-Unis or aux USA.

Voyage d'affaires. Le patron de Michel Maréchal doit aller aux États-Unis en voyage d'affaires. Il invite Michel à l'accompagner.

LE PATRON	Maréchal, je pars aux États-Unis la semaine prochaine. Je vous invite à m'*accompagner*.
MICHEL	Moi ? Vous m'invitez à aller aux USA avec vous ?
LE PATRON	Oui, j'ai besoin de quelqu'un pour m'aider et vous parlez très bien anglais, n'est-ce pas ?
MICHEL	Vous me *flattez*, monsieur !
LE PATRON	Non, non, pas du tout. Je vous trouve dynamique et *débrouillard*. J'aime ça.
MICHEL	Je vous *remercie*.
LE PATRON	*Inutile de* me remercier. Maintenant, je vous quitte. Il y a un client qui veut me voir.

to accompany

flatter

resourceful

thank

no need to

Préparation

A. Est-ce que tu m'aimes ? Danielle's boyfriend is very insecure and needs a lot of reassurance. Give Danielle's answers to his questions.

> **Modèle** Est-ce que tu m'aimes ? → **Mais oui, je t'aime.**

Have students give negative answers : Est-ce que tu m'aimes ? Non, je ne t'aime pas.

1. Est-ce que tu m'aimes beaucoup ?
2. Est-ce que tu m'admires un peu ?
3. Est-ce que tu me comprends ?
4. Est-ce que tu me trouves amusant ?
5. Est-ce que tu vas m'inviter chez tes parents ce week-end ?
6. Est-ce que tu viens me chercher ce soir ?

Substitution : (1) On te demande au téléphone. *(vous / nous / le / les / me)* (2) Ils vous ont invité samedi. *(nous / te / me / les / le)* (3) Ne nous oubliez pas. *(me / les / la / nous)* (4) Ils ne nous ont pas écoutés. *(me / te / la / vous / les / le)* (5) Est-ce qu'ils vont nous quitter ? *(te / vous / me / le / les / la / nous)* (6) Aide-moi. *(nous / le / les / la)* (7) Ne m'embête pas. *(la / les / nous / le / me)*

B. Réciprocité. Violette is talking about what she and her friends do for each other. Complete her statements.

Modèle Je les écoute…
Je les écoute et ils m'écoutent.

1. Je les respecte…

2. Je les aide…

3. Je les aime bien…

4. Je les trouve intéressants…

5. Je les laisse tranquilles…

6. Je ne les oublie pas…

7. Je ne les critique pas…

8. Je ne les embête pas…

C. Ce n'est pas juste. Christophe and Michel are not happy with the way their friends are treating them. Complete their statements.

Modèle Nous les aimons bien…
Nous les aimons bien, mais ils ne nous aiment pas.

1. Nous les respectons…

2. Nous les comprenons…

3. Nous les écoutons…

4. Nous les aidons…

5. Nous les trouvons intéressants…

6. Nous les admirons…

D. L'amitié. Georges has made a list of what he expects from his friends. What would he say to them?

Modèles m'accepter comme je suis
Il faut m'accepter comme je suis.
ou: ne pas m'oublier → **Il ne faut pas m'oublier.**

1. me respecter

2. m'aider de temps en temps

3. m'accepter comme je suis

4. ne pas me critiquer tout le temps

5. ne pas m'embêter

6. ne pas m'insulter

Est-ce que tes amis t'aident… ?

A. For regular verbs it is formed by adding the endings shown below to a stem that is found by dropping the **-ent** from the **ils / elles** form of the present tense.

Regular subjunctive	
Il faut que je parl**e**	que nous parl**ions**
que tu parl**es**	que vous parl**iez**
qu'il / elle / on parl**e**	qu'ils / elles parl**ent**
Il faut que je finiss**e**	que nous finiss**ions**
que tu finiss**es**	que vous finiss**iez**
qu'il / elle / on finiss**e**	qu'ils / elles finiss**ent**
Il faut que je part**e**	que nous part**ions**
que tu part**es**	que vous part**iez**
qu'il / elle / on part**e**	qu'ils / elles part**ent**

Il vaut mieux que tu **partes** tout de suite.
Il vaut mieux qu'ils **finissent** ça maintenant.

B. Several frequently used verbs have irregular stems for the subjunctive. **Faire**, **aller**, and **être** are among these verbs.

Subjunctive of *faire, aller, être*	
Il faut que je **fasse**	que nous **fassions**
que tu **fasses**	que vous **fassiez**
qu'il / elle / on **fasse**	qu'ils / elles **fassent**
Il faut que j'**aille**	que nous **allions**
que tu **ailles**	que vous **alliez**
qu'il / elle / on **aille**	qu'ils / elles **aillent**
Il faut que je **sois**	que nous **soyons**
que tu **sois**	que vous **soyez**
qu'il / elle / on **soit**	qu'ils / elles **soient**

Il faut que j'**aille** au supermarché.
Il faut que nous **soyons** à la gare à une heure.

Note the difference between a general statement where **il faut** is followed by an infinitive and a statement referring to a specific person where **il faut que** is followed by a subjunctive verb clause.

Il faut parler français.
Il faut que vous parliez français.

Mise en situation

Une invitation. Madame Berger désire inviter les Guérin à déjeuner, mais ils sont très occupés en ce moment.

MME BERGER	Je voudrais vous inviter à déjeuner à la maison. Est-ce que vous êtes libres dimanche?
MME GUÉRIN	Non, dimanche, il faut que nous allions voir mes parents.
MME BERGER	Et samedi?
MME GUÉRIN	Samedi, il faut que je finisse un *rapport*.
MME BERGER	Alors, venez dîner un soir.
MME GUÉRIN	Voyons… Lundi, il faut que nous fassions notre *déclaration d'impôts*… Mardi soir, il faut que j'emmène les enfants à leur leçon de piano. Mercredi, André a un *rendez-vous d'affaires*. Jeudi, il faut que nous allions à une *réunion* de parents d'élèves.
MME BERGER	Vous êtes bien *occupés* en ce moment.
MME GUÉRIN	Oui, il vaut mieux que nous *repoussions* ça à la semaine prochaine.

Glosses (right margin):
- report
- income tax return
- business appointment
- meeting
- busy
- postpone

Préparation

A. Obligations. Annick has marked on her calendar the things she has to do next week. What does she say?

Modèle   laver mes vêtements → **Il faut que je lave mes vêtements.**

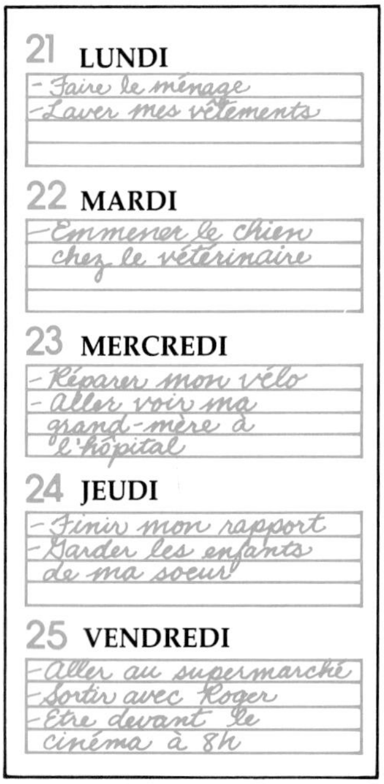

```
21 LUNDI
- Faire le ménage
- Laver mes vêtements

22 MARDI
- Emmener le chien
  chez le vétérinaire

23 MERCREDI
- Réparer mon vélo
- Aller voir ma
  grand-mère à
  l'hôpital

24 JEUDI
- Finir mon rapport
- Garder les enfants
  de ma sœur

25 VENDREDI
- Aller au supermarché
- Sortir avec Roger
- Être devant le
  cinéma à 8h
```

Substitutions : (1) Il faut que je travaille. *(vous / Gérard / les étudiants / Marie et Jeannette / tu / je)* (2) Il vaut mieux que tu finisses ce travail. *(je / vous / nous / les autres / ton amie)* (3) Il faut que nous partions ce matin. *(tu / vous / je / ses cousins / mon amie / nous)* (4) Il faut que j'aille à la bibliothèque. *(nous / tu / vous / le professeur / les étudiants / je)* (5) Il vaut mieux que tu sois ici avant 8 heures. *(je / Chantal / les autres / nous / tu / vous)* (6) Il faut que nous fassions la vaisselle. *(vous / je / ton frère / tes sœurs / nous / tu)*

Il faut que j'aille à la
Bibliothèque nationale.

B. **Ils ne sont pas libres.** Everyone is too busy to go out this weekend.
What do they have to do?

Modèle   Mireille / aller chez le dentiste.
   Il faut que Mireille aille chez le dentiste.

1. nous / faire le ménage
2. Gérard / aller à la bibliothèque
3. je / aller chez ma tante
4. vous / rester à la maison
5. tu / chercher du travail
6. Marcel et Robert / faire le marché

C. **Décisions.** Hélène and her friends are having a party. She is trying to
decide who is best suited for different tasks. What does Hélène say?

Modèle   Madeleine / aller à l'épicerie
   Il vaut mieux que Madeleine aille à l'épicerie.

1. je / faire le ménage
2. tu / aller à la boulangerie
3. Michel / apporter sa guitare
4. nous / faire les courses ensemble
5. Marc et Pascale / être ici à six heures
6. vous / préparer les hors-d'œuvre

Communication et vie pratique

A. Obligations. Make a list of the things you have to do this week.

Exemple   Il faut que je fasse des courses.

B. Questions. Ask another student whether she or he has to do certain things today.

Exemple   — Est-ce qu'il faut que tu ailles à la bibliothèque aujourd'hui ?
— Non, mais il faut que j'aille à la bibliothèque jeudi parce que j'ai un rapport à préparer.

C. Conseils. Some friends have asked you to give them advice about the following problems. What advice would you give them?

Have students come up with other similar problem situations.

Exemple   J'ai envie de quitter l'université.
Il vaut mieux que tu finisses tes études.
ou: **Mais non ! Il faut que tu restes ici.**

1. J'ai un examen la semaine prochaine, mais je n'ai pas envie d'étudier.
2. Mon ami Gérard veut être comptable, mais il n'est pas très fort en maths.
3. Je n'ai pas l'argent pour acheter mes livres pour le trimestre prochain.
4. Nous n'avons pas envie d'aller en classe aujourd'hui.
5. Mes amis m'ont invité(e) à sortir, mais j'ai du travail à faire en ce moment.
6. Je voudrais aller au cinéma, mais je suis très fatigué.

C'est votre tour. Vous êtes invité(e) à dîner. Mais vous ne pouvez pas — ou vous n'avez pas envie — d'accepter l'invitation. Expliquez que vous êtes très occupé(e) en ce moment et indiquez ce que vous devez faire.

Preparation : Have students come up with a variety of tasks and activities that would be appropriate in this situation (e.g., *Non, je regrette, mais il faut que je fasse le ménage. Mes parents viennent ce week-end.*)

Intégration et perspectives

Vive l'initiative personnelle

Si votre *formation* ne vous offre pas les *débouchés* que vous désirez ou si le travail que vous faites ne vous satisfait pas, la solution est peut-être d'inventer votre emploi comme l'ont fait ces jeunes Québécois.

training, education / jobs

CAROLINE DUBOST
Professeur d'histoire dans un CEGEP*, Caroline Dubost a des élèves qui ne sont pas très studieux. Elle est fatiguée d'*enseigner* à des jeunes qui n'ont

teaching

---

*Collège d'enseignement général et professionnel : une école intermédiaire entre l'école polyvalente et l'université.

Have students scan the reading to find out which of the people described (1) rents a boat and serves as a guide ; (2) has a real-estate agency ; (3) has a second-hand clothing store ; and (4) has a catering service.

pas vraiment envie d'apprendre. Elle choisit d'abandonner l'enseignement et de travailler dans une agence *immobilière*. Ça réussit. Les affaires marchent si bien qu'elle décide de créer sa propre agence. Elle a maintenant une douzaine d'employés qui travaillent pour elle. Elle peut organiser son temps comme elle veut et elle gagne quatre fois plus que dans l'enseignement.

real-estate

FRANÇOIS JOYET

François grandit dans un petit village sur la côte de Gaspésie. Il passe des journées entières sur l'eau avec son grand-père. Il est heureux. Mais il doit aussi gagner sa vie. Il quitte son village pour aller faire des études de mathématiques supérieures à l'université. Il entre dans la *marine* dans *l'espoir* de réaliser son rêve : passer sa vie sur un *bateau*. En réalité, il passe presque tout son temps dans un bureau et le travail qu'il fait l'embête. Il décide de quitter son poste et d'acheter un bateau. Pour gagner sa vie il *loue* son bateau et ses services aux visiteurs qui veulent explorer la côte ou faire des *mini-croisières*. Les *débuts* sont difficiles et ses revenus irréguliers mais maintenant il est son propre patron et il *mène* une vie qu'il aime.

navy
hope / boat

rents

mini-cruises / beginnings
leads

MARIE MAGNIEN

Marie Magnien est diplômée d'une grande école de cuisine. Elle travaille *d'abord* dans le restaurant d'un grand hôtel. Mais c'est un travail qu'elle partage avec une dizaine d'autres cuisiniers. Ce n'est pas ce qu'elle veut. Acheter son propre restaurant est un rêve qu'elle n'a pas les *moyens* de réaliser. Que faire ? Elle *finit par* avoir une idée. Beaucoup de gens *n'*ont pas toujours le temps *ni* le talent nécessaire pour préparer les plats qu'ils veulent servir** à leurs invités. Elle place une annonce dans le *journal*. Au début, les clients sont rares. Il faut du temps pour établir sa réputation. Mais maintenant ses affaires marchent si bien qu'elle a une longue *liste d'attente* et elle va *embaucher* plusieurs assistants.

at first

means
ends up by
neither . . . nor
newspaper

waiting list
to hire

ANTOINE CHARBONNEAU

Antoine Charbonneau a son doctorat en philosophie. Il est marié et il a trois enfants. Quand il finit ses études, il cherche un poste dans un collège de la région parce que sa femme ne veut pas abandonner l'entreprise qu'elle a créée. Sans succès. Tous les postes sont déjà occupés. Il passe beaucoup de temps à la maison avec les enfants. Il fait les courses. Il parle avec les autres « mères » de famille. Il *constate* que les enfants grandissent si vite que les vêtements achetés aujourd'hui sont trop petits six mois plus tard. Il a une idée ; créer un centre où les gens peuvent apporter les vêtements qu'ils ne *portent* plus et où d'autres personnes peuvent les acheter.

finds

wear

****Servir** is conjugated like **partir** and **sortir**.

A. Compréhension. Répondez aux questions suivantes selon les renseignements donnés dans le texte.

Option : Have students play the roles of those described in the reading. Other students will ask them questions about their former and present jobs.

1. En quoi consiste le premier travail de Caroline et pourquoi n'est-elle pas satisfaite de ce travail ?
2. Qu'est-ce qu'elle a décidé de faire ? Est-ce qu'elle est contente de son choix ? Pourquoi ou pourquoi pas ?
3. Quel est le rêve de François et comment a-t-il réalisé son rêve ?
4. Pourquoi Marie Magnien n'est-elle pas satisfaite de son premier travail ? Quelle solution finit-elle par trouver ?
5. François et Marie sont-ils contents des postes qu'ils ont créés ? Expliquez votre réponse.
6. Suggérez un nom pour la nouvelle entreprise de François et pour la nouvelle entreprise de Marie.
7. Expliquez pourquoi Antoine a créé sa nouvelle entreprise.

B. Inventez votre emploi ! Alone or with other students, create a job based on your individual or combined talents. Use the guidelines below to assess your possibilities.

Vos qualités	Vos aptitudes	Vos préférences	Solution
Nous sommes très indépendants, etc.	Nous pouvons parler français, etc.	Le prestige social ne compte pas beaucoup pour nous, etc.	Nous pouvons enseigner le français aux enfants le samedi matin.

« Ce travail semble intéressant... »

Notes culturelles: *Les qualités humaines recherchées par les entreprises*

« Quand vous embauchez des diplômés des universités ou des grandes écoles, quelles sont les qualités humaines que vous *recherchez* ? » Voici la question qu'on a posée à 1 500 entreprises françaises. *En plus* on leur a demandé d'indiquer les qualités qui vont devenir de plus en plus importantes à *l'avenir*. Notez qu'être capable de communiquer est la qualité la plus importante maintenant aussi bien que dans cinq ans. « La capacité de négotiation », qui est une forme de communication, va aussi jouer un rôle de plus en plus important.

seek

in addition

future

LE HIT-PARADE DES QUALITÉS

Maintenant	Dans cinq ans	
1er *Sens de la communication*	Sens de la communication 1er	ability to communicate
2e Organisation et méthode	Organisation et méthode 2^{e}	
3e *Implication* dans l'entreprise	Capacité de négociation 3^{e}	involvement
4e Esprit d'innovation	Implication dans l'entreprise 4^{e}	
5e Capacité de négociation	Esprit d'innovation 5^{e}	
6e Aptitude au *commandement*	Aptitude au commandement 6^{e}	leadership
7e Capacité à anticiper	Capacité à anticiper 7^{e}	
8e *Étendue* de la culture générale	Étendue de la culture générale 8^{e}	extent, range
9e Sens de la discipline	Sens de la discipline 9^{e}	

Communication et vie pratique

A. Offres d'emploi. Voici des offres d'emploi pour étudiants. Elles viennent d'un journal français. Remarquez qu'on utilise des abréviations dans ces annonces (e.g., pr. — pour ; ang. — anglais ; sér. — sérieux ; sem. — semaine). Étudiez d'abord ces annonces et ensuite choisissez l'emploi qui vous intéresse le plus. Il faut aussi expliquer votre choix (e.g., intérêts, qualifications, expérience).

Étudiant(e) pr. accomp. dame âgée aller retour Paris Orléans les me. et sa. chaq. sem. juill. et août. tél. 426 46 27 mat.

Étudiant(e) parlant espagnol pr aider mère fam. garder enfs à la campagne et bord de mer, juil., sept., tél. OPE 1973.

Étudiant(e) pour garder 3 enfants, pendt. qq mois, Côte d'Azur, Mme Junot, tél. PAS 22 41.

Étudiant(e) parlant ang. pr réception, hôtel, trav. de nuit. Hôtel Terminus, 42 Rue de Vaugirard, Paris, 15ᵉ.

Étud. aimant livres pr. passer été en famil. Bretagne, contacter Mme Carnot, 764 Rue des Martyrs, Paris, 18ᵉ.

Étudiant sér. énerg. sportif, travail de moniteur pr groupe garçons 12 ans, colonie de vacances Alpes, 3 sem. août. Contacter Directeur, Centre Bel Air, 12 Av. du Mont Blanc, Chamonix.

Ask students to give the gist of each ad : *On cherche un(e) étudiant(e) pour garder des enfants,* etc.

Exemple Je voudrais travailler comme moniteur (monitrice) dans une colonie de vacances parce que j'aime les enfants et je suis très sportif (sportive).

228

B. Interview. Vous avez un rendez-vous avec vos employeurs éventuels. D'autres étudiants vont jouer le rôle des employeurs. Voici quelques questions que vous pouvez utiliser.

Questions que l'employeur peut poser :

1. Quel âge avez-vous ?
2. Quelle est votre nationalité ?
3. Est-ce que vous avez de l'expérience ? Est-ce que vous avez déjà travaillé ?
4. Avez-vous des lettres de recommandation ?
5. Quel salaire espérez-vous gagner ?
6. Est-ce que vous avez des talents particuliers ?
7. Aimez-vous les enfants ? (les livres, les animaux, etc.)
8. ?

Suggestions pour le candidat :

1. Est-ce que je dois travailler tous les jours ?
2. Quelles sont mes heures de travail ?
3. Quel va être mon salaire ?
4. Est-ce que je peux faire des heures supplémentaires ?
5. Quelles vont être mes responsabilités ?
6. Est-ce que vos enfants sont bien sages ?
7. Quelle date est-ce que je peux commencer à travailler ?
8. ?

C. Lettre de demande d'emploi. Vous avez trouvé dans le journal une offre d'emploi qui vous intéresse et vous avez décidé de poser votre candidature. (Choisissez une des offres d'emploi dans la **Communication A** ou bien trouvez dans un journal français une autre offre qui vous intéresse.) Voici le commencement et la fin d'une lettre de demande d'emploi. Complétez le reste de la lettre.

Options : (1) Have several students interview for the same position. Part of the class can serve as interviewers; remaining students can decide who gets the job. (2) Model one or several interviews for students and then have them interview each other in small groups. (3) Other ads from French newspapers and magazines can be used for this activity and for additional reading comprehension practice.

Option : Have students write a letter of recommendation for another student who is interviewing for one of the jobs in Communication A (or another ad from a French newspaper or magazine). They could be asked to talk with the person before writing the letter.

Votre nom et adresse   La date

Le nom et l'adresse de
votre correspondant(e)

Monsieur (Madame),

En réponse à l'annonce d'offre d'emploi que vous avez mise dans le journal, je voudrais me présenter comme candidat(e)...

Veuillez agréer, Monsieur (Madame), mes salutations respectueuses.

Signature

D. **Demande d'emploi.** Vous travaillez dans une administration où vous êtes chargé(e) du recrutement des futurs employés (joués par d'autres étudiants de la classe). Votre rôle est d'interviewer des candidats et de remplir (*fill out*) la fiche de demande d'emploi suivante. Déterminez aussi le genre de travail que les candidats cherchent et les qualifications qu'ils possèdent. Ensuite faites un rapport de l'interview. N'oubliez pas de mentionner votre opinion du candidat.

Preparation : Have students give the questions necessary to obtain the information on the *demande d'emploi* before conducting the interview (*Quel est votre nom ? Quelle est votre nationalité ?*, etc.)

DEMANDE D'EMPLOI

I - ÉTAT CIVIL ET SITUATION DE FAMILLE

Nom : . . . . Prénoms : . . . .

Nationalité : . . . .

Date et lieu de naissance : . . . .

Adresse : . . . .

. . . . Téléphone : . . . .

Situation de famille :   célibataire - marié(e) - séparé(e) -
   divorcé(e) -
Nombre d'enfants :
NOM, Prénoms, sexe, date de naissance des enfants :
1 -   4 -
2 -   5 -
3 -   6 -

II - SITUATION MILITAIRE

Avez-vous accompli votre Service National ?   Oui - Non

Si oui, durée du service accompli : . . . . an (s) . . . . mois

III - ÉTUDES

École fréquentée :

Diplômes obtenus :

IV - SITUATION ACTUELLE

Emploi actuellement occupé par le candidat :

Employeur :

Salaire moyen :

• *Prononciation et orthographe*

A. Certain French vowels are pronounced with the lips rounded and the tongue forward (i.e., resting against the back of the lower front teeth). These vowels in order of increasing openness are :

/y/ as in **du**
/ø/ as in **deux**
/œ/ as in **jeune**

Since these vowels do not exist in English, learning to pronounce them requires special care. Make sure that your tongue is pressed against your teeth when you pronounce these sounds.

Practice repeating the following sequences :

/y/	→ /ø/	→ /œ/
1. su	ceux	seul
2. jus	jeu	jeune
3. pu	peu	peur
4. plu	pleut	pleure

B. The sounds /ø/ and /œ/ are usually written as **eu**. Whereas /œ/ always occurs in a closed syllable (i.e., a syllable ending in a consonant sound), /ø/ occurs in open syllables (i.e., syllables ending in a vowel sound) and in syllables closed by a /z/ sound. Compare and repeat the following pairs. Note the role of the /ø/ versus /œ/ contrast in distinguishing the singular and plural of certain verbs as well as the masculine and feminine of certain adjectives and nouns.

/ø/	/œ/
1. il veut	ils veulent
2. il peut	ils peuvent
3. chanteuse	chanteur
4. vendeuse	vendeur
5. menteuse	menteur

Repeat words containing the sound /ø/ :

il pleut   sérieux   sérieuse   je veux

Repeat words containing the sound /œ/ :

heure   beurre   sœur   moteur

C. Certain French vowels are pronounced with the lips rounded and with the tongue back. These vowels in order of increasing openness are :

/u/   as in **vous**
/o/   as in **vos**
/ɔ/   as in **votre**

Repeat the following sets of words :

/u/   → /o/   → /ɔ/

1. nous   nos   notre
2. doux   dos   dormir
3. sous   sot   sotte
4. tout   tôt   tort

D. The sound /ɔ/ generally corresponds to the spelling **o** and usually occurs in closed syllables. The sound /o/ can also be represented by the spelling **o**, but it occurs in open syllables or in syllables closed by a /z/ sound. The sound /o/ can also be represented by the spellings **o**, **au**, or **eau**.

Compare and repeat :

/o/   /ɔ/

1. faux   fort
2. la côte   le port
3. une rose   une carotte
4. à gauche   la poste
5. un bureau   une école

Repeat words containing the sound /o/ :

beau   chaud   aussi   photo   animaux   tôt

Repeat words containing the sound /ɔ/ :

sport   octobre   sommeil   téléphone   bonne

• *Vocabulaire*

Noms

les métiers et les professions
 (voir pp. 207–208)

d'autres noms

    l'**administration** (f)
    *administration, government
    service*
°   l'**assistant(e)**
   le **bateau** *boat*
   le **bébé** *baby*

le **car** *intercity bus*
le **classement** *ranking*
le **collège** *middle school*
le **commerce** *business, commerce*
° la **condition**
le **congé** *leave*
° le **contact**
le **débouché** *opening,
   opportunity*
le **début** *beginning*
la **dizaine** *about ten*

le **doctorat** *doctorate*
l'**élève** (m, f) *elementary or secondary school student*
l'**emploi** (m) *job*
l'**enquête** (f) *survey*
l'**espoir** (m) *hope*
l'**étude** (f) *study*
le, la **fonctionnaire** *civil servant*
la **formation** *education, training*
la **grève** *strike*
l'**horaire** (m) *schedule, time table*
l'**huile** (f) *oil*
° l'**industrie** (f)
le **journal** *newspaper, journal*
les **loisirs** (m) *leisure time, leisure activities*
le **métier** *occupation, trade*
° le **moment**
la **naissance** *birth*
la **place** *place, room*
le **plombier** *plumber*
le **poste** *job, position*
la **profession libérale** *profession*
° la **promotion**
° la **réputation**
la **réunion** *meeting*
le **salaire** *salary*
° la **sécurité**
le **sentiment** *feeling*
la **société** *company, society*
° la **solution**
le **souci** *worry, care*
° le **talent**
° le **village**

Verbes

° **abandonner**
° **accompagner**
° **admirer**
aider *to help*
apprécier *to appreciate*
critiquer *to criticize*
devoir *to have to, must*
embêter *to annoy*
emprunter *to borrow*

enseigner *to teach*
gagner *to earn, to win*
° **insulter**
intéresser *to interest*
louer *to rent*
mener *to lead*
° **organiser**
porter *to wear*
pouvoir *to be able, can*
réaliser *to achieve, to realize*
remercier *to thank*
° **respecter**
servir *to serve*
vouloir *to want, to wish*

Adjectifs

° **assuré(e)**
content(e) *happy, content, glad*
débrouillard(e) *resourceful*
° **dynamique**
élevé(e) *high*
entier, entière *whole, entire*
° **humain(e)**
° **long(ue)**
° **manuel(le)**
° **nécessaire**
occupé(e) *busy, occupied*
privé(e) *private*
propre *own*
° **public, publique**
° **rare**
satisfait(e) *satisfied*
° **social(e), sociaux**

Divers

d'abord *first*
être de retour *to be back*
finir par *to end up*
gagner sa vie *to earn a living*
il vaut mieux *it's better*
inutile de *no need to*
valoir la peine *to be worth the trouble*
vouloir bien *to be willing*
vouloir rire *to be kidding*

10

CHAPITRE DIX

Communication objectives

Talking about what to buy and where to buy it

1. Talking about buying and selling things

2. Giving orders, suggestions, and advice
3. Indicating how much and how many
4. Showing emphasis

Structures

Les mots et la vie : Les magasins et les marchandises

Vendre et les verbes de la troisième conjugaison

L'impératif

Les expressions de quantité

Les pronoms disjoints

Français! Achetez et consommez!

Mise en scène

Qu'est-ce que tu as acheté?

Jean, je suis très occupée aujourd'hui.

Est-ce que tu peux faire le marché?

Achète: une baguette   loaf of French bread
         un kilo de pommes de terre
         trois boîtes de petits pois
         une douzaine d'oeufs
         une livre de café
         deux tranches de jambon
         une bouteille d'eau minérale

JEAN	Michelle! Michelle! Tu es là?
MICHELLE	Oui. Je suis en train de finir mon article pour le journal.
JEAN	Regarde. J'ai acheté les provisions pour ce soir.
MICHELLE	Merci, tu es gentil! Je vais commencer *tout de suite* à préparer le dîner. Où sont les provisions?

tout de suite — right away

235

JEAN	Ici, sur la table.
MICHELLE	Tu as acheté du pain ?
JEAN	*Zut !* J'ai oublié d'aller à la boulangerie.

Shoot!

| MICHELLE | *Ça ne fait rien.* La boulangerie de la rue Vendôme reste *ouverte* jusqu'à huit heures. |

That doesn't matter / open

JEAN	Je suis allé à la charcuterie…
MICHELLE	Chez qui es-tu allé ?
JEAN	Chez Saclier, rue Voltaire.
MICHELLE	Bon. Tu as acheté du jambon ?
JEAN	Non, j'ai acheté un rôti de porc. J'ai *essayé** de ne pas *dépenser trop d'argent.* Le porc est *bon marché* en ce moment.

tried / to spend
too much / cheap

| MICHELLE | Voyons, Jean, un rôti de porc à huit heures du soir, mais tu es *fou !* C'est trop *lourd* à digérer et c'est bien trop long à préparer. Et tu oublies que j'ai encore cet article à finir pour demain. |

crazy / heavy

| JEAN | *Ne t'en fais pas.* Toi, tu finis ton article et moi, je vais préparer une omelette. |

Don't worry.

Compréhension. Répondez aux questions suivantes selon les renseignements donnés dans le texte.

Options. Ask students to tell : *les provisions que Jean devait* (was to) *acheter ; ce qu'il a acheté en réalité ; ce qu'il a oublié ; ce que Jean et Michelle vont manger au dîner.* Have students create additional titles for the *Mise en scène.*

1. Pourquoi est-ce que Michelle a demandé à Jean de faire le marché aujourd'hui ?
2. Qu'est-ce que Michelle est en train de faire ?
3. Quelle est la profession de Michelle ?
4. Qu'est-ce que Jean a acheté ?
5. Pourquoi est-ce que Jean n'a pas acheté de pain ?
6. Pourquoi est-ce que Michelle n'est pas contente ?
7. Qui va préparer le dîner ?
8. Qu'est-ce que Michelle et Jean vont manger ?

Notes culturelles: *Les petits commerçants*

Have students compare and contrast French and American shopping habits.

Au cours des vingt-cinq dernières années, les habitudes de vie des Français ont beaucoup changé, surtout en ce qui concerne les achats. Par exemple, les petits magasins de quartier ont dû faire face à la *concurrence* des supermarchés, des hypermarchés, des grands magasins et des centres commerciaux qui ont fait leur apparition un peu partout en France. Certains ont été obligés de fermer. *Cependant, en dépit* des prédictions, un grand nombre de petits magasins ont réussi à *survivre. En fait*, au cours des dernières années, il y a eu une augmentation du nombre de petits magasins, surtout des magasins de fruits et de légumes et des boutiques de vêtements. Les Français apprécient le charme, la qualité du

in the course of

competition

however / despite
survive / in fact

***Essayer** and **payer** are **-er** verbs with spelling changes : **j'essaie, tu essaies, il / elle essaie, nous essayons, vous essayez, ils / elles essaient.**

Marché en plein air à Sarlat (Dordogne)

Marché aux puces à Arles

237

service et aussi la proximité de ces petits magasins et cela compense les prix un peu *plus élevés*. Les économistes pensent aussi que l'augmentation du *chômage*, le désir d'être son propre patron, et de meilleures techniques de vente ont contribué au *renouveau* des petits commerces.

    En plus des magasins et supermarchés, la plupart des villes ont une ou deux fois par semaine des marchés *en plein air* où on peut acheter toutes sortes de provisions et même des vêtements et des *chaussures*. Certaines villes ont des halles ou des marchés *couverts* où les *particuliers* et les restaurateurs peuvent venir acheter chaque jour leurs provisions. La variété et la qualité des produits *ainsi que* l'animation de ces marchés offrent un spectacle très pittoresque.

    Les *marchés aux puces* constituent un autre spectacle fascinant. Le marché aux puces de Paris couvre plusieurs hectares* et on peut *y* trouver toutes les marchandises possibles et imaginables.

higher
unemployment
renewal

outdoors
shoes
indoor / individuals

as well as

flea markets
there

*One **hectare** is about 2.5 acres.

Les mots et la vie : *Les magasins et les marchandises*

Étudiez le vocabulaire suivant et faites les activités indiquées. Les choses que vous pouvez acheter :

des bijoux (m) ou une montre (f)

des fleurs (f) et des plantes

des revues (f) et des journaux (m)

des vêtements (m)

des médicaments (m)

des chaussures (f)

des jouets (m)

des cigarettes (m)

du dentifrice, du shampooing, du dé- odorant et d'autres produits (m) pour l'hy- giène personnelle

du parfum

des bonbons (m) et des gâteaux (m)

des livres (m)

des lunettes (f)

du maquillage et des produits de beauté

un sèche-cheveux, un rasoir, et d'autres appareils (m) électriques

un sac à main, un portefeuille, un parapluie

des produits d'en- tretien pour la maison (*household products*)

Pour acheter ce que vous voulez, vous pouvez aller…

dans une pâtisserie / confiserie	chez un opticien
dans une pharmacie*	chez un fleuriste
dans un bureau de tabac	chez un électricien
dans une maroquinerie (*leather goods store*)	dans un magasin de jouets
chez un marchand de journaux	dans une droguerie*
	dans une bijouterie

---

*A **droguerie** sells household and personal hygiene products; prescription drugs and over-the-counter medications must be purchased at a **pharmacie**.

dans une parfumerie *(/)*
dans un magasin de chaussures
dans une librairie / papeterie

dans une boutique de mode
(clothing store)
dans un magasin de vêtements

1. Indiquez dans quel(s) magasin(s) il faut aller pour acheter les produits énumérés dans la première liste.

   Exemple **On peut acheter des vêtements dans une boutique de mode, dans un magasin de vêtements ou dans un grand magasin.**

2. Vous allez partir en voyage. De quoi avez-vous besoin et où pouvez-vous acheter ces choses ?
3. C'est le début de l'année scolaire et vous avez loué un appartement près de l'université. De quoi avez-vous besoin pour l'école et pour l'appartement ? Où allez-vous acheter ces choses ?
4. Vous allez acheter des cadeaux d'anniversaire pour différents membres de votre famille ou pour vos amis. Indiquez ce que vous allez acheter pour chaque personne et où vous allez acheter ce cadeau.

Option: Students indicate that they need a particular item *(J'ai besoin du dentifice)*; other students tell where the item can be purchased *(Il faut aller à la droguerie).*

Explorations
❧ Talking about buying and selling things
Vendre et les verbes de la troisième conjugaison

Présentation

Vendre *(to sell)* belongs to a group of French verbs that have infinitives ending in **-re**. The present tense of these verbs is formed by dropping the **-re** from the infinitive and adding the endings shown. The past participle is formed by dropping the **-re** from the infinitive and adding **u**.

vendre	
je vend**s**	nous vend**ons**
tu vend**s**	vous vend**ez**
il / elle / on vend	ils / elles vend**ent**

passé composé : j'**ai vendu**
subjonctif : il faut que je **vende**

Qu'est-ce qu'on **vend** dans une droguerie ?
Janine **a vendu** son vieux vélo.
Il faut que nous **vendions** notre voiture.

Note that the **d** is not pronounced in the singular **(il vend)** but is pronounced in the plural **(ils vendent)**. In the third-person singular inversion **(vend-il)**, the liaison sound is /t/.

Remind students that the *s* is retained in the second-person singular imperative (e.g., *Vends ton vélo, réponds à sa question*).

Other **-re** verbs that follow this pattern are:

attendre *to wait for, to expect*	Georges **attend** Alice devant la bijouterie.
entendre *to hear*	Répétez, s'il vous plaît. Je n'**ai** pas bien **entendu**.
perdre *to lose, to waste*	Vous ne **perdez** pas votre temps.
répondre (à) *to answer*	Est-ce que tu **as répondu** à sa lettre ?
rendre + NOUN *to hand back, to return*	Est-ce que le prof **a rendu** les examens ?
rendre + NOUN+ADJECTIVE *to make*	L'argent ne **rend** pas les gens heureux.
rendre visite à *to visit (a person)*	Ils **ont rendu** visite à leurs amis canadiens.

Service des Objets Trouvés

Mise en situation

Au bureau des objets trouvés. Catherine a perdu son *portefeuille*. Elle va au bureau des objets trouvés pour voir si quelqu'un l'a trouvé. L'employé est très occupé.   *wallet*

CATHERINE   Monsieur ! Monsieur ! Ça fait un quart d'heure que j'attends !

L'EMPLOYÉ   Ne perdez pas patience, madame ! Je suis à vous dans un instant.
Voilà… Qu'est-ce que je peux faire pour vous ?

CATHERINE   J'ai perdu mon portefeuille.

L'EMPLOYÉ   Où et quand l'avez-vous perdu ?

CATHERINE   Je ne sais pas… Hier soir, j'ai rendu visite à une amie qui est à l'hôpital. Avant ça, je suis allée dans un petit magasin où on vend des *cadeaux*. J'ai payé avec un *billet* de 100 francs. Le marchand m'a rendu la *monnaie*… Ça *veut dire* que c'est après ça que je l'ai perdu.   *gifts / bill, banknote change / means*

L'EMPLOYÉ   Comment est-il, ce portefeuille ?

CATHERINE   C'est un portefeuille rouge, avec mes initiales *dessus* : C. M.   *on it*

L'EMPLOYÉ   Quelles initiales ? Je n'ai pas bien entendu…

CATHERINE   C. M.

L'EMPLOYÉ   Attendez, je vais voir si nous l'avons…

See end-of-chapter Notes culturelles for information on the French monetary system. Have students note the following : un portefeuille (wallet) ; un porte-monnaie (change purse) ; and un sac à main (purse).

Répétition : (1) Je n'entends pas bien, tu n'entends pas bien, etc. (2) Je n'ai pas bien entendu, tu n'as pas bien entendu, etc. Substitution : (1) J'attends un taxi. (mes parents / Jean / tu / vous / nous) (2) Nous avons répondu à la question. (les étudiants / le professeur / vous / tu / je / nous) (3) Est-ce qu'elle perd souvent patience ? (tu / les professeurs / Maurice / vous / nous)

Préparation

A. Au marché aux puces. Some merchants at the flea market in Paris are talking about some of the used items that they are selling. Tell what they say.

Modèle Annette / livres → **Annette vend des livres.**

1. les Leclerc / affiches
2. je / vêtements
3. tu / revues
4. Marcel / bijoux
5. nous / chaussures
6. vous / jouets

Option : Repeat in the interrogative (*Annette vend-elle des livres ?*).

B. Où est-ce qu'ils ont attendu ? André had planned to go shopping with some friends but was unclear about where he would meet them. Using the cues provided, tell where his friends waited.

Modèle Monique / devant le magasin de vêtements
Monique l'a attendu devant le magasin de vêtements.

1. je / près de la pharmacie
2. nous / en face de la charcuterie
3. vous / devant le grand magasin
4. Robert / près du bureau de tabac
5. tu / à côté de la parfumerie
6. les autres / près de la droguerie

Communication et vie pratique

A. Questions / interview. Answer the following questions or use them to interview another student.

1. Est-ce que tu perds souvent patience ?
2. Qu'est-ce que tu aimes faire quand tu as du temps à perdre ?
3. Est-ce que tu réponds toujours aux lettres de tes amis ou de tes parents ?
4. Est-ce que tu attends une lettre aujourd'hui ? De qui ?
5. Est-ce que tu aimes attendre ?
6. Est-ce que l'argent rend les gens heureux ?
7. Qu'est-ce que les étudiants peuvent faire pour rendre les professeurs heureux ?
8. Qu'est-ce que les professeurs peuvent faire pour rendre les étudiants heureux ?
9. Est-ce que tu rends quelquefois visite à tes amis du lycée ?

B. Des produits internationaux. Using vocabulary you know, tell what foreign products (e.g., **chaussures, journaux, voitures**) are sold in your city and in which shops.

Before completing this activity, it might be useful to have students first make a list of foreign products that might be sold in American stores.

Exemple On vend des fromages français et des fromages suisses dans plusieurs magasins.

Optional vocabulary : un sac à main, un parapluie, un passeport, un permis de conduire, des cartes de crédit, une serviette.

C'est votre tour. Imaginez que vous avez perdu quelque chose. Vous expliquez à l'employé(e), joué(e) par un(e) autre étudiant(e), ce que vous avez perdu.

❧ Giving orders, suggestions, and advice
L'impératif

Présentation

Imperative verb forms are used to give orders and advice, to make requests, or to explain how to do something. They are identical to the **tu**, **vous**, and **nous** forms of the present indicative, with one exception : the final **-s** is dropped from the **tu** form of -er verbs, including **aller**. They are used without subject pronouns.

L'impératif		
-er verbs	**-ir** verbs	**-re** verbs
écoute	réfléchis	vends
écoutez	réfléchissez	vendez
écoutons	réfléchissons	vendons

Finis tes études.
Va chez le médecin.
Prends un taxi.

Note that the negative of the imperative is regular ; **ne** precedes the verb and **pas** follows it.

Ne travaillez pas trop.
Ne choisissez pas ce métier.
Ne perds pas ton argent.

A. The **nous** form of the imperative is used for the *let's* form of command.

Finissons notre travail.	*Let's finish our work.*
Ne perdons pas notre temps.	*Let's not waste time!*
N'attendons pas ici.	*Let's not wait here.*

The *nous* form of the imperative is not as commonly used as the present tense (*on va, on fait,* etc.) or the imperfect with *si* (*si on allait au cinéma*). Although students should be able to recognize this form, it does not need to be emphasized in speaking or in writing.

B. The verbs **être** and **avoir** have irregular imperatives.

être	*avoir*
sois	aie
soyez	ayez
soyons	ayons

Sois calme !	*Be calm!*
Soyons prudents.	*Let's be careful.*
N'ayez pas peur.	*Don't be afraid.*

C. In affirmative commands direct object pronouns follow the verb and **moi** and **toi** replace **me** and **te**. In negative commands, the direct object pronoun remains in its usual place before the verb, and its form does not change.

Achetez-**le**.	Ne **l'**achetez pas.
Vendez-**les**.	Ne **les** vendez pas.
Attendez-**moi**.	Ne **m'**attendez pas.

Option. If available, play Jacques Brel's *"Ne me quitte pas."*

D. The imperative is used in common expressions.

Sois sage.	*Be good !*
Sois gentil.	*Be nice !*
Allons-y !	*Let's go !*
Voyons.	*Let's see !*
Ne fais pas l'idiot.	*Don't be an idiot !*
Faites attention !	*Be careful ! (Pay attention !)*
Ne faites pas de bruit.	*Don't make any noise.*

Mise en situation

À l'auto-école. Michel apprend à *conduire.* Il prend des leçons à l'auto-école. Ce n'est pas facile.

to drive

LE MONITEUR	Eh bien, allons-y… et surtout, n'ayez pas peur, je suis là pour vous aider.
MICHEL	Où est-ce que je vais ?
LE MONITEUR	Allez tout droit, jusqu'au *feu rouge.*
MICHEL	Et maintenant ? Qu'est-ce que je fais ?
LE MONITEUR	Tournez à droite… Non, non, pas tout de suite !!! Attendez le *feu vert* ! Faites attention, *voyons* !
MICHEL	Excusez-moi, monsieur ; je fais de mon mieux…
LE MONITEUR	Bon, restons calmes… Ne soyez pas si *crispé*…
MICHEL	C'est facile à *dire* !

instructor

red light

green light / for goodness' sake

tense

to say

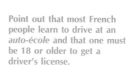

Leçon de conduite

Point out that most French people learn to drive at an *auto-école* and that one must be 18 or older to get a driver's license.

Point out also that *être nerveux* does not mean to be nervous or anxious. It describes a trait of character like "high strung" or "excitable."

Transformation : Tu n'écoutes pas la radio. → Écoute la radio. (1) Tu fais une promenade. (2) Tu fais tes devoirs ce soir. (3) Tu es optimiste. (4) Tu n'as pas peur. (5) Tu attends Michel. (6) Tu prends l'autobus. (7) Tu bois ton lait. (8) Tu vas chez le médecin. Transformation : Vous finissez votre travail. → Finissez votre travail. (1) Vous faites la vaisselle. (2) Vous mangez maintenant. (3) Vous choisissez vos cours. (4) Vous n'obéissez pas. (5) Vous n'êtes pas triste. (6) Vous prenez votre temps. (7) Vous ne perdez pas patience. (8) Vous allez parler avec le professeur. Transformation : Fais tes devoirs ce soir. → Fais-les. Ne fais pas tes devoirs ce soir. → Ne les fais pas ce soir. (1) Écoute le professeur. (2) Ne choisissez pas cet hôtel. (3) Prenez vos vacances en juillet. (4) Prépare le dîner. (5) Ne punis pas les enfants. (6) Finissez votre travail tout de suite. (7) Regardez ce programme. (8) Ne vendez pas ces vieux livres.

Préparation

A. Un homme difficile à satisfaire. Lucette is thinking about things she might want to do. Antoine, who is in a rather contrary mood, objects to each of her statements. Give his responses.

Modele   Je vais rester à la maison. → **Ne reste pas à la maison.**

Option : Have students give affirmative responses (e.g., *Eh bien alors, reste à la maison*).

1. Je vais étudier ce matin.
2. Je vais prendre l'autobus.
3. Je vais faire la cuisine.
4. Je vais aller à la boulangerie.
5. Je vais regarder cette émission.
6. Je vais être en retard.
7. Je vais punir les enfants.
8. Je vais finir mon travail maintenant.

B. À l'agence publicitaire. Some advertising agents are working on an ad campaign for a travel bureau. What are the slogans they come up with ?

Modèles   choisir notre hôtel → **Choisissez notre hôtel.**
          ne pas prendre de risques → **Ne prenez pas de risques.**

1. faire le voyage de vos rêves
2. choisir Air France
3. prendre le train
4. descendre sur la Côte
5. louer une voiture de sport
6. oublier vos soucis
7. ne pas partir sans votre carte de crédit
8. ne pas rester chez vous
9. venir respirer le bon air des montagnes
10. ne pas travailler tout le temps

C. Suggestions. André demande conseil à son ami Daniel. Qu'est-ce que Daniel répond ?

Repeat with *vous* form of the imperative.

Modèle   Je vends ma voiture ? (oui) → **Oui, vends-la.**
          Je vends mon vélo ? (non) → **Non, ne le vends pas.**

1. J'achète cette moto ? (non)
2. Je fais la vaisselle maintenant ? (oui)
3. J'attends Micheline ? (non)
4. Je prends le train ? (oui)
5. J'envoie cette lettre ? (oui)
6. Je finis ce rapport maintenant ? (non)
7. Je t'attends après la classe ? (oui)
8. Je t'attends devant la bibliothèque ? (non)

Communication et vie pratique

A. Conseils. Indicate whether new students at your university should or should not do the following things in order to succeed. Then give them advice from your own experience.

Exemple habiter dans une résidence universitaire
N'habitez pas dans une résidence universitaire.
ou: **Habitez dans un appartement.**

1. avoir peur de poser des questions
2. choisir des cours faciles
3. passer tout votre temps à étudier
4. habiter près de l'université
5. passer votre temps dans les cafés
6. oublier de rendre vos devoirs
7. faire bien attention en classe
8. attendre la fin du trimestre pour étudier

B. Et encore des conseils. What advice would you give to the following groups of people ?

Exemple aux professeurs
Ne donnez pas d'examens le lundi ou le vendredi.

1. aux professeurs
2. aux futurs parents
3. aux enfants
4. aux touristes français aux États-Unis
5. à un(e) ami(e) qui cherche du travail
6. à l'administration de votre université

C. Slogans. Alone or in small groups, choose products and make up short advertising slogans for them.

Exemple **Allez au cinéma sans sortir de chez vous. Achetez un magnétoscope.**

C'est votre tour. Un ami qui vient d'apprendre à conduire a proposé de vous emmener chez vous. Il ne sait pas où vous habitez et vous avez très peur. Imaginez la conversation.

Option : Assign different categories to small groups of students who can then share their advice with the rest of the class. You might also want to spread this activity over several days to allow for re-entry of the material.

Option : Have students come up with advertising slogans about their town, region, or university.

This is a good opportunity for students to review giving street directions. Additional vocabulary that students might want to use : *ralentir, accélérer, freiner* (put on the brakes) ; *respecter la limite de vitesse ; dépasser la limite de vitesse ; klaxonner ; mettre son clignotant.*

Option : Have students continue the conversation between Philippe and the *moniteur.*

❧ Indicating how much and how many
Les expressions de quantité

Présentation

A. Most expressions of quantity are followed by **de (d')** alone, rather than by the full partitive article (**de l', de la, du**) or the plural indefinite article (**des**). The most useful of these expressions are :

assez de *enough*	Nous avons **assez de** pain.
autant de *as much, as many*	Nous n'avons pas **autant de** travail cette semaine.
beaucoup de *much, many, a lot*	Il y a **beaucoup de** magasins près d'ici.
combien de *how much, how many*	**Combien de** boîtes de petits pois voulez-vous ?
moins de *less, fewer*	Il faut dépenser **moins d'**argent.
peu de *little, few*	**Peu de** gens peuvent répondre à cette question.
un peu de *a little of*	Encore **un peu de** vin, s'il vous plaît.
plus de *more*	Passez **plus de** temps à étudier.
tant de *so much, so many*	Ne faites pas **tant de** bruit.
trop de *too much, too many*	Ils ont **trop de** travail.

Option : Introduce the adjectival expressions of quantity : *quelques, certain(e)s, plusieurs.*

Suggestion : Review measures of quantity presented in *chapitre 5.*

Suggestion : Point out that *un peu* is used with mass nouns ; *quelques* with count nouns.

Point out that the *s* in *plus* is often pronounced in the affirmative ; it is never pronounced in the negative.

B. To indicate that there is no more (not any more) of an item, **ne... plus de** is used.

Il **n'**y a **plus de** pain.
Non merci, je **ne** veux **plus de** vin.

C. The partitive article is retained in the expression **la plupart de** (*most, the majority*) and **bien de** (*many*).

La plupart des gens sont satisfaits.
Bien des Français font leur marché tous les jours.

Point out that *la plupart* is used in the singular only with the expression *la plupart du temps* and that *bien des* is used much less often than *beaucoup de.*

Mise en situation

Questions d'argent. Mathieu a besoin d'argent. Il demande à son amie Murielle si elle peut l'aider.

MURIELLE	Tu as l'air préoccupé… *Qu'est-ce qui* ne va pas?… Tu as trop de travail ?	what
MATHIEU	Non, mais j'ai beaucoup de *soucis*… Des soucis d'argent.	worries
MURIELLE	Ne t'en fais pas ! La plupart des gens ont des soucis d'argent !	
MATHIEU	Ne *plaisante* pas ; c'est sérieux. J'ai dépensé trop de *fric* et maintenant, je n'ai pas assez d'argent pour payer mon *loyer*. Est-ce que tu pourrais me *prêter* un peu d'argent jusqu'à la fin du mois ?	joke / money (slang) rent lend

The indirect object pronoun *me* (*Est-ce que tu pourrais me prêter…*) was introduced here because of contextual constraints. Avoid, however, having students use other forms of the pronoun.

Substitutions : (1) J'ai des devoirs à faire. *(beaucoup / trop / peu / moins / assez)* (2) Il y a du lait dans le frigo. *(beaucoup / trop / tant / assez / peu).* (3) J'ai acheté du pain. *(assez / un peu / plus / beaucoup / trop).* (4) Il a des problèmes. *(a lot / enough / few / too many / fewer / so many).*

MURIELLE	Impossible, je suis *fauchée*, moi aussi !	broke
MATHIEU	Pourtant, tu gagnes beaucoup d'argent maintenant?…	
MURIELLE	Oui, mais j'ai plus de *dépenses*, et j'ai encore beaucoup de dettes. Demande à René, il est toujours *bourré de fric.*	expenses / loaded with money (slang)

Préparation

A. Inventaire. Before going shopping, Jean and Michelle check to see what items they may need. What do they say?

> Have students take an inventory of their own refrigerators and food supplies and then make up a shopping list (to review measures of quantity).

Modèle pas beaucoup / cafe → **Nous n'avons pas beaucoup de café.**

1. assez / pommes de terre
2. un peu / fromage
3. un kilo / pommes
4. pas assez / beurre
5. trois bouteilles / vin
6. beaucoup / légumes
7. pas trop / lait
8. trois boîtes / petits pois

B. La vie est difficile. Marie-Pascale is not happy with her part-time job in a supermarket and is complaining to a friend. How would she say these sentences in French?

1. I have a lot of work.
2. I have less free time now.
3. We have so many customers *(clients)*.
4. I don't earn enough money.
5. I do not have as many friends now.
6. Most of the time I'm very tired.

Communication et vie pratique

A. La vie universitaire. Using an expression of quantity, make up questions to ask other students about the following topics. Then choose a partner and ask him or her the questions.

Exemples le travail
> — **Est-ce que tu as autant de travail cette semaine?**
> — **Non, ça va mieux. J'ai moins de travail maintenant. Et toi?**

1. les devoirs
2. les professeurs
3. les amis
4. le temps libre
5. les examens
6. les cours
7. le travail
8. les soucis

B. Votre ville. Using expressions of quantity, describe the following aspects of your town or region.

> Have students use the sentences they prepared for this activity to prepare a written description of their town or region, adding linking words and conjunctions as appropriate and including a short introduction and conclusion.

Exemple parcs → **Il n'y a pas assez de parcs dans notre ville.**

1. théâtres
2. piscines
3. cinémas
4. bons restaurants
5. cafés
6. choses intéressantes à faire
7. supermarchés
8. musées intéressants

C'est votre tour. Imaginez que vous aussi, vous êtes fauché(e) et que vous avez besoin d'emprunter de l'argent pour payer votre loyer (vos livres, votre inscription à l'université, etc.). Vous essayez d'emprunter de l'argent à vos camarades de classe. Soyez convaincant(e) !

❧ Showing emphasis
Les pronoms disjoints

Présentation

The disjunctive, or stress pronouns are :

Les pronoms disjoints	
moi *I, me*	nous *we, us*
toi *you*	vous *you*
lui *he, him, it*	eux *they, them* (m)
elle *she, her, it*	elles *they, them* (f)
soi *one*	

These pronouns are used :

A. After prepositions :

Est-ce que tu peux faire ça **pour moi** ?
Ne partez pas **sans moi**.
Voulez-vous venir **avec nous** ?
Ils sont restés **chez eux**.
Il ne faut pas toujours penser **à soi**.

B. After **c'est** or **ce sont**.

— Qui a fait cela ?
— **C'est moi.**

— Est-ce que c'est Jacques ?
— Oui, **c'est lui.**

C'est nous qui avons fait cela.

— **C'est vous** ?
— Oui, **c'est nous**.

— **Ce sont** les filles de M. Simon ?
— Oui, **ce sont elles**.

Have students note that the verb agrees with the antecedent of *qui*. Have them note also that *c'est* can replace *ce sont* in conversational style *(C'est les filles de Monsieur Simon)*.

C. Alone or in short phrases where there is no verb :

— Qui veut une tasse de café ?
— **Moi.**

— Hélène est fatiguée.
— **Nous aussi.**

— Qui va faire la vaisselle ?
— **Pas moi !**

D. To emphasize the subject of the verb :

Eux, **ils** ont bu du thé, mais **nous**, **nous** avons bu du café.
Moi, **je** suis français. **Lui**, **il** est suisse.

E. In compound subjects where a pronoun is used for at least one of the persons or items :

Philippe et **moi**, nous avons faim.
Elle et **toi**, vous êtes de bonnes amies, n'est-ce pas ?

F. With the expression **être à** to indicate possession :

Ce livre n'**est** pas **à moi** ; il **est à eux.**

G. With **même(s)** to talk about oneself or others (myself, yourself, etc.)* :

Tu l'as fait **toi-même**, n'est-ce pas ?
Ils font leur cuisine **eux-mêmes**.
On ne peut pas tout faire **soi-même**.

Mise en situation

Ce n'est pas moi ! Un des *carreaux* de la fenêtre de la salle à manger est *cassé* et il y a un *ballon* au milieu de la pièce. Qui est responsable ? Monsieur Perret interroge son fils, Bernard, et ses amis.

panes / broken
ball (football or soccer)

M. PERRET	Viens ici, toi.
BERNARD	Qui ? Moi ?
M. PERRET	Oui, toi. Il est à toi, ce ballon ?
BERNARD	Non, il n'est pas à moi.
M. PERRET	Alors, dis-moi qui a cassé ce carreau... C'est un de tes petits copains ?
PHILIPPE	Non, ce n'est pas nous, monsieur, je vous assure... Nous, on fait bien attention quand on joue.
M. PERRET	Alors, c'est peut-être ton petit frère?...
BERNARD	Oui, c'est peut-être lui.
M. PERRET	Ah oui ? Tu penses que c'est lui?... Eh bien, moi, je suis sûr que ce n'est pas lui parce qu'il fait le marché avec ta mère!... Allez, *ça suffit* comme ça. Vous êtes tous des petits *voyous*. Toi, tu montes dans ta chambre et vous, vous rentrez chez vous.

Although *voyou* can be used to describe street "hoods," the word *petit* changes and softens the meaning. You may want to point out to students that the French often use *petit* to describe anything they feel affection for (*On a sa petite maison, on boit un petit pastis*, etc.)

that's enough / scoundrels

Substitution : (1) Ce livre est à moi. *(toi / lui / elle / nous / vous / eux / elles)* (2) Moi, j'ai très faim. *(il / tu / vous / les enfants / nous / elle / les filles)*

---

*For recognition only.

Préparation

A. Je t'invite. Marc is asking Monique whose invitation she is going to accept. What does Marc say?

Modèle   Serge t'invite. → **Veux-tu sortir avec lui?**

1. Je t'invite.
2. Madeleine t'invite.
3. Nous t'invitons.
4. Tes amies t'invitent.
5. Laurent et Emmanuel t'invitent.

B. Quel désordre! Henri and his roommates have decided to clean their apartment. Henri tries to find out which items belong to whom.

Modèle   Jérome, il est à toi ce vieux pull? (non)
            Non, il n'est pas à moi.

1. Ce livre de maths, il est à toi, Alain? (non)
2. Il est à ta petite amie? (oui… peut-être)
3. Cette boîte de chocolats est à vous? (oui)
4. Et ces vêtements, ils sont à toi, Michel? (non)
5. Et ces cassettes, est-ce qu'elles sont à moi? (oui)
6. Elle est à nous, cette affiche? (non)
7. Ces photos sont à Alain? (oui)
8. Et ces disques, est-ce qu'ils sont à tes frères? (oui)

C. Qui a fait cela? Madame Savabarder is not happy this morning because nothing seems to be going right. Use the cues provided to give her children's answers to her questions.

Have students complete this exercise in groups of three or four. Give a student leader the correct responses so that he or she can monitor the responses of the other students in the group. Instructor can circulate and listen to different groups.

Modèle   C'est toi qui as laissé tes vêtements dans la salle de bain? (non)
            Non, maman, ce n'est pas moi.

1. C'est toi qui as pris mes clés? (non)
2. Alors, c'est ta sœur? (oui)
3. C'est toi qui dois faire la vaisselle aujourd'hui? (non)
4. C'est vous, les enfants, qui avez mangé toute la glace? (non)
5. C'est moi qui ai laissé la porte du frigo ouverte? (oui)
6. Ce sont tes amis qui ont appris ce mot à ton frère? (oui)
7. C'est toi qui as cassé ce verre? (non)
8. Alors, c'est ton petit frère? (oui)

Communication et vie pratique

A. **Points communs et différences.** Answer the following questions, using **pronoms disjoints** where appropriate.

Suggested for oral whole-class activity; prior preparation helpful.

Exemple   Certaines personnes dépensent trop d'argent. Et vous?
    Moi aussi, je dépense trop d'argent.

1. Beaucoup d'étudiants vendent leurs livres à la fin du trimestre. Et vous?
2. Certaines personnes perdent toujours leurs affaires. Et vous?
3. Il y a des gens qui détestent attendre. Et vous?
4. Il y a des gens qui sont très impatients. Et vous, perdez-vous souvent patience? Et vos professeurs?
5. La plupart des étudiants détestent les examens. Et vous? Et vos amis?
6. Beaucoup d'étudiants mangent au restaurant universitaire. Et vous?
7. En général, les Français boivent du vin avec leurs repas. Et vous?
8. Il y a des étudiants qui passent peu de temps à étudier. Et vous? Et vos amis?
9. Certains étudiants ont peur de répondre en classe. Et vous?

B. **Ne soyez pas modeste!** In France the **Marseillais** have the reputation of having a tendency to exaggerate and brag. Do some bragging of your own.

Exemples   **Nous, nous n'avons pas besoin d'étudier.**
    ou: **Moi, je suis parfait(e).**

C. **Questions / interview.** Répondez aux questions suivantes ou utilisez-les pour interviewer un(e) autre étudiant(e).

1. Est-ce que tu habites encore chez tes parents?
2. Est-ce que tu passes beaucoup de temps avec eux?
3. Est-ce que tu parles souvent avec eux?
4. De quoi parles-tu quand tu es avec eux?
5. Passes-tu beaucoup de temps avec tes amis?
6. Est-ce que tu les invites souvent chez toi?
7. Est-ce qu'ils t'invitent souvent chez eux?
8. De quoi parles-tu avec tes amis?
9. Est-ce que tu sors souvent avec tes amis pendant le week-end?
10. Où est-ce que tu vas avec eux?

C'est votre tour. Vous habitez avec plusieurs camarades de chambre (joués par d'autres étudiants de la classe). Quelqu'un a pris ou a caché (*hid*) plusieurs choses qui sont à vous (par exemple, votre livre de français, vos chaussures, vos notes de classe). Posez des questions à vos amis pour savoir qui les a.

Intégration et perspectives

La publicité

Pour vendre, il faut de la publicité. Les produits varient mais le message final reste toujours le même : achetez et consommez !

    La publicité vous encourage à dépenser votre argent et elle vous donne toujours de bonnes raisons de ne pas attendre.

Soldes de fin d'année !

Profitez de l'occasion !

Prix réduits !

sales / end

take advantage of / opportunity

Quelquefois, elle vous encourage même à *économiser* :

save money

Ne laissez pas dormir votre argent. Placez-le.

invest

UNE AUTRE FAÇON...
...d'ACHETER !

Si vous n'avez pas l'argent nécessaire pour acheter ce que vous voulez, empruntez-le. Les banques sont là pour vous prêter tout l'argent que vous voulez.

Prêt à 8,7%

loan

Si vous n'avez pas assez d'argent pour acheter une voiture *neuve*, vous pouvez acheter une voiture *d'occasion*.

new
used

Et *si* vous trouvez que c'est trop *cher*, vous pouvez toujours essayer de *marchander* !

if / expensive
to bargain

La publicité est partout : le long des routes, sur les *murs* des maisons, dans les journaux et dans les revues :

walls

Compréhension. Créez un nouveau slogan pour chacun des produits représentés. (*Create a new slogan for each of the products shown.*)

Notes culturelles: *Le porte-monnaie et le portefeuille des Français*

Qu'y a-t-il dans le porte-monnaie d'un Français ? De la monnaie, bien sûr, c'est-à-dire des pièces de monnaie. Voici une photo des principales pièces qui sont maintenant en circulation :

5 centimes, 10 centimes, 20 centimes, 50 centimes

1 franc (1 F), 2 francs (2 F), 5 francs (5 F), 10 francs (10 F)

Et dans un portefeuille, qu'y a-t-il ? Il y a des billets de différentes valeurs. Chaque billet est marqué à l'effigie d'un personnage célèbre, comme vous pouvez le voir sur les photos suivantes.

50 F (à l'effigie de Quentin de La Tour, un peintre du 18ᵉ siècle)

100 F (à l'effigie de Delacroix, un peintre du 19ᵉ siècle)

200 F (à l'effigie
de Montesquieu, un
écrivain du 18ᵉ
siècle.

500 F (à l'effigie de Pascal,
un mathématicien, physicien,
philosophe et écrivain du
17ᵉ siècle)

Dans un portefeuille, on garde aussi ses papiers d'identité et ses cartes
de crédit. Les cartes de crédit américaines (*Visa, Mastercard, American
Express*) sont acceptées dans toutes les banques françaises et dans beaucoup de magasins. Les deux principales cartes de crédit en France sont
Mastercard / Eurocard et CB (carte bancaire).

Communication et vie pratique

A. Soyez persuasif (persuasive)! Using words and phrases from this
chapter and other vocabulary you know, create scripts for thirty-
second radio or television spots for real or imaginary products. Be prepared to present your spots.

B. Au marché. Make a shopping list and then role-play a trip to the market with another student or group of students. One student will play
the role of a difficult customer; another student will play the role of a
person trying very hard to sell the merchandise. Useful sentences include:

Client(e)

Je voudrais une bouteille de…
J'ai besoin de trois kilos de…
C'est combien, s'il vous plaît?
Qu'est-ce que c'est?
Est-ce que les… sont bon
  marché?
Je voudrais un peu de…

Marchand(e)

Que désirez-vous?
Qu'est-ce que je peux faire pour
  vous?
Les… coûtent… le kilo.
Le… coûte… le litre.
Nous n'avons pas de… mais
  nous avons…
Nous n'avons pas beaucoup
  de… aujourd'hui mais ils
  (elles) vont arriver demain.
Avez-vous besoin de…?
Avez-vous assez de…?

C. **Économe ou dépensier (dépensière)?** Do you tend to watch your money or do you tend to spend it easily? In order to find out, answer the following questions and then check the interpretation that follows. Note that the options given represent two extremes possible for each situation; you should therefore pick the answer that best represents your attitude.

1. Quand vous avez de l'argent, en général, est-ce que… ?
   a. vous le placez
   b. vous le dépensez
2. Quand vous avez besoin d'une nouvelle voiture, est-ce que vous achetez… ?
   a. une voiture d'occasion
   b. une voiture neuve
3. Quand votre voiture ne marche pas, est-ce que… ?
   a. vous essayez de la réparer vous-même
   b. vous allez chez le garagiste
4. Quand vous avez envie d'un livre, est-ce que… ?
   a. vous allez à la bibliothèque
   b. vous l'achetez dans une librairie
5. Quand vous avez besoin de nouveaux vêtements, est-ce que vous les achetez… ?
   a. quand ils sont en solde
   b. quand ils sont vendus au prix normal
6. Quand vous cherchez un appartement, est-ce que vous choisissez… ?
   a. un appartement modeste mais confortable
   b. un appartement luxueux qui possède tout le confort moderne
7. Comment organisez-vous votre budget? En général, est-ce que… ?
   a. vous établissez votre budget à l'avance
   b. vous dépensez votre argent sans compter
8. Il y a quelque chose que vous voulez acheter mais votre budget est très limité en ce moment. Est-ce que… ?
   a. vous essayez de gagner l'argent nécessaire
   b. vous l'achetez à crédit ou vous empruntez de l'argent
9. Quand vous utilisez une carte de crédit, est-ce que… ?
   a. vous payez chaque mois ce que vous devez
   b. vous continuez à acheter ce que vous voulez sans penser à vos dettes
10. Quand vous empruntez de l'argent à un(e) ami(e), est-ce que… ?
    a. vous rendez en peu de temps l'argent qu'on vous a prêté
    b. vous oubliez que vous avez emprunté de l'argent
11. À la fin du mois, est-ce que… ?
    a. vous avez toujours assez d'argent pour finir le mois
    b. vous devez emprunter de l'argent ou vous devez faire très attention à ce que vous dépensez
12. Est-ce que… ?
    a. vous payez régulièrement votre loyer
    b. vous oubliez souvent de le payer

Interprétation

Combien de fois avez-vous choisi la réponse « a » ?

10–12   Vous êtes très économe et c'est une bonne chose. Mais ne soyez pas obsédé(e) par les questions d'argent.

7–9   Vous êtes économe, mais sans excès. Et vos amis peuvent compter sur vous quand ils ont besoin d'argent !

4–6   Vous aimez dépenser sans compter, mais n'espérez pas être un jour ministre des Finances.

0–3   Si dépenser de l'argent rend les gens heureux, vous devez être en extase.

● *Prononciation et orthographe*

A. The letter **e** (without an accent mark) is usually pronounced /ə/ , as in the following words:

le   de   me   ce   demain   regarder

The mute **e** is not always pronounced, however. Whether it is pronounced or not depends upon its position in a word or group of words and upon its "phonetic environment." It is not pronounced :

1. At the end of a word :

ouvert¢   chanc¢   voitur¢   anglais¢

2. When it is preceded by only one consonant sound :

sam¢di   tout d¢ suite   seul¢ment   je l¢ sais

Listen and repeat :

ach¢ter	chez l¢ marchand
boulang¢rie	ça n¢ fait rien
épic¢rie	en c¢ moment
heureus¢ment	un kilo d¢ pain
tout l¢ monde	je n'ai pas l¢ temps

B. The mute **e** is pronounced in the following situations :

1. When it is preceded by two consonant sounds and followed by a third :

vendredi   quelque chose   mon propre patron

Listen and repeat :

mercredi	pour demain
quelquefois	ça marche bien
premier	faire le marché
votre livre	pomme de terre
notre voiture	une autre personne

2. When it is in the first syllable of a word or an utterance :

demain   regardez   le marché   ce journal

C. In fast speech, the mute **e** may be dropped even at the beginning of an utterance. This is especially true of the pronoun **je**.

Listen and compare :

Careful speech	Fast speech
je mange /ʒəmɑ̃ʒ/	je mange /ʒmɑ̃ʒ/
je réponds /ʒərepɔ̃/	je réponds /ʒrepɔ̃/
je suis /ʒəsɥi/	je suis* /ʃsɥi/
je pense /ʒəpɑ̃s/	je pense* /ʃpɑ̃s/

In fast, informal speech, the **ne** of the negative may even be omitted entirely.

Careful speech	Fast, informal speech
ça n¢ fait rien	ça fait rien
je n'ai pas l¢ temps	j'ai pas l¢ temps
ce n'est pas possible	c'est pas possible
il n'a pas oublié	il a pas oublié
je n¢ sais pas	j(e) sais pas

D. Repeat the following sentences. Pay special attention to the mute **e**'s.

1. Est-c¢ qu**e** ça march**e** bien en c¢ moment ?
2. Je n¢ sais pas c¢ que j¢ vais fair¢ sam¢di.
3. Je vais ach¢ter quelqu**e** chos¢ à la bouch¢rie ou à l'épic¢rie.
4. Heureus¢ment, il rest**e** du rôti d¢ veau et un kilo d¢ pain.
5. Tout l¢ monde fait l¢ marché l¢ vendr¢di ou le sam¢di.

● *Vocabulaire*

Noms

l'**appareil** (m) *device, machine*
° l'**article** (m)
l'**auto-école** (f) *driving school*
la **baguette** *long loaf of French bread*
le **ballon** *ball (football or soccer)*
le **bijou, les bijoux** *jewel, jewelry*
la **bijouterie** *jewelry store*
le **billet** *bill (currency)*
les **bonbons** (m) *candy*
la **boutique de mode** *clothing store*
le **bureau de tabac** *tobacco shop*
le **cadeau, les cadeaux** *gift*
la **confiserie** *candy store*

le **dentifrice** *toothpaste*
° le **déodorant**
la **dépense** *expense*
la **droguerie** *drugstore*
° l'**électricien(ne)**
le **feu rouge** *red light*
le **feu vert** *green light*
le, la **fleuriste** *florist*
° l'**instant** (m)
le **jouet** *toy*
la **librairie** *bookstore*
le **loyer** *rent*
les **lunettes** (f) *eyeglasses*
le **maquillage** *makeup*
le **marchand, la marchande** *merchant*

*Before an unvoiced consonant, /ʒ/ becomes /ʃ/ .

la **maroquinerie**   *leather goods store*
le **médicament**   *medicine*
le **moniteur, la monitrice**   *instructor*
la **monnaie**   *change*
la **montre**   *watch*
° l'**objet**
° l'**opticien(ne)**
la **papeterie**   *stationery store*
le **parapluie**   *umbrella*
° la **plante**
le **portefeuille**   *wallet*
le **produit**   *product*
les **provisions** (f)   *groceries*
le **rasoir**   *razor*
la **revue**   *magazine*
le **rôti**   *roast*
le **sac à main**   *handbag, purse*
le **sèche-cheveux**   *hair dryer*
le **shampooing**   *shampoo*
le **solde**   *sale*
le **tabac**   *tobacco, tobacco shop*

Verbes

° **assurer**
attendre   *to wait, to wait for*
conduire   *to drive*
dépenser   *to spend*
économiser   *to save (money)*
° **encourager**

entendre   *to hear*
essayer   *to try*
interroger   *to question*
perdre   *to lose, to waste*
° **payer**
plaisanter   *to joke*
prêter   *to lend*
rendre   *to give back, to make*
répondre   *to answer*
vendre   *to sell*

Adjectifs

cassé(e)   *broken*
fou, folle   *crazy*
lourd(e)   *heavy*
ouvert(e)   *open*
réduit(e)   *reduced*

Divers

les expressions de quantité (voir p. 246)

bon marché   *cheap, a good buy*
ça ne fait rien   *it doesn't matter*
ça suffit   *that's enough*
ne... plus de   *no more, not any more*
ne t'en fais pas   *don't worry*
qu'est-ce qui   *what*
rendre visite à   *to visit (a person)*
tout de suite   *right away*
zut   *darn*

11

CHAPITRE ONZE

Communication objectives

Talking about one's health

1. Talking about daily activities
2. Talking about what we intend to do
3. Talking about past activities
4. Giving advice, suggestions, and orders

Structures

Les mots et la vie : Le corps et les maladies

Le présent des verbes réfléchis

L'infinitif des verbes réfléchis

Le passé composé des verbes réfléchis

L'impératif des verbes réfléchis

Santé et habitudes personnelles

Mise en scène

La nouvelle culture, c'est la culture physique

Confessions d'un nouveau converti

J'ai résisté longtemps. Mais c'est fini, j'abandonne. Les *conseils* de mes amis, les messages *étalés* partout sur les pages des magazines et sur les *écrans* de télévision, les livres dans les *vitrines* des librairies, la vue de mes voisins qui, chaque matin, font quinze fois le tour de notre *pâté* de maisons, tout cela a fini par me persuader.

    Je suis maintenant membre d'un club de gymnastique. Je suis parmi les millions de Français qui veulent « *se sentir bien dans leur peau* ».

    Me voilà donc parti à la conquête de mon corps. La route n'est pas facile. Je fais des « *développé-couché* » pour mes muscles pectoraux, des « squatts » pour mes *cuisses*, des abdominaux pour mon *ventre*. Je *soulève* des *poids* pour développer mes biceps. Je fais du jogging pour mes *poumons*, mon *cœur* et mes artères. J'*avale* des vitamines, je bois du ginseng et je mange de la cuisine diététique. Mon médecin m'assure que c'est bon pour ma santé, alors… je *sue*. Je sue *donc* je suis.*

Inspiré d'un article de l'Express.

Glossary (margin):
- advice
- spread out, displayed
- screens / display windows
- block
- to feel good about themselves
- push-ups
- thighs / abdomen, belly / lift
- weights
- lungs / heart / swallow
- sweat / therefore

---

*A play on words based on Descartes' famous statement, **Je pense donc je suis** (*I think therefore I am*).

CLUB DE GYMNASTIQUE

cours de gymnastique
leçons de yoga
gymnastique collective
danse aérobique
piscine
jazz dance

massages
sauna
cure d'amaigrissement   weight-loss program
solarium
bains remous   whirlpool
exercices de respiration   breathing
   et de relaxation

A. Compréhension. Répondez aux questions suivantes selon les renseignements donnés dans le texte.

Have students set up their own health club, giving it a French name and deciding which activities would be offered.

1. Est-ce que l'auteur a toujours été un adepte de la culture physique ?
2. Qu'est-ce qui l'a persuadé de changer son style de vie?
3. Qu'est-ce que ses voisins font chaque matin?
4. À quel club est-ce qu'il appartient maintenant?
5. Selon l'auteur, est-ce que c'est facile de retrouver la forme ?
6. Qu'est-ce qu'il fait pour être en forme et pour développer ses muscles ?
7. Qu'est-ce que son médecin pense de tout ça ?

B. Et vous ? Que faites-vous pour rester en forme ?

1. Est-ce que vous aimez faire de la culture physique ?
2. Est-ce que vous êtes membre d'un club de gymnastique ? Si oui, quel est le nom du club ?
3. Quand vous faites de la gymnastique, quels exercices faites-vous ? Est-ce que vous faites des « développés-couchés » ? Des abdominaux ? Des exercices de respiration ?
4. Est-ce que vous faites de la danse aérobique ? Si oui, combien de fois par semaine ?
5. Est-ce que vous faites du jogging ? Si oui, combien de fois par semaine ?
6. Est-ce que vous soulevez des poids ?
7. Est-ce que vous prenez des vitamines ?
8. Est-ce que vous faites attention à ce que vous mangez ?

Notes culturelles: *Santé et forme*

Est-ce vrai qu'en France la nouvelle culture, c'est la culture physique ? C'est peut-être un peu exagéré mais ce qui est évident c'est que les Français, traditionnellement assez peu sportifs et grands amateurs de bonne cuisine, s'intéressent de plus en plus à leur santé et à leur forme. Par exemple, de récentes statistiques indiquent que 21% des habitants des villes pratiquent régulièrement le jogging. Chaque année, de nouveaux clubs de gymnastique *ouvrent* leur porte et de nombreux livres sur la santé, la forme, les *régimes* et la cuisine *minceur* font leur *apparition* à la vitrine des libraires. Les *stations thermales*, populaires depuis longtemps en France, continuent à *attirer* un grand nombre de gens qui viennent là pour *soigner* leur *foie*, leurs *reins*, leurs *bronches* ou leurs rhumatismes. Chaque jour, ils boivent leur ration d'eau, prennent des bains ou des *douches* d'eau ou de vapeur thermale et *suivent* un régime spécial. À cela, on *ajoute* maintenant tout un programme d'activités physiques.

Ask students to compare and contrast the importance of *santé et forme* in the US and in France.

open

diets / low-calorie / appearance / spas

to attract

to take care of / liver / kidneys / respiratory systems

showers / follow

add

Les mots et la vie : *Le corps et les maladies*

Étudiez les expressions et mots suivants et ensuite faites les activités indiquées.

1. Les parties du corps

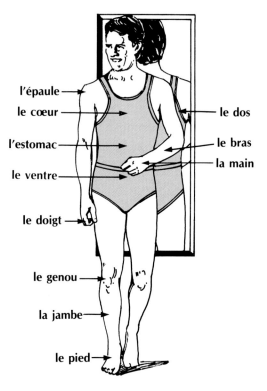

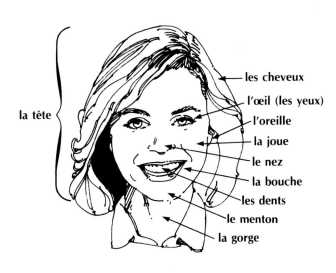

la tête

les cheveux
l'œil (les yeux)
l'oreille
la joue
le nez
la bouche
les dents
le menton
la gorge

l'épaule
le cœur
l'estomac
le ventre
le doigt
le genou
la jambe
le pied

le dos
le bras
la main

2. Les douleurs et les symptômes

avoir mal à la gorge, à la tête, aux pieds,
   à l'estomac, etc.
avoir de la fièvre
avoir la diarrhée
tousser (*to cough*)
vomir
être allergique à
être paralysé(e)

3. Les maladies

un rhume (*cold*)   une crise cardiaque
la grippe (*flu*)   le SIDA (*AIDS*)
une angine (*strep throat*)   le cancer
une bronchite   les oreillons (*mumps*)
une pneumonie   la rougeole (*measles*)
une infection   la varicelle (*chicken pox*)

4. Les remèdes

une ordonnance (*prescription*)   donner une ordonnance
un médicament   prendre un médicament
une pilule (*pill*)   prendre une pilule
un comprimé d'aspirine   prendre un comprimé d'aspirine
   (*aspirin tablet*)
une piqûre (*shot*)   faire une piqûre
une opération   opérer

Optional vocabulary : *le cheville, le cou, la cuisse, la figure, les hanches, les lèvres, les orteils, le poignet, la pouce, les sourcils.*

Le SIDA = Syndrome Immuno-Déficitaire Acquis

A. Chez le médecin. Vous êtes dans la salle d'attente du médecin. Il y a plusieurs autres personnes qui attendent leur tour. Où ont-ils mal?

C'est votre tour. Vous expliquez au médecin (joué(e) par un(e) autre étudiant(e)) où vous avez mal et quels sont vos symptômes. N'oubliez pas de mentionner les maladies et problèmes de santé que vous avez eus dans le passé. Le médecin, de son côté, va vous donner des conseils et des médicaments appropriés.

Explorations
⚜ Talking about daily activities
Le présent des verbes réfléchis

Présentation

In both French and English an action can be performed on an object or on another person.

Je lave la voiture.   *I wash the car.*

When the action is performed on oneself — that is, when the object of the verb is the same as the subject — a reflexive construction is used in French.

Je me lave.   *I wash myself.*
Je m'habille.   *I'm getting dressed.*

Reflexive verbs are conjugated with reflexive pronouns :

se laver (to wash oneself)	
je **me lave**	nous **nous lavons**
tu **te laves**	vous **vous lavez**
il / elle / on **se lave**	ils / elles **se lavent**

s'habiller (to get dressed, to dress oneself)	
je **m'habille**	nous **nous habillons**
tu **t'habilles**	vous **vous habillez**
il / elle / on **s'habille**	ils / elles **s'habillent**

Note that the **e** of the reflexive pronouns **me**, **te**, and **se** is dropped before a vowel sound.

A. Reflexive verbs fall into three main categories.

   1. Certain reflexive verbs, such as **se laver** and **s'habiller**, indicate that the subject performs the action on himself or herself.

s'arrêter *to stop*	Vous **vous arrêtez** à la boulangerie chaque matin ?
se coucher *to go to bed*	Elle **se couche** à onze heures.
se détendre *to relax*	Vous ne **vous détendez** pas assez.
se lever* *to get up*	Je **me lève** à sept heures.
se préparer à *to get ready*	Nous **nous préparons** à partir.
se reposer *to rest*	Ils **se reposent** un peu.
se réveiller *to wake up*	À quelle heure est-ce que tu **te réveilles** d'habitude ?
se soigner *to take care of oneself*	Est-ce que vous **vous soignez** bien ?
se peigner *to comb one's hair*	Il **se peigne** avant de sortir.

---

*Se lever is a regular -er verb except for the spelling changes in its stem. It is conjugated like acheter : je me lève, tu te lèves, il / elle / on se lève, nous nous levons, vous vous levez, ils / elles se lèvent.

2. Many verbs can be used as reflexive verbs to indicate a reciprocal action.

s'aimer *to like, to love each other*	Pierre et Hélène **s'aiment** beaucoup.
s'embrasser *to kiss*	On ne **s'embrasse** pas en public!
se rencontrer *to meet (by accident)*	Nous **nous rencontrons** de temps en temps.
se retrouver *to meet (by prior arrangement)*	Après la classe, nous **nous retrouvons** au café.

3. Certain reflexive verbs have an idiomatic meaning.

s'amuser *to have a good time*	On **s'amuse** bien ici.
s'appeler* *to be named*	Comment **vous appelez**-vous?
se débrouiller *to manage, to get along*	Est-ce que tu **te débrouilles** bien en français?
se dépêcher (de) *to hurry*	Nous **nous dépêchons** de finir notre travail.
s'entendre (avec) *to get along with*	Henri ne **s'entend** pas très bien avec son frère.
s'intéresser à *to be interested in*	Est-ce que tu **t'intéresses** à la politique?
se marier (avec)† *to get married (to)*	Ils **se marient** samedi.
s'occuper de *to be busy with, to take care of*	Qui **s'occupe** des enfants?
se passer *to happen*	Qu'est-ce qui **se passe**?
se préoccuper de *to be concerned with*	Il **se préoccupe** trop de l'opinion des autres.
se souvenir de *to remember*	Je ne **me souviens** pas de son adresse.
se sentir *to feel*	Monique ne **se sent** pas bien aujourd'hui.

B. To form the negative of reflexive verbs, the **ne** is placed before the reflexive pronoun and the **pas** after the verb.

Je me lève très tôt.	Je **ne** me lève **pas** très tôt.
Il se débrouille bien.	Il **ne** se débrouille **pas** bien.
Nous nous entendons bien.	Nous **ne** nous entendons **pas** bien.

---

*Note that **divorcer** is not a reflexive verb: **Ils ont divorcé.**

†**S'appeler** also has spelling changes: **je m'appelle, tu t'appelles, il / elle / on s'appelle, nous nous appelons, vous vous appelez, ils / elles s'appellent.**

C. As with all other verbs, questions can be asked with reflexives by adding **est-ce que** (**Est-ce que tu te souviens de son adresse ?**) or **n'est-ce pas** to the sentence (**Tu t'intéresses à la littérature, n'est-ce pas ?**) or by intonation (**Tu te lèves à six heures demain ?**). To form questions by inversion, the positions of the subject pronoun and the verb are reversed, and the reflexive pronoun remains.

The information on the use of questions by inversion is presented for recognition only and will not be practiced in subsequent exercises because of the general tendency in conversational French to avoid using inversion.

Anne se marie la semaine prochaine.	Anne **se marie-t-elle** la semaine prochaine ?
Ils s'entendent bien.	**S'entendent-ils** bien ?
Vous vous arrêtez ici.	**Vous arrêtez-vous** ici ?

D. Certain reflexive verbs can also be used with parts of the body : **se laver les mains**, **les cheveux**, etc. ; **se brosser** (*to brush*) **les dents**, **les cheveux** ; **se couper** (*to cut*) **le doigt** ; **se casser** (*to break*) **la jambe**, **le bras**, etc. Note that in this case the noun is preceded by an article, not by a possessive adjective as in English.

Elle se lave **les** mains.
Nous nous brossons **les** dents trois fois par jour.

Mise en situation

When talking to a doctor, one says « Oui, docteur, » « Non, docteur, » instead of using monsieur or madame. However, such formality is becoming rarer.

Chez le médecin. Monsieur Verdier ne se sent pas bien. Il vient consulter son médecin, Madame Dupas.

LE MÉDECIN	Comment vous sentez-vous aujourd'hui ?
M. VERDIER	Pas trop bien. Je me sens très fatigué et je n'ai pas d'énergie…
LE MÉDECIN	Vous ne vous reposez pas bien ?
M. VERDIER	Non, je me réveille souvent pendant la nuit.
LE MÉDECIN	À quelle heure vous couchez-vous ?
M. VERDIER	Vers minuit.
LE MÉDECIN	Et à quelle heure vous levez-vous ?
M. VERDIER	À cinq heures.
LE MÉDECIN	Hmmm… Ça ne fait pas beaucoup de sommeil. Vous prenez le temps de déjeuner le matin, j'espère… ?
M. VERDIER	Non, je n'ai pas le temps. Je me lève, je prends une *douche*, et je me dépêche d'aller à mon travail. Quelquefois, je m'arrête *en route* pour prendre une tasse de café…
LE MÉDECIN	Mais ça ne suffit pas, voyons ! *En fait*, je *me demande* comment vous vous débrouillez pour *tenir le coup* ! Le problème, c'est que vous *brûlez la chandelle par les deux bouts* !

Substitution : (1) Je m'amuse bien. (on / vous / nous / Marc / je / tes amis / tu) (2) Elle se couche assez tard. (vous / Jean / tu / nous / je / les autres) (3) Je ne me souviens pas de son nom. (Serge / nous / vous / tu / les professeurs / je) (4) Tu te lèves très tôt. (nous / tu / mon père / mes frères / je / vous)

shower

on the way

in fact / wonder

to hold up (under stress)

burn the candle at both ends

Préparation

A. C'est l'heure! À quelle heure est-ce que ces étudiants se lèvent d'habitude pour aller à l'université?

Have students repeat in negative (e.g., *Paul ne se lève pas à six heures et demie*).

Modèle   Paul / 6 h 30 → **Paul se lève à six heures et demie.**

1. nous / 6 h
2. Catherine / 9 h 15
3. vous / 5 h
4. tu / 7 h 30
5. Roger et Serge / 8 h 45
6. je / 9 h

B. Tout va mal. Monsieur Michalet ne va pas très bien et il décide d'aller chez le médecin. Donnez les réponses de Monsieur Michalet aux questions du médecin.

Assign a student to play the role of the doctor and ask the questions in the exercise. Another student or students will answer using the cues provided. As a variation, have students come up with their own answers to the doctor's questions.

Modèle   Est-ce que vous vous sentez bien aujourd'hui? (non... pas très bien)
Non, je ne me sens pas très bien.

1. Est-ce que vous vous reposez assez? (non)
2. Est-ce que vous vous couchez assez tôt? (non)
3. Est-ce que vous vous intéressez à votre travail? (non... pas vraiment)
4. Est-ce que vos enfants se débrouillent bien à l'école? (non... pas très bien)
5. Est-ce qu'ils se couchent assez tôt? (non)
6. Est-ce que vous vous entendez bien avec vos voisins? (non... pas très bien)
7. Est-ce que vos amis et vous, vous vous retrouvez quelquefois pour parler ensemble? (non... jamais)
8. Est-ce que vous vous amusez bien quand vous sortez avec vos amis? (non)

Communication et vie pratique

A. Êtes-vous d'accord? Si vous n'êtes pas d'accord avec l'opinion exprimée, modifiez la phrase.

Read as statements or ask as questions (e.g., *Est-ce que les médecins s'occupent assez de leurs malades?*). Encourage students to explain their answers.

1. Les médecins ne s'occupent pas assez de leurs malades.
2. Les Américains s'habillent très bien.
3. On se sent bien quand on fait des exercices de relaxation.
4. Les jeunes s'entendent bien avec leurs parents.
5. On se marie trop jeune aux États-Unis.
6. Les Américains ne s'intéressent pas assez à la politique.
7. Les étudiants américains ne se préoccupent pas assez de leur santé.

B. **Questions / interview.** Répondez aux questions suivantes ou utilisez-les pour interviewer un(e) autre étudiant(e).

Have students work in small groups and report back their partner's answers.

1. Est-ce que tu te lèves tard d'habitude ? Et le dimanche ?
2. En général, à quelle heure est-ce que tu te couches ?
3. Est-ce que tu t'amuses bien pendant les week-ends ?
4. Est-ce que tu te souviens toujours de l'anniversaire de tes amis ?
5. Est-ce que tu t'intéresses à la politique ? Et au sport ? Et à la musique ?
6. Est-ce que tu te débrouilles bien en français ? Et en mathématiques ? Et en sciences ?
7. Est-ce que tu t'entends bien avec tes professeurs ? Et avec tes camarades de chambre ?

C. **Votre routine matinale.** Décrivez ce que vous faites généralement chaque matin. Utilisez autant de verbes réfléchis que possible.

Exemple   Je me lève à sept heures et je déjeune immédiatement, etc.

Have students ask each other questions to find out what they do each morning : *Est-ce que tu te lèves tôt ou tard ? À quelle heure est-ce que tu te lèves ? À quelle heure est-ce que tu quittes la maison ?*

Option : Have students ask yes-no questions to find out at what time another student goes to bed (gets up) : *Est-ce que tu te lèves tôt ? Est-ce que tu te lèves avant sept heures ?*, etc.

> **C'est votre tour.** Imaginez une conversation entre une personne qui est un malade imaginaire (*hypochondriac*) et son médecin. Jouez les rôles respectifs.

༝ Talking about what we intend to do
L'infinitif des verbes réfléchis

Présentation

Like all verbs, reflexives can also be used in the infinitive. When used in the infinitive, the reflexive pronoun is always in the same person and number as the subject and precedes the infinitive.

Point out that certain expressions that students already know require the use of the infinitive (*aller, vouloir, pouvoir, avoir envie de, avoir besoin de, avoir l'intention de, avoir l'air de, avoir l'occasion de*). *Avoir l'habitude de* (to be in the habit of, to usually do something) is also useful : *J'ai l'habitude de me coucher assez tôt.*

Je vais **me reposer.**	**Nous** allons **nous reposer.**
Tu vas **te reposer.**	**Vous** allez **vous reposer.**
Elle va **se reposer.**	**Elles** vont **se reposer.**
Il va **se reposer.**	**Ils** vont **se reposer.**

Tu n'as pas l'air de **te sentir** bien.
On va bien **s'amuser.**
Les enfants ne veulent pas **se laver** les mains.
Vous avez besoin de **vous soigner.**

Mise en situation.

Bonne journée ! Denis, Nicolas et des amis ont décidé d'aller passer la journée à la plage. Denis vient chercher Nicolas.

One must be 18 to have a driver's license in France. Thus, fewer French young people have cars than their American counterparts. Mopeds are, however, popular.

DENIS   Bonjour, Madame Martin. Est-ce que Nicolas est prêt ?

MME MARTIN   Non, il vient de se réveiller. Il est en train de se préparer.

Gymnastique sur la plage

NICOLAS   (*dans la salle de bain*) C'est toi, Denis? J'arrive tout de suite. Je finis de m'habiller.

DENIS   Il faut te dépêcher, mon vieux! Les autres vont partir sans nous!

NICOLAS   J'arrive! Je me dépêche de me peigner.

DENIS   Tu peux te peigner dans la voiture.

NICOLAS   Voilà, je suis prêt. Nous allons nous arrêter en route pour déjeuner?

DENIS   Non, on a décidé de ne pas s'arrêter, ça prend trop de temps.

Préparation

A. Les bonnes résolutions. Marc et ses amis pensent qu'il est temps de changer un peu leur style de vie. Qu'est-ce qu'ils disent?

> **Modèle**   se coucher tôt
> — **Je vais me coucher tôt.**
> — **Nous aussi, nous allons nous coucher tôt.**

1. se reposer
2. se lever tôt
3. se dépêcher le matin
4. se brosser les dents trois fois par jour
5. s'amuser un peu
6. se souvenir de faire ses devoirs
7. s'habiller mieux
8. se coucher avant minuit

Substitution : **(1) Est-ce que tu vas te lever tôt? (***nous / je / Jean-Claude / les enfants / vous***) (2) J'ai besoin de me détendre. (***Odile / ses parents / tu / vous / nous / je***) (3) On va s'amuser ce soir. (***nous / Lucien / je / vous / mes amis / tu***) *Transformation :* Je me couche à 11 heures. → Je vais me coucher à 11 heures.
(1) Nous nous reposons un peu. (2) Ils se marient demain. (3) Je me lève assez tard. (4) Tu t'occupes des enfants. (5) Les petits se lavent.**

B. Différences. Il y a des gens qui aiment se coucher tôt et d'autres qui n'aiment pas ça. Utilisez les suggestions suivantes pour donner l'opinion de chaque personne.

> **Modèle** Marc n'aime pas…
>   **Marc n'aime pas se coucher tôt.**

1. Thérèse préfère…
2. Tu as besoin de…
3. Nous ne voulons pas…
4. Je voudrais…
5. Ils ont l'intention de…
6. Vous n'avez pas envie de…

Communication et vie pratique

Habitudes et santé. Nos habitudes de vie ne sont pas toujours très bonnes pour notre santé. Décrivez votre situation, vos habitudes et vos obligations d'une part et d'autre part ce que vous pouvez faire pour éviter de « brûler la chandelle par les deux bouts ». Utilisez des verbes réfléchis et d'autres verbes que vous avez déjà appris.

Have students compare and contrast answers.

> **Exemple** **Je suis obligé(e) de me lever tôt parce que j'ai un cours à huit heures. J'ai besoin de me coucher plus tôt.**

Suggestions : J'ai l'habitude de, je n'ai pas l'habitude de, je voudrais, j'ai besoin de, j'ai envie de, je n'ai pas envie de, j'aime.

C'est votre tour. Imaginez que vous êtes invité(e) à une réception. Vous avez invité un(e) ami(e), joué(e) par un(e) autre étudiant(e), à vous accompagner et vous avez proposé de venir le / la chercher. Quand vous arrivez, il / elle n'est pas prêt(e). Vous n'êtes pas très content(e)… Jouez la scène.

Have students think of possible reasons for not being ready when someone is supposed to pick them up. Have them also think of ways to express politely their irritation with someone who is not ready.

❧ Talking about past activities
Le passé composé des verbes réfléchis

Présentation

The auxiliary verb **être** is used to form the **passé composé** of reflexive verbs. The past participle agrees in gender and in number with the preceding direct object, which is usually the reflexive pronoun.

Le passé composé de *se laver*	
je **me suis lavé(e)**	nous **nous sommes lavé(e)s**
tu **t'es lavé(e)**	vous **vous êtes lavé(e)(s)**
il **s'est lavé**	ils **se sont lavés**
elle **s'est lavée**	elles **se sont lavées**

Ils **se sont mariés** l'été dernier.
Nous **nous sommes** bien **amusés**.
Elle **s'est** bien **débrouillée** à l'examen.

A. The negative is formed by placing the **ne** before the reflexive pronoun and the **pas** after the auxiliary verb.

Je **ne me suis pas souvenu** de son anniversaire.
Nous **ne nous sommes pas réveillés** assez tôt.
Claude **ne s'est pas** bien **reposé**.

B. As with other verbs, questions with reflexives in the **passé composé** can be formed through intonation, by using **est-ce que**, and by using inversion. To form questions using inversion, the subject pronoun is placed after the auxiliary verb and the reflexive pronoun stays before the auxiliary verb.

Marie **s'est-elle** bien **débrouillée** en maths?
Où **vous êtes-vous rencontrés**?
T'es-tu arrêté à la boulangerie ce matin?

C. In some cases, the reflexive pronoun is not a direct but an indirect object. In this case, there is no agreement.*

Ils se sont **téléphoné**. (i.e., on téléphone **à** quelqu'un)
Ils se sont **parlé**. (i.e., on parle **à** quelqu'un)

This is a complex point that need not be taught actively at this time.

Similarly, there is no agreement when the reflexive verb is followed by a direct object. Compare :

Elle s'est **coupé** le doigt. (**Le doigt** is the direct object.)
Elle s'est **coupée**. (The reflexive pronoun **se** is the direct object.)

You may want to point out that reflexives are not used with a part of the body : *Elle a tourné le dos; Levez la main.*

This rule of no agreement applies in particular to expressions indicating that an action is performed on a part of the body :

Ils se sont **brossé** les dents.
Elle s'est **cassé** la jambe.

---
*For recognition only.

Ils viennent de se marier.

76% of French couples get married between the ages of 20 and 30 ; the average age for women is 23 and for men 25. 64% of all marriages take place in a church. In most cases, young couples seem to have a lot in common : age ; education ; social milieu ; profession. More than half the couples indicate that they lived together before getting married.

Mise en situation

Une histoire d'amour. Claude et Josselyne viennent de se marier. Claude parle avec sa cousine Nathalie.

NATHALIE Josselyne et toi, où est-ce que vous vous êtes rencontrés… ?

CLAUDE À une *conférence*. Nous nous sommes regardés, et tout de suite ça a été *le coup de foudre* ! Après cette première rencontre, je me suis débrouillé pour avoir son adresse. Je l'ai invitée à aller faire du ski. Nous nous sommes retrouvés à Chamonix. Nous nous sommes amusés comme des fous… !

NATHALIE C'est à ce moment-là que tu as eu ton accident ?

CLAUDE Oui, je me suis cassé la jambe. Josselyne s'est occupée de moi et après ça, nous ne nous sommes plus jamais quittés !

lecture
love at first sight

Substitution : (1) Je me suis bien débrouillé à l'examen. (*nous / vous / tu / Marc / Monique et Sylvie*) (2) Ils ne se sont pas rasés ce matin. (*tu / je / vous / mon frère / Marc et Serge*) (3) À quelle heure est-ce qu'elle s'est couchée ? (*tu / vous / vos parents / Janine / Pierre*)

Préparation

A. **Un matin comme les autres.** Ce que Marie-José a fait ce matin n'est pas différent de ce qu'elle fait tous les matins. Qu'est-ce qu'elle dit ?

Modèle se réveiller à six heures → **Je me suis réveillée à six heures.**

Repeat using *elle, nous, on.* Give new context (*Un matin pas comme les autres*) and repeat in negative.

1. se lever
2. se préparer
3. se laver
4. se brosser les dents
5. se peigner
6. s'occuper du chat
7. se dépêcher de partir
8. s'arrêter à la boulangerie

B. **Et un matin pas comme les autres.** Marie-Josée est fatiguée de sa routine habituelle et elle a décidé de prendre un jour de repos. Qu'est-ce qu'elle dit ?

Modèle se réveiller avant 10 h
Je ne me suis pas réveillée avant 10 h.

Point out that many people visit Evian, Vichy, and Vittel, where there are mineral waters that are reputed to have therapeutic effects for the liver, kidneys, and arthritis.

1. se lever tout de suite
2. se dépêcher de se préparer
3. se brosser les dents
4. se peigner
5. s'occuper du chat
6. s'habiller pour sortir

C. On va faire une cure à Évian. Il y a beaucoup de choses à faire quand on part en voyage. Indiquez ce que chaque membre de la famille Bertrand a fait le matin de leur départ pour Évian.

Modèle nous / se réveiller à 5 heures
Nous nous sommes réveillés à cinq heures.

1. je / se lever immédiatement
2. nous / se dépêcher
3. Solange / s'occuper des enfants
4. elle / bien se débrouiller
5. les enfants / s'habiller
6. Pierre et Gilles / se brosser les dents
7. tu / se souvenir de fermer les fenêtres
8. vous / s'occuper des valises

D. Mère poule et papa poule. Il y a des parents qui sont de vraies mères poules (*mother hens*). Monsieur Charrier est un de ces parents. Qu'est-ce qu'il dit à sa fille ?

Have students find additional items that might fit this context, using either reflexive or non-reflexive verbs.

Modèle se peigner → **Est-ce que tu t'es peignée ?**

1. se brosser les dents
2. se laver les mains
3. se brosser les cheveux
4. bien s'amuser chez tes amis
5. bien se débrouiller à l'école
6. se dépêcher de rentrer de l'école
7. se reposer un peu
8. se souvenir de ta leçon de piano

E. Au club de gymnastique. Isabelle travaille dans un club de gymnastique. Elle parle de ce qu'elle a fait hier.

Modèle se lever très tôt → **Je me suis levée très tôt.**

1. arriver au club à dix heures
2. faire des exercices de respiration
3. s'occuper de mes clients
4. prendre une douche
5. se reposer un peu
6. quitter le club à six heures et demie
7. s'arrêter chez des amis
8. rentrer chez moi à dix heures
9. boire un verre d'eau minérale
10. se coucher vers onze heures

Communication et vie pratique

A. Interview. Utilisez les phrases suivantes pour formuler des questions à poser à un(e) autre étudiant(e) de votre classe.

Exemple bien s'amuser hier → **Est-ce que tu t'es bien amusé(e) hier ?**

1. bien s'amuser hier
2. se réveiller tôt
3. se lever tout de suite
4. se dépêcher
5. s'arrêter chez des amis après les cours
6. se détendre un peu après le dîner
7. se coucher avant minuit
8. se reposer pendant le week-end

Have students ask yes-no questions to find out the exact time that another student got up or went to bed : e.g., *Est-ce que tu t'es couchée tôt ? Est-ce que tu t'es couché avant minuit ?*)

B. Hier. Racontez votre journée d'hier. Utilisez autant de verbes réfléchis que possible dans votre description. Par exemple, vous pouvez commencer par « Je me suis réveillé(e) à sept heures. Après ça… »

Good for written composition. Hand out page similar to daily calendar to each student. Then have them interview each other in groups of two to find out what the other person did at various times. They should fill out the calendar and use as the basis for an oral or written report.

C'est votre tour. Imaginez que vous êtes un des personnages d'un feuilleton romantique. Décrivez votre petit(e) ami(e), racontez votre histoire et répondez aux questions des autres étudiants. Indiquez, par exemple, où vous vous êtes rencontrés, ce qui s'est passé, etc.

If desired, students can base their conversations on soap opera couples or they could imagine other situations similar to the one described in the *Mise en situation.*

❧ Giving advice, suggestions, and orders
L'impératif des verbes réfléchis

Présentation

In the affirmative imperative, the reflexive pronoun follows the verb. In the negative imperative, it precedes the verb.

Dépêchez-**vous** !	Ne **vous** dépêchez pas !
Mariez-**vous** !	Ne **vous** mariez pas !
Brossez-**vous** les dents !	Ne **vous** brossez pas les dents !

The reflexive pronoun **te** changes to **toi** in the affirmative imperative.

Lève-**toi** !	Ne **te** lève pas !
Amuse-**toi** !	Ne **t'**amuse pas !
Coupe-**toi** les cheveux.	Ne **te** coupe pas les cheveux !

Mise en situation

C'est l'heure ! C'est l'heure de se lever, mais Stéphanie a encore sommeil…

MME CHEVRIER	Réveille-toi, Stéphanie !… Allez, vite, lève-toi, c'est l'heure !
STÉPHANIE	Laisse-moi dormir encore un peu… J'ai sommeil !
MME CHEVRIER	Stéphanie, voyons ! Ne *te recouche* pas… ! Tu exagères !
STÉPHANIE	Bon, bon, ne *te fâche* pas ! Je me lève…
MME CHEVRIER	Dépêche-toi de faire ta toilette.
STÉPHANIE	Je n'ai pas envie de me préparer…
MME CHEVRIER	Arrête-toi de *te plaindre* et brosse-toi les cheveux !
STÉPHANIE	Je ne trouve pas ma brosse…
MME CHEVRIER	*Tant pis !* Habille-toi vite ; tu vas être en retard !

Relationships between French children and their parents are generally good. Principal sources of conflict are clothing, bedtimes, and places children go with friends.

go back to bed

get angry

complaining

Too bad!

Préparation

A. Conseils. Gilbert va partir en vacances parce qu'il a envie de se reposer. Il parle avec ses amis qui lui donnent toutes sortes de conseils.

Modèle   Je vais me réveiller tôt. (mais non)
   Mais non, ne te réveille pas tôt.

   ou: Je vais bien m'amuser. (oui)
   Oui ! Amuse-toi bien.

1. Je vais bien me reposer. (oui)
2. Je vais m'occuper un peu de mon jardin. (mais non)
3. Je vais me préparer à partir. (oui)
4. Je vais me dépêcher de revenir. (mais non)
5. Je vais me détendre. (oui)
6. Je vais me lever tôt. (mais non)

Transformation : Dépêche-toi ! → Ne te dépêche pas. Dépêchez-vous. → Ne vous dépêchez pas. (1) Rase-toi. (2) Repose-toi. (3) Couche-toi. (4) Coupe-toi les cheveux. (5) Lavez-vous. (6) Levez-vous. (7) Amusez-vous bien. (8) Arrêtez-vous de travailler.
Transformation : Ne te réveille pas. → Réveille-toi. Ne vous réveillez pas. → Réveillez-vous. (1) Ne t'arrête pas de travailler. (2) Ne te lève pas. (3) Ne t'amuse pas. (4) Ne te dépêche pas. (5) Ne vous peignez pas. (6) Ne vous couchez pas. (7) Ne vous occupez pas du chat. (8) Ne vous détendez pas.

B. Chez le médecin. Jean-Luc ne se sent pas bien. Quels conseils est-ce que le médecin lui donne ?

Modèles   se coucher tôt → **Couchez-vous tôt.**
   ou :   manger trois repas par jour → **Mangez trois repas par jour.**

1. se détendre un peu
2. faire un peu de sport
3. ne pas boire trop de vin
4. ne pas avoir peur de dire ce que vous pensez
5. ne pas se dépêcher tout le temps
6. sortir plus souvent
7. se débrouiller pour avoir du temps libre
8. oublier vos soucis de temps en temps

Have students role-play situations at the doctor's office. One student (or several) will play the doctor and give advice to the patients who will describe their problems and ailments.

Communication et vie pratique

A. Avez-vous de l'autorité ? Est-ce que vous aimez donner des ordres ? Si oui, profitez de l'occasion et donnez des ordres à un(e) autre étudiant(e). Utilisez autant de verbes réfléchis que possible. L'autre étudiant(e) va décider s'il ou elle va accepter ou refuser ces ordres.

Suggested for oral work. *Option :* Have students give you orders, which you can accept or reject.

Exemple ÉTUDIANT(E) N° 1 : **Lève-toi à cinq heures du matin.**
ÉTUDIANT(E) N° 2 : **Non, je refuse de me lever à cinq heures du matin.**
ou: **Oui, c'est une bonne idée. Je vais me lever à cinq heures du matin.**

B. Conseils. Imaginez qu'un ami français (joué par un autre étudiant) vous parle de ses problèmes de santé. Écoutez-le avec sympathie et donnez-lui quelques conseils.

Exemple — **Je ne me sens pas très bien. J'ai mal à la gorge — c'est peut-être une angine.**
— **C'est dommage. Couche-toi tôt ce soir et va chez le médecin demain matin.**

C'est votre tour. Imaginez que vous êtes moniteur ou monitrice dans une colonie de vacances. Vous êtes chargé(e) d'un groupe de garçons / filles (joués par d'autres étudiants de la classe). C'est l'heure du réveil, mais ils / elles n'ont pas envie de se lever. Imaginez la conversation.

Have students give reasons why the campers wouldn't be ready to get up ; they can also think of good reasons why they should get up. *Option :* Role-play a situation in which students try to talk their roommate into getting up.

Intégration et perspectives

L'A B C des bonnes manières : Ce qu'il faut faire et ne pas faire

En général, on peut dire que la politesse et les bonnes manières sont basées sur le respect des autres. *Cependant*, ce qui constitue les bonnes manières peut varier d'un pays à l'autre. Il est donc bon de savoir ce qu'on doit faire ou ne pas faire pour *éviter* les *malentendus* et les *faux-pas*. Voici quelques conseils pour les étudiants qui se préparent à visiter un pays francophone européen.

however

avoid / misunderstandings / blunders

À table

Tenez-vous bien à table. Ne parlez pas la bouche pleine. Ne posez pas les *coudes* sur la table, *ni* les pieds sur la chaise de votre voisin — *sauf*, peut-être, si vous êtes en famille ou entre jeunes. N'oubliez pas qu'en France, il faut garder les deux mains sur la table pendant le repas. Ne gardez pas la main gauche sous la table comme vous avez l'habitude de le faire aux États-Unis. Ça risque d'amuser vos amis français.

sit up properly

elbows / nor / except

Aux États-Unis, vous devez *repasser* votre *fourchette* dans votre main droite chaque fois que vous avez fini de *couper* un petit morceau de viande. En France, *ça ne se fait pas*. Gardez votre fourchette dans la main gauche. **put back / fork** **cut** **that is not done**

Ne vous servez* pas avant d'être invité à le faire. Quand l'hôte ou l'hôtesse vous demande de vous servir une deuxième fois, répondez : « Oui, avec plaisir » si vous avez envie de reprendre un peu de ce qui vous est proposé. Mais attention, « merci » veut dire « Non, merci, je n'ai plus faim ». Et surtout, ne dites jamais « Je suis plein. » C'est très vulgaire en français.

Quand vous êtes invité à dîner, il est toujours poli — et gentil — d'apporter quelques fleurs, des bonbons ou un petit cadeau. Si vous apportez des fleurs, n'apportez jamais de chrysanthèmes. Ils sont associés avec l'idée de mort et de *deuil*. N'arrivez jamais en avance. En fait, il est bon d'arriver quelques minutes en retard pour laisser à vos hôtes le temps de s'occuper des préparatifs de dernière minute. **grieving**

Rencontres et visites

Ne soyez pas choqué. Les Français, même les hommes quelquefois, s'embrassent sur les joues quand ils rencontrent des parents ou des amis. Par contre, c'est vous qui allez les choquer si vous les embrassez sur la bouche ! Ça ne se fait pas, même entre parents et enfants. C'est réservé aux *amoureux*. Les Français *se serrent* aussi très souvent *la main*. On se serre la main chaque fois qu'on se rencontre et qu'on se quitte, excepté, bien sûr, si on travaille dans le même *endroit* ou si on se rencontre plusieurs fois par jour. **lovers / shake hands** **place**

Ne *tutoyez* pas tout le monde ! On se tutoie entre amis et en famille. Attendez qu'on vous le demande. C'est une marque d'affection et *d'amitié*. **say *tu* (*vouvoyer* : to say *vous*) / friendship**

Un conseil général : quand vous n'êtes pas sûr de ce que vous devez faire, observez d'abord les gens autour de vous et laissez-les prendre l'initiative !

---

*Servir is conjugated like **partir** and **sortir** : je sers, tu sers, il / elle / on sert, nous servons, vous servez, ils / elles servent.

On s'embrasse sur les joues.

Compréhension. Les Johnson, une famille américaine, rendent visite à des Français. Indiquez si, en France, les actions suivantes sont considérées comme de bonnes manières ou non. Expliquez pourquoi.

1. Les Johnson sont invités chez les Grandjean. Ils arrivent dix minutes avant l'heure indiquée parce qu'ils ne veulent pas faire attendre leurs hôtes.
2. Ils se sont arrêtés chez un fleuriste et ils ont acheté de beaux chrysanthèmes pour les Grandjean.
3. Mme Johnson veut montrer ses bonnes manières et elle fait très attention à repasser sa fourchette dans sa main droite chaque fois qu'elle se prépare à porter à sa bouche le morceau de viande qu'elle vient de couper.
4. La conversation tourne à la politique et la discussion devient très animée. M. Johnson commence à tutoyer son voisin de table, le beau-père de M. Grandjean.
5. M. Johnson a envie de reprendre un peu de soufflé. Il se tourne vers sa voisine et dit « Pouvez-vous me passer le soufflé, s'il vous plaît ? »
6. Mme Grandjean remarque que Mme Johnson garde sa main gauche sous la table. Elle est inquiète et elle se demande si Mme Johnson a mal au bras.
7. Mme Grandjean demande à M. Johnson s'il veut reprendre un peu de dessert. M. Johnson a beaucoup mangé et il n'a plus faim. Il répond : « Non merci, madame, votre tarte est délicieuse mais je suis plein. »
8. Le fils des Johnson ne veut pas faire de faux-pas. Il observe les gens autour de lui. Il remarque que le fils des Grandjean tutoie un monsieur d'une trentaine d'années qu'il appelle « tonton Pierre ». Il décide qu'il peut faire la même chose et qu'on vouvoie seulement les gens plus âgés.

Notes culturelles: *Les expressions figuratives*

Un des aspects les plus fascinants d'une langue est l'utilisation de certains mots et expressions dans un sens *figuré*. Leur utilisation est particulièrement fréquente dans la conversation familière. Voici, par exemple, quelques expressions qui se réfèrent au corps humain.

Tu me casses les pieds.   *You're bothering me.*

figurative

Suggestion : Introduce other expressions (*faire du pied, se casser la figure, avoir une dent contre quelqu'un, manger sur le pouce*).

Ne vous cassez pas la tête.   *Don't worry.*

Il a mis les pieds dans le plat.   *He put his foot in his mouth.*

Ça saute aux yeux.   *That's obvious.*

Il a le bras long.   *He has influence (connections).*

C'est un casse-cou.   *He's a daredevil.*

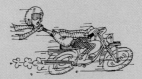

Tu es tombé sur la tête.   *You're crazy.*

Communication et vie pratique

A. Vous êtes invités. Imaginez que vous êtes invité(e) à déjeuner chez des Français. Certains étudiants jouent le rôle des Français et d'autres jouent le rôle des visiteurs américains. Jouez la scène. Les Français vont (1) dire bonjour, serrer la main de leurs amis (ou les embrasser), et indiquer qu'ils sont heureux de voir leurs invités ; (2) inviter leurs amis à entrer et à s'asseoir ; (3) offrir un apéritif à leurs invités ; (4) demander à leurs amis s'ils ont fait un bon voyage, demander des nouvelles de la famille, et parler de chose et autre ; (5) inviter leurs invités à passer à table ; (6) indiquer où chaque personne va s'asseoir.

Extend activity to include simulation of conversation during dinner.

B. L'A B C des bonnes manières. Expliquez à des Français ce qu'il faut faire ou ne pas faire aux États-Unis quand on est à table ou en visite.

Option : L'A B C des bonnes manières pour étudiants.

C. Apprenez à vous débrouiller. Comment allez-vous vous débrouiller si vous vous trouvez dans les situations suivantes ? Si vous n'avez pas encore appris le vocabulaire nécessaire, employez d'autres mots et même quelquefois des gestes si c'est nécessaire.

Remind students that they should try to find alternative ways of saying something that they don't have the vocabulary for instead of trying to translate word for word.

1. You have a bad cold and need to buy some cough medicine.
2. You broke a tooth and need to have it taken care of.
3. You have to explain to a doctor that you have a cut that is infected and that you may need a shot.
4. You have a splinter in your finger and need help to get it out.
5. You have a prescription for airsickness pills that you need to have refilled.
6. You lost your glasses and need to have them replaced.

D. Les photos parlent. Imaginez ce que les personnes sur les photos suivantes sont en train de dire… ou de penser.

Bring in other photos that students can use or have them find their own photos.

● *Vocabulaire*

Noms

les parties du corps (voir p. 264)

les douleurs et les symptômes (voir p. 264)

les maladies et les remèdes (voir p. 264)

le corps et la santé

les **abdominaux** (m)   *sit-ups*
les **bains remous** (m)   *whirlpool*
le **corps**   *body*
le **coude**   *elbow*
la **cure d'amaigrissement**   *weight-loss program*
la **douche**   *shower*
la **gymnastique**   *gymnastics*
° l'**infection** (f)
le **médicament**   *medicine*
le **poids**   *weight*
le **poumon**   *lung*
le **remède**   *treatment, remedy*
la **respiration**   *breathing*
° la **vitamine**
la **vue**   *sight*

d'autres noms

° l'**affection** (f)
l'**amitié** (f)   *friendship*
les **amoureux** (m)   *lovers*
° le **chrysanthème**
° le **club**
° la **confession**
la **conférence**   *lecture*
la **conquête**   *conquest*
le **conseil**   *advice*
le **converti, la convertie**   *convert*
le **coup de foudre**   *love at first sight*
le **deuil**   *grieving*
l'**écran** (m)   *screen*
l'**endroit** (m)   *place*
le **faux-pas**   *blunder*
la **fourchette**   *fork*
l'**habitude** (f)   *habit*
l'**hôte** (m)   *host*
l'**hôtesse** (f)   *hostess*
° le **magazine**
le **malentendu**   *misunderstanding*
° les **manières**
° le **membre**
le **pâté**   *block (of houses)*
le **plaisir**   *pleasure*
la **politesse**   *politeness*

les **préparatifs** (m)   *preparations*
la **route**   *route, way*
la **vitrine**   *display window*

Verbes

les verbes réfléchis (voir pp. 266–267)

d'autres verbes

apporter   *to bring*
avaler   *to swallow*
° **constituer**
couper   *to cut*
se demander   *to wonder*
éviter   *to avoid*
se **fâcher**   *to get angry*
se **plaindre**   *to complain*
se **recoucher**   *to go back to bed*
repasser   *to put back*
risquer   *to risk*
° **résister**
se **serrer la main**   *to shake hands*
se **servir**   *to serve oneself*
soulever   *to lift*
suer   *to sweat*
tousser   *to cough*
tutoyer   *to call someone "tu"*
vouvoyer   *to call someone "vous"*

Adjectifs

° **allergique**
° **associé(e)**
° **basé(e)**
choqué(e)   *shocked*
étalé(e)   *spread out, displayed*
physique   *physical*
plein(e)   *full*
° **réservé(e)**
° **vulgaire**

Divers

avoir mal   *to hurt*
brûler la chandelle par les deux bouts   *to burn the candle at both ends*
ça ne se fait pas   *that is not done*
cependant   *however*
donc   *therefore*
en route   *on the way*
excepté   *except*
faire du jogging   *to jog*
parmi   *among*
tenir le coup   *to hold up (under stress)*

12

CHAPITRE DOUZE

Communication objectives

Describing what we wear and how we look

1. Referring to someone or something already mentioned
2. Talking about what we wear
3. Comparing and contrasting things and people
4. Talking about the best and the worst

Structures

Les mots et la vie : L'habillement

Les compléments d'objet indirect

Les verbes conjugués comme **mettre**

Le comparatif

Le superlatif

L'apparence

Mise en scène

Aux Galeries Lafayette

Micheline et Robert ont décidé d'aller faire des courses aux Galeries Lafayette. Voici les conversations qu'ils ont eues aux différents *rayons*.

Have students scan the conversations and tell what Robert wants to buy and what Micheline needs.

departments

Au *guichet* des renseignements

booth, window

MICHELINE	Excusez-moi, madame, mais est-ce que vous *pourriez* me dire à quel *étage* sont les vêtements de sport?

could
floor

L'EMPLOYÉE	Pour hommes ou pour femmes, madame?
MICHELINE	Pour hommes.
L'EMPLOYÉE	Au troisième étage.
MICHELINE	Et les chaussures?
L'EMPLOYÉE	Au deuxième.
MICHELINE	Merci beaucoup, madame. Eh bien, Robert, tu vas chercher ton jogging et moi, je vais voir ce qu'ils ont comme chaussures.
ROBERT	On se retrouve au restaurant — disons dans une heure.
MICHELINE	D'accord.

Faire du lèche-vitrines — to go window shopping

Au rayon des vêtements de sport

L'EMPLOYÉ	Bonjour, monsieur. Est-ce que je peux vous aider?
ROBERT	Oui, monsieur, je voudrais *essayer* un de ces joggings.

to try on

L'EMPLOYÉ	Quelle *taille*, s'il vous plaît?

size

285

ROBERT	Cinquante-quatre.	
L'EMPLOYÉ	Voici un modèle qui est très populaire. Nos *salons d'essayage* sont à gauche, monsieur… Cette couleur vous va très bien, monsieur, mais c'est peut-être un peu trop grand.	dressing rooms
ROBERT	Non, c'est très confortable — pour faire du sport il vaut mieux que ce ne soit pas trop *serré*.	tight
L'EMPLOYÉ	Alors, monsieur, vous le prenez ?	
ROBERT	Oui. Ça fait combien, s'il vous plaît ?	
L'EMPLOYÉ	Quatre cent dix francs.	

Au rayon des chaussures

L'EMPLOYÉE	Bonjour, madame. *Puis*-je vous aider ?	can
MICHELINE	Je cherche une paire de chaussures. C'est pour porter au bureau. Il faut qu'elles soient *à la fois* élégantes et confortables.	both
L'EMPLOYÉE	Nous avons exactement ce que vous cherchez : des souliers en *cuir* et avec des *talons* pas trop hauts. C'est parfait pour la femme qui travaille. Quelle est votre *pointure* ?	leather / heels
		size
MICHELINE	Trente-huit. Vous les avez en bleu marine ?	
L'EMPLOYÉE	Non, pas dans votre pointure. Mais nous les avons en noir. Vous voulez les essayer ?	
MICHELINE	Oui, s'il vous plaît… Ils sont parfaits. Vous êtes sûre que vous ne les avez pas en bleu ?	
L'EMPLOYÉE	Je vais *vérifier*.	to check

Compréhension. Répondez aux questions suivantes selon les renseignements donnés dans le texte.

Indiquez…

1. où se trouve le rayon des vêtements de sport.
2. où se trouvent les chaussures.
3. ce que Robert a l'intention d'acheter.
4. sa taille ou sa pointure, selon le cas, et ses préférences (style, confort, etc.).
5. ce que Micheline a l'intention d'acheter.
6. sa taille ou sa pointure, selon le cas, et ses préférences.
7. ce que Robert et Micheline vont faire après.

Have students rewrite conversations in which Robert and Micheline each buy different items.

Notes culturelles: *La mode*

La France est depuis longtemps la capitale de la *haute couture* et les noms des grands couturiers et couturières français sont *connus* partout dans le monde. Courrèges, Chanel, Givenchy, Saint-Laurent, Cardin évoquent l'image de vêtements élégants et chers. *[high fashion / known]*

Mais la mode française est en train d'évoluer. Le *fait* que la haute couture coûte très cher et n'est pas *à la portée* de tout le monde explique le développement du « *prêt-à-porter* ». Mais le prêt-à-porter a aussi ses couturiers—Cacharel, Hechter, Sonia Rykiel, par exemple — qui maintiennent la qualité et l'esthétique de leurs créations. *[fact / within reach / ready-to-wear]*

Depuis les années 60, les blue-jeans, les tee-shirts et les sweat-shirts (beaucoup portent le nom d'une université américaine) font partie de la *garde-robe* des jeunes Français. Le blue-jean et le tee-shirt sont des vêtements démocratiques : ils cachent les différences sociales *tandis que* la haute couture les met en évidence. Mais pour les Français, même un tee-shirt *se porte* avec style, et le chic et l'élégance traditionnels des Français n'ont pas *disparu*. *[wardrobe / whereas / is worn / disappeared]*

Les mots et la vie : *L'habillement*

Étudiez le vocabulaire et ensuite faites les activités indiquées.

Les vêtements et les chaussures
Pour compléter l'habillement, il faut ajouter des chaussettes *(socks)* ou un collant *(panty-hose)* et des sous-vêtements *(underwear)* et pour la nuit un pyjama ou une chemise de nuit.

 des jeans
 un pantalon
 une jupe
 une robe
 une chemise
 un tee-shirt
 un pull-over
 un chemisier
 une veste

 un complet
 un tailleur
 un manteau
 des chaussures
 des souliers
 des bottes
 des (chaussures de) tennis

 des sandales
 un short
 un maillot de bain
 un chapeau
 une cravate

Les mesures
La taille : pour les vêtements, on dit : « Quelle est votre **taille** ? »
La pointure : pour les chaussures, on dit : « Quelle est votre **pointure** ? »
Notez que les tailles et les pointures sont différentes en Europe. Pour les équivalents, consultez le tableau suivant.

Table de comparaison de tailles

Robes, chemisiers et *tricots* femmes   knitwear

France	36	38	40	42	44	46
États-Unis	8	10	12	14	16	18

Bas et collants femmes   stockings

France	1	2	3	4	5
États-Unis	8½	9	9½	10	10½

Chaussures femmes

France	36½	37	37½	38	39
États-Unis	5	5½	6	6½	7½

Chaussures hommes

France	41	42	43	44	45
États-Unis	7½	8½	9	10	11

Costumes hommes

France	36	38	40	42	44	46
États-Unis	35	36	37	38	39	40

Chemises hommes

France	37	38	39	40	41	42
États-Unis	14½	15	15½	16	16½	17

Tricots hommes

France	36	38	40	42	44	46
États-Unis	46	48	51	54	56	59

Les couleurs

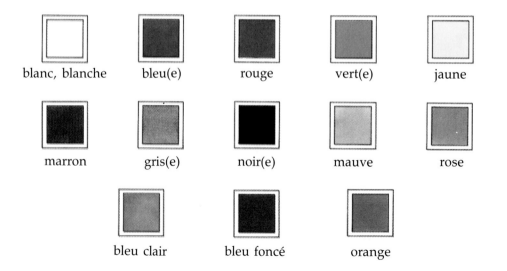

blanc, blanche   bleu(e)   rouge   vert(e)   jaune

marron   gris(e)   noir(e)   mauve   rose

bleu clair   bleu foncé   orange

Note that **marron** and **orange** are invariable.

une robe **marron** des chaussettes **orange**

When modified by **foncé** or **clair**, all colors become invariable.

une veste **bleu foncé**

Pour les cheveux, on dit « Il a les cheveux bruns. » *(dark)*

châtains *(brown)*
roux *(red)*
blonds

Pour les yeux, on dit « Elle a les yeux bleus. »

verts *(green)*
bruns *(brown)*

Les commentaires et les compliments
Ça vous (te) va bien. *(That looks good on you.)*
Cette couleur (ce style) vous (te) va bien.
Ça ne vous (te) va pas bien.
C'est trop grand / petit.
C'est trop long / court *(short)*.
C'est très à la mode *(in fashion)*.
Ce n'est pas à la mode. C'est démodé *(out-of-style)*.
C'est très chic.
C'est très élégant.
C'est très mignon *(cute)*.

Point out that the French have a tendency to downplay compliments, unlike Americans whose typical response is to acknowledge the compliment by smiling and saying thank you (e.g., « *J'aime bien ta veste. Elle est très jolie.* » « *Oh, tu trouves? Je l'ai achetée en solde l'année dernière.* »)

Have students practice giving compliments in various situations (e.g., clothing, dinner, a favor done for them, a gift).

A. Décrivez les vêtements que vous portez dans les circonstances suivantes :

— pour venir à l'université
— quand vous êtes chez vous pendant le week-end
— pour faire du sport
— pour aller dîner dans un restaurant élégant
— quand vous allez à la plage

B. Imaginez que vous êtes dans une boutique de mode. Expliquez au vendeur ou à la vendeuse ce que vous cherchez (pour vous ou pour une autre personne). Répondez aux questions et suggestions du vendeur — joué(e) par un(e) autre étudiant(e) — et donnez votre opinion sur les différents vêtements qu'on vous propose.

C. À la terrasse d'un café. Imaginez que vous êtes à la terrasse d'un café. Vous regardez et vous décrivez les gens qui passent.

Explorations
✤ Referring to someone or something already mentioned
Les compléments d'objet indirect

Présentation

The object of a verb can either be direct

Nous avons vendu **notre voiture**.

or indirect

Nous avons vendu notre voiture **à M. Gérard**.

Indirect objects are introduced by the preposition **à** :

Je donne les livres **à** Pierre.
Elle parle **aux** étudiants.

The following indirect object pronouns can replace **à** + A NOUN :

Les pronoms compléments d'objet indirect	
Il **me** parle.	Il **nous** parle.
Il **te** parle.	Il **vous** parle.
Il **lui** parle.	Il **leur** parle.

Note that only the third-person indirect object pronouns differ from direct object pronouns. **Lui** means either *to him* or *to her*; **leur** means *to them*.

Je parle **à Anne**.	Je **lui** parle.
Je donne le livre **à Paul**.	Je **lui** donne le livre.
Je téléphone **à mes amis**.	Je **leur** téléphone.

A. Indirect object pronouns, like direct object pronouns, are placed directly before the verb of which they are the object.

Il **te** téléphone.	Il **t'**a téléphoné.	Il va **te** téléphoner.
Il ne **te** répond pas.	Il ne **t'**a pas répondu.	Il ne va pas **te** répondre.
Te téléphone-t-il ?	**T'**a-t-il téléphoné ?	Va-t-il **te** téléphoner ?

B. In affirmative commands the indirect object pronoun follows the verb, and **moi** and **toi** replace **me** and **te**. In negative commands, the indirect object pronoun remains in its usual place before the verb, and its form does not change.

Répondez-**lui**.	Ne **lui** répondez pas.
Apportez-**moi** votre livre.	Ne **m'**apportez pas votre livre.
Expliquez-**lui** vos problèmes.	Ne **lui** expliquez pas vos problèmes.
Donnez-**leur** un cadeau.	Ne **leur** donnez pas de cadeau.

C. When both direct and indirect object pronouns occur in the same sentence, they are placed in the following order in all uses except affirmative commands.*

me te nous vous	*before*	le la l' les	*before*	lui leur

---

*For recognition only.

Remind students that in the *passé composé*, only when a direct-object pronoun precedes the verb does the past participle agree with it. The past participle never agrees with an indirect-object pronoun (e.g., *Je vous ai parlé, mademoiselle, et je vous ai invitée à danser.*)

Double-object pronouns are introduced here for the sake of completeness. However, owing to the complexity of the topic and to the fact that use of double-object pronouns can often be circumvented without impeding communication, they are introduced for recognition only.

Il **me l**'a montré.
Je **la leur** ai expliquée.
Nous ne **les lui** avons pas vendus.
Ne **nous les** apporte pas maintenant.

D. In affirmative commands the pronouns are separated by hyphens and
are placed in the following order :*

le la les	before	moi lui nous leur

Expliquez-**le-moi**.   Ne **me l**'expliquez pas.
Apportez-**les-nous**.   Ne **nous les** apportez pas.
Rendez-**le-lui**.   Ne **le lui** rendez pas.
Montrez-**les-leur**.   Ne **les leur** montrez pas.

Mise en situation

Noël approche… Madame et Monsieur Humbert se demandent ce qu'ils
vont acheter comme cadeaux de Noël pour leurs enfants.

M. HUMBERT   Tu as déjà acheté les cadeaux pour les enfants ?

MME HUMBERT   Non, je ne sais pas ce que je vais leur acheter… Ils sont trop
                 grands maintenant pour leur *offrir** des jouets…

M. HUMBERT   Achetons-leur des vêtements…

***Offrir** and **ouvrir** *(to open)* are **-ir** verbs that are conjugated like regular **-er** verbs :
j'offre, tu offres, il / elle / on offre, nous offrons, vous offrez, ils / elles offrent.

Substitution: (1) Chantal me téléphone le samedi. *(te / lui / vous / leur)* (2) Il ne me parle pas. *(lui / nous / leur / vous / te)* (3) Il m'a apporté une glace. *(lui / nous / leur / te / vous)* (4) Donnez-lui votre adresse. *(nous / moi / leur / lui)* (5) Elle ne va pas lui parler. *(leur / vous / me / te / nous). Transformation :* Le professeur explique la leçon aux étudiants. → Le professeur leur explique la leçon. (1) Marc téléphone à Suzanne. (2) Nous rendons visite à nos amis anglais. (3) Je parle souvent à mon voisin. (4) Mon frère a vendu sa moto à Georges. (5) Elle a donné de l'argent à Danielle et Richard. (6) Elle a loué son appartement à M. et Mme Ménard. (7) Téléphone à ton patron. (8) Donnez du lait aux enfants. (9) Ne parlez pas aux autres. (10) Je voudrais donner quelque chose à mes parents.

to offer, give

French people give gifts on birthdays, saint's days, Mother's and Father's days. Gifts are also given at Christmas and for the New Year. A gift of money given to children for the New Year is called *les étrennes.*

Noël à Paris

MME HUMBERT	Ce n'est pas une mauvaise idée. Henri grandit si vite. Les vêtements que je lui ai achetés l'hiver dernier ne lui vont plus…
M. HUMBERT	Alors, achete-lui un *anorak*… Et pour Annette, tu as une idée ?
MME HUMBERT	Je pense que je vais lui acheter une guitare…
M. HUMBERT	Et à toi ? Qu'est-ce que je te donne ?
MME HUMBERT	Si tu veux *me faire plaisir*, offre-moi un lave-vaisselle !

*(marge: **ski jacket**, **to please me**)*

Préparation

A. Générosité. Monsieur Robert, un homme d'affaires, a acheté des cadeaux pour sa famille et ses employés. Qu'est-ce qu'il leur a donné ?

> **Modèle**   à ses parents / un appareil-photo
> **Il leur a donné un appareil-photo.**

1. à son fils / des jouets
2. à sa secrétaire / du parfum
3. à ses clients / du vin
4. à ses employés / des chocolats
5. à sa femme / des bijoux
6. aux enfants du quartier / des bonbons

B. Conversation. Jean interroge Michelle au sujet de ce qui s'est passé pendant la journée. Donnez les réponses de Michelle.

> **Modèle**   Est-ce que tu as téléphoné à tes parents ? (non)
> **Non, je ne leur ai pas téléphoné.**

1. Est-ce que tu as montré ton article à ton patron ? (oui)
2. Est-ce que mon client suisse m'a téléphoné ? (oui)
3. Est-ce qu'il t'a parlé de ses problèmes ? (non)
4. Est-ce qu'il va me téléphoner demain ? (oui)
5. Est-ce que tes parents vont nous rendre visite dimanche ? (non)
6. Est-ce que Paul nous a rendu nos disques ? (non)
7. Est-ce que je t'ai rendu ton argent ? (oui)

C. Indécision. Il y a des gens qui changent d'avis comme de chemise. Jean-Luc est une de ces personnes. Une minute, c'est « oui », l'autre c'est « non ». Qu'est-ce qu'il dit ?

(marge: Repeat, going from negative to affirmative: Ne m'apportez pas de sandwich—Apportez-moi un sandwich.)

> **Modèle**   Apportez-moi un sandwich.
> **Ne m'apportez pas de sandwich.**

1. Téléphone-nous ce soir.
2. Parle-moi de tes voyages.
3. Montre-leur tes revues.
4. Donne-moi ton opinion.
5. Demandez-lui pourquoi elle est triste.
6. Répondez-moi.

Communication et vie pratique

Suggestion: Have students work in small groups and report back their partners' answers.

A. Interview. Utilisez les suggestions suivantes pour poser des questions aux autres étudiants.

> **Exemple**   tes parents / te rendre quelquefois visite à l'université
> **Est-ce que tes parents te rendent quelquefois visite à l'université?**

1. tes amis / te téléphoner souvent
2. ta famille / te rendre souvent visite
3. tes amis / te parler de leurs problèmes
4. tes professeurs / te poser des questions difficiles
5. tes amis / t'acheter quelque chose pour ton anniversaire
6. tes amis / te donner quelquefois des conseils

B. J'ai une autre suggestion. Un(e) ami(e) vous a fait les propositions suivantes. Allez-vous accepter ou suggérer quelque chose d'autre?

> **Exemple**   Est-ce que je peux te parler de mon travail?
> **Oui, parle-moi de ton travail.**
> *ou:*   **Non, ne me parle pas de ton travail. Parle-moi de tes voyages.**

1. Est-ce que je peux te téléphoner ce soir?
2. Est-ce que je peux te montrer mes photos de voyage?
3. Est-ce que je peux te donner mon numéro de téléphone?
4. Est-ce que je peux t'apporter un sandwich?
5. Est-ce que je peux te rendre visite pendant l'été?
6. Est-ce que je peux t'acheter des fleurs?

Students can also be asked to suggest gifts for other members of the class and their teacher.

C'est votre tour. Discutez avec un(e) ami(e) ce que vous allez offrir comme cadeau de Noël ou comme cadeau d'anniversaire à différentes personnes.

La nouvelle mode sportive

❧Talking about what we wear
Les verbes conjugués comme *mettre*

Présentation

The verb **mettre** *(to place, to put, to put on)* is irregular:

mettre	
je **mets**	nous **mettons**
tu **mets**	vous **mettez**
il / elle / on **met**	ils / elles **mettent**
passé composé : j'**ai mis**	

Qu'est-ce que tu vas **mettre** pour sortir?
Mets ton joli complet gris.
Je ne **mets** pas de sucre dans mon café.
Où est-ce que tu **as mis** mon stylo?

A. Mettre has several idiomatic uses:

mettre la table   *to set the table*   Est-ce que tu **as mis** la table?
se mettre à   *to start to*   Il **s'est mis à** pleuvoir.
se mettre à table   *to sit down to*   Nous allons **nous mettre à**
  eat   table.
se mettre en colère   *to get angry*   Il **se met** facilement **en colère**.

B. Other verbs conjugated like **mettre** are:

permettre   *to allow, to permit*   Elle ne **permet** pas à sa fille de
                                       sortir seule.
promettre   *to promise*   J'**ai promis** à mes parents de
                                       leur rendre visite ce soir.
admettre   *to admit*   J'**admets** que j'ai eu tort.
remettre   *to hand in, to postpone*   **Remettez**-moi vos devoirs.
                                    Ne **remettez** pas à demain ce
                                       que vous pouvez faire
                                       aujourd'hui.

Substitution: (1) Je mets la table. *(Pierre et Marc / tu / Janine / vous / nous)*
(2) Qu'est-ce que tu mets pour sortir? *(vous / Jean-Luc / Roger et Martine / tu / je)*
(3) Où est-ce que j'ai mis la lettre? *(nous / vous / on / Patrick / ma sœur)* (4) Il s'est mis en colère. *(je / nous / mon frère / Véronique / ses parents / tu)* (5) Il a promis à Sylvie de préparer le repas. *(je / nous / tu / vous / Marc / les autres).*

  Note that both **permettre** and **promettre** take indirect object pronouns in French: **permettre à quelqu'un de faire quelque chose; promettre à quelqu'un de faire quelque chose.**

Mise en situation

Un compromis acceptable. Martine a envie de sortir ce soir mais Sébastien a déjà d'autres projets. *Heureusement*, ils trouvent une solution.

fortunately

MARTINE	Tu es libre ce soir ?
SÉBASTIEN	Non, j'ai promis à ma sœur de l'accompagner à une *soirée*... Ma mère ne lui permet pas de sortir seule le soir.
MARTINE	Zut... *C'est dommage*...
SÉBASTIEN	Si tu veux, tu peux venir avec nous...
MARTINE	Oui, mais qu'est-ce que je vais mettre ? Je n'ai *rien de joli*.
SÉBASTIEN	Mais si ! Mets ta petite robe bleue ; elle te va si bien... !
MARTINE	Bon, alors... Vous pouvez venir me chercher vers huit heures... ?
SÉBASTIEN	*C'est promis.*

party

that's a pity

nothing pretty

you can count on it

Have students note that although dating customs are changing in France, French young people tend to go out more often in groups and are less likely to pair off than Americans.

Préparation

A. Qu'est-ce qu'on va mettre ? Véronique et ses amis parlent de ce qu'ils vont mettre pour aller au concert ce soir. Qu'est-ce qu'ils disent ?

> **Modèle** Henri / pantalon gris → **Henri met un pantalon gris.**

1. vous / jupe
2. Roger / chemise blanche
3. Suzanne / robe noire
4. nous / cravate
5. je / chemisier
6. tu / complet bleu

Repeat in passé composé (Henri a mis un pantalon gris.)

B. Promesses. Il n'est jamais trop tard pour prendre de bonnes résolutions. Voici ce que différentes personnes ont promis de faire.

> **Modèle** Pierre / sa mère / écrire plus souvent
> **Pierre a promis à sa mère d'écrire plus souvent.**

1. je / ma petite sœur / réparer son vélo
2. nous / le professeur / faire nos devoirs
3. tu / ton patron / arriver à l'heure
4. les enfants / leurs parents / ranger leur chambre
5. Catherine / son fiancé / prendre une décision
6. vous / votre mère / aider un peu à la maison

Have students repeat using indirect object pronouns in their answers (e.g., Pierre lui a promis d'écrire plus souvent.)

Communication et vie pratique

A. On change de rôle. Imaginez que vous êtes le professeur. Qu'est-ce que vous allez permettre et ne pas permettre à vos étudiants de faire ? Par exemple, est-ce que vous allez leur permettre de dormir en classe ? De ne pas remettre leurs devoirs ? D'être souvent en retard ?

Have students become « futurs parents » and indicate what they would permit their children to do and what they would not allow them to do (e.g., Je ne vais pas leur permettre d'avoir leur propre téléphone).

B. Les bonnes résolutions. Le début du trimestre est le temps des bonnes résolutions. Qu'est-ce que vous avez promis de faire ou de ne pas faire ce trimestre ?

> Exemple J'ai promis de mieux écouter en classe et de ne pas remettre mon travail à la dernière minute.

Students might also want to list their New Year's resolutions.

C'est votre tour. Vous avez oublié que vous avez promis à un(e) ami(e) d'aller à un concert avec lui (elle) et à un(e) autre d'aller ensemble à une soirée. Expliquez-leur la situation et essayez de trouver une solution acceptable pour chaque personne.

Have students role-play additional situations where they discuss what they can wear to various functions.

❧ Comparing and contrasting things and people
Le comparatif

Présentation

Comparative constructions are used to compare two things, individuals, or actions. In English, comparatives are formed by adding the suffix *-er (faster, longer)* or by using the adverbs *more, less,* or *as (more quickly, less intelligent, as big)*.

A. In French, comparisons of adjectives can take three forms :

aussi... que	*as . . . as*	Il est **aussi grand que** sa sœur.
plus... que	*more (-er) . . . than*	Il est **plus grand que** son frère.
moins... que	*less (-er) . . . than*	Il est **moins grand que** son père.

Mets cette veste. Elle est beaucoup **plus chaude que** ton pull. Ces chaussures sont **moins confortables que** les autres. Est-ce que Pierre est **aussi sympa que** son frère ?

The same constructions are used to compare adverbs :

aussi... que	Je marche **aussi vite que** Robert.
plus... que	Je marche **plus vite que** Michel.
moins... que	Je marche **moins vite que** Monique.

Est-ce que les vêtements coûtent **aussi cher** en France **qu'**aux États-Unis ?
Mes enfants ne travaillent pas **aussi bien que** leurs cousins.
Vous vous levez beaucoup **plus tôt que** moi.

Point out that *cher* functions as an invariable adverb in the verb phrase *coûter cher*.

B. The following expressions of quantity are combined with **que** to compare amounts of things.

autant de + NOUN + **que** *as much (many) . . . as*	Tu as **autant d'argent que** Jean.
plus de + NOUN + **que** *more . . . than*	Tu as **plus d'argent que** Suzanne.
moins de + NOUN + **que** *less . . . than*	Tu as **moins d'argent que** Mireille.

Est-ce que l'apparence a **autant d'importance** pour les hommes **que** pour les femmes?

Il y a **plus de choix** dans ce magasin **que** dans l'autre.

Nous avons **moins de temps** libre **que** le trimestre passé.

Autant, **plus**, and **moins** are also used in adverbial expressions to compare how much or how little one does something.

Nous travaillons **autant que** Paul.
Nous travaillons **plus que** Serge.
Nous travaillons **moins que** Sophie.

Point out the expressions *de plus en plus* and *de moins en moins*.

C. Bon has an irregular comparative form, which is equivalent to *better* in English.

Le comparatif de *bon*		
	Singular	*Plural*
Masculine	meilleur	meilleurs
Feminine	meilleure	meilleures

Cette boutique de mode est **meilleure que** l'autre.
Les prix sont **meilleurs** ici.

D. The adverb **bien** also has an irregular form, **mieux**, which means *better*.

Est-ce vrai que les Français s'habillent **mieux que** les Américains?
On travaille **mieux** après une bonne nuit de sommeil.
Ça va de **mieux** en **mieux**!

Mise en situation

Dans une boutique de vêtements. Thierry veut acheter une veste. Il a déjà essayé plusieurs modèles.

LE VENDEUR   À mon avis cette veste-ci vous va mieux. Elle est plus longue et elle est moins serrée à la *taille*.

Substitution: (1) Je ne suis pas aussi grand que lui. *(tu / vous / nous / Chantal)* (2) Marie est plus patiente que Philippe. *(Jean-Claude et Lucien / nous / tu / je)* (3) Ce livre est moins intéressant que les autres. *(ces films / cette histoire / ce programme / ces classes)* (4) Ce programme est meilleur que les autres. *(ce livre / ces restaurants / cet hôtel / cette classe / cet étudiant / ces étudiants)* (5) Jean travaille mieux que ces frères. *(chante / parle / travaille / étudie / comprend)*.

waist

Thierry veut acheter une veste.

THIERRY	Oui, mais j'aime mieux l'autre. Le *tissu* est de meilleure qualité et je la trouve plus élégante. Vous ne l'avez pas dans une taille plus grande ?
LE VENDEUR	Non, c'est *tout ce qui nous reste* dans ce modèle. Il n'y a pas autant de choix maintenant qu'au début de la saison.
THIERRY	Qu'est-ce que vous avez d'autre ?
LE VENDEUR	Nous avons d'autres modèles, mais ils sont plus *habillés* et ils coûtent plus cher.
THIERRY	Alors, il vaut peut-être mieux que je regarde *ailleurs*.

fabric

all we have left

dressy

elsewhere

Préparation

A. Paris et la province. Madame Chanet, une Marseillaise qui vient de faire un séjour dans la capitale, a décidé qu'elle préfère la vie en province. Comment compare-t-elle les deux ?

> **Modèle**   les gens / moins heureux
> **Les gens sont moins heureux que chez nous.**

1. la vie / moins agréable
2. les prix / plus élevés
3. les vêtements / aussi chers
4. les restaurants / moins bons
5. les magasins / moins intéressants
6. les gens / plus froids
7. le climat / beaucoup plus froid
8. les maisons / moins jolies

Point out that despite the increasing economic and cultural growth of large French cities, many Parisians still think of Paris as the center of France. Since the 1970s, decentralization and « régionalisation » have been an important part of government priorities.

B. Le nouveau prof. Véronique est assez contente de Mademoiselle Villiers, son nouveau professeur d'anglais, surtout par rapport à ses autres professeurs.

> **Modèles**   Elle est dynamique.
> **Elle est plus dynamique que les autres professeurs.**
> *ou:*   Elle explique bien.
> **Elle explique mieux que les autres professeurs.**

1. Elle est gentille.
2. Elle s'habille bien.
3. Elle parle vite.
4. Elle est sympathique.
5. Elle est facile à comprendre.
6. Elle enseigne bien.
7. Elle est jeune.
8. Elle est amusante.

You may want to teach the colloquial adjective marrante in place of amusante.

C. Évian ou Vittel ? Monsieur Achard fait chaque année une cure à Vittel. Madame Simon préfère aller à Évian. Pourquoi ?

Modèles On mange bien à Vittel. → **On mange mieux à Évian.**
ou: Il y a beaucoup de piscines à Vittel. → **Il y a plus de piscines à Évian.**

1. Les hôtels sont bons à Vittel.
2. L'eau de Vittel est très bonne pour la santé.
3. La vie est très agréable à Vittel.
4. On se repose bien à Vittel.
5. On s'amuse bien à Vittel.
6. Les gens sont très gentils à Vittel.
7. Il y a beaucoup de nouveaux hôtels à Vittel.
8. Il y a beaucoup de jolis parcs à Vittel.
9. Il y a beaucoup de gens qui vont à Vittel.

Point out that Vittel is a spa in the Vosges and that Evian is on Lake Geneva, near Switzerland.

Communication et vie pratique

A. Questions / Interview. Répondez aux questions suivantes ou utilisez-les pour interviewer un(e) autre étudiant(e).

1. Est-ce que tu as l'impression que le français est plus facile ou plus difficile que l'anglais ?
2. Est-ce que ton cours de français est plus facile ou plus difficile que tes autres cours ?
3. Pour toi, est-ce que les maths sont plus faciles que les langues ?
4. Est-ce que tu as autant de travail maintenant qu'à la fin du trimestre ?
5. Est-ce que tes cours à l'université sont plus faciles ou plus difficiles que tes cours au lycée ?
6. Est-ce qu'il y a autant d'étudiants dans ta classe de français que dans tes autres classes ?
7. Est-ce que tu as plus de temps libre ou moins de temps libre ce trimestre ?
8. En comparaison avec le trimestre passé, comment sont tes classes ? Est-ce qu'elles sont plus ou moins intéressantes ? Plus ou moins difficiles ?
9. Et les étudiants, est-ce qu'ils travaillent mieux ou moins bien ?
10. Et les professeurs ? Est-ce qu'ils expliquent mieux ou moins bien ? Est-ce qu'ils sont plus ou moins intéressants ? Plus ou moins sympa ? Est-ce qu'ils donnent autant ou moins de travail ?
11. Et les livres qu'il faut acheter — est-ce qu'ils coûtent plus cher ou moins cher ?
12. Et toi, est-ce que tu comprends mieux ou moins bien ? Est-ce que tu passes plus ou moins de temps à étudier ? Est-ce que tu es plus ou moins satisfait(e) de ton travail ?

B. **Comparaisons.** Utilisez les expressions ou les adjectifs suggérés pour exprimer votre opinion sur les sujets suivants. Notez les différentes possibilités dans l'exemple suivant.

Have students compare two cities, states, universities.

Exemple l'avion ↔ le train
rapide / dangereux / confortable / pratique / cher / bon marché / aller vite / coûter cher / ?
Le train est moins rapide que l'avion.
ou: **Le train n'est pas aussi dangereux que l'avion.**
ou: **Le train coûte moins cher que l'avion.**

1. la cuisine américaine ↔ la cuisine française
variée / bonne / mauvaise / simple / de bonne qualité / ?
2. les Américains ↔ les Européens
accueillants / conformistes / grands / naïfs / optimistes / s'habiller bien / ?
3. les voitures étrangères ↔ les voitures américaines
économiques / chères / confortables / pratiques / de bonne qualité / rapides / coûter cher / marcher bien / ?
4. les hommes ↔ les femmes
courageux (courageuses) / capables / sportifs (sportives) / ambitieux (ambitieuses) / indépendant(e)s / intelligents / ?

C. **Avantages et inconvénients.** Comparez les avantages et les inconvénients des options suivantes.

1. Où préférez-vous faire vos études ? Dans une grande université ou dans un petit collège ? Pourquoi ?
2. Où préférez-vous manger ? Chez vous ou au restaurant ? Pourqoui ?
3. Où préférez-vous habiter ? Dans une résidence universitaire ou dans un appartement ? Pourquoi ?
4. Où préférez-vous faire vos achats ? Dans un grand magasin ou dans une petite boutique ? Pourquoi ?
5. Où préférez-vous passer vos vacances ? Aux États-Unis ou dans un pays étranger ? Où préférez-vous rester ? Dans un camping, chez des amis, ou dans un hôtel ? Pourquoi ?

As preparation, review vocabulary and expressions in the *Les mots et la vie* section of this chapter.

C'est votre tour. Vous allez dans un magasin pour acheter un complet / un tailleur (ou un autre vêtement de votre choix) mais vous avez un peu de difficulté à trouver ce que vous voulez. Vous essayez plusieurs modèles et vous comparez le prix, la qualité, la couleur, etc. Le vendeur ou la vendeuse — joué(e) par un(e) autre étudiant(e) — essaie de vous aider.

☙ Talking about the best and the worst
Le superlatif

Présentation

Superlatives are used to express the idea of *the most*, *the least*, *the best* and to distinguish or set off individuals, people, or things from a group. In French, the superlative of adjectives and adverbs is formed according to the following patterns :

A. Superlatives of adjectives are formed by using the appropriate definite article with **plus** or **moins** before the adjective.

le plus
le moins } joli magasin

la plus
la moins } jolie voiture

les plus
les moins } jolis vêtements

C'est **le plus grand** hôtel **de**   *It's the biggest hotel in Paris.*
   Paris.
Voici **la plus vieille** maison **de**   *Here is the oldest house in town.*
   la ville.

Note in the above examples that **de** after the superlative corresponds to the English *in*. Note also that the group or category can be omitted :

C'est toi qui portes **la plus jolie robe**.

Adjectives in the superlative follow their normal pattern in following or preceding the noun they modify.

C'est une ville intéressante.	C'est **la ville la plus intéressante** de la région.
C'est une petite ville.	C'est **la plus petite ville** de la région.

B. Superlatives can be followed by nouns :

le plus de *(the most)*	C'est Jeanne qui a **le plus de patience**.
le moins de *(the least)*	C'est le magasin où il y a **le moins de choix**.

Note that **le** is invariable and that **de** is not followed by a definite article.

C. When an adverb is used in the superlative, the definite article is always **le** because adverbs do not have gender or number.

C'est la robe que j'aime **le moins**.
Voici les vêtements que je porte **le plus souvent**.

D. To form the superlative of **bon**, simply place the appropriate definite article before the irregular comparative forms you learned in the preceding **Présentation** : **le meilleur** ; **la meilleure** ; **les meilleurs** ; **les meilleures**.

C'est **le meilleur** magasin du quartier.
Andrée est **la meilleure** étudiante de la classe et Jacques est **le plus mauvais**.

E. Le mieux is the superlative of **bien**.

C'est ici qu'on mange **le mieux**.
C'est Mireille qui travaille **le mieux**.

The superlative of *mauvais* can be *le plus mauvais* or *le pire*.

Substitution: (1) C'est le plus beau monument de la ville. *(église / musée / quartier / rue / parc)* (2) Nous avons les plus beaux vêtements. *(jolis / chers / élégants / confortables)* (3) C'est Geneviève qui chante le mieux. *(Paul / moi / mon père / ma sœur / mon ami)* (4) C'est Frédérique qui travaille le mieux. *(chante / parle / comprend / étudie / danse)*

Mise en situation

Qui va gagner le *gros lot* ? Plusieurs personnes participent à un jeu télévisé. C'est le joueur qui est le plus rapide et qui donne le plus de réponses exactes dans chaque catégorie qui a la meilleure chance de gagner le match.

jackpot

LE *MENEUR DE JEU*	Tout le monde est prêt ? Alors on commence. Première catégorie : les superlatifs ! Question numéro un : le plus long *fleuve* d'Europe ?
JOUEUR N° 1	L'Amazone ! Non, non, excusez-moi. Je veux dire la Volga !
LE MENEUR DE JEU	Question numéro deux : le *roi* de France qui a eu le plus long *règne* ?
JOUEUR N° 3	Louis XIV, dit le Roi Soleil !
LE MENEUR DE JEU	Le jour le plus court de l'année ?
JOUEUR N° 1	Le 21 décembre.
LE MENEUR DE JEU	L'avion commercial le plus rapide du monde ?
JOUEUR N° 5	Le Concorde.
LE MENEUR DE JEU	Le pays le plus *peuplé* ?
JOUEUR N° 4	La Chine.
LE MENEUR DE JEU	Fin de cette catégorie. C'est le joueur numéro un qui a le mieux répondu. Nous passons maintenant à la catégorie suivante.

master of ceremonies

river

king
reign

Game shows are also popular in France; they often involve competitions between representatives of cities who are asked to participate in many different types of contests.

populous

Préparation

A. Vendeur aux Galeries Lafayette. Olivier est très content de travailler aux Galeries Lafayette, un des grands magasins de Paris. Qu'est-ce qu'il dit ?

Modèle   un grand choix → **Nous avons le plus grand choix.**

1. de bons prix
2. un magasin moderne
3. de jolies vitrines
4. de jolis vêtements
5. des employés sérieux
6. de bons clients
7. une bonne publicité
8. une clientèle variée

B. Paris. Monsieur Lefort pense que Paris est la plus belle ville du monde. Qu'est-ce qu'il dit?

Modèles   des gens intéressants
          C'est à Paris qu'on trouve les gens les plus intéressants.
     ou: des clubs où on s'amuse bien
          C'est à Paris qu'on trouve les clubs où on s'amuse le mieux.

1. des femmes élégantes
2. de beaux quartiers
3. des restaurants où on mange bien
4. de jolis parcs
5. de bonnes écoles
6. des clubs où on s'amuse bien
7. des musées exceptionnels
8. de bons théâtres
9. des chanteuses qui chantent bien
10. des monuments anciens

C. Le chou-chou du prof. Clarisse fait un stage de formation *(training course)* pour devenir mannequin de mode. Son professeur de danse pense que Clarisse est une de ses meilleures étudiantes. Qu'est-ce qu'elle pense de Clarisse?

Point out that chou-chou is a teacher's pet.

Modèles   Elle est gentille. → **C'est elle qui est la plus gentille.**
     ou: Elle travaille bien. → **C'est elle qui travaille le mieux.**
     ou: Elle a de l'ambition. → **C'est elle qui a le plus d'ambition.**

1. Elle est intelligente.
2. Elle a du talent.
3. Elle danse bien.
4. Elle comprend vite.
5. Elle est sérieuse.
6. Elle a du courage.
7. Elle fait bien son travail.
8. Elle réussit bien.

Communication et vie pratique

A. À votre avis. Utilisez les suggestions suivantes pour formuler des questions que vous allez poser à un(e) autre étudiant(e). L'autre étudiant(e) va répondre à vos questions.

Encourage students to come up with other topics.

Exemple   la plus belle région des États-Unis
          — **À votre avis, quelle est la plus belle région des États-Unis?**
          — **À mon avis, le Sud-Ouest est la plus belle région des États-Unis.**

1. le meilleur chanteur ou la meilleure chanteuse
2. le meilleur acteur ou la meilleure actrice
3. la plus belle ville des États-Unis
4. le meilleur restaurant de la ville
5. le plus mauvais restaurant de la ville
6. le cours le plus difficile
7. le cours le plus facile
8. le film le plus amusant
9. le plus beau pays du monde
10. ?

B. Le plus et le moins. Donnez votre réponse à chacune des questions suivantes ou posez-les à un(e) autre étudiant(e).

Encourage students to explain their answers.

Exemple   le dessert que vous aimez le mieux ?
 — **Quel est le dessert que vous aimez le mieux ?**
 — **La glace est le dessert que j'aime le mieux.**

  1. la personne que vous admirez le plus ?
  2. le dessert que vous aimez le mieux ?
  3. le cours où vous travaillez le plus ?
  4. les légumes que vous aimez le moins ?
  5. le disque que vous aimez le plus ?
  6. le cours ou les matières où vous réussissez le mieux ?
  7. le moment de la journée où vous vous sentez le mieux ?
  8. le ou les mois de l'année que vous aimez le moins ?
  9. le ou les pays que vous avez le plus envie de visiter ?
 10. ?

C. Vérité ou chauvinisme ? Jean Chauvin est un Français qui a des opinions bien définies sur toutes sortes de sujets. Êtes-vous d'accord avec lui ?

Have students come up with other statements that their classmates will agree or disagree with.

  1. C'est en France qu'on boit les meilleurs vins du monde.
  2. Les Françaises sont les plus belles femmes du monde.
  3. Pour être heureux, il faut travailler le moins possible et s'amuser le plus possible.
  4. Les hommes sont plus intelligents et plus capables que les femmes.
  5. La cuisine française est la meilleure du monde.
  6. Paris est la plus belle ville du monde.
  7. Les femmes sont moins courageuses et moins ambitieuses que les hommes.
  8. Les Français s'habillent mieux que les Américains.
  9. La beauté a plus d'importance pour les femmes que pour les hommes.
 10. Les gens les plus intéressants sont aussi les plus modestes (comme moi !).

C'est votre tour. Organisez avec les autres étudiants de votre classe un jeu du même type que dans la **Mise en situation.** Divisez la classe en deux groupes. Chaque groupe pose une question à tour de rôle. Mais attention : il faut pouvoir répondre à votre propre question !

As a class or in small groups, students come up with questions (using the superlative and comparative) and their answers. The instructor can then check over these questions before using them in class.

Intégration et perspectives

Mannequin et maçon... Et pourquoi pas ?

Mannequin et *maçon*. Voilà des métiers qui n'ont rien en commun. Un maçon répare ou construit des maisons. Il doit monter sur des *échaffaudages*, aligner des briques et des *pierres*, *porter* de lourds sacs de ciment. Un mannequin, par contre, ne porte rien de plus lourd qu'un manteau de *fourrure*. Mais il faut le porter avec chic et élégance ! Entre ces deux professions, Laurence n'a pas voulu choisir. Pendant la journée, elle est maçon et porte sur ses épaules des sacs de ciment de 50 kilos. Le soir, elle est mannequin et porte des vêtements *dessinés* par les meilleurs *couturiers* de la ville. Elle est aussi *à l'aise* sur un échaffaudage de cinq étages que dans une présentation de robes de haute couture.

Laurence a 27 ans. Elle est grande et blonde. Elle a les yeux bleus. Elle est pleine de joie de vivre et de santé. Et elle a autant de force et de *volonté* que de charme et d'élégance naturelle !

À l'âge de 17 ans, elle prend la décision de suivre les traces de son père, un maçon italien, plutôt que de faire des études pour devenir avocate. C'est le début d'un *dur* apprentissage. Été comme hiver, il faut être sur les *chantiers*. Elle se trouve plongée dans un univers d'hommes qui se sentent menacés par sa présence. Ils sont plus forts et mieux préparés qu'elle pour ce métier. Mais ça ne l'arrête pas, même si, le soir, elle rentre *épuisée*. « J'ai souvent *pleuré*, admet-elle. Il y a eu des moments difficiles, mais je n'ai jamais abandonné. »

Quand Laurence a fini son apprentissage, elle décide de *se mettre à son compte*. Son père promet de l'aider un peu. Elle embauche plusieurs ouvriers et monte une entreprise spécialisée dans la restauration des maisons anciennes. Son travail lui donne l'occasion de rencontrer des gens de tous les milieux. Elle aime la vie mondaine et les soirées. Parmi ses clients, il y a des directeurs de maisons de haute couture. Ils lui proposent de présenter leurs collections *à temps perdu*. Elle accepte. Et voilà !

Maintenant, sa vie est partagée entre ces deux métiers. Après huit ou dix heures de travail sur les chantiers, elle rentre vite chez elle et change de rôle. Un passage à la salle de bain et la voilà coiffée, maquillée et habillée comme une des plus belles femmes de la ville. Elle porte les créations des plus grands couturiers et elle est en train de devenir un des mannequins les plus *recherchés*.

Adapté d'un article du Progrès

Compréhension. Répondez aux questions suivantes selon les renseignements donnés dans le texte.

1. En quoi Laurence est-elle une personne assez exceptionnelle ?
2. Pourquoi Laurence exerce-t-elle deux métiers si différents l'un de l'autre ? Quels sont les avantages et les inconvénients de ces deux métiers ?
3. Faites le portrait de Laurence. Décrivez sa personnalité et son apparence.
4. Décrivez une journée typique dans la vie de Laurence.

Marginal glosses:

model / mason, builder
scaffolding
stones / carry
fur
designed / fashion designers
at ease
will power
hard
construction sites
exhausted
cried
start her own business
in her spare time
sought after

Have students compare information about *les femmes françaises* with the situation of women in the U.S.

Notes culturelles: *La femme et le travail*

Les femmes françaises ont le droit de vote depuis 1945. En 1946, la loi établit l'égalité entre les sexes et affirme le principe de l'égalité des salaires. Cette loi n'a cependant pas réussi à assurer une égalité de fait et plusieurs lois supplémentaires ont été passées depuis. En 1974 le premier Secrétariat d'État à la condition féminine a été créé. Ce Secrétariat d'État est maintenant devenu un ministère. Son rôle est d'assurer que les lois sont appliquées et de proposer des mesures en faveur des femmes. Il existe aussi un centre national de Renseignements sur les droits des femmes et des Centres Régionaux qui dépendent directement du cabinet du Premier ministre. Le *droit* à l'*avortement* est garanti par la loi depuis 1979.   **right / abortion**

    Le nombre de femmes qui travaillent en dehors de la maison représente entre 40 et 45% de la population *active*. Le nombre de femmes mariées qui travaillent a beaucoup augmenté au cours des dernières années et elles représentent maintenant les 2/5 de la *main-d'œuvre* féminine.   **working**   **work force**

    Quelles sortes de travail les femmes font-elles ? Elles occupent 66,6% des postes administratifs (surtout dans les services) ; 49,7% des emplois dans le commerce et elle représentent 85% des gens qui travaillent à temps partiel. Le chômage est un problème encore plus sérieux pour les femmes que pour les hommes et elles représentent 58% des gens qui cherchent du travail.

    Cependant, les portes des bastions traditionnels de la suprématie masculine s'ouvrent peu à peu aux femmes. Des statistiques récentes indiquent qu'il y a maintenant au moins 7% de femmes à l'École polytechnique, 20% à l'É.N.A. (École nationale d'administration), 43% à H.E.C. (Hautes Études Commerciales) et 54% à l'École nationale de la magistrature. Même l'École militaire de Saint-Cyr compte quelques femmes parmi ses élèves.

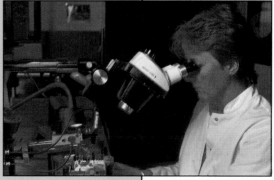

Communication et vie pratique

A. Opinions. Quelle est votre opinion sur les questions suivantes ?

Individual questions can be used as the basis for conversation or composition.

   1. À votre avis, quel métier est le plus facile ? Le plus intéressant ? Le mieux payé ?

   2. En général, est-ce que les femmes gagnent autant que les hommes qui exercent le même métier ?

   3. Est-ce que le travail d'une femme qui choisit de rester à la maison a autant de valeur que le travail d'une femme qui exerce un métier ?

   4. Est-ce qu'il y a autant de femmes que d'hommes qui occupent des postes importants dans le commerce ? Dans l'industrie ? Dans les professions libérales (médecins, avocats, etc.) ? Dans le gouvernement ?

   5. À votre avis, dans quels domaines les femmes ont-elles fait le plus de progrès au cours des 20 dernières années ? Et dans quels domaines y a-t-il des choses qui restent à faire ?

B. Description. Vous avez remarqué un individu suspect dans votre quartier. Faites son signalement (c'est-à-dire, donnez sa description à la police).

Have one student play the role of the *agent de police* who asks questions to find out the description of the *individu suspect.*

Taille? — Les cheveux: couleur? longueur?
Lunettes?
Moustache ou barbe?
Chemise? Couleur? / Veste? Style?

Pantalon: couleur? style?

Chaussures: style? couleur?

Sexe: _____ Age: _____
Taille: _____ Poids: _____
Yeux: _____ Lunettes: _____
Cheveux: _____ Longueur: _____
Chapeau: _____ Veste: _____
Couleur de chemise: _____
Pantalon: _____ Chaussures: _____
Remarques et signes particuliers: _____

C. Portraits. Utilisez les suggestions suivantes (ou ajoutez vos propres idées) et faites le portrait (1) d'une personne que vous connaissez, (2) d'un personnage célèbre ou (3) de la femme idéale ou de l'homme idéal.

Suggested for written homework. If students describe famous people, have them read the descriptions aloud and other students can guess the identity of the person.

D. Opinions. Choisissez une (ou plusieurs) des catégories suivantes et indiquez ce que vous considérez le meilleur et le plus mauvais. Expliquez vos choix.

— Dans votre ville (restaurants, cinémas, parcs, écoles, etc.)
— Dans votre université et près du campus (librairies, cours, restaurants, résidences, etc.)
— À la télévision (acteurs, actrices, jeux télévisés, feuilletons, etc.)

● *Vocabulaire*

Noms

les vêtements (voir p. 287)
d'autres noms

l'**apparence** (f)   *appearance, look*
le **couturier**, la **couturière**   *fashion designer*
le **cuir**   *leather*
le **droit**   *right*
l'**élégance** (f)   *elegance, stylishness*
l'**étage** (m)   *floor*
le **fleuve**   *(major) river*
la **fourrure**   *fur*
le **gros lot**   *jackpot*
le **guichet**   *window, booth*
l'**habillement** (m)   *clothing*
l'**inconvénient** (m)   *inconvenience*
le **jogging**   *jogging, jogging suit*
le **maçon**   *mason, builder*
le **mannequin**   *model*
le **meneur de jeu**   *master of ceremonies*
le **modèle**   *model, style*
Noël (m)   *Christmas*
° la **paire**
la **pierre**   *stone*
la **pointure**   *size (shoes, gloves)*
° la **promesse**
le **rayon**   *department*
le **roi**   *king*
le **règne**   *reign*
le **salon d'essayage**   *dressing room*
la **soirée**   *evening, evening party*
la **taille**   *size (clothing), waist*
le **talon**   *heel*
le **tissu**   *fabric*
la **volonté**   *will power*

Verbes

admettre   *to admit*
dessiner   *to design, to draw*
disparaître   *to disappear*
essayer   *to try, to try on*
mettre   *to place, to put, to put on*

se mettre à   *to start to*
offrir   *to offer, to give*
permettre   *to allow, to permit*
pleurer   *to cry*
porter   *to carry, to wear*
promettre   *to promise*
remettre   *to hand in, to postpone*
vérifier   *to check*

Adjectives

les couleurs (voir p. 288)

d'autres adjectifs

chic   *stylish*
démodé(e)   *out of style*
dur(e)   *hard*
habillé(e)   *dressy, smart*
marin(e)   *navy*
mignon, mignonne   *cute*
peuplé(e)   *populated*
serré(e)   *tight*

Adverbes

ailleurs   *elsewhere*
aussi... que   *as . . . as*
autant de   *as much (many) as*
heureusement   *fortunately, happily*
mieux   *better*

Divers

à la fois   *at the same time, both*
à l'aise   *at ease*
à la mode   *in style*
à temps perdu   *in one's spare time*
ça vous (te) va bien   *that looks good on you*
c'est dommage   *that's a pity*
faire plaisir à quelqu'un   *to please someone*
mettre la table   *to set the table*
se mettre à table   *to sit down to eat*
se mettre en colère   *to get angry*
puis-je   *can I, may I*
rien de joli   *nothing pretty*

13

CHAPITRE TREIZE

Communication objectives

Talking about life events, feelings, and wishes

1. Describing what used to be
2. Saying things more precisely
3. Talking about the past
4. Talking about continuing actions

Structures

Les mots et la vie : Événements, réactions et vœux

L'imparfait

Les adverbes

L'imparfait et le passé composé

Depuis et autres expressions de temps

Le passé et les souvenirs

Mise en scène

Jacques Prévert

Suggestion : Point out the difference between *le petit déjeuner* (also called *le déjeuner*), *le déjeuner*, and *le dîner* and *le souper* as well as corresponding verbs.

Jacques Prévert (1900–1977) a été le poète de la vie de tous les jours, des choses simples et familières, de la solidarité humaine. Il prend le temps d'écouter, de regarder, de sentir les gens et les choses *vivre** autour de lui. Et ensuite il les *exprime* avec des *mots* de tous les jours, dans un style simple et spontané, mais plein de fantaisie et de tendresse.

live

expresses / words

Dans ses poèmes et ses chansons Prévert parle des choses et des gens qu'il aime. *Parfois*, il est aussi le *témoin* discret des drames de la vie, comme, par exemple, dans le poème suivant.

at times / witness

Déjeuner du matin

Have two students act out the poem while another student reads it.

Il a mis le café
Dans la tasse
Il a mis le lait
Dans la tasse de café
Il a mis le sucre
Dans le café au lait
Avec la petite cuiller
Il a tourné

spoon

***Vivre** means *to live*, in the sense of *carrying on one's life*; **habiter** means *to live* or *to reside*. The present tense of **vivre** is : **je vis, tu vis, il / elle vit, nous vivons, vous vivez, ils / elles vivent.** Passé composé : **j'ai vécu**, etc.

Il a bu le café au lait
Et il a reposé la tasse   put back down
Sans me parler
Il a allumé   lit
Une cigarette
Il a fait des ronds   rings
Avec la fumée   smoke
Il a mis les cendres   ashes
Dans le cendrier   ash tray
Sans me parler
Sans me regarder
Il s'est levé
Il a mis
Son chapeau sur sa tête
Il a mis
Son manteau de pluie
Parce qu'il pleuvait   was raining
Et il est parti
Sous la pluie
Sans une parole   Guillaume Apollinaire's   word
Sans me regarder   *Calligrammes* (e.g., « Le
Et moi j'ai pris   Cigare » and « Le Miroir »)
Ma tête dans ma main   can also be used at this point;
                             if desired, students can be
                             asked to prepare their own
Et j'ai pleuré   *calligrammes*.   cried

Jacques Prévert, « Déjeuner du matin » extrait de *Paroles* © Éditions Gallimard.

Have students write a
continuation of the poem.
They can also be asked to
describe the events that
preceded the poem.

Compréhension. Répondez aux questions suivantes selon les renseignements donnés dans le texte.

1. Où et quand ce drame de la vie a-t-il lieu ?
2. À votre avis, qui sont les deux personnages du poème ?
3. Quelles sont les actions principales de l'homme ?
4. Est-ce que ses actions sont des actions ordinaires et habituelles ou des actions inhabituelles ? Donnez des exemples.
5. À votre avis, quelle attitude est-ce que ces gestes et ces actions révèlent ?
6. Quelle est la réaction de l'autre personne ?
7. À votre avis, quel est le problème principal entre ces deux personnes ?
8. Quelle est votre réaction personnelle devant l'attitude de chaque personne ?
9. Est-ce que vous pouvez suggérer une solution à leur problème ?
10. Refaites le poème du point de vue de l'homme qui quitte l'autre personne.

Notes culturelles: *Rites et coutumes*

En France, comme dans la plupart des autres cultures, les *étapes* et les événements importants de la vie sont marqués par des rites particuliers. La France *étant* un pays de tradition catholique, la plupart de ces cérémonies ont une origine religieuse. Les enfants, par exemple, sont généralement baptisés dans les quelques mois qui *suivent* leur naissance. Jusqu'à une époque récente, l'Église *exigeait même* qu'on donne aux enfants des noms de saints, *tels que* Jean, Paul, Thérèse ou Marie. *Ainsi* en France, on célèbre non *seulement* l'anniversaire mais aussi la *fête* d'une personne. Le *baptême* est *suivi d'un* dîner qui réunit toute la famille et le *parrain* et la *marraine*. Il y a *également* une cérémonie religieuse suivie d'un dîner de famille quand l'enfant fait sa première communion, généralement à l'âge de onze ou douze ans. Selon les statistiques, la plupart des Français se marient entre l'âge de vingt et un et vingt-trois ans. Pour être marié légalement, il faut se marier à la mairie mais un grand nombre de couples choisissent également d'avoir une cérémonie religieuse.

Cérémonie civile de mariage

Baptême

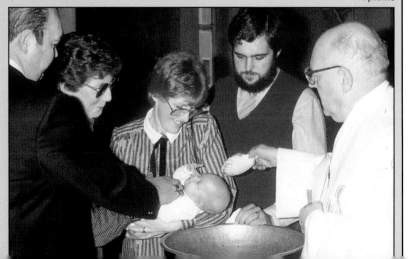

Les mots et la vie : *Événements, réactions et vœux*

Étudiez le vocabulaire présenté et faites les activités indiquées.

A. Les étapes et les événements de la vie

la naissance (il est né / elle est née)
l'enfance *(childhood)*
l'adolescence
la jeunesse *(youth)*
l'âge adulte
la vieillesse *(old age)* (le troisième age)
la mort (il est mort / elle est morte)

le baptême (être baptisé(e))
le mariage (se marier, être marié(e))
le divorce (divorcer, être divorcé(e))
élever *(to raise)* des enfants
la retraite *(retirement)* (prendre sa retraite)
l'enterrement *(funeral)*

Monsieur Ormond Stanford Parke

Madame Daniel M. Boland

ont l'honneur de vous faire part du mariage

de Monsieur Marshall Waite Parke, leur fils,

avec Mademoiselle Véronique de Champvallier,

et vous prient d'assister ou de vous unir par la prière à la cérémonie œcuménique de mariage qui aura lieu le Samedi 28 Décembre 1985, à 15 h. 30 en l'église de Champagne-Mouton (Charente).

4029 North 57th Place, Phoenix, Arizona 85018
286 Dolphin Cove Court, Del Mar, California 92014

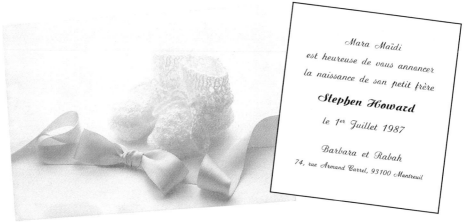

Mara Maïdi
est heureuse de vous annoncer
la naissance de son petit frère

Stephen Howard

le 1er Juillet 1987

Barbara et Rabah
74, rue Armand Carrel, 93100 Montreuil

B. Les réactions et les sentiments

Le plaisir :	J'ai eu le plaisir de la rencontrer.
La satisfaction :	Je suis très content de mon travail.
La joie :	Nous sommes ravis de faire votre connaissance.
Le bonheur *(happiness)* :	Il n'est pas très heureux.
La tristesse :	Pourquoi es-tu si triste ?
L'inquiétude *(worry)* :	Nous sommes très inquiets au sujet de votre santé.
L'espoir :	J'espère que tout ira bien.
La surprise :	Nous avons été surpris d'apprendre cette nouvelle.
La jalousie :	Il est très jaloux.
L'affection :	Elle a beaucoup d'affection pour ses parents.
L'amitié :	Nous sommes amis avec les Laforêt.
L'amour *(love)* :	Jean est amoureux de Suzanne.
La fierté :	Nous sommes très fiers de toi.

C. Les vœux et les condoléances

Félicitations !	Bonne Fête !	Sincères regrets !
Bon anniversaire !	Meilleurs vœux !	Mes condoléances !

1. Choisissez un ou deux personnages célèbres et donnez un résumé de leur vie. (Si vous préférez, vous pouvez raconter la vie d'un membre de votre famille ou d'une personne que vous trouvez particulièrement intéressante.)

2. À votre avis, quels sont les différents sentiments éprouvés par chaque personnage du poème de Prévert ? Quels sentiments semblent absents de leur vie ?

3. Vous envoyez une carte à un(e) ami(e). Qu'allez-vous mettre sur la carte ?

    1. C'est son anniversaire.
    2. C'est sa fête.
    3. C'est le Nouvel An.
    4. Il (elle) vient de réussir à un examen important.

Explorations
⚜ Describing what used to be
L'imparfait

Présentation

The imperfect tense **(l'imparfait)** provides another way of talking about the past. It is formed by dropping the **-ons** ending from the **nous** form of the present tense and adding the endings shown below.

nous parlons	**parl-** + IMPERFECT ENDINGS
nous avons	**av-** + IMPERFECT ENDINGS
nous finissons	**finiss-** + IMPERFECT ENDINGS

Find magazine pictures that illustrate these emotions; then have students identify the emotions. Students could also be asked to find these pictures.

Substitution : (1) D'habitude, je finissais à huit heures. (tes amis / tu / vous / Marcel / je / nous) (2) Autrefois, tu perdais souvent patience. (nous / vous / mon professeur / les étudiants / je) (3) Je n'étais pas fatigué après l'examen. (les étudiants / tu / nous / Véronique / vous / je) Transformation : Je suis fatigué. → J'étais fatigué. (1) Il a beaucoup d'argent. (2) Nous allons en Italie chaque été. (3) Tu es malade. (4) Vous vous levez assez tôt. (5) Ils veulent partir en vacances. (6) Il fait très beau. (7) J'aime beaucoup mon travail. (8) C'est un bon étudiant. (9) Nous l'attendons devant l'école. (10) Je finis le dîner.

Point out that would is often used to express the idea of used to in English.

The only exception is **être**, whose imperfect stem is **ét-**.

L'imparfait de *parler*		L'imparfait d'*être*	
je **parlais**	nous **parlions**	j'**étais**	nous **étions**
tu **parlais**	vous **parliez**	tu **étais**	vous **étiez**
il / elle / on **parlait**	il / elles **parlaient**	il / elle / on **était**	ils / elles **étaient**

All the singular forms and the **ils / elles** form are pronounced the same : [parlɛ] and [etɛ].

Depending on the context used, the imperfect has several translations in English :

j'habitais $\begin{cases} \textit{I was living} \\ \textit{I used to live} \\ \textit{I lived} \end{cases}$

A. There are two main uses of the imperfect :

1. To indicate an habitual past action :

Nous **allions** en Bretagne **tous les étés.**
Chaque matin je **me levais** à huit heures.
Ma mère m'**emmenait** au marché aux poissons.

2. To describe a situation or condition that existed in the past :

Quand il **était petit,** il **était souvent malade.**
J'**étudiais** quand ils sont rentrés.
Ils **avaient** une petite maison à la campagne.
Il **portait** un complet gris.

B. Certain time expressions are often used with the imperfect :

à cette époque-là	*at that time, in those days*
autrefois	*in the past, long ago*
d'habitude	*generally, usually*
chaque année, mois, etc.	*every year, month, etc.*
tous les jours	*every day*

Mise en situation

Souvenirs d'autrefois. Catherine Gagnon, une jeune Québécoise, parle avec son *arrière-grand-mère*, Francine Hébert, âgée maintenant de 83 ans.   great grandmother

CATHERINE   Parle-moi du temps où tu étais petite... Vous habitiez déjà ici, à Jonquière ?

MME HÉBERT   Non, nous habitions près de Roberval. Nous étions huit enfants...

CATHERINE	Tu étais *l'aînée*?	the eldest
MME HÉBERT	Non, non, j'étais *la cadette*. Les autres enfants étaient déjà *grands* quand je suis née. Ma mère était souvent malade, la pauvre, alors les plus âgés faisaient ce qu'ils pouvaient pour l'aider.	the youngest grown up
CATHERINE	Et ton père?	
MME HÉBERT	Il était *bûcheron*. Pendant toute la belle saison, il travaillait dans des camps. Il revenait passer l'hiver avec nous.	logger
CATHERINE	La vie était dure, *hein*…?	*n'est-ce pas* (colloquial)
MME HÉBERT	Oui, mais on n'était pas malheureux… Je me souviens, en hiver, on était bloqué par la neige pendant plusieurs mois. Pour aller à la messe le dimanche, on prenait notre *traîneau*. Moi, je choisissais toujours la meilleure place, entre mon père et ma mère… C'était si beau… On entendait seulement les *pas* du *cheval*…	sleigh footsteps horse

Préparation

A. C'était impossible. Catherine voulait inviter ses amis à dîner mais tout le monde était occupé. Pourquoi ne pouvaient-ils pas venir?

Can be used as listening comprehension by completing the sentences and reading as a paragraph.

Modèle   Serge / avoir mal à la tête → **Serge avait mal à la tête.**

1. tu / être malade
2. vous / ne pas être libres
3. Pierre / attendre la visite de sa mère
4. nous / avoir du travail à faire
5. Hélène / avoir besoin de se reposer
6. je / vouloir regarder une émission spéciale à la télé
7. Bruno / faire le ménage
8. Roger et Claudine / être en voyage

B. Souvenirs d'enfance. Au cours d'une visite dans le quartier du vieux Lyon où il a grandi, Monsieur Berger évoque quelques souvenirs de son enfance.

Modèle   je / jouer souvent dans cette rue
   Je jouais souvent dans cette rue.

1. mes parents / habiter dans ce quartier
2. ma mère / faire son marché chaque matin
3. elle / m'emmener avec elle
4. nous / s'arrêter dans chaque magasin
5. elle / prendre le temps de parler avec les marchands
6. ils / parler de la pluie et du beau temps
7. nous / passer ensuite devant le garage de Monsieur Giraud
8. je / vouloir être mécanicien comme lui
9. il / répondre à toutes mes questions
10. ma mère / attendre patiemment

C. **De bons souvenirs.** Michel et Raymonde ont passé leurs vacances à Antibes. Qu'est-ce qu'ils disent ?

Modèle   Il fait du soleil. → **Il faisait du soleil.**

1. Il fait beau.
2. La mer est bonne.
3. Les gens sont sympathiques.
4. L'hôtel se trouve près de la mer.
5. Nous avons une grande chambre.
6. Notre chambre donne sur la mer.
7. La cuisine est excellente.
8. Nous prenons notre petit déjeuner à l'hôtel.
9. Chaque matin nous faisons une petite promenade.
10. L'après-midi nous allons à la plage.

Communication et vie pratique

A. **Questions / interview.** Répondez aux questions suivantes ou utilisez-les pour interviewer un(e) autre étudiant(e).

1. Où habitait ta famille quand tu étais petit(e) ?
2. Quel était ton programme de télévision favori ?
3. Quelle était ta classe préférée ?
4. Quelles étaient tes distractions favorites ?
5. Quels étaient tes disques et tes livres préférés ?
6. Est-ce que tu avais un chien ou un chat ?
7. Où est-ce que tu allais en vacances ?
8. Qu'est-ce que tu faisais pendant tes vacances ?
9. Qu'est-ce que tu faisais après tes classes ?

B. **Le monde de votre enfance.** Faites une description d'un ou de plusieurs aspects du monde de votre enfance.

1. Un quartier ou une ville où vous avez habité (ou que vous avez visité) autrefois.
2. La maison où vous avez grandi. Comment était-elle ?
3. Un(e) ami(e) d'enfance. Comment était cette personne ?
4. Le lycée où vous avez fait vos études. Comment étaient les étudiants, les professeurs, les cours ?
5. Les dimanches de votre enfance. Que faisiez-vous d'habitude ?

C'est votre tour. Imaginez que dans trente ou quarante ans, un de vos petits enfants vous demande de lui parler du temps où vous étiez étudiant(e). Décrivez-lui votre vie (études, vie universitaire, activités, amis, famille, etc.)

[Marginal notes:]

Have students come up with additional sentences to describe Michel and Raymonde's vacation at Antibes.

Have students note the adding of the e to form the feminine of the name : Raymond — Raymonde ; Pascal — Pascale, René — Renée.

Remind students that they are describing people and places (which requires the imperfect) rather than events that took place at the times mentioned. With students' permission, these descriptions can be modified and used for listening practice. Students can also be asked to keep their descriptions and elaborate on them later in the chapter by describing an event that took place in each situation to help illustrate the distinction between the *passé composé* and the *imparfait*.

Have students work in small groups. One or several students can play the role of the grandchildren and ask questions about student life "back then."

❧ Saying things more precisely
Les adverbes

Présentation

A. Most French adverbs are formed by adding **-ment** to an adjective. This process is similar to the addition of *-ly* to many English adjectives to form adverbs. Most adverbs are formed according to the following rules:

1. Add **-ment** to the masculine singular form of any adjective that ends in a vowel.

facile	**facilement**	vrai	**vraiment**
sincère	**sincèrement**	poli	**poliment**

2. Add **-ment** to the feminine singular form of any adjective whose masculine singular form ends in a consonant.

parfait, parfaite	**parfaitement**
impulsif, impulsive	**impulsivement**
heureux, heureuse	**heureusement** *(fortunately)*
malheureux, malheureuse	**malheureusement** *(unfortunately)*
traditionnel, traditionnelle	**traditionnellement**
premier, première	**premièrement**
franc, franche	**franchement** *(frankly)*

3. If the masculine singular form of an adjective ends in **-ent** or **-ant**, replace the **-ent** with **-emment**, or the **-ant** with **-amment**, to form the corresponding adverb. In both cases the pronunciation of the adverb ending is the same: [amã].

patient	**patiemment**
intelligent	**intelligemment**
constant	**constamment**

B. There are certain common adverbs, a number of which you already know, that are not formed from adjectives :

aujourd'hui	souvent	vite	très
demain	toujours	bien	peu
hier	assez	mal *(badly)*	partout
déjà	beaucoup	aussi	là-bas *(over there)*
quelquefois	dur *(hard)*	pas encore *(not yet)*	

C. Adverbs can be used in several positions within a sentence:

1. Adverbs usually follow immediately a verb in a simple tense, such as the present tense.

Michel parle **constamment**.
Jacqueline attendait **patiemment** la fin de la classe.
Est-ce que le professeur parle **trop vite** ?

2. Short adverbs usually come between the auxiliary verb and the past participle of a verb in a compound tense, such as the **passé composé**. Adverbs that end in **-ment**, however, often follow the past participle.

Il a **déjà** fini ses devoirs.
Vous avez **mal** compris.
Marc a répondu **impulsivement**.
Exception :
J'ai travaillé **dur**.

3. Adverbs of time and place usually are placed at the beginning or end of a sentence.

Les magasins ne sont pas ouverts **aujourd'hui**.
Hier, un de mes amis a eu un accident.

D. Note that **ce que** can be used instead of an adverb of intensity in an exclamation.

Ce que c'est triste !   *It's so sad !*
Ce que je suis fatigué(e).   *I'm so tired.*

Mise en situation

Un concert en plein air. La famille Seguin *assiste à* un concert de rock *en plein air*. Mme Seguin n'apprécie pas beaucoup le rock et elle a envie de rentrer.

are attending / outdoor

MME SEGUIN   *Si on rentrait…?* Je suis terriblement fatiguée.

How about going home ?

CHRISTINE   Déjà…! On vient *à peine* d'arriver !

scarcely

MME SEGUIN   Cette fille chante horriblement mal, et l'orchestre ne vaut pas mieux. Franchement, ça me donne mal à la tête !

Point out the use of *si* + IMPERFECT, which means *What if…, How about…?*

CHRISTINE   Mais non, ils jouent très bien ! Le *batteur* en particulier est vraiment bon. Tu n'es pas d'accord, papa ?

drummer

M. SEGUIN   Pas vraiment… Moi, tu sais, je préfère être bien installé dans un *fauteuil* et lire tranquillement mon journal…

armchair

CHRISTINE   Ce que vous êtes *vieux jeu* tous les deux !

old-fashioned

M. SEGUIN   Premièrement, ma fille, on n'est pas vieux jeu simplement parce qu'on n'a pas les mêmes *goûts* que toi. Deuxièmement, il est l'heure de rentrer. Allez, range vite tes affaires.

tastes

Transformation : Donnez l'adverbe qui correspond à chacun des adjectifs suivants : (1) difficile, (2) final, (3) modeste, (4) courageux, (5) actif, (6) impulsif, (7) heureux, (8) patient, (9) constant, (10) traditionnel, (11) exceptionnel, (12) vrai

Arrêt d'autobus à Kinshasa (Zaïre)

Préparation

Un hold-up. A witness is testifying in court about a recent robbery. Using the cues provided, recreate his answers to the prosecutor's questions.

> **Modèle**   Quand ce hold-up a-t-il eu lieu ? (hier)
> **Il a eu lieu hier.**

1. Est-ce que vous avez observé l'incident ? (oui... bien)
2. Est-ce que la victime a résisté ? (oui... courageusement)
3. Est-ce que la victime a donné son argent à l'homme ? (oui... finalement)
4. Est-ce qu'il y a des crimes dans votre quartier ? (oui... souvent)
5. Est-ce que vous avez téléphoné à la police ? (oui... vite)
6. Quand est-ce que les agents sont arrivés ? (presque immédiatement)
7. Où est maintenant le criminel ? (là-bas)
8. Êtes-vous certain ? (oui... absolument)

Suggestion : Have one student play the role of the witness, another the role of the prosecutor. Another student or instructor can give cues.

Communication et vie pratique

A. Opinions. To express your opinions, choose one of the adverbs provided and, if necessary, make the sentence negative.

Options : Use as direct questions or adapt for directed dialogue (*Demandez à David s'il téléphone souvent à ses amis*, etc.).

1. Mon professeur de français parle...
   bien / vite / tout le temps / ?
2. Mes amis et moi, nous parlons français...
   rarement / souvent / tout le temps / ?
3. Je suis... fatigué(e).
   constamment / assez / très / rarement / un peu / ?
4. J'ai tendance à parler trop...
   impulsivement / franchement / vite / souvent / ?
5. L'année dernière, j'ai... travaillé.
   beaucoup / bien / mal / trop / ?
6. Je téléphone... à mes amis.
   souvent / rarement / quelquefois / tous les soirs / ?

B. La vie d'un(e) étudiant(e). The life of a student is not always easy. Make up sentences describing the problems that students face. Use an adverb in each of your sentences.

> **Exemple**   **Mes camarades de chambre parlent constamment au téléphone.**

Suggestion : Have students work in small groups and compare their statements. Have students repeat, describing the life of a professor, parent, roommate, etc.

> **C'est votre tour.** Vous assistez à un concert avec plusieurs amis. Vous avez des goûts très différents et chaque personne est fermement attachée à son point de vue. Imaginez la conversation.

❧Talking about the past
L'imparfait et le passé composé

Présentation

Although the imperfect and the **passé composé** are both past tenses, they have different purposes. Whether the imperfect or **passé composé** is used depends on the speaker's view or perception of a past action.

Suggestion : Use time line to further contrast *imparfait* vs. *passé composé*.

Have students contrast expressions that are typically used in the *passé composé* (e.g., *hier, la semaine dernière, le mois dernier*) with those used in the *imparfait* (e.g., *autrefois, à cette époque-là*).

Transformation : Je rentre à la maison. → Je rentrais à la maison quand j'ai rencontré Martine. (1) J'attends l'autobus. (2) Nous sommes au café. (3) Il fait des courses. (4) Vous allez à la gare. (5) Tu manges au restaurant. (6) Vous allez au cinéma. *Transformation :* Nous écoutons des disques. Pierre arrive. → Nous écoutions des disques quand Pierre est arrivé. (1) Paul étudie. Jacques téléphone. (2) Je fais du ski. Je me casse la jambe. (3) Patrick finit ses devoirs. Sa sœur entre. (4) Il fait beau. Nous faisons une promenade. (5) Hélène attend l'autobus. Il commence à pleuvoir. (6) Nous allons à la gare. Nous avons un accident.

Imperfect

Background

The imperfect is used to describe a situation that existed in the past. There is no concern for the time when the situation began or ended. For example, it can describe :

- a condition

  Il **pleuvait**.
  It was raining.

- a state of mind

  Elle **était** très malheureuse.
  She was very unhappy.

- an action that was continuing or was in progress

  Il **finissait** ses devoirs.
  He was finishing his homework.
  À cette époque-là, il **travaillait** dans une usine.
  At that time he was working in a factory.

Passé composé

Event

In contrast, the **passé composé** is used to describe specific events. It expresses :

- an action that is a completed event

  Il **a fini** ses devoirs.
  He finished his homework.

- an event that had a known beginning or end, or a specific duration, whether the duration is a few moments or many years

  Nous **avons attendu** pendant deux heurs.
  We waited for two hours.

- a change in state of mind or a reaction to an event

  J'**ai été** très surprise quand j'ai appris la nouvelle.
  I was very surprised when I heard the news.

- a succession of events, each event moving the story forward

  Elle **s'est réveillée**, elle **s'est habillée**, elle **a quitté** la maison.
  She woke up, got dressed, and left the house.

Repeated action

The imperfect describes a habitual action in the past.

> Le samedi, mon père **faisait** la cuisine.
> *My father used to do the cooking on Saturdays.*
> Autrefois, **j'allais** rarement au cinéma.
> *In the past, I rarely went to the movies.*

Specific action

In contrast, the **passé composé** describes what was done or said at a particular time.

> **Hier**, mon père **a fait** la cuisine.
> *Yesterday my father did the cooking.*
> Je **suis allé(e)** quatre fois au cinéma **la semaine dernière**.
> *I went to the movies four times last week.*

One of the most frequent cases where the **passé composé** and the imperfect are contrasted is when a continuing action is interrupted by a specific event.

> Nous **parlions** quand le professeur **est entré**.
> Ils **étaient** en train de manger quand nous **sommes arrivés**.
> Il **faisait** froid quand je **suis sortie** ce matin.

Mise en situation

Un accident de la route. Deux automobilistes, M. Fournier et M. Pessin, ont eu un petit accident. Ils expliquent ce qui s'est passé à l'agent de police.

L'AGENT	Qu'est-ce qui s'est passé ?
M. FOURNIER	Je *roulais* bien tranquillement, quand soudain, cet idiot a *débouché* juste devant moi. J'ai *freiné* mais je n'ai pas pu m'arrêter.
L'AGENT	À quelle vitesse alliez-vous ?
M. FOURNIER	Je n'allais pas vite. Je faisais peut-être du 40 à l'heure, mais pas plus.
L'AGENT	Vos *phares* étaient *allumés* ?
M. FOURNIER	Non, *il faisait encore jour* et la visibilité était bonne.
M. PESSIN	Ce n'est pas vrai. Il commençait à *faire sombre*. Je me suis arrêté au stop, j'ai bien regardé. Il *n'*y avait *rien*... Alors, j'ai tourné... Et vlan ! Il m'est *rentré dedans* !

was driving

pulled out / braked

Point out « *Je faisais du 40 à l'heure* » and have students give the meaning.
headlights / turned on

it was still daylight

to be dark

nothing

ran into me (colloquial)

Un petit accident

Préparation

A. Pourquoi? Bertrand veut toujours savoir pourquoi son ami Philippe fait ce qu'il fait. Donnez ses réponses aux questions de Bertrand.

Ask students to give additional reasons for each question. *Je suis allé chez le médecin parce que j'avais mal à la gorge, etc.*

Modèle   Pourquoi as-tu acheté un sandwich? (avoir faim)
J'ai acheté un sandwich parce que j'avais faim.

1. Pourquoi es-tu allé chez le médecin? (être malade)
2. Pourquoi t'es-tu couché à 9 heures? (être fatigué)
3. Pourquoi t'es-tu levé si tôt? (avoir beaucoup de travail)
4. Pourquoi es-tu allé à la poste? (vouloir envoyer une lettre)
5. Pourquoi as-tu vendu ta vieille voiture? (ne pas marcher bien)
6. Pourquoi es-tu resté à la maison? (avoir mal à la tête)
7. Pourquoi as-tu décidé de faire une promenade? (faire beau)
8. Pourquoi t'es-tu dépêché? (être en retard)

B. Que faisiez-vous? L'accident de la navette spatiale Challenger est un événement qui a choqué beaucoup de gens. Beaucoup se souviennent exactement de ce qu'ils faisaient au moment où ils ont appris la nouvelle.

Modèle   je / être chez des amis
J'étais chez des amis quand j'ai appris la nouvelle.

1. nous / être dans un magasin
2. mon père / venir de rentrer à la maison
3. vous / faire la vaisselle
4. je / servir le dîner
5. tu / s'habiller
6. mes amis / finir leur dîner
7. tu / attendre l'autobus
8. vous / écouter la radio

C. L'histoire de Cendrillon. Pour compléter l'histoire, mettez les verbes suggérés à l'imparfait ou au passé composé selon le cas.

Suggested for individual or small-group writing. Additional paragraph in workbook. Although paragraphs such as these are very helpful, students need also to write their own paragraphs in which the *passé composé* and *imparfait* are contrasted. See activities in this section and in the end-of-chapter *Communication et vie pratique* section.

Il était une fois une jeune fille qui _____ (s'appeler) Cendrillon. Elle _____ (avoir) deux demi-sœurs qui n'_____ (être) pas gentilles avec elle. C'_____ (être) Cendrillon qui _____ (faire) tout le travail à la maison.

Un jour, le prince _____ (décider) de donner un grand bal. Mais Cendrillon ne _____ (pouvoir) pas aller au bal parce qu'elle n'_____ (avoir) pas de jolis vêtements.

Cendrillon _____ (être) en train de pleurer quand sa marraine *(godmother)* _____ (arriver). Elle _____ (posséder) une baguette magique *(magic wand)*. La marraine _____ (toucher) les vêtements de Cendrillon et ils _____ (devenir) très beaux. Cendrillon _____ (promettre) à sa marraine de rentrer avant minuit et elle _____ (partir) au bal.

Le prince _____ (inviter) à danser la mystérieuse jeune fille et ils _____ (danser) pendant tout le bal. Cendrillon _____ (être) si heureuse qu'elle _____ (oublier) l'heure. Quand elle _____ (entendre) minuit sonner *(ring)*, elle _____ (partir) si vite qu'elle _____ (perdre) une de ses chaussures.

Le prince, qui _____ (aimer) Cendrillon, _____ (aller) dans toutes les maisons de son pays pour essayer de la retrouver. Finalement, le prince _____ (venir) à la maison où Cendrillon et ses sœurs _____ (habiter). Les deux sœurs _____ (essayer) la chaussure mais elle _____ (être) beaucoup trop petite pour elles. Timidement, Cendrillon _____ (demander) : « Est-ce que je peux l'essayer ? » La chaussure lui allait parfaitement. Il _____ (être) évident que la belle jeune fille du bal et Cendrillon _____ (être) la même personne. Le prince et Cendrillon _____ (se marier) et ils _____ (avoir) beaucoup d'enfants.

Communication et vie pratique

A. Cendrillon ! Tu viens de loin, ma petite ! L'histoire de Cendrillon appartient au folklore international et reflète les valeurs traditionnelles de notre culture. Transformez-la pour la rendre plus moderne, moins sexiste, plus amusante, etc. Vous pouvez changer les personnages, le pays où l'action a lieu, le développement de l'histoire ou sa conclusion. Si vous préférez, inventez une autre histoire.

B. Alors, raconte... Répondez aux questions suivantes ou utilisez-les pour interviewer un(e) autre étudiant(e). Choisissez un ou plusieurs des sujets suggérés.

Option : Can be used for small-group oral interviews where students write résumés of their partner's answers or as basis for individual student compositions. Topics can be done in one day or spread across several days.

La famille
Où et quand es-tu né(e) ? Est-ce que tu as grandi dans cette ville ? Est-ce que tu avais des frères et des sœurs ? Dans combien de villes différentes est-ce que tu as habité ?
Les amis
Comment s'appelaient tes meilleur(e)s ami(e)s ? Habitaient-ils (elles) près de chez toi ? Est-ce que vous étiez toujours très sages ? Veux-tu me raconter quelques aventures qui vous sont arrivées ? Est-ce que tu es resté(e) en contact avec ces ami(e)s ? Que sont-ils (elles) devenu(e)s ?
Les gens
Est-ce que tu te souviens d'une personne de ton enfance avec un plaisir particulier ? Qui était cette personne ? Pourquoi est-ce que tu te souviens de cette personne ? Est-ce que tu l'admirais beaucoup ? Comment était-il (elle) ?

Les études

Comment était le lycée où tu es allé(e)? Quel âge avais-tu quand tu es entré(e) au lycée? Quels étaient tes cours et tes professeurs préférés? Est-ce que tu avais un travail après l'école? En quoi consistait ce travail? Quelles étaient tes responsabilités à la maison? En quelle année est-ce que tu as fini tes études secondaires? Qu'est-ce que tu as fait après? Pourquoi as-tu décidé de venir faire tes études à cette université?

Les voyages

Raconte-moi un voyage que tu as fait récemment ou quand tu étais petit(e). Où est-ce que tu es allé(e)? Avec qui? Qu'est-ce que tu as fait? Comment est-ce que c'était? Est-ce que tu t'es bien amusé(e)?

C. **Les étapes de la vie.** Racontez votre vie jusqu'au moment présent. Utilisez le vocabulaire présenté dans **Les mots et la vie.**

Suggested for individual written work.

C'est votre tour. Il y a eu un petit accident sur le campus entre un automobiliste et un cycliste. Le cycliste ne s'est pas arrêté au feu rouge et il a été renversé *(knocked down)* par une voiture qui avait la priorité. Imaginez et jouez la scène entre le cycliste, l'automobiliste et les témoins.

Determine (or have students determine) the parameters of the accident (e.g., time of day, description of cyclist and driver, place of accident, witnesses) and then have students role-play the situation.

❧Talking about continuing actions
Depuis et autres expressions de temps

Présentation

To indicate that an action or condition that began in the past is still going on in the present, the present tense is used with the expressions **depuis, il y a... que,** or **ça fait... que.**

A. Depuis, il y a... que, and **ça fait... que** can be used interchangeably when the condition or action that started in the past has lasted a given amount of time. In this case their meaning corresponds to *for* in English. Note that each expression requires a different word order.

Nous habitons ici **depuis** trois mois.
Il y a trois mois **que** nous habitons ici.   *We've been living here for three months.*
Ça fait trois mois **que** nous habitons ici.

Il pleut **depuis** trois jours.
Il y a trois jours **qu'**il pleut.   } *It has been raining for three days.*
Ça fait trois jours **qu'**il pleut.

J'attends **depuis** vingt minutes.
Il y a vingt minutes **que**
  j'attends.   } *I've been waiting for twenty
Ça fait vingt minutes **que**   minutes.*
  j'attends.

B. To indicate that a condition or action started at a particular time in the past, only **depuis** is used; its meaning corresponds in this case to *since* in English.

Suzanne enseigne dans une   *Suzanne has been teaching in a*
  école bilingue **depuis l'année**   *bilingual school since last year.*
  dernière.
André sort avec Lucette **depuis**   *André has been going out with*
  Noël.   *Lucette since Christmas.*

In conversational French, **depuis quand** (*since when*) and **depuis combien de temps** (*how long*) are often used interchangeably.

Depuis quand as-tu ton diplôme? (depuis le mois de juin, depuis deux mois, etc.)
Depuis combien de temps travailles-tu ici? (depuis six mois, depuis le premier mars, etc.)

C. Il y a without **que** is the equivalent of the English word *ago*. In this case a past tense is used.

Il a fini ses études **il y a** deux   *He finished school two years ago.*
  ans.
Raymonde et Pierre se sont   *Raymonde and Pierre got married*
  mariés **il y a** six mois.   *six months ago.*

D. To speak of an action or condition that has a specific beginning and ending, **pendant** (*for, during*) is used.

Pendant combien de temps   *How long did you live in Canada?*
  avez-vous habité au Canada?
Nous avons habité au Canada   *We lived in Canada for two years.*
  pendant deux ans.
Pendant nos vacances nous   *During our vacation we are going*
  allons travailler dans un   *to work in a restaurant.*
  restaurant.

Note the different meanings conveyed by **depuis** and **pendant**:

J'ai étudié à l'université Laval   *I studied at Laval University for*
  pendant trois ans.   *three years.*
J'étudie à l'université Laval   *I've been studying at Laval*
  depuis trois ans.   *University for three years.*

Transformation : Transformez les phrases suivantes selon les modèles donnés. *Modèle :* Je suis ici depuis deux mois. → Il y a deux mois que je suis ici. (1) Ils travaillent depuis une heure. (2) Il neige depuis deux jours. (3) Nous sommes en classe depuis un quart d'heure. (4) Elle a cette voiture depuis trois ans. (5) Ils sont au Canada depuis longtemps. *Modèle :* Il y a une heure que nous attendons ici. → Nous attendons ici depuis une heure. (1) Il y a une semaine qu'il pleut. (2) Il y a une heure qu'elle étudie. (3) Il y a vingt minutes que je regarde la télévision. (4) Il y a quinze ans qu'elle habite à Toronto. (5) Il y a deux jours que ma tante est ici.

Mise en situation

À la plage. Laurence est en vacances sur la Côte d'Azur. Elle est en train de *prendre un bain de soleil*. Un beau jeune homme bien *bronzé* vient *s'asseoir* à côté d'elle.

to sunbathe / tanned / to sit down

THIERRY	Bonjour, mademoiselle. *Vous permettez…*? Il y a longtemps que vous êtes ici?
LAURENCE	Non, seulement deux jours. Nous sommes arrivés dimanche soir. Et vous…?
THIERRY	Je suis ici depuis le début du mois. Mais, malheureusement, je dois repartir dans trois jours. Pendant combien de temps allez-vous rester à Antibes?
LAURENCE	Pendant quinze jours. Après ça, je vais partir en Corse.
THIERRY	Ah oui…? Je suis allé en Corse il y a deux ans. C'était formidable…! Mais, vous partez déjà…?!
LAURENCE	Oui, je ne peux pas rester *au soleil* trop longtemps.
THIERRY	Vous *prenez* facilement *des coups de soleil*?
LAURENCE	Oui. Le premier jour, je suis restée sur la plage pendant tout l'après-midi. Après ça, j'étais rouge comme une tomate!

May I?

in the sun

get sunburned

Préparation

A. Interview. Léon Forestier se présente comme candidat pour un poste dans un service d'administration québécois. On lui pose des questions. Formulez ses réponses selon les indications données.

> **Modèle** Excusez-moi, monsieur, est-ce qu'il y a longtemps que vous attendez? (non… seulement dix minutes)
> **Non, il y a seulement dix minutes que j'attends.**

1. Depuis quand cherchez-vous un nouvel emploi? (janvier)
2. Quand avez-vous fini vos études? (trois ans)
3. Depuis quand habitez-vous à Québec? (deux ans)
4. Pendant combien de temps êtes-vous resté dans votre emploi précédent? (trois mois)
5. Quand avez-vous commencé à travailler pour la première fois? (sept ans)
6. Depuis quand parlez-vous anglais? (l'âge de dix ans)

B. Cours de traduction. Le professeur a demandé à ses étudiants de traduire les phrases suivantes. Comment faut-il les traduire?

1. How long have you been here?
2. How long have you been living in Toronto?
3. I've been studying for four hours.
4. I stayed in the sun for two hours.
5. They got married a week ago.
6. He's been working in this office since 1955.
7. We've been waiting since two o'clock.
8. She retired two years ago.

Communication et vie pratique

A. **Questions/interview.** Répondez aux questions suivantes ou utilisez-les pour interviewer un(e) autre étudiant(e).

1. Depuis quand es-tu étudiant(e) dans cette université?
2. Depuis combien de temps étudies-tu le français?
3. Pendant combien de temps as-tu étudié le français au lycée?
4. Pendant combien de temps as-tu regardé la télévision hier?
5. Où habitais-tu il y a dix ans?
6. Où étais-tu il y a deux heures?
7. Quand as-tu voyagé seul(e) pour la première fois?
8. Est-ce que tu as une voiture? Depuis quand?
9. Où est-ce que tu habites maintenant?
10. Depuis quand habites-tu à cet endroit?

B. **Points communs...** Posez des questions aux autres étudiants pour découvrir qui, dans votre classe, se trouve dans les situations suivantes.

Trouvez un(e) étudiant(e)...

1. qui est allé(e) au Canada pendant ses vacances.
2. qui est marié(e) depuis un an ou plus.
3. qui a habité dans la même ville pendant dix ans.
4. qui est né(e) il y a vingt et un ans.
5. qui est sorti(e) avec la même personne pendant plus de six ans.
6. qui parle une langue étrangère depuis son enfance.
7. qui a habité dans un pays étranger pendant un an ou plus.
8. qui n'a jamais été absent(e) pendant tout le trimestre.

C'est votre tour. Vous êtes à la plage. Vous désirez faire la connaissance d'un jeune homme ou d'une jeune fille que vous trouvez sympathique. Parlez-lui et flirtez un peu. Utilisez la **Mise en situation** comme point de départ.

Intégration et perspectives

Souvenirs d'enfance de Kiwele Shamavu

Kiwele Shamavu, un Africain né au Zaïre, parle de son enfance.

LE REPORTER	Où est-ce que vous avez passé votre enfance?
KIWELE	Je suis né et j'ai grandi dans un petit village du Zaïre. C'était à l'époque où le Congo était encore sous le contrôle de la Belgique.
LE REPORTER	Combien d'habitants y avait-il dans votre village?

KIWELE	C'était un petit village d'environ trois ou quatre cents habitants situé à cinquante kilomètres de Kisangani.	
LE REPORTER	Quelle langue parlait-on dans votre village ?	
KIWELE	Notre tribu parlait le luba. Mais la langue de communication avec les autres tribus était le swahili, et à l'école on parlait français. J'ai donc trois langues *maternelles*.	**native**
LE REPORTER	Il y avait une école dans votre village ?	
KIWELE	Oui, c'était une école *dirigée* par des missionnaires belges. C'est là que je suis allé à l'école jusqu'à l'âge de douze ans.	**directed**
LE REPORTER	Et après, qu'est-ce que vous avez fait ?	
KIWELE	Mon grand-père, qui était le chef du village, m'a envoyé en Belgique pour continuer mes études au lycée. Je suis resté en Belgique pendant six ans et en France pendant quatre ans. Je suis retourné au Congo seulement une fois pendant toute cette période. C'était l'année où j'ai commencé mes études universitaires en France. Au début, cette séparation a été très difficile.	
LE REPORTER	Vous avez des frères et des sœurs ?	
KIWELE	Oui, j'ai cinq frères et trois sœurs, et des multitudes de cousins ! Mes parents habitaient dans une grande maison au centre du village. Oncles, tantes, cousins, cousines, nous formions tous une grande famille. Un de mes cousins était *gardien* dans une réserve d'animaux sauvages. Quelquefois, il m'emmenait avec lui quand il partait en jeep dans la *brousse*. J'avais toujours grand plaisir à l'accompagner.	**guard** **bush**
LE REPORTER	Est-ce que vous avez été très surpris quand vous êtes arrivé à Bruxelles pour la première fois ?	
KIWELE	Oui, c'était en hiver et il y avait de la neige. J'étais absolument *ravi*. J'ai touché la neige. Et puis, j'ai vite *rempli* mes *poches* de neige. La dame qui m'attendait à l'aéroport m'a demandé : « Mais Kiwele, qu'est-ce que tu fais ? Pourquoi mets-tu de la neige dans tes poches ? » Et j'ai répondu : « C'est pour l'envoyer à maman. »	**delighted / filled / pockets**

Texte basé sur une interview avec un Africain originaire du Zaïre.

Compréhension. Répondez aux questions suivantes selon les renseignements donnés.

1. Où est-ce que Kiwele a passé son enfance ?
2. Est-ce qu'il habitait dans une grande ville ?
3. Quelles langues est-ce que Kiwele parle ?
4. Où est-ce qu'il allait à l'école ?
5. Pourquoi est-ce qu'il est parti en Belgique quand il avait douze ans ?
6. Est-ce que Kiwele est resté longtemps sans retourner dans son pays ?
7. Est-ce que Kiwele était le seul enfant de sa famille ?
8. Quelle a été sa réaction quand il est arrivé à Bruxelles ?
9. Pourquoi a-t-il mis de la neige dans ses poches ?

Option : Have students write a description of Kiwele Shamavu using questions as a guide. Have part of the class play the role of Kiwele ; the others ask questions, using those in the *Compréhension* as a point of departure.

Notes culturelles: *Le Zaïre*

La république du Zaïre (ancien Congo belge), avec une population de 28 millions d'habitants, est le deuxième pays d'Afrique. Colonie belge pendant quatre-vingts ans, le Zaïre est devenu indépendant en 1960. Quelques années après, le Zaïre était totalement africanisé : on a demandé à tous les Zaïrois d'adopter un nom africain et on a donné des noms africains aux rues et aux villes. Par exemple, la capitale, Léopold-ville, est devenue Kinshasa.

L'influence de la langue et de la culture françaises est toujours présente au Zaïre *de même que* dans les dix-sept pays d'Afrique noire qui sont devenus indépendants pendant les années soixante. La plupart de ces pays sont membres de la Communauté Franco-Africaine et ont une *monnaie* commune (le franc C.F.A.).

just as

currency

Marché à Kinshasa, capitale du Zaïre

Kinshasa

Communication et vie pratique

A. Souvenirs d'enfance. Racontez vos propres souvenirs d'enfance ou les souvenirs d'une autre personne (parents, grands-parents, ami(e), personne imaginaire).

B. Rapports des témoins. Vous étiez présent(e) quand les événements suivants ont eu lieu. Répondez aux questions de l'agent de police (joué(e) par un(e) autre étudiant(e)). Les autres étudiants écoutent et prennent des notes. Ensuite ils vont préparer un rapport oral ou écrit.

Suggestions :

1. Un piéton *(pedestrian)* qui traversait la rue a été renversé par un cycliste.
2. Il y a eu un cambriolage dans votre quartier.
3. Il y a eu une dispute dans un des bars du quartier.

C. Un événement spécial. Tout le monde se souvient d'un événement spécial avec un plaisir particulier. Décrivez un de vos souvenirs (fête, anniversaire, occasion spéciale). Qu'est-ce que vous avez fait ? Quelles étaient vos réactions et vos sentiments ? Qui était là ? Où étiez-vous ?, etc. N'oubliez pas d'utiliser le vocabulaire présenté dans **Les mots et la vie** de ce chapitre.

D. Portraits. Racontez la vie de différentes personnes célèbres ou de différents personnages historiques sans mentionner leur nom. Les autres étudiants vont deviner l'identité de cette personne.

E. Voyage dans le temps. « Cela se passait il y a vingt siècles sur une planète qui s'appelait la Terre… » Ainsi commence le rapport d'un historien du 40ᵉ siècle décrivant la vie telle qu'elle existait sur la Terre vingt siècles plus tôt. Complétez son rapport.

• *Vocabulaire*

Noms

° l'**adolescence** (f)
l'**aîné(e)** *the eldest*
l'**amour** (m) *love*
l'**arrière-grand-mère** (f) *great-grandmother*
le **baptême** *baptism*
le **batteur** *drummer*
le **bonheur** *happiness*
la **brousse** *brush*
le **bûcheron** *logger*
le **cadet**, la **cadette** *the youngest*
les **cendres** (f) *ashes*
le **cendrier** *ashtray*

le **chagrin** *grief, annoyance*
le **chef** *chief, head*
le **cheval**, les **chevaux** *horse*
les **condoléances** (f) *condolences, sympathy*
la **cuiller** *spoon*
° le **divorce**
° le **drame**
l'**enfance** (f) *childhood*
l'**enterrement** (m) *burial*
° la **fantaisie**
le **fauteuil** *armchair*
la **fête** *patron saint's day*
la **fierté** *pride*

Useful for writing practice. *Option :* Have students prepare a list of questions to ask other students (or instructor) about their childhood. Have them interview each other in small groups and then prepare a written résumé of the conversation.

Have "witnesses" decide on description of the accident and those involved ahead of time.

Option : Have students work in small groups, each group responsible for a different aspect of life in the 20th century. After editing (and perhaps elaboration) by the instructor, the final and longer version could be used for reading or listening practice.

la **fumée**   *smoke*
les **félicitations**
     (f)   *congratulations*
le **gardien**   *guard*
le **goût**   *taste*
l'**inquiétude** (f)   *anxiety, worry, restlessness*
° la **jeep**
la **jeunesse**   *youth*
° la **joie**
le **marriage**   *marriage, wedding*
la **messe**   *mass*
° le, la **missionnaire**
la **mort**   *death*
le **mot**   *word*
la **naissance**   *birth*
la **parole**   *word*
le **pas**   *footstep, step*
la **peine**   *pain*
le **phare**   *headlight*
la **poche**   *pocket*
° le **poète**
° le **regret**
la **retraite**   *retirement*
le **rond**   *ring*
la **réserve**   *reservation*
la **solidarité**   *fellowship*
° la **surprise**
° le **swahili**
la **tendresse**   *tenderness*
le **traîneau**   *sleigh*
la **tribu**   *tribe*
le **témoin**   *witness*
la **vieillesse**   *old age*
° la **visibilité**
les **vœux** (m)   *wishes*

Verbes

allumer   *to light, turn on*
s'asseoir   *to sit down*
assister à   *to attend*
déboucher   *to pull out*

élever   *to bring up, to rear*
éprouver   *to feel*
exprimer   *to express*
freiner   *to brake*
pleurer   *to cry*
remplir   *to fill*
reposer   *to put back down*
rouler   *to go, to drive, to roll*
vivre   *to live*

Adjectifs

° **adulte**
aîné(e)   *elder*
bloqué(e)   *snowed in, blocked*
bronzé(e)   *suntanned*
cadet, cadette   *younger*
dirigé(e)   *directed*
discret, discrète   *discreet, unobtrusive*
dur(e)   *difficult, hard*
installé(e)   *settled*
jaloux, jalouse   *jealous*
maternel(le)   *native*
° **spontané(e)**

Adverbes

(Voir p. 319)

Divers

ça fait... que   *for*
en plein air   *in the open air*
hein?   *isn't it so? (colloquial for n'est-ce pas?)*
il fait jour   *it is daylight*
il fait sombre   *it is dark*
il y a   *ago*
il y a... que   *for*
prendre un bain de soleil   *to sunbathe*
prendre un coup de soleil   *to get sunburned*
rentrer dedans   *to run into*
vieux jeu   *old-fashioned*

CHAPITRE QUATORZE

Communication objectives

Talking about the world we live in

1. Talking about what and whom we know
2. Referring to things already mentioned
3. Talking about intentions and plans for the future
4. Indicating what we see and what we believe

Structures

Les mots et la vie : Le monde où nous vivons

    Les verbes **connaître** et **savoir**

    Les pronoms **y** et **en**

    Le futur

    Les verbes **voir** et **croire**

Face à l'avenir

Mise en scène

L'avenir ? Quel avenir ?

Point out that *à l'avenir* means *in the future.*

Au cours d'une enquête sur les sentiments des jeunes Françaises au sujet de leur *avenir*, une journaliste parle avec Christine, une Parisienne. Elle est plutôt pessimiste.

future

LA JOURNALISTE	À votre avis, est-ce que vos études sont une bonne préparation pour la vie ?
CHRISTINE	Pas particulièrement. Autrefois, on faisait des études et on avait un *boulot* assuré. Maintenant les études ne *mènent* à rien.
LA JOURNALISTE	Est-ce que le *but* principal des études est de préparer à une profession ?
CHRISTINE	Pour moi, oui. On nous dit que c'est pour nous donner une bonne culture générale, pour nous préparer à jouer notre rôle dans la société. Tout ça, *c'est bien beau*, mais ça ne va pas m'aider à gagner ma vie. Et sans boulot, quel rôle peut-on jouer ?
LA JOURNALISTE	Est-ce que vous avez l'intention de vous marier un jour ?
CHRISTINE	Peut-être, mais je ne suis pas *pressée*. Le mariage est une chose sérieuse et je ne veux pas *me tromper*. Être mariée, avoir un ou deux *gosses*, oui, je voudrais bien, éventuellement. Mais, *de toute façon*, je veux avoir un travail intéres-

job (slang) / lead

goal

that's all well and good

in a hurry
make a mistake
kids (slang)
at any rate

sant et raisonnablement bien payé. Je ne veux pas être obli-
gée de *compter sur quelqu'un d'autre*.   count on / someone else

LA JOURNALISTE   Est-ce que vous pensez que les femmes et les hommes ont
les mêmes chances de réussir dans la vie ?

CHRISTINE   En théorie, oui. En réalité, non.

LA JOURNALISTE   Quel *sentiment* avez-vous quand vous pensez à l'avenir ?   feeling

CHRISTINE   Je suis un peu *inquiète*. Avec tous les problèmes qu'il y a   worried
dans le monde, c'est difficile de savoir ce qui va *arriver*.   happen
L'avenir, c'est un gros *point d'interrogation*.   question mark

Compréhension. Quelle est l'opinion de Christine sur les sujets suivants ?

Have students prepare orally
or in writing a paragraph that
describes Christine. Have
them answer personally the
questions in the reading.

1. les études   3. le travail   5. l'avenir
2. le mariage   4. l'égalité entre les sexes

Option : Have students
answer these same questions
(for themselves and / or for
Americans in general) and
then have them compare their
answers with those in the
Notes culturelles.

Notes culturelles: *Questions internationales*

Comment les Français *voient*-ils le monde où ils vivent ? Quels sont leurs   see
espoirs et leurs préoccupations ? Voici les résultats de quelques
sondages *portant sur* ce sujet. Notez que dans certains cas la même ques-   dealing with
tion a été posée dans différents pays, ce qui permet de faire des comparaisons.

1. **Les amis de la France**
   Parmi les pays suivants, quels sont les deux pays que vous considérez comme les meilleurs amis de la France ?

   — la R.F.A. (Allemagne de l'Ouest)   48%
   — la Belgique   38%
   — les États-Unis   33%
   — l'Italie   16%
   — la Grande-Bretagne   16%
   — l'Union Soviétique   2%
   — Sans opinion   16%

Point out that R.F.A. stands
for la République Fédérale
Allemande.

2. **Les grandes préoccupations**
   Quelles sont vos plus grandes préoccupations en ce qui concerne
   votre pays ?

	France	*R.F.A.*	*G.-B.*	*Italie*	*États-Unis*	*Japon*	
Les *menaces* de *guerre* ..	47	14	4056	32	35		threat / war
L'inflation	39	9	18	38	30	26	
Le chômage	78	52	60	69	36	16	
Les armes nucléaires ..	26	15	43	39	28	32	
L'excès des dépenses de l'*État*	21	5	12	19	26	21	state
La médiocrité du gouvernement	24	7	19	25	21	16	

3. Le danger d'une guerre mondiale

Un Francais sur quatre considère qu'une guerre mondiale est inévitable. Cette opinion est partagée par la plupart des habitants des pays *occidentaux*. Les Français et les Américains sont les plus pessimistes de tous.   western

4. Les causes

Selon vous, quels sont, sur cette liste, les facteurs les plus importants pour expliquer les tensions internationales actuelles?

	France	R.F.A.	G.-B.	Italie	États-Unis	Japon
L'*accroissement* du potentiel militaire soviétique	31	50	47	37	37	48
L'accroissement du potentiel militaire américain	20	41	37	26	19	30
Les *taux d'intérêt* américains et le rôle du dollar	19	26	10	22	16	10
L'extension de l'influence soviétique dans le monde	24	19	20	14	21	19
L'*insuffisance* de l'unité européenne	25	32	19	26	8	7

growth

interest rates

inadequacy

5. Les solutions

Selon vous, quels sont, sur cette liste, les objectifs les plus importants pour assurer dans l'avenir la sécurité des pays occidentaux?

	France	R.F.A.	G.-B.	Italie	États-Unis	Japon
Maintenir un *équilibre* des forces militaires avec l'U.R.S.S.	21	33	32	13	22	21
Promouvoir une cooperation *efficace* entre l'Europe et les États-Unis..........	19	34	23	20	28	19
Renforcer l'unité économique de l'Europe	33	32	14	35	14	15
Poursuivre le dialogue et les contacts avec l'U.R.S.S.	18	43	36	18	32	27
Accroître la collaboration des pays de l'Europe de l'Ouest en matière de défense................	19	18	17	23	18	10

balance

promote
effective

carry on

increase

6. La solidarité humaine

Parmi les grands problèmes d'aujourd'hui, la faim dans le monde est le problème qui préoccupe le plus les Français (67%). Viennent ensuite le chômage (65%) et la *course aux armements* (46%). Quant à la possibilité de faire quelque chose pour *résoudre* ces problèmes, la plupart des personnes interrogées sont assez pessimistes. Beaucoup sont personnellement prêtes à aider les gens qui ont faim (on estime qu'une personne sur six a faim, et une personne sur quatre souffre de malnutrition), mais la plupart pensent que le problème doit être traité au *niveau* des gouvernements et des organismes internationaux.

arms race
resolve

level

(Source: *Francoscopie*)

Les mots et la vie : *Le monde où nous vivons*

Étudiez le vocabulaire présenté dans chaque section et répondez aux questions.

Les dangers qui menacent notre planète. La liste suivante représente certains dangers qui menacent l'avenir de notre planète ou la qualité de la vie sur notre planète. À votre avis, quels sont les dangers les plus sérieux et pourquoi ?

Star Wars = *La Guerre des étoiles*

Options : (1) Have students also answer these questions from point of view of their parents' generation and / or for Americans in general. (2) Find headlines or articles relating to the topics given in *Les mots et la vie* ; students can then be asked to read the headline or scan the article to determine the general topic.

les catastrophes naturelles : une inondation *(flood)*, un tremblement de terre *(earthquake)*, une éruption de volcan, un cyclone
le risque d'une guerre nucléaire
le risque d'une catastrophe dans une centrale *(power plant)* nucléaire
la pollution de l'atmosphère et de l'environnement
les conflits et les guerres entre les nations
la course aux armements
la surpopulation
la faim
la crise de l'énergie

Centrale nucléaire à Saint-Laurent-des-Eaux

Les problèmes sociaux et politiques. Chaque pays a ses problèmes. Quels sont, à votre avis, les problèmes les plus sérieux dans votre pays ? Quels sont les problèmes qui vous préoccupent le plus personnellement ? Expliquez.

le chômage
les grèves
l'inflation
la violence et les crimes
les inégalités sociales
le racisme
le sexisme

Point out that *chômeur* / *euse* means an unemployed worker ; *en chômage* means unemployed.

La recherche et le progrès. À votre avis, quels sont les aspects de la recherche et du progrès qui vont apporter le plus de changements dans notre vie ? Expliquez. À quels aspects de la recherche et du progrès vous intéressez-vous le plus personnellement et pourquoi ?

La recherche : la recherche scientifique et médicale
La technologie : le progrès technologique, les technologies nouvelles
— l'informatique, la robotique, l'électronique
L'exploration spatiale : la conquête de l'espace, un satellite, une fusée *(rocket)*, une navette spatiale *(space shuttle)*, un(e) astronaute, un vaisseau spatial *(space ship)*, la lune *(moon)*
L'exploration sous-marine *(undersea)*
La lutte contre la pollution, la maladie, etc.

Point out that *faire des recherches* to do research ; *faire une expérience* is to conduct an experiment.

Lancement d'une fusée *Ariane*

Explorations
❧Talking about what and whom we know
Les verbes *connaître* et *savoir*

The irregular verbs **connaître** and **savoir** correspond to the English verb *to know*; however, they cannot be used interchangeably.

Connaître	
je **connais**	nous **connaissons**
tu **connais**	vous **connaissez**
il / elle / on **connaît**	ils / elles **connaissent**

passé composé : j'**ai connu**
subjonctif : Il faut que **je connaisse**

Savoir	
je **sais**	nous **savons**
tu **sais**	vous **savez**
il / elle / on **sait**	ils / elles **savent**

passé composé : j'**ai su**
subjonctif : Il faut que **je sache**

A. Connaître is used in the sense of *to be familiar with* or *to be acquainted with*. It is always used with a direct object (e.g., people, places, etc.).

> Est-ce que vous **connaissez** le vieux Lyon?
> À cette époque-là, je **connaissais** bien Madame Bertrand.
> Je n'**ai** pas **connu** mon grand-père.

Faire la connaissance de is another frequently used expression meaning *to become acquainted with* in the sense of *to meet*.

> Est-ce que vous **avez fait la connaissance de** mon cousin?
> J'**ai fait sa connaissance** à Paris.

B. Savoir is used in the sense of *to know facts* or *to know how to do something*. It can be used with a direct object, a clause, an infinitive, or by itself.

> **Savez**-vous la date de son anniversaire?
> — Est-ce que tu **sais** qui est Jules Verne? — Non, je ne **sais** pas qui c'est.
> Il ne **sait** pas nager.
> — Paul sort avec Anne. — Oui, je **sais**.

Point out that the circumflex occurs only before the letter *t* in the forms of *connaître*.

Point out the pronunciation of *je ne sais pas* in fast speech : /ʃepa/.

Point out that the noun *savant* refers to a person who is learned or erudite and can also mean a scientist or a scholar.

C. In the **passé composé**, **savoir** and **connaître** may have idiomatic meanings.

J'**ai su** qu'ils étaient en Belgique.	*I learned that they were in Belgium.*
Comment est-ce que tu l'**as su** ?	*How did you find it out ?*
Elle l'**a connu** à Dijon.	*She met him (made his acquaintance) in Dijon.*
Ils **se sont connus** à Dijon.	*They met in Dijon.*

Point out the difference between *rencontrer* (to meet by chance) ; *retrouver* (to meet by appointment) ; and *se connaître* (to meet each other or to make each other's acquaintance).

D. The following verbs are conjugated like **connaître** :

reconnaître *to recognize*	Je l'**ai reconnu(e)** tout de suite.
disparaître *to disappear*	Mon porte-monnaie **a disparu**.
paraître *to appear, to seem, to look*	Vous **paraissez** fatigué(e).

Suggestion : Point out that *il paraît que* (it seems or I've heard that) is used to relate hearsay. One uses, however, *on dirait* instead of *il paraît* in expressions such as *On dirait qu'il va pleuvoir*.

Mise en situation

Des nouveaux venus dans le quartier. Deux habitants du quartier ont remarqué la présence de deux personnes qu'ils ne connaissent pas. Ils se demandent qui sont ces nouveaux-venus.

Point out the role of the concierge as building caretaker and the long-standing reputation that the concierge has of knowing everything that goes on in his or her building.

M. FAVRE	Ce garçon et cette fille, là-bas, vous savez qui c'est… ?
MME THOMAS	Non, je ne sais pas… Je ne les connais pas. *Demandez donc à la concierge*, elle connaît tout le monde…
M. FAVRE	Dites, Madame Lebrun, ces jeunes gens qui sont *assis* à la terrasse du café, vous les connaissez ?
MME LEBRUN	Bien sûr que je les connais ! C'est ma fille et son fiancé. Vous ne la reconnaissez pas ?
M. FAVRE	Eh bien non, je ne l'ai pas reconnue… !
MME THOMAS	Moi non plus ! Où est-ce qu'elle a fait la connaissance de son fiancé ?
MME LEBRUN	Ils se sont connus à l'université…
MME THOMAS	Ah, bon… ?! J'ai su qu'elle était à Paris mais je ne savais pas qu'elle faisait des études !

why don't you ask

building caretaker

seated

Substitution : (1) Je le connais bien. *(vous / mes parents / le professeur / nous / tu)* (2) Tu sais la réponse. *(je / les étudiants / nous / mon ami / vous)* (3) Je connaissais bien les Dupont à cette époque-là. *(mes parents / nous / tu / Anne / vous)* (4) Nous ne savions pas cela. *(vous / ses cousins / tu / je / Marc / nous)*

Préparation

A. **Est-ce que vous les connaissez ?** Catherine veut savoir si les étudiants français connaissent bien leurs professeurs. Qu'est-ce qu'ils répondent ?

> **Modèle** nous / pas très bien
> **Nous ne les connaissons pas très bien.**

1. je / très bien
2. Marc / assez bien
3. certains étudiants / pas du tout
4. nous / un peu
5. tu / pas très bien
6. vous / assez bien

B. Qui sait nager ? Roger veut organiser une excursion en bateau sur le lac d'Annecy et il veut savoir qui sait bien nager. Que répondent ses amis ?

Modèles   Daniel (oui) → **Daniel sait bien nager.**
   ou: Hervé (non) → **Hervé ne sait pas bien nager.**

1. je (oui)
2. Michelle (non)
3. tu (non)
4. nous (oui)
5. Armand (oui)
6. vous (non)
7. les autres (oui)

C. Quelqu'un qui sait toujours tout. Jean-Paul Saitout est une de ces personnes qui sait tout et qui connaît tout le monde. Utilisez les indications données pour formuler ses réactions aux différents sujets mentionnés.

Modèles   la réponse → **Bien sûr que je sais la réponse.**
   ou: Pierre → **Bien sûr que je connais Pierre.**

1. la date de l'examen
2. cette ville
3. les parents de Julien
4. faire la cuisine
5. nager
6. un bon restaurant
7. Marseille
8. l'adresse de Michelle
9. le numéro de téléphone de Françoise
10. la femme de Robert

Communication et vie pratique

A. Savoir n'est pas connaître. Utilisez les suggestions suivantes pour poser des questions aux autres étudiants de votre classe au sujet de ce qu'ils savent et des gens ou des endroits qu'il connaissent.

Put different cues (e.g., peindre, les différents quartiers) on individual note cards. Students circulate asking other students questions using the cues on their cards. They write down answers for use in large-group follow-up (e.g., Michel sait peindre ; Roger et Élise ne savent pas peindre).

Exemples   des Français → **Est-ce que tu connais des Français ?**
   ou: conduire → **Est-ce que tu sais conduire ?**

1. nager
2. les différents quartiers de ta ville
3. où on peut acheter des disques français
4. tes voisins
5. une personne célèbre
6. faire du ski
7. parler chinois
8. ce que tu vas faire l'an prochain
9. qui a inventé la bombe atomique

B. Inventaire. Comparez avec un(e) autre étudiant(e) les gens et les endroits que vous connaissez et que vous ne connaissez pas.

Exemple   **Je ne connais pas le nouveau restaurant près du campus. Et toi, est-ce que tu le connais ?**

C'est votre tour. Imaginez que vous venez d'une petite ville de France où tout le monde se connaît. Vous avez invité quelques ami(e)s américain(e)s que vous avez connu(e)s à l'université à venir vous rendre visite. Tout le monde se demande qui sont ces inconnu(e)s. Utilisez la **Mise en situation** comme guide.

Option : Students ask each other questions to determine whether they know the same things (e.g., *Est-ce que vous savez qui a inventé le téléphone ?*). If the student does not know the answer, he or she can give up (*Je donne ma langue au chat*).

Vary the identity of the visitors to the village (e.g., cousins from Paris, friends from another European country) and where they got acquainted (e.g., while an exchange student, on vacation).

✺Referring to things already mentioned
Les pronoms *y* et *en*

Présentation

Two object pronouns can be used to replace prepositional phrases.

A. The pronoun **y** is used to replace a prepositional phrase indicating location. Its meaning is often approximated by *there*. Like direct and indirect object pronouns, **y** is placed before the verb except in affirmative commands.

Je vais **à Québec** la semaine prochaine.	J'**y** vais la semaine prochaine.
Elle va rester **en Belgique** tout l'été.	Elle va **y** rester tout l'été.
Roland n'est jamais entré **dans ce musée**.	Roland n'**y** est jamais entré.
N'allez pas **chez le dentiste**.	N'**y** allez pas.
Va au cinéma.	Vas-**y**.

Note that an **-s** is added to **va** for the affirmative command with **y** to make it easier to pronounce.

B. Sometimes the preposition **à** is used in a construction where it does not refer to physical location. The pronoun **y** can nevertheless replace the prepositional phrase, as long as the object of the preposition is a thing, not a person.

Je pense **à mon enfance**.	J'**y** pense.
Il réfléchit **au problème**.	Il **y** réfléchit.
As-tu répondu **à sa lettre** ?	**Y** as-tu répondu ?
Je m'intéresse beaucoup **à ça**.	Je m'**y** intéresse beaucoup.
Ne pensez pas trop **à l'avenir**.	N'**y** pensez pas trop.

C. When the object of the preposition **à** is a person, disjunctive pronouns are used instead of **y**. This contrast is especially important when using the verb **penser à**, which means *to think about* or *to have one's mind on someone* or *something*. Compare :

Je pense **à mon travail**.	J'**y** pense.
Je pense **à mes parents**.	Je pense **à eux**.

D. The pronoun **en** replaces the partitive or any other construction with **de, du, de la, de l'** or **des** + A NOUN DENOTING A THING. Its meaning is usually the equivalent of *some, any, not any, of (about, from) it (them)*. Like **y**, **en** is placed before the verb except in affirmative commands.

Nous avons acheté **du pain**.	Nous **en** avons acheté.
Je ne me souviens pas **de l'adresse**.	Je ne m'**en** souviens pas.
Il n'a pas **de chance**.	Il n'**en** a pas.
Elle va m'acheter **des disques**.	Elle va m'**en** acheter.
Prenez **de la salade**.	Prenez-**en**.
Il vient **de l'épicerie**.	Il **en** vient.

E. En is also used to replace a noun modified by a number or by an expression of quantity.

J'ai **un disque**.	J'**en** ai **un**.
Il y a **dix étudiants**.	Il y **en** a **dix**.
Nous avons **beaucoup de travail**.	Nous **en** avons **beaucoup**.
Il n'y a **plus de sucre**.	Il n'y **en** a **plus**.

Note that **moi** contracts to **m'** before **en** :

Donnez-**moi** trois kilos de veau.   Donnez-**m'en** trois kilos.

When the expression of quantity **quelques** is used with the pronoun **en**, it becomes **quelques-unes** if it refers to a feminine noun and **quelques-uns** if it refers to a masculine noun.

Je voudrais **quelques** timbres.	J'**en** voudrais **quelques-uns**.
Achetez **quelques** oranges.	Achetez-**en** **quelques-unes**.

F. En is also used with the verb **penser de** *(to have an opinion about)* when the object of the prepositional phrase is a thing or an idea. When it is a person, disjunctive pronouns are used. Compare :

Qu'est-ce que tu penses **de cette idée** ?	Qu'est-ce que tu **en** penses ?
Qu'est-ce que tu penses **du professeur** ?	Qu'est-ce que tu penses **de lui** ?

Note that **penser de** is used only in the interrogative and that questions using **penser de** are usually answered by **je pense que...**

— Qu'est-ce que tu **penses de** son camarade de chambre ?
— Je **pense qu'**il est assez sympa.

Mise en situation

Point out that in an elegant meal a fish course often precedes the meat course.

On a fait les provisions. Philippe et Catherine adorent les *fruits de mer*. Ils font leurs projets pour le dîner.

seafood

PHILIPPE	Tu es allée chez le marchand de poissons ?
CATHERINE	Oui, j'y suis allée vers midi mais c'était déjà fermé. J'ai été obligée d'y retourner plus tard.
PHILIPPE	Tu as acheté des *crevettes* ?
CATHERINE	Non, il n'y en avait plus. Mais il y avait des *huîtres*. J'en ai acheté deux douzaines.
PHILIPPE	Il faut des *citrons* avec les huîtres. Est-ce que tu en as pris quelques-uns ?
CATHERINE	Non, je n'en ai pas acheté. Mais je pense que nous en avons encore plusieurs dans le frigo.
PHILIPPE	De toute façon, l'épicerie est à côté, *je peux y aller en vitesse* si on n'en a pas assez.

La poissonnerie — fish market, fish shop ; le poissonnier / la poissonnière

Point out that in small towns, stores often still stay closed for an hour or two at noon.

shrimp

oysters

lemons

I can run over there

Other seafood : *les coquilles — scallops ; les harengs — herrings ; le homard — lobster ; la langoustine — prawn ; les maquereaux* (m) *; les moules* (f) *— mussels ; la sole ; le thon — tuna.* Mention also *la bouillabaisse,* well-known provençal fish soup.

Préparation

A. Curiosité. Marguerite veut savoir où ses amis vont ce week-end. Donnez leurs réponses à ses questions.

Modèle Est-ce que Serge va au cinéma ? (oui)
Oui, il y va.

1. Est-ce que tu vas au concert ? (non)
2. Est-ce que Robert et Anne-Marie vont au théâtre ? (oui)
3. Est-ce que vous allez à la campagne ce week-end ? (oui)
4. Est-ce que nous allons à la plage samedi après-midi ? (oui)
5. Est-ce que Bruno va aller à la montagne avec ses amis ? (non)
6. Est-ce que Paul et toi, vous allez à la piscine ? (oui)

Transformations : Transformez les phrases suivantes selon les modèles donnés. *Modèle :* Il travaille dans cette banque. — Il y travaille. (1) J'habite à Lyon. (2) Ne répondez pas à ses questions. (3) Je ne suis jamais retourné dans cette ville. (4) Est-ce que vous passez vos vacances en Suisse ? (5) Tu es resté un an au Mexique, n'est-ce pas ? (6) Ils vont être chez eux à huit heures. *Modèle :* Nous avons acheté des légumes. → Nous en avons acheté. (1) Elle ne mange jamais de viande. (2) Est-ce qu'ils ont vu quelques films français ? (3) Est-ce que vous faites souvent des erreurs ? (4) Est-ce que tu vas m'acheter un livre ? (5) Est-ce que Lisette a envie de sortir ? (6) Avez-vous pris quelques photos ?

B. Différences. Charles et Henri sont deux frères qui sont très différents l'un de l'autre. Décrivez-les.

Modèles son professeur de français
Charles pense souvent à son professeur de français, mais Henri ne pense jamais à lui.
ou: l'avenir
Charles pense souvent à l'avenir, mais Henri n'y pense jamais.

1. la course aux armements
2. les examens
3. sa grand-mère
4. la faim dans le monde
5. son neveu
6. ses parents
7. les menaces de guerre
8. les problèmes sociaux

C. C'est la vie. La vie de Jean n'est pas parfaite mais ça peut aller. Quelle est son opinion sur chacun des sujets suivants ?

Option : Do first without parenthetical cues (*du temps libre* → *Je n'en ai pas*, etc.), then with cues.

Modèle   du temps libre (pas assez) → **Je n'en ai pas assez.**

1. de l'argent (assez)
2. des devoirs (trop)
3. des amis (quelques-uns)
4. de bons profs (plusieurs)
5. des problèmes (pas beaucoup)
6. des disques français (beaucoup)
7. de la chance (un peu)
8. des frères et de sœurs (trois)

D. Curiosité. Colette veut savoir ce que ses amis pensent de sa nouvelle situation.

Modèles   son nouvel appartement → **Qu'est-ce que vous en pensez ?**
   ou: son fiancé → **Qu'est-ce que vous pensez de lui ?**

1. les photos qu'elle a prises
2. son nouveau patron
3. la jupe qu'elle vient d'acheter
4. une actrice qu'elle admire beaucoup
5. un ami qu'elle vient de rencontrer
6. les gens avec qui elle travaille
7. les petites boutiques de son quartier
8. sa nouvelle camarade de chambre

E. Projets de week-end. Des étudiants sont en train de parler de leurs projets pour le week-end. Formulez leurs réponses en utilisant **y** ou **en**.

Have students ask each other whether or not they plan to go to various places this weekend ; ask them to use *y* in their answers (*cinéma* → *Tu vas au cinéma ? Oui, j'y vais vendredi soir avec des amis*, etc.).

Modèle   Est-ce que vous allez chez vos parents ce week-end ? (non, nous…)
   Non, nous n'y allons pas.

1. Est-ce que vous êtes allés chez vos parents récemment ? (non)
2. Est-ce que vous allez chez eux ce week-end ? (oui)
3. Est-ce que tu vas aller au cinéma, Henri ? (oui)
4. Est-ce que tu as vu des films américains récemment ? (oui… deux)
5. Est-ce que Jean était au café hier soir ? (non)
6. Est-ce que vous avez envie d'aller à Versailles ? (non)
7. Est-ce que tu es déjà allé à Versailles ? (non… jamais)
8. Est-ce que vous avez beaucoup de travail ce week-end ? (oui… beaucoup)

Communication et vie pratique

A. Habitudes et activités. Utilisez les suggestions suivantes pour indiquer ce que vous faites et ce que vous ne faites pas. Utilisez le pronom **en** ou le pronom **y** dans vos réponses.

Can be used as direct questions or in small-group work (e.g., *boire du vin* → *Est-ce que tu bois souvent du vin ?*).

Exemples   boire du vin
   Je n'en bois pas souvent.
   ou: **Chez nous, nous en buvons de temps en temps.**

   ou: aller au cinéma
   Je n'y vais pas souvent.

1. acheter des revues françaises
2. faire du sport
3. aller aux matchs de football
4. avoir du travail
5. aller à la bibliothèque
6. manger des légumes
7. boire du lait
8. prendre des vitamines
9. aller chez le dentiste
10. avoir des disques français
11. avoir envie d'aller en France
12. passer quelques semaines à Paris

B. **Questions / interview.** Répondez aux questions suivantes ou utilisez-les pour interviewer un(e) autre étudiant(e). Utilisez **y** ou **en** dans vos réponses.

1. Est-ce que tu achètes quelquefois des journaux français ? Est-ce qu'il y en a dans les librairies de ta ville ?
2. Est-ce qu'il y a des restaurants français dans ta ville ? Est-ce que tu as déjà mangé dans un de ces restaurants ?
3. Est-ce que tu as beaucoup de travail en ce moment ? Est-ce que tu passes beaucoup de temps à la bibliothèque ?
4. Est-ce que tu as envie d'écouter des disques français ? Est-ce que tu sais où on peut en acheter ?
5. Combien d'habitants y a-t-il dans la ville d'où tu viens ? Est-ce que tu y retournes souvent ?
6. Est-ce que tu vas souvent au cinéma ? Est-ce que tu as vu un film français récemment ?
7. Est-ce que tu t'intéresses à la musique ? Est-ce que tu vas souvent au concert ?
8. Est-ce que tu es déjà allé(e) au Québec ? Est-ce que tu as envie d'y retourner ?

C'est votre tour. Vous avez décidé d'organiser un pique-nique avec d'autres étudiants de la classe. Chaque personne est responsable de certains achats. Vérifiez que chaque étudiant(e) est allé(e) acheter les provisions qu'il (elle) a promises d'apporter. Utilisez la **Mise en situation** comme guide.

Preparation : Have students make a list of items needed and who is to buy them.

Variation : Getting ready for a trip and verifying that different items have been packed.

☙ Talking about intentions and plans for the future
Le futur

Présentation

In French, the future tense is a single word formed by adding endings to a stem. It is used both in writing and in speaking, though **aller** + AN INFINITIVE is very commonly used in conversation.

A. Most verbs form the future by adding the endings shown to the infinitive. When the infinitive ends in **-re**, the **-e** is dropped. Note the similarities between the future endings and the present tense forms of **avoir**.

Le futur de *manger*	
je **mangerai**	nous **mangerons**
tu **mangeras**	vous **mangerez**
il / elle / on **mangera**	ils / elles **mangeront**

Le futur de *finir*	
je **finirai**	nous **finirons**
tu **finiras**	vous **finirez**
il / elle / on **finira**	ils / elles **finiront**

Le futur d'*attendre*	
j'**attendrai**	nous **attendrons**
tu **attendras**	vous **attendrez**
il / elle / on **attendra**	ils / elles **attendront**

Je **parlerai** à Jacqueline.
On ne **servira** pas le dîner avant sept heures.
Je suis sûr qu'Anne et Paul se **débrouilleront**.

B. Although the future endings are the same for all French verbs, certain common verbs have irregular stems.

Verb	Future stem	
aller	**ir-**	Je n'**irai** pas en classe demain.
avoir	**aur-**	Vous n'**aurez** pas de difficulté.
être	**ser-**	Nous **serons** ici à six heures.
envoyer	**enverr-**	Est-ce que tu lui **enverras** un télégramme ?
faire	**fer-**	Est-ce que vous **ferez** du ski cet hiver ?
falloir	**faudr-**	Il **faudra** partir à huit heures.
pleuvoir	**pleuvr-**	**Pleuvra**-t-il demain ?
pouvoir	**pourr-**	Je **pourrai** vois aider plus tard.
savoir	**saur-**	Avant la fin de l'été je **saurai** nager.
venir, etc.	**viendr-**	Quand **reviendras**-tu ?
vouloir	**voudr-**	Qu'est-ce qu'ils **voudront** faire ?

C. In French, when a clause begins with **quand** *(when)*, **lorsque** *(when)*, **dès que** *(as soon as)*, or **aussitôt que** *(as soon as)* and future time is implied, the verb is in the future. In English the present tense is used in similar instances.

Faisons une promenade **quand** il **fera** beau.	*Let's take a walk when it's nice.*
Lorsque nous **irons** à Québec, nous visiterons le château Frontenac.	*When we go to Quebec, we'll visit Frontenac Castle.*
Dès qu'ils **arriveront**, nous nous mettrons à table.	*As soon as they arrive, we'll sit down to eat.*
J'achèterai une maison **aussitôt que** j'**aurai** assez d'argent.	*I'll buy a house as soon as I have enough money.*

Notice that either clause can come first and that the verb in the main clause can be either in the future or in the imperative. The meanings of **quand** and **lorsque** and **dès que** and **aussitôt que** are similar. **Lorsque** and **dès que**, however, tend to be used in slightly more formal or literary style. Note also that **lorsque** cannot be used to ask a question.

Mise en situation

Ne repousse jamais à demain... Le *dicton* préféré de Madame Poncin est « Ne repousse jamais à demain ce que tu peux faire aujourd'hui. » Ses enfants, par contre, attendent toujours la dernière minute pour faire ce qu'ils ont à faire. Elle *ne peut pas supporter ça* et elle *en a marre* de toujours être sur leur dos...

MME PONCIN	Est-ce que vous avez sorti* le chien ?
CAROLINE	Bah... Ça peut attendre... On le sortira plus tard.
MME PONCIN	Quand vous le sortirez, n'oubliez pas de descendre la *poubelle*.
CAROLINE	Ne t'inquiète pas, maman, on n'oubliera pas de le faire.
MME PONCIN	Et tes devoirs, Pierre, ils sont faits ?
PIERRE	Presque. Je ne suis pas inspiré... Je les finirai après le dîner. *Au fait*, on dîne bientôt ? J'ai faim.
MME PONCIN	Le dîner...? Ah, oui, le dîner...! Ben, je le préparerai quand je me sentirai inspirée.

Substitution : (1) Nous partirons à onze heures. *(tu / vous / je / Marc / Robert et Véronique)* (2) J'attendrai dix minutes. *(tu / nous / le professeur / vous / les étudiants / je)* (3) Est-ce qu'ils iront au Canada cet été ? *(vous / tu / nous / on / Jeannette / tes amis)* (4) Tu seras en classe, n'est-ce pas ? *(les étudiants / le professeur / nous)* (5) Elle s'en occupera. *(nous / mes amis / tu / je / vous)* (6) Un jour elle aura beaucoup d'argent. *(tu / je / mes amis / vous / nous).*

saying

can't stand that / is fed up

Other related proverbs : *Mieux vaut tard que jamais ; Paris ne s'est pas fait en un jour ; Qui vivra, verra ; Un tiens vaut mieux que deux tu l'auras.*

trash can

by the way

---

*Note that when **sortir** and **descendre** are used with a direct object, they are conjugated with **avoir** in the **passé composé** : J'ai sorti le chien et j'ai descendu la poubelle.

Préparation

A. J'ai confiance... Dominique est assez optimiste quand elle pense à l'avenir. Qu'est-ce qu'elle dit?

Modèle   nous / trouver du travail
> **Je suis sûre que nous trouverons du travail.**

1. Hélène / réussir bien
2. vous / faire des progrès
3. Sylvie et Bertrand / se marier
4. ils / être heureux
5. tu / aller à l'université
6. je / apprendre beaucoup de choses
7. la vie / devenir plus facile
8. vous / avoir de la chance
9. nous / pouvoir trouver une solution
10. tu / revenir nous rendre visite

B. Quand le ferez-vous? Quelques amis parlent des choses qu'ils doivent faire cette semaine. Qu'est-ce qu'ils disent?

Option : Repeat using object pronouns (Je le ferai quand je me sentirai mieux).

Modèle   Quand est-ce que tu vas faire le ménage (quand je me sentirai mieux)
> **Je ferai le ménage quand je me sentirai mieux.**

1. Quand est-ce que vous allez vous occuper du jardin? (quand il fera beau)
2. Quand est-ce que Paul va réparer son vélo? (quand il aura le temps)
3. Quand est-ce que tu vas être plus sérieux? (quand je serai vieux)
4. Quand est-ce que je vais faire une promenade? (quand tu en auras envie)
5. Quand est-ce que Gérard va acheter de nouveaux vêtements? (quand il ira en ville)
6. Quand est-ce que vous allez vous reposer? (quand nous aurons moins de travail)

C. L'amour n'a pas de frontières. Robert, un Américain, a rencontré une jeune Québécoise qu'il a bien envie de revoir. Malheureusement, il ne parle pas français. Il vous a demandé de traduire *(translate)* ce qu'il veut lui dire.

1. When you come to the United States, you can stay with my family.
2. Write to me as soon as you return home.
3. As soon as you write to me, I'll answer.
4. I'll call you when I am at home.
5. I'll come back as soon as I have enough money.
6. We'll get married as soon as we can.

Communication et vie pratique

A. Projets d'avenir. Voici une liste de projets d'avenir. Choisissez-en cinq que vous avez l'intention d'accomplir au cours de votre vie. Si vous préférez, vous pouvez substituer vos propres projets. Ensuite, discutez vos choix avec d'autres étudiants et essayez d'en expliquer les raisons.

Exemple apprendre à parler une autre langue étrangère
J'apprendrai à parler une autre langue étrangère parce que c'est important pour la profession que j'ai choisie.

1. avoir un métier intéressant
2. faire le tour du monde
3. gagner beaucoup d'argent
4. prendre le temps de s'amuser un peu
5. se marier et avoir des enfants
6. faire du sport régulièrement pour rester en bonne forme physique
7. passer plusieurs années de ma vie dans un pays étranger
8. aller habiter à la campagne
9. acheter une maison
10. ?

B. L'été prochain. Posez des questions aux autres étudiants pour savoir ce qu'ils ont l'intention de faire l'été prochain.

Exemple — **Est-ce que tu resteras ici l'été prochain ?**
— **Non, ma famille et moi, nous irons au Canada.**

C Réactions. Complétez les phrases suivantes pour exprimer vos opinions ou vos intentions.

1. Quand j'aurai trente-cinq ans, je…
2. Je partirai en vacances dès que…
3. Quand j'aurai le temps, je…
4. Dès que j'aurai assez d'argent, je…
5. Aussitôt que la classe sera terminée, les étudiants…
6. Les étudiants seront contents quand…
7. Quand j'aurai besoin d'argent, je…
8. Quand il fera froid, nous…
9. Lorsque nous serons au vingt et unième siècle…
10. Je prendrai ma retraite quand…

C'est votre tour. Vos camarades de chambre (joués par d'autres étudiants) essaient toujours de repousser au jour suivant ce qu'ils doivent faire et vous, vous ne pouvez pas supporter ça. Imaginez la conversation. Utilisez la **Mise en situation** comme point de départ.

You may want to begin Communication et vie pratique A, Vous et l'an 2000 in the Intégration et perspectives section at this time.

Have students tell what they will and will not do after graduation.

Preparation : Have students prepare list of tasks that the procrastinating roommate has forgotten to do. Variation : Vary the situation (e.g., classroom where teacher is talking to student ; husband / wife talking about chores ; boss / employee).

❧ Indicating what we see and what we believe
Les verbes *voir* and *croire*

Présentation

The verbs **voir** *(to see)* and **croire** *(to believe)* are irregular :

Note that all uses of *croire* are in the affirmative. The use of *croire* with the subjunctive is introduced later.

Voir	
je **vois**	nous **voyons**
tu **vois**	vous **voyez**
il / elle / on **voit**	ils / elles **voient**
passé composé : j'**ai vu**	
futur : je **verrai**	

Croire	
je **crois**	nous **croyons**
tu **crois**	vous **croyez**
il / elle / on **croit**	ils / elles **croient**
passé composé : j'**ai cru**	
futur : je **croirai**	

Je ne **vois** pas très bien.
Est-ce que tu **as vu** le dernier
  match à la télé ?
Vous **verrez** que c'est facile.

Je **crois** que tu pourras te
  débrouiller.
Personne n'**a cru** cette histoire.

Mise en situation

« **Loin des yeux, loin du cœur.** » Thierry vient de rencontrer une de ses *anciennes* copines qui était aussi la petite amie de Gilbert. Il est impatient d'annoncer la nouvelle à Gilbert.

Related proverb : *Le chat parti, les souris dansent.*

former

Substitution : (1) Je crois que oui. *(nous / Paul / les autres / tu / vous)* (2) Nous ne verrons pas le match. *(mes amis / tu / vous / mon frère / je)* (3) Je n'ai pas vu ce film. *(nous / tu / les autres / Pierre / vous)*

THIERRY Devine qui j'ai vu ce matin. Tu ne le croiras jamais.

GILBERT Dépêche-toi ! Raconte !

THIERRY Sylvie, la fille que tu voyais régulièrement avant ton service mili-
         taire ! Elle est maintenant mariée et mère de famille.

GILBERT *Sans blague ! Tu me fais marcher...*

No kidding ! / You're pulling my leg...
truth

THIERRY Non. C'est la *vérité*, crois-moi.

GILBERT C'est incroyable ! Où est-ce que tu l'as vue ?

THIERRY À la poste. Elle envoyait un paquet. Je voyais qu'elle me regardait
         d'une façon bizarre. Et puis, tout d'un coup, je l'ai reconnue.

in a strange way

GILBERT C'est bête... Je suis parti et nous ne nous sommes jamais revus. *Je
         l'aimais pourtant bien...*

I was quite fond of her, though...

Préparation

A. La coupe du monde de football. Qui va gagner la coupe du monde ? Il y a autant d'opinions que de personnes.

> **Modèle** Pierre / l'équipe du Brésil
> **Pierre croit que c'est l'équipe du Brésil qui va gagner.**

1. nous / l'équipe de France
2. moi / les Italiens
3. tu / les Allemands
4. vous / l'équipe d'Angleterre
5. Cécile / les Espagnols
6. mes amis / les Irlandais

Possible follow-up : Have students give opinions about upcoming sports events (*Je crois que notre équipe va gagner le match dimanche*).

B. Un week-end à Paris. Différentes personnes ont passé une semaine à Paris. Qu'est-ce qu'ils ont vu d'intéressant ?

> **Modèle** Henri / une pièce de théâtre
> **Henri a vu une pièce de théâtre.**

1. nous / un film
2. tu / des amis
3. vous / une pièce de théâtre
4. Michel / un match
5. je / des courses de chevaux
6. Véronique et Serge / beaucoup de gens
7. Marianne / des amis du lycée

Communication et vie pratique

A. Sites et monuments. Posez des questions aux autres étudiants de la classe pour découvrir qui a vu les sites et monuments suivants.

1. la tour Eiffel
2. le Grand Canyon
3. les Alpes
4. les pyramides d'Égypte
5. le Louvre
6. le Vatican
7. le Kremlin
8. le château Frontenac
9. ?

Options : (1) Add (or have students add) other places and monuments. (2) Have students talk about interesting things that they have seen recently (e.g., *J'ai vu un film de Woody Allen vendredi soir*).

B. Je crois que... Demandez aux autres étudiants leur opinion sur les sujets suivants. Mentionnez aussi d'autres sujets qui vous intéressent.

> **Exemple** le « Superbowl »
> — **À ton avis, qui va gagner le « Superbowl » ?**
> — **Je crois que les « Cowboys » vont gagner.**

1. les prochaines élections présidentielles
2. l'Oscar pour le meilleur acteur
3. l'Oscar pour la meilleure actrice
4. l'Oscar pour le meilleur film
5. le « Superbowl »
6. le « World Series »
7. le prochain Tour de France
8. ?

C. Scènes et spectacles. Décrivez ce que vous voyez dans les situations suivantes.

1. de votre fenêtre
2. quand vous traversez le campus
3. dans votre classe de français
4. quand vous venez à l'université ou quand vous rentrez chez vous
5. quand vous imaginez les vacances de vos rêves

C'est votre tour. Vous venez de voir quelqu'un ou quelque chose qui va certainement surprendre *(surprise)* vos amis. Racontez-leur ce que vous avez vu. Ils ont un peu de difficulté à vous croire. Utilisez la **Mise en situation** comme point de départ.

Intégration et perspectives

Demain mon fils

La chanson de Jean Lapointe, un chanteur canadien, intitulée *Demain mon fils* exprime les sentiments d'un père qui voit son fils grandir et qui pense à ce que la vie va lui apporter.

Demain mon fils

Demain tu seras grand, demain t'auras vingt ans
Demain tu pourras faire à ta guise.   **as you wish**
Partir vers les pays dont *tu* rêves *aujourd'hui*   **about which / dream**
Visiter tes châteaux en Espagne.
Et seul comme un nouveau matador,
Tu entreras dans l'arène
Ne craignant *ni la peur ni la mort*   **fearing**
Courant *vers les années qui viennent.*   **running**

Demain tu seras grand, demain t'auras le temps
Demain tu seras fort de *ton âge*   **will draw strength from**
Les années passeront, les rides *sur ton* front   **wrinkles / forehead**
Déjà auront creusé leur sillage   **left their mark (lit., ploughed a furrow)**

Et seul comme un très grand matador
Tu sortiras de l'arène avec des coups *au cœur et au corps*   **bruises**
Marchant vers les années qui traînent.   **drag by**

Demain tu seras vieux, pourtant tu verras mieux
Tu te retourneras en arrière   **turn back**
Alors tu comprendras ce que je sais déjà
Tout comme le savait mon vieux père.   **just as**
Et seul comme un trop vieux spectateur
Voyant ton fils dans l'arène   **seeing**
Alors tu sauras ce qu'est la peur
Tu comprendras combien je t'aime.

Chanson de Jean Lapointe

A. Compréhension. Répondez aux questions suivantes.

Have students imagine that the poet has written a short letter to his son with the same message as the poem. What would the letter say?

1. Comment Jean Lapointe voit-il la vie ? Quelle image utilise-t-il ?
2. Selon Jean Lapointe, quelle est l'attitude de son fils devant la vie ? Est-ce qu'il est impatient d'en découvrir les secrets ou a-t-il peur ?
3. Et le père, est-il entièrement confiant ou a-t-il peur quand il pense à ce que la vie va apporter à son fils ?
4. Est-ce que le fils peut maintenant comprendre les inquiètudes de son père ? Quand pourra-t-il les comprendre ? Pourquoi ?

B. Et vous ?

1. Écrivez un poème ou une histoire qui commencera ainsi : « Demain je serai grand(e), demain j'aurai vingt ans. »
2. Si vous préférez, vous pouvez écrire une histoire ou un poème intitulé : « Demain ma fille… »

Une autre façon de prédire l'avenir

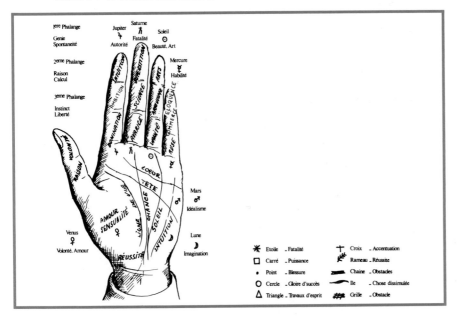

Notes culturelles: *Avenir et technologie*

On a souvent dit que les Français sont plus tournés vers le passé que vers l'avenir. Pour justifier cette opinion, on cite la place accordée à l'enseignement de l'histoire dans les programmes des écoles, l'importance que les Français attachent à leur héritage culturel, et la nostalgie qu'ils *éprouvent* pour « le bon vieux temps ».

    Cependant, la France est aussi un pays qui est à la pointe du progrès dans des domaines technologiques importants, en particulier, les transports, l'énergie nucléaire, l'aéronautique, et les télécommunications. Voici quelques exemples de ces *réalisations*.

    Transports : le T.G.V. (train à grande vitesse) ; VAL (le métro sans chauffeur qui est maintenant en service à Lille).

    Énergie : Du fait qu'elle ne possède pratiquement pas de pétrole, la France a été obligée de se tourner vers l'énergie nucléaire et elle a construit depuis 1973 un grand nombre de centrales nucléaires, *y compris* un centre de recyclage des *déchets* nucléaires.

    Aéronautique : L'industrie aéronautique française occupe la deuxième place mondiale. Elle produit (en coopération avec d'autres pays européens) des avions de tourisme, des avions d'affaires (les Mystères), des avions commerciaux (le Concorde et l'Airbus), des hélicoptères, des avions militaires (les Mirages), des missiles (Exocet), et des fusées (Ariane). Le lancement d'Hermès, la première navette spatiale européenne, est prévu pour 1995.

(marginal glosses:) feel — accomplishments — including — wastes

Carte à mémoire

Aspect moderne de Paris

Télécommunications : La révolution technologique va des cartes électroniques, appelées « *cartes à mémoire* », inventées dès le début des années 70, au Visiophone (un téléphone qui permet de voir la personne à qui on parle) et au Minitel. Le Minitel, qui est en service depuis 1982, se compose d'un *clavier*, d'un *écran* et d'un modem. Le Minitel donne accès à plus de 4 000 services télématiques et *banques de données*. Il donne les numéros de téléphone de toute la France, les horaires des trains et des spectacles, la météo et les informations. Grâce au Minitel, les *abonnés* peuvent payer leurs *factures* et savoir exactement combien d'argent il reste sur leur compte ; ils peuvent communiquer avec les autres abonnés et faire leurs provisions, réserver une chambre d'hôtel ou prendre contact avec un professeur qui aidera directement les enfants à faire leurs devoirs.

"smart cards"

keyboard / screen
data banks

subscribers
bills

Communication et vie pratique

A. Vous et l'an 2000. Et les jeunes Français, comment imaginent-ils l'avenir et quels sont leurs sentiments ? Pour le savoir, on a posé les questions suivantes aux lecteurs de *Phosphore*, un magazine pour les étudiants des lycées. Répondez vous-même aux questions ou faites un petit sondage dans votre classe. Comparez les réponses des jeunes Français avec vos propres idées sur les mêmes sujets.

Have students complete the survey and then compare their individual (or class) responses to those given in the original survey. Questions can be put on notecards and students can circulate among class members asking the question they have been given. You may want to encourage students to explain their answers.

1. La vie / la mort

À votre avis, jusqu'à quel âge vivrez-vous ?

65 ans	10%
75 ans	24
85 ans	34
95 et plus	25
Divers	7

2. Votre cadeau d'anniversaire en l'an 2 000

Pour fêter votre 30ᵉ anniversaire, vous pourrez enfin vous offrir…

Un vieux cottage à la campagne	29%	
Une machine à *remonter* le temps	19	go back in
Un week-end dans l'espace	22	
Une voiture entièrement programmable	16	
Un *abri* antinucléaire	6	shelter
Divers	8	

3. Les plaisirs

Quels seront vos grands plaisirs en l'an 2000 ?

	G	F*
Me promener dans la nature	45%	49%
Faire du sport	48	47
Faire l'amour	38	26
Me baigner dans ma piscine privée	14	29
Voir des films	14	18
Jouer avec mon micro-ordinateur	18	11
Bien manger	12	8

4. La famille

Si vous formez un jour un couple stable, combien d'enfants aurez-vous ?

	G	F	E
Je ne veux pas avoir d'enfants.	4%	4,5%	4%
Un seul suffira	7	7	7
Deux enfants	48	40,5	43
Trois enfants	30	34	32
Quatre et plus	11	14	13
Divers	—	—	1

*G = garçons ; F = filles ; E = ensemble

5. Le travail et la personnalité

En dehors des diplômes, qu'est-ce qui vous sera, à votre avis, le plus utile pour trouver un emploi?

Mes qualités personnelles	69%
La façon de me présenter	18
Les relations de ma famille	10
C'est uniquement une question de chance.	7

6. Le niveau de vie

Par rapport à vos parents, votre niveau de vie en l'an 2000 sera-t-il...

Supérieur au niveau de vie de vos parents	48%
Égal	39
Inférieur	12
Divers	1

7. Les problèmes sociaux

Pensez-vous que vous connaîtrez une période de chômage?

	G	F
Oui, à tout moment il y aura un risque.	46%	50%
Oui, sans doute au début.	31	32
Je pense que non.	23	18

Il y a toujours un risque de chômage.

8. La retraite

Aujourd'hui, la retraite est à 60 ans. Pour vous, qu'en pensez-vous?

	G	F
60 ans, ce sera bien pour moi.	55%	61%
60 ans, c'est trop tôt pour arrêter de travailler.	17	16
60 ans, c'est trop tard pour arrêter de travailler.	26	22
Divers	1	1

9. Le monde où nous vivons

Quel est le problème qui devra être résolu en priorité pour l'an 2000?

La faim dans le monde	45%
Le chômage	18
La prolifération des armes nucléaires	16
Le cancer	11
Le racisme	9
Divers	1

B. Prédictions. Dites ce que vous pensez de chacune des prédictions suivantes. Ensuite, faites vos propres prédictions et demandez aux autres étudiants ce qu'ils en pensent.

Encourage students to explain their answers and to use y or en where appropriate.

Exemple — **Les hommes ne seront jamais parfaits.**
— **C'est vrai, les hommes ne seront probablement jamais parfaits.**

1. On ne pourra jamais éliminer totalement la nécessité de travailler.
2. L'énergie solaire sera notre principale source d'énergie.
3. Dans deux siècles, il n'y aura plus de vie sur cette planète.
4. On pourra habiter sous les mers.
5. Un jour on mangera seulement des aliments artificiels.
6. On n'aura pas besoin de travailler. Ce sont les robots qui feront tout.
7. On ne pourra jamais résoudre le problème des inégalités sociales.
8. Il n'y aura plus de guerre.

C. Dans dix ans... Essayez d'imaginer comment sera votre vie dans dix ans.

Exemple   **Je serai probablement plus riche que maintenant.**

• *Vocabulaire*

Noms

    l'**arène** (f) *arena, bull ring*
°   l'**atmosphère** (f)
    l'**avenir** (m) *future*
    le **boulot** *job* (slang)
    le **but** *goal*
°   la **catastrophe**
    la **centrale** *power plant*
    le **citron** *lemon*
 le, la **concierge** *building caretaker*
°   le **conflit**
°   la **conquête**
    le **coup** *bruise, blow*
    la **course aux armements** *arms race*
    la **crevette** *shrimp*
°   la **crise**
°   le **cyclone**
    le **dicton** *saying*
°   la **douzaine**
    l'**électronique** (f) *electronics*
°   l'**environnement** (m)
    l'**espace** (m) *space*
    le **front** *forehead*
    la **fusée** *rocket*
 le, la **gosse** *kid* (slang)
    la **guerre** *war*
    l'**huître** (f) *oyster*
    l'**inondation** (f) *flood*
    l'**inégalité** (f) *inequality*
    la **lune** *moon*
    la **lutte** *struggle*
    le **matador** *bullfighter*
    la **navette spatiale** *space ship, space shuttle*
    le **nouveau venu** *newcomer*
    le **point d'interrogation** *question mark*
    la **poubelle** *trashcan*
    la **recherche** *research*
    le **ride** *wrinkle*
    la **robotique** *robotics*
    le **sillage** *wake, track*
    la **surpopulation** *overpopulation*
    la **terrasse** *terrace, outdoor area of café*
°   la **théorie**
    le **tremblement de**
        terre *earthquake*
    la **vérité** *truth*

Verbes

arriver *to happen*
compter *to count*
connaître *to know, to be acquainted with*
courir *to run*
craindre *to fear, to be afraid of*
creuser *to groove, to plough*
croire *to believe, to think*
deviner *to guess*
repousser *to put off, to repulse, to*
  push back
se **tromper** *to make a mistake*
supporter *to stand, to put up with*

Adjectifs

assis(e) *seated*
assuré(e) *assured, guaranteed*
d'autre *else, other*
bizarre *strange*
incroyable *unbelievable, incredible*
inquiet, inquiète *worried*
° **nucléaire**
pressé(e) *in a hurry*
sous-marin(e) *underwater*
spatial(e), spatiaux *space, spacial*

Divers

à ta guise *as you wish*
au fait *by the way*
aussitôt que *as soon as*
autrefois *formerly, in the past*
c'est bien beau *that's all well and good*
de toute façon *in any case*
donc *so, then*
dont *of which, of whom*
dès que *as soon as*
en arrière *behind, back*
en avoir marre *to be fed up*
éventuellement *eventually*
faire la connaissance de *to meet, to*
  make the acquaintance of
lorsque *when*
puis *then*
sans blague *no kidding*
tout d'un coup *suddenly*
tu me fais marcher *you're pulling my leg*

15

CHAPITRE QUINZE

Communication objectives

Talking about college life

1. Talking about what we read, write, and say
2. Asking questions
3. Telling what you would do
4. Saying what you would do if...

Structures

Les mots et la vie: Les cours et la vie universitaire

Les verbes **lire, écrire** et **dire**

Les pronoms interrogatifs

Le conditionnel

L'emploi de **si** dans la phrase conditionnelle

Le Québec

Mise en scène
Portrait des étudiants québécois

Que pensent les étudiants québécois de leurs études universitaires?
Quelles sont leurs ambitions? Comment imaginent-ils leur *avenir*? Que   future
veulent-ils faire dans la vie? Quelles sont leurs relations avec leurs parents? Pourquoi étudient-ils? Sont-ils obligés de travailler? Comment
s'habillent-ils? Quelle est leur attitude *au sujet de* l'amour et du mariage?   toward, on the subject of
Que pensent-ils de la politique et de la religion?

Pour avoir des réponses à ces questions, un éducateur canadien a organisé un sondage d'opinion. Il a interrogé mille étudiants et étudiantes de
seize à vingt-trois ans. Cette étude *a duré* dix ans.   lasted

Leur *but* dans la vie   goal

Quand on les a interrogés sur leur idéal dans la vie, la plus grande
partie des jeunes (32%) ont choisi la *réussite* personnelle et le *bonheur* (17%)   success / happiness
plutôt que la réussite financière ou le désir d'être *utile* à la société.   rather than / useful

Leurs qualités et leurs *défauts*   shortcomings

Quand on leur a présenté une liste de qualités et qu'on leur a demandé
d'indiquer la qualité principale qu'ils possédaient, ils ont choisi la
sociabilité (14%) et la *franchise* (13%). Ces résultats sont restés constants   sincerity, frankness
pendant les dix dernières années. Ils pensent que leur principal défaut est
l'*orgueil*.   pride

Point out that *qualité* in
French has a positive
connotation; *défaut* is the
equivalent of a negative
quality. You might have to
explain the use of *que* for
quand in the above
paragraph.

Leur avenir

Cinquante-neuf pour cent des étudiants québécois sont optimistes au sujet de leur avenir. Peu d'étudiants se sont déclarés pessimistes ou indifférents. Ces réponses n'ont pas changé au cours des années.

Leur orientation professionnelle

Les professions libérales attirent de plus en plus de jeunes (44%). Un fait intéressant est que la proportion de jeunes qui désirent devenir *agriculteurs augmente* chaque année. Par contre, l'intérêt pour le travail de commerçant diminue chaque année.

farmers

increases

La famille

Les jeunes ont des relations *plus profondes* avec leur mère qu'avec leur père. En général aussi, ils s'entendent mieux avec leur mère. Ils parlent plus souvent avec elle qu'avec leur père. Quand ils étaient petits, ils *se confiaient* plus facilement à leur mère (43%) qu'à leur père (11%).

deeper

confided

Les études

À la question « Pourquoi continuez-vous vos études », la majorité des jeunes (71%) ont répondu que c'est parce qu'ils veulent réussir dans la vie. La proportion de jeunes qui ont choisi cette réponse a augmenté d'année en année. Mais 10% *disent* qu'ils continuent leurs études parce qu'ils aiment étudier.

say

Le travail

La majorité des jeunes (50%) disent que leurs parents *ne* leur donnent *aucune* aide financière. Seulement 23% disent qu'ils travaillent pour pouvoir continuer leurs études, et 43% disent qu'ils travaillent pour avoir de l'argent de poche.

no, not any

Les vêtements

La majorité des jeunes disent qu'ils s'habillent comme ils veulent. En fait, presque tous les jeunes portent des jeans. Est-ce que cela veut dire qu'ils ont les mêmes goûts ou qu'ils sont conformistes ?

L'amour

La plupart des jeunes (69%) pensent que l'amour donne un *sens* à la vie; mais pour eux il n'y a pas de *partenaire* prédestiné et l'amour dure rarement toute la vie.

meaning

partner

La politique

En général, les jeunes qui s'intéressent à la politique préfèrent le Parti québécois.

Follow-up : Do *Communication D (Le Portrait de l'étudiant américain)* in the *Communication et vie pratique* section at the end of the chapter. Students might also be asked to compare what they know about French students and French-Canadian students.

La religion

Seulement un tiers des jeunes pratiquent une religion, mais 81% pensent qu'il existe un Être Suprême.

Extrait et adapté d'un article du *Québec en Bref.*

Compréhension. Selon les renseignements donnés, est-ce que les phrases suivantes sont vraies ou fausses ? Corrigez le sens de la phrase s'il est faux.

1. La réussite financière est moins importante pour les jeunes Québécois que la réussite personnelle et le bonheur.
2. Selon eux, le principal défaut des jeunes est la franchise.
3. L'intérêt pour les professions libérales diminue chaque année.

Et pour vous ?

Et selon vous ?

Êtes-vous d'accord ?

4. Le travail de commerçant intéresse de moins en moins les jeunes Québécois.
5. Il y a de moins en moins de jeunes qui veulent devenir agriculteurs.
6. En général, les jeunes s'entendent moins bien avec leur père qu'avec leur mère.
7. La majorité des jeunes Québécois continuent leurs études parce qu'ils aiment étudier.
8. Presque la moitié des jeunes sont obligés de travailler pour gagner leur argent de poche.
9. Le parti politique que les jeunes Québécois préfèrent est le Parti libéral.
10. Plus de deux tiers des jeunes pratiquent une religion.

Et les Américains ?
Êtes-vous d'accord ?

Êtes-vous d'accord ?

Est-ce votre cas ?

Et vous ?
Et aux États-Unis ?
Et aux États-Unis ?

Have students compare French, French-Canadian, and U.S. systems of education.

Notes culturelles: *L'enseignement au Québec*

A La maternelle. La maternelle prépare les enfants de 5 ans à leur vie d'écolier. Elle facilite leur passage de la maison à l'école. Les enfants fréquentent la maternelle pendant un an, une demi-journée par jour.

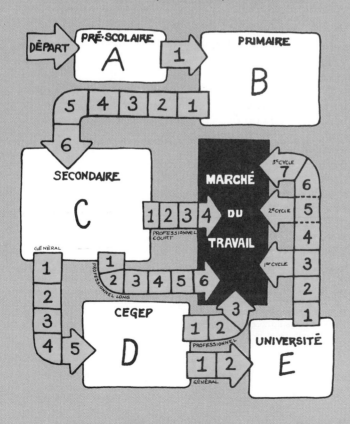

De l'école au travail
(Les chiffres correspondent à la durée de chaque formation)

B **L'école primaire.** Par une multitude d'activités, l'école primaire développe la personnalité des enfants de six à douze ans et leur donne une formation de base : langue écrite et parlée, mathématiques, sciences et arts.

C **L'école secondaire.** Lorsque les élèves atteignent le cycle secondaire, ils sont intégrés à un système polyvalent : cours obligatoires, cours à option, formation professionnelle ou générale.

D **Le CÉGEP.** Le Collège d'Enseignement Général et Professionnel (ou CÉGEP) vient après les études secondaires. La formation générale s'adresse aux étudiants qui continueront leurs études à l'université. La formation professionnelle prépare plus directement au marché du travail.

E **L'université.** L'enseignement supérieur vous prépare à l'exercice d'une profession, à la recherche ou à l'enseignement. Le 1er cycle correspond au baccalauréat, le 2e cycle à la maîtrise, le 3e cycle au doctorat.

Les mots et la vie : *Les cours et la vie universitaire*

Étudiez le vocabulaire et ensuite décrivez votre vie universitaire. Utilisez les questions suggérées comme point de départ.

Les cours qu'il faut suivre
Quels cours désirez-vous suivre* le semestre prochain ?
— les sciences : l'astronomie, la biologie, la chimie (*chemistry*), la physique, la géologie, l'ingénierie (électrique, aéronautique, agricole), l'informatique
— les sciences politiques, les sciences économiques, la comptabilité (*accounting*), la gestion et l'administration des entreprises (*business administration*), le marketing
— les mathématiques : la géométrie, le calcul, l'algèbre
— les sciences humaines : l'anthropologie, la psychologie, la sociologie
— l'histoire, la littérature, la philosophie
— les langues : le chinois, le grec, le latin, etc.
— l'architecture, le dessin industriel
— les arts : la peinture, la photographie, la sculpture, la musique, etc.
— les arts ménagers (*home economics*)
— le journalisme et les relations publiques
— la pédagogie (*education*)

---

*suivre (*to follow*) ; **suivre un cours** (*to take a course*). This verb is irregular. Its forms are **je suis, tu suis, il / elle / on suit, nous suivons, vous suivez, ils / elles suivent** ; passé composé : **j'ai suivi** ; futur : **je suivrai** ; subjonctif : **que je suive**.

Le métier d'étudiant
— assister aux cours et aux conférences
— assister à des séances de travaux pratiques (*lab sessions*)
— prendre des notes
— faire des recherches à la bibliothèque
— faire des lectures (*readings*)
— faire des expériences (*experiments*) en laboratoire
— participer aux discussions
— présenter des exposés
— écrire des comptes rendus (*reports*) ou des compositions

Le budget de l'étudiant
Les dépenses
    les frais d'inscription (*tuition*)
    le loyer
    les livres et les fournitures (*supplies*) scolaires
    la nourriture (les tickets de restaurant)
    l'argent de poche
Les ressources
    avoire une bourse (*scholarship*)
    travailler à temps partiel (à mi-temps, à plein temps)
    avoir un prêt (faire une demande de prêt, emprunter de l'argent)
    être à la charge de ses parents

Types of courses : les conférences ; les séances de travaux pratiques ; les discussions dirigées ; les cours télévisés ; les cours programmés (computerized) ; les travaux en groupe ; les présentations enregistrées sur magnétoscope.

1. Quels cours suivez-vous ce trimestre ou ce semestre ? Et le trimestre prochain, quels cours suivrez-vous ? Quels sont les cours obligatoires que vous avez déjà suivis, ou que vous devez suivre ? Quand espérez-vous obtenir votre diplôme ?
2. Quelles sont vos activités et vos obligations habituelles ?
3. Comment organisez-vous votre budget ? Quelles sont vos dépenses principales ?

Université de Montréal : résidences universitaires

Explorations
✤ Talking about what we read, write, and say
Les verbes *lire*, *écrire* et *dire*

The verbs **lire** (*to read*), **écrire** (*to write*), and **dire** (*to tell, to say*) are irregular but resemble each other in several ways.

lire	
je **lis**	nous **lisons**
tu **lis**	vous **lisez**
il / elle / on **lit**	ils / elles **lisent**

passé composé : j'**ai lu**
futur : je **lirai**
subjonctif : que je **lise**

Things to read : des livres de classe ; des romans ; des romans de science-fiction ; le journal ; des bandes dessinées ; des revues, des nouvelles, des poèmes, des pièces de théâtre.

       D'habitude je **lis** *Montréal-Martin.*
       Hier j'**ai lu** le dernier livre d'Anne Hébert.
       Il faut que vous **lisiez** ce livre.
       Je **lirai** le livre que vous m'avez suggéré.

Suggestion : Point out that Anne Hébert, author of *Le Seigneur de Kamouraska,* is a 20th century French-Canadian novelist and that Gilles Vigneault (see Chapter 2) is a French-Canadian poet and singer.

écrire	
j'**écris**	nous **écrivons**
tu **écris**	vous **écrivez**
il / elle / on **écrit**	ils / elles **écrivent**

passé composé : j'**ai écrit**
futur : j'**écrirai**
subjonctif : que j'**écrive**

       Demain j'**écrirai** au centre d'orientation professionnelle.
       Ses enfants lui **écrivaient** toutes les semaines.
       Gilles Vigneault **a écrit** un très beau poème sur le Canada.
       Il faut que j'**écrive** une composition ce soir.

dire	
je **dis**	nous **disons**
tu **dis**	vous **dites**
il / elle / on **dit**	ils / elles **disent**

passé composé : j'**ai dit**
futur : je **dirai**
subjonctif : que je **dise**

Qu'est-ce que vous **dites** ?
Sais-tu qui a **dit** « Vive le Québec libre » ?
Dis à Yvonne de ne pas nous attendre.
Je crois qu'ils **diront** oui.
Il faut que tu **dises** la vérité.

Charles de Gaulle said, « Vive le Québec libre. »

Dire des mots doux = to say sweet nothings

Another verb like **écrire** is **décrire** (*to describe*).

Décrivez la maison où vous habitez.

Substitution (écrire) : (1) J'écris bien. (nous / vous / ce journaliste / les étudiants / tu) (2) Elle n'a pas écrit sa composition. (je / mon ami / nous / tu / Christophe / vous) (3) Nous avons lu ce livre. (tu / le professeur / je / vous / les autres) (4) J'écrivais peu mais je lisais beaucoup. (vous / tu / on / nous / les enfants) (5) Je crois que oui. (nous / vous / sa femme / tu / ses parents) (6) Il faut que je lise ce livre. (tu / vous / nous / les étudiants / Michel)

Mise en situation

Le courrier des lecteurs. Sabine et Bernard ont participé à une manifestation organisée par l'U.N.E.F. (Union Nationale des Étudiants de France). Sabine vient de lire un compte rendu de l'événement dans le journal.

demonstration (*manifestation*)

SABINE	Dis, tu as lu le journal?
BERNARD	Non, pas encore.
SABINE	Lis ce qu'ils disent au sujet de la *manif*…
BERNARD	Eh bien, dis donc ! Il n'aime pas beaucoup les étudiants, le *type* qui a écrit ça !
SABINE	Ça, c'est son droit. Mais il ne dit pas la vérité sur ce qui s'est passé.
BERNARD	Si nous leur écrivions une lettre et si nous leur disions ce que nous pensons… ?
SABINE	Bonne idée. Je vais d'abord faire un *brouillon* et tu me diras si ça va.

guy

rough draft

Préparation

A. Sujets de composition. Les étudiants de Madame Degagne parlent des compositions qu'ils écrivent. Qu'est-ce qu'ils disent ?

Repeat in the future tense. Option : Ask students what compositions and papers they have written recently or are planning to write and for what courses.

Modèle   Jean-Marie / la musique québécoise
Jean-Marie écrit sa composition sur la musique québécoise.

1. nous / le problème du chômage au Québec
2. je / l'histoire du Québec
3. vous / le rôle de la religion au Québec
4. Jean et Roger / le roman québécois
5. Madeleine / l'histoire du Parti québécois
6. tu / la chanson québécoise
7. nous / le dernier livre d'Antonine Maillet
8. Armand / le français qu'on parle au Québec

Antonine Maillet is a contemporary French-Canadian novelist. Her historical novel about French Canada, Pélagie-la-Charrette, is mentioned in the next exercise.

B. **Au Québec.** Deux étudiants québécois parlent de ce qu'ils aiment lire. Formulez leurs réponses selon les indications données.

Modèle Est-ce que tu lis les journaux? (oui… plusieurs)
Oui, je lis plusieurs journaux.

1. Quel journal est-ce que tu lis le matin? (*Montréal-Matin*)
2. Et tes parents, quel journal est-ce qu'ils lisent? (*La Presse*)
3. Quand vous habitiez à Québec, quel journal est-ce que vous lisiez? (*Le Soleil*)
4. Est-ce que tu as lu *Maria Chapdelaine* quand tu étais jeune? (oui)
5. Est-ce que tu lis souvent des revues américaines? (oui… de temps en temps)
6. Quelles revues françaises est-ce que tu lis? (*L'Express* et *Le Nouvel Observateur*)
7. Est-ce que ta mère lit une revue féminine? (oui… *Châtelaine*)
8. Et les jeunes, qu'est-ce qu'ils lisent? (*Vidéo-Presse*)
9. Est-ce que tu as lu un bon roman récemment? (oui… *Pélagie-la-Charrette*)

C. **On dit ce qu'on pense.** Certaines personnes disent toujours ce qu'elles pensent; d'autres, non.

Modèle Claude (jamais) → **Claude ne dit jamais ce qu'il pense.**

1. je (toujours)
2. Anne (quelquefois)
3. vous (jamais)
4. mes amis (toujours)
5. tu (rarement)
6. nous (tout le temps)

Communication et vie pratique

A. **Questions / interview.** Répondez aux questions suivantes ou utilisez-les pour interviewer un(e) autre étudiant(e).

1. Est-ce que tu écris bien?
2. Est-ce que tu écris beaucoup de lettres? À qui?
3. Qui t'écrit des lettres?
4. Aimes-tu écrire des poèmes? As-tu jamais écrit un poème en français?
5. Est-ce que tu aimes lire? Qui est ton auteur préféré?
6. Quels livres as-tu lus cette année?
7. Est-ce que tu lis le journal tous les jours? Est-ce que tu le lis le matin ou le soir?
8. Est-ce que tu lisais beaucoup quand tu étais petit(e)? Qu'est-ce que tu lisais?
9. Est-ce que tu as déjà lu un livre en français? Et dans une autre langue étrangère?
10. Qu'est-ce que tu aimes lire quand tu as du temps libre?

B. **Qu'est-ce que vous dites?** Répondez aux questions suivantes.

1. Est-ce que vous dites toujours la vérité?
2. Est-ce que vous dites toujours ce que vous pensez?

3. Comment dit-on bonjour en espagnol? Et en italien? Et dans d'autres langues?
4. Qu'est-ce que vous dites au professeur quand vous ne comprenez pas? Et quand vous n'avez pas fait vos devoirs?
5. Quel est le premier mot que vous avez dit?

C'est votre tour. Vous venez de lire, dans le journal de votre école, une nouvelle ou un article qui vous met en colère. Informez un(e) autre étudiant(e) de son contenu et discutez ce que vous pouvez faire.

Preparation : Have students identify a possible topic for the article or have them find an article in their school newspaper or elsewhere to use as a point of departure for the article.

❧ Asking questions
Les pronoms interrogatifs

Présentation

Since the early chapters of this book you have been forming questions using **qu'est-ce que** and **qui** as interrogative words meaning *what* and *who*. **Qu'est-ce que** and **qui** are part of a larger group of interrogative pronouns that includes :

A. Pronouns referring to persons.
These correspond to *who* and *whom* in English. The pronoun **qui** is always used to refer to persons.

1. **Qui** can function as the subject of a sentence. **Qui** can be replaced by the longer form **qui est-ce qui**.

   Qui a fondé la ville de Québec?
   Qui est-ce qui a fondé la ville de Québec?

2. **Qui** can function as a direct object or as the object of a preposition. It can be used with **est-ce que** or with inversion.

   Qui avez-vous rencontré pendant votre promenade?
   Qui est-ce que vous avez rencontré pendant votre promenade?
   Avec **qui** as-tu voyagé?
   Avec **qui est-ce que** tu as voyagé?

3. **Qui est-ce** is used to ask the identity of a person.

   —**Qui est-ce**? — C'est Jean.

B. Pronouns referring to things.
These correspond to *what* in English.

1. **Qu'est-ce qui** is used as the subject of a sentence.

   Qu'est-ce qui est arrivé?   **Qu'est-ce qui** te préoccupe?

   A useful expression used with **qu'est-ce qui** is **Qu'est-ce qui se passe**?
(What's going on?).

2. Either **qu'est-ce que** or **que** is used as the direct object of a sentence. With **que** inversion is required.

Qu'est-ce que vous faites ?   **Qu'est-ce qu'**elle a vu ?
Que faites-vous ?   **Qu'**a-t-elle vu ?

3. **Quoi** (*what*) is used after a preposition when there is not a specific antecedent.

De **quoi** est-ce qu'il a parlé ?   À **quoi** est-ce que tu penses ?
De **quoi** a-t-il parlé ?   À **quoi** penses-tu ?

4. **Qu'est-ce que c'est** or **qu'est-ce que c'est que** is used to ask someone to identify or define something.

— **Qu'est-ce que c'est ?** — C'est une tarte au sucre. C'est une spécialité québécoise.
— **Qu'est-ce que c'est qu'**une 2CV ? — C'est une petite voiture française.

The following table summarizes the uses of the interrogative pronouns.

Les pronoms interrogatifs

	Subject	*Object*	*Object of a preposition*	*Definition or identification*
Persons	qui qui est-ce qui	qui qui est-ce que	qui	qui est-ce
Things	qu'est-ce qui	que qu'est-ce que	quoi	qu'est-ce que c'est qu'est-ce que c'est que

Mise en situation

Comment ça finit ? Bernadette *a manqué* le dernier épisode d'une série policière. Elle demande à François comment finit l'histoire.

BERNADETTE   Qu'est-ce qui s'est passé ? Comment finit l'histoire ?

FRANÇOIS   Comme toutes les histoires policières ! Le *coupable* monte dans le *panier à salade* et deux policiers l'emmènent en prison.

BERNADETTE   Oui, mais qui est le coupable ? Qui est-ce que les policiers ont arrêté ?

FRANÇOIS   Denise de Beauchemin, la nièce de la vieille dame.

BERNADETTE   C'est Denise qui… ? Ah ça, alors !

FRANÇOIS   Qui est-ce que tu *soupçonnais* ?

BERNADETTE   Le jardinier. Mais, dis-moi, qu'est-ce qui a mis les policiers *sur la piste* ?

Transformation : Pour chaque série de phrases, donnez les questions correspondantes. *Modèle :* Dominique a apporté ses disques. → Qu'est-ce que Dominique a apporté ? (1) Tu as lu ce livre. (2) Ils ont acheté une carte de la région. (3) Vous avez vu un bon film. (4) Robert attendait l'autobus. (5) Vous avez regardé le match à la télé. *Modèle :* Nadine a apporté ses disques. → Qui a apporté ses disques ? (Utilisez les phrases de l'exercice précédent.) *Modèle :* Tu as vu Claude au match. → Qui as-tu vu au match ? (1) Nous avons invité les Dupont. (2) Elle a emmené ses enfants à la plage. (3) Jean a retrouvé ses amis en ville. (4) Ils ont rencontré Michelle au cinéma. (5) Nous avons vu Bernard au match. *Modèle :* Tu as vu Claude au match. → Qui a vu Claude au match ? (Utilisez les phrases de l'exercice précédent.)

missed

guilty one

paddy wagon

Option : Mention the famous Belgian mystery writer, Georges Simenon, whose books featuring *l'inspecteur Maigret* are popular around the world.

suspected

on the right track

FRANÇOIS   Un coup de téléphone anonyme.

BERNADETTE   Et qu'est-ce que Denise a dit quand les policiers sont venus
l'arrêter ?

FRANÇOIS   Elle *a* tout *avoué*.   **confessed**

Préparation

A. Un vrai fiasco. André était responsable de l'organisation d'une randonnée (*hike*) dans les Laurentides. Malheureusement, le résultat est
un vrai fiasco. D'après ses réponses, quelles sont les questions que les
autres membres du club lui ont posées ?

> **Modèle**   C'est moi qui devais apporter une carte.
> **Qui devait apporter une carte ?**

1. C'est moi qui ai décidé de partir à quatre heures du matin.
2. C'est moi qui ai acheté les provisions.
3. C'est moi qui ai promis d'apporter une carte.
4. C'est moi qui suis responsable de tout ça.
5. C'est moi qui ai choisi cette auberge.

> **Modèle**   Je ne sais pas ce qu'on va faire ce soir.
> **Qu'est-ce qu'on va faire ce soir ?**

1. Je ne sais pas ce qu'on va manger.
2. Je ne sais pas ce qu'on va boire.
3. Je ne sais pas ce qu'on va trouver à l'auberge.
4. Je ne sais pas ce qu'on va faire demain.
5. Je ne sais pas ce qu'il faut faire maintenant.

B. Au bureau des inscriptions. Les employés du bureau des inscriptions
de l'université Laval sont obligés de répondre à toutes sortes de questions. Voici quelques-unes de leurs réponses. Quelles sont les questions qu'on leur a posées ? Remplacez les mots en italique par l'interrogatif approprié.

> **Modèle**   Vous aurez besoin d'*une copie de vos diplômes.*
> **De quoi aurons-nous besoin ?**

1. Vous avez besoin d'*une demande d'inscription.*
2. Vous donnez la demande d'inscription à *la secrétaire.*
3. C'est *un de nos professeurs.*
4. Il faudra apporter *des lettres de référence.*
5. Vous pouvez écrire à *vos anciens professeurs.*
6. C'est *un plan du campus.*
7. C'est *Madame Laforge* qui s'occupe de cette question.
8. Vous pouvez payer *vos droits d'inscription* au bureau d'à côté
9. Vous pouvez les payer par *chèque*, si vous voulez.
10. Vous devez parler *au directeur.*

The *Laurentides* are
characterized by numerous
lakes, rivers, and forests. The
great plateau of Canada (also
known as the Canadian shield)
extends southeast from the
Mackenzie River Basin
through southern Ontario and
Quebec (passing through the
Great Lakes Region) and
northeast to the Laborador
Sea. The area is known for its
beautiful scenery, resorts, and
year-round sporting activities.

Option : Have students repeat
using the long form of *qui*
(*Qui est-ce qui devait
apporter une carte ?*) and the
short form of *que* (*Que va-t-
on faire ce soir ?*).

C. **Des Américains au Québec**. Des amis américains sont en voyage au Québec. Ils ont toutes sortes de questions à poser. Malheureusement, ils ne parlent pas français. Pouvez-vous les aider?

1. What do we need for this trip?
2. Who told you about this restaurant?
3. What are we going to do tomorrow?
4. Who wrote this book?
5. What's an "érable"?
6. What are they playing over there?
7. Whom did you talk to?
8. What did you talk about?

Communication et vie pratique

A. **Des oreilles indiscrètes**. Vous êtes candidat(e) pour un emploi de moniteur (monitrice) dans une colonie de vacances. Le directeur de la colonie est en train d'interviewer un autre candidat. Vous entendez seulement les réponses du candidat. Quelles questions le directeur a-t-il posées?

Option : Oral or written.
Follow-up : Have students role-play a job interview.

LE DIRECTEUR : _____ ?
LE CANDIDAT : Je m'appelle Charles Girard.
LE DIRECTEUR : _____ ?
LE CANDIDAT : J'ai vingt ans.
LE DIRECTEUR : _____ ?
LE CANDIDAT : Un de mes amis m'a parlé de ce travail.
LE DIRECTEUR : _____ ?
LE CANDIDAT : Je veux être professeur de gymnastique.
LE DIRECTEUR : _____ ?
LE CANDIDAT : En ce moment je suis étudiant et je travaille dans un restaurant.
LE DIRECTEUR : _____ ?
LE CANDIDAT : J'ai travaillé comme secrétaire dans un bureau de l'université.
LE DIRECTEUR : _____ ?
LE CANDIDAT : Parce que j'aime les enfants et j'ai besoin d'argent.
LE DIRECTEUR : _____ ?
LE CANDIDAT : Je m'intéresse à tous les sports.

B. **Impressions**. Imaginez que vous venez de faire la connaissance d'un groupe de Français qui voyagent aux États-Unis. Demandez-leur leurs impressions des Américains et de la vie américaine.

If possible, have students ask a native speaker these questions and those in the next communication, C — Préparations. You might also want them to write a letter in French to a French university and include these or similar questions in the letter.

Exemples Qu'est-ce que vous pensez de la cuisine américaine?
Qu'est-ce qui vous a surpris le plus?

C. **Préparations**. Vous vous préparez à partir en France pour passer un an dans une université française. Quelles sont les questions que vous poserez à un(e) ami(e) français(e) (études, logement, prix, transports, loisirs et vie sociale, etc.)?

Have students pick a topic of interest (e.g., les sports, la vie universitaire, les vacances) and then prepare a series of questions that they would ask another student. Students can then ask each other these questions in small groups.

Exemple Que font les jeunes pendant leur temps libre?

> **C'est votre tour.** Le dialogue entre Bernadette et François ne donne pas beaucoup de détails sur l'histoire policière en question. Certains étudiants vont jouer le rôle de l'auteur et compléter les détails qui manquent (par exemple, où et quand l'histoire se passe-t-elle, qui sont les personnages principaux, qu'est-ce qu'ils ont fait, etc.). Les autres étudiants vont leur poser des questions pour apprendre autant de détails possibles.

Preparation : The first group provides the missing details while the second group prepares questions to ask. If time permits, roles can be reversed.

❧ Telling what you would do
Le conditionnel

Présentation

The use of the conditional in *si* clauses is explained in the next section of this chapter.

In English a conditional verb can usually be recognized by the word *would* in the verb phrase : *I would like to study in Quebec* ; *he would like to buy a new car.*

Have students review the future stems presented in Chapter 14.

In French the conditional is formed by adding the endings of the imperfect tense to the future stem of a verb. There are no exceptions to this pattern.

Le conditionnel d'*aimer*	
j'**aimerais**	nous **aimerions**
tu **aimerais**	vous **aimeriez**
il / elle / on **aimerait**	ils / elles **aimeraient**

The conditional is used :

A. To express a wish or a suggestion :

| J'**aimerais** partir demain. | *I'd like to leave tonight.* |
| Nous **voudrions** faire une promenade. | *We'd like to go for a walk.* |

B. When a condition is stated or implied :

À votre place, je ne **dirais** pas ça.	*In your place, I wouldn't say that.*
Dans ce cas-là, tu **pourrais** venir demain.	*In that case, you could come tomorrow.*
Si j'avais le temps, je **lirais** davantage.	*If I had the time, I'd read more.*

C. In order to be less direct and more polite in :

1. Making requests or suggestions : **je voudrais...** ; **pourriez-vous...** ; **voudriez-vous...** ; **accepteriez-vous...** ; **aimeriez-vous...** ; **est-ce que cela vous arrangerait de...** (*would it suit you to...*) ; **est-ce que cela vous dérangerait si...** (*would it bother you if...*) ; etc.

2. Accepting invitations : **ça me ferait plaisir** ; **je serais ravi(e)** ; **ce serait une excellente idée** ; **j'aimerais bien**.

> —**Aimeriez**-vous venir dîner à
> la maison ?
> —Oui, ça me **ferait** plaisir.   *I'd love to. (Yes, that would please*
>   *me very much.)*

D. In indirect style, to relate what somebody has said :

> Il a dit qu'il **parlerait** au   *He said that he would speak to the*
> professeur.   *instructor.*
> Ils ont répondu qu'ils   *They answered that they'd rather*
> **aimeraient** mieux attendre ici.   *wait here.*

Remind students that the imperfect, not the conditional, is used to express the idea of *would* in the sense of *used to*.

Mise en situation

Projets de voyage. Jean-Claude et Robert sont des amis de Liliane, une Québécoise qu'ils ont connue quand elle faisait un séjour à Paris. Ils aimeraient bien la revoir et lui rendre visite dans son pays.

JEAN-CLAUDE   Je voudrais aller au Canada cet été. C'est un pays que j'aimerais bien connaître. Qu'est-ce que tu en penses ?

ROBERT   Ce serait une bonne idée ! Nous pourrions rendre visite à Liliane…

JEAN-CLAUDE   Oui, ça me ferait vraiment plaisir de la revoir.

ROBERT   Je suis en vacances *à partir du* 1er août. Nous pourrions partir la semaine suivante.

JEAN-CLAUDE   Oui, mais il faudrait vite lui écrire. Elle n'est peut-être pas libre.

ROBERT   Dans sa dernière lettre elle m'a dit qu'elle resterait chez elle tout l'été et que ses parents seraient très heureux de nous recevoir.

JEAN-CLAUDE   Tu crois vraiment que ça ne les *dérangerait* pas ?

Substitution : (1) J'aimerais sortir. (tu / nous / Christophe / mes amis / vous) (2) Tu voudrais regarder la carte. (nous / vous / cette personne / je / les autres) (3) Elle a dit qu'elle attendrait. (tu / je / son ami / Michel et Raymond / nous / vous) (4) Dans ce cas-là, vous pourriez rester à la maison. (Pierre / je / on / tu / Claude et son ami / nous)

starting on

Point out that *aller voir quelqu'un* and *rendre visite à quelqu'un* (more formal) are used to talk about visiting people ; *visiter* is used only with places.

would disturb

Préparation

A. **Chacun a ses responsabilités**. Plusieurs amis ont décidé de faire un voyage au Canada. Voici ce que chaque personne a promis de faire.

> **Modèle**   Luc va choisir l'itinéraire.
>   **Luc a dit qu'il choisirait l'itinéraire.**

1. Nous allons louer une voiture.
2. Tu vas acheter une carte.
3. Je vais retenir des chambres dans les hôtels.
4. Michel va consulter un agent de voyage.
5. Catherine va écrire à ses cousins québécois.
6. Vous allez acheter les billets d'avion.
7. Mes amis vont me prêter une valise.

B. Je me suis trompée. Monique a mal compris ce que les autres ont dit. Elle est surprise quand on lui dit qu'elle s'est trompée.

Modèle   Il viendra demain. (aujourd'hui)
Ah, oui ? Moi, je croyais qu'il viendrait aujourd'hui.

1. Le concert aura lieu vendredi. (samedi)
2. Nous irons au cinéma. (au théâtre)
3. Nos amis arriveront lundi. (dimanche)
4. On mangera à la maison. (au restaurant)
5. Tu m'attendras devant le musée. (dans le parc)
6. On sera de retour à huit heures. (à sept heures)

C. Politesse. Monsieur Bourru n'a pas toujours le succès qu'il aimerait avoir avec ses employés parce qu'il est souvent trop direct. Pourriez-vous l'aider à être plus poli ?

Modèles   Je veux parler au directeur.
Je voudrais parler au directeur.
Aidez-moi.
Pourriez-vous m'aider ?

1. Je veux voir le rapport que vous avez écrit.
2. Jeune homme, apportez-moi un café.
3. Je veux une réponse aujourd'hui même.
4. Soyez ici à huit heures pour votre interview.
5. Dites à Georges que je veux le voir tout de suite.
6. Téléphonez à Bernard et dites-lui que je veux lui parler.

Option : Have students make polite requests in various settings (*au restaurant, à table,* etc.) Also introduce *auriez-vous l'obligeance (la bonté) de ; vous serait-il possible de ; pourrais-je.*

Communication et vie pratique

A. À votre place, moi, je… Que feriez-vous à la place de la personne qui parle ?

Exemple   Je vais me coucher à trois heures du matin parce que j'ai un examen demain matin.
Moi, à votre place, je me coucherais avant minuit.
ou: **Moi, à votre place, je ferais la même chose.**
ou: **À votre place, je ne me coucherais pas à trois heures du matin.**

1. Je vais aller faire une promenade. J'irai en classe un autre jour.
2. J'ai besoin de perdre quelques kilos. Je vais manger un seul repas par jour.
3. Je n'ai pas envie d'écrire à mes parents aujourd'hui. Je leur écrirai un autre jour.
4. Je n'ai pas assez d'argent en ce moment. Mais j'ai vraiment envie d'une nouvelle stéréo. Je vais l'acheter à crédit.
5. J'ai déjà bu trois verres de vin mais j'ai encore soif. Je vais en boire un autre.
6. Je vais regarder la télévision. Je finirai mes devoirs demain.
7. Moi, je ne permettrai pas à mes enfants de sortir seuls le soir.

B. Invitations. On dit que la façon de donner est aussi importante que ce qu'on donne. La façon de répondre à une invitation est importante aussi. Posez les questions suivantes (ou d'autres questions) à un(e) autre étudiant(e) qui va accepter — ou refuser — aussi gentiment que possible.

Exemple   Demandez-lui si vous pourriez l'emmener à l'aéroport.
         — **Est-ce que je pourrais t'emmener à l'aéroport?**
         — **Oui, ce serait gentil de ta part.**
    ou: — **Ce serait gentil mais Pierre a déjà dit qu'il m'y em-**
           mènerait.
Demandez-lui…

1. s'il / si elle voudrait boire quelque chose.
2. s'il / si elle aimerait aller au cinéma ce soir.
3. si cela lui ferait plaisir de venir au match avec vous.
4. s'il / si elle aimerait jouer au tennis cet après-midi.
5. s'il / si elle aurait le temps de vous aider à faire vos devoirs.
6. s'il / si elle pourrait vous prêter ses notes de classe.
7. s'il / si elle aurait envie de faire une petite promenade.
8. ?

C'est votre tour. Quelques amis et vous avez décidé de voyager ensemble cet été. Explorez les possibilités. Utilisez la **Mise en situation** comme guide.

❧ Saying what you would do if...
L'emploi de *si* dans la phrase conditionnelle

Présentation

As already noted, sentences with **si** clauses in the present can be followed by a result clause that uses the present, the future, or the imperative.

Si vous **êtes** fatigué, vous **pouvez** vous reposer.
Si vous **allez** à Québec, **n'oubliez pas** de visiter le château Frontenac.
Si vous **partez** maintenant, vous **aurez** le temps de tout faire.

Sentences with the **si** clause in the imperfect and the result clause in the conditional indicate what would happen if certain conditions were met. Although different tenses can be used in the *if* clause in similar English constructions, only the imperfect tense is used in French.

Si Jean **étudiait** plus, il **réussirait** mieux.	*If John studied more,* *If John were to study more,*	*he would do better.*

Note that in French, as in English, either clause can come first.

Si j'avais assez d'argent, j'achèterais un ordinateur.

or: J'achèterais un ordinateur **si j'avais assez d'argent.**

Je suis sûr que ça coûterait moins cher **si tu choisissais un autre modèle.**

or: **Si tu choisissais un autre modèle,** je suis sûr que ça coûterait moins cher.

Mise en situation

Si on achetait une maison…? Francine et Antoine Rhéault, un jeune couple de Montréal, *envisagent* la possibilité d'acheter une maison en banlieue plutôt que de continuer à louer un appartement. **are considering**

ANTOINE Si on achetait une petite maison en banlieue? Qu'est-ce que tu en penses?

FRANCINE J'aimerais bien ça, si nous en avions les *moyens*… Mais malheureusement, ce n'est pas le cas! **means**

ANTOINE Oui, je sais bien… Mais si tes parents pouvaient nous aider, nous pourrions peut-être y arriver…

FRANCINE Si tu crois que c'est une bonne idée, je leur écrirai.

ANTOINE Ce serait si agréable d'avoir notre propre maison…

FRANCINE Je suppose que si on pouvait trouver quelque chose de pas trop cher, ce ne serait pas une mauvaise idée… *agent immobilier = real-estate agent*

ANTOINE Si on en parlait à ton cousin Henri? Il est dans l'*immobilier*. Il saurait peut-être où on peut trouver ce que nous cherchons. **real estate**

FRANCINE Si tu veux, je lui en parlerai la prochaine fois qu'il viendra nous voir.

Substitution : (1) S'il faisait mauvais, nous resterions à la maison. (je / vous / mes amis / Claire / tu) (2) Si Jacques travaillait plus, il aurait de meilleures notes. (vous / nous / les étudiants / mon frère / je / tu) (3) Pierre viendrait s'il avait le temps. (vous / mes parents / nous / je / Nadine)

Préparation

A. Interview. Un reporter a interviewé des Français et il leur a posé la question suivante : « Que feriez-vous si vous aviez plus d'argent? » Donnez leurs réponses.

Modèle je / aller aux États-Unis
J'irais aux États-Unis si j'avais plus d'argent.

1. je / prendre de longues vacances
2. Paul et sa femme / acheter une maison à la campagne
3. ma femme / prendre sa retraite
4. nous / faire un voyage au Canada
5. Pierre / acheter un bateau
6. Jean et moi, nous / mettre un peu d'argent à la banque
7. je / en donner une partie aux autres
8. nous / aller à Tahiti

B. Si c'était possible... Serge Lefèvre est un jeune Québécois qui parle des choses qu'il aimerait faire.

> **Modèle** chercher un autre travail
> **Si je pouvais, je chercherais un autre travail.**

1. continuer mes études
2. suivre des cours de comptabilité
3. habiter dans un autre quartier
4. apprendre un autre métier
5. vendre ma vieille voiture
6. m'acheter une nouvelle voiture
7. rendre visite à nos amis français

Communication et vie pratique

A. Que feriez-vous ? Que feriez-vous si vous étiez dans les situations suivantes ? Complétez les phrases selon vos préférences.

1. S'il n'y avait pas de cours aujourd'hui…
2. Si j'avais besoin d'une nouvelle voiture…
3. Si je pouvais être une autre personne…
4. Si j'avais soixante ans…
5. Si j'étais millionnaire…
6. Si j'habitais dans un autre pays…

Have students put themselves in the place of a French or French-Canadian student and imagine different aspects of their lives (e.g., university life, family, leisure-time activities, town) : Si j'étais un(e) étudiant(e) français(e), je ferais mes études à l'université de Grenoble.

B. Changez de rôle. Que feriez-vous si vous étiez à la place des personnes suivantes.

1. le professeur
2. le président des États-Unis
3. le président de votre université
4. une vedette de cinéma
5. ?

Add other professions and have students respond.

> **C'est votre tour.** Vous envisagez la possibilité de faire un achat assez important (voiture, meubles, équipement audio-visuel, ordinateur, par exemple). Vous discutez les différentes possibilités avec un(e) ami(e). Utilisez la **Mise en situation** comme guide.

Bring in ads from French or Canadian magazines or newspapers for students to use in completing this activity.

Intégration et perspectives

Une invitation à visiter Québec

La ville de Québec possède un charme unique en Amérique du Nord. Ce charme vient en grande partie de son atmosphère européenne et de ses traditions françaises. Capitale de la province du même nom, la ville de Québec a été fondée en 1608 par Samuel de Champlain, qui était à la fois

Have students skim reading and find three or more reasons why a tourist should visit Quebec.

Option : Have students research Montreal and report on its history and attractions.

Québec : la vieille ville et le château Frontenac

soldat, navigateur et explorateur. Elle est située sur une *colline* qui domine
le Saint-Laurent.

    L'accès de la ville est facile. On peut y arriver par la *route*, par le train,
par l'avion, ou même par bateau. Le port est équipé pour recevoir les plus
gros bateaux transatlantiques, et de l'aéroport partent de fréquents vols
vers Montréal et vers les diverses régions de la province. Québec possède
tout ce qu'il faut pour recevoir les visiteurs : d'excellents hôtels, des restaurants réputés, des *boîtes de nuit* et des discothèques, des salles de concert et
des musées, et toutes sortes d'activités et de compétitions sportives.

    La ville de Québec a une population d'environ 575 000 habitants ; envi-
ron 95 pour cent d'entre eux sont de langue française.

    L'université Laval, fréquentée par plus de 20 000 étudiants, est située à
l'ouest de la ville. C'est la plus vieille université de langue française en
Amérique du Nord. En été des étudiants de presque tous les pays du
monde viennent y suivre des cours de français. C'est à Québec aussi que se
trouve le campus principal de l'université du Québec, créée en 1968, et qui
est organisée selon les concepts les plus modernes.

    Les rivières et les montagnes qui *entourent* la ville en font un lieu idéal
pour la pratique des sports d'été et d'hiver, mais c'est pendant le Carnaval
que l'exubérance générale est à son plus haut point. Pendant les jours de
festivités populaires qui précèdent le *Carême*, on peut voir toutes sortes de
défilés et de danses dans les rues décorées de monuments de *glace*. On peut
aussi assister à la célèbre *course* de canots parmi les glaces du Saint-
Laurent, à une compétition internationale de hockey pee-wee, à des
courses de chiens, et à bien d'autres choses encore.

(marginal glosses)
hill
road
nightclubs
surround
Lent
parades / ice
race

381

Château de neige construit
pour le Carnaval

Course de canots sur le Saint-Laurent

Québec est une ville moderne qui est restée *fidèle* à son passé et qui a | faithful
protégé son riche héritage historique. Toute visite de la ville est un petit
voyage dans l'histoire : monuments, architecture traditionnelle, vieilles
églises — tout y *rappelle* son passé. Intimement associé à l'histoire du Can- | recalls
ada depuis l'arrivée des premiers explorateurs, Québec a conservé une
façon de vivre et une ambiance française qui en font une des grandes villes
touristiques du monde.

Extrait et adapté d'une publication de *Tourisme Québec*.

Compréhension. Répondez aux questions suivantes selon les renseigne- | *Have students write postcards (or letters) in French describing their visit to Québec.*
ments donnés dans le texte.

1. Quand et par qui la ville de Québec a-t-elle été fondée ?
2. Quels sont les différents moyens de transport qu'on peut utiliser pour aller à Québec ?
3. Pourquoi est-ce que la ville de Québec est bien équipée pour recevoir des touristes ?
4. Quel est le pourcentage de gens qui parlent français à Québec ?
5. Dans quelle sorte de région la ville de Québec est-elle située ?
6. Quels sont les principaux événements qui ont lieu à Québec pendant le Carnaval ?
7. Qu'est-ce qui fait le charme particulier de la ville de Québec ?

Notes culturelles: *Le Québec en bref*

Voici quelques dates importantes dans l'histoire du Canada et plus particulièrement du Canada français.

1497	Jean Cabot *découvre* le Canada.	*discovers*
1535	Jacques Cartier découvre le golfe du Saint-Laurent et remonte le Saint-Laurent jusqu'à Montréal.
1608	Samuel de Champlain crée le premier établissement à Québec et s'allie avec les tribus indiennes.
1630	Le cardinal Richelieu envoie des missionnaires jésuites pour con-vertir les ''sauvages''.
1663	La Nouvelle-France est proclamée une province royale par Louis XIV.
1759	Les Français sont battus par les Anglais à la bataille des plaines d'Abraham et abandonnent toute la Nouvelle-France à l'Angleterre. À la suite de cette défaite, un grand nombre d'Acadiens doivent s'exiler. Ils finissent par s'installer en Louisiane (les Cajuns).
1960	Formation du FLQ (Front pour la Libération du Québec).
1970	Le gouvernement établit le bilinguisme : le français et l'anglais sont les deux langues officielles.
1974	Le gouvernement du Québec établit le français comme la seule langue officielle de cette province.
1979	Le Parlement canadien rejette un *projet de loi visant à* donner son indépendance au Québec.	*bill / aiming to*

Communication et vie pratique

A. Agence de voyages. Imaginez que vous travaillez pour une agence de voyages canadienne. Vous répondez aux questions des touristes éventuels (*prospective*) et vous leur décrivez les charmes du Québec pour les persuader de venir y passer leurs vacances. Jouez le rôle de l'employé(e) et essayez de décrire le Québec. D'autres étudiant(e)s peuvent être les touristes éventuels.

Works well as a small-group activity.

B. Une brochure touristique. Vous êtes chargé(e) de préparer une brochure qui décrit les différentes attractions de la ville où vous habitez pour les touristes francophones qui visiteront cette ville. Quels sont les monuments et les attractions touristiques que vous leur suggérez de visiter ? Quels sont les meilleurs restaurants et les meilleurs hôtels de la ville ? Y a-t-il des parcs, des théâtres, des concerts, des compétitions sportives, des musées ou des activités folkloriques susceptibles d'intéresser des touristes étrangers ?

Suggested for individual or small-group writing. Option : Have students prepare a brochure for their university, town, or region for French-speaking tourists.

C. Imaginez que… Imaginez que vous êtes dans les situations suivantes. Que ferez-vous ?

Option : Have class choose the five most useful phrases.

   1. Vous avez un(e) ami(e) qui part au Québec dans quinze jours. Vous avez très peu de temps pour lui apprendre quelques phrases utiles. Quelles sont, à votre avis, les dix ou quinze phrases les plus utiles pour se débrouiller dans un pays où on parle français ?

   2. Vous avez un(e) ami(e) québécois(e) qui va passer un an dans votre université. Il (elle) ne parle pas bien l'anglais. Quelles sont les dix ou quinze phrases les plus utiles dans la vie d'un(e) étudiant(e) américain(e) et que vous allez lui apprendre ? Bien entendu, il (elle) a besoin de comprendre ces phrases. Comment allez-vous les lui expliquer en français ?

D. Le portrait de l'étudiant américain. Est-ce que les étudiants américains ressemblent aux étudiants québécois ? Par exemple, est-ce qu'ils ont les mêmes buts dans la vie ? À quelles professions s'intéressent-ils le plus ? Sont-ils satisfaits de leurs relations avec leur famille ? etc.

Option : Have students compare American and French-Canadian (and / or French) students.

Optional role-play : Several students play the role of French-speaking students who are planning to study at this college or university and ask questions about various aspects of campus life ; remaining students answer these questions.

● *Vocabulaire*

Noms

les cours (voir p. 366)

d'autres noms

   l'**accès** (m)   *access, approach*
   l'**agriculteur** (m), l'**agricultrice** (f)   *farmer*
° l'**attitude** (f)
   la **boîte de nuit**   *nightclub*
   la **bourse**   *scholarship*
   le **brouillon**   *rough draft*

   le **canot**   *canoe*
° le **charme**
   la **colline**   *hill*
   la **composition**   *composition, paper*
   le **compte rendu**   *report*
° le, la **conformiste**
   le, la **coupable**   *guilty person*
   la **course**   *race*
   le **défaut**   *fault, shortcoming*
   le **défilé**   *parade*

° la **discothèque**
° la **discussion**
° l'**éducateur** (m), l'**éducatrice** (f)
l'**être** (m) *being*
l'**événement** *event*
l'**expérience** (f) *experiment*
l'**exposé** (m) *report, paper*
° l'**exubérance**
les **fournitures** (f pl) *supplies*
les **frais** (m pl) *expenses, cost*
la **franchise** *sincerity, frankness*
la **glace** *ice, ice cream*
° l'**idéal** (m)
l'**immobilier** (m) *real estate*
l'**inscription** (f) *registration*
° le **laboratoire**
la **lecture** *reading*
la **manifestation** *demonstration*
° la **nièce**
la **nourriture** *food*
l'**orgueil** (m) *pride*
° l'**orientation** (f)
le **panier à salade** *police van, paddy wagon*
° le, la **partenaire**
la **poche** *pocket*
° le **port**
le **prêt** *loan*
la **qualité** *good quality*
les **ressources** (f pl) *means, resources*
la **réussite** *success*
la **séance de travaux pratiques** *lab sessions*
le **sens** *meaning, sense*
la **sociabilité** *sociability*
le **ticket** *ticket*
le **type** *guy, character*

la **vérité** *truth*
le **vol** *flight*

Verbes

augmenter *to increase*
avouer *to confess*
se **confier** *to confide*
décrire *to describe*
déranger *to disturb, to trouble*
durer *to last*
écrire *to write*
entourer *to surround*
envisager *to consider*
lire *to read*
rappeler *to recall*
soupçonner *to suspect*
suivre *to follow, to take* (a course)

Adjectifs

° **anonyme**
fidèle *faithful*
financier, financière *financial*
obligé(e) *obligated*
partiel(le) *part-time*
prédestiné(e) *predestined*
profond(e) *deep*
° **suprême**
unique *unique, only*
utile *useful*

Divers

au cours de *during*
au sujet de *on the subject of*
intimement *intimately*
mettre sur la piste *to put on the right track*
ne... aucun(e) *not any, no*
plutôt que *rather than*
quoi *what*

CHAPITRE SEIZE

Communication objectives

Talking about sports

1. Expressing relationships between two actions
2. Expressing negative facts or ideas
3. Using verbs with prepositions : Differences in usage and meaning
4. Linking several ideas

Structures

Les mots et la vie : Les sports

Le participe présent et l'infinitif

La négation

L'emploi des prépositions après les verbes

Les pronoms relatifs

Sports et loisirs

Mise en scène
Les plaisirs de la marche à pied

Have students read through and tell what the pleasures of walking are, according to the article.

Quel est le sport le plus populaire en France ? Est-ce que c'est le football ? Le ski ? Le cyclisme ? Peut-être... , si on considère seulement les reportages sportifs à la télévision. Mais si on parle du sport que les Français pratiquent vraiment, c'est peut-être tout simplement la *marche à pied*. Même les gens qui ne pratiquent aucun sport régulièrement font fréquemment une petite promenade à pied en famille le dimanche après-midi.

walking, hiking

De plus en plus, la marche devient un sport. Sa popularité correspond à un désir général de retour à la nature et à la simplicité, et à un besoin d'effort physique. Il y a en France un comité national des *Sentiers* qui est responsable de l'*entretien* de 22 000 kilomètres de sentiers. Il y a soixante-trois itinéraires qui traversent la France, et parmi les cinq sentiers européens, il y en a trois qui passent par la France.

paths, trails
maintenance

Le Comité national organise aussi des conférences et des présentations du film *La France et ses sentiers*. Il a même organisé un marathon de 4 000 kilomètres qui a duré d'avril à octobre. Chaque équipe de *randonneurs* marchait pendant quinze jours avant d'être remplacée par une autre équipe. À chaque *ville-étape*, il y avait des activités et des jeux organisés par les municipalités locales.

hikers

stopover

L'*ouverture* de ces sentiers est due non seulement aux services publics mais aussi à des initiatives privées. Certains individus, et même dans certains cas des familles entières, qui *sont tombés amoureux* d'une région, passent leur temps libre à créer de nouveaux *réseaux* de sentiers. Chaque

opening

have fallen in love
systems

week-end ils emportent leurs pots de peinture et installent les *pancartes* qui montreront le *chemin* à d'autres randonneurs.

signs

way, road

Pour pratiquer ce sport, on n'a pas besoin d'avoir beaucoup d'argent ni d'être très jeune. Les jeunes randonneurs peuvent passer la nuit dans des auberges de jeunesse qui sont très bon marché. L'équipement n'est ni très cher ni très compliqué non plus. Une bonne paire de chaussures, des chaussettes, un pantalon, une chemise, un pull-over, un *anorak*, et un *sac à dos* suffisent. Mais pour être un bon randonneur, il ne suffit pas d'être bien équipé, il faut aussi être très prudent et connaître ses possibilités et ses limites. Et surtout, il faut respecter la nature. Voici les dix commandements du randonneur :

Option : Do activity B, Les Dix Commandements, in the Communication et vie pratique of the Intégration et perspectives section.

windbreaker, ski jacket / backpack

1. Tu porteras de bonnes chaussures.
2. Tu seras en bonne condition physique.
3. Tu étudieras ton itinéraire sur la carte.
4. Tu t'informeras sur la nature du terrain.
5. Tu éviteras les *randonnées* qui sont *au-dessus de* tes forces.

hikes / above, beyond

6. Tu ne partiras jamais seul au-dessus de 1000 mètres d'altitude.
7. Tu emporteras des vêtements chauds ; les nuits sont froides en toute saison dans les montagnes.
8. Tu feras attention aux *vipères*.

poisonous snakes

9. Tu n'oublieras pas que tu es toujours sur la propriété de quelqu'un d'autre.
10. Tu respecteras la nature.

Compréhension. Répondez aux questions suivantes selon les renseignements donnés dans le texte.

1. Quel est le sport qu'on pratique le plus en France ?
2. Pourquoi est-ce que les Français marchent beaucoup ?
3. Qu'est-ce que beaucoup de Français font le dimanche après-midi ?
4. Quelles sont les raisons principales de la popularité de la marche à pied en France ?
5. Est-ce que la France est bien équipée en sentiers ?
6. Comment est organisé le marathon qui dure d'avril à octobre ?
7. Selon les dix commandements du randonneur, quelles sont les choses principales qu'il faut emporter ?
8. Quelles sont les précautions qu'il faut prendre avant de partir ?

1. Et aux États-Unis ?

2. Les Américains marchent-ils autant ?

3. Et les Américains ?

4. Est-ce la même chose aux États-Unis ?

5. Et les États-Unis ?

6. Êtes-vous d'accord ?

7. Êtes-vous d'accord ?

Notes culturelles: *Les Français et le sport*

Les Français s'intéressent beaucoup aux sports et, comme les Américains, ils aiment regarder les compétitions sportives à la télévision ou les écouter à la radio. Le football (ce que nous appelons le « soccer » aux États-Unis) est très populaire, et les Français regardent avec intérêt, et même passion, les matchs de leurs équipes favorites. Les équipes des

In 1973, 41% of French men and 28% of the women engaged in sports regularly ; the numbers have now risen to 52% for men and 40% for women. The number of French people jogging or doing aerobic exercise has doubled in the last ten years.

Match de football à Paris

grandes villes comme Saint-Étienne, Clermont-Ferrand et Lille jouent non seulement dans des compétitions régionales mais aussi dans des compétitions nationales et internationales comme la Coupe de France et le Championnat d'Europe.

Une différence importante entre la France et les USA est que les universités françaises n'ont pas leurs propres équipes sportives et que les « intercollegiate sports » n'existent pas en France. Le sport est une activité personnelle qui ne fait pas partie de la vie universitaire.

Le cyclisme est un sport très populaire aussi. Parmi les différentes courses cyclistes, c'est le Tour de France qui est suivi avec le plus de passion par les Français. Le Tour de France, comme son nom l'indique, fait le tour de presque toute la France *y compris* les régions montagneuses comme les Alpes ou les Pyrénées. Les Français s'intéressent aussi aux courses automobiles — surtout aux Vingt-Quatre Heures du Mans et au rallye de Monte-Carlo.

En plus de ces sports internationaux, il y a des sports typiquement français : la pétanque, ou les boules, un jeu qui ressemble un peu au « bowling » et qui *se joue* surtout dans le sud de la France, et la pelote basque (ce que nous appelons « jai alai ») qui se joue au Pays basque dans le sud-ouest de la France.

including

besides

is played

Partie de boules à Paris

Les mots et la vie : Les sports

Étudiez le vocabulaire et ensuite faites les activités indiquées.

Option : Also introduce *faire de la natation, du footing, du ski de randonnée, du judo, de la danse, du tir à la carabine, du tire à l'arc ; jouer au ping-pong.*

Les sports

jouer
| au tennis
| au football
| au base-ball
| au basket-ball
| au golf
| au rugby
| à la pétanque
| au hockey

faire
| du ski
| du ski nautique *(water skiing)*
| de l'alpinisme *(moutain climbing)*
| du patinage *(roller skating)*
| du patinage sur glace *(ice skating)*
| de la gymnastique *(exercise or gymnastics)*
| de l'athlétisme *(track and field)*
| de la boxe
| de la lutte *(wrestling)*
| de la marche à pied
| de la course automobile *(racing)*
| de la course à pied *(running)*
| du cheval *(hourseback riding)*
| de la bicyclette / du vélo
| de la natation *(swimming)*
| de la voile *(sailing)*
| de la planche à voile *(wind surfing)*
| du surfing

aller
| à la chasse *(hunting)*
| à la pêche *(fishing)*

Les compétitions sportives
un match
un championnat
une course à pied, d'automobile, de chevaux, cycliste
un marathon
un tournoi
Les résultats
gagner
perdre
être battu(e)(s) *(to be beaten)*
faire match nul *(to tie)*

A. **Sports et sportifs.** Donnez le nom d'un(e) athlète. Les autres étudiants diront quel sport cette personne pratique (ou pratiquait).

   Exemple   Babe Ruth → **Babe Ruth jouait au base-ball.**

B. **Quels sports pratiquez-vous?** Indiquez si vous pratiquez régulièrement, de temps en temps, rarement ou jamais les sports indiqués
dans la liste précédente.

Exemple **Je joue souvent au tennis, mais je fais rarement du cheval.**
Je ne vais jamais à la pêche ou à la chasse.

C. **Vous et le sport.** Répondez aux questions suivantes ou utilisez-les pour
interviewer un(e) autre étudiant(e).

1. Quels sports pratiquez-vous?
2. Quels autres sports aimeriez-vous pratiquer?
3. Préférez-vous les sports d'équipe ou les sports individuels?
4. Faites-vous du sport surtout pour la compétition, pour le plaisir ou
   pour rester en forme?
5. Y a-t-il un(e) athlète ou un(e) champion(ne) que vous admirez particulièrement? Si oui, pourquoi?
6. À quelles compétitions sportives avez-vous assisté ou participé?
   Quels ont été les résultats?

D. **Qui suis-je?** Imaginez que vous êtes un(e) athlète célèbre. Les autres
étudiants vont vous poser des questions pour trouver qui vous êtes.

Explorations
❧ Expressing relationships between two actions
Le participe présent et l'infinitif

Présentation

The present participle is used to indicate that an action taking place is
closely related to the action of the main verb. It is equivalent to English
forms ending in *-ing* such as *speaking, walking, finding, choosing*. In French
the present participle always ends in **-ant**. It is formed by adding **-ant** to the
stem of the present-tense **nous** form of the verb.

nous parlons → **parlant**   nous faisons → **faisant**
nous finissons → **finissant**   nous commençons →
nous attendons → **attendant**   **commençant**
                                  nous mangeons → **mangeant**

There are only three irregular present participles in French :

être → **étant**   savoir → **sachant**   avoir → **ayant**

Sachant cela, nous avons pris la décision de rester.
L'avion **arrivant** de Paris aura un retard de trente minutes.
Étant étudiant, je n'avais pas beaucoup d'argent.

A. The most common use of the present participle is after the preposition **en**. It is used to indicate :

1. That two actions are taking place at the same time. English equivalents to this use are *while* or *upon* plus the *-ing* form of the verb.

J'écoute de la musique **en faisant** du jogging.	*I listen to music while jogging.*
En entrant dans le stade nous avons remarqué qu'il y avait peu de spectateurs.	*Upon entering (as we entered), we noticed that there were few spectators.*
Elle s'est cassé la jambe **en faisant** du ski.	*She broke her leg skiing.*

2. The manner in which an action is done or the means by which an end is achieved. This use of the present participle is equivalent to using *by*, *in*, or *through* plus the *-ing* form of an English verb. Sometimes no preposition is used in English.

C'est **en jouant** tous les jours qu'on apprend à bien jouer.	*It is by playing every day that one learns to play well.*
Je me détends **en écoutant** de la musique classique.	*I relax by listening to classical music.*

B. Present participles are occasionally used as adjectives. In this case, they agree with the noun modified.

Ils ont gagné le match **suivant**.	*They won the next game.*
Les réactions du public sont **encourageantes**.	*The reactions of the public are encouraging.*
C'est un événement **intéressant**.	*That's an interesting event.*

C. When prepositions other than **en** are used with verb forms, the verb is always in the infinitive.

Venez me voir **avant de partir**.	*Come to see me before leaving.*
Lisez lentement **pour** bien **comprendre**.	*Read slowly in order to understand well.*
Ne décidez pas **sans réfléchir**.	*Don't decide without thinking.*

D. After the preposition **après**, the past infinitive must be used. It is composed of the infinitive **avoir** or **être** plus the past participle. Note that the past participle agrees with the subject when the verb is conjugated with **être**.

Après avoir joué au tennis, tout le monde était fatigué.	*After playing (having played) tennis, everyone was tired.*
Elle a fait la connaissance de Jean-Claude **après être revenue** d'Europe.	*She met Jean-Claude after returning (having returned) from Europe.*
Nous avons fini le match **après nous être reposés**.	*We finished the game after resting (having rested).*

Transformation : Modèle : Je regarde la télévision quand je mange. → Je regarde la télévision en mangeant. (1) quand je fais mes devoirs ; (2) quand je m'habille ; (3) quand j'étudie ; (4) quand je lis le journal ; (5) quand je prépare le dîner ; (6) quand je finis mon dîner. Modèle : Je regarde la télévision quand je mange. → Je regarde la télévision avant de manger. (Utilisez les phrases de l'exercice précédent.) Modèle : Je regarde la télévision quand je mange. → Je regarde la television après avoir mangé. (Utilisez les phrases de l'exercice précédent.)

Mise en situation

Vacances de ski. Comme beaucoup de Français, Véronique a passé ses vacances d'hiver dans une station de ski. Mais elle n'a pas eu de chance et elle est revenue avec une jambe cassée. Ses camarades de bureau la *taquinent*.

CAROLINE   Qu'est-ce qui t'est arrivé ? Tu t'es cassé la jambe en faisant du ski ?

VÉRONIQUE   Eh bien, non. Ce n'est pas en descendant une belle *pente* que je me suis fait ça, mais en sortant de l'hôtel.

JOSETTE   Tu *plaisantes*, non ?

VÉRONIQUE   Non. Après être arrivée à Chamonix, je suis montée dans ma chambre pour me changer. Après avoir fait cinq heures de route, j'étais très fatiguée. J'ai donc décidé de me reposer un peu avant d'*affronter* les belles *pistes* neigeuses.

CAROLINE   Et alors ?

VÉRONIQUE   Quand je suis sortie, il commençait à faire sombre. Je n'ai pas vu qu'il y avait du verglas. J'ai *glissé* et je me suis cassé la jambe en tombant.

Chamonix is a popular ski and mountain climbing resort in the French Alps at the foot of Mont Blanc. Skiing is so popular that French students get a week off in February for ski vacations.
tease

slope

are joking

tackling / trails

slipped, slid

Préparation

A. Activités. On peut facilement écouter de la musique en faisant autre chose. Quand les personnes suivantes écoutent-elles de la musique ?

    Modèle   moi / quand je fais de la gymnastique
           Moi, j'écoute de la musique en faisant de la gymnastique.

1. nous / quand nous préparons le dîner
2. mon père / quand il lit son journal
3. moi / quand je m'habille
4. nous / quand nous prenons notre petit déjeuner
5. mes amis / quand ils font du jogging
6. toi / quand tu fais le ménage
7. moi / quand je reviens de mon travail
8. vous / quand vous faites de la marche à pied
9. ma sœur / quand elle va à l'université
10. toi / quand tu finis ton travail

It might be helpful to have students first give the present participle for each of the verbs given before putting them in a complete sentence. (e.g., en préparant le dîner, en lisant son journal, etc.)

Randonnée dans les Alpes

B. **Assez d'excuses.** Madame Lebrun est fatiguée d'entendre des excuses. Qu'est-ce qu'elle dit?

> **Modèle**   Faites la vaisselle. Vous écouterez vous disques après.
> **Faites la vaisselle avant d'écouter vos disques.**

1. Rangez votre chambre. Vous jouerez après.
2. Finis tes devoirs. Tu iras à la piscine après.
3. Va à la boulangerie. Tu boiras ton café après.
4. Lavez la voiture. Vous vous reposerez après.
5. Aide-moi un peu. Tu sortiras après.
6. Apprends à conduire. Tu achèteras une voiture après.
7. Lavez-vous les mains. Vous mangerez après.
8. Brosse-toi les dents. Tu te coucheras après.

C. **Plus tard.** Monsieur Lebrun veut savoir quand les différents membres de sa famille vont faire certaines choses. Qu'est-ce qu'ils répondent?

Have students give the forms of the past infinitive before making complete sentences (e.g., après avoir fini ses devoirs, après avoir fini leur jeu, etc.)

> **Modèle**   Quand est-ce que tu vas faire la vaisselle?
> (Je veux d'abord me reposer un peu.)
> **Je la ferai après m'être reposé(e) un peu.**

1. Quand est-ce que Pierre va faire le marché? (Il veut d'abord finir ses devoirs.)
2. Quand est-ce que les enfants vont ranger leurs jouets? (Ils veulent d'abord finir leur jeu.)
3. Quand est-ce que Josette va faire la vaisselle? (Elle veut d'abord aller à la bibliothèque.)
4. Quand est-ce que tu vas commencer à préparer le dîner? (Je veux d'abord me laver les mains.)
5. Quand est-ce que vous allez laver la voiture? (Nous voulons d'abord nous reposer.)
6. Quand est-ce que tu vas prendre une décision? (Je veux d'abord parler avec René.)
7. Quand est-ce que Claude va aller à la boulangerie? (Il veut d'abord réparer son vélo.)
8. Quand est-ce que ton ami Raymond va se marier? (Il veut d'abord trouver un travail.)

D. **Différences.** Laurent aime écouter de la musique en faisant autre chose. Colette préfère finir son travail pour pouvoir mieux se concentrer. Quant à Nadine et Paul, ils sont trop impatients pour attendre. Quand Laurent, Colette, Nadine et Paul écoutent-ils de la musique?

This exercise can be done as shown in the modèles or each series can be done separately.

> **Modèles**   faire ses devoirs
> **Laurent écoute de la musique en faisant ses devoirs.**
> *et*:   **Colette écoute de la musique après avoir fait ses devoirs.**
> *et*:   **Nadine et Paul écoutent de la musique avant de faire leurs devoirs.**

1. lire le journal	4. manger	7. faire le ménage
2. aller à l'université	5. faire la cuisine	8. finir ses devoirs
3. se préparer le matin	6. s'habiller	

Communication et vie pratique

A. **Pendant, avant ou après ?** Quelles sont les choses que vous aimez faire en même temps ou l'une après l'autre ? Faites des phrases qui expriment vos préférences personnelles.

Written or oral. Have students compare their sentences. Written preparation may be helpful.

Exemples regarder la télévision
> **Je n'aime pas manger en regardant la télévision.**
> *ou:* **Je préfère regarder la télévision après avoir mangé.**
> *ou:* **La plupart du temps, je ne peux pas regarder la télévision avant de manger parce que je rentre trop tard.**

1. regarder la télévision
2. faire ses devoirs
3. lire le journal
4. se détendre
5. écouter de la musique
6. faire du sport

B. **Est-ce que tu peux... ?** Répondez aux questions suivantes ou utilisez-les pour interviewer un(e) autre étudiant(e).

Can be asked as direct questions or adapted for directed dialogue. Students can work in small groups and report back their partner's answers.

1. Est-ce que tu peux faire tes devoirs en regardant la télévision ?
2. Est-ce que tu peux aller en classe après avoir passé une nuit sans dormir ?
3. Est-ce que tu peux répéter une phrase en français après l'avoir entendue seulement une fois ?
4. En général, est-ce que tu peux finir tout ton travail avant de te coucher ?
5. Est-ce que tu peux faire les exercices de grammaire avant de lire les explications ?
6. Est-ce que tu peux expliquer dix fois la même chose sans te mettre en colère ?
7. Est-ce que tu peux marcher droit après avoir bu toute une bouteille de vin ?
8. Est-ce que tu peux traverser le campus la nuit sans avoir peur ?

C. **Moi, je...** Complétez les phrases suivantes selon votre expérience personnelle.

Student responses can be elicited by asking *Quand avez-vous peur ?*, etc.

1. J'ai peur avant de...
2. J'ai mal à la tête après avoir...
3. Je suis content(e) après avoir...
4. Je lis les journaux pour...
5. Je suis prudent(e) avant de...
6. Je suis fatigué(e) après avoir...

C'est votre tour. Racontez un accident (réel ou imaginaire) qui vous est arrivé. Expliquez quand et comment cet accident est arrivé. Utilisez la **Mise en situation** comme guide.

As preparation, have students prepare the sequence of events that led up to the accident and the events pertaining to the accident. Students can also be asked to discuss sequence of events of a trip, week-end outing, etc.

❧Expressing negative facts or ideas
La négation

Présentation

In addition to **ne... pas** and **ne... jamais**, there are several other ways to express negative meanings. All such negative expressions are composed of **ne** and another element :

ne... plus *no longer*

ne... pas du tout *not at all*

ne... rien *nothing*

ne... personne *nobody*

ne... que *only*

ne... aucun(e) *none, not a single*

ne... ni... ni *neither ... nor*

A. Ne... jamais, ne... plus, and **ne... pas du tout** function in the same way as **ne... pas. Ne** precedes the verb, and the second part of the negative expression follows the verb or the auxiliary in a compound tense. When the partitive follows the negative, its form is **de** or **d'.**

Tu **ne** penses **jamais** à nous.
Ce sport **ne** m'intéresse **plus.**
Il **ne** se préoccupe **pas du tout**
de son avenir.

Nous **n'**avons **plus d'**argent.
Il **ne** se trompe **jamais.**
Je **n'**ai **jamais** visité Paris.

Jamais without **ne** means *ever* :

Avez-vous **jamais** perdu un
match ?

Have you ever lost a game ?

B. Personne and **rien** used with **ne** can be either subjects or objects of the verb and are sometimes objects of prepositions.

Nous **ne** faisons **rien** cet après-midi.
Il **n'**y avait **personne** en classe vendredi.
Elle **n'**a parlé **à personne.**
Je **ne** me souviens **de rien.**

When **rien** and **personne** are direct object pronouns, the word order differs in a compound tense. **Rien** comes before the past participle and **personne** comes after it.

Je n'ai **rien** vu.
Je n'ai vu **personne.**

When **rien** and **personne** are subjects, both come at the beginning of the sentence.

Rien n'est simple.
Personne n'est venu.

C. With **ne... que** and **ne... aucun(e),** the second part of the negative is placed directly before the item modified. Notice that **aucun(e)** is an adjective used only in the singular. Notice also that the partitive article is retained after **ne... que**.

Il **n'**y a **qu'**un choix possible.
Je **ne** mange **que** des légumes.
Je **n'**ai **aucune** idée.
Aucun magasin **n'**est ouvert.

D. In response to a question, **jamais**, **personne**, **rien**, and **aucun(e)** can be used alone.

— Quand vas-tu prendre une décision? — **Jamais!**
— Qui a téléphoné? — **Personne.**
— Qu'est-ce qui est arrivé? — **Rien.**

E. In the expression **ne... ni... ni**, **ne** is placed before the verb, and **ni** is placed before each item negated. After **ni**, the indefinite and partitive articles are not used, but the definite articles are retained.

Compare :

Elle a un frère et une sœur.
Nous avons acheté des légumes
  et des fruits.
Il aime la bière et le vin.
Victor et Alfred ont répondu à
  notre invitation.

Elle **n'**a **ni** frère **ni** sœur.
Nous **n'**avons acheté **ni**
  légumes **ni** fruits.
Il **n'**aime **ni** la bière **ni** le vin.
Ni Victor **ni** Alfred **n'**a répondu
  à notre invitation.

F. Aussi is used to agree with a positive statement; **non plus** is used to agree with a negative statement.

— Christine joue très bien. — **Moi aussi.**
— Ils n'ont jamais été battus. — **Nous non plus.**

G. To disagree with a negative statement, **si** is used instead of **oui**.

Compare :

— Tu as fait tes devoirs? — **Oui**, je les ai faits.
— Tu n'as pas fait tes devoirs? — **Si**, je les ai faits.

Mise en situation

Un cambriolage. En rentrant de vacances, les Perretti ont eu la surprise de découvrir que leur maison a été cambriolée pendant leur absence. Ils parlent avec leurs voisins, les Darmon.

MME PERRETTI   Est-ce que vous avez vu ou entendu quelque chose de suspect?

M. DARMON   Non, nous n'avons rien entendu et nous n'avons vu personne. Tout était très calme dans le quartier.

Point out that prepositions are also retained : Il n'est allé ni en Espagne ni au Portugal.

Transformation : Mettez les phrases suivantes au passé composé. *Modèle :* Nous ne voyons rien. → Nous n'avons rien vu. (1) Il ne voit personne. (2) Elle ne mange que des légumes. (3) Vous ne vous souvenez plus de son nom. (4) Personne ne vient ici. (5) Je ne parle à personne. (6) Nous n'avons aucun problème. (7) Nous n'achetons ni légumes ni fruits. *Transformation :* Mettez les phrases suivantes à la forme négative en utilisant les expressions négatives indiquées. *Modèle :* Nous avons peur de voyager en avion. (ne... plus) → Nous n'avons plus peur de voyager en avion. (1) Il fait du vent au mois de juin. (ne... jamais) (2) Hélène sort avec Patrick. (ne... plus). (3) Ils boivent du lait. (ne... que) (4) Elle aime les haricots et les petits pois. (ne... ni... ni) (5) J'ai une chance de réussir. (ne... aucune) (6) Nous comprenons ses idées. (ne... pas du tout).

Remind students that some neighborhoods are almost deserted in August because of the annual vacation exodus.

MME DARMON	En fait, la semaine dernière il n'y avait presque personne ici. Tout le monde était en vacances. *Il ne restait que* les Giraud, les Dumont et nous.
M. PERRETTI	Et ils n'ont rien remarqué de suspect, eux, non plus ?
MME DARMON	Non, rien. Je leur ai demandé. Personne n'a rien vu.
MME PERRETTI	Et personne d'autre n'a été cambriolé ?
M. DARMON	Non, personne. Du moins je ne crois pas. Au fait, qu'est-ce qu'on vous a volé ?
M. PERRETTI	Notre télé et notre stéréo. À part ça, il ne manquait rien.
M. DARMON	Et comment sont-ils entrés dans la maison ?
M. PERRETTI	Ils n'ont laissé aucune trace. Il n'y a ni *vitre* cassée ni porte forcée. Rien. C'est *bizarre, vous ne trouvez pas* ?

Margin notes:
there were only

window

strange / don't you think

Préparation

A. Que la vie est cruelle ! Jean se sent abandonné et négligé par ses amis. Retrouvez les réponses négatives que Jean a données aux questions qu'on lui a posées.

Margin note: English cues can be given.

Modèle   Qui as-tu vu cet après-midi ? (personne)
   Je n'ai vu personne cet après-midi.

1. Qui est venu te voir hier soir ? (personne)
2. Est-ce qu'on te téléphone quelquefois ? (non… jamais)
3. Qu'est-ce qu'on t'a donné pour ton anniversaire ? (rien)
4. Est-ce que ton père t'envoie encore de l'argent ? (non… plus)
5. Est-ce qu'André et toi, vous avez aimé le film ? (non… pas du tout)
6. Est-ce que tu as des projets pour le week-end ? (non… aucun)
7. Est-ce que quelque chose a changé dans ta vie ? (non… rien)
8. Est-ce que tu as jamais été vraiment heureux ? (non… jamais)

B. Mais non, ne t'inquiète pas. Bernard est inquiet au sujet de tout le monde. Mireille le rassure.

Margin note: Repeat, going from negative to affirmative (e.g., *Personne n'est malade.* → *Tout le monde est malade.*) Remind students that the negative answer to a question with encore is *ne… plus.*

Modèle   Tout le monde est malade.
   Mais non, personne n'est malade.

1. Isabelle a beaucoup de problèmes en ce moment.
2. Quelque chose lui est arrivé.
3. Tu as toujours l'air triste.
4. Tout le monde est inquiet à ton sujet.
5. Pierre est encore à l'hôpital.
6. Il y a eu plusieurs accidents dans notre quartier.
7. Les enfants ont tout cassé.
8. Tout a été volé.

C. Ni l'un ni l'autre. Martine pose des questions à Raymond qui n'est jamais satisfait. Comment répond-il aux questions de Martine ?

> **Modèles**   Est-ce que tu préfères le café ou le thé ?
> **Je n'aime ni le café ni le thé.**
> Tu bois du vin ou de la bière ?
> **Je ne bois ni vin ni bière.**

1. Est-ce tu préfères le poulet ou le poisson ?
2. Est-ce que tu veux du fromage ou des fruits pour le dessert ?
3. Est-ce que tu prends un café ou un digestif après le dîner ?
4. Est-ce que tu veux regarder la télé ou écouter la radio ?
5. Est-ce que tu as envie d'aller au café ou d'aller au cinéma ?
6. Est-ce que tu connais Jean-Luc et Sylvie ?
7. Est-ce que tu as invité Philippe et Gérard à venir ce soir ?

D. Ce n'est pas formidable. Les enfants des Hunt, une famille anglaise qui passe des vacances en France, ne sont pas très contents de l'endroit que leurs parents ont choisi. Donnez l'équivalent français de ce qu'ils disent.

Written preparation may be helpful.

1. No one plays with us.
2. The meals are never very good.
3. There is nothing to do in the evening.
4. We never have enough time to play.
5. We haven't seen anyone we know.
6. There is only one movie theater in town.
7. There isn't a pool or a café near the hotel.

Communication et vie pratique

A. Questions / interview. Répondez aux questions suivantes ou utilisez-les pour interviewer un(e) autre étudiant(e). Si votre réponse est négative, utilisez l'expression négative appropriée.

Ask questions or adapt as directed dialogue. Then ask what students have said (e.g., Est-ce que Jean a jamais voyagé au Japon ?).

1. Est-ce que tu as encore les jouets que tu avais quand tu étais petit(e) ?
2. Est-ce que tu te souviens du nom de ton premier professeur à l'école élémentaire ?
3. Est-ce que tu regardes encore les dessins animés pour les enfants ?
4. Est-ce que tu as jamais voyagé au Japon ou en Chine ?
5. Est-ce que tu as jamais étudié une langue asiatique ?
6. Est-ce que quelqu'un est venu te voir hier soir ?
7. Est-ce que tu te mets souvent en colère ?

B. Rien ne va plus. Il y a des jours où tout va mal. Imaginez ce que les personnes suivantes peuvent dire un de ces jours où tout va mal.

> **Exemple**   vous-même
> **Personne ne s'est souvenu de mon anniversaire.**
> **Je n'ai rien fait d'intéressant pendant le week-end.**

Option : Assign a different category to small groups of students who will make up sentences that these individuals might say. Their complaints can then be shared with the whole class. Class can choose the group with the best complaints.

1. un(e) étudiant(e) typique
2. votre professeur de français
3. les étudiants de votre classe
4. les parents d'un enfant qui n'est pas sage
5. l'entraîneur (*coach*) d'une équipe sportive

C. J'en ai marre ! Comme tout le monde, vous rencontrez quelquefois des contrariétés. Mais cette fois vous avez décidé de dire ce que vous pensez, même si ce n'est pas agréable. Imaginez que vous êtes dans les situations suivantes.

1. Vous êtes dans un restaurant où le service et la cuisine laissent beaucoup à désirer.
2. Vous n'êtes pas content(e) de l'hôtel ou de la région où vous passez vos vacances.
3. Vous essayez de préparer un bon dîner, mais c'est un vrai fiasco.
4. Vous désirez acheter des vêtements mais il ne reste presque rien.
5. Votre petit(e) ami(e) et vous, vous avez des goûts très différents. Il / elle n'aime aucune des choses que vous aimez.
6. Vous êtes très déçu(e) par l'équipe de football de votre école.

C'est votre tour. Un appartement dans votre quartier a été cambriolé. Vous parlez avec des voisins, joués par d'autres étudiants, mais personne n'a rien remarqué de suspect. Imaginez les conversations. Utilisez la **Mise en situation** comme guide.

Use the situations in Communication C (J'en ai marre) for additional role-plays.

❧ Using verbs with prepositions : Differences in usage and meaning
L'emploi des prépositions après les verbes

Présentation

As you have already seen, some verbs are followed by the preposition **de**, others by **à**, and still others by no preposition at all. The use of prepositions with verbs you have already learned can be summarized as follows :

Remind students that they are already familiar with these verbs and with the prepositions that accompany them. The goal of this section is to help review and consolidate this information.

A. Verbs followed by an infinitive :

1. The following verbs take no preposition at all before an infinitive :

aimer	désirer	espérer	penser	préférer	venir
aller	détester	laisser	pouvoir	savoir	vouloir

Je **voudrais aller** à la piscine.
Il **préfère ne pas parler** de ça.

2. The following verbs take **de** before an infinitive :

accepter	se dépêcher	persuader
s'arrêter	dire	permettre
choisir	essayer	promettre
décider	éviter	refuser
défendre	finir	regretter
demander	oublier	rêver

Il **rêve de jouer** dans une équipe professionnelle.
Vous **avez promis de vous dépêcher de finir** votre travail.

Demander, **dire**, **permettre**, and **promettre** can also take an indirect object.

Nous avons promis **à nos amis** de sortir avec eux.
Elle **nous** a demandé de l'aider.

3. The following verbs take **à** before an infinitive :

aider	avoir	hésiter	résister
s'amuser	commencer	inviter	réussir
apprendre	continuer	se mettre	tenir
arriver			

Il **s'est mis à pleuvoir**.
Nous **avons appris à jouer** à la pétanque.

Avoir, **aider**, and **inviter** usually take a direct object, which precedes the preposition.

J'ai **beaucoup de choses** à vous dire.
On a invité **les étudiants** à participer à la discussion.
Elle a aidé **Pierre** à apprendre à jouer au tennis.

B. Verbs followed by a noun :

1. Some verbs that take a preposition in English do not take one in French.

attendre *to wait for*	Nous **attendons** les résultats.
chercher *to look for*	Je **cherche** l'entrée.
demander *to ask for*	Il faut **demander** la permission.
écouter *to listen to*	Tu **écoutes** des disques ?
regarder *to look at*	Elle te **regarde**.

2. Some verbs that take a preposition in French do not take one in English.

assister à *to attend, be present at*	Est-ce que vous avez l'intention d'**assister au** match ?
changer de *to change*	Tu **changes d'**avis comme tu changes de chemise.
entrer dans *to enter*	Nous sommes **entrés dans** un café.
se marier avec *to marry*	Josette va **se marier avec** un footballeur professionnel.
obéir à *to obey*	**Obéissez à** vos parents.
répondre à *to answer*	Est-ce que tu **as répondu à** sa lettre ?
ressembler à *to resemble*	Elle **ressemble à** son père.
se souvenir de *to remember*	Te **souviens-tu des** résultats ?
téléphoner à *to telephone*	Je vais **téléphoner à** ma mère.
jouer à *to play a sport*	Nous **jouons** souvent **au** tennis.
jouer de *to play a musical instrument*	Il **joue de la** clarinette.

Remind students that one does not use *assister* to talk about attending class. Instead, one uses *aller en classe, aller à mon cours de...* , etc.

3. Some verbs take different prepositions in French and in English.

s'intéresser à *to be interested in*	Ils ne **s'intéressent** pas **aux** sports.
s'occuper de *to be busy with, to take care of*	**Occupez-vous de** vos propres problèmes.
participer à *to participate in*	Nous **avons participé à** un marathon.

Mise en situation

Le Tour de France. Les Français s'intéressent beaucoup aux courses cyclistes et, en particulier, au Tour de France. Il y a toujours de nombreux spectateurs qui attendent son passage et dans chaque ville-étape il y a des *foules* de gens qui se *bousculent* pour assister à l'arrivée des coureurs et savoir qui va porter le fameux « maillot jaune ».

SPECTATEUR NO. **1** Ne poussez pas, voyons, moi aussi, je veux essayer de voir !

SPECTATEUR NO. **2** Regardez, les voilà ! Ils entrent dans le stade.

SPECTATEUR NO. **1** Philippi est *en tête*, mais Schwartz cherche à le dépasser !

SPECTATEUR NO. **3** Philippi refuse de le laisser passer. Bravo, Philippi !

SPECTATEUR NO. **2** Schwartz va réussir à le dépasser. Vas-y, Schwartz, encore un effort !

SPECTATEUR NO. **1** Arrêtez de gesticuler comme ça, je ne peux rien voir. Ça commence à m'*énerver* !

SPECTATEUR NO. **3** Ne te fâche pas, Antoine ! Regarde, Philippi reprend la tête. Il est d'ici. Il a promis à ses supporters de gagner cette étape.

crowds / jostle

ahead

to annoy

From its first run in 1903, Tour de France (also called Grande Boucle), has taken place every year except during the Second World War (from 1940–1947). This world famous bicycle race is held from the end of June to mid-July in 22 *étapes* and covers approximately 3,800 kilometers. The route goes around the periphery of France with runs into Germany, Switzerland, Italy, Spain, and / or Belgium depending on the year. It always ends in Paris. The winner of each day's *étape* is entitled to wear *le maillot jaune*. Multiple winners in recent years have been two Frenchmen (Jacques Anquetil with 5 wins and Bernard Hinault with 4 wins) and Eddy Merckx from Belgium with 5 wins. In 1986, Greg Lemond was the first American to win the Tour de France.

Le Tour de France: Bernard Hinault porte le maillot jaune.

Substitution : (1) Elle a oublié de venir. *(refusé / essayé / décidé / accepté / promis / choisi)* (2) Nous avons promis à Pierre d'aller au match. *(demandé / dit / permis)* (3) Est-ce que tu continues à parler français ? *(commences / hésites / apprends / réussis)* (4) Il apprend à jouer au tennis. *(rêve / veut / sait / essaie / refuse / a envie / espère)* (5) Il s'est arrêté de faire du jogging. *(s'est mis / préférait / a décidé / voulait / a hésité / a continué)*.

Préparation

A. Il faut faire de la gymnastique. Plusieurs personnes ont décidé qu'elles avaient besoin de faire un peu de gymnastique pour être en forme. Qu'est-ce qu'ils / elles disent ?

Ask students to describe their own reactions to this statement or those of family members or friends.

Modèle J'ai décidé...
J'ai décidé de faire de la gymnastique.

1. Nous voulons...
2. Marc a promis...
3. J'ai commencé...
4. Elle a accepté...
5. J'ai persuadé mes amis...
6. Vous avez choisi...
7. Nous aimerions...
8. Catherine espère...
9. Mes amis désirent...
10. Moi, je préfère...

B. Le nouvel entraîneur. François s'est présenté comme candidat pour un poste d'entraîneur d'une équipe sportive. Voici pourquoi on l'a choisi.

Modèle s'intéresser vraiment / football
Il s'intéresse vraiment au football.

1. promettre / faire beaucoup de changements
2. savoir / écouter
3. écouter / les conseils des autres
4. répondre / nos besoins
5. accepter / commencer tout de suite
6. ne pas hésiter / dire ce qu'il pense
7. connaître / beaucoup de reporters

C. C'est dommage, mais... Un des joueurs de l'équipe a été renvoyé (*fired*). Voici les raisons.

Modèle rêver / devenir célèbre → **Il rêvait de devenir célèbre.**

1. vouloir / être beaucoup mieux payé
2. refuser / faire comme tout le monde
3. se dépêcher / partir après les matchs
4. ne pas écouter / les conseils de l'entraîneur
5. ne pas pouvoir / reconnaître ses erreurs
6. essayer / impressionner les spectateurs
7. commencer / embêter tout le monde

Communication et vie pratique

A. Vous et le sport. Quelles sont vos préférences et habitudes en ce qui concerne le sport ? Utilisez les verbes présentés dans cette section et les suggestions suivantes pour exprimer votre situation ou vos préférences dans chaque cas.

> **Exemple**   passer mon temps à regarder des matchs à la télé
> **Je refuse de passer mon temps à regarder des matchs à la télé.**

— faire régulièrement du jogging
— faire du cheval
— apprendre à jouer au golf
— aller à un match de boxe
— aller à la chasse
— aller à la pêche
— jouer dans une équipe professionnelle
— passer mon temps à regarder des matches à la télé
— être membre d'un club de gymastique
— ?

Can be asked as questions (Est-ce que vous faites régulièrement du jogging ?, etc.) in a whole-class or small-group activity.

B. Interview. Utilisez les verbes suivants pour formuler des questions que vous poserez à un(e) autre étudiant(e) au sujet du sport ou sur un autre sujet de votre choix.

> **Exemples**   apprendre
> **Est-ce que tu as appris à jouer au tennis quand tu étais jeune ?**
> *ou:*   **Est-ce que tu aimerais apprendre à faire de la voile ?**

Preparation : Assign as homework or have students prepare questions in class before having them ask each other questions.

1. rêver	5. savoir	9. décider
2. aimer	6. réussir	10. refuser
3. apprendre	7. préférer	11. se souvenir
4. essayer	8. aller	12. ?

C'est votre tour. Vous assistez avec vos amis à un match de votre équipe favorite. Décrivez ce qui se passe et exprimez vos réactions.

Preparation : Have students decide the sports event(s) in question and practice phrases that can be used to react to events.

❧ Linking several ideas
Les pronoms relatifs

Présentation

Relative pronouns are used to connect two clauses, a main clause and a dependent clause. They are never omitted in French, whereas in English we may say either *There is the girl I met*, or *There is the girl that I met*.

Point out that, unlike interrogatives, qui and que can refer to both persons and objects.

A. Qui and **que** *(who, that, which)* are used to refer to both persons and things.

1. **Qui** is used when the relative pronoun is the subject of the dependent clause.

   Voilà une étudiante. Elle parle espagnol.   Voilà une étudiante **qui** parle espagnol.

   Ce sont les athlètes **qui** ont participé aux Jeux Olympiques.
   Avez-vous vu le match **qui** a eu lieu dimanche?

2. **Que** is used when the relative pronoun is the direct object in the dependent clause.

   Où est le ballon? J'ai acheté le ballon.   Où est le ballon **que** j'ai acheté?

   Quel est le sport **que** vous préférez?
   Voici les championnes **que** nous avons interviewées.

   Note again that the past participles of verbs conjugated with **avoir** agree with preceding direct objects.

B. Dont *(of whom, of which, whose)* is used to replace **de** plus a noun. It can refer to people or to things.

Point out that the antecedent of *dont* takes the definite article.

   Voici l'équipement. Nous aurez besoin **de cet équipement**.   Voici l'équipement **dont** vous aurez besoin.

   J'ai rencontré la femme **dont** vous m'avez parlé.
   Ce sont les gens **dont** le fils a gagné le marathon.

C. Ce qui, **ce que** *(what, that which)*, and **ce dont** *(that of which)* are indefinite relative pronouns. They refer to ideas that do not have number or gender.

1. **Ce qui** is used as the subject of the dependent clause.

   Je ne comprends pas **ce qui** est arrivé.
   Ce qui m'impressionne le plus, c'est son style.
   Elle aime **ce qui** est beau.

2. **Ce que** is used as the direct object of the dependent clause.

   Il dit toujours **ce qu'**il pense.
   Nous ne savons pas **ce que** les autres vont faire.
   Voici tout **ce que** nous avons pu savoir.

3. **Ce dont** is used as the object of a verb or verb phrase that is used with the preposition **de** (**parler de**, **avoir besoin de**, etc.).

   Je sais **ce dont** tu as envie.
   Nous ne savons pas **ce dont** il est capable.
   Ce dont vous parlez est intéressant.
   Je te donnerai tout **ce dont** tu as besoin.

Transformation : Modèle : J'ai lu les journaux. Les journaux sont sur la table. → J'ai lu les journaux qui sont sur la table. (1) Nous avons regardé le programme. Il commence à six heures. (2) Je connais une vieille dame. Elle fait de la marche à pied. (3) Nous avons assisté à un concert. Il était intéressant. *Modèle :* J'ai lu les journaux. Mon frère m'a apporté ces journaux. → J'ai lu les journaux que mon frère m'a apporté. (1) J'ai perdu le disque. Vous m'avez donné le disque. (2) Nous avons trouvé la revue. Vous cherchiez cette revue. (3) Avez-vous lu la lettre ? Je vous ai écrit cette lettre.

406

Ce qui and **ce que** are frequently used in answers to questions beginning with **qu'est-ce qui** and **qu'est-ce que**.

— **Qu'est-ce qui** intéresse les jeunes ?
— Je ne sais pas **ce qui** les intéresse.
— **Qu'est-ce que** tu penses de cette équipe ?
— Je préfère ne pas dire **ce que** j'en pense.

Ce qui, **ce que**, and **ce dont** are also used when suggesting to someone what he or she should say or ask.

Demandez à Alain **ce qu'**il a pensé de ce reportage.
Expliquez-nous **ce que** vous avez l'intention de faire.
Dites-moi **ce dont** vous avez besoin.

Mise en situation

C'est sérieux ? Xavier passe des vacances en Bretagne chez sa grand-mère. Il vient de faire la connaissance d'une jeune fille qui lui *plaît*.

XAVIER	Regarde la fille, là-bas, devant la vitrine de la librairie.
GRAND-MÈRE	La fille qui porte des jeans ?
XAVIER	Oui, c'est la fille dont je t'ai parlé.
GRAND-MÈRE	La jeune fille dont les parents ont une villa près d'ici ?
XAVIER	Oui, la fille avec qui j'ai déjeuné la semaine dernière.
GRAND-MÈRE	Ah oui ! Je me souviens ! La jeune fille que tu as rencontrée chez Corrine… et dont tu es tombé follement amoureux !
XAVIER	Mais non, mémé. Ce n'est pas ce que je t'ai dit ! Je t'ai dit que je la trouvais sympa. *Un point*, c'est tout.
GRAND-MÈRE	Si elle te plaît, c'est tout ce qui compte !

Préparation

A. Un amoureux bien malheureux. Bruno n'a pas de chance. Il aime Natacha mais elle n'a pas les mêmes goûts que lui. Qu'est-ce qu'il dit ?

Modèle   J'ai écrit des chansons.
   Elle n'aime pas les chansons que j'ai écrites.

1. J'ai acheté des disques.
2. Je lui ai apporté des fleurs.
3. J'ai composé des poèmes.
4. Je lui ai donné un cadeau.
5. Je lui ai écrit une lettre.
6. J'ai pris des photos.
7. Je lui ai envoyé une carte.
8. J'ai acheté de nouveaux vêtements.

Modèle : J'ai lu les journaux. Vous m'avez parlé de ces journaux. → J'ai lu les journaux dont vous m'avez parlé. (1) J'ai acheté un disque. J'avais très envie de ce disque. (2) Voici la liste des livres. Vous avez besoin de ces livres. (3) Dites-nous les détails. Vous vous souvenez des détails. *Modèle :* Je connais des gens. Leur fils est diplomate. → Je connais des gens dont le fils est diplomate. (1) Voici des Français. J'ai fait leur connaissance à Paris. (2) Je connais un homme. Sa fille travaille en Suisse. (3) Voilà un copain. Son frère est champion de tennis.

pleases (**elle te plaît = you like her**)

period (that's all !)

Point out that *la Bretagne,* the westernmost area of France, is located on the English Channel and the Atlantic Ocean. Because of its proximity to the ocean, many Bretons have become sailors ; in addition, fishing and shipbuilding are important industries. Bretons have a strong sense of identity which is different from the rest of France, mainly due to their Celtic past and traditions. There is even a separatist movement. Although French is spoken everywhere, many Bretons still speak *le breton,* a Celtic language. Major cities are Brest, Nantes, Rennes, and Quimper.

Repeat, having students use the appropriate form of the demonstrative pronoun : *J'ai écrit des chansons. Elle n'aime pas celles que j'ai écrites.*

B. Elle a bon goût. Brigitte a répondu à un questionnaire au sujet de ses préférences dans différents domaines en donnant les indications suivantes. Dites ce qu'elle aime et ce qu'elle n'aime pas.

Have students give their own opinions and preferences about the subjects given in this exercise.

> **Modèles** les chanteurs / Ils ont quelque chose à dire.
> **Elle aime les chanteurs qui ont quelque chose à dire.**
>
> *et*: les chanteurs / Ils imitent les chanteurs anglais.
> **Elle n'aime pas les chanteurs qui imitent les chanteurs anglais.**

Les domaines	Traits positifs	Traits négatifs
1. les chanteurs	Ils ont quelque chose à dire.	Ils imitent les chanteurs anglais.
2. les hommes	Ils ont l'esprit ouvert.	Ils se croient supérieurs.
3. les femmes	Elles savent ce qu'elles veulent.	Elles ne sont jamais contentes.
4. les vêtements	Ils sont de bonne qualité.	Ils ne sont pas bien coupés.
5. les gens	Ils s'intéressent aux sports.	Ils passent leur temps à regarder les matchs à la télé.

C. J'ai suivi tes conseils. Véronique a suivi les conseils que son amie Bernadette lui a donnés. Qu'est-ce qu'elle dit ?

> **Modèle** écouter les disques
> **J'ai écouté les disques dont tu m'as parlé.**

1. aller au concert
2. lire le livre
3. consulter le médicin
4. aller chez le dentiste
5. acheter le disque
6. assister au spectacle

D. Snobisme. Certaines personnes sont très fières de connaître, même indirectement, des gens célèbres. Qu'est-ce que les personnes suivantes disent ?

> **Modèle** avoir des amis / leur fils est champion de ski
> **Nous avons des amis dont le fils est champion de ski.**

1. connaître des gens / leur fille est journaliste
2. rencontrer un vieux monsieur / son petit-fils a participé au Tour de France
3. parler avec un ami / sa femme connaissait Édith Piaf
4. voir un ami / son frère a acheté un château
5. rencontrer une personne / sa famille descend des Bourbon

E. **On va faire une randonnée.** Alain pose toutes sortes de questions à Geneviève. Donnez les réponses de Geneviève en utilisant le pronom relatif approprié.

Modèle Qu'est-ce qu'on va faire s'il pleut ?
Je ne sais pas ce qu'on va faire.

1. Qu'est-ce qu'on va faire ce soir ?
2. Qui va nous accompagner ?
3. Qu'est-ce que Jacques va apporter à manger ?
4. Qu'est-ce qui va arriver si quelqu'un tombe malade ?
5. Qu'est-ce que tu vas porter ?
6. Qu'est-ce qu'on va boire ?
7. De quoi avons-nous besoin ?
8. Qu'est-ce qu'on va manger ?
9. Qui va acheter les provisions ?
10. Qui va choisir l'itinéraire ?

Communication et vie pratique

A. **Vos opinions.** Indiquez les types de gens et de choses que vous appréciez et ceux que vous n'appréciez pas du tout.

> Elicit student answers by asking questions (*Quelles sortes de chansons préférez-vous ?*, etc.) in small- or large-group activity.

Exemple **J'apprécie les cours qui sont intéressants même s'ils sont un peu difficiles.**

1. les chansons
2. les hommes
3. les femmes
4. les chanteurs / chanteuses
5. les livres
6. les amis
7. les vêtements
8. les professeurs
9. les voitures
10. les sports

B. **Descriptions.** Seul(e) ou avec un groupe d'étudiants, décrivez un(e) sportif(ive), une équipe, un match, etc. Utilisez autant de pronoms relatifs que possible dans votre description.

> Suggested for writing activity. Have students prepare initial descriptions (individually or in small groups) and then, if necessary, suggest additional ways that relative pronouns could be used to enhance their descriptions.

C. **Enrichissez votre style.** Quand on ne connaît pas très bien une langue, on a souvent tendance à s'exprimer d'une façon un peu trop simple. Réfléchissez aux mots, expressions et constructions que vous pourriez utiliser pour enrichir les phrases suivantes.

Exemple C'était un bon match.
Je viens de voir un match qui m'a beaucoup impressionné(e).

1. J'ai aimé ce film.
2. Paris est une très belle ville.
3. C'est un joueur exceptionnel.
4. Ce vin n'est pas bon.
5. J'ai besoin d'une voiture.
6. C'est un très bon restaurant.

C'est votre tour. Vous désirez présenter un(e) ami(e) — joué(e) par un(e) autre étudiant(e) — à une personne qu'il / elle ne connaît pas. Expliquez qui est cette personne.

> Students can use their own identities or they can create (or be given) French identities.

The Saguenay, an important waterway in Quebec, begins at the eastern end of Lake Saint-Jean in Quebec, flows eastward 100 miles, and empties into the St. Lawrence 120 miles northeast of Quebec city. Although the first 35 miles are not navigable, this branch of the river has become an important hydro-electric source. Tourist cruises have been conducted on the Lower Saguenay since the middle of the 19th century. Tadoussac, at the mouth of the river, is a well-known resort area.

Intégration et perspectives

Le Saguenay à la rame

Voyager en canot sur le Saguenay comme le faisaient autrefois les voyageurs, préparer ses repas sur un bon *feu de bois*, écouter la chanson *reposante* des *oiseaux* dans les arbres, dormir sous les *étoiles* en respirant un air très pur, avancer *en ramant* à l'unisson comme le faisaient les Indiens… Est-ce une expérience dont vous rêvez mais que vous croyiez impossible à notre *époque*? Rassurez-vous, tout cela est possible, même de nos jours, *grâce à* un groupe de jeunes que vous trouverez à Tadoussac, une petite localité située à la jonction du Saint-Laurent et du Saguenay. C'est de Tadoussac aussi que vous partirez pour une des longues et heureuses randonnées sur l'eau qu'ils organisent.

  wood fire / *restful / birds / stars* / *rowing* / *time* / *thanks to*

C'est Daniel qui a eu l'idée d'organiser ces randonnées. Depuis longtemps, il cherchait un moyen de naviguer le Saguenay, un moyen qui serait adapté à la rapidité de son courant et à ses *rives* sauvages. Il ne voulait pas *se servir d*'un gros bateau, ni d'un canot en *fibre de verre*, et encore moins d'un canot motorisé.

  banks / *to use / fiberglass*

Après avoir cherché en vain pendant plusieurs années, Daniel a réussi à mettre la main sur des *barques* qu'on utilisait autrefois dans la région pour transporter les voyageurs, les sacs de *courrier*, et presque tout ce dont on avait besoin pour vivre dans ces îles isolées. Ces « canots d'hiver » ainsi appelés parce qu'ils pouvaient aussi naviguer en hiver, mesurent une *vingtaine* de pieds de *longueur*. Pointus aux deux *bouts*, ils sont construits du meilleur bois et ils sont équipés d'une *plaque* de métal qui leur permet de glisser sur la glace.

  boats / *mail* / *about 20 / length / ends* / *plate*

Au début, Daniel et quelques amis qui travaillaient avec lui ne proposaient à leurs clients que de petits voyages sur le Saguenay. Voyant que ces vieilles barques donnaient de très bons résultats, ils ont peu à peu *allongé* la *durée* de leurs voyages, multipliant les *escales* dans les sites sauvages qu'ils découvraient au cours de leurs expéditions.

  lengthened / duration / stops

Aujourd'hui, leur groupe *accueille* pour une somme très modeste tous les gens qui sont tentés par ce *genre* d'aventure et qui veulent redécouvrir le plaisir de vivre en harmonie avec la nature. Chaque expédition dure cinq jours et se compose de dix personnes, cinq dans chaque barque. Même si personne ne se connaît au début, on devient vite des amis quand on partage les mêmes *tâches* et les mêmes joies. Les barques glissent *côte à côte*, sans faire de *bruit* et pénètrent une nature qui respire encore. En plus de la beauté naturelle du paysage, ces expéditions donnent aux voyageurs modernes l'occasion de découvrir des plaisirs uniques : des bains de *glaise* à *marée basse* près de Gagnon; l'exploration de *grottes* qui, il y a trois cents ans, servaient de refuge aux Amérindiens. Souvent, on a même la chance d'être escorté par des *marsouins*. Ils jouent autour des barques mais ils n'essaient jamais de les *renverser*.

  receives, welcomes / *type* / *tasks / side by side* / *noise* / *clay* / *low tide / cave* / *porpoises* / *tip over*

Daniel et ses compagnons envisagent maintenant de plus longs séjours où les voyageurs pourront étudier les nombreuses *espèces* d'oiseaux qui habitent le Saguenay ou *faire de l'escalade* dans les montagnes voisines.

  species / *go climbing*

Ces barques ne naviguent pas seulement pendant l'été, mais aussi au printemps et en automne quand le rouge des *feuilles* offre au regard un spectacle inoubliable. Et en hiver… ? Eh bien, on répare les barques et les *rames*, on rêve aux expéditions futures et on commence à préparer la saison suivante. Et quelquefois même Daniel et ses amis partent sur le Saguenay *gelé*, le cœur *battant*, comme le faisaient autrefois les voyageurs et les habitants des îles.

leaves

oars

frozen / beating

Compréhension. Répondez aux questions suivantes selon les renseignements donnés dans le texte.

1. Quelle sorte de randonnée Daniel et ses compagnons offrent-ils aux voyageurs ?
2. Dans quelle région du Canada ces randonnées ont-elles lieu et comment est cette région ?
3. Pour quel type de personnes ce genre d'expérience a-t-il un attrait particulier et pourquoi ?
4. Qu'est-ce qu'on peut faire et voir d'intéressant pendant ces randonnées ?
5. À quel moment de l'année Daniel et ses compagnons organisent-ils ces randonnées et que font-ils le reste du temps ?
6. Quelle sorte d'équipement Daniel a-t-il choisi pour ces randonnées et pourquoi ?
7. Quels sont les projets de Daniel et de ses compagnons ?

Have several students role-play Daniel; the rest of the class asks questions about his venture. Have students imagine that they are Daniel (or someone working with him) and write a description of the area, their job, their reactions, etc.

Notes culturelles:
Le Québec : Sports et activités de loisir

Randonnées à pied, à cheval ou sur l'eau, pêche, chasse, sports d'été ou sports d'hiver : le Québec offre une multitude de possibilités et constitue un véritable paradis pour les amoureux de la nature.

Un des événements qui vient chaque année mettre une note de joie et de couleur dans le long hiver canadien est le Carnaval de Québec. Le Carnaval, qui dure onze jours, attire plus d'un million et demi de visiteurs venant de tous les coins du monde. L'inauguration au Palais de neige du roi du Carnaval, le Bonhomme Carnaval, marque le début des festivités. Le programme comprend de nombreuses activités : des soirées de danse populaire et folklorique, des concours, des expositions et des événements sportifs, la course de canots sur le Saint-Laurent gelé, la course de motos sur glace, la course internationale de chiens de traîneaux *(dog sleds)*, des courses de ski et de patins et surtout le tournoi international de hockey Pee-Wee.

Le hockey sur glace est probablement le sport le plus populaire au Canada et les équipes canadiennes jouissent d'une renommée mondiale. Chaque année le tournoi de la Coupe Canada réunit les meilleurs

Défilé pendant le Carnaval

Match de hockey Pee Wee

équipes du monde. Le Canada tient aussi une place importante sur la scène sportive internationale. C'est à Montréal qu'ont eu lieu les Jeux Olympiques de 1976 et la ville de Calgary en Alberta a été choisie pour les Jeux Olympiques d'hiver en février 1988.

Communication et vie pratique

A. Description. Imaginez que vous avez participé soit à une randonnée à pied sur un des sentiers français soit à une randonnée en bateau sur le Saguenay. Décrivez ce que vous avez fait et ce que vous avez vu.

B. Les dix commandements. Prenez les « dix commandements du randonneur » comme modèle et écrivez (1) les dix commandements pour rester en bonne condition physique, (2) les dix commandements de l'étudiant, (3) ? .

C. Interview. Imaginez que vous êtes un reporter et que vous allez interviewer des athlètes célèbres. Quelles questions allez-vous leur poser ? Trouvez un(e) autre étudiant(e) qui jouera le rôle d'un(e) athlète de son choix.

Have students make up short sports reports, giving the results of sports events and/or announcing future events. If available, have students examine the sports section of a French or Canadian newspaper.

Have students take notes during the interview and then write up the results of the interview. If one or several groups role-play the interview in front of the class, have remaining class members take notes.

• *Vocabulaire*

Noms

les sports et les compétitions sportives (voir p. 390)

d'autres noms

l'**anorak** (m)   *ski jacket, windbreaker*
le **bois**   *wood*
le **bout**   *end*
le **bruit**   *noise*
le **chemin**   *road, way*
le **courant**   *current*
le **courrier**   *mail*
la **durée**   *duration*
l'**entretien** (m)   *maintenance, upkeep*
l'**époque** (f)   *time, epoch*
l'**équipe** (f)   *team*
l'**escale** (f)   *stop, intermediate landing*
l'**espèce** (f)   *species, type*
l'**étoile** (f)   *star*
le **feu**   *fire*
la **feuille**   *leaf*
la **fibre de verre**   *fiberglass*
la **foule**   *crowd*
le **genre**   *type*
la **glaise**   *clay*

la **grotte**   *cave*
l'**itinéraire** (m)   *route*
la **longueur**   *length*
la **marche**   *walking*
la **marée**   *tide*
le **marsouin**   *porpoise*
l'**oiseau** (les **oiseaux**) (m)   *bird*
l'**ouverture** (f)   *opening*
la **pancarte**   *sign*
la **pente**   *slope*
la **piste**   *trail, track*
la **plaque**   *plate, sheet (of metal)*
la **propriété**   *property*
la **rame**   *oar*
la **randonnée**   *hike*
le **randonneur**, la **randonneuse**   *hiker*
le **regard**   *sight, look*
la **rive**   *bank (of river)*
le **réseau**   *system, network*
le **sentier**   *footpath*
le **supporter**   *supporter, fan (sports)*
la **tâche**   *task*
la **ville-étape**   *stopover (in race)*
la **vipère**   *poisonous snake*

412

Verbes

affronter   *to tackle, to confront*
allonger   *to lengthen, to prolong*
battre   *to beat*
° **considérer**
correspondre   *to agree, to correspond*
créer   *to create*
dépasser   *to overtake, to go beyond*
emporter   *to carry*
énerver   *to annoy, to get on someone's nerves*
glisser   *to slide*
naviguer   *to navigate, to sail*
pratiquer   *to practice*
pénétrer   *to penetrate, to enter*
rassurer   *to reassure*
se servir de   *to use*
taquiner   *to tease*

Adjectifs

bas, basse   *low*
bizarre   *strange*
escorté(e)   *escorted*
gelé(e)   *frozen*
motorisé(e)   *motorized*
tenté(e)   *tempted*

Divers

à l'unisson   *in unison*
à part   *except for*
au-dessus   *above, beyond*
côte à côte   *side by side*
faire de l'escalade   *to go climbing*
grâce à   *thanks to*
il ne restait que...   *there was (were) only...*

17

CHAPITRE DIX-SEPT

Communication objectives

Talking about art and music

1. Expressing opinions

2. Expressing wants, emotions, and doubts

3. Telling which one
4. Talking about possessions

Structures

Les mots et la vie : Les arts et la musique

Le subjonctif avec les
expressions impersonnelles

Le subjonctif avec les verbes
de volition, d'émotion et de doute

Les pronoms démonstratifs

Les pronoms possessifs

L'humour et les arts

Mise en scène

L'humour et la bande dessinée

Point out that *bandes dessinées* are commonly referred to as *les B.D.* in French, and that *le Nouvel Observateur,* like *l'Express,* is a weekly news magazine.

La *bande dessinée* est une forme d'art *si* populaire en France qu'elle a même son festival et qu'elle fait l'objet de très sérieuses thèses de doctorat. Auteur de la bande dessinée intitulée *Les Frustrés,* Claire Bretécher est une des *dessinatrices* les plus remarquables de notre époque. Pendant plusieurs années les Français ont pu lire chaque semaine ses bandes dessinées dans le *Nouvel Observateur.* Elle a aussi publié plusieurs albums qui ont été traduits en plusieurs langues.

Ses lecteurs les plus enthousiastes sont souvent les gens qu'elle ridiculise dans ses dessins : les *soi-disant* intellectuels, les libéraux, les femmes émancipées — *autrement dit,* les gens de son propre milieu. Elle donne à *chacun* l'occasion de rire de ses propres prétentions, de ses complexes et de ses *névroses.* « Mes dessins représentent des épisodes de la vie de tous les jours, dit-elle. J'observe et j'écoute les gens autour de moi, je *me moque de* mes propres problèmes. »

Les personnages masculins des *Frustrés* sont des nouveaux riches *poseurs,* des intellectuels qui se prennent trop au sérieux, des chauvinistes condescendants, des *névrosés* de la vie moderne. Ses personnages féminins sont des femmes qui se croient émancipées mais ne le sont pas toujours, des *ménagères opprimées,* des intellectuelles insatisfaites.

Dans ses bandes dessinées, Claire Bretécher se moque des femmes aussi bien que des hommes, mais elle pense que les femmes apprécient ses dessins plus que les hommes. « Les femmes savent *rire* d'elles-mêmes,

comic strip / so

cartoonists

so-called
in other words
each one
neuroses
make fun of, laugh at

who put on airs, affected
neurotics

homemakers / oppressed

to laugh at

415

dit-elle. Les hommes se sentent *blessés*. Leur fierté est offensée. » Claire Bretécher vient d'une famille de femmes fortes et, bien que mariée maintenant, elle a toujours pensé qu'il valait mieux rester célibataire plutôt que de se marier avec *n'importe qui*. Mais elle n'a pas beaucoup de patience avec les féministes *non plus*. « Il y a longtemps que j'ai *résolu* ces problèmes-là, dit-elle. Et puis mon mari est un homme qui sait très bien qu'il ne faut pas compter sur moi pour faire le ménage, que mon argent est à moi et que je ne veux pas avoir d'enfants. »

Elle a décidé de ne pas utiliser ses bandes dessinées pour exprimer ses idées féministes. « J'avais le choix, dit-elle. Je pouvais *lutter* pour les femmes, mais c'est fatigant et ça me limitait trop. Ou bien je pouvais oublier tout cela et m'adresser à tout le monde. » Voyant qu'elle n'est pas toujours *tendre* pour les femmes, certains hommes l'accusent de détester les femmes. « Ça, c'est idiot, explique-t-elle. Ils n'ont absolument rien compris et je suis fatiguée de tout leur expliquer. »

En effet, Claire Bretécher s'identifie à ses propres personnages : la femme aux *hanches* trop grosses en train d'essayer des blue-jeans trop petits, la femme qui boit un verre *en cachette* pendant la visite de sa *belle-mère*, la femme qui a peur de *vieillir* et la femme qui pense que personne ne l'aime ni la comprend. « Elles sont toutes moi, » dit-elle.

Avec la permission de Claire Bretécher

hurt

just anyone
neither / resolved

fight

kind, sympathetic

You may also wish to mention *beau-père, beau-frère, belle-sœur*.
hips
on the sly / mother-in-law
growing old

CRÉATION

Have students describe orally or in writing the cartoon, *Création*. They might also want to create a *"monologue intérieur"* to accompany the cartoon. Useful vocabulary : *allumer une cigarette, enlever les toiles d'araignées, faire une petite lessive dans le lavabo, se faire une tasse de café, une lampe de chevet, une machine à écrire, manquer d'inspiration, passer l'aspirateur, regarder (compter) les mouches au plafond, se ronger les ongles, taper à la machine.*

Compréhension. Selon les renseignements donnés dans le texte, est-ce que les phrases suivantes sont vraies ou fausses ? Si le sens de la phrase est faux, corrigez-le.

1. Claire Bretécher est un personnage de bande dessinée qui est très populaire en France.
2. Les situations que Claire Bretécher décrit représentent des faits qu'elle a observés dans la vie de tous les jours.
3. Elle se moque surtout des gens qui se prennent trop au sérieux.
4. Claire Bretécher se moque aussi bien des femmes que des hommes.
5. Elle a l'intention de rester célibataire toute sa vie.
6. Elle a décidé d'utiliser ses bandes dessinées pour faire défendre la cause des femmes.
7. Certains hommes pensent que Claire Bretécher déteste les femmes, mais ils se trompent.
8. Quand Claire Bretécher se moque des autres femmes, c'est un peu une façon de se moquer d'elle-même.

Notes culturelles: *L'art et la musique*

Même si les Français ne s'intéressent pas tous à l'art, d'une façon générale, on accorde une assez grande importance à l'art en France. Ce respect de l'art est évident dans les institutions mêmes du pays; il existe un ministère de la Culture dont le rôle est de protéger et de développer le *patrimoine* culturel national et d'intéresser le public à l'art.

Le gouvernement accorde aussi d'assez généreuses subventions aux différentes entreprises culturelles : théâtres, musées, salles de concert, expositions, maisons de la culture, etc. Chaque année, on organise aussi des festivals qui attirent des artistes et des spectateurs du monde entier : le festival d'art dramatique d'Avignon, le festival de Cannes (cinéma), le festival d'Aix (musique), par exemple.

Montmartre : artiste de rue

If available, have students listen to examples of the music of different French composers. Students can also be shown examples of paintings by various French artists and asked to describe the paintings and their reactions to them.

heritage

Thionville: concert en plein air

Pour les Français, l'art est aussi dans la rue. À Paris, *ainsi que* dans la plupart des villes françaises, il y a partout de magnifiques exemples d'architecture ancienne, des jardins et des places ornées de statues, des galeries d'art et même des artistes qui travaillent dans la rue sous les yeux des curieux. On peut passer quelques minutes (ou quelques heures) à regarder les *gravures* des *bouquinistes* installés sur les quais de la Seine; on peut aller faire un tour au marché aux fleurs et si on est fatigué, on peut se reposer tranquillement à l'*ombre* de Notre Dame, dans le jardin des Tuileries ou sur les *bancs* des places et des parcs publics.

Un certain nombre de musiciens et compositeurs français ont leur place parmi les grands noms de la musique. Par exemple, le *Boléro* de Maurice Ravel (1875–1937) et le *Prélude à l'après-midi d'un faune* de Claude Debussy (1862–1918) sont des classiques de l'impressionnisme. À l'époque moderne, le groupe des Six, fondé en 1918 et parmi *lesquels* figuraient Francis Poulenc, Darius Milhaud, et Arthur Honegger, un Suisse — ainsi que des compositeurs comme Olivier Messiaen, Érik Satie et plus récemment Pierre Boulez — ont beaucoup contribué à l'évolution de la musique classique moderne.

Les amateurs d'opéra ont probablement eu l'occasion d'entendre *Carmen*, *Les Pêcheurs de perles* ou *L'Arlésienne* de Georges Bizet (1838–1875) ou un opéra de Charles Gounod (1818–1893) *tel que Faust* ou *Mireille*. Même le jazz, dont les origines sont typiquement américaines, occupe une place importante dans la vie musicale française. Au jazz américain *s'ajoute* le jazz européen que des musiciens comme Stéphane Grappelli et Jean-Luc Ponty ont beaucoup contribué à développer.

as well as

prints / outdoor booksellers

shade
benches

whom

such as

is added

418

Les mots et la vie : *Les arts et la musique*

Étudiez le vocabulaire présenté et répondez aux questions qui suivent.

Les arts et les artistes

dessiner	un dessin	un dessinateur, une dessinatrice
peindre	un tableau / une peinture	un peintre
sculpter	une sculpture / une statue	un sculpteur
composer	une symphonie / un opéra	un compositeur, une compositrice
jouer	un morceau de musique	un musicien, une musicienne
danser	un ballet (classique ou moderne)	un danseur, une danseuse
prendre des photos	une photo, un portrait	un(e) photographe
chanter	une chanson	un chanteur, une chanteuse

Les instruments de musique
jouer…

de la guitare	du trombone
du violon	de la clarinette
du piano	de la flûte
de la guitare électrique	du saxophone
de la trompette	du violoncelle *(cello)*
du tambour *(drum)*	du banjo

Point out that *electronic synthesizer* is *un synthétiseur (un synthé)* and that *faire du synthétiseur* means to play an electronic synthesizer.

Les préférences musicales
la musique classique
la musique moderne
la musique populaire
la musique folklorique
le rock
le jazz
l'opéra

Have students rank the types of music given in the order of their preference.

Les événements artistiques
une exposition
un festival
un concert
un récital
la première d'un film, d'une pièce de théâtre
un spectacle son et lumière

Tell students that a *spectacle de son et lumière* is a show usually presented at a historical site such as *Notre-Dame, les Invalides* (Napoleon's tomb), *Chambord*. These spectacles involve narration, dramatization, and special effects with sound and light.

A. Interview. Répondez aux questions suivantes ou utilisez-les pour interviewer un(e) autre étudiant(e).

1. Quelles sont vos activités artistiques préférées ?
2. Quels sont vos peintres et vos musiciens préférés ?
3. De quel instrument de musique jouez-vous ? Est-ce qu'il y a d'autres instruments dont vous aimeriez apprendre à jouer ?
4. Quel genre de musique préférez-vous ? Quels sont vos chanteurs et vos chanteuses préférés ?
5. À quels événements artistiques avez-vous assisté récemment ?
6. Allez-vous souvent au théâtre ?
7. Avez-vous déjà composé un morceau de musique ou écrit une chanson ?

B. Connaissez-vous la musique ? Préparez des questions que vous poserez aux autres étudiants de votre classe ou à votre professeur pour savoir s'ils connaissent bien la musique et les musicien(ne)s.

Exemples   **De quel instrument James Galway joue-t-il ?**
                Qui est Linda Ronstadt ?
                Quelle est la chanson la plus populaire en ce moment ?

Le nouveau musée d'Orsay à Paris

Explorations
✤ Expressing opinions
Le subjonctif avec les expressions impersonnelles

You have already seen that the subjunctive is used in clauses following **il faut que** and **il vaut mieux que** to express necessity or judgment.

A. The subjunctive is also used after other expressions that indicate uncertainty, impossibility, judgment, or necessity.

Judgment

il vaut mieux que
il vaudrait mieux que
il est préférable que
il est dommage que (*it is too bad that*)
il est temps que
il est naturel que
il est important que
il est bon que
il est juste que

Uncertainty or impossibility

il est possible que
il est impossible que
il est rare que
il est peu probable que (*it is unlikely that*)
il semble que

Necessity

il faut que
il faudrait que
il est nécessaire que

Point out that il est probable and il paraît take the indicative.

Il est peu probable que nous assistions à cette conférence.	*It's unlikely that we'll attend that lecture.*
Il serait préférable que tu **répondes** à sa lettre toi-même.	*It would be preferable if you answered his letter yourself.*
Il vaudrait mieux qu'ils **attendent.**	*It would be better for them to wait.*
Il n'est pas nécessaire que vous **payiez** à l'avance.	*You don't have to pay in advance.*

Note that **il n'est pas nécessaire que** has a meaning similar to *it's not necessary*, or *one doesn't have to*, but **il ne faut pas** means *one must not*.

Il ne faut pas que tu oublies de faire tes devoirs.	*You must not forget to do your homework.*
Il faudra aussi que tu lises cette histoire, mais **il n'est pas nécessaire** que tu comprennes tous les mots.	*You will also have to read this story, but it is not necessary for you to understand every word.*

B. In conversation, **il est** is often replaced by **c'est**.

C'est dommage qu'ils ne soient pas ici.	*It's too bad that they are not here.*

C. You have already seen that some verbs have irregular subjunctive stems (e.g., **aller**, **être**, **faire**). Some additional verbs with irregular stems are:

pouvoir → **puiss-**   Il est dommage que vous ne
                              puissiez pas venir.
savoir → **sach-**   Il est important que nous
                              sachions la vérité.

D. Several other irregular verbs form their subjunctive regularly (from the present tense **ils / elles** form) in the **je**, **tu**, **il / elle / on**, and **ils / elles** persons, but base the **nous** and **vous** forms on the present tense **nous** form.

Le subjonctif de *venir*	
que je **vienne**	que nous **venions**
que tu **viennes**	que vous **veniez**
qu'il / elle / on **vienne**	qu'ils / elles **viennent**

Le subjonctif de *prendre*	
que je **prenne**	que nous **prenions**
que tu **prennes**	que vous **preniez**
qu'il / elle / on **prenne**	qu'ils / elles **prennent**

Le subjonctif de *devoir*	
que je **doive**	que nous **devions**
que tu **doives**	que vous **deviez**
qu'il / elle / on **doive**	qu'ils / elles **doivent**

Il serait bon que tu **viennes** demain.
Il est possible que nous **prenions** une décision aujourd'hui.
Il est dommage que vous **deviez** rentrer si tôt.

E. **Avoir** and **vouloir** each have two irregular stems.

Le subjonctif d'*avoir*	
que j'**aie**	que nous **ayons**
que tu **aies**	que vous **ayez**
qu'il / elle / on **ait**	qu'ils / elles **aient**

Le subjonctif de *vouloir*

que je **veuille**	que nous **voulions**
que tu **veuilles**	que vous **vouliez**
qu'il / elle / on **veuille**	qu'ils / elles **veuillent**

Substitution : (1) Il faut que je travaille. *(tu / les étudiants / mon ami / vous / je / nous)* (2) Il est temps que vous appreniez ces verbes. *(nous / tu / je / Georges et Guy / Raoul)* (3) Il serait bon que nous soyons ici. *(je / vous / Marie-Claire / Louise et Jacques / tu)* (4) Il est préférable que vous fassiez du ski. *(nous / je / Michèle / Alain et Richard / vous)* (5) Il est dommage que Jean n'ait pas de patience. *(ses parents / nous / tu / son professeur / je / vous)*

Il est peu probable que nous **ayons** le temps.
Il est possible qu'ils **veuillent** nous accompagner.

Mise en situation

On va au théâtre ? On joue une nouvelle pièce à la maison de la Culture de la ville. Thierry pense que c'est une occasion à ne pas manquer. Il essaie de persuader Maryse.

THIERRY   Il faut absolument que tu ailles voir cette pièce.

MARYSE   Je voudrais bien, mais il est peu probable que j'aie le temps cette semaine.

THIERRY   Fais un effort ! *Ça en vaut* vraiment *la peine.* Et puis, tu travailles trop. Il serait bon que tu prennes le temps de te détendre un peu.

MARYSE   Attends. Il est possible que je sois libre vendredi soir. Je vais regarder dans mon *agenda...* Zut, j'ai une *dissertation* à rendre lundi. Il vaudrait mieux que je la finisse cette semaine.

THIERRY   C'est dommage que tu ne puisses pas venir... Il est si rare que nous ayons l'occasion de voir une pièce de cette qualité.

The idea of the *maisons de la culture* began in the 1930s and represents an attempt to bring culture to people who would not normally be inclined to go to the theater, concerts, etc. Most towns of any importance have a *maison de la culture.* In large cities, professional groups often volunteer their services and give plays, etc.

It's worth the effort.

appointment book / term paper

Préparation

A. Un étudiant à l'école des Beaux-Arts. Marcel parle de ce qu'il doit faire comme étudiant dans les Beaux-Arts. Qu'est-ce qu'il dit ?

Modèle   aller aux expositions
Il est important que nous allions aux expositions.

1. assister aux conférences
2. étudier beaucoup
3. apprendre à dessiner
4. prendre le temps de réfléchir
5. visiter les différents musées de la ville
6. participer à la vie culturelle de l'école
7. choisir bien nos cours
8. vouloir travailler dur
9. s'entendre avec nos professeurs
10. s'intéresser aux nouveaux artistes

Point out that the admission to the *école des Beaux-Arts* (one of France's *Grandes Écoles*) is through a competitive, selective examination. Once admitted, students often have to complete additional courses before beginning their studies. The *école des Beaux-Arts* concentrates on painting, sculpture, etc. Talented musical students study at the *Conservatoire.*

After completing this exercise, do *Communication C (Changeons de rôle)* if students are ready.

B. **Vous venez à l'exposition?** Armand essaie de persuader ses amis d'aller à une exposition. Mais ils ont tous quelque chose d'autre à faire. Qu'est-ce qu'ils disent?

Have students imagine that someone has asked them to go to an exhibit and they don't want to go. Have them give their excuses.

Modèle Véronique / aller chez le dentiste.
Il faut que Véronique aille chez le dentiste.

1. nous / écrire un rapport
2. Gérard / être de retour à cinq heures
3. je / aller voir ma grand-mère
4. vous / lire plusieurs articles
5. tu / finir ton travail
6. je / prendre ma leçon de piano
7. Marcel et Robert / faire le marché
8. nous / rendre visite à des amis

C. **Au conservatoire de musique.** Des professeurs du conservatoire de musique parlent avec leurs étudiants et leur donnent quelques conseils.

Modèle Il faudra / donner un récital à la fin de l'année
Il faudra que vous donniez un récital à la fin de l'année.

1. il serait bon / choisir un morceau très classique
2. il faudrait / apprendre à jouer d'un autre instrument
3. il est naturel / avoir un peu peur
4. il ne faut pas / abandonner maintenant
5. il est important / être prêts
6. il est nécessaire / faire des progrès
7. il serait préférable / savoir ce que vous voulez faire
8. il n'est pas nécessaire / prendre une décision maintenant
9. il vaudrait mieux / se mettre au travail

Communication et vie pratique

A. **Décisions.** La liste qui suit représente certaines habitudes, intentions ou préoccupations que vous pouvez avoir. Exprimez votre réaction envers chacune de ces suggestions en utilisant les expressions suivantes.

Exemples finir mon travail
Il faut que je finisse mon travail ce soir.
ou: **Il est peu probable que je finisse mon travail ce soir.**

Expressions	**Suggestions**
Il faut que	finir mon travail
Il vaudrait mieux que	répondre aux lettres qu'on m'a
Il est temps que	écrites
Il est rare que	vendre mes vieux livres
Il est peu probable que	aller en classe tous les jours
Il n'est pas nécessaire que	sortir ce soir
Il est possible que	me reposer un peu
	choisir mes cours pour le
	trimestre prochain

B. **Projets et obligations.** Indequez ce que vous devez faire cette semaine.

  Exemples   Il faut que j'aille chez le dentiste.
    ou: **Il serait bon que j'écrive à mes parents.**

Have students describe other situations (e.g., *le week-end prochain, les prochaines vacances, l'été prochain*).

C. **Changeons de rôle.** Vous êtes professeur. Dites à vos étudiants ce qu'il faut qu'ils fassent.

  Exemple   Il est important que vous étudiiez régulièrement.

Have students tell a roommate, teacher, etc., what he or she must do.

C'est votre tour. Essayez de persuader un(e) autre étudiant(e) de prendre le temps d'aller voir une pièce de théâtre (ou si vous préférez un film, un concert, une exposition, ou un spectacle de ballet) que vous jugez important. Utilisez la **Mise en situation** comme guide.

Bring in the movie / culture section of a French magazine or newspaper that students can use in role-playing this situation.

❧ Expressing wants, emotions, and doubts
Le subjonctif avec les verbes de volition, d'émotion et de doute

Présentation

The subjunctive is used after certain verbs and expressions of volition, emotion, and doubt. Thus, the use of the subjunctive is not always a question of rigid grammatical rules; it is partly a matter of the meaning or feeling the speaker wants to convey (i.e., doubt, desire, emotion, or opinion of some kind).

A. The subjunctive is always used following verbs or expressions of wanting or wishing (**vouloir, désirer, préférer, aimer mieux,** etc.).

Other verbs in this category are *accepter* and *permettre*, which are generally used in the negative, and *vouloir bien*.

Ils ne **veulent** pas que je **sorte** seule le soir.	*They don't want me to go out alone at night.*
Nous **voudrions** qu'il y **ait** moins de violence à la télévision.	*We wish there were less violence on television.*
Jeannette et Daniel **préfèrent** que nous les **accompagnions.**	*Jeannette and Daniel prefer that we accompany them.*
J'**aimerais mieux** que vous **finissiez** vos devoirs immédiatement.	*I prefer that you finish your homework immediately.*

B. The subjunctive is always used following verbs or expressions of emotion (**avoir peur, être content, regretter, être triste, être surpris, être déçu,** etc.).

J'**ai peur** qu'ils **aient** un accident.	*I'm afraid that they might have an accident.*
Il **regrette** que nous ne **puissions** pas y venir.	*He is sorry that we can't come.*
Tout le monde **est content** que vous vous **sentiez** mieux.	*Everyone is happy that you are felling better.*
Les amis de Charles **sont tristes** qu'il ne leur **écrive** plus.	*Charles' friends are sad that he doesn't write to them anymore.*
Il **est surpris** que je ne **veuille** pas faire ça.	*He is surprised that I don't want to do that.*

C. The subjunctive is used following verbs or expressions of uncertainty or doubt.

Je **doute** qu'ils **viennent.**	*I doubt that they're coming.*
Je **ne crois pas** que tu le **saches.**	*I don't believe that you know it.*
Ne penses-tu pas que la situation **soit** grave ?	*Don't you think the situation is serious ?*
Je **ne suis pas sûr** qu'ils **comprennent.**	*I'm not sure they understand.*

Croire and **penser** are followed by the subjunctive only when used in the negative and interrogative — that is, when doubt is implied.

Point out that *croire* and *penser* can be followed by a second clause in which the subject is the same as the main clause.

Compare :

Je crois qu'ils viendront.	Je **ne crois pas** qu'ils **viennent.**
Tu penses qu'il pourra se débrouiller.	**Penses-tu** qu'il **puisse** se débrouiller ?

The verb **espérer** is never followed by the subjunctive.

Nous **espérons** que vous vous **amuserez** bien.

D. The subjunctive is used only when the subject of the first clause is not the same as the subject of the second clause. When there is only one subject, an infinitive is used instead of the subjunctive.

Compare the following sentences :

Mon père veut que **je** finisse mes études.	**Je** veux **finir** mes études.
Elle est contente que **nous** partions.	**Elle** est contente de **partir.**

Mise en situation

Il faut retenir nos places. Jean-Pierre Rampal, le célèbre flûtiste, va donner un concert. Sébastien et Nathalie voudraient bien y aller, mais est-ce qu'il y a encore des *places*?

Important concert halls for classical music in Paris are *La Salle Pleyel* and *Les Concerts Lamoureux*; the most famous popular music hall in Paris is *L'Olympia.*

seats

NATHALIE   Téléphone vite, j'ai peur qu'il n'y ait plus de places si on attend trop.

SÉBASTIEN   J'aimerais mieux que tu le fasses toi-même. Je ne sais jamais quelle place choisir.

NATHALIE   Je doute que nous ayons beaucoup de choix! J'espère qu'il reste encore quelque chose… Allô, allô. Nous voulons *retenir* deux places pour le concert de Jean-Pierre Rampal.

to reserve

L'EMPLOYÉ   À l'orchestre ou au balcon?

NATHALIE   Au premier rang du balcon de préférence.

L'EMPLOYÉ   Je ne crois pas que ce soit possible. Non, tout est pris. Il ne nous reste que deux places au quinzième *rang*.

row

NATHALIE   Sébastien, les seules places qui restent sont au quinzième rang. Tu veux que je les prenne quand même?

Préparation

A. Opinions. Paul Lefranc donne ses opinions sur les activités culturelles de sa famille. Qu'est-ce qu'il dit?

Modèle   Nous allons si rarement au théâtre. (je regrette)
Je regrette que nous allions si rarement au théâtre.

1. Mon fils apprend à jouer du saxophone. (je suis content)
2. Il fait des progrès. (je voudrais)
3. Il n'a pas beaucoup de talent. (j'ai peur)
4. Ma femme a envie de visiter cette exposition. (je ne crois pas)
5. Nous pouvons aller au concert ce soir. (je doute)
6. Nous passons des heures devant la télé. (c'est dommage)
7. Nous allons à un concert de rock. (les enfants aimeraient)
8. Je ne m'intéresse pas à ce genre de musique. (les enfants sont déçus)
9. Nous n'avons pas de magnétoscope. (je regrette)
10. Nous pouvons en acheter un cette année (je ne crois pas)

Substitution : (1) Je préfère que vous alliez à la banque maintenant. *(je veux / je ne crois pas / je doute / j'aimerais mieux / je suis surpris)* (2) Elle est triste que vous soyez malade. *(elle ne pense pas, elle n'est pas sûre, elle est surprise / elle regrette)* (3) Est-ce que vous regrettez que Lucien ne puisse pas venir? *(Est-ce que vous êtes content / Est-ce que vous avez peur / Est-ce que vous êtes surpris)*

Le Monde sur minitel

CINEMA

Tous les programmes.
Toutes les salles. Tous les horaires.

36.15 TAPEZ LEMONDE

Mardi 5 mai

B. **Différences d'opinion.** Jean-Luc et ses parents ne sont pas toujours d'accord. Quelle est sa situation ?

Students may need to go through each phase of the exercise before doing it together.

> **Modèle**   Ses préférences : aller à l'université de Nice
> **Il voudrait aller à l'université de Nice.**
> Les préférences de ses parents : aller à l'université de Lille
> **Ils voudraient qu'il aille à l'université de Lille.**

Ses préférences	Les préférences de ses parents
1. louer un appartement	1. habiter dans une résidence universitaire
2. acheter une moto	2. utiliser son vieux vélo
3. apprendre à conduire	3. apprendre à jouer du piano
4. être musicien	4. être comptable
5. faire des études de médecine	5. faire des études de droit
6. sortir tous les soirs	6. sortir moins souvent
7. choisir des cours intéressants	7. suivre des cours plus pratiques
8. s'amuser	8. être plus sérieux

C. **Iront-ils au concert ou non ?** Les Petitjean iront-ils au concert ou non ? Il y a autant d'opinions que de personnes. Qu'est-ce que chaque personne dit ?

Add other expressions to the list. Can also be repeated with model sentences : *il prend des leçons de piano, elle fait des études à l'école des Beaux Arts*, etc.

> **Modèles**   je crois
> **Je crois qu'ils vont au concert.**
> *ou:*   je ne crois pas
> **Je ne crois pas qu'ils aillent au concert.**

1. je doute	6. je ne crois pas	11. ce n'est pas sûr
2. je voudrais	7. il vaudrait mieux	12. je regrette
3. j'espère	8. je crois	13. je pense
4. je suis sûr(e)	9. je suis content(e)	14. croyez-vous
5. je ne suis pas sûr(e)	10. je ne pense pas	

Communication et vie pratique

Have students come up with other statements for class discussion.

Êtes-vous d'accord ? Êtes-vous d'accord avec les opinions exprimées ? Indiquez votre opinion en commençant la phrase avec **je crois, je suis sûr(e), je ne suis pas sûr(e)**, ou **je doute**, etc.

> **Exemples**   On peut être à la fois riche et heureux.
> *ou:*   **Je crois qu'on peut être à la fois riche et heureux.**
> *ou:*   **Je doute qu'on puisse être à la fois riche et heureux.**

1. Nous accordons beaucoup d'importance aux arts et à la culture.
2. Nous nous intéressons plus aux sports qu'à l'art.
3. Les femmes ont autant de talent artistique que les hommes.
4. Les jeunes sont bien préparés pour la vie.
5. Les parents donnent trop de liberté à leurs enfants.
6. Les vieilles traditions sont en train de disparaître.
7. Les journalistes disent toujours la vérité.
8. Les Français sont plus cultivés que les Américains.

Have students imagine things they would say to the ticket agent to explain their situation; have them also come up with what the employee might say about the ticket situation. You might also give the employee information about where tickets are available and how much each costs.

> **C'est votre tour.** Vous essayez de réserver des places pour un concert qui va avoir lieu dans votre ville. Malheureusement, vous avez attendu un peu trop longtemps pour faire vos réservations. Un(e) autre étudiant(e) va jouer le rôle de l'employé(e). Utilisez la **Mise en situation** comme guide.

❧ Telling which one
Les pronoms démonstratifs

Présentation

Demonstrative pronouns can replace nouns. They reflect the number and gender of the nouns they replace.

Les pronoms démonstratifs			
	Masculine	**Feminine**	
Singular	celui	celle	*the one, this one, that one*
Plural	ceux	celles	*the ones, these, those*

Demonstrative pronouns cannot stand alone.

A. Demonstrative pronouns can be followed by prepositional phrases.

A mon avis, les meilleures peintures sont **celles des impressionnistes**.	*In my opinion, the best paintings are those of the impressionists.*
Il prend l'avion pour Strasbourg, et moi, je prends **celui pour Lyon**.	*He's taking the plane for Strasbourg, and I'm taking the one for Lyon.*
Les vêtements de Monoprix sont moins chers que **ceux des Galeries Lafayette**.	*Monoprix's clothes are less expensive than those of Galeries Lafayette.*

The preposition **de** used with a demonstrative pronoun frequently indicates possession.

À qui est cette affiche? C'est **celle de** Jacques.	*Whose poster is this? It's Jack's.*
Cet appareil photo est très bon marché mais **celui d'**Anne est meilleur marché.	*This camera is very cheap, but Anne's is cheaper.*
— Est-ce que tu as vu les nouveaux manteaux de Christian Dior?	*Did you see Dior's new coats?*
— Oui, mais j'aime mieux **ceux d'**Yves Saint-Laurent.	*Yes, but I prefer those of Yves Saint-Laurent.*

B. Demonstrative pronouns can be followed by relative pronouns.

Quel tableau voulez-vous? Je préfère **celui qui** coûte le moins cher.	*Which painting do you want? I prefer the one that costs the least.*
Je préfère cette affiche à **celle que** Paul a achetée.	*I prefer this poster to the one that Paul bought.*
Ces gravures et **celles qu'**on a exposées l'année passée sont très belles.	*These prints and the ones that were shown last year are very beautiful.*
Ceux qui arriveront les premiers au musée attendront les autres.	*Those (the people) who arrive first at the museum will wait for the others.*

C. Demonstrative pronouns can be used with the suffixes **-ci** and **-là**.

Je ne sais pas quel dessin choisir. **Celui-ci** est moins cher, mais **celui-là** est plus joli.	*I don't know which drawing to choose. This one is less expensive, but that one is prettier.*

You may want to tell students that *-ci* generally refers to the nearer item and *-là* to the more distant item.

D. Ceci *(this)* and **cela** *(that)* and the more informal **ça** *(that)* are used to refer to ideas or unspecified things rather than to specifically named items. Thus, they do not indicate gender and number.

Ceci va vous intéresser.	*This is going to interest you.*
Je ne comprends pas **cela**.	*I don't understand that.*
Ça, c'est formidable!	*That's great!*
Ça ne veut rien dire.	*That doesn't mean anything.*
Ça alors!	*Really! (You've got to be kidding!)*
C'est **ça**.	*That's it.*

Mise en situation

Confusion. Françoise et Christophe ont un peu de difficulté à communiquer. La conversation porte sur certaines reproductions. Mais de quelles reproductions *s'agit-il*?

FRANÇOISE	Qu'est-ce que tu penses de mes nouvelles reproductions?
CHRISTOPHE	Quelles reproductions? Celles que tu as achetées à la galerie d'art?
FRANÇOISE	Non, celles que mon cousin m'a envoyées.
CHRISTOPHE	Quel cousin? Celui de Lyon ou celui de Dijon?
FRANÇOISE	Mais non! Celui dont je t'ai parlé. Tu sais, celui qui est peintre.
CHRISTOPHE	Ah oui! Je me souviens! Ses tableaux ressemblent à ceux de Monet.
FRANÇOISE	Mais non! *Tu n'y connais rien!* Son style ressemble beaucoup plus à celui de Pissarro qu'à celui de Monet.

Transformation : Modèle :
C'est le manteau de Jacques. → C'est celui de Jacques.
(1) C'est la cravate du professeur. (2) Ce sont les chaussures de Guy. (3) Ce sont les étudiants de notre classe. (4) Ce sont les vêtements des enfants. (5) C'est la voiture de mon père. (6) C'est la mode de l'année passée. (7) C'est le train pour Madrid. (8) C'est la robe que je préfère.

is it about

Point out that Pissarro (1830–1903) and Monet (1840–1926) are both impressionists. You may want to show reproductions of some of their paintings to point out differences in their style.

You don't know anything about it!

Préparation

A. Contradictions. Jeannette et Paul ont des goûts très différents. Chaque fois que Jeannette donne son opinion sur quelque chose, Paul est de l'opinion opposée.

Modèle — Cette reproduction est très jolie.
— **Ah non, celle-ci est beaucoup plus jolie.**

1. Cette exposition est très bien organisée.
2. Ce peintre est très célèbre.
3. Ces tableaux sont bien faits.
4. Ces photos sont très belles.
5. Cet article est passionnant.
6. Cette affiche est amusante.
7. Cette danseuse a beaucoup de talent.
8. Ce château est très beau.

B. La nostalgie du bon vieux temps. Il y a des gens — même des personnes assez jeunes — qui pensent toujours que le passé était bien plus agréable que le présent. Honoré Regret est une de ces personnes. Qu'est-ce qu'il dit ?

Have students react to these statements (e.g., Moi, je n'aime pas la mode d'il y a dix ans ; je préfère celle d'aujourd'hui).

Modèles Je n'aime pas ma nouvelle maison. (la maison où nous habitions autrefois)
J'aimais mieux celle où nous habitions autrefois.
ou: Je n'aime pas ma nouvelle maison. (la maison de mes parents)
J'aimais mieux celle de mes parents.

1. Je n'aime pas la musique qu'on entend à la radio. (la musique qu'on entendait autrefois)
2. Je n'aime pas les vêtements d'aujourd'hui. (les vêtements qu'on portait quand j'étais jeune)
3. Je n'aime pas les jeux qu'on joue aujourd'hui. (les jeux de mon enfance)
4. Je n'aime pas les cours que je suis ce trimestre. (les cours que je suivais le trimestre passé)
5. Je n'aime pas mes professeurs. (les professeurs que j'avais au lycée)
6. Je n'aime pas la mode d'aujourd'hui. (la mode d'il y a dix ans)
7. Je n'aime pas ma nouvelle chambre. (la chambre ou j'habitais l'année dernière)
8. Je n'aime pas les derniers tableaux de Picasso. (les tableaux de la période bleue)
9. Je n'aime pas mon nouveau camarade de chambre. (le camarade de chambre que j'avais l'année dernière)

Communication et vie pratique

Préférences. Répondez aux questions suivantes.

1. Quels romans préférez-vous ? Les romans d'aventure ou ceux de science-fiction ?
2. Quelles chansons françaises préférez-vous ? Les chansons de Johnny Halliday ou celles d'Édith Piaf ?
3. Quelle peinture aimez-vous le mieux ? La peinture des impressionnistes ou celle des cubistes ?
4. Quels types de musée préférez-vous ? Ceux où il y a seulement des tableaux ou ceux où on peut voir toutes sortes d'objets d'art ?
5. Préférez-vous les sculptures d'Auguste Rodin ou celles d'Henry Moore ?

> **C'est votre tour.** Vous parlez de certains objets ou de certaines personnes (livres, disques, peintres, écrivains, etc.) mais la personne avec qui vous parlez ne sait jamais exactement de quel objet ou de quelle personne vous parlez. Utilisez la **Mise en situation** comme guide.

Ask questions, having students answer orally. Have them explain their choices.

Option : Have students imagine that they are sitting at an outdoor café and want to point out someone (another student in the class). The other students try to guess which one by asking questions : *C'est le garçon aux cheveux bruns près de la porte. Non, c'est celui aux cheveux blonds à côté de toi.*

❧ Talking about possessions
Les pronoms possessifs

Présentation

Possessive pronouns are used to replace nouns and possessive adjectives. They therefore have the same number and gender as the nouns they replace.

Les pronoms possessifs				
Singular		**Plural**		
Masculine	**Feminine**	**Masculine**	**Feminine**	
le mien	la mienne	les miens	les miennes	*mine*
le tien	la tienne	les tiens	les tiennes	*yours*
le sien	la sienne	les siens	les siennes	*his, hers, its*
le nôtre	la nôtre	les nôtres	les nôtres	*ours*
le vôtre	la vôtre	les vôtres	les vôtres	*yours*
le leur	la leur	les leurs	les leurs	*theirs*

—Avez-vous apporté votre programme ? — Moi, j'ai apporté **le mien**.
Nous avons fait nos devoirs, mais Nadine n'a pas fait **les siens**.
Je vous raconterai mes secrets si vous me racontez **les vôtres**.
Nous avons encore notre vieille voiture, mais Marie a vendu **la sienne**.

Remind students that they already know several ways to express possession : possessive adjectives and the NOUN + *de* construction (*c'est la maison de Fabien*) and that possessive pronouns are shortcuts that they can use in communication in the same way as direct / indirect objects pronouns.

A. It is important to remember that the pronoun agrees in number and gender with the noun possessed and not with the possessor.

> la chambre de Paul → **la sienne**
> le chien de Suzanne → **le sien**

B. When the possessive pronoun is preceded by **à** or **de**, the forms are contracted in the usual way.

> Je ne suis pas très content de mon appareil photo, mais eux, ils
>   sont très satisfaits **du leur**.
> Je pense à mes problèmes et elle, elle pense **aux siens**.

Mise en situation

Rangez vos affaires. Les camarades de chambre de Philippe ont la mauvaise habitude de *laisser traîner leurs affaires* partout. Philippe en a marre.

leave their things lying around

PHILIPPE	J'ai *rangé* mes affaires ; c'est votre tour de ranger les vôtres.

put away

EMMANUEL	Moi, je remets toujours mes affaires à leur place ; c'est Pierre et Nicolas qui ne rangent pas les leurs.
PHILIPPE	Ces vêtements dans la salle de bain, ce sont les tiens ou ceux de Nicolas ?
EMMANUEL	Je crois que ce sont les siens ; j'ai rangé les miens hier.
PHILIPPE	Et ces chaussures, elles sont à toi ?
EMMANUEL	Non, je ne crois pas que ce soit les miennes... Ah si ! Ce sont celles que je viens d'acheter. Elles ressemblent beaucoup aux tiennes ; je me suis trompé.
PHILIPPE	Au fait, cette cravate que tu portes, tu es sûr que c'est la tienne ?

Transformation : Modèle :
Voilà ma maison. → Voilà la mienne. (1) Voilà mes suggestions. (2) Voilà mes chaussures. (3) Voilà ton livre. (4) Voilà ta cravate. (5) Voilà son appartement. (6) Voilà sa robe. (7) Voilà notre village. (8) Voilà leurs examens.

Préparation

A. Visite des châteaux de la Loire. Un groupe d'amis sont en train de visiter les châteaux de la Loire. Valérie veut savoir ce que les autres ont apporté.

> **Modèle** — Qui a apporté son appareil photo ? (moi)
>   — **Moi, j'ai apporté le mien.**

1. Qui a apporté sa caméra ? (Marc)
2. Qui a déjà acheté son billet d'entrée ? (Laurent)
3. Qui a apporté un *Guide Michelin* ? (nous)
4. Qui a apporté sa carte de la région ? (toi)
5. Qui a déjà vu sa chambre d'hôtel ? (moi)
6. Qui a déjà retenu une table au restaurant ? (mes amis)
7. Qui a apporté des lunettes de soleil ? (nous)

Point out to students that the Guide Michelin (rouge) contains information about hotels and restaurants in French towns, each accompanied by a rating (four-star, three-star, etc.), current prices, and a description of available amenities. The Guide Michelin (vert), on the other hand, describes a particular region and suggests places of interest and possible itineraries.

B. **Il ne faut pas se tromper!** Les habitants d'une petite ville ont prêté leurs tableaux et d'autres objets d'art pour une exposition organisée par la ville. Maintenant il faut les rendre. Ce n'est pas facile.

Modèle —Est-ce que ce tableau est à Madame Sabatier? (Non, Monsieur Lejeune)
— **Non, ce n'est pas le sien, c'est celui de Monsieur Lejeune.**

1. Est-ce que cette gravure est à vous? (non, Madame Verneuil)
2. Est-ce que ces dessins sont à toi, Élise? (non, mon frère)
3. Est-ce que cette petite gravure est à vos voisins? (non, Mademoiselle Pasteur)
4. Est-ce que ces affiches sont à vous? (non, Monsieur Girard)
5. Est-ce que ce tableau est à Monsieur Denis? (non, Madame Boivin)
6. Est-ce que cette sculpture est à Monsieur Dumas? (non, Monsieur Lambert)

Communication et vie pratique

A. **Vous et moi.** Choisissez un(e) autre étudiant(e) avec qui vous allez parler et utilisez les suggestions suivantes pour guider la conversation.

1. Dites-lui quelle est votre boisson préférée et demandez-lui quelle est la sienne.
2. Dites-lui quels sont vos peintres préférés et demandez-lui quels sont les siens.
3. Dites-lui quels sont vos écrivains préférés et demandez-lui quels sont les siens.
4. Dites-lui comment est décoré votre appartement et demandez-lui comment est décoré le sien.
5. Dites-lui quel est votre musée préféré et demandez-lui quel est le sien.
6. Dites-lui quand est votre anniversaire et demandez-lui quand est le sien.
7. Donnez-lui votre numéro de téléphone et demandez-lui quel est le sien.
8. Donnez-lui votre adresse et demandez-lui quelle est la sienne.

B. **Questions / interview.** Répondez aux questions suivantes ou utilisez-les pour interviewer un(e) autre étudiant(e).

1. Beaucoup d'Américains ont des ancêtres qui viennent d'Europe. D'où viennent les tiens?
2. L'anniversaire de George Washington est le 22 février. Quand est celui de Lincoln? Et le tien? Et celui de ton (ta) meilleur(e) ami(e)?
3. Certaines personnes préfèrent les grosses voitures, d'autres les petites voitures. Comment est la tienne? Et celle de tes parents?
4. Beaucoup d'étudiants passent leurs vacances de printemps en Floride. Et toi, où passes-tu les tiennes? Et tes parents, où passent-ils les leurs? Et ton professeur, sais-tu où il passe les siennes?

5. À ton avis, les vins français sont-ils meilleurs que les nôtres ?
6. Il y a des étudiants qui font toujours leurs devoirs à la dernière minute. Quand fais-tu les tiens ?
7. À ton avis, est-ce que les voitures étrangères sont plus économiques que les nôtres ?

C'est votre tour. Êtes-vous parmi ceux qui rangent leurs affaires ou parmi ceux qui les laissent traîner ? Choisissez le rôle qui vous convient et imaginez la conversation avec un(e) camarade de chambre ou avec un membre de votre famille qui a des habitudes opposées aux vôtres.

Intégration et perspectives

Comment va le cinéma français ?

Si vous me demandiez comment va le cinéma français, je vous répondrais qu'il va très bien, merci. Bien sûr, vous me diriez qu'on ne va *plus guère* au cinéma, que les gens se contentent de regarder la télévision confortablement installés dans leur *fauteuil*, que le cinéma connaît depuis les années 60 une crise longue et difficile.

    Vous auriez en partie raison. Mais je vous *ferais remarquer* qu'on *tourne* plus de films en France qu'aux États-Unis et que quatre *milliards* de spectateurs par an, ce n'est pas si mal que ça.

hardly anymore

armchair

would point out / shoot, make

billion

Le cinéma reste populaire.

Vous me demanderiez alors où sont tous ces spectateurs et pourquoi les salles sont souvent *à moitié vides*. Je serais bien obligée de *reconnaître* qu'il y a de moins en moins de gens qui *fréquentent* les salles de cinéma. Mais cela ne veut pas dire que les Français ne s'intéressent plus au cinéma. S'ils ne s'y intéressaient pas, pourquoi y aurait-il quinze millions de téléspectateurs qui chaque dimanche soir s'installent devant leur télévision pour regarder un film ? La vérité est que les Français vont au cinéma, qu'ils y vont souvent, et qu'ils aiment ça, mais la plupart préfèrent voir les films chez eux !

half / empty / admit
frequent, go often to

Voici leurs réponses aux questions qu'on leur a posées au cours d'un récent sondage.

1. Allez-vous au cinéma…

plusieurs fois par semaine ?	2,2%
une fois par semaine ?	10,7
une fois par mois ?	34
moins souvent ?	51,3
sans réponse	1,7

Point out that in spoken French, *virgule* is equivalent to *point* (e.g., *quinze virgule un pour cent* = *fifteen point one percent*).

2. Parmi les genres de films suivants, quels sont…

	Ceux que vous préférez ?	Et ceux que vous détestez ?
Les films comiques	40,3%	5,2%
Les films policiers	29,5	7,5
Les films de science-fiction	23,9	25,9
Les films d'aventure	23,9	1,8
Les comédies dramatiques	17,7	17,2
Les grands classiques	17	12,6
Les westerns	15,3	19,3
Les dessins animés	13,9	5
Les comédies musicales	13,6	21,8
Les films à grand spectacle	12,2	11,8
Les films historiques	11,7	10,8
Les films politiques	10,3	27,8
Les films X	2,6	46
Sans réponse	0,8	

The French rating system for films includes the following : (1) *ouvert à tous les publics* ; (2) *interdit au moins de 18 ans* ; (3) *interdit au moins de 13 ans*. The last two ratings are for films with excessive violence or explicit sexual content or language. The rating *Classe X* is used for films with pornographic content.

François Truffaut tourne un film.

3. Préférez-vous voir les films étrangers…

en version originale avec *sous-titres*?	23%
en version française?	68,3
pas de préférence	7,3
sans réponse	1,4

subtitles

4. Comment choisissez-vous les films que vous allez voir? Qu'est-ce qui vous influence le plus dans vos choix?

Le sujet du film	48,7%
La vedette	39,3
Les commentaires de vos amis	37,5
Les critiques des journaux	24
Les émissions à la télévision	16,8
Le *metteur en scène*	15,1
L'affiche	13,4
Le titre	10,1
La proximité de la salle	9,7
Les *prix* obtenus par le film	3,1
Sans raison	7,9
Sans réponse	2,8

director

awards

5. Quels sont vos acteurs et actrices préférés? Donnez trois noms.
Alain Delon
Jean-Paul Belmondo
Jean Gabin

6. Quels sont vos metteurs en scène préférés? Donnez trois noms.
Claude Lelouche
François Truffaut
Federico Fellini

Inspiré d'un article de *L'Express*.

Point out that the responses listed for questions 5 and 6 represent the top three choices of people responding to the survey.

A. Compréhension. Répondez aux questions suivantes selon les renseignements donnés dans le texte.

1. Est-ce que l'auteur pense que le cinéma français est en assez bonne santé ou qu'il est très malade?
2. Où est-ce qu'on tourne le plus de films chaque année, en France ou aux États-Unis?
3. Est-ce que les Français fréquentent beaucoup les salles de cinéma?
4. Comment font-ils pour voir les films qui les intéressent?
5. Qu'est-ce que beaucoup de Français font le dimanche soir?
6. Quel genre de film les Français préfèrent-ils?
7. Et quels sont les films qu'ils aiment le moins?
8. Est-ce qu'ils préfèrent voir les films étrangers en version française ou en version originale avec sous-titres?
9. Qu'est-ce qui les influence le plus dans leur choix d'un film?
10. Quels sont leurs acteurs et actrices préférés?

Have students use the responses of the French people surveyed to write a résumé of French film preferences (e.g., *La majorité des Français vont au cinéma moins d'une fois par mois*).

B. Et vous, aimez-vous le cinéma? Répondez vous-même aux questions du sondage. Ensuite, comparez vos réponses à celles des autres étudiants ou bien à celles des Français.

Have students choose the film that they consider the best of the year. Individual choices and the reasons for them can be presented to the class and a vote taken to decide on the choice of the class.

Notes culturelles: *Le cinéma français*

La France a toujours joué un rôle important dans l'histoire du cinéma aussi appelé « le septième art. » Cette histoire a commencé en 1895 quand Louis Lumière a présenté ses premières projections animées à une assemblée de 120 personnes. C'est seulement deux ans plus tard que Georges Méliès a construit le premier studio du monde et a commencé à inventer des *truquages*. À partir de ce moment-là, la vogue du cinéma *s'est répandue* dans le monde entier.

    Les Français moyens sont loin d'être tous des *cinéphiles*. Beaucoup vont au cinéma surtout pour se distraire, et un grand nombre d'entre eux préfèrent rester à la maison pour regarder la télévision. Mais il existe aussi un assez large public bien informé qui *recherche* la qualité. Les ciné-clubs, groupés en sept fédérations nationales, contribuent beaucoup à éduquer le public et attirent chaque année cinq millions de spectateurs. Les critiques des films occupent une place importante dans les principales revues françaises et il existe plusieurs revues spécialisées telles que *Les Cahiers du cinéma*.

special effects
spread
film lovers

seeks

Communication et vie pratique

A. Testez vos connaissances. Pouvez-vous répondre aux questions suivantes ? Si non, consultez les réponses à la fin du test.

    1. Parmi les trois architectes français suivants, quel est celui qui a dessiné les plans de la ville de Washington ?
       a. Le Corbusier **b.** Pierre L'Enfant **c.** André Le Nôtre

    2. Parmi les peintres suivants, quel est celui qui est considéré comme le principal représentant de l'école impressionniste ?
       a. Auguste Renoir **b.** Eugène Delacroix **c.** Bernard Buffet

    3. C'est un musicien du début du vingtième siècle dont l'œuvre la plus connue est le *Boléro*. Qui est-ce ?
       a. Pierre Boulez **b.** Camille Saint-Saëns **c.** Maurice Ravel

    4. Auteur de la célèbre phrase « une rose est une rose est une rose est une rose », cette femme de lettres américaine a passé une grande partie de sa vie en France où elle a connu et encouragé les artistes de son temps. Qui est-ce ?
       a. Mary Cassatt **b.** Gertrude Stein **c.** Virginia Woolf

    5. Parmi les trois artistes suivants, quel est celui qui a peint le tableau intitulé Guernica ?
       a. Édouard Manet **b.** Paul Gauguin **c.** Pablo Picasso

    6. Cet auteur d'origine roumaine est un des principaux représentants du théâtre de l'absurde. Qui est-ce ?
       a. Jean Cocteau **b.** Jean Anouilh **c.** Eugène Ionesco

Useful for listening practice.

New cognate vocabulary used in this activity is not intended to be active.

Have students complete short research projects on the names mentioned in this activity and / or make up additional items about francophone culture.

7. Il est généralement considéré comme un des plus grands poètes de l'époque romantique. Qui est-ce ?
   a. Victor Hugo   **b.** Jean de La Fontaine   **c.** Pierre de Ronsard
8. Parmi les trois villes suivantes, quelle est celle où il y a chaque année un festival d'art dramatique qui attire des jeunes du monde entier ?
   a. Avignon   **b.** Cannes   **c.** Strasbourg
9. Un des trois peintres suivants a décoré l'Opéra de Paris et celui de New York. Qui est-ce ?
   a. Henri Matisse   **b.** Marc Chagall   **c.** Vincent Van Gogh
10. Auteur de nombreux livres, cette femme a aussi écrit des scénarios de films et dirigé ses propres films. Qui est-ce ?
    a. Simone de Beauvoir   **b.** Marguerite Duras   **c.** George Sand*

B. **Votre culture.** Chaque pays et même chaque génération a sa propre culture. Pensez aux artistes et aux œuvres que les gens de votre génération connaissent et apprécient et composez un petit test culturel que vous présenterez au reste de la classe (ou à votre professeur).

*Réponses : 1. b ; 2. a ; 3. c ; 4. b ; 5. c ; 6. c ; 7. a ; 8. a ; 9. b ; 10. b

Musicien de rue

C. Une soirée musicale. Choisissez parmi les spectacles et concerts suivants ceux que vous aimeriez aller voir. Choisissez au moins cinq endroits qui seraient des choix possibles pour vous. Ensuite, avec un groupe d'étudiants, décidez (en respectant les préférences respectives des étudiants de votre groupe) où vous allez passer la soirée ensemble.

Exemple Moi, je voudrais aller écouter « Un soir de fête aux Antilles » parce que je ne connais pas du tout la musique créole et je voudrais bien avoir l'occasion d'en écouter un peu.

MUSIQUE

GENEVIEVE ET BERNARD PICAVET, pianos. Œuvres de Chopin, Brahms, Herz, Lefebure, Wely. 19h30. **Lucernaire Forum.** Pl : 20 et 30 F.
MARIANNE CLEMENT, flûte avec **Raul Sanchez,** guitare. Œuvres de Bach, Haendel. 17h45. **Conciergerie du Palais.** Pl : 30 F. Etud : 15 F.

SAINTE CHAPELLE
FESTIVAL DE MUSIQUE SACREE
9 CONCERTS
du 29 mars au 7 avril
Voir calendrier
Loc. sur place   278.67.46
Tous les jours (10h à 18h)   887.12.41

ENSEMBLE DE CORDES ET PERCUSSIONS. Avec **Georges Schmitt,** flûte de pan. Œuvres de Bach, Vivaldi. 21h. **Eglise Saint-Germain-des-Près.** Pl : 20 à 50 F.
EAST RIDGE HIGH SCHOOL VARSITY CHORUS. 33 chanteurs et musiciens. Madrigaux et négro-spirituals. 16h. **Kiosque à musique du jardin du Luxembourg.** Entrée libre.
PREMIERE RENCONTRE INTERNATIONALE D'ORCHESTRES DE JEUNES. Dir. **Alfred Loewenguth.** Concerts symphoniques d'orchestres français et étrangers. De 10h à 18h. **Parc Floral de Vincennes.** Entrée libre.
LINETTE DALMASSO, chanteuse-accordéoniste dans « écologiste et c'est pas triste ». Dimanche 6 à 21h. **Point Virgule,** 7, rue Ste-Croix-de-la-Bretonnerie (M° Hôtel-de-Ville). Pl : 30 F. Etud : 25 F.

un soir de FETE aux Antilles

20h30 : DINER au Rythme des ANTILLES avec le Trio Créole
22h30 : Orchestre et Attractions
LA CANNE A SUCRE - 222.23.25
4, rue St-Beuve - F. Dim. et Lun.

CLUB DES POÈTES
JEAN-PIERRE ROSNAY
POEMES DITS, POEMES CHANTES
2 spect. 22h15 et 23h30 (f. dim. et lun.)
30, rue de BOURGOGNE - 705.06 03

LA LOUISIANE, 176, rue Montmartre. 236.58.98. Déj. Dîn. soupers. Jazz New-Orléans. En alternance : **Maxime Saury, Christian Morin** ou **High Society Jazz Band.**
RIVER BOP, 67, rue Saint-André-des-Arts (M° Saint-Michel). 325.93.71. Tls sf Dim et Lun. A 22h : **Aldo Romano** en quintette. Avec **Philippe Petit, Dominique Bertram, Patrick Gauthier, Jean-Pierre Fouquey, Benoît Wideman.**
CLUB SALSA LATINE (à la Talmouse), 1, rue Laplace (5°). M° Panthéon. 326.29.83. Tls de 21h30 à 2h mat. Orchestre tropical.

SLOW·CLUB
130, rue de Rivoli 233.84.30
LA CELEBRE CAVE DE JAZZ
T.l.j. 21h30 à 2h du matin
Du mardi au vendredi
CLAUDE LUTER
Le samedi **RENE FRANC** et son orchestre
Fermé dimanche et lundi

D. En direct d'Amérique... Seul(e) ou avec un groupe d'étudiants, préparez une émission spéciale d'environ deux heures pour une station de radio française. Le but de ce programme est de donner aux Français une idée de ce que c'est que la musique américaine. Préparez un programme aussi varié que possible et avec un grand choix de chanteurs, de groupes et de genres différents. Expliquez les choix que vous avez faits.

Exemple   **7 h 00 – 7 h 30 Concert George Gershwin**
De sept heures à sept heures et demie, nous allons présenter quelques morceaux de George Gershwin. C'est un des compositeurs américains les plus célèbres.

● *Vocabulaire*

Noms

les instruments de musique (voir p. 419)

d'autres noms

l'**agenda** (m) *appointment book*
la **bande dessinée** *comic strip*
la **belle-mère** *mother-in-law*
le **dessinateur,** la **dessinatrice** *cartoonist*
la **dissertation** *term paper*
l'**époque** (f) *epoch, era*
le **fauteuil** *armchair*
la **hanche** *hip*
la **ménagère** *homemaker*
le **metteur en scène** *director*
le **milliard** *billion*
la **névrose** *neurosis*
le **névrosé,** la **névrosée** *neurotic*
la **place** *seat*
le **poseur,** la **poseuse** *pretender, show off*
le **préfet** *prefect*
le **prix** *award, prize, price*
le **rang** *row*
le **récital** *recital, performance*
le **sous-titre** *subtitle*
° la **version**

Verbes

s'agir de *to be a question of*
°**composer**
faire remarquer *to point out*
fréquenter *to frequent, go to often*
laisser traîner *to leave lying around*
lutter *to fight*
se **moquer de** *to make fun of*
peindre *to paint*

ranger *to put away, arrange*
ressembler à *to resemble*
retenir *to reserve, hold, retain*
ridiculiser *to ridicule*
rire *to laugh*
sculpter *to sculpt, carve*
tourner *to shoot (movie)*
traduire *to translate*
vieillir *to grow old*

Adjectifs

blessé(e) *hurt, wounded*
condescendant(e) *condescending*
déçu(e) *disappointed*
°**émancipé(e)**
enthousiaste
fort(e) *strong*
intitulé(e) *entitled*
opprimé(e) *oppressed*
soi-disant (invariable) *so-called*

Pronoms

ceci *this*
celui, celle, ceux, celles *this (that) one, these, those*
chacun(e) *each one*

Divers

à moitié *half*
autrement *otherwise, differently*
bien que *although*
ça en vaut la peine *it's worth the effort*
dommage, il est dommage, c'est dommage *it's a pity, it's too bad*
en cachette *secretly*
n'importe qui *no matter who, anyone*

18

CHAPITRE DIX-HUIT

Communication objectives

Talking about rights and obligations

1. Referring to unspecified people and things
2. Talking about what was and what could have been
3. Talking about future events
4. Expressing opinions about past events

Structures

Les mots et la vie : Les devoirs et les responsabilités des citoyens

    Les pronoms indéfinis

    Le plus-que-parfait et le conditionnel passé

    Le futur antérieur

    Le subjonctif passé

Vivre en France

Mise en scène

À chacun sa vérité

CHRISTIAN ET MONIQUE

Christian et Monique ont décidé de quitter la ville pour aller vivre à la campagne.

« Il y a sept ans, raconte Christian, j'étais avocat et ma femme était professeur. Nous avions un très joli appartement à Paris. Un jour, en nous promenant dans la campagne, nous avons trouvé une vieille ferme qui était *à vendre*. Nous l'avons achetée pour aller y passer les week-ends. Pendant l'été nous avons commencé à la réparer avec l'aide de quelques amis qui, eux aussi, *en avaient marre* des *embouteillages* parisiens. On était heureux ici, on a eu envie de rester et c'est ce qu'on a fait.

Et puis aussi, ma femme et moi, nous voulions avoir des enfants, mais nous ne voulions pas qu'ils grandissent dans l'atmosphère stérile et *déprimante* d'une ville. Nous voulions qu'ils puissent grandir libres et heureux, qu'ils apprennent en regardant vivre les gens et les *bêtes* autour d'eux. Nous voulions qu'ils sachent que le travail peut être un plaisir si on aime ce qu'on fait. Ici, nous produisons presque tout ce dont nous avons besoin et *au lieu de* vendre nos produits nous *faisons des échanges* avec nos voisins. Nous redécouvrons la joie du travail et la joie de vivre. »

SYLVIANE

Sylviane, elle, voudrait vivre dans une *communauté* urbaine.

« Moi, dit-elle, je voudrais vivre dans une communauté, mais pas tout de suite. Je veux d'abord terminer mes études. Mes parents voudraient que

---

for sale

where fed up / traffic jams

depressing

animals

instead of / barter

commune

je me marie, que j'aie des enfants et que j'aille habiter dans une banlieue tranquille. Mais ce genre de vie n'est pas pour moi. Je veux que ma vie serve à quelque chose. Personnellement, j'aimerais bien vivre à la campagne, mais je pense que c'est dans les villes que l'avenir du monde va être décidé. Je ne pense pas que nous ayons le droit d'abandonner ces décisions aux politiciens. Mais il est *également* important que nous apprenions à vivre et à lutter ensemble. »

just as, equally

MARIE-HÉLÈNE

Marie-Hélène, elle, est fille de *cultivateurs*. Elle a quitté la ferme pour aller faire ses études en ville, mais maintenant, elle a décidé de revenir au village pour *prendre la succession de* son père.

farmers

take over for

« Les gens ne croient pas que je puisse m'occuper d'une ferme parce que je suis une femme, dit-elle. Mais je suis en bonne santé et je n'ai pas peur de travailler dur. *D'ailleurs*, une femme peut conduire un tracteur tout aussi bien qu'un homme. Et puis, à la campagne, on a besoin de gens jeunes, enthousiastes et ouverts aux idées nouvelles. Mais dans la plupart des petits villages, surtout dans les régions où le *sol* n'est pas très riche, il n'y a que les vieux qui restent. Et les jeunes, eux, n'ont qu'une envie : quitter la ferme et aller vivre en ville où la vie est plus facile. Moi aussi, surtout avec les études que j'ai faites, je pourrai avoir une bonne situation en ville, mais je doute que ma vie y soit plus heureuse ou plus utile qu'ici.

besides

soil

Je ne regrette pourtant pas d'avoir fait des études. Le baccalauréat, *à quoi ça sert* ? me direz-vous. Je crois que les choses que j'ai apprises à l'école pourront m'être utiles ici. Et même si elles ne sont pas directement utiles, je ne crois pas que ce soit une *perte* de temps. Il est toujours bon qu'une personne soit aussi *cultivée* que possible. Je crois que c'est surtout pour ça que mes parents voulaient que je fasse des études ; pour ça et pour que j'aie la liberté de choisir ce que je voudrais vraiment. Ils ne voulaient pas m'influencer, mais maintenant ils sont bien contents que je revienne au village. Et moi aussi. »

what good is it ?

waste
cultured, educated

MICHEL

Le père de Michel voulait que son fils fasse des études de droit et qu'il prenne ensuite sa succession à la tête de la compagnie qu'il *dirige*. Au début, Michel ne s'y est pas opposé, mais maintenant il a des doutes.

runs, directs

« J'ai *fait mon droit* parce que mon père le voulait. Mais je ne suis pas sûr que ce soit ce que je veux vraiment. Je pourrais gagner beaucoup d'argent, c'est vrai, mais je ne suis pas sûr d'être *taillé* pour ce rôle. Le commerce m'ennuie. Ma *véritable* vocation, c'est l'*enseignement*. Je sais bien que c'est un travail difficile et mal payé, mais dans la vie, ce qui compte c'est de faire un métier qu'on aime. Mais j'ai peur que mes parents soient terriblement *déçus*. C'est *bête* d'ailleurs, parce que ma sœur, elle, s'intéresse aux *affaires* et je suis sûr qu'elle serait bien plus capable que moi de diriger une compagnie. Mais mon père ne veut pas *en entendre parler*. Il va *falloir* que nous essayions de le persuader. »

studied law

cut out
true, real / teaching

disappointed / stupid / business

hear about it / *falloir* = infinitive of *il faut*

Compréhension. Répondez aux questions suivantes selon les renseignements donnés dans le texte.

1. Qu'est-ce que Christian et Monique faisaient avant d'aller vivre à la campagne ?

Have students prepare brief oral or written descriptions of one or several of the people described. Students can also be asked to role-play one of these people ; other students can ask them questions.

2. Pourquoi ont-ils décidé de quitter Paris ?
3. Qu'est-ce qui leur plaît dans leur nouvelle vie ?
4. Qu'est-ce que les parents de Sylviane voulaient qu'elle fasse ?
5. Et elle, que veut-elle faire dans la vie ?
6. Pourquoi Marie-Hélène a-t-elle décidé de revenir à la ferme quand la plupart des autres jeunes quittent la campagne ?
7. Pourquoi Marie-Hélène ne regrette-t-elle pas d'avoir fait des études ?
8. Quel conflit existe-t-il entre les désirs de Michel et ceux de son père ?
9. En quoi Michel et sa sœur sont-ils différents l'un de l'autre ?

Notes culturelles: *L'individualisme français*

Les Français pour qui l'individualisme est une vertu (bien qu'ils soient souvent assez conformistes dans leur vie de tous les jours) ont une admiration particulière pour ceux qui ont eu le courage de dire non. *Que ce soit* dans le domaine des arts, de la politique ou de la science, il y a eu au cours des siècles des hommes et des femmes qui ont eu le courage de *mettre en question* les idées établies. Ainsi, dans le domaine scientifique, la ténacité de Pasteur a ouvert la *voie* à la biologie moderne. Dans le domaine artistique, des peintres *tels que* Cézanne et Matisse ont révolutionné notre *sensibilité* artistique. À la fin du siècle dernier, l'*écrivain* Émile Zola s'est opposé à l'antisémitisme *voilé* du gouvernement en prenant la défense de Dreyfus dans sa célèbre lettre intitulée « J'accuse ».

    Quelquefois ce sont des gens humbles et obscurs qui ont changé le cours de l'histoire. C'est le cas, par exemple, de la petite paysanne Jeanne d'Arc qui a su persuader le *roi* de lui *confier* une armée pour aller défendre la France contre les Anglais. Plus récemment, il y a l'exemple des *milliers* de Français qui, pendant l'occupation allemande, ont répondu à l'*appel* du général de Gaulle et ont lutté dans la Résistance, même quand tout semblait perdu.

whether it

challenge
way
such as
sensitivity
writer / veiled

king / to give

thousands
call, appeal

Les mots et la vie : *Les devoirs et les responsabilités des citoyens*

Étudiez le vocabulaire et ensuite faites les activités indiquées.

Les devoirs *(duties)* **du citoyen**
Il faut...   obéir aux lois   voter
faire son service national   se tenir au courant
payer ses impôts *(taxes)*   *(keep up-to-date)* de ce qui se passe

Les représentants du gouvernement et de l'administration
le maire *(mayor)*   le Premier ministre
le conseiller municipal *(city council member)*   le président de la République
le député   le préfet du département
le sénateur   le fonctionnaire *(civil servant)*

Les infractions
commettre un crime
commettre une infraction à la loi
commettre une infraction au code de la route *(driving rules and regulations)*
*recevoir une contravention *(to get a ticket)*
aller en prison

Les règles et les contraintes dans la vie de tous les jours

Défense de stationner

no parking

Défense de fumer

no smoking

Poussez

push

Priorité à droite

yield to the vehicle
on the right

Défense d'afficher

post no bills

Porte de secours

emergency exit

Il est interdit de marcher sur les pelouses

forbidden / lawns

Sens unique

one-way street

Prière de sonner avant d'entrer

please ring

Point out that *prière de* is a formal way to say *s'il vous plaît.*

Tirez

pull

Entrée interdite

Prière de ne pas déranger

please do not disturb

Frappez, s.v.p.

please knock

Explain that *s.v.p.* is the abbreviation for *s'il vous plaît.*

Chien méchant

beware of the dog (méchant
= bad, mean, naughty)

Défense de parler au chauffeur

Stationnement réservé aux taxis

parking

Sortie obligatoire

this way out

Propriété privée

private

---

*Recevoir is an irregular verb whose present tense forms are : **je reçois, tu reçois, il /
elle / on reçoit, nous recevons, vous recevez, ils / elles reçoivent.** Passé composé : **j'ai
reçu,** etc. ; **futur : je recevrai,** etc. ; **subjonctif : que je reçoive, que nous recevions.**

L'Assemblée nationale dans la Chambre des Députés

A. **Opinions.** Quelle est votre opinion sur chacun des points suivants ?

1. **Les lois :** Êtes-vous satisfait(e) des lois que nous avons dans ce pays ? Y en a-t-il qu'il faudrait changer ? Si oui, lesquelles et pourquoi ?

2. **Le service militaire :** Êtes-vous pour ou contre le service militaire pour les hommes ? Et pour les femmes ? Que pensez-vous des objecteurs de conscience ? Que pensez-vous des alternatives civiles au service militaire (comme le Corps de la Paix) ?

3. **L'information :** Est-ce que vous vous tenez au courant de ce qui se passe dans votre ville ? Dans votre état ? Dans votre pays ? Dans le monde ? Comment est-ce que vous vous tenez au courant ?

4. **Le choix des représentants :** Savez-vous le nom de votre maire ? De vos conseillers municipaux ? De votre député ? De vos sénateurs ? Est-ce que vous êtes content(e) d'eux ? Aimeriez-vous occuper un de ces postes ? Si oui, lequel et pourquoi ?

Have students campaign for various offices and have an election following the French system.

B. **Prière de répondre.** Parmi les inscriptions présentées dans la dernière partie de **Les mots et la vie**, quelles sont celles qu'on peut voir… ?

sur une autoroute
sur une porte
dans une pièce

dans la rue
sur le mur d'un bâtiment
dans un train ou dans un autobus

Have students think of signs that could be used in the classroom (e.g., *Prière de ne pas fumer*).

Tell students that in France one must always yield the right of way to the person on the right unless otherwise indicated.

Explorations
❧Referring to unspecified people and things
Les pronoms indéfinis

Présentation

Indefinite pronouns can be used when there is no specific antecedent. The principal indefinite pronouns are :

This presentation integrates indefinite pronouns, some of which have been used receptively already. Since this is basically a review section, it could be omitted if necessary.

A. Quelqu'un (someone), **quelque chose** (something), **quelque part** (somewhere). These forms are considered masculine and are always singular.

> **Quelqu'un** m'a téléphoné.
> — Avez-vous rencontré **quelqu'un** ? — Non, je n'ai rencontré personne.
> Je ne les vois **nulle part** ; ils sont allés **quelque part**, mais je ne sais pas où.
> — Avez-vous **quelque chose** à boire ? — Non, nous n'avons rien à boire.

Note the negative counterpart of these pronouns : **quelqu'un — personne** ; **quelque chose — rien** (nothing) ; **quelque part — nulle part** (nowhere).

When **quelqu'un** and **quelque chose** and their negative counterparts are modified by adjectives, the adjectives are preceded by **de** and are always masculine singular.

> Nous avons fait la connaissance de **quelqu'un d'intéressant**.
> Est-ce que vous avez découvert **quelque chose de nouveau** ?
> Il n'y a **rien d'amusant** à faire ici.

One of the most frequently used adjectives that can modify indefinite pronouns is **autre** (else) :

quelqu'un d'autre *someone else*	personne d'autre *no one else*
quelque chose d'autre *something else*	rien d'autre *nothing else*

> Nous ne savons **rien d'autre** à leur sujet.
> Connaissez-vous **quelqu'un d'autre** ?

Note, however, that the word for *elsewhere* or *somewhere else* is **ailleurs**.

B. Quelques-uns, **quelques-unes** (some, a few) can refer to people or things :

> **Quelques-unes** de ces vieilles maisons sont à vendre.
> Il nous a présenté **quelques-uns** de ses amis.

The pronoun **en** is used with **quelques-uns** and **quelques-unes** when they are direct objects.

Ils ont acheté quelques livres. Ils **en** ont acheté **quelques-uns**.
Nous avons visité **quelques-unes de** ces villes. Nous **en** avons visité **quelques-unes**.

C. Plusieurs (*several*) :

Plusieurs de mes ancêtres viennent de France.
Parmi les restaurants de cette ville, **plusieurs** sont excellents.

The partitive pronoun **en** is used when **plusieurs** is a direct object.

Elles ont gagné plusieurs matchs.   Elles **en** ont gagné **plusieurs**.

J'ai déjà entendu plusieurs de ces chansons.   J'**en** ai déjà entendu **plusieurs**.

D. Un(e) autre (*another one*), **d'autres** (*others*), **certain(e)s** (*certain ones, some*) :

Un de mes ancêtres vient d'Afrique et **un autre** vient d'Espagne.
Certaines de ces lois sont injustes.
Certains se passionnent pour la politique ; **d'autres** ne s'y intéressent pas du tout.

The pronoun **en** is used with **autre(s)** and **certain(e)s** when they are direct objects.

Je voudrais un autre sandwich. Apportez-m'**en un autre**, s'il vous plaît.

E. Chacun, chacune (*each one*) :

Chacun a le droit de faire ce qu'il veut.
J'ai écrit à **chacune** de mes amies, mais aucune n'a répondu.

Note that the negative counterpart of **chacun, chacune** is **aucun, aucune** (*none, not one*). **Aucun, aucune** also contrasts with **plusieurs, quelques-uns, certains**, and **tous**.

J'ai envoyé **plusieurs** lettres, mais je n'en ai reçu **aucune**.
Aucun des députés n'a assisté à cette réunion.

Transformation : Modèle : Nous avons étudié plusieurs documents. → Nous en avons étudié plusieurs. (1) Ils ont visité quelques châteaux. (2) Tu as écrit une autre lettre. (3) On va lire quelques romans. (4) Elle a visité plusieurs pays européens. *Modéle :* Est-ce que quelqu'un veut sortir? → Non, personne ne veut sortir. (1) Est-ce que quelque chose t'intéresse ? (2) Certaines de ces lois sont-elles injustes ? (3) Est-ce qu'il y a quelqu'un à la porte ? (4) Avez-vous quelque chose d'autre à dire ? (5) Est-ce que vous avez vu quelque chose d'amusant ? (6) A-t-il compris quelque chose ? (7) Est-ce qe tu veux aller quelque part ?

Mise en situation

À la pharmacie. Arnaud ne se sent pas très bien. Il demande à la pharmacienne si elle pourrait lui donner quelque chose.

ARNAUD	Est-ce que vous pourriez me donner quelque chose *contre* le *rhume des foins*? Voici les comprimés que je prends d'habitude. J'en ai encore quelques-uns...
LA PHARMACIENNE	Je regrette, mais je ne peux rien vous donner sans une ordonnance du médecin.

against
hay fever

Unlike the American Social Security system, *la Sécurité Sociale* in France refers to a government-run system financed by contributions from employers and employees and by special taxes. It covers expenses such as medical insurance, prescriptions, retirement pensions, family allocations, job-related accidents, unemployment, and funds for the low-income elderly. In 1981, an additional 1% tax was levied ; the revenues from this tax are used to supplement the social security pension for those who have no retirement income other than social security. From 60% to 100% of prescription medicine costs are reimbursed through the *Sécurité Sociale* and medical expenses from 80% to 100%.

ARNAUD	Je crois que j'en ai une. Elle doit être quelque part dans mon portefeuille. Ah, la voilà !
LA PHARMACIENNE	Nous n'avons pas ce médicament. Mais je peux vous donner quelque chose d'autre qui a à peu près le même effet. Est-ce qu'il y a des médicaments auxquels vous êtes allergique ?
ARNAUD	Non, aucun.
LA PHARMACIENNE	Chacun *réagit* différemment. Certains tolèrent très bien ce médicament ; d'autres disent que ça leur donne des *brûlures d'estomac*.
ARNAUD	Ne vous inquiétez pas. J'ai un estomac de *fer* !

reacts

heartburn

iron

Préparation

A. La passion de la généalogie. Deux amis parlent de leurs recherches généalogiques et de ce qu'ils ont appris à propos de leurs ancêtres. Qu'est-ce qu'ils disent ?

Option : English cues can be used.

> **Modèle**   Est-ce que vous avez trouvé des documents qui étaient intéressants ? (oui, quelques-uns)
> **Oui, j'en ai trouvé quelques-uns.**

1. Est-ce que vous avez des ancêtres français ? (oui, plusieurs)
2. Est-ce que vous avez des ancêtres célèbres ? (non, aucun)
3. Est-ce que vous avez des parents qui habitent en Louisiane ? (oui, quelques-uns)
4. Est-ce qu'il y a quelqu'un d'autre qui s'intéresse à l'histoire de votre famille ? (non, personne)
5. Est-ce que vous avez trouvé quelque chose d'intéressant dans vos recherches ? (non, rien)

B. Tout le monde n'est pas dans la même situation. Jean-Luc est de mauvaise humeur et il a l'impression que tout le monde est contre lui. Son amie Catherine, par contre, est de très bonne humeur et tout va bien pour elle. Donnez les réponses de Catherine.

Options : (1) Give students these statements in English and have them give the French equivalents. They can then compare their sentences with those in the exercise. (2) Give an affirmative response (*J'ai rencontré quelqu'un d'intéressant*) and have students give the negative (*Je n'ai rencontré personne d'intéressant*).

> **Modèle**   Je n'ai rencontré personne d'intéressant hier.
> **Moi, j'ai rencontré quelqu'un d'intéressant.**

1. Je n'ai rien mangé de bon au restaurant universitaire.
2. Personne ne m'a téléphoné ce matin.
3. Je n'ai rien vu de nouveau.
4. Rien d'intéressant ne m'est arrivé hier.
5. Je n'ai rien acheté de nouveau en ville.
6. Je n'ai rien d'autre à te dire.
7. Je n'ai écrit aucune lettre cette semaine.
8. Aucun de mes amis n'est venu me voir.

Communication et vie pratique

Questions / interview. Répondez aux questions suivantes ou utilisez-les pour interviewer un(e) autre étudiant(e).

Option : If used in small groups, encourage students to ask related questions.

1. Est-ce que tu as téléphoné à quelqu'un hier soir ? Est-ce que quelqu'un t'a téléphoné ?
2. Est-ce que tu as fait quelque chose d'intéressant pendant le week-end ?
3. Est-ce que quelques-uns de tes amis ont déjà voyagé en Europe ? Si oui, quels pays ont-ils visités ?
4. Est-ce que tu aimes travailler avec quelqu'un d'autre ou est-ce que tu préfères travailler seul(e) ?
5. Est-ce que tu as fait la connaissance de quelqu'un d'intéressant récemment ?
6. Est-ce que quelque chose d'amusant t'est arrivé cette semaine ?
7. Est-ce que tu penses que certaines de nos lois soient injustes ? Si oui, lesquelles ?
8. Est-ce que tu connais bien chacun de tes professeurs ?

C'est votre tour. Vous êtes en France et vous avez un petit problème de santé (mal à la gorge, rhume, allergie, etc.). Vous demandez au pharmacien ou à la pharmacienne — joué(e) par un(e) autre étudiant(e) — s'il / si elle peut vous donner quelque chose. Utilisez la **Mise en situation** comme guide.

Preparation : Have students review the vocabulary in *Les mots et la vie* of chapter 11 before doing their role-plays.

❧ Talking about what was and what could have been
Le plus-que-parfait et le conditionnel passé

Présentation

A. The **plus-que-parfait** (*pluperfect*, or *past perfect tense*) is used to indicate that one past action occurred before a second past action. The second past action is sometimes stated and sometimes simply understood : *I didn't know you had finished already. They had not performed yet.*

The **plus-que-parfait** is formed by using the imperfect of **avoir** or **être** plus the past participle.

Le plus-que-parfait de *vendre*	
j'avais vendu	nous avions vendu
tu avais vendu	vous aviez vendu
il / elle / on avait vendu	ils / elles avaient vendu

Le plus-que-parfait de *partir*

j'étais parti(e)	nous étions parti(e)s
tu étais parti(e)	vous étiez parti(e)(s)
il / elle / on était parti(e)	ils / elles étaient parti(e)s

Elle **avait déjà publié** plusieurs albums quand elle est devenue célèbre.

Ils ont visité la Grèce l'été dernier parce qu'ils n'y **étaient jamais allés** avant.

Je **m'étais coupé** le doigt en ouvrant une boîte.

Elle **n'avait jamais pensé** à se marier.

Nous **n'avions jamais entendu** parler d'eux.

B. The **conditionnel passé** (*past conditional tense*) is used to describe a past hypothetical event or condition (e.g., *They would have preferred to stay*). It is composed of the conditional tense of **avoir** or **être** and the past participle.

Le conditionnel passé de *parler*

j'aurais parlé	nous aurions parlé
tu aurais parlé	vous auriez parlé
il / elle / on aurait parlé	ils / elles / auraient parlé

Le conditionnel passé d'*aller*

je serais allé(e)	nous serions allé(e)s
tu serais allé(e)	vous seriez allé(e)(s)
il / elle / on serait allé(e)	ils / elles seraient allé(e)s

À votre place, je **n'aurais pas dit** ça.	*If I were you, I wouldn't have said that.*
Dans ce cas-là, il **aurait mieux valu** que vous partiez.	*In that case, it would have been better for you to leave.*
Moi, je **n'aurais jamais pu** faire ça.	*I would never have been able to do that.*
Je suis sûr qu'elle **se serait bien débrouillée**.	*I'm sure that she would have gotten along nicely.*

C. In French, as in English, the past conditional frequently occurs in sentences that contain a **si** clause. In such cases, the verb in the **si** clause is in the **plus-que-parfait** and the verb in the result clause in the **conditionnel passé**.

S'il **avait fait** beau, nous **serions allés** à la plage.

Ça **ne serait pas arrivé** si tu **avais fait** attention.

Si vous **aviez écouté**, vous **auriez compris**.

Ils **se seraient bien amusés** s'ils **étaient venus**.

You may want to point out the difference between sentences such as *Ils ont dit qu'ils préféreraient venir un autre jour* and *Ils ont dit qu'ils auraient préféré venir un autre jour*. Both express the idea of the future in relation to the past, but the *conditionnel passé* implies that what they would have preferred is impossible to realize.

You may want to review the tense sequences used with si clauses.

Substitution (plus-que-parfait) : (1) Je n'avais jamais fait cela. *(nous / vous / tu / on / nos amis)* (2) Nous étions déjà arrivés. *(vous / tu / les invités / mon oncle / je)* (3) Le jour précédent, je m'étais réveillé à dix heures. *(tu / ma mère / nous / vous / les autres)* *Substitution (conditionnel passé)* : (1) Moi, j'aurais fait la même chose. *(tu / nous / ma sœur / les autres / vous)* (2) À sa place, je serais venue plus tôt. *(nous / je / vous / tu / Micheline) Substitution* (les phrases avec *si)* : (1) S'il avait fait beau, nous serions allés à la plage. *(je / Marie et moi / mes amis / vous / Jean-Pierre)* (2) Cela ne serait pas arrivé si tu avais fait attention. *(je / nous / les enfants / vous / mon petit frère)* (3) Si j'avais eu plus d'argent, j'aurais acheté une voiture de sport. *(tu / les Charpentier / vous / nous / Céline)*.

Mise en situation

À l'hôtel. Les Verdier vont passer quelques jours au Pays basque où ils ont une petite propriété. Ils ont l'habitude de s'arrêter pour passer la nuit dans un petit hôtel qu'ils connaissent.

MME VERDIER	Bonjour, Madame Duchêne. Nous voici encore une fois ! Vous avez quelque chose pour la nuit ?
MME DUCHÊNE	Non, je regrette. Il n'y a plus rien. Si vous nous *aviez prévenu* de votre arrivée, j'aurais pu vous *garder* quelque chose.
M. VERDIER	Et à côté, à l'auberge du Vieux-Pont, c'est plein aussi ?
MME DUCHÊNE	Je crois qu'ils viennent de louer leur dernière chambre à des Anglais qui sont arrivés juste avant vous. Si vous étiez arrivés dix minutes plus tôt, vous auriez pu l'avoir.
M. VERDIER	*Je te l'avais bien dit !* Nous aurions dû réserver une chambre à l'avance.
MME VERDIER	Oui, mais si tu n'avais pas insisté pour qu'on déjeune en route, nous ne serions pas arrivés si tard, et tout n'aurait pas été pris.
M. VERDIER	On ne peut jamais compter sur toi. Si j'avais su, je me serais occupé de tout ça moi-même.
MME VERDIER	C'aurait été une excellente idée.

Point out that the *Pays Basque* is located in the southwesternmost corner of France, near the *Pyrénées*. The costal region is a popular tourist area, especially Biarritz. When speaking of *les Basques,* one refers not only to those living in France in

had warned

to hold

the department of the *Basses Pyrénées* but also to those living in Spanish Basque country. Fiercely independent, some Basques, particularly in Spain, have formed a vocal

I told you so !

(and sometimes violent) separatist movement. The Basques are known to be the descendants of one of the oldest peoples who inhabited France. Their ancient language, customs, and traditions distinguish them from other Europeans. *La pelote basque* (jai alai) originated there and is a very popular sport in the area.

Préparation

A. Sur la piste des ancêtres. Philippe Laforêt, un « Cajun » de Louisiane, a retrouvé la trace d'un de ses ancêtres, Jean-Baptiste Laforêt, qui a émigré au Canada quand il était jeune.

Modèle   Jean-Baptiste / naître en France
Jean-Baptiste était né en France.

1. il / vivre les premières années de sa vie en Normandie
2. il / venir au Canada quand il avait seize ans
3. il / s'installer en Acadie
4. il / apprendre le métier de boulanger
5. il / rencontrer Angèle, sa future femme, quelques années plus tard
6. Angèle / grandir en Acadie
7. ses parents / mourir quand elle avait douze ans
8. elle / s'occuper de ses petits frères et sœurs
9. elle / se débrouiller toute seule pour les élever
10. Jean-Baptiste et Angèle / se marier en 1750
11. ils / réussir à acheter une boutique
12. ils / devoir tout quitter quelques années plus tard

Nearly 6,000 Acadians (French colonists who had settled in Acadia) were forced to flee to—or were deported to—Louisiana between 1765 and 1780 after Acadia was taken over by the British. Longfellow memorialized this tragic exodus in his long poem "Evangeline." The Canadian singer Angèle Arsenault has also treated this topic in her song, "Évangéline."

B. Une réunion de famille. À une réunion de famille, les différents membres de la famille échangent des nouvelles et parlent de leur vie.

Modèle Il a fait très froid l'hiver passé. (l'hiver précédent, assez beau)
L'hiver précédent, il avait fait assez beau.

1. L'été passé nous avons fait de l'alpinisme. (l'été précédent, du ski nautique)
2. Nous avons loué une petite maison. (l'été précédent, rester à l'hôtel)
3. L'année dernière mon fils a travaillé dans un restaurant. (avant ça, dans un hôpital)
4. Nous avons acheté notre bateau il y a deux ans. (l'année précédente, notre voiture)
5. L'année dernière ma fille a gagné le marathon. (l'année d'avant, une course cycliste)
6. Le trimestre passé j'ai suivi un cours de biologie (le trimestre précédent, un cours de chimie)
7. Cette saison, notre équipe a gagné trois matchs. (la saison précédente, six matchs)

C. À votre place. Il y a toujours des gens qui pensent que leurs idées sont meilleures que celles des autres. Jean-Marie Dubourg est une de ces personnes et il n'a pas peur de dire ce que lui, il aurait fait s'il s'était trouvé dans la situation en question. Qu'est-ce qu'il dit ?

Follow-up : Change to *nous, il(s), elle(s),* etc.

Modèle prendre le train
À votre place, j'aurais pris le train.

1. téléphoner à la police
2. me coucher plus tôt
3. venir à huit heures
4. m'arrêter immédiatement
5. réagir d'une autre façon
6. dire ce que je pensais
7. ne pas me mettre en colère
8. ne rien répondre

D. Si j'avais eu plus de temps… Un groupe d'Américains parlent de leurs voyages récents en France et chacun dit ce qu'il / elle aurait fait s'ils avaient eu plus de temps. Qu'est-ce qu'ils disent ?

Modèle je / rendre visite à des amis
Si j'avais eu plus de temps, j'aurais rendu visite à des amis.

1. nous / rester plus longtemps à Paris
2. tu / aller à Chamonix
3. nous / visiter les châteaux de la Loire
4. vous / passer deux semaines en Provence
5. je / se promener le long de la Seine
6. Robert / faire du camping en Bretagne

Communication et vie pratique

A. Questions / interview. Répondez aux questions suivantes ou utilisez-les pour interviewer un(e) autre étudiant(e).

1. Est-ce que tu avais choisi ta future profession avant de commencer tes études à l'université?
2. Est-ce que tu avais déjà visité le campus avant de venir ici?
3. Est-ce que tu avais consulté d'autres personnes avant de prendre la décision de venir ici?
4. Est-ce que tu avais déjà rencontré d'autres étudiants de cette université avant de venir ici?
5. Est-ce que tu avais étudié le français avant de venir à l'université?
6. Est-ce que tu avais déjà étudié une autre langue avant de commencer l'étude du français?
7. Est-ce que tu avais déjà parlé avec ton professeur avant de commencer ce cours?

Option : Have two students interview each other in front of the class. The rest of the class listens and takes notes. Then have listeners prepare a written or oral summary of the conversation.

B. Si... Imaginez ce qui se serait passé si les événements suivants avaient eu lieu.

1. Si j'étais né(e) en France...
2. Si la guerre de Sécession (la guerre civile) avait été gagnée par le Sud plutôt que par le Nord...
3. Si Christophe Colomb n'avait pas découvert l'Amérique...
4. Si on n'avait pas inventé l'automobile...
5. Si je n'avais pas décidé de faire mes études ici...
6. Si j'avais été totalement libre de choisir mes cours...
7. Si j'étais né(e) il y a deux cents ans...
8. Si les Indiens avaient été mieux traités par les pionniers...

Written preparation helpful. Elicit student responses through questions (e.g., *Qu'est-ce que vous auriez fait si vous étiez né(e) en France ?*).

C. Réactions. Nous avons tous des réactions différentes. Qu'est-ce que vous auriez fait si vous aviez été à la place des personnes décrites dans les paragraphes suivants?

1. Paulette Dufour, une dame de soixante ans, se promenait dans la rue quand un jeune garçon lui a volé son sac. Elle a réussi à attraper le voleur et elle l'a emmené au poste de police. Et vous, qu'est-ce que vous auriez fait si vous aviez été à sa place?
2. Giselle avait besoin de faire réparer sa voiture. Elle a pris rendez-vous chez le garagiste pour sept heures et demie. Elle y est arrivée à sept heures et demie précises. Elle a attendu pendant plus d'une heure. Furieuse, elle a finalement quitté le garage pour aller à son travail. Si vous aviez été dans la même situation, qu'est-ce que vous auriez fait?
3. Les Duroc conduisaient sur une petite route de campagne quand ils ont vu un jeune homme dont la voiture était apparemment tombée en panne. Monsieur Duroc ne voulait pas s'arrêter mais Madame Duroc a insisté qu'ils aident le jeune homme. Qu'est-ce que vous auriez fait à leur place?

Assign as homework or allow students time to think about what they would have done. Have them compare and contrast their answers and come up with what would have been the best course of action in each of these situations. If desired, each situation could be used for role-plays.

4. Quand Monsieur et Madame Rochefort ont gagné vingt mille francs à la loterie nationale, ils ont mis tout cet argent à la banque. Si vous aviez gagné cet argent, qu'est-ce que vous auriez fait ?

5. Robert vient de s'acheter une guitare. Il paie et le vendeur lui rend la monnaie. En sortant du magasin, il vérifie sa monnaie et il réalise que le vendeur lui a rendu cinquante francs de trop. « C'est mon jour de chance, » pense-t-il. Qu'est-ce que vous auriez fait à sa place ?

C'est votre tour. Vous voyagez avec des amis français (joués par d'autres étudiants). Vos amis devaient s'occuper de tous les préparatifs : réservations de chambres, achat des billets, etc., mais ils ne l'ont pas fait. Imaginez la conversation (à l'hôtel, à la gare, à l'aéroport, au restaurant). Utilisez la **Mise en situation** comme guide.

Have students think of ways to blame the other person (e.g., Si tu avais réservé nos places, nous aurions du partir aujourd'hui) and ways to excuse oneself (e.g., Si j'avais su que c'était si important, je l'aurais certainement fait).

✿ Talking about future events
Le futur antérieur

Présentation

The future perfect tense is used to indicate that an action will have taken place prior to another future time (*We will have finished by noon*) or prior to another future action (*They will have eaten when we get home*). It is therefore used most frequently in clauses beginning with **quand** (*when*), **lorsque** (*when*), **aussitôt que** (*as soon as*), or **dès que** (*as soon as*). It is formed by using the future of **avoir** or **être** plus the past participle.

May be taught for recognition only.

Remind students that although the meanings of quand and lorsque are essentially identical, lorsque is slightly more literary and that only quand can be used in questions.

Le futur antérieur de *parler*	
j'**aurai parlé**	nous **aurons parlé**
tu **auras parlé**	vous **aurez parlé**
il / elle / on **aura parlé**	ils / elles **auront parlé**

Le futur antérieur d'*aller*	
je **serai allé(e)**	nous **serons allé(e)s**
tu **seras allé(e)**	vous **serez allé(e)(s)**
il / elle / on **sera allé(e)**	ils / elles **seront allé(e)s**

Est-ce que vous **aurez fini** ce travail avant la fin de la semaine ?
Téléphone-moi aussitôt que tu **seras rentré**.
Nous nous mettrons à table dès que vous vous **serez lavé** les mains.
Elle vous téléphonera lorsqu'elle **se sera reposée** un peu de son voyage.

Note that while in English one does not always use the future or future perfect tense after conjunctions such as *when* or *as soon as*, in French the future or future perfect tense must be used to refer to future time. For example, **Je vous écrirai quand je serai rentré de vacances** might be expressed in English as *I'll write you when I return from vacation.*

Mise en situation

Au salon de coiffure. Madame Nathan voudrait que sa coiffeuse lui fasse un shampooing, mais elle a oublié de *prendre un rendez-vous*.

MME NATHAN	Bonjour, Madame Simon. Est-ce que vous pourriez me faire un shampooing et un brushing ce matin ?
MME SIMON	Vous avez un rendez-vous ?
MME NATHAN	Non, mais j'espérais que vous pourriez peut-être me prendre quand même…
MME SIMON	Oui, mais il faudra attendre. Je pourrai m'occuper de vous quand j'aurai fini cette permanente.
MME NATHAN	Et Josyane, elle n'est pas libre ?
MME SIMON	Non, elle est allée chercher de la monnaie. Dès qu'elle sera revenue, il faudra qu'elle fasse une *coupe*.
MME NATHAN	J'ai quelques courses à faire dans le quartier. Je pourrais revenir quand je les aurai faites ?
MME SIMON	C'est ça. Revenez quand vous aurez fini vos achats.

Related words : le coiffeur / la coiffeuse ; une coiffure ; être bien / mal coiffé ; salon de coiffure, se coiffer.

make an appointment

Substitution : (1) Vous aurez vite oublié ces problèmes. *(nous / tu / Chantal / les autres / je)* (2) Quand vous aurez fini, vous pourrez partir. *(je / nous / tu / Geneviève / les enfants)* (3) Téléphone-lui dès que tes amis seront arrivés. *(ta sœur / tu / tes grands-parents / nous / je)*

haircut

Bureau de vote

Préparation

A. Il faudra attendre un peu. Madame Ronchamps doit souvent rappeler à sa famille qu'on ne peut pas toujours avoir ce qu'on veut immédiatement. Qu'est-ce qu'elle dit?

Prior preparation helpful.

> **Modèle** Nous ne pouvons pas acheter une nouvelle voiture maintenant. Il faut d'abord que nous fassions des économies.
> **Nous achèterons une nouvelle voiture quand nous aurons fait des économies.**

1. Tu ne peux pas sortir tout de suite. Il faut d'abord que tu finisses ton travail.
2. Tu ne peux pas aller jouer tout de suite. Il faut d'abord que tu fasses tes devoirs.
3. Je ne peux pas m'occuper de ça maintenant. Il faut d'abord que je prépare le dîner.
4. Vous ne pouvez pas commencer à manger tout de suite. Il faut d'abord que tes frères finissent de mettre la table.
5. Tu ne peux pas déjeuner tout de suite. Il faut d'abord que tu t'habilles.
6. Tu ne peux pas quitter la table maintenant. Il faut d'abord que tu boives ton lait.
7. Le plombier ne peut pas venir tout de suite. Il faut d'abord qu'il finisse un autre travail.
8. Nous ne pouvons pas jouer avec toi maintenant. Il faut d'abord que nous rentrions à la maison.

B. Ne remettez pas à demain ce que vous pouvez faire aujourd'hui. Marianne a toujours une excuse pour remettre à plus tard les choses qu'elle doit faire. Donnez l'équivalent français des phrases qu'elle a prononcées.

Written preparation may be helpful.

1. I'll do my homework when I've finished reading this magazine.
2. As soon as you return, we'll talk about that.
3. I'll write you as soon as I arrive in Paris.
4. I'll look for the recipe as soon as I've rested.
5. When I buy the book, I'll begin to study.
6. I'll go home when I finish my coffee.

Communication et vie pratique

Questions / interview. Répondez aux questions suivantes ou utilisez-les pour interviewer un(e) autre étudiant(e).

1. Lorsque tu auras fini tes études, est-ce que tu chercheras du travail ou est-ce que tu voyageras pendant quelque temps?
2. Quand tu seras rentré(e) chez toi ce soir, est-ce que tu te reposeras ou est-ce que tu auras encore du travail à faire?
3. Quand tu auras gagné un peu d'argent, est-ce que tu le dépenseras ou est-ce que tu le mettras à la banque?

4. Quand tu auras fini tout ton travail ce soir, est-ce que tu liras un bon livre ou est-ce que tu te coucheras tout de suite?
5. Lorsque tu auras quitté l'université, est-ce que tu y reviendras quelquefois, ou est-ce que tu n'y reviendras jamais?
6. Lorsque tu seras arrivé(e) à l'âge de la retraite, est-ce que tu continueras à travailler ou est-ce que tu prendras ta retraite?

C'est votre tour. Imaginez que vous êtes en France et que vous allez chez le coiffeur. Expliquez au coiffeur ou à la coiffeuse — joué(e) par un(e) autre étudiant(e) — ce que vous voulez. Lui / elle de son côté, va indiquer quand il / elle pourra le faire.

Related words : une mise en plis, un séchoir, une manicure, une frange, une boucle, un rinçage, un shampooing, une coloration. Have students practice describing the type of haircut they want, using vocabulary they know.

✿ Expressing opinions about past events
Le subjonctif passé

The past subjunctive of all verbs is composed of the present subjunctive of **avoir** or **être** plus the past participle. It is used when the verb in the dependent clause represents a time period before the time of the verb in the independent clause.

Le subjonctif passé de *parler*

que j'**aie parlé**	que nous **ayons parlé**
que tu **aies parlé**	que vous **ayez parlé**
qu'il / elle / on **ait parlé**	qu'ils / elles **aient parlé**

Review present subjunctive of *avoir* and *être*.

Substitution : (1) C'est dommage que j'aie perdu. *(nous / l'équipe / vous / les garçons / tu)* (2) Je suis content que tu sois venu me voir. *(Claude / mes amis / tu / vous / quelqu'un)* (3) Je regrette que vous vous soyez mis en colère. *(le professeur / les ouvriers / tu / nous / vous)* *Transformation :* Mettez les phrases suivantes au passé du subjonctif. (1) Je regrette que vous ne puissiez pas venir. (2) C'est dommage que tu ne sortes pas avec nous. (3) Elle est surprise que nous nous levions si tôt. (4) Nous sommes contents que tu ailles en vacances avec nous. (5) Je ne suis pas sûre qu'ils s'amusent à la soirée. (6) Je suis heureuse que tu fasses des progrès.

Le subjonctif passé d'*aller*

que je **sois allé(e)**	que nous **soyons allé(e)s**
que tu **sois allé(e)**	que vous **soyez allé(e)(s)**
qu'il / elle / on **soit allé(e)**	qu'ils / elles **soient allé(e)s**

Je regrette que vous **ne soyez pas venu**.	*I'm sorry that you didn't come.*
Je suis content qu'elles **aient réussi**.	*I'm happy that they have succeeded.*
Il est possible que je **me sois trompé**.	*It's possible that I made a mistake.*

Mise en situation

Regrets. Un groupe d'amis avaient l'intention de se réunir pour passer la soirée ensemble, mais plusieurs personnes n'ont pas pu venir.

PIERRE   On a passé une soirée formidable. Mais c'est dommage que tu n'aies pas pu venir.

PHILIPPE   Oui, c'est dommage ; mais je suis content que vous vous soyez bien amusés.

JEAN-CLAUDE   Annick *a demandé de tes nouvelles*. Elle était déçue que tu ne sois pas venu.   asked about you

PHILIPPE   Ah oui ? Moi aussi, ça m'aurait fait plaisir de la revoir. Et Chantal, elle était là ?

JEAN-CLAUDE   Non, je ne l'ai pas vue. Mais il est possible qu'elle soit partie avant notre arrivée.

PIERRE   J'ai peur qu'elle *se soit trompée de jour*. Elle avait l'intention d'y aller.   got the dates confused

JEAN-CLAUDE   Tu sais, il est possible qu'*elle ait eu un empêchement* à la dernière minute.   something came up

Préparation

Réactions. Olivier donne son opinion sur ce qui est arrivé récemment à ses amis. Qu'est-ce qu'il dit ?

> Point out that *Polytechnique* refers to the *École polytechnique* in Paris. One of the most prestigious of the *Grandes Écoles,* it prepares individuals for high-level government, military, and civilian posts.

> **Modèle**   Pierre a réussi à tous ses examens. (je suis heureux)
> **Je suis heureux que Pierre ait réussi à tous ses examens.**

1. Il a été accepté à Polytechnique. (je suis content)
2. Son cousin n'a pas été accepté. (j'ai peur)
3. André a décidé d'abandonner ses études. (je ne pense pas)
4. Tu as pu trouver du travail. (je suis ravi)
5. Elle s'est trompée de route. (il est possible)
6. Vous êtes partis trop tôt. (je regrette)
7. Tu n'es pas allé voir ce film. (c'est dommage)
8. Ils sont rentrés à quatre heures du matin. (je ne crois pas)
9. Ils se sont bien amusés. (je ne suis pas sûr)
10. Nous n'avons pas pu aider Monique. (c'est dommage)

Défilé du 14 juillet

Communication et vie pratique

A. Réactions. Exprimez vos réactions ou opinions vis-à-vis des événements suivants en utilisant des expressions telles que **je suis content(e) que**, **je regrette que**, **c'est dommage que**, etc.

> **Exemple** Les Russes ont vendu l'Alaska aux États-Unis.
> **Je suis content(e) que les Russes aient vendu l'Alaska aux États-Unis.**

1. Alexander Graham Bell a inventé le téléphone.
2. On a inventé la bombe atomique.
3. On a construit beaucoup de centrales nucléaires.
4. On a ouvert beaucoup de restaurants « self-service ».
5. On a dépensé beaucoup d'argent pour l'exploration de l'espace.
6. Les frais de l'université ont augmenté.
7. Beaucoup de gens ont commencé à s'intéresser à l'environnement.
8. On a inventé l'ordinateur.

Have students make two separate lists; the first beginning with *je suis content(e) que*, the second *je regrette que*. Encourage them to add other items to their lists and then compare and contrast with other students.

B. En fin de compte… En fin de compte *(everything considered)* quelles sont vos raisons d'être satisfait(e) et quels sont vos regrets quand vous pensez à la situation présente — ou passée — dans votre pays ?

Written preparation helpful.

> **Exemples** **En fin de compte, je suis bien content que mes grands-parents aient choisi de venir vivre aux États-Unis.**
> *ou:* **Je regrette qu'on ait détruit tant de beaux paysages naturels en construisant des autoroutes et des villes.**

C'est votre tour. Vous aussi, vous aviez l'intention de passer une soirée avec des amis, mais vous avez eu un empêchement à la dernière minute. Le jour suivant vous rencontrez des amis qui étaient à la soirée. Imaginez la conversation.

Intégration et perspectives

Les Français et les Américains

L'Express a interviewé Laurence Wylie, professeur de civilisation française à Harvard et auteur de plusieurs livres sur les Français. Voici quelques-unes des conclusions *auxquelles** il est arrivé après avoir passé plusieurs années en France.

at which

LE REPORTER Vous vous intéressez beaucoup à la communication non verbale, au langage du corps et des gestes. Qu'avez-vous découvert en nous regardant vivre ?

***Lequel, laquelle, lesquels,** and **lesquelles** *(which, who, which ones)* can function as interrogative or relative pronouns. They also combine with **à** and **de**, just like the definite article.

WYLIE	Beaucoup de choses. Parlons d'abord de l'aspect physique. Les Français peuvent *reconnaître* un Américain simplement à sa façon de marcher. Un Américain a besoin de plus d'espace qu'un Français. La *démarche* d'un Français est beaucoup plus contrôlée que celle d'un Américain. Le *buste* doit être droit, les épaules immobiles, les bras près du corps. D'ailleurs, ne dit-on pas toujours aux enfants « *Tiens-toi droit !* » « Ne *traîne* pas les pieds ! » ? Bien que votre *éducation* vous enseigne à ne pas faire de *gestes*, vous ne pouvez pas résister à en faire pour amplifier l'effet de la *parole*. Mais ce sont essentiellement des gestes des mains et de l'*avant-bras*. Les Français expriment beaucoup avec leur bouche, le plus souvent *arrondie*, *sans cesse* en mouvement : le *mépris* (Peuh !), le doute (Bof !), l'admiration (Au poil !).	recognize way of walking upper body Stand up straight ! / drag upbringing gestures spoken word forearm rounded / constantly scorn
LE REPORTER	Quels sont, à votre avis, les principaux aspects de notre tempérament national ?	
WYLIE	Si vous m'aviez posé cette question il y a vingt-cinq ans, je vous aurais dit : l'attachement au passé. Les Français pensaient toujours au passé comme à une époque idéale. Aujourd'hui, je crois qu'ils vivent *davantage* dans le présent. Mais malgré tout, vous restez beaucoup plus tournés vers le passé que les Américains, pour lesquels seul le présent existe.	 more

Les vacances en famille sont importantes.

Les familles françaises sont très unies.

Un autre trait fondamental de la culture française, à mon avis, est le besoin de *définir*. Les Français ont un besoin esthétique de définitions claires et rigoureuses. Cela vous *conduit* à créer des catégories rigides, des divisions, des subdivisions, des différentiations subtiles. Prenez par exemple l'enseignement de la géographie : vous partez du *tout* — le monde — et vous le divisez en continents, à l'intérieur desquels vous étudiez successivement chacun des pays qui le composent. L'enfant américain, lui, fera des *études de cas* : comment vit un petit Argentin d'aujourd'hui, en quoi il ressemble à un petit Américain malgré les différences régionales.

define

leads

whole

case studies

LE REPORTER *En somme*, vous *insistez sur* les ressemblances ; nous insistons sur les différences.

all things considered / stress

WYLIE Oui, moi, j'aime les généralisations. Mais dans une conversation avec des Français, il y a toujours quelqu'un pour me dire : « Je ne suis pas du tout de votre avis. Vous simplifiez beaucoup trop. »

LE REPORTER Mais les Français adorent généraliser ! Même sur des sujets qu'ils ne connaissent pas !

WYLIE C'est vrai que les Français aiment bien avoir leur petite idée sur tout… Si on rencontre un médecin américain, il voudra toujours parler de médecine. Un médecin français vous parlera de musique, de littérature, de tout, sauf de médecine !

LE REPORTER Parlez-nous de vos idées sur l'éducation des enfants français.

WYLIE Je crois qu'il faut commencer par la famille. On a souvent dit que la famille était *en train de* se désintégrer. Je dirais exactement le contraire. Mais la différence est qu'elle repose aujourd'hui sur des *liens* plus *affectifs*, plus ouverts, moins autoritaires, mais *tout aussi* solides que dans le passé. Les familles françaises sont beaucoup plus *unies* que les familles américaines. Vous ne verriez pas aux États-Unis des mères et des filles se promener *bras-dessus, bras-dessous*. Ni des enfants qu'on tient par la main pour les conduire à l'école. Ni ces dimanches et ces vacances « en famille ». Cette unité-là n'existe pas chez nous. Il y a en France un effort réel de compréhension des enfants *alors qu*'en Amérique on se contente généralement de les traiter comme des *copains*.

Ce qui, *en revanche*, choque souvent les Américains, c'est le *côté* négatif de l'éducation des petits Français. La base de l'éducation française, c'est le « non » : « Non, on ne fait pas cela. Non, c'est dangereux. Non, ce n'est pas comme ça que ça se fait ! » On *empêche* l'enfant de faire des erreurs, d'apprendre par lui-même. Chez nous, c'est le contraire : l'enfant est encouragé, stimulé : « C'est bien ! Continue ! » L'enfant américain est plus *entreprenant*. En revanche, il dépend davantage des autres. La méthode française a, bien sûr, des avantages. Elle forme des enfants plus riches intérieurement, des personnalités plus fortes, qui ne comptent que sur elles-mêmes.

LE REPORTER Est-ce vrai aussi pour les adultes ?

WYLIE Dans une certaine mesure. Vous êtes *habitués à* vous *protéger* contre les autres. Vous *entourez* vos maisons d'un *mur* aussi haut que possible. Le soir, vous fermez vos *volets*. Ça se voit même dans le langage. Quand on demande à quelqu'un comment il va, il est fréquent qu'il réponde : « Je me défends. »

Vous, Français, vous vivez à l'intérieur d'un système de cercles, chaque cercle étant entouré d'un mur : le cercle de la personnalité, le cercle de la famille, le cercle des amis, le cercle des *relations* du travail… Cette importance du cercle se traduit dans le langage. Le pronom « nous » s'applique à ceux qui sont à l'intérieur du cercle ; le « ils » s'applique à tous ceux qui sont à l'extérieur. « Ils », c'est toujours « l'ennemi » — c'est-à-dire, « les autres ».

Ces cercles n'existent pas aux États-Unis. En Amérique on change d'amis et de relations quand on change de maison ou de travail. Prenez un cas typique : Un Américain rencontre un Français qui vient d'arriver aux États-Unis. Immédiatement, il l'invite à dîner chez lui. Le Français pense : « Comme les Américains sont ouverts et *accueillants* ! » La semaine suivante, il reverra cet Américain qui ne le reconnaîtra peut-être pas. Ou il verra cet Américain tous les jours pendant deux ans et

---

in the process of

ties / emotional

just as

close

arm in arm

whereas
friends, pals
on the other hand
side

prevents

enterprising

used to / protect
surround / wall
shutters

acquaintances

welcoming

leurs relations resteront au même point. Les Français ne comprennent pas ça. En France, il est difficile de pénétrer dans un de ces cercles, mais *une fois* accepté, c'est pour la vie!   **once**

Extrait et adapté d'un article de *L'Express*.

A. Compréhension. Répondez aux questions suivantes, selon les renseignements donnés dans le texte.

1. Selon Wylie, comment est-ce que les Français peuvent reconnaître un Américain dans la rue?
2. Selon Wylie, quels sont deux des principaux aspects du caractère français?
3. Qu'est-ce qui caractérise la conversation des Français? En quoi est-ce que les Américains sont différents?
4. Quels changements récents Wylie a-t-il observés dans la structure de la famille française?
5. Selon Wylie, les familles françaises sont plus unies que les familles américaines. Donnez quelques exemples de cette unité.
6. En quoi l'éducation d'un petit Français est-elle différente de celle d'un petit Américain?
7. Quels sont les avantages de chaque système d'éducation?
8. Selon Wylie, les Français ont tendance à se protéger contre les autres. Donnez quelques exemples de cette attitude.
9. Décrivez le système de cercles qui existe dans la société française.
10. Les Américains sont assez ouverts et accueillants dès qu'ils font la connaissance de quelqu'un. En quoi les Français sont-ils différents?

B. Et vous?

1. À votre avis, quels sont les traits principaux du caractère américain?
2. Qu'est-ce que vous aimeriez changer dans la façon de vivre des Américains?
3. Quelles sont vos propres idées sur l'éducation des enfants?
4. Si un Français visitait les États-Unis pour la première fois, quelles observations pourrait-il faire au sujet du style de vie des Américains?

Notes culturelles: *Le peuple et le tempérament français*

Comparée à la population américaine, la population française *paraît* très homogène et très stable. Il n'est pas rare, en effet, qu'une famille ait vécu pendant plusieurs siècles dans le même village et même quelquefois dans la même maison.   **seems**

On ne peut cependant pas parler d'une « race » française car le peuple français est le résultat de l'assimilation de groupes ethniques très divers. En effet, la France étant située à la pointe occidentale de l'Europe, c'est là que les différentes migrations est-ouest se sont arrêtées. On peut donc dire que la France est le « melting pot » de l'Europe.

Aux temps préhistoriques, trois races différentes sont venues s'installer sur le sol français : (1) la race méditerranéenne composée de chasseurs et de nomades ; (2) la race nordique dont les représentants sont grands et blonds ; (3) la race alpine (les Celtes) composée surtout d'agriculteurs. Les Celtes qui se sont fixés sur le territoire français s'appelaient les Gaulois et leur pays, la Gaule.

Plus tard, d'autres invasions ont accentué encore la richesse ethnique et la variété de la population : les Romains au premier siècle avant J.-C. ; les Francs, d'origine germanique, arrivés au cinquième siècle et qui ont donné leur nom à la France ; les Normands, d'origine scandinave, au dixième siècle. Depuis un siècle, la France connaît *de nouveau* une importante immigration de travailleurs étrangers, surtout Nord-Africains et Italiens.

Parmi les noms « bien » français, on trouve donc de nombreux noms d'origine étrangère. Les noms français les plus communs représentent des traits physiques (Legrand, Petit, Leroux, Leblanc) ; des traits psychologiques (Lesage, Lefranc) ; ou des noms de lieux (Laforêt, Dubourg, Fontaine, Deschamps, Dumont).

Selon le *Nouveau Guide France* (Guy Michaud et Georges Torrès ; Classiques Hachette) le caractère français a deux composantes principales : le Français *moyen* qui est surtout un « sanguin » et le Parisien qui est surtout un « nerveux ».

Le Français moyen	Le Parisien
Il est...	Il est...
jovial : C'est le type du *bon vivant*, souvent optimiste, *amateur* de bon vin et de bonne cuisine.	**insouciant** : Son humeur est capricieuse et frivole. Il est assez bohème.
ingénieux : Il a le sens pratique ; il sait se débrouiller. Il s'adapte facilement. Sa présence *d'esprit* en fait un brillant improvisateur.	**curieux** : Ouvert à tout, il aime jouer et voir jouer. Il paraît toujours pressé mais il aime prendre son temps. Il aime suivre la mode ou même la précéder.
sociable : Il est l'ami de tout le monde. Il se sent *bien* en compagnie.	**moqueur** : Il a l'esprit *vif* et il est toujours prêt à se moquer de quelque chose — ou de lui-même. Il aime les jeux de mots. En France on dit encore que « le ridicule *tue* ».

again

Ask students if a similar comparison can be made in the United States, e.g., between the average American and someone from a particular large city. Are there other comparisons that could be made ? If so, have students use the *Nouveau Guide France* descriptions as a guide and prepare similar ones for the U.S.

average

fun-loving / carefree
one who appreciates

of mind

quick
comfortable

kills

466

Communication et vie pratique

A. Proverbes et dictons. Bien que les proverbes et dictons fassent partie de l'héritage culturel d'un peuple et bien qu'ils reflètent dans une certaine mesure l'identité d'un peuple, beaucoup représentent aussi une sorte de sagesse sans frontière.

Introduce other proverbs.

Pouvez-vous donner l'équivalent américain des proverbes suivants ou en paraphraser le sens ? Pouvez-vous les utiliser dans un petit dialogue qui en illustre le sens ?

Quelques proverbes africains :
« Ne repoussez pas du pied la pirogue qui vous a aidé à traverser. »
« Si tu élèves un serpent, c'est sur toi-même qu'il apprendra à *mordre*. »   bite
« Tous ces coqs qui chantent, hier encore étaient des œufs. »
Quelques proverbes français :
« Les absents ont toujours tort. »
« Tel père, tel fils. »
« Petit à petit, l'oiseau fait son *nid*. »   nest
« Qui se ressemble, s'assemble. »
« Loin des yeux, loin du cœur. »
« Comme on fait son lit, on se couche. »
« Il n'y a que la vérité qui *blesse*. »   hurts
« Il n'y a que le premier *pas* qui coûte. »   step

B. Pensées et maximes. La Rochefoucauld, un écrivain français du 17ᵉ siècle, est célèbre pour ses *Maximes* dans lesquelles il expose sans indulgence nos petits et nos grands défauts. Beaucoup d'autres écrivains ou autres personnages célèbres ont aussi exprimé leurs pensées et leurs observations dans des phrases qui sont restées célèbres.

Encourage students to write their own *maximes* and share them with the class.

Indiquez si vous êtes d'accord avec ces pensées et maximes. Ensuite, écrivez vos propres maximes.

« *L'amour-propre* est le plus grand des *flatteurs*. »   self-esteem / flatterers
« On ne donne rien si généreusement que ses *conseils*. »   advice
« La *faiblesse* est plus opposée à la vertu que le vice. »   weakness
« *Il y va du* véritable amour comme de l'apparition des *esprits* ; tout le   the same goes for / spirits
monde en parle, mais peu de gens en ont vu. »
« Nous aurions souvent honte de nos plus belles actions si le monde voyait tous les motifs qui les produisent. »
« Quelque bien qu'on dise de nous, on ne nous apprend rien de nouveau. »

La Rochefoucauld, moraliste du 17ᵉ siècle

« Il faudrait essayer d'être heureux, ne serait-ce que pour donner l'exemple. »

Jacques Prévert, poète français, mort en 1977

« L'homme qui a le plus vécu n'est pas celui qui a compté le plus d'années, mais celui qui a le plus senti la vie. »

Jean-Jacques Rousseau, philosophe français du 18ᵉ siècle

C. Le français familier. Dans la conversation de tous les jours les Français utilisent souvent des mots familiers. Pouvez-vous deviner *(guess)* d'après le contexte le sens des mots en italique dans les phrases suivantes.

1. Je viens d'acheter les *bouquins* dont j'ai besoin pour mon cours d'histoire. Ils étaient *vachement* chers : ça m'a coûté 150 *balles*. Maintenant je suis complètement *fauché* et mes parents ne m'enverront pas de *fric* avant la fin du mois.

2. Il faut que je fasse réparer ma *bagnole*. Il y a toutes sortes de *trucs* qui ne marchent pas dans le moteur. Heureusement, je connais un *mec* qui est mécanicien. C'est un de mes *copains*. Comme ça, ça ne coûtera pas trop cher.

3. Je vais passer mon *bac* l'année prochaine. Il va falloir que je *bosse* parce que je ne suis pas très *calé* en *philo*. Après ça, je ne sais pas si j'irai à l'université ou si je chercherai du *boulot*. J'aimerais bien travailler dans une agence de voyage.

4. Moi, j'ai *rudement* faim ; je n'ai rien *bouffé* depuis ce matin. Il n'y avait plus rien dans le *frigo*. Vous n'avez pas envie d'aller *bouffer* quelque chose avec moi ? Il y a un petit restaurant *vachement chouette* tout près d'ici. On pourrait y aller tous ensemble. Je connais le patron ; vous verrez ; il est *sympa*.*

D. Tour d'horizon. Vous voulez laisser pour les générations futures un document qui décrive les principaux aspects de la vie contemporaine. Comment allez-vous la décrire ? Pourriez-vous aussi décrire quelques aspects de la vie en France ou dans d'autres pays francophones ?

Have students prepare descriptions of life in the United States and in France, including both differences and similarities. They should draw not only on the information provided in the Wylie text but also from what they have already learned.

*bouquins = livres ; **vachement** = très ; **balles** = francs ; **fauché** = sans argent ; **fric** = argent ; **bagnole** = voiture ; **trucs** = choses ; **mec** = homme ; **copains** = amis ; **bac** = baccalauréat ; **bosse** = travaille ; **calé** = fort ; **philo** = philosophie ; **boulot** = travail ; **rudement** = très ; **bouffé** = mangé ; **frigo** = réfrigérateur ; **bouffer** = manger ; **vachement chouette** = très bien ; **sympa** = sympathique.

• *Vocabulaire*

Noms

les représentants du gouvernement
(voir p. 445)

d'autres noms

les **affaires** (f) *business*
° l'**attachement** (m)
la **bête** *animal*
la **brûlure d'estomac** *heartburn*
° le **brushing**
le **buste** *upper body*
° le **cercle**
le **citoyen,** la **citoyenne** *citizen*

le **code de la route** *driving regulations*
le **coiffeur,** la **coiffeuse** *hairdresser, barber*
la **communauté** *community, commune*
le **contraire** *opposite*
la **contravention** *driving or parking ticket*
le **cultivateur,** la **cultivatrice** *farmer*
la **démarche** *walk, gait*
l'**effet** (m) *effect*
l'**embouteillage** (m) *traffic jam*

l'**empêchement** (m) *delay*
l'**enseignement** (m) *teaching*
le **fer** *iron*
la **ferme** *farm*
les **impôts** (m) *taxes*
l'**infraction** (f) *infraction, violation*
l'**intérieur** (m) *interior, inside*
la **loi** *law*
le **mépris** *contempt*
la **pelouse** *lawn*
° la **permanente**
la **perte** *waste, loss*
° la **prison**
le **rhume des foines** *hay fever*
le **secours** *help*
le **sens** *direction*
le **sol** *soil*
la **sortie** *exit*
° le **tempérament**
le **volet** *shutter*

Verbes

afficher *to post*
amplifier *to amplify, increase*
choquer *to shock*
commettre *to commit*
se **défendre** *to get along*
définir *to define*
désintégrer *to disintegrate*
diriger *to direct, manage*
empêcher *to hinder, keep from*
entendre parler de *to hear about*
frapper *to knock*
garder *to hold, keep*
insister *to insist, stress*
pousser *to push, press*
prévenir *to warn, tell ahead of time*
se **promener** *to walk, take a walk*
réagir *to react*
reconnaître *to recognize*
réparer *to repair*
se **réunir** *to get together*
° **simplifier**
stationner *to park*
terminer *to end*

tirer *to pull*
tolérer *to tolerate*
traîner *to drag*
traiter *to treat*
° **voter**

Adjectifs

arrondi(e) *round, rounded*
autoritaire *authoritarian*
bête *stupid*
cultivé(e) *cultured*
déprimant(e) *depressing*
entreprenant(e) *enterprising*
° **esthétique**
interdit(e) *forbidden*
méchant(e) *mean, naughty*
privé(e) *private*
° **rigoureux, -euse**
° **subtil(e)**
taillé(e) *cut out*
uni(e) *united*
véritable *true, real*

Adverbes

d'ailleurs *moreover*
davantage *more*
également *equally, likewise*

Divers

à quoi ça sert? *what good is it?*
au courant de *up to date, aware*
au lieu de *instead of*
bras dessus, bras dessous *arm in arm*
défense de *it is forbidden to*
en revanche *on the other hand*
faire des échanges *to barter*
faire son droit *to study law*
je te l'avais bien dit *I told you so*
prendre la succession de *to take over from*
prendre un rendez-vous *to make an appointment*
prière de *please*

Invitation à la lecture

Introduction

You have now mastered most of the basic forms of the French language and are ready to enjoy literary works in their original form. In order to understand literature, other kinds of formal writing, and very formal speech, a knowledge of the **passé simple** is often necessary. The **passé simple** often replaces the more conversational **passé composé** in these types of writing. Thus, reading in French requires the recognition and understanding of the forms of the **passé simple**.

Présentation

A. The forms of the **passé simple** for regular verbs are:

-er verbs, including *aller*	
je parl**ai**	nous parl**âmes**
tu parl**as**	vous parl**âtes**
il / elle / on parl**a**	ils / elles parl**èrent**

-re verbs	
je perd**is**	nous perd**îmes**
tu perd**is**	vous perd**îtes**
il / elle / on perd**it**	ils / elles perd**irent**

You may wish to suggest that students look at the full forms of irregular verbs, particularly *avoir* and *être*, in the tables in the Appendix.

470

-ir verbs, including those like *dormir*

je chois**is**	nous chois**îmes**
tu chois**is**	vous chois**îtes**
il / elle / on chois**it**	ils / elles chois**irent**

Un grand nombre de gens **perdirent** leur vie pendant la guerre.

Charles de Gaulle **organisa** la Résistance française.

Beaucoup de Français **participèrent** à la Résistance directement ou indirectement ; d'autres **choisirent** la coopération ou le silence.

B. The following endings are added to the stems of irregular verbs : **-s, -s, -t, -ˆmes, -ˆtes, -rent.**

Verb	Stem	Verb	Stem	Verb	Stem	Verb	Stem	Verb	Stem
avoir	**eu-**	croire	**cru-**	faire	**fi-**	pouvoir	**pu-**	valoir	**valu-**
boire	**bu-**	devoir	**du-**	lire	**lu-**	prendre	**pri-**	venir	**vin-**
conduire	**conduisi-**	dire	**di-**	mettre	**mi-**	rire	**ri-**	vivre	**vécu-**
connaître	**connu-**	écrire	**écrivi-**	mourir	**mouru-**	savoir	**su-**	voir	**vi-**
courir	**couru-**	être	**fu-**	naître	**naqui-**	suivre	**suivi-**	vouloir	**voulu-**

Benjamin Franklin **vécut** à Paris pendant plusieurs années.

Lafayette **se mit** au service de la Révolution américaine.

Alexis de Tocqueville **écrivit** *De la démocratie en Amérique.*

Un grand nombre d'Acadiens qui **furent** exilés du Canada **trouvèrent** refuge en Louisiane.

Les premiers Jeux Olympiques modernes **eurent** lieu en 1896.

Activités

A. Personnages et événements historiques. Les phrases suivantes décrivent certains personnes ou événements qui sont importants dans l'histoire de la France. Mettez les verbes au passé composé.

1. Madame Marie Curie obtint le prix Nobel de chimie en 1911.
2. Jacques Cartier découvrit le Saint-Laurent.
3. La France envoya une armée commandée par le comte de Rochambeau pour aider le général Washington.
4. Les États-Unis achetèrent la Louisiane à Napoléon en 1803.
5. Marcel Proust écrivit *À la recherche du temps perdu.*
6. Les Anglais furent battus par les Américains à la bataille de Yorktown.
7. Henri IV établit la liberté de religion en France en 1598.
8. Après la défaite de Waterloo, Napoléon fut exilé à l'île de Sainte-Hélène où il mourut.
9. Albert Camus, auteur du célèbre roman *La Peste*, naquit à Mondovi en Algérie.
10. Les Romains colonisèrent tout le sud de la France et construisirent des villes, des routes et des monuments.

B. **Connaissez-vous l'histoire?** Avec quel fait historique les personnages de la colonne à gauche sont-ils associés?

  1. Ferdinand de Lesseps
  2. Sarah Bernhardt
  3. Antoine-Laurent de Lavoisier
  4. Frédéric Bartholdi
  5. Louis XIV
  6. Auguste Rodin
  7. Georges Bizet
  8. Paul Gauguin
  9. Jean-François Champollion
  10. Claude-Joseph Rouget de Lisle
  11. Claude Monet
  12. Pierre de Coubertin

  a. composa l'opéra intitulé *Carmen*
  b. découvrit l'oxygène
  c. sculpta la statue du *Penseur*
  d. construisit le canal de Suez
  e. sculpta la Statue de la Liberté
  f. vécut une partie de sa vie à Tahiti
  g. fut le rénovateur des Jeux Olympiques
  h. fit construire le château de Versailles
  i. devint la plus grande actrice de son temps
  j. fut un des fondateurs de l'école impressionniste
  k. traduisit les hiéroglyphes égyptiens
  l. écrivit l'hymne national français

Réponses: 1.d; 2.i; 3.b; 4.e; 5.h; 6.c; 7.a; 8.f; 9.k; 10.l; 11.j; 12.g

Lectures

Présence française en Amérique du Nord

Il y a aujourd'hui plus de 130 millions de francophones. Le français est donc loin d'être une simple langue de culture littéraire comme on le croit souvent. Il est utilisé *à travers* le monde, non seulement par plusieurs peuples mais également par de nombreux organismes internationaux et diplomatiques. Ainsi, à l'UNESCO, les chefs de délégation qui s'expriment en français sont aussi nombreux que ceux qui s'expriment en anglais. Et aux Nations-Unies, une délégation sur trois utilise régulièrement le français.

     Sur le continent américain, c'est le Québec qui constitue le cœur de la francophonie avec ses cinq millions de francophones et son *réseau* d'institutions politiques, économiques, sociales et culturelles. Les États-Unis eux-mêmes comptent plusieurs millions de gens qui sont d'origine canadienne française.

     Bien que ce soit à New York que les Français *mirent pied à terre* pour la première fois en Amérique, c'est du Québec que partirent la plupart des explorateurs du Canada et des États-Unis. La ville de Québec elle-même fut fondée en 1608 par Samuel de Champlain. Mais avant de fonder le premier établissement permanent en Amérique, Champlain avait *parcouru*

throughout

network

set foot

traveled

Samuel de Champlain
fonde le Québec.

les *côtes* de la Nouvelle-Angleterre jusqu'à la *Nouvelle-Écosse*. Il avait ex-   coasts / Nova Scotia
ploré ce qui est aujourd'hui Boston. C'est lui aussi qui découvrit les mon-
tagnes du Vermont et le lac qui porte maintenant son nom.

    C'est du Québec aussi qu'Étienne Brûlé partit à la découverte du lac
Supérieur en 1628. Et à Red Banks dans le Wisconsin se trouve un monument qui commémore la découverte du lac Michigan par Jean Nicolet en
1634. Ce sont deux missionnaires canadiens, les pères Galinée et Dollier de
Casson qui établirent les premières cartes de l'Érié. Jolliet et Marquette
explorèrent le Mississippi jusqu'à l'Arkansas, et un monument dans le
Wyalusing State Park dans le Wisconsin honore encore leur mémoire.
L'Ohio fut découvert par Cavelier de La Salle, dont la mémoire est honorée
à South Bend dans l'Indiana. C'est lui aussi qui explora le Mississippi
jusqu'à son *embouchure* et qui construisit le premier *navire* qui naviqua sur   mouth / ship
les Grands Lacs.

On pourrait mentionner beaucoup d'autres explorateurs encore : Daniel Duluth, dont une ville du Minnesota porte le nom ; Jean-Baptiste Le Moyne de Bienville, qui fonda La Nouvelle-Orléans et qui traça les plans du *Vieux Carré* ; son frère Pierre Le Moyne d'Iberville, qui fonda les villes de Biloxi et de Mobile et qui fut le premier colonisateur de la Louisiane. Il y eut aussi Longueuil, qui explora le Tennessee et le Kentucky ; Pierre LeSueur, qui découvrit la rivière Minnesota ; les frères La Vérendrye, qui explorèrent le Dakota, le Montana et le Wyoming où beaucoup de localités portent encore des noms français ; et beaucoup d'autres qu'il serait trop long d'énumérer.

French Quarter

La colonisation du Nouveau Monde a donc été fortement marquée par la présence française. Et on peut *se demander* ce que seraient les États-Unis aujourd'hui si Napoléon n'avait pas vendu la Louisiane en 1803.

wonder

Extrait et adapté d'un discours prononcé par Gilles La Montagne, ancien maire de la ville de Québec. Le texte a paru dans le *AATF National Bulletin*.

Compréhension. Répondez aux questions suivantes selon les renseignements donnés dans le texte. Bien que le texte soit au passé simple, utilisez le passé composé dans vos réponses où il convient de l'utiliser.

1. Pourquoi peut-on dire que le français n'est pas seulement une langue de culture et qu'il garde une importance internationale ?
2. Quel rôle le Québec joue-t-il en Amérique du Nord ?
3. Est-ce qu'il y a beaucoup de gens d'origine française aux États-Unis ?
4. Quel a été le point de départ de la plupart des explorateurs du Canada et des États-Unis ?
5. Qui a fondé la ville de Québec et en quelle année ?
6. Qui a découvert le lac Supérieur et en quelle année ?
7. Pourquoi y a-t-il à South Bend un monument qui honore la mémoire de Cavelier de La Salle ?
8. Quelle a été la contribution des deux frères Le Moyne ?
9. Quelle partie des États-Unis les frères La Vérendrye ont-ils explorée ?

Les Français et la Guerre d'Indépendance

L'influence française aux États-Unis ne se limite pas à celle des explorateurs et des pionniers. Une partie des principes démocratiques sur lesquels la nation américaine est fondée ont leur origine dans les idées que les philosophes français du dix-huitième siècle — Montesquieu, Rousseau, Voltaire, Diderot, d'Alembert et d'autres — avaient exprimées dans leurs écrits. Les idées des philosophes français furent ainsi mises en pratique aux États-Unis avant même que la Révolution française de 1789 puisse imposer ces mêmes principes sur le *sol* français.

soil

Au temps de la Guerre d'Indépendance, d'autre part, les Français apportèrent une aide à la fois économique et militaire aux treize colonies qui luttaient pour leur indépendance. Une des premières missions politiques de Benjamin Franklin fut d'obtenir l'aide financière de la France. Le marquis de LaFayette de son côté, se passionna immédiatement pour la cause américaine, et après avoir équipé à ses propres *frais* un navire baptisé *La Victoire*, il vint se mettre au service de la révolution américaine.

expense

Le marquis de Lafayette pendant la bataille de Monmouth

Il faut dire *cependant* que l'aide de la France n'était pas uniquement motivée par la générosité et par l'amour de la liberté car le gouvernement français voyait là un moyen de combattre indirectement les Anglais. Il *cédait* aussi dans une certaine mesure à la pression de l'intelligentsia française qui se passionnait pour les idées des philosophes et qui voyait dans la révolution américaine l'espoir d'une victoire des idées nouvelles.

Compréhension. Selon les renseignements donnés dans le texte, comment la France a-t-elle aidé les États-Unis pendant la Guerre d'Indépendance et pourquoi est-elle venue à l'aide des Américains ?

however

gave in

475

Le lion et le rat

Il faut autant qu'on peut, obliger tout le monde :
On a souvent besoin d'un plus petit que soi.
De cette vérité deux fables feront foi, — will attest
    Tant la chose en preuves abonde. — proofs
    Entre les pattes d'un lion — paws
Un rat sortit de terre assez à l'étourdie. — dazed
Le roi des animaux, en cette occasion,
Montra ce qu'il était, et lui donna la vie.
    Ce bienfait ne fut pas perdu. — good deed
    Quelqu'un aurait-il jamais cru
    Qu'un lion d'un rat eût affaire ? — had any need
Cependant il advint qu'au sortir des forêts — came to pass / at the exit
    Ce lion fut pris dans des rets — nets
Dont ses rugissements ne le purent défaire. — roars
Sire Rat accourut, et fit tant par ses dents — came running
Qu'une maille rongée emporta tout l'ouvrage. — mesh / gnawed
    Patience et longueur de temps
    Font plus que force ni que rage.

Jean de La Fontaine (1621–1695)

Compréhension. Répondez aux questions suivantes selon les renseignements donnés dans la fable.

1. Quel conseil La Fontaine donne-t-il dans cette fable aux gens importants et puissants?
2. Quel conseil donne-t-il aux gens qui sont toujours pressés?
3. Qu'est-ce que le lion a fait quand le rat est apparu entre ses pattes?
4. Qu'est-ce qui est arrivé au lion quelque temps plus tard?
5. Qu'est-ce que le rat a fait pour l'aider?

Le lion et le rat (gravure
de Gustave Doré)

International phonetic alphabet

Vowels

i midi
u nous
a la
y du
e été
ɛ fête
o dos
ɔ votre
ø deux
œ leur
ə le
ɑ pâte
ɛ̃ vin
ɔ̃ mon
ɑ̃ dans
œ̃ un

Consonants

p petit
t tête
k quand
b beau
d danger
g gare
f fin
v victoire
s sa
z zéro
m maman
n non
l livre
ʃ chien
ʒ juge
ɲ montagne
r rêve

Semivowels

j famille, métier, crayon
w Louis, voici
ɥ lui, depuis

Verbs

Regular Verbs

Infinitif Participes	Indicatif				
	Présent	Imparfait	Passé composé	Passé simple	Plus-que-parfait
parler parlant parlé	parle parles parle parlons parlez parlent	parlais parlais parlait parlions parliez parlaient	ai parlé as parlé a parlé avons parlé avez parlé ont parlé	parlai parlas parla parlâmes parlâtes parlèrent	avais parlé avais parlé avait parlé avions parlé aviez parlé avaient parlé
finir finissant fini	finis finis finit finissons finissez finissent	finissais finissais finissait finissions finissiez finissaient	ai fini as fini a fini avons fini avez fini ont fini	finis finis finit finîmes finîtes finirent	avais fini avais fini avait fini avions fini aviez fini avaient fini
rendre rendant rendu	rends rends rend rendons rendez rendent	rendais rendais rendait rendions rendiez rendaient	ai rendu as rendu a rendu avons rendu avez rendu ont rendu	rendis rendis rendit rendîmes rendîtes rendirent	avais rendu avais rendu avait rendu avions rendu aviez rendu avaient rendu
partir (dormir, s'endormir, mentir, sentir, servir, sortir) partant parti	pars pars part partons partez partent	partais partais partait partions partiez partaient	suis parti(e) es parti(e) est parti(e) sommes parti(e)s êtes parti(e)(s) sont parti(e)s	partis partis partit partîmes partîtes partirent	étais parti(e) étais parti(e) était parti(e) étions parti(e)s étiez parti(e)(s) étaient parti(e)s

		Conditionnel		**Impératif**	**Subjonctif**	
Futur	Futur antérieur	Présent	Passé		Présent	Passé composé du subjonctif
parlerai	aurai parlé	parlerais	aurais parlé		parle	aie parlé
parleras	auras parlé	parlerais	aurais parlé	parle	parles	aies parlé
parlera	aura parlé	parlerait	aurait parlé		parle	ait parlé
parlerons	aurons parlé	parlerions	aurions parlé	parlons	parlions	ayons parlé
parlerez	aurez parlé	parleriez	auriez parlé	parlez	parliez	ayez parlé
parleront	auront parlé	parleraient	auraient parlé		parlent	aient parlé
finirai	aurai fini	finirais	aurais fini		finisse	aie fini
finiras	auras fini	finirais	aurais fini	finis	finisses	aies fini
finira	aura fini	finirait	aurait fini		finisse	ait fini
finirons	aurons fini	finirions	aurions fini	finissons	finissions	ayons fini
finirez	aurez fini	finiriez	auriez fini	finissez	finissiez	ayez fini
finiront	auront fini	finiraient	auraient fini		finissent	aient fini
rendrai	aurai rendu	rendrais	aurais rendu		rende	aie rendu
rendras	auras rendu	rendrais	aurais rendu	rends	rendes	aies rendu
rendra	aura rendu	rendrait	aurait rendu		rende	ait rendu
rendrons	aurons rendu	rendrions	aurions rendu	rendons	rendions	ayons rendu
rendrez	aurez rendu	rendriez	auriez rendu	rendez	rendiez	ayez rendu
rendront	auront rendu	rendraient	auraient rendu		rendent	aient rendu
partirai	serai parti(e)	partirais	serais parti(e)		parte	sois parti(e)
partiras	seras parti(e)	partirais	serais parti(e)	pars	partes	sois parti(e)
partira	sera parti(e)	partirait	serait parti(e)		parte	soit parti(e)
partirons	serons parti(e)s	partirions	serions parti(e)s	partons	partions	soyons parti(e)s
partirez	serez parti(e)(s)	partiriez	seriez parti(e)(s)	partez	partiez	soyez parti(e)(s)
partiront	seront parti(e)s	partiraient	seraient parti(e)s		partent	soient parti(e)s

Spelling-Changing Verbs

Infinitif Participes	Indicatif				
	Présent	Imparfait	Passé composé	Passé simple	Plus-que-parfait
acheter (lever, mener, promener) achetant acheté	achète achètes achète achetons achetez achètent	achetais achetais achetait achetions achetiez achetaient	ai acheté as acheté a acheté avons acheté avez acheté ont acheté	achetai achetas acheta achetâmes achetâtes achetèrent	avais acheté avais acheté avait acheté avions acheté aviez acheté avaient acheté
préférer (considérer, espérer, exagérer, inquiéter, répéter) préférant préféré	préfère préfères préfère préférons préférez préfèrent	préférais préférais préférait préférions préfériez préféraient	ai préféré as préféré a préféré avons préféré avez préféré ont préféré	préférai préféras préféra préférâmes préférâtes préférèrent	avais préféré avais préféré avait préféré avions préféré aviez préféré avaient préféré
manger (arranger, changer, corriger, déranger, diriger, encourager, nager) mangeant mangé	mange manges mange mangeons mangez mangent	mangeais mangeais mangeait mangions mangiez mangeaient	ai mangé as mangé a mangé avons mangé avez mangé ont mangé	mangeai mangeas mangea mangeâmes mangeâtes mangèrent	avais mangé avais mangé avait mangé avions mangé aviez mangé avaient mangé
payer (essayer) payant payé	paie paies paie payons payez paient	payais payais payait payions payiez payaient	ai payé as payé a payé avons payé avez payé ont payé	payai payas paya payâmes payâtes payèrent	avais payé avais payé avait payé avions payé aviez payé avaient payé
commencer commençant commencé	commence commences commence commençons commencez commencent	commençais commençais commençait commencions commenciez commençaient	ai commencé as commencé a commencé avons commencé avez commencé ont commencé	commençai commenças commença commençâmes commençâtes commencèrent	avais commencé avais commencé avait commencé avions commencé aviez commencé avaient commencé
appeler (rappeler) appelant appelé	appelle appelles appelle appelons appelez appellent	appelais appelais appelait appelions appeliez appelaient	ai appelé as appelé a appelé avons appelé avez appelé ont appelé	appelai appelas appela appelâmes appelâtes appelèrent	avais appelé avais appelé avait appelé avions appelé aviez appelé avaient appelé

		Conditionnel		Impératif	Subjonctif	
Futur	Futur antérieur	Présent	Passé		Présent	Passé composé du subjonctif
achèterai	aurai acheté	achèterais	aurais acheté		achète	aie acheté
achèteras	auras acheté	achèterais	aurais acheté	achète	achètes	aies acheté
achètera	aura acheté	achèterait	aurait acheté		achète	ait acheté
achèterons	aurons acheté	achèterions	aurions acheté	achetons	achetions	ayons acheté
achèterez	aurez acheté	achèteriez	auriez acheté	achetez	achetiez	ayez acheté
achèteront	auront acheté	achèteraient	auraient acheté		achètent	aient acheté
préférerai	aurai préféré	préférerais	aurais préféré		préfère	aie préféré
préféreras	auras préféré	préférerais	aurais préféré	préfère	préfères	aies préféré
préférera	aura préféré	préférerait	aurait préféré		préfère	ait préféré
préférerons	aurons préféré	préférerions	aurions préféré	préférons	préférions	ayons préféré
préférerez	aurez préféré	préféreriez	auriez préféré	préférez	préfériez	ayez préféré
préféreront	auront préféré	préféreraient	auraient préféré		préfèrent	aient préféré
mangerai	aurai mangé	mangerais	aurais mangé		mange	aie mangé
mangeras	auras mangé	mangerais	aurais mangé	mange	manges	aies mangé
mangera	aura mangé	mangerait	aurait mangé		mange	ait mangé
mangerons	aurons mangé	mangerions	aurions mangé	mangeons	mangions	ayons mangé
mangerez	aurez mangé	mangeriez	auriez mangé	mangez	mangiez	ayez mangé
mangeront	auront mangé	mangeraient	auraient mangé		mangent	aient mangé
paierai	aurai payé	paierais	aurais payé		paie	aie payé
paieras	auras payé	paierais	aurais payé	paie	paies	aies payé
paiera	aura payé	paierait	aurait payé		paie	ait payé
paierons	aurons payé	paierions	aurions payé	payons	payions	ayons payé
paierez	aurez payé	paieriez	auriez payé	payez	payiez	ayez payé
paieront	auront payé	paieraient	auraient payé		paient	aient payé
commencerai	aurai commencé	commencerais	aurais commencé		commence	aie commencé
commenceras	auras commencé	commencerais	aurais commencé	commence	commences	aies commencé
commencera	aura commencé	commencerait	aurait commencé		commence	ait commencé
commencerons	aurons commencé	commencerions	aurions commencé	commençons	commencions	ayons commencé
commencerez	aurez commencé	commenceriez	auriez commencé	commencez	commenciez	ayez commencé
commenceront	auront commencé	commenceraient	auraient commencé		commencent	aient commencé
appellerai	aurai appelé	appellerais	aurais appelé		appelle	aie appelé
appelleras	auras appelé	appellerais	aurais appelé	appelle	appelles	aies appelé
appellera	aura appelé	appellerait	aurait appelé		appelle	ait appelé
appellerons	aurons appelé	appellerions	aurions appelé	appelons	appelions	ayons appelé
appellerez	aurez appelé	appelleriez	auriez appelé	appelez	appeliez	ayez appelé
appelleront	auront appelé	appelleront	auraient appelé		appellent	aient appelé

Auxiliary Verbs

Infinitif Participes	Indicatif				
	Présent	Imparfait	Passé composé	Passé simple	Plus-que-parfait
être	suis	étais	ai été	fus	avais été
étant	es	étais	as été	fus	avais été
été	est	était	a été	fut	avait été
	sommes	étions	avons été	fûmes	avions été
	êtes	étiez	avez été	fûtes	aviez été
	sont	étaient	ont été	furent	avaient été
avoir	ai	avais	ai eu	eus	avais eu
ayant	as	avais	as eu	eus	avais eu
eu	a	avait	a eu	eut	avait eu
	avons	avions	avons eu	eûmes	avions eu
	avez	aviez	avez eu	eûtes	aviez eu
	ont	avaient	ont eu	eurent	avaient eu

Futur	Futur antérieur	**Conditionnel** Présent	Passé	**Impératif**	**Subjonctif** Présent	Passé composé du subjonctif
serai	aurai été	serais	aurais été		sois	aie été
seras	auras été	serais	aurais été	sois	sois	aies été
sera	aura été	serait	aurait été		soit	ait été
serons	aurons été	serions	aurions été	soyons	soyons	ayons été
serez	aurez été	seriez	auriez été	soyez	soyez	ayez été
seront	auront été	seraient	auraient été		soient	aient été
aurai	aurai eu	aurais	aurais eu		aie	aie eu
auras	auras eu	aurais	aurais eu	aie	aies	aies eu
aura	aura eu	aurait	aurait eu		ait	ait eu
aurons	aurons eu	aurions	aurions eu	ayons	ayons	ayons eu
aurez	aurez eu	auriez	auriez eu	ayez	ayez	ayez eu
auront	auront eu	auraient	auraient eu		aient	aient eu

Irregular Verbs

Each verb in this list is conjugated like the model indicated by number. See the table of irregular verbs for the models.

admettre 13	découvrir 17	paraître 4	reconnaître 4	satisfaire 11
(s')apercevoir 22	décrire 9	permettre 13	redire 8	souffrir 16
apprendre 21	devenir 27	poursuivre 25	relire 12	se souvenir 27
commettre 13	disparaître 4	prévoir 29	remettre 13	surprendre 21
comprendre 21	inscrire 9	produire 3	retenir 27	se taire 18
construire 3	introduire 3	promettre 13	revenir 27	tenir 27
couvrir 17	obtenir 27	reconduire 3	revoir 29	traduire 3
décevoir 22				

Infinitif Participes			Indicatif		
	Présent	Imparfait	Passé composé	Passé simple	Plus-que-parfait
1 **aller** allant allé	vais vas va allons allez vont	allais allais allait allions alliez allaient	suis allé(e) es allé(e) est allé(e) sommes allé(e)s êtes allé(e)(s) sont allé(e)s	allai allas alla allâmes allâtes allèrent	étais allé(e) étais allé(e) était allé(e) étions allé(e)s étiez allé(e)(s) étaient allé(e)s
2 **boire** buvant bu	bois bois boit buvons buvez boivent	buvais buvais buvait buvions buviez buvaient	ai bu as bu a bu avons bu avez bu ont bu	bus bus but bûmes bûtes burent	avais bu avais bu avait bu avions bu aviez bu avaient bu
3 **conduire** conduisant conduit	conduis conduis conduit conduisons conduisez conduisent	conduisais conduisais conduisait conduisions conduisiez conduisaient	ai conduit as conduit a conduit avons conduit avez conduit ont conduit	conduisis conduisis conduisit conduisîmes conduisîtes conduisirent	avais conduit avais conduit avait conduit avions conduit aviez conduit avaient conduit
4 **connaître** connaissant connu	connais connais connaît connaissons connaissez connaissent	connaissais connaissais connaissait connaissions connaissiez connaissaient	ai connu as connu a connu avons connu avez connu ont connu	connus connus connut connûmes connûtes connurent	avais connu avais connu avait connu avions connu aviez connu avaient connu

Futur	Futur antérieur	Conditionnel Présent	Conditionnel Passé	Impératif	Subjonctif Présent	Passé composé du subjonctif
irai	serai allé(e)	irais	serais allé(e)		aille	sois allé(e)
iras	seras allé(e)	irais	serais allé(e)	va	ailles	sois allé(e)
ira	sera allé(e)	irait	serait allé(e)		aille	soit allé(e)
irons	serons allé(e)s	irions	serions allé(e)s	allons	allions	soyons allé(e)s
irez	serez allé(e)(s)	iriez	seriez allé(e)(s)	allez	alliez	soyez allé(e)(s)
iront	seront allé(e)s	iraient	seraient allé(e)s		aillent	soient allé(e)s
boirai	aurai bu	boirais	aurais bu		boive	aie bu
boiras	auras bu	boirais	aurais bu	bois	boives	aies bu
boira	aura bu	boirait	aurait bu		boive	ait bu
boirons	aurons bu	boirions	aurions bu	buvons	buvions	ayons bu
boirez	aurez bu	boiriez	auriez bu	buvez	buviez	ayez bu
boiront	auront bu	boiraient	auraient bu		boivent	aient bu
conduirai	aurai conduit	conduirais	aurais conduit		conduise	aie conduit
conduiras	auras conduit	conduirais	aurais conduit	conduis	conduises	aies conduit
conduira	aura conduit	conduirait	aurait conduit		conduise	ait conduit
conduirons	aurons conduit	conduirions	aurions conduit	conduisons	conduisions	ayons conduit
conduirez	aurez conduit	conduiriez	auriez conduit	conduisez	conduisiez	ayez conduit
conduiront	auront conduit	conduiraient	auraient conduit		conduisent	aient conduit
connaîtrai	aurai connu	connaîtrais	aurais connu		connaisse	aie connu
connaîtras	auras connu	connaîtrais	aurais connu	connais	connaisses	aies connu
connaîtra	aura connu	connaîtrait	aurait connu		connaisse	ait connu
connaîtrons	aurons connu	connaîtrions	aurions connu	connaissons	connaissions	ayons connu
connaîtrez	aurez connu	connaîtriez	auriez connu	connaissez	connaissiez	ayez connu
connaîtront	auront connu	connaîtraient	auraient connu		connaissent	aient connu

Infinitif Participes	Présent	Imparfait	Passé composé	Passé simple	Plus-que-parfait
5	cours	courais	ai couru	courus	avais couru
	cours	courais	as couru	courus	avais couru
courir	court	courait	a couru	courut	avait couru
courant	courons	courions	avons couru	courûmes	avions couru
couru	courez	couriez	avez couru	courûtes	aviez couru
	courent	couraient	ont couru	coururent	avaient couru
6	crois	croyais	ai cru	crus	avais cru
	crois	croyais	as cru	crus	avais cru
croire	croit	croyait	a cru	crut	avait cru
croyant	croyons	croyions	avons cru	crûmes	avions cru
cru	croyez	croyiez	avez cru	crûtes	aviez cru
	croient	croyaient	ont cru	crurent	avaient cru
7	dois	devais	ai dû	dus	avais dû
	dois	devais	as dû	dus	avais dû
devoir	doit	devait	a dû	dut	avait dû
devant	devons	devions	avons dû	dûmes	avions dû
dû	devez	deviez	avez dû	dûtes	aviez dû
	doivent	devaient	ont dû	durent	avaient dû
8	dis	disais	ai dit	dis	avais dit
	dis	disais	as dit	dis	avais dit
dire	dit	disait	a dit	dit	avait dit
disant	disons	disions	avons dit	dîmes	avions dit
dit	dites	disiez	avez dit	dîtes	aviez dit
	disent	disaient	ont dit	dirent	avaient dit
9	écris	écrivais	ai écrit	écrivis	avais écrit
	écris	écrivais	as écrit	écrivis	avais écrit
écrire	écrit	écrivait	a écrit	écrivit	avait écrit
écrivant	écrivons	écrivions	avons écrit	écrivîmes	avions écrit
écrit	écrivez	écriviez	avez écrit	écrivîtes	aviez écrit
	écrivent	écrivaient	ont écrit	écrivirent	avaient écrit
10	envoie	envoyais	ai envoyé	envoyai	avais envoyé
	envoies	envoyais	as envoyé	envoyas	avais envoyé
envoyer	envoie	envoyait	a envoyé	envoya	avait envoyé
envoyant	envoyons	envoyions	avons envoyé	envoyâmes	avions envoyé
envoyé	envoyez	envoyiez	avez envoyé	envoyâtes	aviez envoyé
	envoient	envoyaient	ont envoyé	envoyèrent	avaient envoyé
11	fais	faisais	ai fait	fis	avais fait
	fais	faisais	as fait	fis	avais fait
faire	fait	faisait	a fait	fit	avait fait
faisant	faisons	faisions	avons fait	fîmes	avions fait
fait	faites	faisiez	avez fait	fîtes	aviez fait
	font	faisaient	ont fait	firent	avaient fait

Indicatif

		Conditionnel		Impératif	Subjonctif	
Futur	Futur antérieur	Présent	Passé		Présent	Passé composé du subjonctif
courrai	aurai couru	courrais	aurais couru		coure	aie couru
courras	auras couru	courrais	aurais couru	cours	coures	aies couru
courra	aura couru	courrait	aurait couru		coure	ait couru
courrons	aurons couru	courrions	aurions couru	courons	courions	ayons couru
courrez	aurez couru	courriez	auriez couru	courez	couriez	ayez couru
courront	auront couru	courraient	auraient couru		courent	aient couru
croirai	aurai cru	croirais	aurais cru		croie	aie cru
croiras	auras cru	croirais	aurais cru	crois	croies	aies cru
croira	aura cru	croirait	aurait cru		croie	ait cru
croirons	aurons cru	croirions	aurions cru	croyons	croyions	ayons cru
croirez	aurez cru	croiriez	auriez cru	croyez	croyiez	ayez cru
croiront	auront cru	croiraient	auraient cru		croient	aient cru
devrai	aurai dû	devrais	aurais dû		doive	aie dû
devras	auras dû	devrais	aurais dû	dois	doives	aies dû
devra	aura dû	devrait	aurait dû		doive	ait dû
devrons	aurons dû	devrions	aurions dû	devons	devions	ayons dû
devrez	aurez dû	devriez	auriez dû	devez	deviez	ayez dû
devront	auront dû	devraient	auraient dû		doivent	aient dû
dirai	aurai dit	dirais	aurais dit		dise	aie dit
diras	auras dit	dirais	aurais dit	dis	dises	aies dit
dira	aura dit	dirait	aurait dit		dise	ait dit
dirons	aurons dit	dirions	aurions dit	disons	disions	ayons dit
direz	aurez dit	diriez	auriez dit	dites	disiez	ayez dit
diront	auront dit	diraient	auraient dit		disent	aient dit
écrirai	aurai écrit	écrirais	aurais écrit		écrive	aie écrit
écriras	auras écrit	écrirais	aurais écrit	écris	écrives	aies écrit
écrira	aura écrit	écrirait	aurait écrit		écrive	ait écrit
écrirons	aurons écrit	écririons	aurions écrit	écrivons	écrivions	ayons écrit
écrirez	aurez écrit	écririez	auriez écrit	écrivez	écriviez	ayez écrit
écriront	auront écrit	écriraient	auraient écrit		écrivent	aient écrit
enverrai	aurai envoyé	enverrais	aurais envoyé		envoie	aie envoyé
enverras	auras envoyé	enverrais	aurais envoyé	envoie	envoies	aies envoyé
enverra	aura envoyé	enverrait	aurait envoyé		envoie	ait envoyé
enverrons	aurons envoyé	enverrions	aurions envoyé	envoyons	envoyions	ayons envoyé
enverrez	aurez envoyé	enverriez	auriez envoyé	envoyez	envoyiez	ayez envoyé
enverront	auront envoyé	enverraient	auraient envoyé		envoient	aient envoyé
ferai	aurai fait	ferais	aurais fait		fasse	aie fait
feras	auras fait	ferais	aurais fait	fais	fasses	aies fait
fera	aura fait	ferait	aurait fait		fasse	ait fait
ferons	aurons fait	ferions	aurions fait	faisons	fassions	ayons fait
ferez	aurez fait	feriez	auriez fait	faites	fassiez	ayez fait
feront	auront fait	feraient	auraient fait		fassent	aient fait

Infinitif Participes					Indicatif
	Présent	Imparfait	Passé composé	Passé simple	Plus-que-parfait
12 **lire** lisant lu	lis lis lit lisons lisez lisent	lisais lisais lisait lisions lisiez lisaient	ai lu as lu a lu avons lu avez lu ont lu	lus lus lut lûmes lûtes lurent	avais lu avais lu avait lu avions lu aviez lu avaient lu
13 **mettre** mettant mis	mets mets met mettons mettez mettent	mettais mettais mettait mèttions mettiez mettaient	ai mis as mis a mis avons mis avez mis ont mis	mis mis mit mîmes mîtes mirent	avais mis avais mis avait mis avions mis aviez mis avaient mis
14 **mourir** mourant mort	meurs meurs meurt mourons mourez meurent	mourais mourais mourait mourions mouriez mouraient	suis mort(e) es mort(e) est mort(e) sommes mort(e)s êtes mort(e)(s) sont mort(e)s	mourus mourus mourut mourûmes mourûtes moururent	étais mort(e) étais mort(e) était mort(e) étions mort(e)s étiez mort(e)(s) étaient mort(e)s
15 **naître** naissant né	nais nais naît naissons naissez naissent	naissais naissais naissait naissions naissiez naissaient	suis né(e) es né(e) est né(e) sommes né(e)s êtes né(e)(s) sont né(e)s	naquis naquis naquit naquîmes naquîtes naquirent	étais né(e) étais né(e) était né(e) étions né(e)s étiez né(e)(s) étaient né(e)s
16 **offrir** offrant offert	offre offres offre offrons offrez offrent	offrais offrais offrait offrions offriez offraient	ai offert as offert a offert avons offert avez offert ont offert	offris offris offrit offrîmes offrîtes offrirent	avais offert avais offert avait offert avions offert aviez offert avaient offert
17 **ouvrir** ouvrant ouvert	ouvre ouvres ouvre ouvrons ouvrez ouvrent	ouvrais ouvrais ouvrait ouvrions ouvriez ouvraient	ai ouvert as ouvert a ouvert avons ouvert avez ouvert ont ouvert	ouvris ouvris ouvrit ouvrîmes ouvrîtes ouvrirent	avais ouvert avais ouvert avait ouvert avions ouvert aviez ouvert avaient ouvert
18 **plaire** plaisant plu	plais plais plaît plaisons plaisez plaisent	plaisais plaisais plaisait plaisions plaisiez plaisaient	ai plu as plu a plu avons plu avez plu ont plu	plus plus plut plûmes plûtes plurent	avais plu avais plu avait plu avions plu aviez plu avaient plu

Futur	Futur antérieur	Conditionnel Présent	Conditionnel Passé	Impératif	Subjonctif Présent	Passé composé du subjonctif
lirai	aurai lu	lirais	aurais lu		lise	aie lu
liras	auras lu	lirais	aurais lu	lis	lises	aies lu
lira	aura lu	lirait	aurait lu		lise	ait lu
lirons	aurons lu	lirions	aurions lu	lisons	lisions	ayons lu
lirez	aurez lu	liriez	auriez lu	lisez	lisiez	ayez lu
liront	auront lu	liraient	auraient lu		lisent	aient lu
mettrai	aurai mis	mettrais	aurais mis		mette	aie mis
mettras	auras mis	mettrais	aurais mis	mets	mettes	aies mis
mettra	aura mis	mettrait	aurait mis		mette	ait mis
mettrons	aurons mis	mettrions	aurions mis	mettons	mettions	ayons mis
mettrez	aurez mis	mettriez	auriez mis	mettez	mettiez	ayez mis
mettront	auront mis	mettraient	auraient mis		mettent	aient mis
mourrai	serai mort(e)	mourrais	serais mort(e)		meure	sois mort(e)
mourras	seras mort(e)	mourrais	serais mort(e)	meurs	meures	sois mort(e)
mourra	sera mort(e)	mourrait	serait mort(e)		meure	soit mort(e)
mourrons	serons mort(e)s	mourrions	serions mort(e)s	mourons	mourions	soyons mort(e)s
mourrez	serez mort(e)(s)	mourriez	seriez mort(e)(s)	mourez	mouriez	soyez mort(e)(s)
mourront	seront mort(e)s	mourraient	seraient mort(e)s		meurent	soient mort(e)s
naîtrai	serai né(e)	naîtrais	serais né(e)		naisse	sois né(e)
naîtras	seras né(e)	naîtrais	serais né(e)	nais	naisses	sois né(e)
naîtra	sera né(e)	naîtrait	serait né(e)		naisse	soit né(e)
naîtrons	serons né(e)s	naîtrions	serions né(e)s	naissons	naissions	soyons né(e)s
naîtrez	serez né(e)(s)	naîtriez	seriez né(e)(s)	naissez	naissiez	soyez né(e)(s)
naîtront	seront né(e)s	naîtraient	seraient né(e)s		naissent	soient né(e)s
offrirai	aurai offert	offrirais	aurais offert		offre	aie offert
offriras	auras offert	offrirais	aurais offert	offre	offres	aies offert
offrira	aura offert	offrirait	aurait offert		offre	ait offert
offrirons	aurons offert	offririons	aurions offert	offrons	offrions	ayons offert
offrirez	aurez offert	offririez	auriez offert	offrez	offriez	ayez offert
offriront	auront offert	offriraient	auraient offert		offrent	aient offert
ouvrirai	aurai ouvert	ouvrirais	aurais ouvert		ouvre	aie ouvert
ouvriras	auras ouvert	ouvrirais	aurais ouvert	ouvre	ouvres	aies ouvert
ouvrira	aura ouvert	ouvrirait	aurait ouvert		ouvre	ait ouvert
ouvrirons	aurons ouvert	ouvririons	aurions ouvert	ouvrons	ouvrions	ayons ouvert
ouvrirez	aurez ouvert	ouvririez	auriez ouvert	ouvrez	ouvriez	ayez ouvert
ouvriront	auront ouvert	ouvriraient	auraient ouvert		ouvrent	aient ouvert
plairai	aurai plu	plairais	aurais plu		plaise	aie plu
plairas	auras plu	plairais	aurais plu	plais	plaises	aies plu
plaira	aura plu	plairait	aurait plu		plaise	ait plu
plairons	aurons plu	plairions	aurions plu	plaisons	plaisions	ayons plu
plairez	aurez plu	plairiez	auriez plu	plaisez	plaisiez	ayez plu
plairont	auront plu	plairaient	auraient plu		plaisent	aient plu

Infinitif Participes				Indicatif	
	Présent	Imparfait	Passé composé	Passé simple	Plus-que-parfait
19 **pleuvoir** pleuvant plu	pleut	pleuvait	a plu	plut	avait plu
20 **pouvoir** pouvant pu	peux peux peut pouvons pouvez peuvent	pouvais pouvais pouvait pouvions pouviez pouvaient	ai pu as pu a pu avons pu avez pu ont pu	pus pus put pûmes pûtes purent	avais pu avais pu avait pu avions pu aviez pu avaient pu
21 **prendre** prenant pris	prends prends prend prenons prenez prennent	prenais prenais prenait prenions preniez prenaient	ai pris as pris a pris avons pris avez pris ont pris	pris pris prit prîmes prîtes prirent	avais pris avais pris avait pris avions pris aviez pris avaient pris
22 **recevoir** recevant reçu	reçois reçois reçoit recevons recevez reçoivent	recevais recevais recevait recevions receviez recevaient	ai reçu as reçu a reçu avons reçu avez reçu ont reçu	reçus reçus reçut reçûmes reçûtes reçurent	avais reçu avais reçu avait reçu avions reçu aviez reçu avaient reçu
23 **rire** riant ri	ris ris rit rions riez rient	riais riais riait riions riiez riaient	ai ri as ri a ri avons ri avez ri ont ri	ris ris rit rîmes rîtes rirent	avais ri avais ri avait ri avions ri aviez ri avaient ri
24 **savoir** sachant su	sais sais sait savons savez savent	savais savais savait savions saviez savaient	ai su as su a su avons su avez su ont su	sus sus sut sûmes sûtes surent	avais su avais su avait su avions su aviez su avaient su
25 **suivre** suivant suivi	suis suis suit suivons suivez suivent	suivais suivais suivait suivions suiviez suivaient	ai suivi as suivi a suivi avons suivi avez suivi ont suivi	suivis suivis suivit suivîmes suivîtes suivirent	avais suivi avais suivi avait suivi avions suivi aviez suivi avaient suivi

		Conditionnel		Impératif	Subjonctif	
Futur	Futur antérieur	Présent	Passé		Présent	Passé composé du subjonctif
pleuvra	aura plu	pleuvrait	aurait plu		pleuve	ait plu
pourrai	aurai pu	pourrais	aurais pu	(pas d'impératif)	puisse	aie pu
pourras	auras pu	pourrais	aurais pu		puisses	aies pu
pourra	aura pu	pourrait	aurait pu		puisse	ait pu
pourrons	aurons pu	pourrions	aurions pu		puissions	ayons pu
pourrez	aurez pu	pourriez	auriez pu		puissiez	ayez pu
pourront	auront pu	pourraient	auraient pu		puissent	aient pu
prendrai	aurai pris	prendrais	aurais pris		prenne	aie pris
prendras	auras pris	prendrais	aurais pris	prends	prennes	aies pris
prendra	aura pris	prendrait	aurait pris		prenne	ait pris
prendrons	aurons pris	prendrions	aurions pris	prenons	prenions	ayons pris
prendrez	aurez pris	prendriez	auriez pris	prenez	preniez	ayez pris
prendront	auront pris	prendraient	auraient pris		prennent	aient pris
recevrai	aurai reçu	recevrais	aurais reçu		reçoive	aie reçu
recevras	auras reçu	recevrais	aurais reçu	reçois	reçoives	aies reçu
recevra	aura reçu	recevrait	aurait reçu		reçoive	ait reçu
recevrons	aurons reçu	recevrions	aurions reçu	recevons	recevions	ayons reçu
recevrez	aurez reçu	recevriez	auriez reçu	recevez	receviez	ayez reçu
recevront	auront reçu	recevraient	auraient reçu		reçoivent	aient reçu
rirai	aurai ri	rirais	aurais ri		rie	aie ri
riras	auras ri	rirais	aurais ri	ris	ries	aies ri
rira	aura ri	rirait	aurait ri		rie	ait ri
rirons	aurons ri	ririons	aurions ri	rions	riions	ayons ri
rirez	aurez ri	ririez	auriez ri	riez	riiez	ayez ri
riront	auront ri	riraient	auraient ri		rient	aient ri
saurai	aurai su	saurais	aurais su		sache	aie su
sauras	auras su	saurais	aurais su	sache	saches	aies su
saura	aura su	saurait	aurait su		sache	ait su
saurons	aurons su	saurions	aurions su	sachons	sachions	ayons su
saurez	aurez su	sauriez	auriez su	sachez	sachiez	ayez su
sauront	auront su	sauraient	auraient su		sachent	aient su
suivrai	aurai suivi	suivrais	aurais suivi		suive	aie suivi
suivras	auras suivi	suivrais	aurais suivi	suis	suives	aies suivi
suivra	aura suivi	suivrait	aurait suivi		suive	ait suivi
suivrons	aurons suivi	suivrions	aurions suivi	suivons	suivions	ayons suivi
suivrez	aurez suivi	suivriez	auriez suivi	suivez	suiviez	ayez suivi
suivront	auront suivi	suivraient	auraient suivi		suivent	aient suivi

Infinitif Participes					Indicatif
	Présent	Imparfait	Passé composé	Passé simple	Plus-que-parfait
26	vaux	valais	ai valu	valus	avais valu
	vaux	valais	as valu	valus	avais valu
valoir	vaut	valait	a valu	valut	avait valu
valant	valons	valions	avons valu	valûmes	avions valu
valu	valez	valiez	avez valu	valûtes	aviez valu
	valent	valaient	ont valu	valurent	avaient valu
27	viens	venais	suis venu(e)	vins	étais venu(e)
	viens	venais	es venu(e)	vins	étais venu(e)
venir	vient	venait	est venu(e)	vint	était venu(e)
venant	venons	venions	sommes venu(e)s	vînmes	étions venu(e)s
venu	venez	veniez	êtes venu(e)(s)	vîntes	étiez venu(e)(s)
	viennent	venaient	sont venu(e)s	vinrent	étaient venu(e)s
28	vis	vivais	ai vécu	vécus	avais vécu
	vis	vivais	as vécu	vécus	avais vécu
vivre	vit	vivait	a vécu	vécut	avait vécu
vivant	vivons	vivions	avons vécu	vécûmes	avions vécu
vécu	vivez	viviez	avez vécu	vécûtes	aviez vécu
	vivent	vivaient	ont vécu	vécurend	avaient vécu
29	vois	voyais	ai vu	vis	avais vu
	vois	voyais	as vu	vis	avais vu
voir	voit	voyait	a vu	vit	avait vu
voyant	voyons	voyions	avons vu	vîmes	avions vu
vu	voyez	voyiez	avez vu	vîtes	aviez vu
	voient	voyaient	ont vu	virent	avaient vu
30	veux	voulais	ai voulu	voulus	avais voulu
	veux	voulais	as voulu	voulus	avais voulu
vouloir	veut	voulait	a voulu	voulut	avait voulu
voulant	voulons	voulions	avons voulu	voulûmes	avions voulu
voulu	voulez	vouliez	avez voulu	voulûtes	aviez voulu
	veulent	voulaient	ont voulu	voulurent	avaient voulu

Futur	Futur antérieur	Conditionnel Présent	Conditionnel Passé	Impératif	Subjonctif Présent	Passé composé du subjonctif
vaudrai	aurai valu	vaudrais	aurais valu		vaille	aie valu
vaudras	auras valu	vaudrais	aurais valu	vaux	vailles	aies valu
vaudra	aura valu	vaudrait	aurait valu		vaille	ait valu
vaudrons	aurons valu	vaudrions	aurions valu	valons	valions	ayons valu
vaudrez	aurez valu	vaudriez	auriez valu	valez	valiez	ayez valu
vaudront	auront valu	vaudraient	auraient valu		vaillent	aient valu
viendrai	serai venu(e)	viendrais	serais venu(e)		vienne	sois venu(e)
viendras	seras venu(e)	viendrais	serais venu(e)	viens	viennes	sois venu(e)
viendra	sera venu(e)	viendrait	serait venu(e)		vienne	soit venu(e)
viendrons	serons venu(e)s	viendrions	serions venu(e)s	venons	venions	soyons venu(e)s
viendrez	serez venu(e)(s)	viendriez	seriez venu(e)(s)	venez	veniez	soyez venu(e)(s)
viendront	seront venu(e)s	viendraient	seraient venu(e)s		viennent	soient venu(e)s
vivrai	aurai vécu	vivrais	aurais vécu		vive	avais vécu
vivras	auras vécu	vivrais	aurais vécu	vis	vives	avais vécu
vivra	aura vécu	vivrait	aurait vécu		vive	avait vécu
vivrons	aurons vécu	vivrions	aurions vécu	vivons	vivions	avions vécu
vivrez	aurez vécu	vivriez	auriez vécu	vivez	viviez	aviez vécu
vivront	auront vécu	vivraient	auraient vécu		vivent	avaient vécu
verrai	aurai vu	verrais	aurais vu		voie	aie vu
verras	auras vu	verrais	aurais vu	vois	voies	aies vu
verra	aura vu	verrait	aurait vu		voie	ait vu
verrons	aurons vu	verrions	aurions vu	voyons	voyions	ayons vu
verrez	aurez vu	verriez	auriez vu	voyez	voyiez	ayez vu
verront	auront vu	verraient	auraient vu		voient	aient vu
voudrai	aurai voulu	voudrais	aurais voulu		veuille	aie voulu
voudras	auras voulu	voudrais	aurais voulu	veuille	veuilles	aies voulu
voudra	aura voulu	voudrait	aurait voulu		veuille	ait voulu
voudrons	aurons voulu	voudrions	aurions voulu	veuillons	voulions	ayons voulu
voudrez	aurez voulu	voudriez	auriez voulu	veuillez	vouliez	ayez voulu
voudront	auront voulu	voudraient	auraient voulu		veuillent	aient voulu

Vocabulaire
Français-Anglais

The vocabulary contains all words that appear in the **Mise en scène, Présentation, Mise en situation,** and **Intégration et perspectives** sections except articles, identical cognates, and vocabulary appearing in the **Notes culturelles** and the **Invitation à la lecture**. Irregular noun plurals are included, as are irregular feminine and plural forms of adjectives.

Abbreviations

adj	adjective	*m*	masculine
coll	colloquial	*pl*	plural
f	feminine	*pp*	past participle
irr	irregular	*s*	singular

A

à at, in, to; — **côté de** beside, next to; — **demain** see you tomorrow; — **l'aise** at ease; — **l'appareil** speaking on the phone; — **l'étranger** abroad; — **l'heure** on time; — **l'unisson** in unison, in keeping with; — **la fois** at the same time; — **la mode** in style; — **part** except for, besides; — **peine** hardly, scarcely; — **ta guise** as you

wish; — **temps perdu** in one's spare time; — **tout à l'heure** see you later; — **votre avis** in your opinion; — **votre santé** cheers, to your health
abandonner to abandon
abdominal (abdominaux) *m* sit-up
accepter to accept
accès *m* access, approach
accident *m* accident
accompagner to accompany

accomplir to accomplish
accord *m* **agreement; être d'** — to agree
accueillant friendly, hospitable
achat *m* purchase
acheter to buy
acteur *m*, **actrice** *f* actor, actress
actif, active active
activité *f* activity
actualités *f pl* news
actuel, actuelle present, current
addition *f* bill

adieu good-bye
admettre to admit, to allow
administration *f* administration, government service
admirer to admire
adolescence *f* adolescence
adorable adorable
adorer to adore, to like a great deal
adresse *f* address
adulte *m,f* adult
adversaire *m,f* adversary
aéronautique aeronautical
aéroport *m* airport
affaire *f* deal, business matter
affection *f* affection
affiche *f* poster
afficher to post, put up a sign
affronter to tackle, to confront
afin que in order that
africain African
Afrique *f* Africa
âge *m* age
agence *f* agency; — **de voyage** travel agency; — **immobilière** *f* real estate agency
agenda *m* appointment book
agent de police *m* police officer
agent publicitaire *m,f* advertising agent
s'agir de to be a question of, to be a matter of
agréable pleasant
agricole agricultural
agriculteur *m* farmer
aide *f* help
aider to help, assist
ailleurs elsewhere; **d'—** besides
aimer to like, to love
aimer bien to like
aimer mieux to prefer, to like better
aîné(e) *m,f* elder, eldest
ainsi thus, so
air *m* air; **avoir l'—** to seem, appear; **en plein —** outdoors
aise *f* ease; **à l'—** at ease
aisé well-to-do
ajouter to add
album *m* album

alcool *m* alcohol
algèbre *f* algebra
aliment *m* food, food item
aller to go; — **bien** to be fine; **ça vous va bien** that looks good on you
allergique allergic
allô hello (on the phone)
allonger to lengthen
allumer to light
alors then, well, then
alors que while, when, whereas
alpinisme *m* mountain climbing
alpiniste *m,f* mountain climber
amateur *m* enthusiast
ambitieux, ambitieuse ambitious
améliorer to improve
américain American
ami(e) *m,f* friend
amitié *f* friendship
amnésique *m* amnesia victim
amour *m* love
amoureux *m,* **amoureuse** *f* in love, lover
amour-propre *m* self-esteem
amplifier to amplify, to increase
amusant funny
amuser to amuse; **s'—** to have a good time
an *m* year
ancêtre *m* ancestor
ancien, ancienne old; former
angine *f* strep throat
anglais English
anglais *m* English language
animal (animaux) *m* animal
animé lively; **les dessins —s** cartoons
année *f* year
anniversaire *m* birthday
annoncer to announce
anonyme anonymous
anorak *m* ski jacket, windbreaker
anthropologie *f* anthropology
août *m* August
apercevoir to notice; **s'—** to realize
apéritif *m* before-dinner drink

appareil *m* device, machine; **à l'—** speaking (on the phone)
appareil-photo *m* camera
appartement *m* apartment
appeler to call; **s'—** to be named
appétit *m* appetite; **bon —** enjoy your meal
apporter to bring
apprécier to appreciate
apprendre to learn
apprentissage *m* apprenticeship
approprié appropriate
après after
après-midi *m* afternoon
araignée *f* spider
arbre *m* tree; — **généalogique** family tree
architecte *m* architect
architecture *f* architecture
arène *f* arena, bull ring
argent *m* money
armée *f* army
arrêt d'autobus *m* bus stop
arrêter to stop, arrest; **s'—** to stop (oneself)
arrière: en — behind, backwards
arrière-grand-mère *f* great-grandmother
arrivée *f* arrival
arriver to arrive, to happen, to succeed
arrondi rounded
arrondissement *m* administrative division of Paris
art *m* art; **—s ménagers** *m pl* home economics
artichaut *m* artichoke
article *m* article
artisan *m,* **artisane** *f* craftsperson
artiste *m,f* artist
ascension *f* ascent, climbing
aspirateur *m* vacuum cleaner
aspirine *f* aspirin
s'asseoir to sit down
asseyez-vous sit down
assez rather, enough
assis seated
assistant(e) *m,f* assistant
assister à to attend

associé associated

assuré assured, guaranteed

astronaute *m,f* astronaut

astronomie *f* astronomy

athlétisme *m* track and field

atmosphère *f* atmosphere

attachement *m* attachment

attendre to wait, to wait for

attention *f* attention; —! watch out!; **faire —** to pay attention

attitude *f* attitude

au to, at, in; **— courant** aware, up to date; **— cours de** during, in the course of; **— fait** by the way; **— milieu de** in the middle of; **— revoir** good-bye; **— sujet de** on the subject of

au-dessus above

auberge *f* hostel, inn; **— de jeunesse** *f* youth hostel

aucune no, none

audio-visuel, audio-visuelle audiovisual

augmenter to increase

aujourd'hui today

aussi also, too

aussi... que as . . . as

aussitôt que as soon as

autant as much, as many

auteur *m* author

auto *f* car

autobus *m* bus

auto-école *f* driving school

automne *m* autumn

automobile *f* automobile, car

automobiliste *m,f* motorist

autoritaire authoritarian, strict

autoroute *f* freeway

autour de around

autre other, another; **d'—** else, other; **d'— part** on the other hand

autrefois in the past, formerly, long ago

autrement otherwise, differently

aux to, in, at

avaler to swallow

avance: en — early; **à l'—** in advance

avant before

avantage *m* advantage

avec with

avenir *m* future

aventure *f* adventure

avenue *f* avenue

avion *m* plane

avis *m* opinion; **à votre —** in your opinion; **changer d'—** to change one's mind

avocat *m,* **avocate** *f* lawyer

avoir to have; **— besoin de** to need; **— de la chance** to be lucky; **— envie de** to feel like, to want to; **— faim** to be hungry; **— honte** to be ashamed; **— l'air** to seem, to appear; **— l'intention de** to intend to; **— l'occasion de** to have the chance to; **— mal** to hurt; **— peur** to be afraid; **— raison** to be right; **— soif** to be thirsty; **— sommeil** to be sleepy; **— tort** to be wrong; **—... ans** to be . . . years old; en **— marre** to be fed up

avouer to confess

avril *m* April

B

baccalauréat *m* French high school diploma

bagarre *f* brawl

baguette *f* long loaf of French bread

bain *m* bath; **la salle de —** bathroom; **—s remous** *m pl* whirlpool

ballon *m* ball (football or soccer)

banane *f* banana

bande dessinée *f* cartoon, comic strip

banjo *m* banjo

banlieue *f* suburb

banque *f* bank

baptême *m* baptism

barque *f* boat

bas *m pl* hose

bas, basse low

basé based

base-ball *m* baseball

basket-ball *m* basketball

bataille *f* battle

bateau (-x) *m* boat

batteur *m,* **batteuse** *f* drummer

battu beaten

bavarder to chat

beau, bel, belle, beaux, belles beautiful, handsome; **il fait —** the weather is nice; **c'est bien —** that's all well and good

beaucoup much, many, a lot

bébé *m* baby

beige beige

belge Belgian

belle-mère *f* mother-in-law

besoin *m* need; **avoir — de** to need

bête stupid

bête *f* animal

beurre *m* butter

bibliothèque *f* library

bicyclette *f* bicycle

bien fine, well; **— des** many; **— entendu** of course; **— que** although; **— sûr** of course; **eh —** well, so

bientôt soon; **à —** see you soon

bière *f* beer

bijou (-x) *m* jewel

bijouterie *f* jewelry store

bilingue bilingual

billet *m* banknote, bill, ticket

biologie *f* biology

bizarre strange

blanc, blanche white

blessé hurt, wounded

bleu blue; **— marin** navy blue

blond blond

bloqué snowed in, blocked

boeuf *m* beef

boire to drink

bois *m* wood

boisson *f* drink, beverage

boîte *f* can, box; **— de nuit** *f* nightclub

bon, bonne good; **bon appétit** have a good meal; **bon**

marché cheap, a good buy;
le bon vieux temps the good
old days
bonbon *m* candy
bonheur *m* happiness
bonjour hello
bonsoir good evening
botte *f* boot
bouche *f* mouth
boucher *m*, bouchère *f*
butcher
boucherie *f* butcher shop
boulangerie *f* bakery
boulevard *m* boulevard
boulot *m* job (coll.)
bourse *f* scholarship, purse
bout *m* end
bouteille *f* bottle
boutique de mode *f* clothing
store
boxe *f* boxing
bras *m* arm
bras-dessus, bras-dessous arm
in arm; avoir le bras long to
have connections
Bretagne *f* Brittany
brique *f* brick
bronchite *f* bronchitis
bronzé suntanned
se brosser to brush
brouillard *m* fog
brouillon *m* rough draft
brousse *f* brush
bruit *m* noise
brûler to burn
brûler la chandelle par les deux
bouts to burn the candle at
both ends
brûlure d'estomac *f* heartburn
brun dark, brown
brushing *m* brushing
bruyant noisy
bûcheron *m* logger
bulletin météorologique *m*
weather report
bureau (-x) *m* desk, office; —
de poste *m* post office; —
de tabac tobacco shop
buste *m* upper body
but *m* goal, aim

C

ça that
ça va, ça va bien things are
fine
cacher to hide
cachette : en — on the sly
cadeau (-x) *m* gift
cadet *m*, cadette *f* the
younger, youngest, junior
cadre *m* business executive
café *m* coffee, café
cahier *m* notebook
calcul *m* calculus
calculatrice *f* calculator
calme *m* calm
camarade *m,f* pal, friend; —
de chambre *m,f* roommate
cambrioler to burglarize
cambrioleur *m*, cambrioleuse
f burglar
caméra *f* movie camera,
videotape camera
campagne *f* country,
countryside
camping *m* camping,
campground; faire du — to
go camping
campus *m* campus
canadien, canadienne Canadian
canal *m* canal, channel
cancer *m* cancer
canot *m* canoe
capacité *f* ability, capacity
capitale *f* capital
car *m* bus
car for, because
carafe *f* carafe
carême *m* Lent
carnaval *m* carnival
carnet *m* notebook
carotte *f* carrot
carte *f* map, card; — postale
postcard; — de crédit *f*
credit card
cas *m* case
casser to break; — les pieds à
to bother; se — la tête to
rack one's brains
casserole *f* pan
cassette *f* cassette tape
catastrophe *f* catastrophy

catégorie *f* category
catholique Catholic
cauchemar *m* nightmare
cause *f* cause; à — de
because of
causerie *f* talk show, chat
ce it, that, he, she, they
ce(t), cette, ces this, that, these,
those
ce que that which
ce qui what, which
ceci this
cela that
célèbre famous
célibataire unmarried
celui, celle, ceux, celles this
(that) one, these, those; the
one(s)
cendre *f* ash
cendrier *m* ashtray
cent *m* hundred
centaine *f* about a hundred
centimètre *m* centimeter
centrale *f* power-station
centre *m* center; —
commercial shopping center
centre-ville *m* downtown area
cependant however
cercle *m* circle
cerise *f* cherry
certain certain
c'est-à-dire that is to say
chacun(e) each (one)
chagrin *m* grief, sorrow
chaîne *f* channel
chaîne stéréo *f* stereo
chaise *f* chair
chalet *m* chalet
chambre *f* bedroom; camarade
de — roommate
champignon *m* mushroom
champion *m*, championne *f*
champion
championnat *m* championship
chance *f* luck; avoir de la —
to be lucky
changement *m* change
chanson *f* song
chanter to sing
chanteur *m*, chanteuse *f*
singer
chantier *m* construction site

chapeau (-x) *m* hat
chaque each, every
charcuterie *f* pork shop, deli
charmant charming, delightful
charme *m* charm
chasse *f* hunting
chat *m* cat
châtain brown
château (-x) *m* chateau, castle
chaud hot; **avoir** — to be warm, hot (of persons); **faire** — to be warm, hot (of weather)
chauffeur *m* driver
chaussette *f* sock
chaussure *f* shoe
chef *m* chief, head, cook
chemin *m* road
chemise *f* shirt; — **de nuit** *f* nightshirt, nightgown
chemisier *m* blouse
chèque *m* check
cher, chère dear, expensive
chercher to look for, to seek
chercheur *m*, **chercheuse** *f* researcher
cheval (chevaux) *m* horse; **faire du** — to go horseback riding
cheveux *m pl* hair
chez at the home of, at the business of
chic stylish
chien *m* dog
chimie *f* chemistry
chinois *m* Chinese
chirurgien *m*, **chirurgienne** *f* surgeon
chocolat *m* chocolate
choisir to choose
choix *m* choice
chômage *m* unemployment
choqué shocked
choquer to shock
chose *f* thing
chouette neat, great (*coll.*)
chrysanthème *m* chrysanthemum
ciel *m* sky; **le** — **est couvert** it's cloudy
cigarette *f* cigarette
cinéma *m* movie theater

circuit *m* circuit, route
citoyen *m*, **citoyenne** *f* citizen
citron *m* lemon; — **pressé** *m* lemonade
clair light, pale
clarinette *f* clarinet
classe *f* class
classement *m* ranking
classique classic
clé *f* key
client *m*, **cliente** *f* customer
climat *m* climate, weather
club *m* club
coca-cola *m* Coca-Cola
code de la route *m* driving regulations
code postal *m* zip code, postal code
cœur *m* heart
cognac *m* cognac
coiffé with hair styled, coiffed
coiffeur *m*, **coiffeuse** *f* hairdresser, barber
coin *m* corner
colère *f* anger; **se mettre en** — to become angry
collant *m* panty-hose
collège *m* college, secondary school
colline *f* hill
colonie de vacances *f* summer camp
combien how much, how many; — **de temps** how long
comédien *m*, **comédienne** *f* comedian
commander to order
comme like, as; — **dessert** for dessert; — **d'habitude** as usual
commémorer to commemorate
commencer to start
comment how; — **vous appelez-vous** what's your name
commerçant *m*, **commerçante** *f* small-business person, shopkeeper
commerce *m* business, commerce

commettre to commit
commode *f* chest of drawers, cabinet
commun common
communauté *f* community, commune
communiquer to communicate
compagnie *f* company
comparaison *f* comparison; **en** — **de** in comparison with
compétent competent
complet *m* men's suit
complet, complète full, complete
complètement completely
compliqué complicated
comportement *m* behavior
composer to compose
compositeur *m*, **compositrice** *f* composer
composition *f* composition, paper
comprendre to understand, to include
comprimé *m* pill, tablet
compris included; **y** — including
comptabilité *f* accounting
comptable *m,f* accountant
compte rendu *m* report, review
compter to count
concerner to concern; **en ce qui concerne** concerning
concert *m* concert
concierge *m,f* building caretaker
condescendant condescending
condition *f* condition
condoléances *f pl* condolences, sympathy
conduire to drive, to lead; **permis de** — driver's license
conférence *f* lecture
confession *f* confession
confiance *f* confidence, trust
se confier to confide
confirmer to confirm
confiserie *f* candy store
confiture *f* jam
conflit *m* conflict
conformiste *m,f* conformist

confortable comfortable

congé *m* leave, holiday

connaissance *f* knowledge, acquaintance; **faire la — de** to meet

connaître to know, to be acquainted with

conquête *f* conquest

conseil *m* advice, counsel, council

conseiller *m*, **conseillère** *f* counselor

conséquent, par — consequently

considérer to consider

consommation *f* consumption, use

consommer to consume, use

constater to find, to note

constituer to constitute

construire to build, construct

contact *m* contact

conte *m* story, tale

content happy, glad, content

continuer to continue

contradiction *f* contradiction

contraire *m* opposite; **au —** on the contrary

contraste *m* contrast

contre against; **par —** on the other hand

converti(-e) *m,f* convert

coopérative *f* cooperative

copain *m*, **copine** *f* pal, buddy

copie *f* copy

corps *m* body

correspondre to agree with, to correspond

côte *f* coast; **côté** *f* side, direction, way; **à — de** beside, next to

côte à côte side by side; **la Côte d'Azur** Riviera

coteau (-x) *m* slope, hill

côtelette de porc *f* pork chop

cou *m* neck

se coucher to go to bed

coude *m* elbow

couleur *f* color

coup *m* blow, wound — **de foudre** *m* love at first sight

coupable *m,f* guilty person

coupe *f* cup, cut

couper to cut

cour *f* court, courtyard

courageux, courageuse courageous, brave

courant *m* current; **au —** up to date

courir to run

courrier *m* mail

cours *m* course, class; **au — de** during, in the course of

course *f* race; **— aux armements** *f* arms race

courses *f pl* errands; **faire les —** to go food shopping

court short

cousin *m*, **cousine** *f* cousin

couteau *m* knife

coûter to cost

coutume *f* custom, habit

couturier *m*, **couturière** *f* couturier, dressmaker

couvert covered, cloudy

couvrir to cover

craindre to fear, to be afraid (of)

cravate *f* tie

crayon *m* pencil

crèche *f* nursery

credo *m* prayer, I believe

créer to create

crème *f* cream

creuser to plough, to groove

crevette *f* shrimp

crime *m* crime

crise *f* crisis; **— cardiaque** *f* heart attack

crispé tense

critiquer to criticize

croire to believe

croisière *f* cruise

cuiller (*or* **cuillère**) *f* spoon, tablespoon

cuir *m* leather

cuire to cook

cuisine *f* kitchen, cooking

cuit cooked

cultivateur *m* farmer

cultivé educated, cultured

culturel, culturelle cultural

cure d'amaigrissement *f* weight-loss program

cyclisme *m* cycling

cyclone *m* cyclone

D

d'abord first

d'accord okay, agreed

d'ailleurs moreover, besides

dame *f* lady, woman

danger *m* danger

dangereux, dangereuse dangerous

dans in

danse *f* dance

danser to dance

danseur, danseuse dancer

date *f* date

d'autre else, other

davantage more

de of, from, by; (*as partitive*) some, any; **— moins en moins** less and less; **— rien** you're welcome; **— toute façon** in any case

débouché *m* job opening, opportunity

déboucher to pull out, to clear

débrouillard resourceful

se débrouiller to manage, get along

début *m* beginning; **au —** in the beginning

décembre *m* December

décevoir to deceive

décider to decide

décision *f* decision; **prendre une —** to make a decision

déclaration d'impôts *f* income tax return

déclarer to declare

découpé jagged, rough

découverte *f* discovery; **découvrir** to discover

décrire to describe

déçu disappointed

défaut *m* fault, shortcoming

se défendre to get along

défilé *m* parade

définir to define

degré *m* degree

dehors outside

déjà already, yet

déjeuner *m* lunch; **petit —** breakfast
délicieux, délicieuse delicious
déluge *m* flood
demain tomorrow; **à —** see you tomorrow
demande *m* application, request
demander to ask, to ask for; **se —** to wonder
démarche *f* walk, gait
demi *m* one half, mug of beer
démocratie *f* democracy
démodé out of style
dent *f* tooth
dentifrice *m* toothpaste
dentiste *m,f* dentist
déodorisant *m* deodorant
départ *m* departure
département *m* department
dépasser to overtake, to go beyond
se dépêcher to hurry
dépense *f* expense
dépenser to spend
déplaire to displease, offend
déposer to drop off
déprimant depressing
depuis since
député *m* delegate, deputy
déranger to disturb, to trouble
dernier, dernière last
derrière behind
des some, any
dès que as soon as
désagréable unpleasant
descendre to go down
désintégrer disintegrate
désirer to want, desire
désobéir to disobey
dessert *m* dessert
dessin *m* design, drawing; **— animé** *m* cartoon
dessinateur *m*, **dessinatrice** *f* cartoonist
dessiner to design, to draw; **bande dessinée** comic strip
dessus above, on it
se détacher to move away
se détendre to relax
détester to hate
dette *f* debt
deuil *m* grieving
devant in front of

devenir to become
deviner to guess
devoir to have to, must
devoirs *m pl* homework, assignment
d'habitude usually
diagnostic *m* diagnosis
diarrhée *f* diarrhea
dictionnaire *m* dictionary
dicton *m* saying
dieu *m* god
différent different
difficile difficult, hard
difficulté *f* difficulty, trouble
digérer to digest
digestif *m* after-dinner drink
diminuer to lessen, diminish
dîner to have dinner
dîner *m* dinner
diplômé(e) de graduated from
dire to say, to tell; **c'est-a-— que** that is to say; **vouloir —** to mean
direct direct
diriger to direct
discothèque *f* discotheque
discours *m* speech
discret, discrète discreet, unobtrusive
discussion *f* discussion
discuter to discuss
disparaître to disappear
disque *m* record
dissertation *f* term paper
divisé par divided by
division *f* division
divorcé divorced
divorce *m* divorce
dizaine *f* about ten
d'occasion used
docteur *m* doctor
doctorat *m* doctorate
documentaire *m* documentary
doigt *m* finger
domicile *m* residence, home
dommage, il est dommage it's a pity, it's too bad
donc therefore, then, so
dont whose, of which, of whom
dormir to sleep
dos *m* back; **sac à —** backpack

douane *f* customs office
douche *f* shower
doute *m* doubt; **sans —** probably
douter to doubt
d'outre-mer overseas
doux, douce sweet, mild
douzaine *f* dozen
drame *m* drama
droguerie *f* drug store
droit *m* law, right; **faire son —** to study law
droit, droite right, straight; **tout droit** straight ahead; **à droite** to the right
dur difficult, hard
durée *f* duration
durer to last
dynamique dynamic

E

eau *f* water; **— d'érable** *f* maple sap
échafaudage *m* scaffolding
échalote *f* shallot
échange *m* exchange, barter; **faire des échanges** to barter
échanger to exchange
école *f* school
écologie *f* ecology
économiser to save (money)
écouter to listen
écran *m* screen
écrire to write
éducateur *m*, **éducatrice** *f* educator
éducation physique *f* physical education
effet *m* effect; **en —** in fact
également equally, likewise
égalité *f* equality
église *f* church
eh bien well, so
électricien *m*, **électricienne** *f* electrician
électrique electric
électronique *f* electronics
élégant elegant
élémentaire elementary
élève *m,f* pupil
élevé high, raised
élever to bring up, to rear

éliminer to eliminate
elle she, it, her; **elles** they, them; **elle-même** herself; **elles-mêmes** themselves
émancipé emancipated
embaucher to hire, to sign on
embêtant annoying
embêter to annoy
embouchure *f* mouth of a river
embouteillage *m* traffic jam
embrasser to kiss, hug; **s'—** to kiss
émigrer to emigrate
émission *f* broadcast, program
emmener to take (along), to lead
empêcher to hinder, to keep from
empêchement *m* delay
s'empiler to pile up
emploi *m* employment, job
employé *m*, **employée** *f* employee
employer to use
employeur *m*, **employeuse** *f* employer
emporter to carry, to take along
emprunter to borrow
en in, to, at; of it, of them, some, any; **— arrière** behind, backwards; **— avoir marre** to be fed up; **— espèces** in cash; **— face de** facing, across from; **— fait** in fact; **— panne** broken down; **— plein air** in the open air; **— route** on the way
encore still, yet, again
encourager to encourage
endroit *m* place, spot
énergie *f* energy
énerver to get on someone's nerves, to weaken
enfance *f* childhood
enfant *m,f* child
enfin finally, at last, after all
ennui *m* trouble, difficulty
ennuyer to bore
ennuyeux, ennuyeuse boring
énorme enormous
enquête *f* survey

enquêteur *m*, **enquêtrice** *f* pollster
enrichir to enrich
enseignement *m* teaching
enseigner to teach
ensemble together
ensuite then, next
entendre to hear; **— parler de** to hear about; **s'—** to get along; **bien entendu** of course
enterrement *m* burial, funeral
enthousiaste enthusiastic
entier, entière entire
entourer to surround
entraîner to carry away
entre between
entrée *f* entrance
entreprenant enterprising
entreprise *f* business, company
entrer to enter, to go in
entretien *m* upkeep, maintenance
envers toward, in regard to
envie *f* desire; **avoir — de** to feel like, want to
environ approximately, about
environnement *m* environment
envisager to consider
envoyer to send
épaule *f* shoulder
épicerie *f* grocery store
épinards *m pl* spinach
épisode *m* episode
époque *f* epoch, era; **à cette —-là** at that time, in those days
éprouver to feel, to experience
épuisé exhausted
équilibre *m* balance
équipe *f* team
équipement *m* equipment
équivalent *m* equivalent
érable *m* maple; **eau d'—** maple sap
erreur *f* error, mistake
éruption *f* eruption
escale *f* stop, intermediate landing, place of call
escorté escorted
espace *m* space

espagnol Spanish
espèce *f* species, type; **en —s** in cash
espérance *f* hope
espérer to hope
espoir *m* hope
esprit *m* mind, spirit
essayer to try, to try on
essentiel *m* essential
est *m* east
esthétique aesthetic
estomac *m* stomach
et and
établir to establish
étage *m* floor, story
étalé spread out, displayed
étape *f* stage
état *m* state
été *m* summer
étoile *f* star
étranger, étrangère foreign, foreigner; **à l'étranger** abroad
être to be
étroit narrow
étude *f* study; **faire des —s** to study
étudiant *m*, **étudiante** *f* student
étudier to study
européen, européenne European
eux, elles them, to them; **—-mêmes** themselves
évaluer to evaluate
événement *m* event
éventuellement eventually
évidemment evidently
éviter to avoid
évoluer to evolve
exact exact
examen *m* test, exam
excellent excellent
excepté except
exceptionnel, exceptionnelle exceptional
excès *m* excess
excusez-moi excuse me
exemple *m* example; **par —** for example
exercer to practice (a profession)
exercice *m* exercise
exil *m* exile

exister to exist
expérience *f* experiment
expert *m* expert
explication *f* explanation
expliquer to explain
explorateur *m*, **exploratrice** *f* explorer
exposé *m* report, paper
exposition *f* exhibition, exhibit
exprimer to express
extra super, excellent
exubérance *f* exuberance

F

face *f* face; **en — de** across from
se fâcher to get angry
facile easy
façon *f* way, manner; **de toute — in any case**
faible light, weak
faim *f* hunger; **avoir —** to be hungry
faire to do, to make; **— beau** to be fine weather; **— de son mieux** to do one's best; **— des courses** to run errands; **— du camping** to go camping; **— du jogging** to jog; **— du ski** to go skiing; **— du sport** to play sports; **— la connaissance de** to meet, to become acquainted with; **— la cuisine** to cook, to do the cooking; **— la vaisselle** to do the dishes; **— le marché** to go grocery shopping; **— le ménage** to do housework; **— le tour de** to go around, to make a tour of; **— les courses** to go shopping; **— mal** to hurt; **— match nul** to tie; **— plaisir à quelqu'un** to please someone; **— remarquer** to point out; **— ses devoirs** to do one's homework; **— sombre** to be dark (night); **— son lit** to make one's bed; **— un voyage** to take a trip; **— une promenade** to go for a walk; **ça ne fait rien** it

doesn't matter; **ça ne se fait pas** that is not done; **ne t'en fais pas** don't worry; **tu me fais marcher** you're pulling my leg
fait *m* fact, act; **au —** by the way; **en —** in fact
falloir to be necessary
familial (*m pl* **familiaux**) family
famille *f* family
fantaisie *f* fantasy
fascinant fascinating
fatigant tiring
fatigué tired
fatigue *f* fatigue
fauché (*coll.*) broke, out of money
fauteuil *m* armchair
faux, fausse false
faux pas *m* blunder
favori, favorite favorite
félicitations *f* congratulations
féminité *f* femininity
femme *f* woman, wife
fenêtre *f* window
fer *m* iron
ferme *f* farm
fermé closed, locked
fermer to close
fête *f* holiday, patron saint's day
fêter to celebrate
feu *m* fire
feu rouge red light
feu vert green light
feuille *f* leaf
feuilleton *m* soap opera, story
février *m* February
fibre de verre *f* fiberglass
fidèle faithful
fier, fière proud
fierté *f* pride
fièvre *f* fever
fille *f* girl, daughter
film *m* film, movie
fils *m* son
fin *f* end
finalement finally
financier, financière financial
finir to finish, end; **— par** to end up, finally
flatter to flatter
fleur *f* flower

fleuriste *m,f* florist
fleuve *m* major river
flûte *f* flute
foi *f* faith, belief
fois *f* time; **à la —** at the same time
folklorique popular, folk
foncé dark
fonctionnaire *m* civil servant, government worker
fonder to found
football *m* soccer
force *f* force, strength
forcer to force, make
forêt *f* forest
formation *f* training, education
forme *f* form, shape, kind
formidable great, wonderful
formuler to formulate
fort strong
fou, folle crazy
foule *f* crowd
fourchette *f* fork
fournitures *f pl* supplies
fourrure *f* fur
frais *m pl* expenses, cost
frais, fraîche fresh, cool
français French
franchement frankly
franchise *f* sincerity, frankness
francophone French-speaking
frapper to hit, knock
freiner to apply the brakes
fréquemment frequently
fréquenter to frequent, go to often
frère *m* brother
frigo *m* (*coll.*) refrigerator
frites *f pl* french fries
froid cold; **avoir —** to be cold (persons); **faire —** to be cold (weather)
fromage *m* cheese
front *m* forehead
frontière *f* border
fruit *m* fruit
frustré frustrated
fumée *f* smoke
fumer to smoke
furieux, furieuse furious
fusée *f* rocket
futur *m* future

G

gagner to earn, to win; — **sa vie** to earn one's living
garage *m* garage
garçon *m* boy, waiter
garde : de — on duty
garder to keep, hold, to watch over
gardien *m*, **gardienne** *f* guard; — **d'enfants** baby-sitter
gare *f* railway station
gâteau (-x) *m* cake
gauche *m* left; **à —** to the left
gazeux, gazeuse carbonated
gelé frozen
généalogique : arbre — family tree
général (*m pl* **généraux**) general; **en —** in general, generally
genou (-x) *m* knee
genre *m* type
gens *m pl* people
gentil, gentille nice
géographie *f* geography
géologie *f* geology
géométrie *f* geometry
geste *m* gesture
gesticuler to gesture
gestion *f* management
gibier *m* wild game
glace *f* ice cream, ice
glaise *f* clay
glisser to slide, slip
golf *m* golf
gorge *f* canyon, throat
gosse *m, f* (*coll.*) kid
goût *m* taste
goûter *m* snack
gouvernement *m* government
grâce à thanks to
gramme *m* gram
grand big, tall, great, large, grown up
grand magasin *m* department store
grandir to grow, to grow up
grand-mère *f* grandmother
grand-parents *m pl* grandparents

grand-père *m* grandfather
gratuit free
grave serious
grec, grecque Greek
grève *f* strike
grippe *f* flu
gris grey
gros, grosse large, big, fat
gros lot *m* jackpot
groupe *m* group
grotte *f* cave
guerre *f* war; — **mondiale** world war
guichet *m* booth, window
guise, à sa — as one wishes
guitare *f* guitar
gymnase *m* gymnasium
gymnastique *f* gymnastics; **faire de la —** to exercise

H

habillé dressy
habillement *m* clothing
habiller to dress; **s'—** to get dressed
habiter to live
habitude *f* habit, custom
habituel, habituelle usual, habitual
***hanche** *f* hip
***haricots verts** *m pl* green beans
harmonie *f* harmony
***hasard** *m* chance; **par —** by chance
***haut** high
***haute couture** *f* high fashion
***hein** equivalent of **n'est-ce pas**, Eh
herbe *f* grass, herb
***héros** *m* hero
heroïne *f* heroine
hésiter to hesitate
heure *f* hour, o'clock; **à l'—** on time; **à tout à l'—** see you later; **quelle — est-il** what time is it; **de bonne —** early
heureusement fortunately, happily

heureux, heureuse happy, fortunate
heureusement fortunately
hier yesterday; — **soir** last night
histoire *f* history, story
hiver *m* winter
***hockey** *m* hockey
***homard** *m* lobster
homme *m* man
honnête honest
***honte** *f* shame; **avoir —** to be ashamed
hôpital *m* hospital
horaire *m* schedule, time table
***hors de** outside
hôte *m* host
hôtel *m* hotel
hôtesse *f* hostess
huile *f* oil
huître *f* oyster
humain human
hygiène *f* hygiene

I

ici here
idéal *m* ideal
idée *f* idea
identifier to identify
identité *f* identity
il he, it; — **y a** there is, there are; ago
île *f* island
ils they
image *f* picture, image
imaginer to imagine
imiter to imitate, copy
immédiatement immediately
immeuble *m* apartment building
immobilier *m* real estate
impatient impatient
impossible impossible
impôts *m pl* taxes
impressionnant impressive
impressionner to impress
impulsif, impulsive impulsive
inconvénient *m* disadvantage, inconvenience
incroyable unbelievable
indépendance *f* independence
indépendant independent

---

* An asterisk indicates an aspirate *h*.

indiqué indicated
indiquer to indicate, show
individu *m* individual
industrie *f* industry
industriel, industrielle industrial
inégalité *f* inequality
infection *f* infection
infirmier *m*, **infirmière** *f* nurse
inflation *f* inflation
informatique *f* computer science
infraction *f* infraction, violation
ingénierie *f* engineering
ingénieur *m* engineer
initiale *f* initial
initiative *f* initiative
injuste unfair
inondation *f* flood
inquiet, inquiète uneasy, worried
inquiétude *f* anxiety, restlessness
inscription *f* registration
insister to insist, to stress
inspection *f* inspection
installé settled
installer to install, to set up
instant *m* instant, moment
instituteur *m*, **institutrice** *f* elementary school teacher
insulter to insult
intellectuel, intellectuelle intellectual
intelligent intelligent
intention *f* intention; **avoir l'—** to intend
intéressant interesting
intéresser to interest
s'intéresser à to be interested in
intérêt *m* interest
intérieur *m* interior, inside; **à l'—** inside
interroger to question
interview *f* interview
interviewer to interview
intimement intimately
intitulé entitled
inutile de no need to
inventer to invent

invité *m*, **invitée** *f* guest
inviter to invite
irrésistible irresistible
italien, italienne !talian
italique : en — in italics
itinéraire *m* route, itinerary
ivre intoxicated

J

jaloux, jalouse jealous
jamais never, ever; **ne... —** never
jambe *f* leg
jambon *m* ham
janvier *m* January
jardin *m* garden; **— d'enfants** *m* kindergarten
jaune yellow
je (j') I
jeans *m* jeans
jeep *f* jeep
jeu (-x) *m* game; **les Jeux Olympiques** the Olympic Games
jeune young
jeunesse *f* youth; **auberge de —** youth hostel
jogging *m* jogging, jogging suit
joie *f* joy
joli pretty
jonction *f* junction
joue *f* cheek
jouer to play
jouet *m* toy
joueur *m*, **joueuse** *f* player
jour *m* day; **tous les —s** every day; **huit —s** one week; **quinze —s** two weeks
journal (journaux) *m* newspaper, journal
journalisme *m* journalism
journaliste *m,f* journalist
journée *f* day
juge *m* judge
juillet *m* July
jupe *f* skirt
jus d'orange *m* orange juice
jusqu'à as far as, until; **— ce que** until
juste fair, exact
justifier to justify

K

kilogramme *m* kilogram
kilomètre *m* kilometer

L

la the, her, it
là there; **ce jour-—** that day; **—-bas** over there
laboratoire *m* laboratory
lac *m* lake
laid ugly
laisser to leave, to let, allow
lait *m* milk
lampe *f* lamp, light
langage *m* language
langue *f* language, tongue
laquelle which one; **lesquelles** which ones
large wide
latin *m* Latin
laver to wash; **se —** to wash (oneself)
le the, it, him
leçon *f* lesson
lecture *f* reading
légume *m* vegetable
lent slow
lequel which one; **lesquels** which ones
les the, them
lettre *f* letter; **—s** humanities
se lever to get up
libéral (*m pl* **libéraux**) liberal
librairie *f* bookstore
libre free
lien *m* tie
lieu *m* place; **au — de** instead of; **avoir —** to take place
ligne *f* line
limite *f* limit; **— de vitesse** speed limit
liqueur *m* liquor
lire to read
liste d'attente *f* waiting list
lit *m* bed
litre *m* liter
littérature *f* literature
livre *f* pound
livre *m* book
logement *m* housing

loi *f* law
loin far
loisirs *m pl* leisure activities, recreation
long, longue long; **le — de** along
longtemps a long time
longueur *f* length
lorsque when
loterie *f* lottery
louer to rent
lourd heavy
loyer *m* rent
lui (to, for) him, (to, for) her; **—-même** himself
lune *f* moon
lunettes *f pl* eyeglasses
lutte *f* struggle, wrestling
lutter to fight, struggle
lycée *m* French secondary school

M

ma my
machine *f* machine; **— à écrire** *f* typewriter; **— à laver** *f* washing machine
maçon *m* mason, bricklayer, builder
madame Mrs., ma'am
mademoiselle Miss, ma'am
madère *f* madeira wine
magasin *m* store; **— de chaussures** *m* shoe store
magazine *m* magazine
magnétophone *m* tape recorder
magnétoscope *m* video-recorder
magnifique magnificent, terrific, great
maillot de bain *m* bathing suit
main *f* hand
maintenant now
maire *m* mayor
mairie *f* city hall
mais but
maison *f* house; **à la —** at home
majorité *f* majority
mal *m* evil, wrong, pain; **avoir — à** to have pain in

mal badly, poorly, ill
malade ill
maladie *f* illness, sickness
malentendu *m* misunderstanding
malgré in spite of
malheur *m* misfortune
malheureusement unfortunately
manger to eat
manières *f pl* manners
manifestation *f* demonstration
mannequin *m* model
manquer to lack, miss
manteau (-x) *m* coat
manuel, manuelle manual, blue collar
maquillage *m* make-up
maquillé made-up
marathon *m* long-distance race, marathon
marchand *m*, **marchande** *f* merchant
marche *f* walking
marché *m* market; **bon —** cheap, inexpensive
marcher to walk, run (of a machine); **tu me fais —** you're pulling my leg
marée *f* tide
mari *m* husband
mariage *m* marriage, wedding
marié married
se marier to get married
marin navy, marine
marine *f* navy
maroquinerie *f* leather goods store
marraine *f* godmother
marron (*invariable*) brown
marsouin *m* porpoise
matador *m* bullfighter
match *m* game, match
maternel, maternelle native
maternité *f* maternity
mathématiques (maths) *f pl* mathematics
matin *m* morning; **le —** in the morning
mauvais bad; **il fait —** the weather is bad
mauve mauve
mécanicien *m*, **mécanicienne** *f* mechanic

méchant bad, wicked, naughty
médecin *m* physician, medical doctor
médecine *f* medicine (profession)
médical (*m pl* **médicaux**) medical
médicament *m* medicine
meilleur best, better
melon *m* melon
membre *m* member
même same, even, very; -self
menacer to threaten
ménagère *f* homemaker
mener to lead
meneur de jeu *m* master of ceremonies
mensonge *m* lie
menton *m* chin
menu *m* menu, bill of fare
mépris *m* contempt
mer *f* sea; **au bord de la —** at the seashore
merci thank you
mère *f* mother
mériter to deserve, earn
merveilleux, merveilleuse marvelous
mes my
message *m* message
messe *f* mass
métal (métaux) *m* metal
météo *f* weather report
méthode *f* method
métier *m* trade, occupation, profession
mètre *m* meter
métro *m* subway
metteur en scène *m* director
mettre to put, to place, to put on; **— la table** to set the table; **— sur la piste** to put on the right track
se mettre à to start to; **se mettre à table** to sit down to eat
meublé furnished
meubles *m pl* furniture
micro-ordinateur *m* microcomputer
midi *m* noon
Midi *m* South (of France)
mien, mienne mine

mieux better, best; **aimer —** to prefer; **valoir —** to be better
mignon cute
mijoter to simmer
militaire military
milieu *m* middle, environment; **au — de** in the middle of
mille *m* thousand
millier *m* around a thousand
million *m* million
minéral mineral (*m pl* **mineraux**)
mini-croisière *f* mini-cruise
minuit *m* midnight
missionnaire *m* missionary
mode *f* fashion, style; **à la —** in style
modèle *m* model, style
modéré moderate
moderne modern
modeste modest
moi me, I; **—-même** myself
moins minus, less; **à — que** unless; **le —** least; **— de** less than; **au —** at least; **de — en —** less and less; **plus ou —** more or less; **deux heures — dix** ten minutes to two
mois *m* month
moisson *f* harvest
moitié *f* half
moment *m* moment; **à ce —-là** at that moment, at that time; **en ce —** now
mon my
monde *m* world; **tout le —** everybody
mondial (*m pl* **mondiaux**) world
moniteur *m*, **monitrice** *f* instructor, camp counselor
monnaie *f* change, coins
monotonie *f* monotony
monsieur (*m pl* **messieurs**) mister, sir, gentleman
mont *m* mountain, mount
montagne *f* mountain
monter to go up, rise, to climb, get in, get on
montre *f* watch
montrer to show

monument *m* monument
se moquer de to make fun of
morceau (-x) *m* piece, chunk
mort dead
mort *f* death
mot *m* word; **—s doux** sweet nothings
moto *f* motorcycle
motorisé motorized
mourir to die
moyens *m pl* means
moyenne *f* the average
multiplication *f* multiplication
municipalité *f* municipality, town
mûr ripe, mature
mur *m* wall
musée *m* museum
musicien *m*, **musicienne** *f* musician
musique *f* music

N

nager to swim
naïf, naïve naive
naissance *f* birth
naître to be born
natation *f* swimming
nation *f* nation
nationalité *f* nationality
nature *f* outdoors, nature
naturel, naturelle natural
nautique : le ski — water skiing
navet *m* turnip
navette spatiale *f* space craft, space shuttle
naviguer to navigate
ne no, not; **—... aucun(e)** not one; **—... guère** hardly; **—... jamais** never; **—... ni... ni** neither . . . nor; **—... pas** not; **—... pas du tout** not at all; **—... personne** no one; **—... plus** no more, no longer; **—... que** only; **—... rien** nothing
nécessaire necessary
neige *f* snow
neiger to snow
nerveux, nerveuse edgy
n'est-ce pas? isn't it so?

nettoyer to clean
neuf, neuve brand new
neveu (-x) *m* nephew
névrose *f* neurosis
névrosé(e) *m,f* neurotic
nez *m* nose
ni... ni neither . . . nor
nièce *f* niece
n'importe qui anyone, no matter who
niveau (-x) *m* level
Noël *m* Christmas
noir black
nom *m* name, last name
nombre *m* number
nommer to name
nord *m* north
nos our
note *f* grade, mark
noter to note
notre our
nôtre ours
nourriture *f* food, meals
nous we, us
nouveau (-x), nouvel, nouvelle new; **de nouveau** again, anew
nouveau venu *m* newcomer
nouvelles *f pl* news
nuage *m* cloud
nuageux, nuageuse cloudy
nucléaire nuclear
nuit *f* night; **boîte de —** nightclub
numéro *m* number

O

obéir to obey
objet *m* object
obligé obligated
occasion *f* chance; **d'—** used; **avoir l'— de** to have a chance to
occupé occupied, busy
s'occuper de to take care of
octobre *m* October
œil (-yeux) *m* eye
œuf *m* egg
œuvre *f* (literary or art) work
officiel, officielle official
offrir to offer, to give
oignon *m* onion

oiseau (-x) *m* bird
on one, they, we
oncle *m* uncle
ongle *m* fingernail
opéra *m* opera
opération *f* operation
opinion *f* opinion
opposé opposite, opposed
opprimé oppressed
optimiste optimistic
orage *m* storm
orangeade *m* orange drink
orchestre *m* band, orchestra
ordinaire ordinary
ordinateur *m* computer
ordonnance *f* prescription
ordre *m* order
oreille *f* ear
oreillons *m* mumps
organiser to organize
orgueil *m* pride, arrogance
orientation *f* orientation,
   direction
origine *f* origin, descent
ou or
où where
oublier to forget
ouest *m* west
oui yes; **mais** — of course
ouverture *f* opening
ouvrier *m*, **ouvrière** *f* worker
ouvrir to open

P

pain *m* bread
paire *f* pair
palais *m* palace
pancarte *f* sign
panier à salade *m* paddy
   wagon, police van
panne *f* breakdown; **en** —
   broken down
pantalon *m* pants
papeterie *f* stationery store,
   office supply store
papier *m* paper
paquet *m* pack, package
par by, through; —
   conséquent consequently
par contre on the other hand;
   — **exemple** for example

paradis *m* paradise
paraître to appear, seem
paralysé paralyzed
parapluie *m* umbrella
parc *m* park
parce que because
pardon pardon me
pardonner to forgive
parent *m* parent, relative
paresseux, paresseuse lazy
parfait perfect
parfois at times
parfum *m* perfume, scent
parier bet
parisien, parisienne Parisian
parking *m* parking lot
parler to speak, to talk
parmi among
parole *f* (spoken) word; *pl*
   lyrics
part *f* part; **d'une** — on one
   hand; **d'autre** — on the
   other hand; **à** — except for
partager to share
partenaire *m,f* partner
parti *m* party
participation *f* participation
particulier, particulière
   particular, special
partie *f* part; **faire** — to be a
   part
partiel, partielle partial
partir to leave
partout everywhere
pas no, not; **ne...** — not, no;
   — **de** no; — **du tout** not at
   all
pas *m* step; **faux** — blunder
passage *m* passing through,
   crossing
passé *m* past
passé last, past
passeport *m* passport
passer to spend, pass; — **un**
   examen to take a test; **se** —
   to happen
passionné(e) *m,f* fan
passionnant exciting
pâté *m* block of houses
patient patient
patinage *m* skating
pâtisserie *f* pastry, pastry shop
patron *m*, **patronne** *f* boss

pause *f* pause
pauvre poor
payer to pay
pays *m* country
paysage *m* countryside
peau *f* skin
pêche *f* peach, fishing
pédagogie *f* education
se peigner to comb one's hair
peindre to paint
peine *f* trouble, difficulty; **ça**
   vaut la — it's worth the
   effort; **à** — hardly, scarcely
peintre *m* painter
peinture *f* painting
pelouse *f* lawn
pendant during; — **que** while
pénétrer to penetrate, to enter
penser to think; — **à** to think
   about; — **de** to think of
   (have an opinion); **je pense**
   que non I don't think so; **je**
   pense que oui I think so
pension de famille *f* rooming
   house
pente *f* slope
perdre to lose; to waste (time);
   à temps perdu in one's spare
   time
père *m* father
période *f* period, time
permanente *f* permanent
permettre to allow, to permit
permis permitted
permis *m* permit, license; —
   de conduire driver's license
personnage *m* character
personnalité *f* personality
personne *f* person; **ne...** —
   no one; — **ne** no one
personnel, personnelle
   personal
persuader to persuade
perte *f* loss
pessimiste pessimist
pétanque *f* game of balls
petit small, short; — **ami**
   boyfriend
petit déjeuner *m* breakfast
petite amie *f* girlfriend
petits pois *m pl* peas
peu little; — **de** few; **un** —
   a little; — **probable** unlikely

peuple *m* people, nation
peuplé populated
peur *f* fear; **avoir —** to be afraid
peut-être perhaps
phare *m* headlight
pharmacie *f* drug store
pharmacien *m*, **pharmacienne** *f* pharmacist
philosophe *m,f* philosopher
philosophie *f* philosophy
photo *f* photograph
phrase *f* sentence
physique physical
physique *f* physics
piano *m* piano
pièce *f* room
pièce de théâtre *f* play, drama
pied *m* foot; **à —** on foot
pierre *f* rock, stone
pilule *f* pill
pique-nique *m* picnic
pique-niquer to picnic
piqûre *f* injection, shot
pire worse
piscine *f* swimming pool
piste *f* trail, track
placard *m* cupboard, closet
place *f* place, seat, room, square; **à votre —** if I were you
plafond *m* ceiling
plage *f* beach
plaindre to pity; **se —** to complain
plaine *f* plain
plaire to please; **s'il vous (te) plaît** please
plaisanter to joke
plaisir *m* pleasure; **faire — à** to please
plan *m* plan, map
planche à voile *f* wind surfing
planète *f* planet
plantation *f* plantation
plante *f* plant
plaque *f* plate, sheet
plat *m* dish, course; **— du jour** *m* daily special; **mettre les pieds dans le —** to put one foot in one's mouth
plein full; **en — air** outdoor(s)

pleurer to cry
pleuvoir to rain; **il pleut** it's raining
plombier *m* plumber
plongé plunged
pluie *f* rain
plupart *f* most
plus plus, and, more; **— de** besides; **de — en —** more and more; **en —** in addition; **le —** the most; **ne... —** no longer; **non —** not . . . either; **— ou moins** more or less; **— que** more than
plusieurs several
plutôt rather; **— que** rather than
pneumonie *f* pneumonia
poche *f* pocket
poème *m* poem
poésie *f* poetry
poète *m* poet
poids *m* weight
point *m* period; **— d'interrogation** question mark
pointure *f* size (shoes and gloves)
poire *f* pear
pois : petits — peas
poisson *m* fish
poivre *m* pepper
poli polite
police *f* police; **agent de —** police officer; **poste de —** police station
policier, policière police, detective
politesse *f* politeness
politique politics; political
pollution *f* pollution
pomme *f* apple; **— de terre** *f* potato
populaire popular
porc *m* pork
port *m* port
porte *f* door
portefeuille *m* billfold
porter to carry, to wear; **— sur** to bear upon, to relate
poser to ask, to place
poseur, poseuse phony, snobbish

posséder to possess, own, have
possibilité *f* possibility
possible possible
poste *f* post office
poste *m* job, position; **— de police** *m* police station
pot *m* drink
poubelle *f* trashcan
poulet *m* chicken
poumon *m* lung
pour for, in order to; **— que** in order, that; **— cent** percent
pourcentage *m* percentage
pourquoi why
pourriez-vous could you
pourtant however
pourvu que provided that
pousser to push, press
pouvez-vous can you
pouvoir to be able, can
pratique practical; **travaux —** lab
pratiquer to practice
précédent preceding, former
prédestiné predestinated, fated
prédire to foretell, predict
préférer prefer
préfet *m* prefect
premier, première first; **premier ministre** prime minister; **premier étage** *m* second floor
prendre to take, to have; **— un bain de soleil** to sunbathe; **— un coup de soleil** to get sunburned; **— une décision** to make a decision; **— un pot** to have a drink; **— un rendez-vous** to make an appointment; **— la succession de** to take over from
prénom *m* first name
se préoccuper to be concerned
préparatif *m* preparation
préparer to prepare; **se —** to get ready
près near, close; **— de** near, close to
présentateur *m*, **présentatrice** *f* anchorperson
présenter to introduce, present
presque almost

pressé in a hurry
prestige *m* prestige
prêt ready
prêt *m* loan
prêter to lend
prévenir to warn, to tell ahead of time
prière *f* prayer; **— de** please
principal (*m pl* **principaux**) main
printemps *m* spring
priorité *f* priority; **— à droite** yield to the right
prison *f* prison
prisonnier *m* **prisonnière** *f* prisoner
privé private
prix *m* award, prize, price
probable probable; **peu —** unlikely
probablement probably
problème *m* problem
prochain next
produire to produce
produit *m* product
professeur *m* teacher, professor
profession *f* profession
professionnel, professionnelle professional
profiter to profit, to take advantage of
profond deep
programme *m* program
progrès *m* progress
progresser move, progress
projet *m* plan, project
promenade *f* walk; **faire une — ** to take a walk
se promener to take a walk
promesse *f* promise
promettre to promise
promotion *f* promotion
pronom *m* pronoun
prononcer to pronounce, say
proposer to propose
propre own; clean
propriétaire *m,f* owner
propriété *f* property
protéger to protect
provençal of Provence
proverbe *m* proverb
province *f* province

provisions *f pl* groceries
prudent prudent
psychiatrique psychiatric
psychologie *f* psychology
psychologue *m,f* psychologist
public, publique public
publicité *f* advertising
publier to publish
puis then
puis-je can I
pull-over *m* pullover sweater
punir punish
pur pure
pyjama *m* pyjamas

Q

qualité *f* good quality
quand when; **— même** anyway, just the same
quant à as for, as to
quantité *f* quantity
quart *m* one fourth, quarter; **neuf heures et —** a quarter after nine
quartier *m* neighborhood
que (qu') that, what, than, which, whom; **ce —** what, that which; **ne... —** only; **qu'est-ce —** what; **qu'est-ce qui** who
québécois pertaining to Quebec
quel, quelle what, which
quelque(s) some, any; **— chose** something; **—s minutes** a few minutes; **— part** somewhere; **quelqu'un** someone; **quelques-un(e)s** some people
quelquefois sometimes
question *f* question
qui who, whom, that; **— est-ce** who is that, who is it
quitter to leave
quoi what, which
quotidien, quotidienne daily

R

racisme *f* racism
raconter to tell, to recount
radio *f* radio

raffiné refined
raisin *m* grape
raison *f* reason; **avoir —** to be right
rame *f* oar
randonnée *f* hike
randonneur *m*, **randonneuse** *f* hiker
rang *m* row
ranger to put away, to arrange
rapide fast
rappeler to recall; **se —** to remember
rapport *m* report, relationship, rapport
rare rare
rarement rarely
rasoir *m* razor
rassurer to reassure
ravi delighted
rayon *m* department
réaliser to achieve, to realize
réalité *f* reality
récent recent
recette *f* recipe
recevoir to receive
recherche *f* research
recherché sought after
récital *m* recital, performance
recommander to recommend
reconnaître to recognize
se recoucher to go back to bed
réduit reduced
réel, réelle real, authentic
réfléchir to reflect, to consider, think
reflet *m* reflection
réflexion *f* reflection
réfrigérateur *m* refrigerator
refuser to refuse
regard *m* sight
regarder to watch, to look at
région *f* region
règne *m* reign
regret *m* regret
regretter to regret, to be sorry
régulier, régulière regular
relations *f* relationships
religion *f* religion
remarquable remarkable
remarquer to notice, observe
remède *m* treatment, remedy
remercier to thank

remettre to hand in, to postpone
remplir to fill
rencontre *f* meeting
rencontrer to meet, to run into
rendez-vous *m* appointment
rendre to hand back, to make; — **visite à** to visit (a person)
renseignements *m pl* information
rentrer to return (home); — **dedans** to run into
renverser to tip over
réparer to repair
repas *m* meal
repasser to put back
répéter to repeat
répondre to answer
réponse *f* answer, response
reportage *m* report
reporter *m* reporter
reposer to put back down; **se — ** to rest
repousser to postpone, to put off, to push back
représentant(e) *m,f* representative
réputation *f* reputation
réputé famous, known
réseau (-x) *m* system, network
réserve *f* reservation
réservé reserved
résidence universitaire *f* dormitory
résigné resigned
résister to resist
résoudre to resolve
respecter to respect
respiration *f* breathing
respirer to breathe
responsabilité *f* responsibility
ressembler à to resemble
ressources *f pl* means, resources
restaurant universitaire *m* university food service
reste *m* rest
rester to stay, remain
résultat *m* result
retard *m* delay; **en — ** late
retenir to reserve, to hold, retain
retour *m* return; **de — ** back

retourner to return
retraite *f* retirement
se retrouver to meet (by arrangement)
réunion *f* meeting
se réunir to get together
réussir to succeed, to pass (exam)
réussite *f* success
revanche : en revanche on the other hand
rêve *m* dream
se réveiller to wake up
révéler to reveal
revendication *f* demand
revenir to come back, to return
rêver to dream
revoir to see again; **au — ** good-bye
revue *f* magazine
rez-de-chaussée *m* ground floor, first floor
rhume *m* cold; — **des foins** *m* hay fever
riche rich
ride *m* wrinkle
ridiculiser to ridicule
rien nothing, anything; **ne... — ** nothing; — **ne** nothing; — **de joli** nothing pretty; **de — ** you're welcome
rigoureux rigorous
rire to laugh; **tu veux — ** you're kidding
risquer to risk
rive *f* bank
rivière *f* river
robe *f* dress
robotique *f* robotics
rock *m* rock music
roi *m* king
rôle role, part; **à tour de — ** in turn
roman *m* novel
rond *m* ring
rose pink
rôti *m* roast
rouge red
rougeole *f* measles
rougir to blush
rouler to roll
route *f* road, route, way; **en — ** on the way

roux, rousse red (of hair)
rue *f* street
rugby *m* rugby

S

sa his, her, its, one's
sable *m* sand
sac *m* bag; — **à dos** backpack; — **à main** *m* handbag, purse
sage well-behaved
saison *f* season
salade *f* salad
salaire *m* salary
salle *f* room; — **à manger** *f* dining room; — **de bain** *f* bathroom; — **de séjour** *f* living room
salon d'essayage *m* fitting room
salut hi, hello
salutation *f* greeting
sandale *f* sandal
sandwich *m* sandwich
sans without; — **blague** no kidding; — **cesse** constantly; — **doute** probably; — **que** without
santé *f* health; **à votre — ** cheers, to your health
satellite *m* satellite
satisfaire to satisfy
satisfait satisfied
sauce *f* sauce
saucisson *m* salami
sauf except
sauter to jump; **ça saute aux yeux** that's obvious
sauvage wild
savoir to know, know how
saxophone *m* saxophone
sceptique sceptical
science *f* science; **—s économiques** home economics
scolaire school
sculpter to sculpt, to carve
sculpteur *m*, **sculpteuse** *f* sculptor
sculpture *f* sculpture
se (to, for) himself, herself, themselves, each other

séance *f* showing, session; — **de travaux pratiques** lab session

sec, sèche dry

sèche-cheveux *m* hair dryer

secours *m* help; **porte de —** emergency exit

secrétaire *m,f* secretary

sécurité *f* security

séjour *m* stay; **salle de —** living room

sel *m* salt

sélection *f* selection

selon according to

semaine *f* week

semblable similar

sembler to seem, appear

semestre *m* semester

sénateur *m* senator

sens *m* meaning, sense; direction

sensationnel, sensationnelle sensational

sensibilité *f* sensitivity

sentier *m* footpath, trail

sentiment *m* feeling

sentir to smell; feel; **se —** to feel

séparer to separate

série *f* series

sérieux, sérieuse serious

serpent *m* snake

serré tight

se serrer la main to shake hands

service *m* service

serviette *f* napkin; briefcase

servir to serve; **se —** to serve oneself; **se — de** to use

ses his, her, its

seul alone, only; **tout —** all by himself

seulement only

sévère strict

sexisme *m* sexism

sexiste sexist

shampooing *m* shampoo

short *m* shorts

si yes, if, whether; yes

SIDA *m* AIDS

siècle *m* century

sien, sienne his, hers

signaler to report

signe *m* sign

signifier to mean

sillage *m* wake, track

simple simple

simplifier to simplify

sincère sincere

sinon if not, or else

situation *f* situation, position, job

situé situated, located

ski *m* skiing, ski; **— nautique** *m* water-skiing

sociabilité *f* sociability

social (*m pl* **sociaux**) social

société *f* company, society

sociologie *f* sociology

sœur *f* sister

soi oneself

soi-disant (*invariable*) so-called

soif *f* thirst; **avoir —** to be thirsty

se soigner to take care of oneself

soin *m* care

soir *m* evening

soirée *f* evening, party

soit... soit either . . . or

sol *m* soil

soldat *m* soldier

solde *m* sale

soleil *m* sun; **bain de —** sunbath; **coup de —** sunburn

solidarité *f* fellowship

solution *f* solution

sommeil *m* sleep; **avoir —** to be sleepy

son his, her, its

son *m* sound

sondage *m* poll

sonner to ring

sorte *f* kind, sort, type

sortie *f* outing, exit

sortir to go out, take out

souci *m* worry, care

souffrir to suffer

soulever to lift

soulier *m* shoe

soupçonner to suspect

soupe *f* soup

souple flexible

sourire *m* smile

sous below

sous-marin underwater

sous-sol *m* basement

sous-titre *m* subtitle

sous-vêtements *m pl* underwear

souvenir *m* souvenir, memory

se souvenir de to remember

souvent often

spatial (*m pl* **spatiaux**) space

spécial (*m pl* **spéciaux**) special

se spécialiser to major

spécialité *f* specialty

spectacle *m* show

spontané spontaneous

sportif, sportive athletic

sport *m* sport

stable stable

stade *m* stadium, athletic field

station de métro *f* subway station

stationnement *m* parking

stationner to park

stéréo *f* stereo

studieux, studieuse studious

stylo *m* pen

subtil subtle

substituer to substitute

succès *m* success

succession *f* inheritance, estate

sucre *m* sugar

sud *m* South

suer to sweat

suffire to be enough

suggérer to suggest

suisse Swiss

suite : tout de — immediately

suivant *m* next one, following

suivre to follow, to take (a course)

sujet *m* subject; **au — de** about, concerning

superficiel, superficielle superficial

supérieur higher

supermarché *m* supermarket

supporter to stand, to put up with

supporter *m* supporter

suprême supreme

sur on

sûr sure, certain; **bien —** of course

514   surfing

surfing *m* surfing
surgelé frozen
surpopulation *f* overpopulation
surprendre to surprise
surprise *f* surprise
surprise-partie *f* party
surtout especially
suspect *m* suspect
swahili *m* Swahili
symbole *m* symbol
sympathique (sympa) nice
système *m* system

T

ta your
tabac *m* tobacco; **bureau de —** tobacco shop
table *f* table; **à —** at the table, seated; **mettre la —** to set the table
tableau (-x) *m* chalkboard; painting
tâche *f* task
taille *f* size (clothing); waist
taillé cut out
tailleur *m* women's suit
se taire to be silent
talent *m* talent
talon *m* heel
tambour *m* drum
tant so much, so many
tante *f* aunt
taquiner to tease
tard late
tarte *f* pie, tart
tas *m* a lot
tasse *f* cup
te (to, for) you
technique technical
technologie *f* technology
tee-shirt *m* tee-shirt
tel, telle such
télé *f* TV
téléfilm *m* TV movie
téléphone *m* telephone
téléphoner to telephone
téléviser to televise
téléviseur *m* television set
télévision *f* television
tellement so, so much

témoin *m* witness
tempérament *m* temperament
température *f* temperature
temps *m* time; weather; **à — perdu** in one's spare time; **de — en temps** from time to time; **en même —** at the same time; **tout le —** always; **le bon vieux —** the good old days
tendre tender
tendresse *f* tenderness
tenir to keep, hold; **se — droit** to stand up straight; **— le coup** to hold up (under stress)
tennis *m* tennis; sneaker
tentant tempting
tenté tempted
terminer to end
terrasse *f* terrace, outside area of café
terre *f* land, earth; **pomme de —** potato
tes your
tête *f* head; **se casser la —** to rack one's brain
thé *m* tea
théâtre *m* theater; **pièce de —** play
théorie *f* theory
ticket *m* ticket
tien, tienne yours
tiens hey, look
tiers *m* one third
timbre *m* stamp
timide shy
tirer to pull
tissu *m* fabric
toi you
toile d'araignée *f* spider web
tolérer to tolerate
tomate *f* tomato
tomber to fall; **— en panne** to break down
ton your
tort *m* wrong; **avoir —** to be wrong
tôt early, soon
toujours always, still, ever
tour *m* trip, turn
tour *f* tower
touriste *m,f* tourist

tourner to turn, to produce (a movie)
tournoi *m* tournament
tous all
tousser to cough
tout, toute, tous, toutes all, every; quite; **en tout cas** at any rate; **à tout à l'heure** see you later; **de toute façon** in any case; **tout d'un coup** all at once; **tout de suite** right away; **tout droit** straight ahead; **tout le monde** everyone; **tout le temps** all the time
tout *m* whole (thing)
traduire to translate
train *m* train; **en — de** in the process of
traîneau (-x) *m* sleigh
traîner to drag
trait *m* feature
traiter to treat
tranche *f* slice
tranquille calm, peaceful
transport *m* transportation
transporter to transport
travail (travaux) *m* job, work
travailler to work
traverser to cross
tremblement de terre *m* earthquake
très very
tribu *f* tribe
trimestre *m* quarter
triste sad
tristesse *f* sadness
se tromper to be wrong, to make a mistake
trompette *f* trumpet
trop too; **— de** too much, too many
tropical (m pl tropicaux) tropical
trottoir *m* sidewalk
trouver to find; **se —** to be located, be found
truquage *m* special effects
tu you
tutoyer to say "tu"
type *m* character, chap
typique typical

U

un, une a, an; one
uni united
unique unique, only
unisson : à l'— in unison
univers *m* universe
universitaire pertaining to university
université *f* university
usine *f* factory
utile useful
utiliser to use

V

vacances *f pl* vacation; **colonie de —** summer camp; **bonnes —** have a good vacation; **en — ** on vacation
vague *f* wave
vaisselle; faire la — to do the dishes
valeur *f* value
valise *f* suitcase
valoir to be worth; **ça vaut la peine** it's worth the trouble; **— mieux** to be better
vanille *f* vanilla
variable variable
varicelle *f* chicken pox
varier to vary
variété *f* variety, variety show
veau (-x) *m* veal
vedette *f* star, celebrity
végétation *f* vegetation
vélo *m* bicycle
vélomoteur *m* moped
vendre to sell; **à —** for sale
venir to come; **— de** to have just
vent *m* wind; **il fait du —** it's windy
vente *f* sale
ventre *m* belly, abdomen
verglas *m* ice, frost
vérifier to check

véritable real, true, genuine
vérité *f* truth
verre *m* glass, drink
vers toward, around
version *f* version
vert green
veste *f* jacket
vêtements *m pl* clothing
vétérinaire *m* veterinarian
viande *f* meat
victime *f* victim
vide empty
vidéo-cassette *f* videotape
vie *f* life
vieillesse *f* old age
vieux, vieil, vieille old; **vieux jeu** old-fashioned; **le bon vieux temps** the good old days
village *m* village
ville *f* city
ville-étape *f* town-stage
vin *m* wine
vingtaine *f* about twenty
violence *f* violence
violent violent
violon *m* violin
violoncelle *m* cello
vipère *f* poisonous snake
visage *m* face
vis-à-vis concerning
visibilité *f* visibility
visite *f* visit; **rendre — à** to visit (a person)
visiter to visit
vitamine *f* vitamin
vite quickly
vitesse *f* speed
vitre *f* window pane
vitrine *f* display window
vivant living
vivre to live
vœux *m pl* wishes
voici here is (are)
voilà there is (are); here is (are)
voile *f* sailing
voisin neighboring

voisin *m*, **voisine** *f* neighbor
voiture *f* automobile
voix *f* voice
vol *m* flight
volcan *m* volcano
volcanique volcanic
voler to steal
volet *m* shutter
volonté *f* will, will power
vomir to vomit
vos your
voter to vote
votre your
vôtre yours
vouloir to want, to wish; **— bien** to be willing; **— rire** to be kidding
vous you
vouvoyer to say "vous"
voyage *m* trip; **faire un —** to take a trip
voyager to travel
voyons let's see
voyou *m* scoundrel
vrai true
vraiment really, truly
vue *f* sight, view
vulgaire vulgar

W

w-c *m pl* toilet
week-end *m* weekend

Y

y in it, at it, to it, there; **il — a** there is (are); ago
yeux *m* eyes

Z

zaïrois from Zaire
zéro *m* zero
zone *f* zone
zut darn

Vocabulaire
Anglais-Français

Abbreviations

adj	adjective	*n*	noun
adv	adverb	*pl*	plural
f	feminine	*pron*	pronoun
m	masculine	*v*	verb

A

a(n) un, une
abandon abandonner
ability capacité *f*
able : to be pouvoir
about (approximately) environ;
  (*in expressions of time*) vers
above au-dessus, dessus
abroad à l'étranger
accept accepter
access accès *m*
accident accident *m*
accompany accompagner
accomplish accomplir
according to selon
accountant comptable *m,f*
accounting comptabilité *f*
achieve réaliser
across from en face de

activity activité *f*
actor acteur *m*
actress actrice *f*
add ajouter
address adresse *f*
admire admirer
admit admettre
adorable adorable
adore adorer
adult adulte *m*
advantage avantage *m*
advertising publicité *f*
advice conseil *m*
afraid : to be avoir peur
after après
afternoon après-midi *m*
again de nouveau, encore
against contre
age âge *m*; **to age** vieillir

ago il y a
agree être d'accord
AIDS SIDA *m*
airport aéroport *m*
album album *m*
algebra algèbre *f*
all tout, toute, tous, toutes
allow permettre
almost presque
alone seul(e)
along le long de
already déjà
also aussi; également
although bien que, quoique
always toujours
ambitious ambitieux,
  ambitieuse
among parmi
and et

animal animal (animaux) *m*
announce annoncer
annoy embêter
annoying embêtant(e)
another un(e) autre
answer *v* répondre; *n* réponse *f*
anthropology anthropologie *f*
anxiety inquiétude *f*
any du, de la, de l', des; quelque(s); en
anyway quand même
apartment appartement *m*
apartment building immeuble *m*
appear paraître, apparaître, sembler, avoir l'air
apple pomme *f*
application demande *m*
appreciate apprécier
appropriate approprié(e)
approximately environ
architect architecte *m*
architecture architecture *f*
arm bras *m*
arm chair fauteuil *m*
around autour de, vers
arrival arrivée *f*
arrive arriver
article article *m*
as . . . as aussi... que
as far as jusqu'à
as for quant à
as much (many) as autant de
as soon as aussitôt que, dès que
ashamed : to be avoir honte
ask demander; poser (une question)
aspirin aspirine *f*; — **tablet** comprimé d'aspirine *m*
assistant assistant *m*
astronaut astronaute *m,f*
astronomy astronomie *f*
at à, en, dans; — **ease** à l'aise; — **the house of** chez; — **least** au moins; — **once** tout de suite
athletic sportif, sportive
attend assister à
attention attention *f*; **to pay —** faire attention
attitude attitude *f*

aunt tante *f*
automobile voiture *f*, automobile *f*
autumn automne *m*
avenue avenue *f*
average *n* moyenne *f*; *adj* moyen, moyenne
avoid éviter
aware au courant de

B

baby bébé *m*
baby-sitter gardien, gardienne, d'enfants
back dos *m*; **in — of** derrière
bad mauvais(e); **it's too —** il est (c'est) dommage; **the weather is —** il fait mauvais
badly mal
bakery boulangerie *f*
ball ballon *m*
banana banane *f*
bank banque *f*
baseball base-ball *m*
based basé
basement sous-sol *m*
basketball basket-ball *m*
bathing suit maillot de bain *m*
bathroom salle de bain *f*
be être; — **able** pouvoir; — **better** valoir mieux; — **worth** valoir; — **. . . years old** avoir... ans
beach plage *f*
beans (green) haricots verts *m pl*
beautiful beau, bel, belle, beaux, belles
because parce que; car; — **of** à cause de
become devenir
bed lit *m*; **go to —** se coucher
bedroom chambre *f*
beef bœuf *m*
beer bière *f*
before (*time*) avant, avant de, avant que; devant (*place*)
begin commencer à; se mettre à
beginning début *m*; commencement *m*

behind derrière
beige beige
believe croire
below sous
beside à côté de
besides à part; d'ailleurs; de plus
best *adj* meilleur(e); *adv* mieux
bet parier
better *adj* meilleur(e); *adv* mieux; **be —** valoir mieux
between entre
bicycle vélo *m*; bicyclette *f*
big grand(e); gros, grosse
bill addition *f*; (money) billet *m*
billfold portefeuille *m*
biology biologie *f*
bird oiseau (oiseaux) *m*
birth naissance *f*
birthday anniversaire *m*
black noir(e)
blond blond(e)
blouse chemisier *m*
blue bleu(e)
blush rougir
boat bateau (-x) *m*
body corps *m*
book livre *m*
bookstore librairie *f*
boot botte *f*
booth guichet *m*
bore ennuyer; **be bored** s'ennuyer
born : to be naître
boring ennuyeux, ennuyeuse
borrow emprunter
boss patron *m*, patronne *f*
bother déranger
bottle bouteille *f*
boulevard boulevard *m*
box boîte *f*
boxing boxe *f*
boy garçon *m*
brand new neuf, neuve
brave courageux, courageuse
bread pain *m*
break casser
breakfast petit déjeuner *m*
breathe respirer
breathing respiration *f*
brick brique *f*

bring apporter
bring up élever
broadcast émission *f*
broken cassé(e)
broken down en panne
brother frère *m*
brown marron (*invariable*)
brush (se) brosser
build construire
burglar cambrioleur *m,*
  cambrioleuse *f*
burn brûler
bus autobus *m,* car *m*
bus stop arrêt d'autobus *m*
business affaires *f pl,*
  commerce *m;* entreprise *f*
busy : be — with s'occuper de
but mais
butcher shop boucherie *f*
butter beurre *m*
buy acheter
by par, de

C

café café *m*
cake gâteau (-x) *m*
calculator calculatrice *f*
calculus calcul *m*
call appeler
calm tranquille
camera appareil-photo *m;*
  movie — caméra
camp faire du camping
campground camping *m*
campus campus *m*
can (be able to) pouvoir
cancer cancer *m*
candy bonbon *m*
candy store confiserie *f*
canoe canot *m*
capital capitale *f*
car voiture *f,* auto *f*
carafe carafe *f*
card carte *f*
care : take care of s'occuper de
careful prudent(e)
carrot carotte *f*
carry emporter, porter
cartoon bande dessinée *f,*
  dessin animé *m*
case cas *m;* **in any —** en tout
  cas, de toute façon

cassette tape cassette *f*
cat chat *m*
catastrophy catastrophe *f*
cello violoncelle *m*
center centre *m*
century siècle *m*
chair chaise *f*
chalkboard tableau (-x) *m*
champion champion *m,*
  championne *f*
championship championnat *m*
chance occasion *f,* hasard *m*
change *n* monnaie *f; v*
  changer
channel chaîne *f*
character personnage *m*
charm charme *m*
charming charmant(e)
cheap bon marché
check *v* vérifier; *n* chèque *m*
cheek joue *f*
cheese fromage *m*
chemistry chimie *f*
cherry cerise *f*
chicken poulet *m*
chief chef *m*
child enfant *m,f*
childhood enfance *f*
chin menton *m*
chocolate chocolat *m*
choice choix *m*
choose choisir
Christmas Noël *m*
church église *f*
circle cercle *m*
citizen citoyen *m,* citoyenne *f*
city ville *f*
clarinet clarinette *f*
class classe *f,* cours *m*
clean *v* nettoyer, ranger; *adj*
  propre
climate climat *m*
climb monter
close fermer
closed fermé
closet placard *m*
clothing vêtement *m*
cloud nuage *m*
cloudy nuageux, nuageuse; **it's**
  — le ciel est couvert
club club *m*
coast côte *f*
coat manteau (-x) *m*

coffee café *m*
cold *n* rhume *m; adj*
  froid(e); **be —** (*person*) avoir
  froid; **be —** (*weather*) faire
  froid
color couleur *f*
come venir
come back revenir, rentrer
comedian comédien *m,*
  comédienne *f*
comfortable confortable
comic strip dessin animé *m*
commune communauté *f*
community communauté *f*
company société *f*
comparison comparaison *f*
competent compétent(e)
complain se plaindre
complicated compliqué(e)
compose composer
composition composition *f*
computer science informatique *f*
concerned : be — with se
  préoccuper de
concerning sur, en ce qui
  concerne
concert concert *m*
confession confession *f*
confirm confirmer
congratulations félicitations *f*
consider considérer
constantly sans cesse;
  constamment
continue continuer
contrast contraste *m*
cook faire la cuisine
cool frais, fraîche; **it is —**
  (*weather*) il fait frais
corner coin *m*
correct corriger
cost coûter
cough tousser
count compter
country pays *m,* campagne *f*
countryside paysage *m*
courageous courageux,
  courageuse
course cours *m;* **in the — of**
  au cours de
cousin cousin *m,* cousine *f*
cover couvrir
craftsperson artisan *m,*
  artisane *f*

crazy fou, folle
cream crème *f*
create créer
credit card carte de crédit *f*
crime crime *m*
crisis crise *f*
criticize critiquer
cross traverser
crowd foule *f*
cry pleurer
cup tasse *f*
customer client *m*, cliente *f*
customs office douane *f*
cut couper
cute mignon, mignonne
cycling cyclisme *m*

D

daily quotidien, quotidienne
dance danser
danger danger *m*
dark (*color*) foncé; be —
(*night*) faire sombre
dark (haired) brun(e)
darn zut
date date *f*
day jour *m*; journée *f*
dead mort(e)
deal affaire *f*
dear cher, chère
debt dette *f*
deceive décevoir
decide décider
defend défendre
define définir
degree degré *m*
delighted ravi
democracy démocratie *f*
demonstration manifestation *f*
dentist dentiste *m,f*
deodorant déodorisant *m*
department département *m*
describe décrire
desk bureau (-x) *m*
dessert dessert *m*
device appareil *m*
dictionary dictionnaire *m*
die mourir
different différent(e)
difficult difficile
dine dîner
dining room salle à manger *f*

dinner dîner *m*; to have —
dîner
direct *adj* direct(e); *v* diriger
disadvantage inconvénient *m*
disappear disparaître
disappointed déçu
discover découvrir
discovery découverte *f*
discuss discuter, parler (de)
discussion discussion *f*
dish plat *m*, assiette *f*
disobey désobéir
display window vitrine *f*
disturb déranger
divided by divisé par
divorce divorce *m*
do faire; — housework faire
le ménage; — one's best
faire de son mieux; — the
dishes faire la vaisselle
doctor docteur *m*; médecin *m*
doctorate doctorat *m*
documentary documentaire *m*
dog chien *m*
dollar dollar *m*
door porte *f*
dormitory résidence
universitaire *f*
doubt douter
downtown area centre-ville *m*
dozen douzaine *f*
drag traîner
drama drame *m*
dream *n* rêve *m*; *v* rêver
dress *n* robe *f*; *v* s'habiller
dressy habillé
drink *v* boire; *n* boisson *f*
drive conduire
driver chauffeur *m*;
conducteur, conductrice
driving school auto-école *f*
drugstore pharmacie *f*;
droguerie *f*
drum tambour *m*
during pendant, au cours de
dynamic dynamique

E

each chaque
ear oreille *f*
early de bonne heure, tôt; be
— être en avance

earn gagner
east est *m*
easy facile
eat manger
education formation *f*,
éducation *f*, instruction *f*
educator éducateur *m*,
éducatrice *f*
effect effet *m*
either ou
elbow coude *m*
electric électrique
electronics électronique *f*
else d'autre
elsewhere ailleurs
employee employé *m*,
employée *f*
employer employeur *m*,
employeuse *f*
employment emploi *m*
encourage encourager
end *n* bout *m*; fin *f*; *v*
terminer
energy énergie *f*
engineer ingénieur *m*
engineering ingénierie *f*
English anglais
enormous énorme
enter entrer
enthusiastic enthousiaste
entire entier, entière
environment environnement
m
equally également
equipment équipement *m*
errands courses *f pl*
especially surtout
essential essentiel *m*
establish établir
even *adv* même
evening soir *m*
event événement *m*
eventually éventuellement
every chaque; tout(e), tous,
toutes; — day tous les jours
everybody tout le monde
everyone tout le monde
everywhere partout
examination examen *m*; pass
an — réussir à un examen;
take an — passer un examen
example: for — par exemple
excellent excellent(e)

except excepté, sauf
exchange échanger
exercise exercice *m*
expense dépense *f*
expenses frais *m pl*
expensive cher, chère
experiment expérience *f*
expert expert *m*
explain expliquer
explanation explication *f*
express exprimer

F

facing en face de
fact fait *m*; **in —** en effet, en
  fait
fail échouer; **— an exam**
  échouer à un examen
fall *v* tomber; *n* automne *m*
family famille *f*
famous célèbre
fantasy fantaisie *f*
far loin; **— from** loin de
farm ferme *f*
farmer agriculteur *m*
fascinating fascinant(e)
fatigue fatigue *f*
fault défaut *m*
favorite préféré(e); favori,
  favorite
fear craindre; avoir peur de
feel sentir, éprouver; **— like**
  avoir envie de
femininity féminité *f*
fever fièvre *f*
few peu (de); **a —** quelques
fight *v* lutter; *n* lutte *f*
fill remplir
film film *m*
finally enfin
find trouver
fine bien
finger doigt *m*
finish finir
first premier, première; **— of
  all** d'abord
floor étage *m*
flower fleur *f*
flu grippe *f*
flute flûte *f*
fog brouillard *m*
follow suivre

food aliment *m*; nourriture *f*
for pour; pendant; il y a...
  que; ça fait... que; depuis; car
forbid défendre
forehead front *m*
foreign étranger, étrangère
forest forêt *f*
forget oublier
fork fourchette *f*
former ancien, ancienne
formerly autrefois
fortunately heureusement
free libre; gratuit(e)
freeway autoroute *f*
fresh frais, fraîche
friend ami *m*, amie *f*; (*coll.*)
  copain *m*, copine *f*
friendly accueillant(e)
friendship amitié *f*
from de
front : in — of devant
fruit fruit *m*
full complet, complète; plein(e)
funny amusant(e)
furniture meubles *m pl*
future *n* avenir *m*; *adj*
  futur(e)

G

game jeu *m*; match *m*
garage garage *m*
garden jardin *m*
geography géographie *f*
geology géologie *f*
geometry géométrie *f*
get obtenir; (**become**) devenir;
  — acquainted connaître; **—
  along (manage)** se
  débrouiller; **— married** se
  marier; **— off** descendre; **—
  on** monter; **— up** se lever
gift cadeau (-x) *m*
girl fille *f*
give donner; offrir; **— up**
  abandonner
glad content(e)
go aller; **— around** faire le
  tour de; **— back** retourner;
  — down descendre; **— for a
  walk** faire une promenade;
  — grocery shopping faire le
  marché; **— home** rentrer; **—

out sortir; **— shopping** faire
  les courses; **— to bed** se
  coucher; **— up** monter
goal but *m*
golf golf *m*
good bon, bonne
good-bye au revoir
government gouvernement *m*
grade note *f*
grandfather grand-père *m*
grandmother grand-mère *f*
grandparent grand-parent *m*
grass herbe *f*
gray gris(e)
great grand(e), formidable
great-grandmother arrière-
  grand-mère *f*
grief chagrin *m*
grocery store épicerie *f*
group groupe *m*
grow grandir
guard gardien *m*, gardienne *f*
guess deviner
guilty coupable
guitar guitare *f*
gymnastics gymnastique *f*

H

habit habitude *f*; **be in the —
  of** avoir l'habitude de
hair cheveux *m pl*
hairdresser coiffeur *m*,
  coiffeuse *f*
half moitié *f*; demi
ham jambon *m*
hand in remettre
happen arriver, se passer
handsome beau, bel, belle,
  beaux
happiness bonheur *m*
happy heureux, heureuse;
  content(e)
hard dur(e), difficile
hardly à peine
harmony harmonie *f*
hat chapeau (-x) *m*
hate détester
have avoir; **— dinner** dîner;
  — just venir de; **— to**
  devoir
he il, lui
head tête *f*

headache : have a — avoir mal à la tête
hear entendre ; **— about** entendre parler de
heart cœur *m* ; **— attack** crise cardiaque *f*
heavy lourd(e)
hello bonjour
help aider
her (*dir obj*) la ; (*ind obj*) lui ; (*after prep*) elle ; *adj* son, sa, ses
here ici ; **— is** voici, voilà
hero *héros *m*
heroine héroïne *f*
hi salut
hide cacher
high haut(e), élevé(e)
hike randonnée *f*
hill colline *f*
hinder empêcher
hire embaucher
history histoire *f*
holiday fête *f*
home : at the — of chez
homework devoirs *m pl*
honest honnête
hope *v* espérer ; *n* espoir *m*
horse cheval (chevaux) *m*
hose bas *m pl*
hospital hôpital *m*
host hôte *m*
hostel auberge *f* ; **youth —** auberge de jeunesse
hostess hôtesse *f*
hot chaud(e) ; **be —** (*person*) avoir chaud ; **be —** (*weather*) faire chaud
hotel hôtel *m*
hour heure *f*
house maison *f* ; **apartment —** immeuble *m*
how comment ; **— long** depuis quand, depuis combien de temps ; **— many, — much** combien (de) ; **— old is she ?** quel âge a-t-elle ? ; **— are you ?** comment allez-vous ?, comment ça va ?
however cependant, pourtant
human humain(e)

*Denotes an aspirate *h*.

hundred cent *m*
hungry : be — avoir faim
hunting chasse *f*
hurry se dépêcher ; **in a —** pressé(e)
hurt *v* avoir mal ; *adj* blessé
husband mari *m*

I

I je
ice glace *f*
ice cream glace *f*
idea idée *f*
ideal idéal *m*
identify identifier
identity identité *f*
if si ; **— not** sinon
immediately tout de suite, immédiatement
important important(e)
impossible impossible
improve améliorer
impulsive impulsif, impulsive
in à, en, dans ; **— back of** derrière ; **— front of** devant ; **— spite of** malgré ; **— style** à la mode ; **— your opinion** à votre avis
included compris(e)
including y compris
increase augmenter
independent indépendant(e)
industry industrie *f*
inequality inégalité *f*
infection infection *f*
infraction infraction *f*
inhabit habiter
initial initiale *f*
initiative initiative *f*
insist insister
inspection inspection *f*
install installer
instance : for — par exemple
instant instant *m*
instead of au lieu de
insult insulter
intellectual intellectuel, intellectuelle
intelligent intelligent(e)
intend to avoir l'intention de
interest *v* intéresser ; *n* intérêt *m* ; **be —ed in** s'intéresser à

interesting intéressant(e)
interrogate interroger
intimately intimement
into dans, en, à ; **go —** entrer dans
intoxicated ivre
invent inventer
invite inviter
irresistible irrésistible
island île *f*
it il, elle, ce ; (*dir obj*) le, la ; **— is** (+ weather expression) il fait
it's c'est
it's going well ça marche bien
its son, sa, ses

J

jackpot gros lot *m*
jam confiture *f*
jealous jaloux, jalouse
jewel bijou (bijoux) *m*
job emploi *m*, poste *m* ; (*coll.*) boulot *m*
jog faire du jogging
journalist journaliste *m,f*
just juste ; **have —** venir de

K

keep garder
key clé *f*
kid gosse *m,f*
kill tuer
kind sorte *f*, espèce *f* ; *adj* sympathique ; gentil, gentille
kiss embrasser
kitchen cuisine *f*
know (something) savoir ; **(be acquainted with)** connaître ; **— how to** savoir

L

lady dame *f*
language langue *f*, langage *m*
large grand(e) ; gros, grosse
last *v* durer ; *adj* dernier, dernière ; **— night** hier soir ; **at —** enfin
late tard ; **be —** être en retard
laugh rire
law loi *f* ; droit *m*
lawyer avocat *m*, avocate *f*
learn apprendre

leather cuir *m*
leave (something somewhere)
  laisser; **(a place)** quitter, partir
  de, sortir de
lecture conférence *f*
left gauche *f*; **to the —** à
  gauche
leg jambe *f*
lemon citron *m*
lemonade citron pressé
lend prêter
less moins; **— and —** de
  moins en moins
lesson leçon *f*
let's *verb stem* + -ons *ending*
letter lettre *f*
library bibliothèque *f*
life vie *f*
light allumer
like aimer; **feel —** avoir envie
  de
like comme
lip lèvre *f*
listen (to) écouter
literature littérature *f*
little *adj* petit(e); *adv* peu; **a
  —** un peu
live habiter; vivre
living room salle de séjour *f*
located : be — se trouver, être
  situé
long long, longue; **how —**
  depuis quand; **no —er** ne...
  plus; **— ago** autrefois; **—
  time** longtemps
look for chercher
lose perdre
lot : a — beaucoup (de)
love *n* amour *m*; *v* aimer,
  adorer; **in —** amoureux,
  amoureuse
luck chance *f*
lucky : be — avoir de la
  chance
lunch déjeuner *m*

M

magazine revue *f*, magazine
  m
magnificent magnifique
mail courrier *m*

main principal(e), principaux
make faire
man homme *m*
manage (get along) se
  débrouiller
many beaucoup (de); bien des;
  how — combien (de); **too —**
  trop (de)
map carte *f*
market marché *m*
marriage mariage *m*
marry se marier (avec)
mathematics mathématiques *f
  pl*
may pouvoir
maybe peut-être
mayor maire *m*
me me, moi
meet faire la connaissance de,
  connaître; *(by appointment)*
  retrouver; *(by chance)*
  rencontrer; *(together)* se réunir
middle : in the — of au milieu
  de
mild doux, douce
mind : change one's —
  changer d'avis
mine le mien, la mienne, etc.
Miss mademoiselle, Mlle
modern moderne
money argent *m*
month mois *m*
more davantage; plus
moreover d'ailleurs
morning matin *m*
most le plus; le, la, les plus
  adj; la plupart de
mother-in-law belle-mère *f*
motorcycle motocyclette *f*;
  (coll.) moto *f*
mountain montagne *f*; **—
  climber** alpiniste *m,f*
mouth bouche *f*
movie film *m*; **the —s** le
  cinéma; **— camera** caméra *f*;
  — theater cinéma *m*
Mr. monsieur, M.
Mrs. madame, Mme
much beaucoup (de); **how —**
  combien (de); **too —** trop
  (de); **as —** autant de; **so —**
  tant de
museum musée *m*

mushroom champignon *m*
music musique *f*
must devoir, falloir
my mon, ma, mes

N

name nom *m*; *v* nommer;
  my — is je m'appelle
narrow étroit(e)
natural naturel, naturelle
near près (de)
necessary nécessaire; **it is —**
  il faut, il est nécessaire
need avoir besoin (de)
neighbor voisin(e) *m,f*
neither . . . nor ne... ni... ni
never ne... jamais
new nouveau, nouvel,
  nouvelle, nouveaux,
  nouvelles; **brand —** neuf,
  neuve
news actualités *f pl*;
  informations *f pl*
newspaper journal (journaux)
  m
next prochain(e); **— to** à côté
  de
nice sympathique; gentil,
  gentille; agréable
night nuit *f*; **— club** boîte de
  nuit; **last —** hier soir
nightmare cauchemar *m*
no non, pas (de), aucun, ne...
  aucun; **— longer** ne... plus;
  — more ne... plus; **— one**
  personne, ne... personne,
  personne ne...
noise bruit *m*
noisy bruyant(e)
none aucun
noon midi *m*
north nord *m*
not ne... pas; **— at all** ne...
  pas du tout
notebook cahier *m*
nothing rien, rien ne..., ne...
  rien
notice remarquer
novel roman *m*
now maintenant
nuclear nucléaire
nurse infirmier *m*, infirmière *f*

O

obey obéir (à)
obligated obligé
occupation métier *m*
o'clock heure(s)
of de
offer offrir
office bureau (-x) *m*; **post —** bureau de poste
often souvent, fréquemment
oil huile *f*
okay d'accord
old vieil, vieux, vieille; ancien, ancienne
on sur; — **TV** à la télé; — **foot** à pied; — **time** à l'heure
once une fois; **at —** tout de suite
one un(e); on; **that —** celui-là, celle-là; **this —** celui-ci, celle-ci
one fourth quart *m*
one half demi *m*
one third tiers *m*
onion oignon *m*
only *adj* seul(e); *adv* seulement; ne... que
only seulement
open *v* ouvrir; *adj* ouvert(e)
opening ouverture *f*
opinion opinion *f*, **avis** *m*; **in my —** à mon avis
opportunity occasion *f*
opposite contraire *m*
or ou
orange drink orangeade *m*
orange juice jus d'orange *m*
order commander; **in — that** pour que; **in — to** pour
other autre, d'autre; **on the — hand** d'autre part, par contre
otherwise autrement
our notre, nos
ours le, la nôtre; les nôtres
outside dehors
over there là-bas
owe devoir
own *adj* propre; *v* posséder
owner propriétaire *m,f*

P

package paquet *m*
paint peindre
painting peinture *f*, tableau *m*
pal copain *m*, copine *f*
pan casserole *f*
pants pantalon *m*
panty hose collant *m*
paper papier *m*
parade défilé *m*
paradise paradis *m*
parent parent *m*
park parc *m*
parking lot parking *m*
part partie *f*
part-time à temps partiel
party surprise-partie *f*
pass passer; **— a test** réussir à un examen
past passé *m*
pastry shop pâtisserie *f*
pay payer
peach pêche *f*
pear poire *f*
peas petits pois *m pl*
pen stylo *m*
pencil crayon *m*
people gens *m pl*; on
pepper poivre *m*
percent pour cent
perfect parfait(e)
perfume parfum *m*
perhaps peut-être
permit *n* permis *m*; *v* permettre
person personne *f*
physical education éducation physique *f*
physician médecin *m*
physics physique *f*
piano piano *m*
picnic pique-niquer
pie tarte *f*
piece morceau (-x) *m*
pill pilule *f*
pink rose
place endroit *m*, lieu *m*; **take —** avoir lieu
plan projet *m*
plane avion *m*

play *v* jouer (à, de); *n* pièce de théâtre *f*; **— sports** faire du sport
pleasant agréable
please s'il vous (te) plaît; *v* plaire à
pleasure plaisir *m*
plumber plombier *m*
plus plus
pocket poche *f*
police officer agent de police *m*
police station poste de police *m*
polite poli
politeness politesse *f*
political politique
poll sondage *m*
poor pauvre
popular populaire
populated peuple
pork porc *m*
pork shop charcuterie *f*
position situation *f*
possess posséder
post office bureau de poste *m*, poste *f*
poster affiche *f*
potato pomme de terre *f*
pound livre *f*
practice pratiquer
prefer préférer, aimer mieux
preparation préparatif *m*
prepare préparer
prescription ordonnance *f*
present actuel, actuelle
pretender poseur *m*
pretty joli(e)
prevent empêcher (de)
price prix *m*
private privé(e)
prize prix *m*
probably probablement; sans doute
problem problème *m*
product produit *m*
program émission *f*
promise promesse *f*
promise promettre
property propriété *f*
public public, publique
pull out déboucher

pullover sweater pull-over *m*
punish punir
purchase achat *m*
purse sac à main *m*
put mettre
put back down reposer; **put on**
   mettre

Q

quarter quartier *m*; **— to**
   moins le quart; **— after** et
   quart
question interroger; **be a — of**
   s'agir de; **ask a —** poser une
   question
quickly vite
quite tout

R

race course *f*
racism racisme *m*
radio radio *f*
railroad station gare *f*
rain *v* pleuvoir; *n* pluie *f*
raise lever, élever
rapid rapide
rather assez; plutôt
razor rasoir *m*
read lire
ready prêt(e)
real véritable, vrai(e)
really vraiment
reassure rassurer
recall rappeler
receive recevoir
recently récemment
recipe recette *f*
recognize reconnaître
record disque *m*
red rouge
reflect réfléchir
refrigerator réfrigérateur *m*,
   frigo *m*
regret regretter
regular régulier, régulière
relationships relations *f pl*
relative parent *m*
relax se détendre
remain rester
remember se souvenir de

rent *v* louer; *n* loyer *m*
repair réparer
repeat répéter
reply *n* réponse *f*; *v*
   répondre
report rapport *m*
request demander
research recherches *f pl*
resemble ressembler à
reservation réserve *f*
reserve retenir
residence domicile *m*
rest *v* se reposer; *n* reste *m*
restaurant restaurant *m*
result résultat *m*
retire prendre sa retraite
retirement retraite *f*
return (go back) retourner;
   (come back) revenir
return (home) rentrer; **(give
   back)** rendre; *n* retour *m*
rich riche
ridicule ridiculiser
right (*direction*) droite *f*; droit
   m; **be —** avoir raison
right away tout de suite
rigorous rigoureux, rigoureuse
ripe mûr(e)
risk risquer
river fleuve *m*, rivière *f*
road chemin *m*
roast rôti *m*
rock pierre *f*
rock music rock *m*
roll rouler
roller skating patinage *m*
room pièce *f*; **living —** salle
   de séjour *f*
rooming house pension de
   famille *f*
roommate camarade de
   chambre *m,f*
round arrondi(e)
route itinéraire *m*
row rang *m*
run courir
run errands faire des courses

S

sad triste
sailing voile *f*

salad salade *f*
salary salaire *m*
salt sel *m*
same même
sand sable *m*
sandal sandale *f*
satisfied satisfait(e)
save (*money*) économiser
say dire
schedule horaire *m*
scholarship bourse *f*
school école *f*
sciences sciences *m pl*
scoundrel voyou *m*
sculpture sculpture *f*
sculptor sculpteur *m*
sea mer *f*
season saison *f*
seated assis
second deuxième; second(e)
second floor premier étage *m*
see voir; **— you soon** à
   bientôt; **— you tomorrow** à
   demain
seem sembler, avoir l'air,
   paraître
sell vendre
send envoyer
sentence phrase *f*
separate séparer
series série *f*
serious sérieux, sérieuse; grave
serve servir
several plusieurs
sexism sexisme *m*
share partager
she elle
shirt chemise *f*
shock choquer
shoe chaussure *f*, soulier *m*
shoe store magasin de
   chaussures *m*
shop boutique; **tobacco —**
   bureau de tabac *m*; *v* faire le
   marché
shopping center centre
   commercial *m*
short court(e), petit(e)
shorts short *m*
shoulder épaule *f*
show montrer
show spectacle *m*

shower douche *f*
shrimp crevette *f*
shutter volet *m*
shy timide
sick malade; **to get —** tomber malade
sickness maladie *f*
side côté *m*
sidewalk trottoir *m*
sight vue *f*
sign pancarte *f*
since depuis; puisque
sincere sincère
singer chanteur *m*, chanteuse *f*
sister sœur *f*
sit (down) s'asseoir; **— to eat** se mettre à table
sit-up abdominal (abdominaux) *m*
situated situé
ski ski *m*; *v* faire du ski; **— jacket** anorak *m*
skirt jupe *f*
sky ciel *m*
sleep dormir
sleepy : be — avoir sommeil
slice tranche *f*
slope pente *f*
slow lent(e)
slowly lentement
small petit(e)
smoke *v* fumer; *n* fumée *f*
snack (*after-school*) goûter *m*
snow *v* neiger; *n* neige *f*
so ainsi, donc, alors; **— (much)** tellement; **— that** pour que
soap opera feuilleton *m*
soccer football *m*
social social
sociology sociologie *f*
sock chaussette *f*
some quelque(s)
someone quelqu'un
something quelque chose *f*
sometimes parfois, quelquefois
son fils *m*
song chanson *f*
soon bientôt; **as — as** dès que, aussitôt que
sorrow chagrin *m*, peine *f*
sorry : be — regretter
soup soupe *f*

south sud *m*; **— of France** Midi *m*
space espace *m*
speak parler
special spécial(e), spéciaux
spend dépenser (*money*), passer (*time*)
spider araignée *f*
spinach épinards *m pl*
spite : in — of malgré
spoon cuiller *or* cuillère *f*
sport sport *m*
spring printemps *m*
stadium stade *m*
stamp timbre *m*
stand supporter
star étoile *f*; **vedette** *f*
start commencer
state état *m*
stay rester
stay séjour *m*
steal voler
step pas *m*
stereo chaîne-stéréo *f*
still encore
stomach estomac *m*
stop (s')arrêter
store magasin *m*
storm orage *m*
story histoire *f*, conte *m*
straight (ahead) tout droit
strange bizarre
street rue *f*
strict sévère
strike grève *f*
strong fort(e)
struggle lutte *f*
student étudiant *m*, étudiante *f*
studious studieux, studieuse
study étude *f*
study étudier, faire des études
stupid bête
stylish chic
subject sujet *m*; **academic —** matière *f*
suburb banlieue *f*
subway métro *m*
subway station station de métro *f*
succeed réussir
success réussite *f*
sugar sucre *m*

suit (*women's*) tailleur *m*
suit (*men's*) complet *m*
suitcase valise *f*
summer été *m*
summer camp colonie de vacances *f*
sun soleil *m*
sunbathe prendre un bain de soleil
sunny : be — faire du soleil
suntanned bronzé
supreme suprême
sure sûr(e)
surgeon chirurgien *m*, chirurgienne *f*
surprise *n* surprise *f*; *v* surprendre, étonner
surround entourer
survey enquête *f*
suspect soupçonner
swim nager
swimming natation *f*
swimming pool piscine *f*
symbol symbole *m*

T

table table *f*; **set the —** mettre la table
take prendre; emmener; emporter; **— an exam** passer un examen; **— a course** suivre un cours; **— a trip** faire un voyage; **— out** sortir
talent talent *m*
talk parler
talk show causerie *f*
tape recorder magnétophone *m*
taste goût *m*
taxes impôts *m pl*
tea thé *m*
teach enseigner
teacher professeur *m*
team équipe *f*
tease taquiner
technology technologie *f*
tee-shirt tee-shirt *m*
telephone *n* téléphone *m*; *v* téléphoner
television télévision (télé) *f*
television set téléviseur *m*

tell raconter; dire
temperature température *f*
tempting tentant
tennis tennis *m*
tennis shoe chaussure de tennis *f*
term paper dissertation *f*
terrace terrasse *f*
terrific formidable
thank remercier
thank you merci
thanks to grâce à
that ça; *adj* ce, cet, cette; *pron* celui, celle; **— means** ça veut dire; **— which** ce que
the le, la, les
theater théâtre *m*
their leur, leurs
theirs le leur, la leur, les leurs
them les; leur; eux, elles
then alors, ensuite, puis, donc
there là(-bas); y
there is, are il y a; voilà
therefore donc
these ces; ceux, celles
they ils, elles
thing chose *f*
think penser; réfléchir; croire; **— about** penser à; **— of** penser de
thirsty : to be — avoir soif
this ce, cet, cette; celui, celle
those ces; ceux, celles
thousand mille *m*
threaten menacer
ticket billet *m*, ticket *m*
tie cravate *f*
tight serré
time temps *m*, heure *f*; **on —** à l'heure; **what — is it?** quelle heure est-il?; **from — to —** de temps en temps; **have a good —** s'amuser; **at that —** à ce moment-là, à cette époque-là; **at —s** parfois
timid timide
tired fatigué(e)
tiring fatigant(e)
tobacco tabac *m*; **— shop** bureau de tabac *m*
today aujourd'hui
together ensemble
tolerate tolérer

tomato tomate *f*
tomorrow demain
too trop; **it's — bad** il est (c'est) dommage; **— many, — much** trop (de)
tooth dent *f*
town ville *f*
toy jouet *m*
trail piste *f*
train train *m*
translate traduire
trashcan poubelle *f*
travel voyager
treat traiter
treatment remède *m*
tree arbre *m*
trip voyage *m*
trouble ennui *m*
true vrai(e)
trumpet trompette *f*
truth vérité *f*
try essayer
turn tourner
type sorte *f*; genre *m*, espèce *f*
typewriter machine à écrire *f*
typical typique

U

umbrella parapluie *m*
unbelievable incroyable
uncle oncle *m*
under sous
understand comprendre
underwear sous-vêtements *m pl*
unemployment chômage *m*
unfair injuste
unfortunately malheureusement
unique unique
university université *f*
unless à moins que
unmarried célibataire
unpleasant désagréable
until jusqu'à ce que
upkeep entretien *m*
us nous
use utiliser, se servir de
used d'occasion
useful utile
usual habituel habituelle
usually d'habitude

V

vacation vacances *f pl*
vanilla vanille *f*
variety variété *f*
vary varier
veal veau *m*
vegetable légume *m*
very très, bien; **— much** beaucoup
victim victime *f*
video-recorder magnétoscope *m*
videotape vidéo-cassette *m*
village village *m*
violin violon *m*
visit visiter; rendre visite à (*person*)
vitamin vitamine *f*
vote voter

W

wait (for) attendre
wake up se réveiller
walk démarche *f*
walk se promener, marcher
walking marche *f*
wall mur *m*
wallet portefeuille *m*
want vouloir, désirer
war guerre *f*
warm chaud; **be —** (*persons*) avoir chaud; **be —** (*weather*) faire chaud
warn prévenir
wash laver, se laver
washing machine machine à laver *f*
watch *v* regarder; *n* montre *f*; **— out!** attention!
water eau *f*
water closet w-c *m pl*
way façon *f*; manière *f*; **on the —** en route; **by the —** au fait
we nous
wear porter
weather temps
weather report bulletin météorologique *m*; météo *f*
week semaine *f*
weekend week-end *m*

weight poids *m*
well bien; **I am —** je vais
  bien
west ouest *m*
what qu'est-ce qui; que; qu'est-
  ce que; quel, quelle, quoi,
  que; ce qui, ce que
what's that qu'est-ce que c'est
when quand
where où
which quel(s), quelle(s); **— one**
  lequel, laquelle
while pendant que, alors que
white blanc, blanche
who qui
why pourquoi
wide large
wife femme *f*
win gagner
wind vent *m*

windy : it is — il fait du vent
window fenêtre *f*
wine vin *m*
winter hiver *m*
with avec
without sans; sans que
woman femme *f*
wonder se demander
wood bois *m*
word mot *m*; (*spoken*) parole *f*
work travailler
worker ouvrier *m*, ouvrière *f*
world monde *m*
worried inquiet, inquiète
worse pire
worth : be — valoir
wrinkle ride *m*
write écrire
wrong : to be — avoir tort

Y

year an *m*, année *f*; **to be**
  . . . years old avoir... ans
yellow jaune
yes oui, si
yesterday hier
yet encore
you vous, tu; te; toi
young jeune
your votre, vos, ton, ta, tes
yours le vôtre, etc; le tien, etc.
youth jeunesse *f*

Z

zero zéro *m*

Index

528

Photo Credits